Lecture Notes in Artificial Intelligence 10501

Subseries of Lecture Notes in Computer Science

LNAI Series Editors

Randy Goebel
University of Alberta, Edmonton, Canada
Yuzuru Tanaka
Hokkaido University, Sapporo, Japan
Wolfgang Wahlster
DFKI and Saarland University, Saarbrücken, Germany

LNAI Founding Series Editor

Joerg Siekmann
DFKI and Saarland University, Saarbrücken, Germany

T0171835

More information about this series at http://www.springer.com/series/1244

Renate A. Schmidt · Cláudia Nalon (Eds.)

Automated Reasoning with Analytic Tableaux and Related Methods

26th International Conference, TABLEAUX 2017
Brasília, Brazil, September 25–28, 2017
Proceedings

Editors
Renate A. Schmidt
University of Manchester
Manchester
UK

Cláudia Nalon
University of Brasília
Brasília D.F.
Brazil

ISSN 0302-9743   ISSN 1611-3349   (electronic)
Lecture Notes in Artificial Intelligence
ISBN 978-3-319-66901-4   ISBN 978-3-319-66902-1   (eBook)
DOI 10.1007/978-3-319-66902-1

Library of Congress Control Number: 2017951311

LNCS Sublibrary: SL7 – Artificial Intelligence

Printed on acid-free paper

This Springer imprint is published by Springer Nature
The registered company is Springer International Publishing AG
The registered company address is: Gewerbestrasse 11, 6330 Cham, Switzerland

Preface

This volume contains the proceedings of the 26th International Conference on Automated Reasoning with Analytic Tableaux and Related Methods, held at the Universidade de Brasília (UnB) in Brasília, Brazil, during September 25–28, 2017. TABLEAUX is the main international conference at which research on all aspects – theoretical foundations, implementation techniques, systems development, and applications – of the mechanization of tableaux-based reasoning and related methods is presented.

TABLEAUX 2017 was co-located with the 11th International Symposium on Frontiers of Combining Systems (FroCoS 2017) and the 8th International Conference on Interactive Theorem Proving (ITP 2017), whose proceedings also appeared in the Lecture Notes in Artificial Intelligence Series of Springer (Volumes 10483 and 10499).

We received 27 submissions (35 abstracts) out of which 19 papers were accepted (including one system description). Four of these papers were accepted under conditions from the reviewers and the Program Committee. After an accelerated re-evaluation, all four papers were accepted and are included in the program. All submissions were subject to academic peer review by at least three reviewers. The selection criteria included accuracy and originality of ideas, clarity and significance of results, possible implementability, and quality of presentation. The reviewing and selection of the papers was the responsibility of the TABLEAUX 2017 Program Committee, which consisted of 35 members from 18 countries in America, Asia, Europe, and Oceania. In addition, 18 external reviewers were consulted.

TABLEAUX 2017 offered an interesting and diverse program, which, in addition to the technical papers, included six invited talks by leading experts: Carlos Areces on Tableau Calculus for Hybrid Xpath with Data, Wolfgang Bibel on A Vision for Automated Deduction Rooted in the Connection Method, Reiner Hähnle on Locally Abstract, Globally Concrete Semantics of Concurrent Programming Languages, Katalin Bimbó on The Perimeter of Decidability (with Sequent Calculi on the Inside), Jasmin Blanchette on Foundational (Co)Datatypes and (Co)Recursion for Higher-Order Logic, and Cezary Kaliszyk on Automating Formalization by Statistical and Semantic Parsing of Mathematics. The invited talks of Katalin Bimbó, Jasmin Blanchette, and Cezary Kaliszyk were joint with FroCoS and ITP. FroCoS contributed with two invited talks given by Cesare Tinelli and Renata Wassermann. Moa Johansson and Leonardo de Moura gave the invited talks for ITP. There was a shared poster session with FroCoS and ITP for the presentation of work in progress. Fifteen abstracts were accepted for presentation as short talks and posters.

This year marks the 25th anniversary of the TABLEAUX conference, a series of meetings which started with a workshop on Theorem Proving with Analytic Tableaux and Related Methods held in Lautenbach, Germany, in March 1992. Since then it has been organized on an annual basis; in 2001, 2004, 2006, 2008, 2010, 2012, 2014, 2016 as a constituent of IJCAR. The invited talks of Wolfgang Bibel and Reiner Hähnle were part of a special session celebrating the achievements of TABLEAUX. Posters, proceedings, pictures, and memorabilia of past editions, together with testimonies of several of chairs of previous TABLEAUX conferences, were displayed in an exhibition held during TABLEAUX 2017.

This year's Best Paper Award was presented to Ori Lahav and Yoni Zohar for their paper Cut-Admissibility as a Corollary of the Subformula Property. All three reviews highlighted the novelty and fundamental importance of the results, and the Program Committee voted unanimously to give the award to this paper. The TABLEAUX Best Paper Award was established as a permanent initiative of TABLEAUX in 2015.

There are a lot of people we need to thank. We thank all authors who submitted papers and all participants of the conference for their contributions and presentations. We are grateful to the invited speakers for their participation and invited lectures as well as for contributing papers to the proceedings, and we thank the tutorial presenters and workshop organizers. We thank everyone who contributed to the celebration and exhibition commemorating 25 years of TABLEAUX. We are extremely grateful to the Program Committee and the additional reviewers for their assistance and hard work in ensuring a high-quality program. For advice and support, we thank the members of the TABLEAUX Steering Committee. Special thanks must go to the program chairs of FroCoS, Clare Dixon and Marcelo Finger, and the program chairs of ITP, César Muñoz and Mauricio Ayala-Rincón, for the friendly cooperation in coordinating the programs and joint sessions.

It is our pleasure to acknowledge and thank a number of organizations for supporting the conference. The Association for Automated Reasoning (AAR), the European Association for Computer Science Logic (EACSL), and the Association for Symbolic Logic (ASL) provided scientific support. We received financial support from CNPq (ARC 03/2016), CAPES (PAEP 03/2017), and FAP-DF (02/2017). We are also very grateful to the European Association for Artificial Intelligence (EurAI) for sponsoring the talks of Wolfgang Bibel and Reiner Hähnle. Special thanks go to everyone in the Departments of Computer Science (CIC) and Mathematics (MAT) at the Universidade de Brasília (UnB) and the Departments of Informatics and Applied Mathematics (DIMAp) and Mathematics (DMAT) at the Universidade Federal do Rio Grande do Norte (UFRN), who contributed to the organization of the conference. Also, we greatly appreciate Springer's continuing support in publishing the proceedings.

Last but not least, we are indebted to Daniele Nantes, Elaine Pimentel, and João Marcos for their tremendous effort in organizing TABLEAUX, FroCoS, ITP, and all co-located events. Their support was essential for the success of the conferences, and making our lives as chairs much easier.

July 2017   Cláudia Nalon
                                                                             Renate A. Schmidt

Organization

TABLEAUX 2017 was organized by the Departments of Computer Science (CIC) and Mathematics (MAT) at the Universidade de Brasília (UnB) and by the Departments of Informatics and Applied Mathematics (DIMAp) and Mathematics (DMAT) at the Universidade Federal do Rio Grande do Norte (UFRN).

Conference Chair

Cláudia Nalon   Universidade de Brasília, Brazil

Program Chairs

Renate A. Schmidt   The University of Manchester, UK
Cláudia Nalon   Universidade de Brasília, Brazil

Poster Session Chairs

Elaine Pimentel   Universidade Federal do Rio Grande do Norte, Brazil
Daniele Nantes Sobrinho   Universidade de Brasília, Brazil

Organizing Committee

Cláudia Nalon   Universidade de Brasília, Brazil
Daniele Nantes Sobrinho   Universidade de Brasília, Brazil
Elaine Pimentel   Universidade Federal do Rio Grande do Norte, Brazil
João Marcos   Universidade Federal do Rio Grande do Norte, Brazil

Steering Committee

Agata Ciabattoni   Technische Universität Wien, Austria
Martin Giese   Universitetet i Oslo, Norway
Neil V. Murray   State University of NY at Albany, USA
Cláudia Nalon (Ex-officio)   University of Brasília, Brazil
Hans de Nivelle   University of Wrocław, Poland
Nicola Olivetti (Ex-officio)   Aix-Marseille Université, LSIS, France
Jens Otten (President)   Universitetet i Oslo, Norway
Renate A. Schmidt   The University of Manchester, UK

Program Committee

Peter Baumgartner   Data61/CSIRO, Australia
Maria Paola Bonacina   Università degli Studi di Verona, Italy

Laura Bozzelli	Universidad Politécnica de Madrid, Spain
Torben Braüner	Roskilde University, Denmark
Serenella Cerrito	Ibisc, Université d'Evry Val d'Essonne, France
Agata Ciabattoni	Technische Universität Wien, Austria
Clare Dixon	University of Liverpool, UK
Pascal Fontaine	LORIA, Inria, Université de Lorraine, France
Didier Galmiche	LORIA, Université de Lorraine, France
Martin Giese	Universitetet i Oslo, Norway
Laura Giordano	DISIT, Università del Piemonte Orientale, Italy
Rajeev Goré	The Australian National University, Australia
Volker Haarslev	Concordia University, Canada
George Metcalfe	Universität Bern, Switzerland
Angelo Montanari	Università degli Studi di Udine, Italy
Barbara Morawska	Ahmedabad University, India
Boris Motik	University of Oxford, UK
Leonardo de Moura	Microsoft Research, USA
Neil V. Murray	State University of NY at Albany, USA
Linh Anh Nguyen	Uniwersytet Warszawski, Poland
Hans de Nivelle	Uniwersytet Wrocławski, Poland
Nicola Olivetti	LSIS, Aix-Marseille Université, France
Jens Otten	Universitetet i Oslo, Norway
Valeria de Paiva	Nuance Communications, USA
Nicolas Peltier	CNRS, Laboratoire d'Informatique de Grenoble, France
Elaine Pimentel	Universidade Federal do Rio Grande do Norte, Brazil
Giselle Reis	Carnegie Mellon University in Qatar
Philipp Rümmer	Uppsala Universitet, Sweden
Katsuhiko Sano	Hokkaido University, Japan
Cesare Tinelli	The University of Iowa, USA
Alwen Tiu	Nanyang Technological University, Singapore
David Toman	University of Waterloo, Canada
Josef Urban	Czech Technical University in Prague, Czech Republic

Additional Reviewers

James Brotherston	Daniel Méry	Dmitriy Traytel
Chad Brown	Marianna	Irene Lobo Valbuena
Harley Eades III	Nicolosi-Asmundo	Laurent Vigneron
Nicola Gigante	Carlos Olarte	Aleksandar Zeljić
Ullrich Hustadt	Zixi Quan	
Nikoo Karahroodi	Revantha Ramanayake	
Dominique	Pietro Sala	
Larchey-Wendling	Loredana Sorrentino	

Sponsors of the 25th Anniversary Exhibition

Peter Baumgartner
David Basin
Krysia Broda
Kai Brünnler
Marta Cialdea Mayer
Roy Dyckhoff
Uwe Egly
Christian Fermüller
Bertram Fronhöfer
Ullrich Furbach
Didier Galmiche
Martin Giese
Reiner Hähnle

Dominique Larchey-Wendling
George Metcalfe
Ugo Moscato
Daniele Mundici
Neil V. Murray
Mario Ornaghi
Fiora Pirri
Joachim Posegga
Steve Reeves
Peter H. Schmitt
Harrie de Swart
Arild Waaler

Sponsoring Institutions

Association for Automated Reasoning (AAR)
European Association for Computer Science Logic (EACSL)
Association for Symbolic Logic (ASL)
European Association for Artificial Intelligence (EurAI)
National Council for Scientific and Technological Development (CNPq)
Coordination for the Improvement of Higher Education Personnel (CAPES)
Federal District Research Foundation (FAP-DF)

Contents

Transitive Closure and Cyclic Proofs

Formalization and Complexity

Invited Papers

A Vision for Automated Deduction Rooted in the Connection Method

Wolfgang Bibel[✉]

Darmstadt University of Technology, Darmstadt, Germany
bibel@gmx.net

Abstract. The paper presents an informal overview of the Connection Method in Automated Deduction. In particular, it points out its unique advantage over competing methods which consists in its formula-orientedness. Among the consequences of this unique feature are three striking advantages, viz. uniformity (over many logics), performance (due to its extreme compactness and goal-orientedness, evidenced by the lean-CoP family of provers), and a global view over the proof process (enabling a higher-level guidance of the proof search). These aspects are discussed on the basis of the extensive work accumulated in the literature about this proof method. Along this line of research we envisage a bright future for the field and point out promising directions for future research.

Keywords: Automated deduction · Automated theorem proving · Connection method · leanCoP · Logic · Learning

1 Introduction

This year we are celebrating a quarter of a century enriched by TABLEAUX conferences. It is a great honour for the author to be invited for the present contribution to this anniversary.

This conference series was born in Germany a year after the Deutsche Forschungsgemeinschaft (German Research Council) agreed to fund a major national research programme on Automated Deduction (AD) for a period of six years, initiated and coordinated by the present author. My pertinent activities might well have furthered the birth of this new conference series, although I was not directly and personally involved in the TABLEAUX initiative. In consequence, the history of this series will play merely a marginal role in the following (see [30,35]).

Rather I would like for the TABLEAUX community to bring to bear my expertise in AD and Logic which by now has been accumulated in more than half a century. In particular, I want to share my views of our field taken from some distance, both looking back and forth, and thereby envision a promising future development of our field.

In the mid-seventies of the last century Peter Andrews and the author independently developed a new approach to AD (see eg. [2,3],[12, Formula 6.5, p. 24,

© Springer International Publishing AG 2017
R.A. Schmidt and C. Nalon (Eds.): TABLEAUX 2017, LNAI 10501, pp. 3–21, 2017.
DOI: 10.1007/978-3-319-66902-1_1

and Appendix], [18,19],[10, eg. p. 325, 353]). He characterized it by the term *mating* while I eventually introduced the term *Connection Method* (CM) for it. It took quite a long time until the community began to take a closer notice of the advantages of this approach, which to Peter and me have seemed so obvious. I understood this invitation also as an opportunity to remind us of the virtues of this method deserving a more prominent role in a prospering future AD.

As this conference series has derived its name from a different AD method, viz. tableaux, it is a natural question how the CM actually fits under its umbrella. Let us answer this question by looking somewhat deeper into the history of our field.

Among the logicians in the early twentieth century Jacques Herbrand was undoubtedly the first who focussed on ways for *finding* proofs of formulas in first-order logic (fol) [37]. His work therefore became the theoretical basis for AD systems which I would therefore term Herbrand-systems, or simply *H-systems*. Resolution systems are of this category. The initial successes of resolution in the mid-sixties of the last century provided this approach with a big push towards its popularity, supported further by the simplicity of acquiring a basic understanding of resolution.

Shortly after Herbrand it was Gerhard Gentzen who published his formal fol systems which up to this day are judged to be the most adequate systems for modeling human mathematical reasoning [32]. On this theoretical basis a number of researchers in AD took an alternative route towards developing AD systems which I therefore would term Gentzen-systems, or simply *G-systems*. Tableaux systems are G-systems in this sense as is the first proof system developed by the author in 1970 [11]. In fact, it turns out that the CM is just an extremely compressed form of the tableaux method [23], thus answering our question.

In terms of popularity H-systems despite their known disadvantages continued to dominate G-systems for several decades. This can be seen in an analysis of the contributions to the leading AD conference series CADE. Frustrated by the bias in acceptance rates in CADE in favor of H-systems papers, G-systems researchers around 1991 started to think about a workshop specialized on the most popular G-systems, viz. tableaux. This might be taken as a crude historic outline of how and why the TABLEAUX series got started in 1992. By now our field has become so rich that there is room enough for several AD conferences. While they all continue to preserve their specific characteristics, they in these days are all open for either G-systems or H-systems among others and indeed are collocated within IJCAR every second year.

Among all approaches to AD the CM is unique in that it performs the proof search in terms of the structural features of the very formula which is to be proved rather than destroying this original structure in one way or another. This *formula-orientedness* involves on the one hand connections, ie. unordered pairs of certain literal occurrences in the formula, which provide the basis for the propositional part of the search. On the other hand the selection of a connection for a possible proof depends upon a unificational part applied to connections which takes into account the structural occurrences of the logical junctors making up the formula. While the basic propositional part based on connections is identical for a wide variety of logics, it is the unificational part which differs from one logic to the other. While the unificational part can be solved by fast algorithms for many logics, it is the propositional part which, in dependence of the unificational part of course, still requires intensive efforts for achieving further progress, and any such progress can be applied to all logics. Due to the strict *goal-orientedness* during the *connection-driven* proof search, both suggested by the formula-orientedness, systems based on the CM exhibit a comparatively strong performance.

It is the uniformity of the proof search covering many logics and the resulting impressive performance which eventually raised the interest of the AD community in the CM, because there is no competing method covering many logics with the same powerful proof technique in a uniform way. Both, the *uniformity* and the *performance* of CM-based proof systems are consequences of the unique formula-orientedness as just indicated. There is a third, yet hardly exploited major advantage of the CM over the competitive AD methods. Namely, the formula-orientedness enables the proof process to take a *global* view over the object of analysis, an aspect which still offers a great potential for being tapped and exploited in our future research. It is the main purpose of the present paper to outline some of the possibilities in this direction.

In detail the paper is organized in the following way. The subsequent Sect. 2 introduces in an illustrative way the CM. There are by now so many excellent sources for the formal details of the CM that here we may prefer a high-level view of the features and virtues of this particular approach to AD. This is followed by Sect. 3 briefly reviewing CM-based connection calculi and their implementations. They impressively demonstrate the CM's unique features of uniformity and performance through a large family of uniformly and powerful provers. Section 4 demonstrates the great potential of taking advantage of meta-level features in proof search which could be realized on top of the CM due to its global view of the search for proofs. Thereby we distinguish between recursive, intrinsically and extrinsically complex features in the connection structure of problem classes and suggest high-level approaches for each of these. In particular, we favor in this context the use of learning techniques (such as deep learning which recently led to spectacular successes in other applications). In Sect. 5 we outline in more detail the relationship between the CM and tableaux, and in consequence point out CM's striking advantage. Similarly, we argue why the CM is more adequate for achieving further progress than H-systems like resolution. The final Sect. 6 draws some conclusions out of these expositions envisioning a bright future for AD on their basis.

2 Recollection of the Connection Method

Before entering into any discussion on future research lines for Automated Deduction (AD) we want to make sure that the reader has an understanding of the Connection Method (CM) and its basic features. This is important since the views on AD may differ considerably depending on which basic proof method one bears in mind. The present section thus introduces in an illustrative way the approach to AD taken by the CM. For the underlying theoretical basis, ie. precise definitions, theorems and algorithms, the reader is referred to the literature (eg. [19, 20, 23]).

At this point of the paper we take it as understood that, firstly, the usual language of logic is useful for representing in a formal way a variety of problems. Secondly, we take it for granted here that many problems may suitably be formulated in such a way that their solutions consist in proving the validity of the representing logical formulas. We will briefly discuss these assumptions in Sect. 6.

So assume we are given – to begin with say – a simple formula in first-order logic (fol), viz. $\exists a(Pa \lor \neg\exists x\, Qx) \to \exists y\, Py \lor \forall b\, \neg Qfb$, or shortly F_1. In order to determine whether or not the formula is valid we may think of a connection calculus which tries to find a proof by locating in the formula a spanning and unifiable set of connections. Since the formula is simple enough it turns out that the two obvious connections are both spanning and unifiable establishing the connection proof as displayed in Fig. 1.

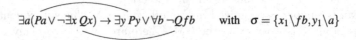

$$\exists a(Pa \lor \neg\exists x\, Qx) \to \exists y\, Py \lor \forall b\, \neg Qfb \qquad \text{with} \quad \sigma = \{x_1 \backslash fb, y_1 \backslash a\}$$

Fig. 1. The connection proof for F_1.

In order for the reader to grasp the gist of what is going on in the search for such a proof let us add a few comments. First of all, our formulas are written in a standard fol language. In order to minimize parentheses we follow the widely used order of precedence among the logical operators (defined eg. in the literature cited above) and in addition we write eg. Qfb instead of the cumbersome $Q(f(b))$. The connection prover in some algorithmic way analyzes the structure of the formula in exactly the form as presented focusing on connections in it. Once it has found a spanning and unifiable set of such connections it reports success.

It is exclusively for our human understanding that usually the details of the underlying algorithmic search are explained by way of a simplified and more intuitive representation of the information coded in such a formula. This so-called *matrix representation* is obtained by dispensing of quantifiers altogether in a standard way, transforming the resulting formula into one containing only literals, conjunctions, and disjunctions (by applying basic laws from propositional logic), and displaying disjunctions horizontally and conjunctions vertically. Our formula in the resulting representation along with its connection proof in matrix representation looks as displayed in Fig. 2.

In the matrix representation the notion of connections and the spanning property can nicely be illustrated. A *path* through such a matrix can be regarded as a walk through it strictly from left to right, thereby collecting exactly one literal

$$\left[\left[\begin{array}{c}\neg Pa\\ Qx\end{array}\right]\ [Py]\ [\neg Qfb]\right]\qquad \sigma=\{x_1\backslash fb, y_1\backslash a\}$$

Fig. 2. The connection proof from Fig. 1 in matrix representation.

from each column. If this is done for our example matrix, we see that it has exactly two different paths, $\{\neg Pa, Py, \neg Qfb\}$ and $\{Qx, Py, \neg Qfb\}$. (Formally, a path may be defined as an unordered set of occurrences in the formula or in the matrix.) An unordered pair of elements in a path through such a matrix with identical predicate symbols, one negated the other unnegated, is called a *connection*. (If paths are defined as occurrences the same applies to connections.) Connections are depicted the way illustrated in our examples in either representation. As already mentioned, our matrix features exactly two connections, viz. $\{\neg Pa, Py\}$ and $\{Qx, \neg Qfb\}$. If each path through a matrix contains at least one connection from a set U of connections, U is called *spanning* for the matrix, which thus is the case for the set consisting of the two displayed connections in each of the two figures. A connection is called *complementary* if its literals are identical up to the negation sign. If the displayed substitution is applied to our two connections they turn out to become complementary. It is exactly these two properties, spanning and complementary, which establish the validity of a connection proof. Thus the matrix and with it the formula from which it is derived both turn out to be valid.

Obviously, these explanations of the basic CM features are understood much more easily with the matrix representation than with the linear formula representation in mind. This psychological aspect is however completely irrelevant for a realization in the machine. The notions of paths through a formula and of connections can of course be defined also directly for formulas such as F_1 (as done eg. in [23]), so that the search for a spanning and unifiable set of connections can be carried out as well and as efficiently by the machine directly in such a formula and without any reference to matrices and such, as illustrated in Fig. 1. In the following we will therefore restrict ourselves to exactly this view on the CM as a method able to analyze a given formula in its standard representation and without any preparatory manipulation to it.

This lack of any manipulation to the given formula applies to the proof process as well. This process accumulates additional information about the formula's structure but leaves the formula itself as the object of the analysis completely intact during the entire process. It is this *formula-orientedness*, already mentioned in the Introduction, which makes the CM unique among all its competitors. As we will discuss in Sect. 5 this allows a much more focussed search than in competitive methods.

Due to the very nature of logic, connection proofs may require multiple instances of connections. Let us illustrate this feature with the formula $N0 \wedge \forall x(Nx \rightarrow Nfx) \rightarrow Nff0$, shortly F_2, for which Fig. 3 shows a connection proof. As is indicated with the indices 1 and 2 attached to the ends of the three connections, two instances of the universally quantified rule are required to establish the proof. But note that despite this requirement the object of the analysis, ie. the given formula, is still not changed in any way since these instances are simply coded as indices attached to the connections in the additional information accumulated by the proof search. For the formal details the reader again is referred to the literature (eg. [23]).

$$N0 \wedge \forall x(Nx \to Nfx) \to Nff0 \quad \text{with} \quad \sigma = \{x_1 \backslash 0, x_2 \backslash f0\}$$

Fig. 3. The connection proof for formula F_2.

This example also illustrates the reason why we have attached indices to the variables occurring in the substitutions of all three figures. In the first two the index was just 1 since only a single instance was needed for the proofs therein. We further remark that logically the instances are generated by the quantifiers, more precisely by existential quantifiers with polarity 0 or by universal quantifiers with polarity 1. In the notational convention used in this paper (as in the author's earlier publications) the variables bound by these types of quantifiers are denoted by $x, y, \ldots$ while those bound by the remaining types of quantifiers are denoted by $a, b, \ldots$.

Already this simple example opens an initially disquieting perspective for the proof search requirements. This is because in principle there is no limit on the number of instances of the occurring rule which might be required to achieve the proof thus opening up an unlimited search space already for this simple example. Note that this is an intrinsic feature of fol, not one of the CM. One strategy for coping with this challenge consists in iteratively increasing the number of instances taken into account in the proof search. Another one consists in taking global structures of sets of connections into account and it is this one which serves particularly well in the present case.

Namely assume that the conclusion of the formula reads Nf^n0 (or $Nf \ldots f0$ or Nn for that matter) with $n \geq 1$ then n instances of the rule and $n-1$ instances of the lower connection would be needed for the proof of the formula, named $F_2(n)$, as illustrated in Fig. 4. The $n-1$ lower connections in this proof may be regarded as a connection scheme, say $S(n)$, rather than a set of independent connections. The scheme inherently goes along with the underlying universally quantified premise. This view suggested by the rule in the premise reduces the search space drastically in general. In the example it eliminates search completely since the two upper connections along with $S(n)$, which can be regarded as a single macro connection, establish the proof for all n. In order to appreciate the drastic reduction note that the n instances of the rule without the scheme view would require considering some n^2 unifiable connections in the proof search rather than just three.

$$N0 \wedge \forall x(Nx \rightarrow Nfx) \rightarrow Nf^n 0 \quad \sigma = \{x_1 \backslash 0, \; x_{i+1} \backslash fx_i, i = 1,\ldots,n-1\}$$

Fig. 4. The connection proof for formula $F_2(n)$.

This example teaches us a first important lesson for AD. In contrast to Mathematics where the ellipsis notation "$\ldots$" plays a fundamental role as a meta-language feature, AD so far has failed completely to integrate into proofs such meta-language features for describing crucial meaning from a global perspective. The language describing connection proofs naturally suggests such meta-language constructs like the one just illustrated with $F_2(n)$ leading to drastic reductions of the search space.

How can our principle of avoiding any preparatory manipulation to the given formula cope with quantifiers in the context of unification in general? Consider the formula $\exists x \forall a(Qax \rightarrow Qxa)$ which for arbitrary Q of course is not valid, although the obvious connection is spanning. Usually, the formula is transformed into Skolem normal form which introduces a Skolem function fx replacing a, so that unification obviously fails. The same can be achieved by introducing an ordering relation $<$ on the quantified variables, $x < a$ in the case of the present example, reflecting the relative occurrence of the quantifiers within the formula, ie. quantifier $\exists x$ dominates quantifier $\forall a$ in the formula. This by now well-known technique has been introduced in [19, Sect. 4.8]. Unification $\{x \backslash a\}$ implies $a < x$, reflecting the well-known Eigenvariable condition in tableaux or Gentzen-type formal systems, and succeeds if it does not lead to cycles. Hence unification does not succeed in this example since the attempted unification obviously leads to the cycle $x < a < x$.

This *ordering approach* to unification as an alternative to skolemization has recently become attractive in the context of combining deduction with learning. Namely, *"techniques like skolemization can destroy some explicit similarities useful for learning"* [59], a topic further discussed in Sect. 4.

The ordering approach may involve also occurrences of junctors like $\wedge$. One may think of attaching to such an occurrence sort of a variable in analogy with those attached to quantifiers (or to modal operators as mentioned below). Traditionally, these variables are denoted by attaching indices to the junctor like in $\wedge_1$.

$$\forall b(\forall a \exists z(\exists x\, Paxz \wedge_1 \exists y\, Pbyz) \vee \forall c \exists u\, \neg Puuc \wedge_2 \forall d \exists v\, \neg Pvbd)$$

$$\wedge_2 <\cdot z, \; \wedge_1 <\cdot u \text{ and } \wedge_1 <\cdot v$$
$$\sigma = \{x \backslash a, x' \backslash b, y \backslash a, y' \backslash b, z \backslash c, z' \backslash d, u \backslash a, u' \backslash b, v \backslash a, v' \backslash b\}$$

Fig. 5. The connection proof for F_3.

With this additional feature we may realize a form of splitting by need as illustrated with formula F_3 in Fig. 5 (presented first in [12, Appendix, p.16]). Namely, each of its four variables, due to the displayed occurrence relation generated by need, may adopt two different values resulting in a non-cyclic unification and thus in a remarkably straightforward proof of the formula. Unfortunately, the details of this generalization are somewhat involved (see [19, Sect. 4.10] and [8,36]).

The CM has proved to provide an adequate approach to proving formulas in many logics other than fol. For example, the following proof illustrates its application to modal logic.

$$\overbrace{\Box\,man(Plato) \;\rightarrow\; \Diamond\,man(Plato)}$$

Again the proof is established by a spanning and unifiable set of connections. The unificational part in modal logic involves, in addition to that of the occurring quantified variables (none in the simple example), the unification of so-called prefixes. These code the occurrences of the modal operators in relation to all other junctors (propositional, quantifiers, modal operators) within the formula. In building these prefixes the modal operators are formally treated like quantifiers and artificially generated prefix variables and prefix constants are attached to them (like those attached to the junctors above). The resulting prefixes (ie. strings of prefix variables and prefix constants) attached to the connected literals need to be unified similarly as the terms in the literals. Otherwise everything works as in fol. Different modal logics just differ in the specifics of the prefix unification (see [51,52,54] for details and [56] for an overview of the different calculi and systems).

This prefix unification technique, as realized in current systems like Mlean-CoP, ileanCoP, nanoCoP-M and nanoCoP-i, involves a kind of skolemization similar to that in classical fol. Alternatively, this could be realized by the ordering approach to unification through an appropriate extension of the ordering relation $<$ introduced above to include the occurrences of the modal operators in addition to those of the classical logical junctors. This way the unificational part of proofs would be handled in a completely uniform process. But no one sofar has worked out this more elegant approach in detail.

Further logics which have been studied under the CM include intuitionistic, linear, transition, description, paraconsistent, and even higher-order logic (see [7,22,29,31,43–45,47] and [19, Sect. 5.6] as well as further literature on higher-order logic listed further below). In order to illustrate a connection proof in higher-order logic (hol), assume that equality is defined by way of the Leibniz characterization. The commutativity of equality can then be stated as the following formula.

$$\forall ab\forall P\exists X[\overbrace{(Xa \rightarrow Xb)} \rightarrow \underbrace{(Pb \rightarrow Pa)}]$$

The picture at the same time shows part of the formula's connection proof which, in addition, requires the underlying substitution $\sigma = \{X\backslash\lambda z\neg Pz\}$. This shows that the substitution affects even the connection structure which complicates matters substantially, due to the inherent nature of hol.

So we see that the CM spans a wide variety of logics in a completely uniform way. What is needed for a proof in any of these logics is a spanning set of connections along with some unification rendering the connection set complementary whereby the specifics of the latter differs from one logic to the other.

3   Connection Calculi and Their Implementations

In the previous section we have illustrated the basic features of the connection method (CM) for proving formulas in various logics. These illustrations did not yet indicate how proofs are actually found. In the present section we therefore briefly discuss connection calculi, the adequate tools for proof search.

As we have demonstrated connection proofs consist of two components, viz. a set of connections and a unificational part. As is well-known the latter enjoys fast solutions and will more or less be taken for granted in what follows. There are exceptions to this statement because, for instance, higher-order unification is highly complex. Therefore we exclude higher-order logic (hol) from our discussions and refer to the pertinent literature in this regard [4–7,24,25,42]. So, we are left with the main task of identifying spanning sets of connections in formulas (along with the necessary substitutions).

This task is a truly hard and challenging one since in more complex problems the spanning set might be a rather small subset picked out of a sea of connections, so that we are in a situation like searching for the needle in a haystack. Decades of AD research have accumulated insights into the features of this task which have led to a number of quite powerful connection calculi. These guarantee the success of the search in case of valid formulas, unless the time-limit cuts off the search, ie. they are sound and complete.

Since the area of connection calculi is a rather wide one, we restrict ourselves here to a few comments. First of all, if a problem is coded into a logical formula, this formula may naturally be separated into the core problem description D and the prerequisites or assumptions A from which D logically follows. Therefore any connection-driven search should start with connections involving literals in D in order to focus it on the given problem. Second, if at any stage the search has selected a number of connections, say U, then for any clause C connected by one of these connections, say $c \in U$, involving some literal $L \in C$, it holds that each other literal in C needs to be contained in some connection in the final connection set, if this is to involve c for establishing the proof.

Already these two principles lead to the goal-orientedness mentioned in the Introduction and give rise to a reasonably performing connection calculus. One of its basic operations, called extension, may be illustrated with formula $F_2(n)$ and its proof shown in Fig. 3. There the core problem D is $Nff0$ so that a proof attempt would look for a connection involving this literal and would identify the single possible one shown in the picture. The connected literal Nfx shares the clause with literal Nx so that the second principle would bring us to look for a connection involving this literal and would identify two possible ones shown in the picture, of which only the lower one turns out to be unifiable, thereby activating a second instance of the clause. Note that by generating the proof in a recursive way as we do here, the sequence of indices needs to be reversed in comparison with the inductive way shown in the picture, so that 1 and 2 in the picture would have to be exchanged. The second instance of the clause would, again due to the second principle, lead us to look for a connection involving the literal Nx. Among the again two alternatives the one with $N0$ would complete the proof.

As this simple example already demonstrates, backtracking may be required if the wrong choice among alternatives had been taken. The basic algorithm, additionally involving an operation called reduction, can be enhanced considerably by the technique of *restricted backtracking* [49]. The resulting connection calculus for fol was developed and implemented in high-level PROLOG by Jens Otten. The program, called leanCoP, although comprising only a few PROLOG clauses, shows a performance comparable to competitive theorem provers consisting of hundreds of thousands of lines of code (loc) [48,55]. Due to its high-level code its correctness in contrast to the large systems can be and has been verified which we regard as an important issue for proof systems [56]. leanCoP, in contrast to our examples shown in the previous section, operates on formulas in clause form. A variant of leanCoP has been realized as an OCaml version [41].

A crucial step towards a connection calculus envisioned in the previous section, namely one operating on standard fol formulas, has been made again by Otten. He developed a connection calculus for skolemized, but non-clausal fol formulas and implemented it in the style of leanCoP as a system called nanoCoP [50,53] showing again a comparatively impressive performance. There is only a relatively small step left from nanoCoP to a system envisaged in the previous section. The step consists of allowing all standard logical operators including, for instance, "$\rightarrow$" as well as replacing the standard unification by that described in the previous section, both amounting to relatively simple changes to the system. From a scientific point of view these changes are of a cosmetic nature and of minor urgency to be worked out. Under this view the illustration of the CM as done in the previous section therefore reflects the state of the art as achieved by now — up to the minor extra feature just described.

In the Introduction we pointed out the two major consequences of the formula-orientedness of the CM which are uniformity and performance. The CM's unique uniformity bears its fruits in porting the proof-search technology developed in one logic into other logics. This way Jens Otten has ported the fol technologies built into leanCoP and nanoCoP to many other logics resulting in systems such as ileanCoP, MleanCoP, nanoCoP-i and nanoCoP-M for a variety of logics, thus forming a large family of uniformly designed and powerful provers [48,51,52,54]. The CM is the unique and unrivalled proof-method in AD which features such a wide variety of systems, many of which are outperforming any of its competitors.

4   The Unexploited Potential of the CM

Except for a few attempts most AD systems operate on the lowest logical level, executing some logical rules in a relatively blind way. In contrast, mathematical reasoning is done on a much higher conceptual level. I am convinced that AD systems will not be able to compete with human mathematical reasoning unless they incorporate such higher-level features. It is the CM's formula-orientedness explained in Sect. 2 which lends itself to such a form of higher-level reasoning in a natural way. Some of the possibilities in this direction will be discussed in the present section.

Recall the connection proof for formula $F_2(n)$ in Fig. 4. Its antecedent part will structurally be the same for any n in the conclusion. Hence we could abbreviate the entire antecedent part simply by Nf^z0 so that for a given conclusion Nf^n0 just a single connection along with sort of a meta-unification between z and n would be required thus reducing the search space for a spanning set of connections drastically. Note that inductive (or recursive) features abound in reasoning so that the same *abbreviation* technique would apply to numerous other examples and thus, if integrated, would enhance existing provers. Although this technique has already been introduced in the book [19, Sect. 5.5] and formally worked out in [26] and [15, Sect. 2.10] under the term *connection structure calculi* I am not aware of any system which would take advantage of such an obvious structural feature on the meta-level of proof search although it would result in a straightforward improvement.

The recursive connection structure in $F_2(n)$ is what in [13] was called a *recursive cycle* whereby cycles are sets of connections which taken as a sequence start with a literal in one clause and end up in the same clause, as do the $n - 1$ connections in the middle of Fig. 4. In general cycles may be much more complicated than the one in $F_2(n)$. For example, consider the following formula originally studied by Łukasiewicz.

$$Pi(i(ixy, z), i(izx, iux)) \land (Pv \land Pivw \to Pw) \to Pi(iab, i(ibc, iac))$$

The function symbol i represents logical implication, ie. iab codes $a \to b$, so that the rule in the antecedent expresses modus ponens. The formula has five connections each of which may be required in several instances for the proof. Although there is a known 29-step proof for the formula involving a few dozens of instances of those five connections, a system like OTTER, operating on the lowest proof search level determined by resolution, needed to generate a gigantic number of 6.5 million clauses in order to eventually discover some proof.[1] Only a more intelligent analysis of the connection structure made up by the five original connections would lead us more directly to a proof as proposed already in [14] and further pursued in [16].

---

[1] Josef Urban was so kind to run the formula with several state-of-the-art provers. E processes still 1.2 million clauses which can be reduced to 36.1 thousand by automatically learned strategies (with BliStr [39]), while Prover9 succeeds already with 3.3 thousand clauses.

For the present formula such an analysis would have to take into account the effect of each of these connections thereby measuring the change in the difference between the axiom literal and the goal literal. For instance, one could in a breadth-first iteratively deepening search, starting from the goal literal, calculate all different initial fragments of an attempted connection proof and, before deepening the search limit, strategically select out of all combinations those for further exploration which came closest to the axiom literal according to such a difference measure. Given that we know of a 29-step proof we could even limit the index to 29 and would be guaranteed to find a proof. But even if we would not know in advance such a limit, an iterative deepening of such a limit on the index would guarantee success, as already proposed in 1970 [11]. Instead of the index one could use the size of the generated terms in the resulting substitution for the same purpose and again apply iterative deepening. None of these alternatives, which in the context of the CM are obvious ones, have been used, to the best of the author's knowledge. Rather all existing provers continue to blindly search for a proof of this and similar formulas without any such considerations at a higher *mathematical* level above the level of clauses, resolvents, extensions or whatever.

AD practitioners typically argue that these high-level strategies are too time-consuming in comparison with the straightforward execution of brute-force operations. They overlook that the proofs of many hard theorems may never be found automatically except with such sophisticated high-level approaches. An example like the present one by Łukasiewicz may guide the search for such sophisticated strategies.

This Łukasiewicz formula is an extreme example of an *intrinsically complex* theorem. At the other extreme there are formulas which are *extrinsically complex* because they involve large theories and hence are huge in terms of size and number of connections. Think, for example, of a theorem F_4 to be proved in the context of a mathematical theory like linear algebra. This means that we are actually faced with the task of proving $F_5 \rightarrow F_4$ where F_5 combines the body of knowledge consisting of axioms, theorems and lemmas known for linear algebra. This might be a very large formula indeed since there are many theorems in linear algebra. A mathematician would immediately have a feeling for what kind of known theorems might apply in the proof, given F_4. Translated into CM-terms this means that some connections would rate much higher than others as to their usefulness for the required proof. In other words, the set of available connections in $F_5 \rightarrow F_4$ bears with it a logical/mathematical semantics that is tapped by mathematicians in their work. In AD the underlying task has been termed *premise selection* (or relevance filtering) but should rather be considered as *connection selection* in order to account for the finer grain of this task. So as in the case of intrinsically complex examples strategies at the higher *mathematical* level seem highly needed.

These are just some examples illustrating the need for an analysis of the structures on the higher mathematical level of proof search to be integrated in advanced systems. Many other aspects of this kind have been studied by the author and his collaborators as well as by other AD researchers. Thereby a wealth of detailed enhancements with great potential for more powerful calculi and high-level strategies has been accumulated in the last three decades. In addition to the references mentioned sofar, some out of the many sources for such information are the books [17,19,38] and the chapter [21]. Integrating an appropriate selection of these improvements in detail into a single system of the kind like leanCoP amounts to an intellectual challenge still waiting to be attacked in a major scientific project and investment. A prerequisite for such an attack would be the growing conviction within the AD community with regard to the advantages of the CM. While the interest fortunately is growing, it has deplorably not yet reached the deserved degree of enthusiasm.

The recent spectacular successes in Artificial Intelligence in game-playing like GO and Poker have been made possible through the use of deep learning techniques. It is therefore a natural idea to engage such techniques also in the context of AD. However, it is a non-trivial question what kind of unlabeled data would be appropriate to learn feature representations for supporting proof search. In any rate it seems much more promising to apply learning techniques at the *mathematical* level, ie. to the formulas to be proved rather than to data such as clause sets in which crucial features are deeply buried.

The recent papers [1,28,40,46] along with earlier and similar work referenced in the ones just cited are first and encouraging steps into the application of learning techniques to AD. However, with two very recent exceptions most of these approaches are using standard learning techniques like naïve Bayes learning, kernel methods, various versions of distance-weighted k-nearest neighbor, random forests, some basic ensemble or clustering methods, hand-engineered learning features and similarity functions, etc. rather than deep learning. One of the exceptions uses convolutional neural networks (CNN) but only up to a shallow depth of three layers rather than the full power currently possible. Only some of them use leading frameworks like Caffe, CNTK, Tensorflow or Torch.

Probably even more important is the choice of the level where the learning applies which in most approaches so far is the low operational level of proof systems rather than the mathematical level, characterized by the formulas to be proved, at which human mathematicians excel in their learning. If we wish to enrich our systems with the meta-knowledge of the kind used by mathematicians the focus of deep learning algorithms should be on learning feature representations of this unstructured meta-knowledge on the mathematical level which would then guide the search for spanning sets of connections.

As a historical note I mention that connectionist approaches to deduction were initiated already around 1990 in the two major research groups founded by the author. In the group at the Technical University Munich which persisted there for nearly two decades after the author's move to UBC, Wolfgang Ertel, Christoph Goller, Johann Schumann and Christian Suttner engaged to develop connectionist learning techniques for deduction systems and and applied them to the prover SETHEO [27,34]. Goller for good reasons can be regarded as one of the early pioneers in deep learning. In my group at Darmstadt University of Technology it was Steffen Hölldobler whose Habilitation thesis, completed in 1993, was entitled *"Automated Inferencing and Connectionist Models"* (see eg. [9]).

Besides extracting meta-knowledge out of data by learning, our systems should as well lend themselves to interactive guidance provided by the expert which can only be done at the level familiar to the expert, hence again the mathematical level. *"Ease of use is the 'license to operate'"* [57]. Exactly for this reason mathematicians in their daily work will not take advantage of AD systems to a considerable extent unless these cooperate at the mathematical level familiar to them.

Thus we are still facing the great, but promising challenge to apply deep learning in its full power to AD as well as to enable human interaction at this mathematical level. Only the CM among the various proof methods offers the possibility to realize learning and interaction at this higher level of formalization in a direct way, hence opening extremely promising perspectives.

5   The CM in Relation with Other AD Methods

In [23, Sect. 2] the evolution of the CM out of Gentzen's fol system has been demonstrated in a rather compact form based on the results contained in [19]. This evolution consists in a stepwise extraction of all redundancy from the formal systems which leads to a radical compression to their very essence. Tableaux occur in this line of evolution at a rather early stage which is evidence for two important facts.

First, tableaux and CM share the same heritage for which reason they are both termed G-systems in Sect. 1. Any connection proof can be transformed into a tableaux proof in a straightforward way, and vice versa. The same applies to strategies and other features in proof search. So at first sight it seems that both are equally adequate for research in AD. But there is this second fact which definitely favors the CM over tableaux. Namely, tableaux carry with them a burden which is completely redundant and slows down performance substantially. It is exactly this redundancy which has been extracted in the evolution of the CM resulting in the strict formula-orientedness already pointed out in Sect. 1 and further explained in Sect. 2. Its consequence is an enhanced performance of CM systems over comparable tableaux systems which has been demonstrated in competitions in a spectacular way. Since we all aim at high performance, in comparison with tableaux without any doubt the CM is the technique of choice in AD.

Herbrand's great achievement was the reduction of fol proof search to the ground level modulo term unification. This reduction is not without a price, especially if it is exploited further by destroying even the propositional structure of the original formula as is done in any H-system like those based on resolution. The technical simplification resulting from this reduction helped a lot in getting experiments in AD running during AD's initial years. But these initial years are long gone. Eventually, the price for the simplification had to be payed which happened for instance when logics other than classical fol were taken into consideration for automation. For this purpose the relative occurrences of all junctors in the formulas became crucial for appropriate proof methods while resolution was built on the idea of their elimination. Hence the rebirth of G-systems which excel in this respect due to the uniformity pointed out in Sects. 1 through 3. But the price to be payed included also disadvantages like the comparatively huge search space resulting in excessive storage and operations requirements and thus impairing performance.

As already mentioned in Sect. 1 there is another aspect favoring G-systems, notably the CM, which is its global view. Recall the Łukasiewicz formula of the previous section with its five basic connections along with our meta-level and global considerations for finding a short proof. Contrast this strict focus on the formula's very structure, ie. the formula-orientedness, with the sea of 6.5 million clauses, which resulted in a run of Otter, in order to see the obvious weakness of resolution in comparison with the CM. This weakness is highlighted further by the fact that none of the high-level options discussed in the previous section in the context of the Łukasiewicz formula come to mind in the context of resolution. Further, the use of simplified formula representations like CNF, being a standard in H-systems, *"significantly influences also the performance of high-level heuristic guidance methods in large theories"* [59].

But do not competitions like CASC continue to demonstrate that resolution systems are superior in performance in comparison with CM systems? In fact, these competitions while stimulating research a lot, do not say much about the *potential* of the different underlying proof methods. If system S_1 featuring *several hundreds of thousands* lines of code (loc) written in a low-level programming language and optimized towards CASC competitions proves some theorems not proved by system S_2 consisting of *a dozen* of loc written in high-level programming language PROLOG, what lesson does this teach about the different methods used, especially if S_2 inversely proves some theorems not proved by S_1? The only lesson I can draw from such a comparison is that the method used for S_2 seems to be so powerful that it is able to compensate for the exorbitant, several orders of magnitude higher investment put into S_1. The theoretical insights into the competing methods available in the literature including the present paper are reveiling much more about their relative potentials than superficially interpreted CASC competition results.

Of course, there is plenty of room for speeding-up the systems from the leanCoP or nanoCoP family by compiling these high-level programs into much faster low-level and optimized code. Once such codes are produced also for CM systems then the CASC results will reflect the comparative performance of the different methods used in the competing systems in a fairer way than done at present where apples are compared with pears in a blind way. Unfortunately, so far there is not yet a more general and adequate performance measure available in AD like, for instance, the one based on g-factors or IQs in psychology.

6   Conclusions

Logic has widely been agreed to provide a formal basis for much of Computer Science (CS) and Artificial Intelligence (AI). In applications like correctness of hardware and software, for instance, it has become indispensible [56]. Often it is used thereby in such a way as to prove the validity of a formula representing some problem, be it a mathematical or other problem. These observations justify the two assumptions stated at the beginning of Sect. 2. As a consequence Automated Deduction (AD) is considered to be of fundamental importance for CS and AI.

The last decades have witnessed remarkable progress in AD and in the performance of its proof systems. However, if compared with the progress in other AI subfields (like eg. learning) AD might be rated as not quite as successful. In the present paper the author has pointed to possible reasons for the absence of a more startling progress.

Perhaps the most important reason is that the work in AD is still diverted to a number of different proof methods, although some of these are evidently less promising than others. In particular, we have reminded the community of the fact that the Connection Method (CM) enjoys unique advantages in comparison with its competitors. While the acceptance of this fact obviously is growing, too many researchers seem still to be stuck in working on less promising approaches. In order to speed up this change of mind in the community, we have summarized the features of the CM in Sects. 2 and 3. In particular we have demonstrated that the unique feature of the CM, viz. the formula-orientedness, provide it with three striking advantages which are uniformity (over many logics), performance (due to the extreme compactness), and a global view over the proof process. Especially the last point was illustrated in Sect. 4 and the CM's approach was compared with its competitors wrt. all three points in Sect. 5.

In this comparison it becomes clear that our field needs to take a major step towards a higher-level guidance of the search for proofs which could and should be supported by deep learning techniques. While competing methods are hardly suited for such higher-level guidance, the CM lends itself to supporting it as illustrated in the paper. We thus envision a new revival and rising profile of AD with spectacular breakthroughs in the near future.

Acknowledgement. I greatly appreciate a very careful reading and many suggestions by Peter Andrews, Cezary Kaliszyk, Jens Otten and Renate Schmidt as well as helpful comments and generous information on system run-times by Josef Urban. David Plaisted independently suggested in a private communication the use of deep learning techniques in AD.

References

1. Alemi, A.A., Chollet, F., Een, N., Irving, G., Szegedy, C., Urban, J.: Deepmath - Deep sequence models for premise selection. In: Lee, D., Sugiyama, M., Luxburg, U., Guyon, I., Garnett, R. (eds.) Advances in Neural Information Processing Systems 29 (NIPS 2016), pp. 2235–2243 (2016)
2. Andrews, P.B.: Refutations by matings. IEEE Trans. Comput. **C−25**, 193–214 (1976)
3. Andrews, P.B.: Theorem proving via general matings. J. ACM **28**, 193–214 (1981)
4. Andrews, P.B.: An Introduction to Mathematical Logic and Type Theory: To Truth through Proof. Academic Press, Orlando (1986)

5. Andrews, P.B.: On connections and higher-order logic. J. Autom. Reas. **5**, 257–291 (1989)
6. Andrews, P.B.: Classical type theory. In: Robinson, A., Voronkov, A. (eds.) Handbook of Automated Reasoning, vol. 2, pp. 965–1007. Elsevier Science, Amsterdam (2001). Chap. 15
7. Andrews, P.B., Bishop, M., Issar, S., Nesmith, D., Pfenning, F., Xi, H.: TPS: a theorem proving system for classical type theory. J. Autom. Reas. **16**, 321–353 (1996)
8. Antonsen, R., Waaler, A.: Liberalized variable splitting. J. Autom. Reas. **38**, 3–30 (2007)
9. Beringer, A., Hölldobler, S., Kurfeß, F.: Spatial reasoning and connectionist inference. In: Bajcsy, R. (ed.) Proceedings of the International Joint Conference on Artificial Intelligence, IJCAI-95, pp. 1352–1357. IJCAII. Morgan Kaufmann, San Mateo (1995)
10. Bibel, L.W.: Reflexionen vor Reflexen - Memoiren eines Forschers. Cuvillier Verlag, Göttingen (2017)
11. Bibel, W.: An approach to a systematic theorem proving procedure in first-order logic. Computing **12**, 43–55 (1974). First presented to the GI Annual Conference in 1971; also available as Bericht Nr. 7207. Technische Universität Mänchen, Abteilung Mathematik (1972)
12. Bibel, W.: Programmieren in der Sprache der Prädikatenlogik. (Rejected) thesis for "Habilitation" presented to the Faculty of Mathematics. Technische Universität München, January 1975
13. Bibel, W.: Advanced topics in automated deduction. In: Nossum, R.T. (ed.) ACAI 1987. LNCS, vol. 345, pp. 41–59. Springer, Heidelberg (1988). doi:10.1007/3-540-50676-4_9
14. Bibel, W.: Perspectives on automated deduction. In: Boyer, R.S. (ed.) Automated Reasoning: Essays in Honor of Woody Bledsoe, pp. 77–104. Kluwer Academic, Utrecht (1991)
15. Bibel, W., Eder, E.: Methods and calculi for deduction. In: Gabbay, D.M., Hogger, C.J., Robinson, J.A. (eds.) Handbook of Logic in Artificial Intelligence and Logic Programming, vol. 1, pp. 71–193. Oxford University Press, Oxford (1993). Chap. 3
16. Bibel, W., Hölldobler, S., Würtz, J.: Cycle unification. In: Kapur, D. (ed.) CADE 1992. LNCS, vol. 607, pp. 94–108. Springer, Heidelberg (1992). doi:10.1007/3-540-55602-8_158
17. Bibel, W., Schmitt, P.H. (eds.): Automated Deduction - A Basis for Applications. Volume I: Foundations - Calculi and Methods. Applied Logic Series. Kluwer, Dordrecht (1998)
18. Bibel, W.: Matings in matrices. Comm. ACM **26**, 844–852 (1983)
19. Bibel, W.: Automated Theorem Proving, 2nd edn. Vieweg Verlag, Braunschweig (1987). First edition 1982
20. Bibel, W.: Deduction: Automated Logic. Academic Press, London (1993)
21. Bibel, W.: Research perspectives for logic and deduction. In: Stock, O., Schaerf, M. (eds.) Reasoning, Action and Interaction in AI Theories and Systems. LNCS, vol. 4155, pp. 25–43. Springer, Heidelberg (2006). doi:10.1007/11829263_2
22. Bibel, W.: Transition logic revisited. Logic J. IGPL (Interest Group Pure Appl. Logic) **16**(4), 317–334 (2008)
23. Bibel, W., Otten, J.: From Schütte's formal systems to modern automated deduction. In: Kahle, R., Rathjen, M. (eds.) The Legacy of Kurt Schütte. Springer (2017, to appear)

24. Bishop, M.: A breadth-first strategy for mating search. CADE 1999. LNCS, vol. 1632, pp. 359–373. Springer, Heidelberg (1999). doi:10.1007/3-540-48660-7_32

25. Brown, C.E.: Automated Reasoning in Higher-Order Logic: Set Comprehension and Extensionality in Church's Type Theory. Studies in Logic: Logic and Cognitive Systems, vol. 10. College Publications, London (2007)

26. Eder, E.: Relative Complexities of First Order Calculi. Vieweg, Braunschweig (1992)

27. Ertel, W., Schumann, J.M.P., Suttner, C.B.: Learning heuristics for a theorem prover using back propagation. In: Retti, J., Leidlmair, K. (eds.) 5. Österreichische Artificial-Intelligence-Tagung, vol. 208, pp. 87–95. Springer, Heidelberg (1989). doi:10.1007/978-3-642-74688-8_10

28. Färber, M., Kaliszyk, C., Urban, J.: Monte carlo tableau proof search. In: de Moura, L. (ed.) Automated Deduction - CADE 26. CADE 2017. LNCS, vol. 10395, pp. 563–579. Springer, Cham (2017). doi:10.1007/978-3-319-63046-5_34

29. Freitas, F., Otten, J.: A connection calculus for the description logic $\mathcal{ALC}$. In: Khoury, R., Drummond, C. (eds.) AI 2016. LNCS, vol. 9673, pp. 243–256. Springer, Cham (2016). doi:10.1007/978-3-319-34111-8_30

30. Fronhöfer, B.: Memories of the tableaux workshop 1992. Personal communication, January 2017

31. Galmiche, D.: Connection methods in linear logic and proof nets construction. Theoret. Comput. Sci. **232**, 231–272 (2000)

32. Gentzen, G.: Untersuchungen über das logische Schließen. Math. Z. **39**, 176–210 and 405–431 (1935). English transl. in [58]

33. Herbrand, J.J.: In: Goldfarb, W.D. (ed.) Logical Writings. Reidel, Dordrecht (1971)

34. Goller, C.: A Connectionist Approach for Learning Search-Control Heuristics for Automated Deduction Systems. Akademische Verlagsgesellschaft AKA, Berlin (1999)

35. Hähnle, R.: Early Tableaux, presented to the Conference TABLEAUX 2017 (2017)

36. Hansen, C.M.: A Variable Splitting Theorem Prover. Ph.D. thesis. University of Oslo (2012)

37. Herbrand, J.: Recherches sur la théorie de la démonstration. Travaux Soc. Sciences et Lettres Varsovie, Cl. 3 (Mathem. Phys.) (1930). English transl. in [33]

38. Hölldobler, S. (ed.): Intellectics and Computational Logic - Papers in Honor of Wolfgang Bibel. Applied Logic Series. Kluwer Academic Publishers, Dordrecht (2000)

39. Jakubuv, J., Urban, J.: BliStrTune: hierarchical invention of theorem proving strategies. In: Proceedings of the 6th ACM SIGPLAN Conference on Certified Programs and Proofs, pp. 43–52. ACM (2017)

40. Kaliszyk, C., Urban, J.: FEMaLeCoP: fairly efficient machine learning connection prover. In: Davis, M., Fehnker, A., McIver, A., Voronkov, A. (eds.) LPAR 2015. LNCS, vol. 9450, pp. 88–96. Springer, Heidelberg (2015). doi:10.1007/978-3-662-48899-7_7

41. Kaliszyk, C., Urban, J., Vyskočil, J.: Certified connection tableaux proofs for HOL light and TPTP. In: CPP 2015 Proceedings of the 2015 Conference on Certified Programs and Proofs, pp. 59–66. ACM (2015)

42. Kohlhase, M.: Automated Deduction - A Basis for Applications, Vol. I: Foundations - Calculi and Methods, Applied Logic Series. In: Higher-Order Automated Theorem Proving, vol. 8, pp. 431–462. Kluwer, Dordrecht (1998). Chap. 13

43. Krause, D., Nobre, E., Musicante, M.: Bibel's matrix connection method in para consistent logic: general concepts and implementation. In: 21st International Con-

ference of the Chilean Computer Science Society, SCCC 2001, pp. 161–167. IEEE (2001)

44. Kreitz, C., Otten, J.: Connection-based theorem proving in classical and non-classical logics. J. Univ. Comput. Sci. **5**(3), 88–112 (1999)

45. Kreitz, C., Otten, J., Schmitt, S., Pientka, B.: Matrix-based constructive theorem proving. In: Hölldobler, S. (ed.) Intellectics and Computational Logic. Applied Logic Series. Kluwer Academic Publishers, Dordrecht (2000). doi:10.1007/978-94-015-9383-0_12

46. Loos, S., Irving, G., Szegedy, C., Kaliszyk, C.: Deep network guided proof search. In: Eiter, T., Sands, D. (eds.) LPAR-21. 21st International Conference on Logic for Programming, Artificial Intelligence and Reasoning. EPiC Series in Computing, vol. 46, pp. 85–105, EasyChair (2017). https://easychair.org/publications/paper/340345

47. Otten, J.: Clausal connection-based theorem proving in intuitionistic first-order logic. In: Beckert, B. (ed.) TABLEAUX 2005. LNCS (LNAI), vol. 3702, pp. 245–261. Springer, Heidelberg (2005). doi:10.1007/11554554_19

48. Otten, J.: leanCoP 2.0 and ileanCoP 1.2: high performance lean theorem proving in classical and intuitionistic logic (System Descriptions). In: Armando, A., Baumgartner, P., Dowek, G. (eds.) IJCAR 2008. LNCS, vol. 5195, pp. 283–291. Springer, Heidelberg (2008). doi:10.1007/978-3-540-71070-7_23

49. Otten, J.: Restricting backtracking in connection calculi. AI Commun. **23**, 159–182 (2010)

50. Otten, J.: A non-clausal connection calculus. In: Brünnler, K., Metcalfe, G. (eds.) TABLEAUX 2011. LNCS (LNAI), vol. 6793, pp. 226–241. Springer, Heidelberg (2011). doi:10.1007/978-3-642-22119-4_18

51. Otten, J.: Implementing connection calculi for first-order modal logics. In: Ternovska, E., Korovin, K., Schulz, S. (eds) 9th International Workshop on the Implementation of Logics (IWIL 2012), Merida, Venezuela (2012)

52. Otten, J.: MleanCoP: a connection prover for first-order modal logic. In: Demri, S., Kapur, D., Weidenbach, C. (eds.) IJCAR 2014. LNCS (LNAI), vol. 8562, pp. 269–276. Springer, Cham (2014). doi:10.1007/978-3-319-08587-6_20

53. Otten, J.: nanoCoP: a non-clausal connection prover. In: Olivetti, N., Tiwari, A. (eds.) IJCAR 2016. LNCS (LNAI), vol. 9706, pp. 302–312. Springer, Cham (2016). doi:10.1007/978-3-319-40229-1_21

54. Otten, J.: Non-clausal connection calculi for non-classical logics. In: Schmidt, R., Nalon, C. (eds.) TABLEAUX 2017. LNAI, vol. 10501, pp. 209–227. Springer, Cham (2017)

55. Otten, J., Bibel, W.: leanCoP: lean connection-based theorem proving. J. Symb. Comput. **36**, 139–161 (2003)

56. Otten, J., Bibel, W.: Advances in connection-based automated theorem proving. In: Bowen, J., Hinchey, M., Olderog, E.R. (eds.) Provably Correct Systems, pp. 211–241. Springer, London (2016). doi:10.1007/978-3-319-48628-4_9

57. Smith, R.G., Eckroth, J.: Building AI applications: yesterday, today, and tomorow. AImagazine **38**(1), 6–22 (2017)

58. Szabo, M.E. (ed.): The Collected Papers of Gerhard Gentzen. North-Holland, Amsterdam (1969)

59. Urban, J., Vyskočil, J.: Theorem proving in large formal mathematics as an emerging AI field. In: Bonacina, M.P., Stickel, M.E. (eds.) Automated Reasoning and Mathematics. LNCS, vol. 7788, pp. 240–257. Springer, Heidelberg (2013). doi:10.1007/978-3-642-36675-8_13

Locally Abstract, Globally Concrete Semantics of Concurrent Programming Languages

Crystal Chang Din[2], Reiner Hähnle[1]($\boxtimes$), Einar Broch Johnsen[2], Ka I Pun[2], and Silvia Lizeth Tapia Tarifa[2]

[1] Department of Computer Science, Technische Universität Darmstadt, Darmstadt, Germany
haehnle@cs.tu-darmstadt.de
[2] Department of Informatics, University of Oslo, Oslo, Norway
{crystald,einarj,violet,sltarifa}@ifi.uio.no

Abstract. Language semantics that is formal and mathematically precise, is the essential prerequisite for the design of logics and calculi that permit automated reasoning about programs. The most popular approach to programming language semantics—small step operational semantics (SOS)—is not modular in the sense that it does not separate conceptual layers in the target language. SOS is also hard to relate formally to program logics and calculi. Minimalist semantic formalisms, such as automata, Petri nets, or π-calculus are inadequate for rich programming languages. We propose a new formal trace semantics for a concurrent, active objects language. It is designed with the explicit aim of being compatible with a sequent calculus for a program logic and has a strong model theoretic flavor. Our semantics separates sequential and object-local from concurrent computation: the former yields abstract traces which in a second stage are combined into global system behavior.

1 Introduction

Our goal in this paper is a new kind of trace semantics for concurrent OO programming languages with cooperative scheduling, no more, no less. It is designed with the explicit aim of being compatible with a sequent calculus for a program logic and has a strong model theoretic flavor. The semantics separates sequential and object-local from concurrent computations. This is achieved by keeping traces of local computations inside an abstract context. Only in a second stage these abstract traces are combined into global system behavior.

Motivation. Conspicuously, semantics is mostly absent in program logics, starting with the early work of Hoare [1] and Dijkstra [2] and extending to contemporary approaches, such as the program logic of the KeY system [3]. Generally, the rules of a calculus of a program logic are taken to *be* the (axiomatic) semantics and this is considered to be a major advantage: "axioms enable the language designer to express his general intentions quite simply and directly, without the mass of detail which usually accompanies algorithmic descriptions" [1, p. 583].

© Springer International Publishing AG 2017
R.A. Schmidt and C. Nalon (Eds.): TABLEAUX 2017, LNAI 10501, pp. 22–43, 2017.
DOI: 10.1007/978-3-319-66902-1_2

Ample work on formalizing the semantics of programming languages has been performed. Many recent accounts are based on Plotkin's structural operational semantics (SOS).[1] In SOS the behavior of a program is formalized as transition rules that transform a given state of execution and a given program statement into a result state (which might be an abort state). The traces, i.e. the state sequences resulting from all possible sequences of rule applications from a given initial configuration, constitute a program's semantics.

Local SOS configurations contain runtime infrastructure, such as frame stacks, etc. The rules are schematic and need to cover all well-formed programs, in particular, the composition mechanisms of the target programming language, such as sequential composition, method calls, and synchronization. In essence, the SOS rules represent an interpreter.

Large fragments of industrial programming languages have been formalized in this style, including Java [5], C [6], but also the ABS language targeted here [7].

Yet, semantics based on transition systems tends not to be very modular. Often, there are dozens, if not hundreds of rules, and it is hard to judge the consequences if some of them are changed. It is also very difficult to relate SOS rules to modern verification calculi based on symbolic execution [3] or verification condition generation [8,9]. As noted above, the consequence is that the calculi of verification tools for mainstream languages generally lack a corresponding formal semantics relative to which soundness can be proven. Minimalist semantic formalisms, such as automata, Petri nets, or the π-calculus are frequently used in theoretical investigations, but they are inadequate for mainstream programming languages.

Contribution. A main contribution of our work is a new trace semantics for concurrent programs that exhibits a denotational, compositional flavor and strictly separates local from interleaving and parallel computations. It has a number of important advantages: 1. The semantics is concise: it has exactly one rule per statement. 2. Consequences of changes are local and easy to analyze. 3. It is denotational: Semantic objects (i.e. traces) directly result from application of semantic rules and not indirectly from their interpretation. 4. One can easily map semantic rules to rules of the program logic.

Below we introduce several new mechanisms into our trace semantics: Local computations cannot know their parallel execution context, therefore, we execute them in an *abstract* environment and we work with *continuations* to handle local suspension and blocking. This enables us to completely separate sequential from interleaving and parallel computations by means of *synchronization* events whose well-formedness is ensured when local, sequential behavior is composed into global, concurrent behavior. This can be viewed as a generalization of Brookes' action traces [10].

Specifically, our work targets the active object language ABS [7], but we expect that the principle is applicable to languages based on asynchronous communication in general and probably to other concurrent languages as well.

---

[1] The official citation is [4], but the approach goes back to the early 1980s.

$scope ::= \{block\}$
$block ::= T \; \ell = exp; block \mid stmt$
$stmt ::= block \mid \textbf{skip} \mid \ell = rhs \mid \textbf{if} \; bexp \; \textbf{then} \; stmt \; \textbf{else} \; stmt \; \textbf{fi} \mid \textbf{return} \; exp$
$\qquad \mid \textbf{suspend} \mid stmt; stmt \mid \textbf{await} \; gexp \mid \textbf{while} \; bexp \{ \, stmt \, \}$
$\;\; rhs ::= exp \mid \textbf{new} \; C \, (\bar{\ell}) \mid cm$
$\;\;\; cm ::= \ell! mth(\bar{\ell}) \mid \ell.mth(\bar{\ell}) \mid \ell.\textbf{get}$
$gexp ::= bexp \mid \ell?$
$bexp ::= exp \; brel \; exp \mid \text{tt} \mid \text{ff}$
$\;\; brel ::= == \mid < \mid > \mid \leq \mid \geq$
$\;\;\; exp ::= exp + exp \mid exp - exp \mid exp \star exp \mid exp \, / \, exp \mid \ell \mid \textbf{this} \mid \textbf{destiny} \mid 0 \mid 1 \mid \cdots$
$\;\;\;\; \ell ::= identifier \mid \textbf{this}.identifier$

Fig. 1. ABS Program Syntax.

2   ABS: The Abstract Behavioral Specification Language

The Abstract Behavioral Specification language (ABS) [7] is an object-oriented modeling language for concurrent and distributed systems, which has been designed with a focus on analyzability. Its syntax and semantics are similar to Java to maximize usability. The grammar is given in Fig. 1. Expressions and imperative statements are standard. We slightly deviate from official ABS syntax and assume that local variables are introduced inside blocks before any other statement. This can be easily achieved by adding suitably scoped block statements. For simplicity, we only include integer and Boolean typed expressions, and we assume that all methods have a return value. The declaration of interfaces, classes, and methods is completely straightforward and omitted. We briefly discuss the main language features that are non-standard and the statements associated with them (for a full account, see [7]). The features considered here are explained by an example below.

Rigorous Encapsulation. Communication between different objects is only possible via method calls. The fields of an object are strictly private and inaccessible even to other instances of the same class and there are no static fields. There is no code inheritance and only interfaces constitute valid object types. This enforces the programming to interfaces discipline [11] and ensures that the heap of an object is only accessed by its own processes.

Asynchronous Communication with Futures. Asynchronous calls are dispatched with the statement Fut<T> f = o!m(e), where method m is called on the object o with parameters e. Upon making this call, a *future* is bound to f and the caller continues its execution uninterrupted. A future is a handle to the called process and may be passed around; in particular, a process may refer to its own associated future using the keyword destiny. Upon process termination, its return value may be accessed via the associated future. To read a value from a future, the statement T i = f.get; is used.

Cooperative Scheduling. In ABS at most one process is active per object. Active processes cannot be preempted, but give up control when they suspend

```
1   interface IC { Int n(); }
2   class C implements IC {
3     Int i = 0;
4     Int m(Int x) {
5       this.i = x; return x;
6     }
7     Int n() {
8       Int y = 10;
9       Fut<Int> l₁ = 0;
10      l₁ = this ! m(3);
11      if y == 0 then y = this.m(1) else await l₁? fi;
12      y = this.i+y;
13      return y;
14    }
15  }
16  { // Main block
17    Fut<Int> l = 0;
18    Int v = 0;
19    IC o = null;
20    o = new C();
21    l = o!n();
22    v = l.get;
23  }
```

Fig. 2. An example in ABS.

or terminate. Hence the ABS modeler has explicit control over interleaving. The active process suspends itself either by a suspend statement or by waiting for a guard. A guard can be a future—then the suspension statement has the form await f?; and the process may become active again once f has been resolved (i.e. its process terminated). Otherwise, a guard can be a side-effect-free Boolean expression—then the suspension statement has the form await e; and the process may become active again if e evaluates to true. If a future is accessed with f.get before it has been resolved, then the whole object blocks until f is resolved. When blocked, an object may still receive method calls, but it will not execute them.

The code between the start and the end of a method, as well as between suspension statements, can be reasoned about as if it were executed sequentially, because of cooperative scheduling: the active process is guaranteed to have exclusive access to the local heap of its object.

Given in Fig. 2 is an ABS example covering most ABS syntax categories. It declares an interface IC with a single public method, implemented in class C and called in the program's Main block. After declaring a future l and variables v, o, a new C object is created and stored in o. As o is new, it runs on a separate processor from Main. The asynchronous call to n returns a future that is stored in l and the following get is immediately executed. If the call to n is not yet completed, the main process blocks until it is. As there is no other process waiting on o, the call to n will be scheduled provided the scheduler is fair.

Local variable declarations of y and l_1 are followed by an asynchronous self call to m. This cannot start yet, because the execution of n continues with the conditional, where the second branch is taken. At this point, the execution of n suspends, and the execution of m can commence. In m the field i is set to the call parameter, hence this.i $== 3$ holds when n resumes. Consequently, n returns the value 13, which will also be assigned to v.

3   Abstract Traces

Our goal is a denotational trace semantics for ABS that, given a piece of ABS code, yields all possible traces for any local context, where a trace is a finite or infinite sequence of computation states. By *local* we mean an arbitrary initial state, an object this (including the heap), and a future destiny. Since ABS is non-deterministic, it is clear that we require a *collecting semantics*, i.e. a set of traces. More importantly, we want the semantics to be *local* in the sense that the evaluation of a given piece of ABS code is *independent* of the evaluation of other pieces. In a second stage, the local evaluations will be composed into well-formed traces that constitute the global system behavior. At first glance, this seems completely impossible. Look at the following code snippet (closely related to the example in Fig. 2):

$$v = f.\text{get}; \text{ if } (v == 0) \text{ then } o.m() \text{ else await } f'? \tag{1}$$

Behavior of this code depends, for example, on whether the futures f and f' have been resolved or not. Moreover, we need to know on which object o the method m is called. The branch taken in the conditional depends on the value of v, which is in turn the result of a previous asynchronous computation. So how can we achieve locality? The central idea is to abstract away from the unknowns during the evaluation of local statements:

1. As we cannot know which execution branch is taken, we simply generate traces for all of them. Hence, the evaluation of a statement yields a *set* of traces. This is standard in cumulative semantics [12].
2. Likewise, we don't know the values of parameters and attributes and, in particular, of the initial state, so the semantic evaluation will be *symbolic*.
3. Likewise, as we don't know the identity of this object, nor that of the future destiny, evaluation is *parametric* in them.

Yielding from these ideas is a formalization where we define, for any ABS statement s, a valuation function $\text{val}_\sigma^{O,F}(s)$ that returns the *set* of possible traces resulting from s when started in (a symbolic) initial state σ on object O with destiny F. Throughout the paper we assume a fixed domain D of semantic values and drop it from the valuation function to improve readability. We further assume that all expressions are well-typed and that their evaluation on D is fixed in a standard manner (e.g., $+$ is addition on the integers, etc.). As indicated above, we need to be able to evaluate the semantics in symbolic states:

Definition 1 (Memory location, symbolic/concrete state). Consider the set of all objects $\mathcal{O}$, all futures $\mathcal{F}$, the set of local variables and parameters $\mathcal{V}$, the set of attributes (fields) $\mathcal{A}$, and let $\mathcal{C}$ be an infinite supply of symbolic constants. Denote by $\mathcal{L} = \{O.a \mid O \in \mathcal{O},\, a \in \mathcal{A}\} \cup \mathcal{V} \cup \mathcal{C} \cup \mathcal{F}$ the *set of all memory locations* and by $\mathsf{Exp}(\mathcal{L})$ the ABS *expressions* over $\ell \in \mathcal{L}$. A *symbolic state* σ is a function $\sigma : \mathcal{L} \to \mathsf{Exp}(\mathcal{L})$. Without loss of generality we assume that $\sigma(\ell)$ is fully evaluated whenever $\sigma(\ell)$ contains no symbol from $\mathcal{L}$, i.e. $\sigma(\ell) \in D$. A state is called a *concrete state* if its range is in D and a trace is called a *concrete trace* if all its states are concrete.

Our evaluation of (1) starts in a state where $\sigma(v) = v_0$ and $v_0 \in \mathcal{C}$ is a fresh constant. Semantic evaluation of a statement returns a set of traces τ over symbolic states. Allowing symbolic constants in states amounts to a restricted form of *symbolic execution*. In order to decide which traces are feasible and which are not, it is necessary to record *path conditions* whenever a trace splits, such as for the conditional statement in the example above. Therefore, we work with *conditioned, symbolic traces* of the form $pc \triangleright \tau$, where pc is a path condition that must be satisfiable for the trace τ to be feasible. Path conditions are sets of quantifier-free Boolean expressions over $\mathcal{L}$. For (1) we would obtain path conditions of the form $\{v_0 = 0\}$ and $\{v_0 \neq 0\}$.

Now, during the semantic evaluation, we ensure that the value $\sigma(\ell)$ of each symbol ℓ in the path condition and in the symbolic states of a trace τ is correctly maintained relative to the initial state in τ [13]. Consequently, the symbolic traces can be easily concretized:

Definition 2 (Concretization of symbolic trace). Conditioned, symbolic traces are denoted by $pc \triangleright \tau$ and concrete states by σ. The *concretization* τ_σ of τ is obtained by replacing each σ' in τ with $\sigma \circ \sigma'$ and pc with $\sigma(pc)$. We can assume that path conditions are automatically evaluated, so that $\sigma(pc)$ is either true or false (where empty path conditions are considered to be true).

Notation for Traces. Represent symbolic traces in the sequel by variables τ, ω, where τ is typically finite and ω infinite. We use sh for concrete traces, i.e. traces in the usual sense (the letters stand for "shining trace"). Path conditions, if present, are explicitly given, but we identify $\mathsf{true} \triangleright sh$ with sh. The constructors for traces (symbolic or concrete) are as follows: The empty trace is written ε. Given a (possibly empty) trace τ, we extend it with a single state σ by writing $\tau \curvearrowright \sigma$. A singleton trace consisting of the state σ is written $\langle \sigma \rangle = \varepsilon \curvearrowright \sigma$. Concatenation of two traces τ, ω is written as $\tau \cdot \omega$ and only defined when τ is finite. The final state of a non-empty, finite trace τ is obtained as $\mathsf{last}(\tau)$.

Extend sequential composition of programs to traces as follows: Assume that τ is a trace of statement r and ω a trace of s. To obtain the trace corresponding to the sequential composition of r and s, the last state of τ and the first state of ω must be identical, but the resulting trace should not contain a doubled state. Hence, we define the *semantic chop* $**$ (inspired by [14]):

$$(pc_\tau \triangleright \tau) \underline{**} (pc_\omega \triangleright \omega) = \begin{cases} pc_\tau \triangleright \tau & \text{if } \tau \text{ is infinite or } \tau = \tau' \cdot starve(O) \\ (pc_\tau \cup pc_\omega) \triangleright \tau \cdot \omega' & \text{if } last(\tau) = \sigma, \ \omega = \langle \sigma \rangle \cdot \omega' \end{cases}$$

$$(2)$$

This definition takes into account a possibly non-terminating first trace, either because it is infinite or it represents a starving process ($starve(O)$ is a starvation marker defined below). The definition can be specialized to traces without path conditions in the obvious way: $\tau \underline{**} \omega$ is $(\emptyset \triangleright \tau) \underline{**} (\emptyset \triangleright \omega)$.

4   The Local Semantics of ABS Programs

Execution of ABS will now be formalized using denotational and compositional local semantics; the main challenge here is the suspension of local control flow. To meet this challenge, we introduce continuations. We first consider statements which do not need continuations, before we discuss the continuation mechanism.

4.1   Statements Without Continuations

Syntactic structure of programs guides the definition of the valuation function $\mathrm{val}_\sigma^{O,F}(s)$. As explained above, given a symbolic state σ, $\mathrm{val}_\sigma^{O,F}(s)$ yields the set of all possible symbolic traces when s is executed from the initial state σ on object O with destiny F. We explain it case by case, beginning with the valuation of scopes that start with local variable declarations; here, bs may contain further variable declarations, followed by a statement, see Fig. 1:

$$\mathrm{val}_\sigma^{O,F}(\{T\,\ell = e; bs\}) = \{pc \triangleright \langle \sigma \rangle \cdot \omega \mid \sigma' = \sigma[\ell' \mapsto \mathrm{val}_\sigma^{O,F}(e)], \tag{3}$$
$$pc \triangleright \omega \in \mathrm{val}_{\sigma'}^{O,F}(\{bs[\ell'/\ell]\}), isFresh(\ell')\}.$$

Evading name clashes between variable names is achieved by replacing ℓ with a fresh name ℓ' throughout the scope and evaluate the resulting scope in the state σ', where ℓ' has been initialized with the evaluation of e. The evaluation function for side effect-free expressions $\mathrm{val}_\sigma^{O,F} : \mathrm{Exp}(\mathcal{L}) \to \mathrm{Exp}(\mathcal{L})$ is completely standard, except $\mathrm{val}_\sigma^{O,F}(\mathtt{this}) = O$ and $\mathrm{val}_\sigma^{O,F}(\mathtt{destiny}) = F$. The traces of the form $pc \triangleright \omega$ resulting from evaluation of the renamed scope start with σ', so we need to prepend σ. The next rule evaluates scopes without leading local variable declarations. These become simply statements after stripping the delimiting braces:

$$\mathrm{val}_\sigma^{O,F}(\{s\}) = \mathrm{val}_\sigma^{O,F}(s)$$

Meanwhile, the skip statement yields a trace of length one with empty path condition:

$$\mathrm{val}_\sigma^{O,F}(\mathtt{skip}) = \{\emptyset \triangleright \langle \sigma \rangle\} \tag{4}$$

Assignment of expressions results in a single trace of length two: from the initial state σ to the state where ℓ has been updated with the value of e:

$$\mathrm{val}_\sigma^{O,F}(\ell = e) = \{\emptyset \triangleright \langle \sigma \rangle \curvearrowright \sigma[\ell \mapsto \mathrm{val}_\sigma^{O,F}(e)]\} \tag{5}$$

Notation for Events in Traces. To model concurrency in our semantics we use *event markers* in traces. For example, an object must have been created before its methods can be called. With event markers it is easy to ensure such properties via well-formedness conditions over events. For example, each invocation event on an object o in a given trace must be preceded by a creation event for o. Let $ev(\overline{v})$ be an event marker with arguments $\overline{v}$. To insert $ev(\overline{v})$ into a trace that continues with σ, we define an *event trace* $ev_\sigma(\overline{v})$ of length three as follows:

$$ev_\sigma(\overline{v}) = \langle \sigma \rangle \curvearrowright ev(\overline{v}) \curvearrowright \sigma.$$

This notation has the advantage that it is "choppable" with preceding or trailing traces and it ensures that no trace begins or ends with an event marker. Evaluation of the assignment of new objects is now straightforward:

$$\mathrm{val}_\sigma^{O,F}(\ell = \mathtt{new}\ C\,(\overline{e})) = \{pc \triangleright newEv_\sigma(O, o, \mathrm{val}_\sigma^{O,F}(\overline{e})) \cdot \tau \mid$$
$$isFresh(o),\ class(o) = C,\ \sigma' = C.\epsilon(o) \circ \sigma,$$
$$pc \triangleright \tau \in \mathrm{val}_{\sigma'}^{O,F}(\ell = o)\} \tag{6}$$

Insertion of the event marker *newEv* happens at the initial state σ. This creation event is attached to the current object O and represents the creation of a new object o whose class must be C. To initialize o, define an *abstract* initial state $C.\epsilon(o)$ such that $(C.\epsilon(o))(a) = a_0$ for each attribute a of C, where a_0 is a fresh symbol of the same type as a, and let σ' extend σ with those initial assignments. The assignment of the newly created object can then be evaluated by rule (5). The construction is deterministic and results in a single trace of length five. *Asynchronous* method calls follow a similar schema:

$$\mathrm{val}_\sigma^{O,F}(\ell = e'!m(\overline{e})) = \{pc \triangleright invEv_\sigma(O, \mathrm{val}_\sigma^{O,F}(e'), f, m, \mathrm{val}_\sigma^{O,F}(\overline{e})) \underset{*}{*} \tau \mid$$
$$isFresh(f),\ method(f) = m,\ pc \triangleright \tau \in \mathrm{val}_\sigma^{O,F}(\ell = f)\} \tag{7}$$

An event marker *invEv* from the caller O to the evaluated callee $\mathrm{val}_\sigma^{O,F}(e')$ is inserted at state σ. The invocation event is associated with a fresh future f, the name m of the called method, and the evaluated call arguments $\mathrm{val}_\sigma^{O,F}(\overline{e})$. The call does not change the state and does not suspend, so we can assign the future to ℓ and proceed. Here the local semantics shows its strength: the called method is evaluated separately; only later will we take care of synchronization. *Synchronous* method calls are not handled using futures, but by inlining:

$$\mathrm{val}_\sigma^{O,F}(\ell = e'.m(\overline{e})) = \{pc \triangleright \langle \sigma \rangle \cdot \omega \mid O' = \mathrm{val}_\sigma^{O,F}(e'),$$
$$lookup(m, class(O')) = T\ m(\overline{T}\ \overline{\ell'})\{s; \mathtt{return}\ e\},$$
$$pc \triangleright \omega \in \mathrm{val}_{\sigma'}^{O',F}(\{\overline{T}\ \overline{\ell'} = \mathrm{val}_\sigma^{O,F}(\overline{e}); s; \ell'' = e\}; \ell = \ell''),$$
$$\sigma' = \sigma[\ell'' \mapsto v_0],\ isFresh(\ell'', v_0)\} \tag{8}$$

We get all traces $pc \triangleright \omega$ of the called method, whose implementation is obtained from a class table lookup of the callee O'. Observe that even when O' is a symbolic value, we can still determine its type statically. We initialize the formal parameters with the call parameters and put the resulting code into a scope. Consequently, the formal parameters are treated as local variables and automatically renamed. A fresh variable ℓ'' will hold the return value and assign it to ℓ. This causes the only slight complication, because ℓ'' needs to be initialized with a fresh value in the state σ' from where the inlined code is executed. Here, the predicate *isFresh* expresses that one or more variable names are (globally) fresh.

For the evaluation of conditionals, we take the union of the sets of behaviors of the branches and add appropriate path conditions for each branch:

$$\mathrm{val}_\sigma^{O,F}(\texttt{if } e \texttt{ then } s_1 \texttt{ else } s_2 \texttt{ fi}) =$$
$$\{\{\mathrm{val}_\sigma^{O,F}(e) = \mathtt{tt}\} \cup pc_1 \triangleright \omega_1 \mid pc_1 \triangleright \omega_1 \in \mathrm{val}_\sigma^{O,F}(s_1)\} \ \cup \ (9)$$
$$\{\{\mathrm{val}_\sigma^{O,F}(e) = \mathtt{ff}\} \cup pc_2 \triangleright \omega_2 \mid pc_2 \triangleright \omega_2 \in \mathrm{val}_\sigma^{O,F}(s_2)\}$$

We discuss two further cases for sequential statements, before we turn to rules with continuations. The `return` statement emits an event marker *compEv* for completion, given the current object and future to contain the returned value.

$$\mathrm{val}_\sigma^{O,F}(\texttt{return } e) = \{\emptyset \triangleright compEv_\sigma(O, F, \mathrm{val}_\sigma^{O,F}(e))\} \qquad (10)$$

Finally, consider execution of a method m declared in class C, running on object O with future F: it starts with an event marker *invREv* representing the reaction to an asynchronous invocation from an unknown caller O' and with unknown argument values $\overline{v_0}$. This is followed by any of the possible traces for the method's implementation. The formal parameters are handled as local variables initialized with $\overline{v_0}$ that are put into a scope over the method body s.

$$\mathrm{val}_\sigma^{O,F}(C.m) = \{pc \triangleright invREv_\sigma(O', O, F, m, \overline{v_0}) \ \underline{**} \ \omega \mid$$
$$pc \triangleright \omega \in \mathrm{val}_\sigma^{O,F}(\{\overline{T} \ \overline{\ell'} = \overline{v_0}; s\}), \qquad (11)$$
$$lookup(m, C) = T \ m(\overline{T} \ \overline{\ell'})\{s\}, \ isFresh(O', \overline{v_0})\}$$

4.2   Statements with Continuations

All remaining statements may involve suspension, the intermittent scheduling of other processes, and resumed execution of the suspended statement. Two problems must be addressed: first, we cannot know the computation state upon resumption. Second, when we later combine local into global traces, we require interleaving points. Both are addressed by continuations. We start with the simplest case, the unconditional `suspend` statement:

$$\mathrm{val}_\sigma^{O,F}(\texttt{suspend}) = \{\emptyset \triangleright relEv_\sigma(O) \cdot starve(O)\} \cup$$
$$\{\emptyset \triangleright relEv_\sigma(O) \cdot relCont(O, F, \texttt{skip})\} \qquad (12)$$

Release of control of the currently executing process is captured by an event marker *relEv*. It has the current object as argument to identify which object was released, when global system behavior is composed. Execution after suspension has two cases. First, the current object may suffer from starvation and never regain control. This situation is captured by the marker $starve(O)$, which can only occur as the final element of a trace. Second, control is regained but we do not know what happened "in between" while other processes were executing on O. Without knowing the state in which execution will continue, it is not meaningful to evaluate the rest of the process. This is only achieved later, when we combine the local, sequential evaluation into the global one. Technically, we address this problem by ending the trace with a *continuation marker* $relCont$, which captures the return of control after suspension. The arguments of a continuation marker are the currently executing object, the future associated with the computation, and the code to be executed after control is regained. For unconditional suspension this is just a `skip` statement. The `get` statement, which retrieves the value of an asynchronous computation, can also introduce a continuation marker. There are two branches:

$$\mathrm{val}_\sigma^{O,F}(\ell = \ell'.\texttt{get}) = \{pc \triangleright compREv_\sigma(O, \mathrm{val}_\sigma^{O,F}(\ell'), v_0) \underline{**} \tau \mid$$
$$isFresh(v_0),\ pc \triangleright \tau \in \mathrm{val}_\sigma^{O,F}(\ell = v_0)\} \cup \qquad (13)$$
$$\{\emptyset \triangleright blkEv_\sigma(O, \mathrm{val}_\sigma^{O,F}(\ell')) \cdot blkCont(O, F, \ell = \ell'.\texttt{get})\}$$

In the first branch, the future bound to ℓ' has been resolved. We introduce an event marker $compREv$ to capture a completion reaction in the current object O. The actual result is unknown at this point, so we assign a fresh, symbolic value to ℓ, to represent it. This causes no problem in a symbolic setting, and the value will be later resolved during composition of global behavior. In the second branch, the process is scheduled to retrieve the value of an unresolved future. The process is blocked until the future is resolved, i.e. local control is not released. This is captured by an event marker $blkEv$, associated to the current object O and the future. Similar to unconditional suspension, we do not know how the state evolves while the process is blocked and put a continuation marker $blkCont$ at the end of the local trace to enable the correct composition of global traces.

In the sequel we use the convention that traces denoted with τ do *not* contain any continuation marker. To fully understand the continuation mechanism it is useful to look at last branches of the evaluation of sequential composition:

$$\mathrm{val}_\sigma^{O,F}(r;s) =$$
$$\{(pc_r \triangleright \tau_r) \underline{**} (pc_s \triangleright \omega_s) \mid pc_r \triangleright \tau_r \in \mathrm{val}_\sigma^{O,F}(r), pc_s \triangleright \omega_s \in \mathrm{val}_{\sigma'}^{O,F}(s),$$
$$\text{where } \sigma' = \mathrm{last}(\tau_r) \text{ if } \tau_r \text{ is finite, arbitrary otherwise}\} \cup \qquad (14)$$
$$\{pc_r \triangleright \tau_r \cdot relCont(O, F, r'; s) \mid pc_r \triangleright \tau_r \cdot relCont(O, F, r') \in \mathrm{val}_\sigma^{O,F}(r)\} \cup$$
$$\{pc_r \triangleright \tau_r \cdot blkCont(O, F, r'; s) \mid pc_r \triangleright \tau_r \cdot blkCont(O, F, r') \in \mathrm{val}_\sigma^{O,F}(r)\}$$

Let us evaluate `suspend; s`. By (12) we obtain a set of traces for `suspend` that end with $relCont(O, F, \texttt{skip})$. By (14) the evaluation of `suspend; s` is a set of traces that end with $relCont(O, F, \texttt{skip}; s)$. All evaluations accumulate the remaining commands in this way, so the top-level continuation contains all code remaining to be executed. For $\ell = \ell'$.get we similarly obtain from (13) a set of traces that end with $blkCont(O, F, \ell = \ell'.\text{get})$, which can be sequenced with s to $blkCont(O, F, \ell = \ell'.\text{get}; s)$. This shows that the get statement is re-evaluated before the process can proceed with the remaining statements. The first branch of sequential composition covers the sequential case: r runs without suspension or blocking. This includes the case when r starves or does not terminate (2).

$$\text{val}_\sigma^{O,F}(\text{await } \ell?) = \{\emptyset \triangleright compREv_\sigma(O, \text{val}_\sigma^{O,F}(\ell), v_0) \mid isFresh(v_0)\} \cup$$
$$\{\emptyset \triangleright relEv_\sigma(O, \text{val}_\sigma^{O,F}(\ell)) \cdot starve(O)\} \cup \qquad (15)$$
$$\{\emptyset \triangleright relEv_\sigma(O, \text{val}_\sigma^{O,F}(\ell)) \cdot relCont(O, F, \text{await } \ell?)\}$$

Awaiting a future is similar to suspension (12). Its second and third branch are almost the same, but in addition to the executing object we need to record the identity of the future ℓ in the release event marker $relEv$, to ensure well-formedness of traces in the global semantics. In the third branch, the await statement is re-evaluated in the continuation. This models await as a loop that repeatedly suspends and checks whether the future is available. The latter is treated in the first branch: to capture the completion reaction, we insert an event marker $compREv$, for the future in ℓ and record its value. This value is yet unknown and set to a symbolic term v_0. But how do we know that the future was actually completed in the first branch? In the local evaluation we cannot know and we might create ill-formed traces at this point; such traces will be removed later when we compose the global behavior. Await on fields can be defined as: $\text{val}_\sigma^{O,F}(\text{await } e) = \text{val}_\sigma^{O,F}(\text{if } e \text{ then skip else suspend; await } e \text{ fi})$. An inductive version of loop evaluation can be defined similarly, using the rules above: $\text{val}_\sigma^{O,F}(\text{while } e \{s\}) = \text{val}_\sigma^{O,F}(\text{if } e \text{ then } s; \text{ while } e \{s\} \text{ else skip fi})$.

4.3   Local Traces by Example

Figure 3 summarizes the local, abstract traces of the example from Fig. 2. Denote the empty state by ϵ and a state σ such that $\sigma(\ell) = v$ by $[\ell \mapsto v]$; i.e. states are unnamed and only relevant parts of their domain are listed. The evaluation of method m in $\text{val}_{C.\epsilon(O)}^{O,F}(\text{C.m})$ gives a set with one symbolic trace (note that parameter x was renamed to x'), while the evaluation of method n in $\text{val}_{C.\epsilon(O)}^{O,F}(\text{C.n})$ gives a set with four symbolic traces due to the if−then−else and await statements.

We discuss the traces for method n in detail. The first trace occurs when the condition of the if−then−else statement is true, and we proceed with the execution of the synchronous call to method m, which has no release points. The next three cases occur when the condition of the if−then−else statement is false, and we evaluate the await statement. In the second trace the future has been resolved; we do not have a release point and the trace contains a completion event. The third trace occurs when the future is unresolved. After release, the process never regains control, i.e. the scheduler is unfair, so the trace ends with a starvation marker. The fourth trace happens when the process regains control with a release continuation $relCont(O, F, \ldots)$. The evaluation of

$\mathrm{val}^{O,F}_{\mathsf{C}.\mathsf{e}(O)}(\mathsf{C}.\mathsf{m}) =$
$\{ \quad \emptyset \quad \blacktriangleright \langle [O.i \mapsto v_i] \rangle \curvearrowright invREv(O',O,F,\mathsf{m},v_0) \curvearrowright \cdots \curvearrowright [O.i \mapsto v_i, x' \mapsto v_0] \qquad \}$

$\mathrm{val}^{O,F}_{\mathsf{C}.\mathsf{e}(O)}(\mathsf{C}.\mathsf{n}) =$
$\{ \{(10 = 0)\} \triangleright \langle [O.i \mapsto v_j] \rangle \curvearrowright invREv(O',O,F,\mathsf{n},\_) \curvearrowright \cdots$
$\quad \{(10 \neq 0)\} \triangleright \langle [O.i \mapsto v_j] \rangle \curvearrowright invREv(O',O,F,\mathsf{n},\_) \curvearrowright \cdots \curvearrowright compEv(O,F,v_j + 10) \curvearrowright$
$\qquad\qquad [O.i \mapsto v_j, y' \mapsto v_j + 10, l'_1 \mapsto f_1],$
$\quad \{(10 \neq 0)\} \triangleright \langle [O.i \mapsto v_j] \rangle \curvearrowright invREv(O',O,F,\mathsf{n},\_) \curvearrowright \cdots starve(O),$
$\quad \{(10 \neq 0)\} \blacktriangleright [O.i \mapsto v_j] \curvearrowright \cdots \curvearrowright relEv(O,f_1) \curvearrowright [O.i \mapsto v_j, y' \mapsto 10, l'_1 \mapsto f_1]$
$\qquad \cdot relCont(O,F,\mathbf{await}\ l'_1?; y' = \mathbf{this}.i + y'; \mathbf{return}\ y';) \qquad \}$

$\mathrm{val}^{O,F}_{[O.i \mapsto v_{j'}, y' \mapsto v_{y'}, l'_1 \mapsto v_2]}(O,F,\ \mathbf{await}\, l'_1?; y' = \mathbf{this}.i + y'; \mathbf{return}\ y';) =$
$\{ \{(v_{y'} \neq 0)\} \blacktriangleright \langle [O.i \mapsto v_{j'}, y' \mapsto v_{y'}, l'_1 \mapsto v_2] \rangle \curvearrowright \cdots \curvearrowright compEv(O,v_2,v'_j + v'_y) \curvearrowright$
$\qquad\qquad [O.i \mapsto v_{j'}, y' \mapsto v'_j + v'_y, l'_1 \mapsto v_2],$
$\quad \{(v_{y'} \neq 0)\} \triangleright \langle [O.i \mapsto v_{j'}, y' \mapsto v_{y'}, l'_1 \mapsto v_2] \rangle \curvearrowright \cdots starve(O),$
$\quad \{(v_{y'} \neq 0)\} \triangleright \langle [O.i \mapsto v_{j'}, y' \mapsto v_{y'}, l'_1 \mapsto v_2] \rangle \curvearrowright \cdots$
$\qquad\qquad relCont(O,F,\mathbf{await}\ l'_1?; y' = \mathbf{this}.i + y'; \mathbf{return}\ y';) \qquad \}$

$\mathrm{val}^{\mathsf{Main},f_0}_{\epsilon}(\{\mathbf{Fut}\langle\mathsf{Unit}\rangle\ l = \mathsf{null};\ \mathsf{Int}\ v = 0;\ \mathsf{IC}\ o = \mathsf{null};\ o = \mathbf{new}\ \mathsf{C}();\ l = o!\mathsf{n}();\ v = l.\mathbf{get};\}) =$
$\{ \quad \emptyset \quad \triangleright \varepsilon \curvearrowright [l' \mapsto null] \curvearrowright \cdots \curvearrowright invEv(\mathsf{Main},o'',f,\mathsf{n},\_) \curvearrowright$
$\qquad\qquad compREv(\mathsf{Main},f,v_1) \curvearrowright \cdots \curvearrowright [l' \mapsto f, v' \mapsto v_1, o' \mapsto o'', o''.i \mapsto 0],$
$\quad\quad \emptyset \quad \blacktriangleright \varepsilon \curvearrowright \cdots \curvearrowright invEv(\mathsf{Main},o'',f,\mathsf{n},\_) \curvearrowright \cdots \curvearrowright blockEv(\mathsf{Main},f) \curvearrowright$
$\qquad\qquad [l' \mapsto f, v' \mapsto 0, o' \mapsto o'', o''.i \mapsto 0] \cdot blkCont(\mathsf{Main},f_o,v = l.\mathbf{get};) \qquad \}$

$\mathrm{val}^{\mathsf{Main},f_0}_{[l' \mapsto v_3, v' \mapsto v_4, o' \mapsto o'', o''.i \mapsto v_5]}(\{v = l.\mathbf{get};\}) =$
$\{ \quad \emptyset \quad \triangleright \langle [l' \mapsto v_3, v' \mapsto v_4, o' \mapsto o'', o''.i \mapsto v_5] \rangle \curvearrowright compREv(\mathsf{Main},v_3,v_6) \curvearrowright \cdots \curvearrowright$
$\qquad\qquad [l' \mapsto v_3, v' \mapsto v_6, o' \mapsto o'', o''.i \mapsto v_7],$
$\quad\quad \emptyset \quad \blacktriangleright \langle [l' \mapsto v_3, v' \mapsto v_4, o' \mapsto o'', o''.i \mapsto v_5] \rangle \curvearrowright blockEv(\mathsf{Main},f) \curvearrowright$
$\qquad\qquad [l' \mapsto v_3, v' \mapsto v_4, o' \mapsto o'', o''.i \mapsto v_5] \cdot blkCont(\mathsf{Main},f_o,v = l.\mathbf{get};) \qquad \}$

Fig. 3. Examples of local traces. The filled triangle $\blacktriangleright$ identifies those traces that become part of the global trace in Sect. 5.4.

$\mathrm{val}^{O,F}_{[O.i \mapsto v_{j'}, y' \mapsto v_{y'}, l'_1 \mapsto v_2]}(O,F,\ \mathbf{await}\ l'_1?; \ldots)$ results in three traces due to the await statement, following a similar pattern as the three last traces of n.

The evaluation of the main block in $\mathrm{val}^{\mathsf{Main},f_0}_{\epsilon}(\{\mathbf{Fut}\langle\mathsf{Unit}\rangle\ l = \mathsf{null}; \ldots\})$ produces two traces due to the get statement. In the first trace, the future is resolved and the main block finishes execution. In the second trace, the future is not resolved and we get a blocking continuation $blkCont(\mathsf{Main},f_0,\ldots)$, marking the object as blocked until the future is resolved. The evaluation of $\mathrm{val}^{\mathsf{Main},f_0}_{[l' \mapsto v_3, v' \mapsto v_4, o' \mapsto o'', o''.i \mapsto v_5]}(\{v = l.\mathbf{get};\})$ again produces two traces, similar as above. Note that some of these symbolic traces will never result in a concrete trace of the global system, because they will be eliminated by well-formedness requirements at the global level or due to inconsistencies in their path conditions.

5   The Global Semantics of ABS Programs

The local semantics of ABS yields for each object $O \in \mathcal{O}$, future $F \in \mathcal{F}$, and statement s a set of conditioned, symbolic traces $\omega \in \mathrm{val}^{O,F}_{\sigma}(s)$ that describe all possible behaviors of s when started in state σ. We now construct, for a given ABS program P, a set of *concrete* traces sh without path conditions describing the possible *global* behaviors of the system; i.e. these traces consist of *global states* that fix the value of each variable and each attribute of each object.

5.1   From Locally Abstract to Globally Concrete Behavior

An ABS execution starts from an executable main block $\{\overline{T}\ \overline{\ell} = \overline{v}; s\}$ of an ABS program P in a concrete global state ϵ, where each attribute and variable is initialized with the concrete default value of its type. We assume that the main block is executed on object Main that is associated with a future f_0.[2] Our semantics works as follows: we start to evaluate the main block by picking a trace from $\mathcal{M} = \text{val}_\epsilon^{\text{Main},\ f_0}(\{\overline{T}\ \overline{\ell} = \overline{v}; s\})$. As long as we don't suspend execution, this results in a *concrete* trace with path condition either true or false, because s is executable and fresh values are only introduced upon suspension. We only produce traces with feasible path condition, i.e. true, which can be discarded. Hence, the result is an initial trace sh of P.

Two technical issues need to be addressed. The first is *suspension*, given by continuation markers in the symbolic traces. When we encounter a continuation in a symbolic trace, other traces on O and on other objects should have a chance to be inserted in the global trace. Where do these other traces come from? In addition to $\mathcal{M}$ we have the following symbolic traces at our disposal:

$$\mathcal{G} = \{\text{val}_{\mathsf{C}.\epsilon(O)}^{O,\,F}(C.m) \mid class(O) = \mathsf{C},\ m \in mtd(\mathsf{C}),\ O \in \mathcal{O},\ F \in \mathcal{F},\ \mathsf{C} \in P\}(16)$$

Symbolic traces represent possible executions on different objects, started in abstract states (6) for all objects, all futures, and for each method of each class in P. Assume that our initial concrete trace sh contains an invocation event $invEv_\sigma(O, v, F, m, \overline{v})$ and that we have suspended trace generation. Note that v and $\overline{v}$ are *concrete* values in D. We select a symbolic trace in $\text{val}_{\mathsf{C}.\epsilon(O)}^{O,\,F}(C.m) = \Omega \in \mathcal{G}$ and instantiate it with v and $\overline{v}$. In addition, we start it with the *concrete* state $last(sh)$ instead of $\mathsf{C}.\epsilon(O)$. Well-formedness conditions over event sequences will ensure that only valid ABS traces can be generated in this way.

We formalize this idea in *global trace composition rules*. These define a relation $\rightarrow$ that takes a concrete initial trace sh and a queue q of sets of local symbolic traces, extends sh by concretizing one such trace, and modifies q accordingly. Exhaustive, non-deterministic application of these rules yields one of the possible global system traces of P. The initial state of that global execution is given by:

$$\varepsilon, \{\mathcal{M}\} \cup \mathcal{G}$$

The second technical issue is *non-termination*. Starvation is straightforward, due to the event markers in the local semantics. When we encounter a starving object, we can simply discard all traces associated with it, and let other objects continue execution. However, non-terminating statements, such as loops or synchronous recursive calls, contain neither continuation nor starvation markers.

---

[2] This future is never retrieved by any completion reaction event and can be thought of as the client who started P's execution.

To produce a global system trace, we need to interrupt the generation of such infinite traces "from time to time" so that other objects in the global system (except the diverging object) can proceed. Our solution to this problem is to let the generation of concrete traces be preempted after some finite number of steps, but we need to exclude arbitrary interleaving of traces, which is not permitted by the cooperative concurrency model of ABS. Technically, this can be done by means of *interleaving events* and *interleaving reaction events* that contain enough information to exclude unwanted traces. It has previously been shown that local scheduling information of this kind is needed to obtain a complete proof system for cooperative concurrency [15].

5.2   The Rules of the Global Semantics

The correct global composition of traces is governed by *events* over futures and objects, which are related by a *well-formedness predicate* over global traces. While the correct interaction with futures depends on the communication events introduced in Sect. 4, the interleaving of different executions is captured by two kinds of scheduling events, related to internal and external interleaving of execution. Internal interleaving reflects the cooperative concurrency of ABS objects, with suspend and await. We let the event $schEv_\sigma(O)$ express that O has scheduled a process in state σ. External interleaving reflects how the execution in different objects may be interleaved in the global trace. This is captured in the semantics by a pair of interleaving events, $ilEv_\sigma(O)$ and $ilREv_\sigma(O)$, expressing that object O permits the execution of other objects to be observed in state σ and that object O continues its execution after such an observation, respectively.

We define the execution relation $\rightarrow$ for global execution by five composition rules. The first rule captures *external interleaving* in the global trace by preempting the local execution:

$$\frac{\begin{array}{ccc} pc \rhd \tau \cdot \omega \in \Omega & \Omega \in q & object(\Omega) = O & last(sh) = \sigma \\ \tau \neq \varepsilon & \omega \notin \{\varepsilon, blkCont(O, \_, \_), relCont(O, \_, \_), starve(O)\} \\ pc_\sigma = \mathsf{true} & wf(sh \mathbin{\underline{**}} \tau_\sigma) & q' = q \setminus \Omega \cup \{\emptyset \rhd ilREv_{last(\tau)}(O) \cdot \omega\} \end{array}}{sh, q \rightarrow sh \mathbin{\underline{**}} \tau_\sigma \mathbin{\underline{**}} ilEv_{last(\tau_\sigma)}(O), q'} \quad (17)$$

Select a candidate set Ω of symbolic traces representing the abstract behaviors of a method in object O with a given associated future F, and a specific local candidate trace $pc \rhd \tau \cdot \omega$ from that set. From this trace, we select a non-empty prefix τ which we concretize with the last state σ of sh and require that the concretized path condition pc_σ holds. This rule captures interleaving, so we require that the rest ω of the trace does not introduce an internal scheduling point or diverges. This is expressed by the condition $\omega \notin \{\ldots\}$; these cases are handled by other rules below. If the extension of sh by the concrete candidate trace τ_σ is well-formed, expressed by the predicate $wf(sh \mathbin{\underline{**}} \tau_\sigma)$, the interleaving step succeeds, and the rule produces a new concrete trace $sh \mathbin{\underline{**}} \tau_\sigma \mathbin{\underline{**}} ilEv_{last(\tau_\sigma)}(O)$ and a new queue q' of behaviors. The new trace ends in an interleaving event to record that τ_σ only represents a prefix of the full execution $\tau \cdot \omega$. In the new queue q', the other possible behaviors of the current method execution in Ω are replaced by the continuation ω of the selected behavior, prefixed by the dual interleaving reaction event $ilREv_{last(\tau)}(O)$. This prefixing ensures that other behaviors of O cannot be selected for execution before this method has completed its execution.

Now consider the case where the selected behavior is a *blocking continuation* marker $blkCont(O, F, s)$, which expresses that a `get` statement is blocked while waiting for a future to be resolved.

$$\frac{pc \triangleright \tau \cdot blkCont(O,F,s) \in \Omega \quad \Omega \in q \quad object(\Omega) = O \\ \tau \neq \varepsilon \quad pc_\sigma = \text{true} \quad wf(sh \ast\!\ast \tau_\sigma) \quad last(sh) = \sigma \\ q' = q \setminus \Omega \cup \{pc' \triangleright ilREv_{last(\tau)}(O) \ast\!\ast \omega \mid pc' \triangleright \omega \in \mathrm{val}^{O,F}_{last(\tau)}(s)\}}{sh, q \to sh \ast\!\ast \tau_\sigma \ast\!\ast ilEv_{last(\tau_\sigma)}(O), q'} \quad (18)$$

In contrast to rule (17), the set Ω of behaviors is here replaced by the behaviors obtained by expanding the marker to exclude local interleaving at the blocked `get` statement. Note that trace $sh \ast\!\ast \tau_\sigma$ ends with an event trace $blkEv_{last(\tau_\sigma)}(O, F)$.

Next consider the case when the continuation of the selected behavior has an *internal scheduling point*, as expressed by the requirement $\omega \in \{\ldots\}$:

$$\frac{pc \triangleright \tau \cdot \omega \in \Omega \quad \Omega \in q \quad object(\Omega) = O \\ \tau \neq \varepsilon \quad pc_\sigma = \text{true} \quad wf(sh \ast\!\ast \tau_\sigma) \quad last(sh) = \sigma \\ \omega \in \{\varepsilon, relCont(O, \_, \_), starve(O)\} \quad q' = q \setminus \Omega \cup \{\emptyset \triangleright \omega\}}{sh, q \to sh \ast\!\ast \tau_\sigma, q'} \quad (19)$$

Interleaving events are not required, as the local semantics ensures that τ ends with a release or completion event that allows internal scheduling to happen.

Now consider the case where the selected behavior is a *release continuation* marker $relCont(O, F, s)$. In the following rule, the set Ω of behaviors is replaced by the behaviors obtained by expanding the marker at the concrete state $last(sh)$. After scheduling the trace we add an interleaving event, which allows the previous rules to concretize and decompose ω.

$$\frac{relCont(O, F, s) \in \Omega \quad \Omega \in q \quad last(sh) = \sigma \\ pc_\sigma = \text{true} \quad q' = q \setminus \Omega \cup \{\emptyset \triangleright ilREv_\sigma(O) \ast\!\ast \omega \mid pc \triangleright \omega \in \mathrm{val}^{O,F}_\sigma(s)\}}{sh, q \to sh \ast\!\ast schEv_\sigma(O) \ast\!\ast ilEv_\sigma(O), q'} \quad (20)$$

Finally, consider the case where the selected behavior is *starvation*, the starving process can never be re-scheduled. This is captured by the final rule:

$$\frac{starve(O) \in \Omega \quad \Omega \in q \quad wf(sh \ast\!\ast schEv_{last(sh)}(O)) \quad q' = q \setminus \Omega}{sh, q \to sh, q'} \quad (21)$$

In this case the concrete trace sh ends with an interleaving event trace, i.e. object O is in the middle of a sequential execution, a scheduling event for object O is technically added to sh for well-formedness checking. In addition, the set of abstract traces Ω associated to the starving method is removed from q to capture that the process never gets rescheduled.

5.3 Well-Formed Global Traces

Events in traces must obey certain ordering restrictions to ensure that only valid traces of a given program can be obtained. This is captured in the composition rules by a well-formedness predicate. Only the well-formedness of finite, concrete traces sh needs to be checked and only the information relating to events is of relevance. We use auxiliary functions $filter(sh, f)$ and $filter(sh, o)$ to filter the events related to a specific future f and to a specific object o in a finite trace sh, respectively. The output of these functions is a finite sequence η of events in which the ordering is the same as in sh. Their definition is obvious and omitted here. Well-formedness is defined inductively over the length of event sequences of a trace sh, using auxiliary predicates $wff(\eta, f)$ and $wfo(\eta, o)$:

$$wf(sh) \triangleq \forall o \in obj(sh), f \in fut(sh). wfo(filter(sh, o), o) \wedge wff(filter(sh, f), f) \quad (22)$$

Here, $obj(sh)$ and $fut(sh)$ return the set of all object and future identities found in trace sh, respectively. Thus, a global trace is well-formed if and only if the projection of its event trace on any object and any future is well-formed. We use $ew(\eta, o)$ and $ew(\eta, f)$ to return the last event in a non-empty event sequence η related to o and f, respectively. For example, $ew(\eta \cdot schEv(o), o) = schEv(o)$. We define the most interesting cases of $wff(\eta, f)$ and $wfo(\eta, o)$.

In a well-formed trace, a release event related to a future f can never be preceded by a completion event for f, indicating that the future is resolved. Obviously, the same holds for blocking events.

$$wff(\eta \curvearrowright relEv(o, f), f) \triangleq wff(\eta, f) \wedge compEv(o, f, \_) \notin \eta \quad (23)$$

$$wff(\eta \curvearrowright blkEv(o, f), f) \triangleq wff(\eta, f) \wedge compEv(o, f, \_) \notin \eta \quad (24)$$

We use the symbol "_" for "don't care" (implicitly universally quantified) values. To ensure cooperative scheduling (no local preemption), an interleaving event related to object o must be immediately followed by the corresponding interleaving reaction event:

$$wfo(\eta \curvearrowright ilREv(o), o) \triangleq wff(\eta, o) \wedge ew(\eta, o) = ilEv(o) \quad (25)$$

To prevent scheduling a different process after an interleaving event relating to an object o, an invocation reaction event or a scheduling event for o should not directly succeed an interleaving event.

$$wfo(\eta \curvearrowright invREv(\_, o, \_, \_, \_), o) \triangleq wff(\eta, o) \wedge (ew(\eta, o) \neq ilEv(o)) \quad (26)$$

$$wfo(\eta \curvearrowright schEv(o), o) \triangleq wff(\eta, o) \wedge (ew(\eta, o) \neq ilEv(o)) \quad (27)$$

The remaining cases are similar and express that, e.g., an invocation reaction happens after an invocation, scheduling only after a release or a completion, etc.

$\varepsilon \curvearrowright \cdots \curvearrowright newEv(\mathsf{Main}, o'', \_) \curvearrowright \cdots \curvearrowright invEv(\mathsf{Main}, o'', f, \mathsf{n}, \_) \curvearrowright \cdots \curvearrowright blockEv(\mathsf{Main}, f) \curvearrowright$
$[l' \mapsto f, v' \mapsto 0, o' \mapsto o'', o''.i \mapsto 0] \curvearrowright ilEv(\mathsf{Main}) \curvearrowright [l' \mapsto f, v' \mapsto 0, o' \mapsto o'', o''.i \mapsto 0]$
$\curvearrowright$
$invREv(\mathsf{Main}, o'', f, \mathsf{n}, \_) \curvearrowright \cdots \curvearrowright invEv(o'', o'', f_1, \mathsf{m}, 3) \curvearrowright \cdots \curvearrowright$
$relEv(o'', f_1) \curvearrowright [l' \mapsto f, v' \mapsto 0, o' \mapsto o'', o''.i \mapsto 0, y' \mapsto 10, l'_1 \mapsto f_1]$
$\curvearrowright$
$invREv(o'', o'', f_1, \mathsf{m}, 3) \curvearrowright \cdots \curvearrowright$
$compEv(o'', f_1, 3) \curvearrowright [l' \mapsto f, v' \mapsto 0, o' \mapsto o'', o''.i \mapsto 3, y' \mapsto 10, l'_1 \mapsto f_1, x' \mapsto 3]$
$\curvearrowright$
$schEv(o'') \curvearrowright [l' \mapsto f, v' \mapsto 0, o' \mapsto o'', o''.i \mapsto 3, y' \mapsto 10, l'_1 \mapsto f_1, x' \mapsto 3] \curvearrowright ilEv(o'') \curvearrowright$
$[l' \mapsto f, v' \mapsto 0, o' \mapsto o'', o''.i \mapsto 3, y' \mapsto 10, l'_1 \mapsto f_1, x' \mapsto 3] \curvearrowright ilREv(o'') \curvearrowright$
$[l' \mapsto f, v' \mapsto 0, o' \mapsto o'', o''.i \mapsto 3, y' \mapsto 10, l'_1 \mapsto f_1, x' \mapsto 3] \curvearrowright compREv(o'', f_1, 3) \curvearrowright \cdots \curvearrowright$
$compEv(o'', f, 13) \curvearrowright [l' \mapsto f, v' \mapsto 0, o' \mapsto o'', o''.i \mapsto 3, y' \mapsto 13, l'_1 \mapsto f_1, x' \mapsto 3]$
$\curvearrowright$
$ilREv(\mathsf{Main}) \curvearrowright [l' \mapsto f, v' \mapsto 0, o' \mapsto o'', o''.i \mapsto 3, y' \mapsto 13, l'_1 \mapsto f_1, x' \mapsto 3] \curvearrowright$
$compREv(\mathsf{Main}, f, 3) \curvearrowright \cdots \curvearrowright [l' \mapsto f, v' \mapsto 3, o' \mapsto o'', o''.i \mapsto 3, \boldsymbol{y' \mapsto 13}, l'_1 \mapsto f_1, x' \mapsto 3]$

Fig. 4. A summary of a global trace for the example.

5.4 Global Traces by Example

Figure 4 shows a possible global trace for the example in Fig. 2, by composing the local traces from Fig. 3. Note that the trace renames all declared variables and fields. The trace starts with an empty state ε in the main block, then object o is created and an asynchronous method call to method n in o is invoked. The Main object is blocked while waiting for the termination of the invoked method n (i.e. until future l is resolved). There is no local interleaving in object Main. Interleaving events are used to enable global interleaving at the blocking get statement. The global trace continues with the execution of method n while Main is blocked. Since the trace for method n contains a release event relating to its await statement, method m in object o can be selected for execution. After completion of m the remaining code of n is scheduled and once that is completed, the Main process resumes, fetches the value from future l and the program terminates when the get statement retrieves the value 13. Other possible global traces can be generated by varying the global interleaving at the get statement in the Main block and the await statement in method n.

6   Calculus

The main point of a modular, denotational semantics for ABS is to drive the development of program logics for deductive reasoning. Although this will largely be the topic of future work, we sketch some opportunities. Starting points are (i) the dynamic logic for *sequential* Java implemented in KeY [3], (ii) the dynamic logic for the ABS version of KeY [16] that permits *object-local* reasoning about class invariants, and (iii) a dynamic logic for a sequential language that uses symbolic trace formulas to specify program behavior [17]. Trace formulas are the syntactic counterpart to symbolic traces. All three logics implement a *symbolic interpreter* for the sequential language fragments in their calculus. Therefore, they are an excellent match for the semantics developed here—in fact, program logics were the motivation for the work presented in this paper. We will merge these program logics into a single one that is sufficient for *invariant* reasoning on *local objects* with *symbolic traces*. The logic outlined here is relatively weak, because global behavior or pre- and postconditions (specifically, return values) are not addressed, but it is designed with suitable extensions in mind.

6.1 Symbolic Trace Formulas

Our semantics uses symbolic traces to specify the behaviors of local computations of ABS programs. It is, therefore, natural to have a syntactic representation of them in the logic. Symbolic trace formulas are due to Nakata & Uustalu [14], and were intended for an abstract Hoare calculus with co-inductive reasoning about non-terminating programs. Trace formulas were generalized to dynamic logic over trace modality formulas in [17]. For our purposes, it is sufficient to leave trace formulas completely abstract, i.e., a *trace formula* is an expression Θ that describes a possibly infinite set of (concrete) traces. There is a semantic evaluation function such that $\mathrm{val}_\tau^{O,F}(\Theta)$ is true iff τ is one of the traces on O, F described by Θ. We give an informal example of a typical trace formula:

$$invREv(\_, \texttt{this}, f, m, v) \ll invEv(\texttt{this}, \_, \_, n, w) ** \lceil \phi(v, w) \rceil \ll compEv(\texttt{this}, f, m)$$

Here, $\ll$ represents a "happens after" relation (i.e. an arbitrary, finite trace between the events), $**$ is the syntactic equivalent of $\underline{**}$, and $\lceil \phi \rceil$ denotes the occurrence of a state in which ϕ holds. The trace formula above might be paraphrased as: "whenever the current object 'this' completes method m, then during the execution of m there was a call to n such that the arguments v of m and w of n were in relation ϕ." This is a typical example of a class invariant that can be succinctly expressed via symbolic trace formulas.

Trace modality formulas Ψ are defined on top of trace formulas by taking them as atomic building blocks that are syntactically closed with respect to the usual propositional/first-order connectives and the following modalities:

1. If s is an ABS statement and Ψ a trace modality formula, then $[\![s]\!]\Psi$ is a trace modality formula.
2. If $\{u\}$ is a trace update and Ψ a trace modality formula, then $\{u\}\Psi$ is a trace modality formula.

Trace updates [17] are expressions $\{\ell := exp\}$ or $\{ev(\bar{e})\}$ recording state change effected by assignments (with semantics $\langle\sigma\rangle \curvearrowright \sigma[\ell \mapsto \mathrm{val}_\sigma(exp)]$) or the occurrence of communication events. Let $\mathcal{U}$ denote a finite sequence of trace updates.

The semantics $\mathrm{val}_\tau([\![s]\!]\Psi)$ of a trace modality formula $[\![s]\!]\Psi$ and a trace τ is formally defined as: if τ is finite, $O \in \mathcal{O}$, $F \in \mathcal{F}$, and $\tau' \in \mathrm{val}_{\mathrm{last}(\tau)}^{O,F}(s)$, then $\tau \underline{**} \tau'$, if well-formed, is in $\mathrm{val}_\tau^{O,F}(\Psi)$. In words, any valid trace of s that extends

τ must be a trace of Ψ. If τ is infinite, s is never reached, and τ must be a trace of Ψ. The semantics of $\{u\}\Psi$ is similar, by first extending τ according to the trace update u.

6.2 Selected Reasoning Rules

We define a sequent calculus where antecedents and succedents range over multisets of trace modality formulas. For trace modality formulas Γ and $[\![s]\!]\Psi$, and trace updates $\mathcal{U}$, the sequent $\Gamma \Rightarrow \mathcal{U}[\![s]\!]\Psi$ expresses: if the execution of s on $\mathtt{this}$ with future $\mathtt{destiny}$ begins in the last state of a finite trace τ described by Γ and after applying $\mathcal{U}$, then Ψ must contain any trace generated by the execution of s and the effect of the updates $\mathcal{U}$ that extends τ. For an infinite trace τ in Γ, s is not executed, but Ψ must contain τ.

We now discuss four proof rules in more detail. In the rule for *assignments*,

$$\text{assign} \;\; \frac{\Gamma \Rightarrow \mathcal{U}\{\ell := e\}[\![r]\!]\Psi}{\Gamma \Rightarrow \mathcal{U}[\![\ell = e; \, r]\!]\Psi}$$

ℓ is a program variable and e a pure (side effect-free) expression. This rule rewrites the formula by moving the assignment from the program into an update to capture the state change, here $\{\ell := e\}$. Symbolic execution continues with the remaining program r. Updates can be viewed as explicit substitutions accumulated in front of the modality during symbolic program execution. Once the program has been completely executed and the modality is empty, the accumulated updates are applied to the formula after the modality, resulting in an update- and program-free trace modality formula. In the rule for *asynchronous method calls*

$$\text{asyncCall} \;\; \frac{\Gamma, isFresh(f) \Rightarrow \mathcal{U}\{invEv(O, \mathtt{this}, f, m, \overline{e}')\}\{\ell := f\}[\![r]\!]\Psi}{\Gamma \Rightarrow \mathcal{U}[\![\ell = e!m(\overline{e}'); \, r]\!]\Psi}$$

the premise introduces a constant f representing the future associated with this method invocation. The left side of the implication ensures that f is fresh. The right side adds two trace updates, an invocation event generated by this call and a binding of ℓ to the fresh future f. In the rule for the *await* statement

$$\text{await} \;\; \frac{\Gamma, class(\mathtt{this}) = C \Rightarrow \mathcal{U}\, I_C}{\Gamma, \mathcal{U}\mathcal{U}_a\, I_C \Rightarrow \mathcal{U}\mathcal{U}_a\, \{compREv(\mathtt{this}, \ell, v_0)\}[\![r]\!]\Psi}{\Gamma \Rightarrow \mathcal{U}[\![\mathtt{await}\; \ell?; \, r]\!]\Psi}$$

I_C denotes a trace modality formula that serves as the invariant of class C. This rule has two premises: the first expresses that I_C should hold at the process release point and the second expresses the situation where future ℓ has been resolved. This is captured by the completion reaction event. Update $\mathcal{U}_a$ represents the unknown trace updates from other processes on the same object. This is achieved by initializing any location that might be changed by another process with a fresh constant. Since class invariant I_C is guaranteed by the latest released process, I_C is true by assumption. The rule for the *get* statement is

$$\text{get} \; \frac{\Gamma, isFresh(v_0) \Rightarrow \mathcal{U}\{compREv(\text{this}, \ell', v_0)\}\{\ell := v_0\}[\![r]\!]\Psi}{\Gamma \Rightarrow \mathcal{U}[\![\ell = \ell'.\text{get}; \; r]\!]\Psi}$$

For partial correctness, we can assume that future ℓ' has been resolved. The right side of the implication adds two trace updates, a completion reaction event for ℓ' with some value v_0 and a binding of ℓ to v_0. Note that v_0 is a fresh variable because ℓ' might be resolved on a different object, which makes the value of v_0 invisible. Any information about the value of ℓ must be put into the class invariant. However, support from pre- and postcondition reasoning in future work may provide more information about the return value v_0.

7 Related Work

This paper is motivated by our aim to devise compositional proof systems to verify protocol-like behaviors for asynchronously communicating objects. The general field of trace semantics is too vast to cover here. For languages with ABS-like features, Din et al. [16,18,19] introduced 4-event trace semantics for asynchronous method calls and shared futures, which, together with the trace modality formulas of Nakata et al. [14,17], underlies our work. Recent work [20] on similar communication structures for ASP/ProActive, using parametrized labelled transition systems with queues, models interaction with futures in a very detailed, operational way. In contrast, our work with traces allows futures to be abstracted into communication events and well-formedness conditions.

Brookes' action traces [10] bear some similarity to our work. He aims at denotational semantics using collecting semantics, explicitly represents divergence, and synchronizes communication using events. Action traces have been used as a semantics for concurrent separation logic [21], where scheduling is based on access to shared resources with associated invariants (so-called "mutex fairmerge"). In contrast, we use conditioned traces and continuations, cover procedure calls by *abstract* traces, and extend the use of dual events from communication to different scheduling situations, resulting in a compositional denotational semantics for asynchronous method calls and cooperative concurrency.

8 Conclusion and Future Work

We presented a denotational semantics for an OO concurrent language with cooperative scheduling that is streamlined for the development of program logics with trace formulas. The main advantages of the semantics are its compositionality and the separation of local and global computations. Technical innovations include abstract, conditioned traces permitting symbolic evaluation as well as event pairs to keep track of schedulability. We sketched a simple program logic with trace formulas that is sufficient for local invariant reasoning. In future work we will extend it to a calculus that allows to reason about global properties, including liveness, and that supports method-local specification with contracts.

Acknowledgement. We are grateful to Dave Sands for useful hints and feedback and to Georges P. for inspiring our use of constraints.

References

1. Hoare, C.A.R.: An axiomatic basis for computer programming. Commun. ACM **12**(10), 576–580 (1969). (583)
2. Dijkstra, E.W.: A Discipline of Programming. Prentice-Hall, Upper Saddle (1976)
3. Beckert, B., Klebanov, V., Weiß, B.: Dynamic logic for Java. In: Ahrendt, W., Beckert, B., Bubel, R., Hähnle, R., Schmitt, P., Ulbrich, M. (eds.) Deductive Software Verification–The KeY Book: From Theory to Practice. LNCS, vol. 10001, pp. 49–106. Springer, Heidelberg (2016). doi:10.1007/978-3-319-49812-6
4. Plotkin, G.D.: A structural approach to operational semantics. J. Log. Algebraic Program. **60–61**, 17–139 (2004)
5. Drossopoulou, S., Eisenbach, S.: Describing the semantics of Java and proving type soundness. In: Alves-Foss, J. (ed.) Formal Syntax and Semantics of Java. LNCS, vol. 1523, pp. 41–82. Springer, Heidelberg (1999)
6. Krebbers, R., Wiedijk, F.: A typed C11 semantics for interactive theorem proving. In: Conference on Certified Programs and Proofs, 15–27. ACM (2015)
7. Johnsen, E.B., Hähnle, R., Schäfer, J., Schlatte, R., Steffen, M.: ABS: a core language for abstract behavioral specification. In: Aichernig, B.K., de Boer, F.S., Bonsangue, M.M. (eds.) 9th International Symposium on Formal Methods for Components and Objects (FMCO 2010), vol. 6957, pp. 142–164. Springer, Berlin (2011). doi:10.1007/978-3-642-25271-6_8
8. Filliâtre, J.C., Marché, C.: The Why/Krakatoa/Caduceus platform for deductive program verification. In: Damm, W., Hermanns, H. (eds.) 19th International Conference on Computer Aided Verification, CAV 2007. LNCS, vol. 4590, pp. 173–177. Springer, Berlin (2007). doi:10.1007/978-3-540-73368-3_21
9. Leino, K.R.M.: Dafny: an automatic program verifier for functional correctness. In: Clarke, E.M., Voronkov, A. (eds.) LPAR 2010. LNCS, vol. 6355, pp. 348–370. Springer, Heidelberg (2010). doi:10.1007/978-3-642-17511-4_20
10. Brookes, S.: Traces, pomsets, fairness and full abstraction for communicating processes. In: Brim, L., Křetínský, M., Kučera, A., Jančar, P. (eds.) CONCUR 2002. LNCS, vol. 2421, pp. 466–482. Springer, Heidelberg (2002). doi:10.1007/3-540-45694-5_31
11. Meyer, B.: Applying "design by contract". IEEE Comput. **25**(10), 40–51 (1992)
12. Nielson, F., Nielson, H.R., Hankin, C.L.: Principles of Program Analysis. Springer, Heidelberg (1999). doi:10.1007/978-3-662-03811-6
13. Hentschel, M., Hähnle, R., Bubel, R.: Visualizing unbounded symbolic execution. In: Seidl, M., Tillmann, N. (eds.) TAP 2014. LNCS, vol. 8570, pp. 82–98. Springer, Cham (2014). doi:10.1007/978-3-319-09099-3_7
14. Nakata, K., Uustalu, T.: A Hoare logic for the coinductive trace-based big-step semantics of While. Log. Methods Comput. Sci. **11**(1), 1–32 (2015)
15. Boer, F.S., Clarke, D., Johnsen, E.B.: A complete guide to the future. In: Nicola, R. (ed.) ESOP 2007. LNCS, vol. 4421, pp. 316–330. Springer, Heidelberg (2007). doi:10.1007/978-3-540-71316-6_22

16. Din, C.C., Bubel, R., Hähnle, R.: KeY-ABS: a deductive verification tool for the concurrent modelling language ABS. In: Felty, A.P., Middeldorp, A. (eds.) CADE 2015. LNCS, vol. 9195, pp. 517–526. Springer, Cham (2015). doi:10.1007/978-3-319-21401-6_35

17. Bubel, R., Din, C.C., Hähnle, R., Nakata, K.: A dynamic logic with traces and coinduction. In: Nivelle, H. (ed.) TABLEAUX 2015. LNCS, vol. 9323, pp. 307–322. Springer, Cham (2015). doi:10.1007/978-3-319-24312-2_21

18. Din, C.C., Dovland, J., Johnsen, E.B., Owe, O.: Observable behavior of distributed systems: component reasoning for concurrent objects. J. Logic Algebraic Program. **81**(3), 227–256 (2012)

19. Din, C.C., Owe, O.: Compositional reasoning about active objects with shared futures. Formal Asp. Comput. **27**(3), 551–572 (2015)

20. Ameur-Boulifa, R., Henrio, L., Kulankhina, O., Madelaine, E., Savu, A.: Behavioural semantics for asynchronous components. J. Logical Algebraic Methods Program. **89**, 1–40 (2017)

21. Brookes, S.: A semantics for concurrent separation logic. Theor. Comput. Sci. **375**(1–3), 227–270 (2007)

On the Decidability of Certain Semi-Lattice Based Modal Logics

Katalin Bimbó$^{(\boxtimes)}$ ⓘD

Department of Philosophy, University of Alberta, Edmonton, AB T6G 2E7, Canada
bimbo@ualberta.ca
http://www.ualberta.ca/~bimbo

Abstract. Sequent calculi are proof systems that are exceptionally suitable for proving the decidability of a logic. Several *relevance logics* were proved decidable using a technique attributable to Curry and Kripke. Further enhancements led to a proof of the decidability of *implicational ticket entailment* by Bimbó and Dunn in [12,13]. This paper uses a different adaptation of the same core proof technique to prove a group of *positive modal logics* (with disjunction but no conjunction) decidable.

Keywords: Sequent calculi · Modal logic · Decidability · Relevance logic · Heap number · Semi-lattice based logic

1 Modal Logics

The well-known modal logic **S4** is arguably one of the most successful modal systems ever invented. It is a system that grew out of Lewis's original system of strict implication defined in [29] by the addition of the axiom $\neg\Diamond\neg p \dashv3 \neg\Diamond\neg\neg\Diamond\neg p$, where $\dashv3$ is strict implication (see [15]). **S4** was given the nowadays standard formulation of a normal modal logic as an explicit extension of classical propositional logic by Gödel in [24]. **S4** has a close connection to intuitionistic logic and topology, and it has a straightforward relational semantics over pre-ordered (or partially ordered) frames. The list of remarkable features goes on and on.

S4 can be formulated by adding two rules, namely, ($\Box\Vdash$) and ($\Vdash\Box$) to the propositional part of **LK** from [23].

$$\frac{\Gamma^\Box \Vdash \varphi}{\Gamma^\Box \Vdash \Box\varphi} \ (\Vdash\Box) \qquad\qquad \frac{\varphi, \Gamma \Vdash \Delta}{\Box\varphi, \Gamma \Vdash \Delta} \ (\Box\Vdash) \qquad\qquad (1)$$

This formulation assumes that the other modality, which is often denoted by $\Diamond$ is defined (i.e., $\Diamond\varphi$ is simply an abbreviation for $\neg\Box\neg\varphi$). This is unproblematic in the case of classical logic, however, we do not always want to have a negation in a logic or we simply want to have both these modalities as primitives.[1]

The sequent calculus formulation of **S4** with both modalities amends ($\Vdash\Box$) to permit multiple formulas in the succedent. The new ($\Vdash\Box$) rule and the rules for $\Diamond$ were introduced in Kripke [27], and they are as follows:

---

[1] See for example Dunn [20] and Kripke [27].

© Springer International Publishing AG 2017
R.A. Schmidt and C. Nalon (Eds.): TABLEAUX 2017, LNAI 10501, pp. 44–61, 2017.
DOI: 10.1007/978-3-319-66902-1_3

$$\frac{\Gamma^\square \Vdash \Delta^\lozenge, \varphi}{\Gamma^\square \Vdash \Delta^\lozenge, \square\varphi} \ (\Vdash\square) \qquad\qquad \frac{\Gamma \Vdash \Delta, \varphi}{\Gamma \Vdash \Delta, \lozenge\varphi} \ (\Vdash\lozenge) \qquad\qquad \frac{\varphi, \Gamma^\square \Vdash \Delta^\lozenge}{\lozenge\varphi, \Gamma^\square \Vdash \Delta^\lozenge} \ (\lozenge\Vdash)$$

Our goal in this paper is to investigate the problem of decidability for logics that contain a pair of modalities that have introduction rules analogous to the ones above, but they lack much of what an underlying 2-valued calculus gives. We are not concerned with interpretations here, however, we note that it is clear that once we start to drop rules from **LK**, the "meanings" of the connectives change. In order to preclude confusions stemming from connotations, we will use a pair of neutral symbols—▷ and ◁—for the two unary connectives we take to be modalities. Another effect of omitting rules from **LK** is that space opens up for new versions of connectives—even without the introduction of multiple structural connectives. We will take advantage of this opportunity by including both ∨ and + in all our logics.

Our strategy is to fix a common set of connective rules for a group of logics. The choice of the connectives and of the rules for them is motivated by relevance logic (see, for example, [1,2]). We will vary the structural rules and we will select 9 logics to scrutinize. We will refer to the whole group of these logics or to an arbitrary element of the group as $L\mathfrak{X}^*$.

Definition 1. The *signature* for $L\mathfrak{X}^*$ is $\langle \circ^2, \to^2, +^2, \vee^2, \triangleright^1, \triangleleft^1 \rangle$ (with the arities indicated in the superscripts). The *set of formulas* is generated by the following context-free grammar (CFG) in Backus–Naur form (BNF).

$$\varphi := \mathsf{Prop} \mid (\varphi \circ \varphi) \mid (\varphi \to \varphi) \mid (\varphi + \varphi) \mid (\varphi \vee \varphi) \mid \triangleright\varphi \mid \triangleleft\varphi,$$

where Prop is a non-terminal symbol that can be rewritten as any of the denumerably many propositional letters.[2]

REMARK 1. Occasionally, it is convenient to be able to refer to the connectives by names, which are somewhat mnemonic. We call ∘ *fusion*, → *implication*, + *fission*, ∨ *disjunction*, ▷ *solid modality* and ◁ *fluid modality*. The latter two terms are chosen to keep the usual modal connotations at bay.

In the $L\mathfrak{X}^*$ logics, we want ∘ and + to be connectives that are commutative and associative. Then, it is felicitous to formulate the notion of sequents using multisets. In order to make this paper more or less self-contained (and to minimize the chance of terminological confusions), we include the definition of a multiset as well as an illustration of the concept.

Definition 2. A *multiset* is the set of finite sequences comprising the same elements that is closed under permutation.[3]

---

[2] We may use other letters than φ, from the latter part of the Greek alphabet, as variables for formulas.

[3] In this paper, we only have use for *finite* multisets; thus, we use the term in a narrower sense than it is used elsewhere in the literature.

An essentially equivalent definition of multisets can be given as certain functions—see, for example, the definition of multisets in [10]. We are not interested in the reconstruction of sequences or multisets as sets here, and we take sets, multisets and sequences to be different ways of collecting objects together. Thus, informally speaking, a multiset is a finite set, in which the elements may appear more than once, hence, the number of listings matters.

EXAMPLE 2. If the multiset $\mathbb{A}$ has two a's and b's as its elements, then we could list the elements of $\mathbb{A}$ as a, a, b, b, or equivalently, as b, a, a, b, etc. Of course, $\langle a, a, b, b \rangle$ may be a different 4-tuple than $\langle b, a, a, b \rangle$ is, but a permutation transforms one into the other. On the other hand, $\{a, b\} = \{a, a, b, b\}$. The latter specification of a set is not only informal, but unnecessarily repetitive.

NOTATION 3. Obviously, we can describe a multiset by listing its elements. To distinguish an array from a multiset, we may enclose the latter into [ ], and we use ; as the separator, because our multisets of formulas are associated to fusions or fissions of formulas. The letters $\alpha, \beta, \gamma, \ldots$ range over multisets of formulas of the $L\mathfrak{X}^*$ logics. If φ is an element of α thrice, then we may say that the *type* φ is in α, and the *tokens* φ, φ and φ are in α.

Definition 3. If α and β are multisets, then $\alpha \cap \beta$ (the *intersection* of α and β) and $\alpha \uplus \beta$ (the *union* of α and β) are multisets. $\alpha \cap \beta$ has all the types that are in both α and β, and the number of tokens for each type is the lesser number of tokens of that type in the two. $\alpha \uplus \beta$ has all the types that are either in α or in β, and the number of tokens for a type is the sum of the number of tokens of that type in α and that in β.

We defined both $\cap$ and $\uplus$ to stress the lack of (informal) duality between them. $\cap$ is min on the number of tokens, whereas $\uplus$ is *not* max, rather +. For our purposes, $\uplus$ is the important operation.

Definition 4. A *sequent* is an ordered pair of multisets of formulas. We write $\alpha \Vdash \beta$ instead of $\langle \alpha, \beta \rangle$. α is the *antecedent* and β is the *succedent* of the sequent.

NOTATION 4. The empty set is unique and so is the empty multiset, which we denote by $\varnothing$. However, when $\varnothing$ appears in a sequent, we replace it with space. To formulate the rules of our calculi, we will use $\alpha; \varphi$ (or $\varphi; \alpha$) instead of $\alpha \uplus [\varphi]$. Similarly, $\alpha; \beta$ is a shorthand for $\alpha \uplus \beta$.

Definition 5. The $L\mathfrak{X}^*$ *logics* comprise axiom (1) and rules from among the following.

$$\varphi \Vdash \varphi \quad (1)$$

$$\frac{\alpha \Vdash \varphi; \beta}{\alpha \Vdash \varphi \vee \psi; \beta} \;(\Vdash\vee_1) \qquad \frac{\alpha \Vdash \psi; \beta}{\alpha \Vdash \varphi \vee \psi; \beta} \;(\Vdash\vee_2) \qquad \frac{\alpha; \psi \Vdash \beta \quad \alpha; \varphi \Vdash \beta}{\alpha; \varphi \vee \psi \Vdash \beta} \;(\vee\Vdash)$$

$$\frac{\alpha \Vdash \varphi; \beta \quad \gamma \Vdash \psi; \delta}{\alpha; \gamma \Vdash \psi \circ \varphi; \beta; \delta} \;(\Vdash\circ) \qquad \frac{\alpha; \psi; \varphi \Vdash \beta}{\alpha; \varphi \circ \psi \Vdash \beta} \;(\circ\Vdash)$$

$$\frac{\alpha;\psi \Vdash \varphi;\beta}{\alpha \Vdash \psi \to \varphi;\beta} \ (\Vdash\to) \qquad \frac{\alpha \Vdash \psi;\beta \quad \gamma;\varphi \Vdash \delta}{\alpha;\gamma;\psi \to \varphi \Vdash \beta;\delta} \ (\to\Vdash)$$

$$\frac{\alpha \Vdash \psi;\varphi;\beta}{\alpha \Vdash \varphi + \psi;\beta} \ (\Vdash+) \qquad \frac{\alpha;\psi \Vdash \beta \quad \gamma;\varphi \Vdash \delta}{\alpha;\gamma;\varphi + \psi \Vdash \beta;\delta} \ (+\Vdash)$$

$$\frac{\alpha^{\triangleright} \Vdash \varphi;\beta^{\triangleleft}}{\alpha^{\triangleright} \Vdash \triangleright\varphi;\beta^{\triangleleft}} \ (\Vdash\triangleright) \qquad \frac{\alpha;\varphi \Vdash \beta}{\alpha;\triangleright\varphi \Vdash \beta} \ (\triangleright\Vdash)$$

$$\frac{\alpha \Vdash \varphi;\beta}{\alpha \Vdash \triangleleft\varphi;\beta} \ (\Vdash\triangleleft) \qquad \frac{\alpha^{\triangleright};\varphi \Vdash \beta^{\triangleleft}}{\alpha^{\triangleright};\triangleleft\varphi \Vdash \beta^{\triangleleft}} \ (\triangleleft\Vdash)$$

$$\frac{\alpha \Vdash \psi;\psi;\beta}{\alpha \Vdash \psi;\beta} \ (\Vdash W) \qquad \frac{\alpha;\varphi;\varphi \Vdash \beta}{\alpha;\varphi \Vdash \beta} \ (W\Vdash)$$

$$\frac{\alpha \Vdash \triangleleft\varphi;\triangleleft\varphi;\beta}{\alpha \Vdash \triangleleft\varphi;\beta} \ (\Vdash\triangleleft W) \qquad \frac{\alpha;\triangleright\psi;\triangleright\psi \Vdash \beta}{\alpha;\triangleright\psi \Vdash \beta} \ (\triangleright W\Vdash)$$

$$\frac{\alpha \Vdash \beta}{\alpha \Vdash \triangleleft\varphi;\beta} \ (\Vdash\triangleleft K) \qquad \frac{\alpha \Vdash \beta}{\alpha;\triangleright\psi \Vdash \beta} \ (\triangleright K\Vdash)$$

$$\frac{\alpha \Vdash \beta}{\alpha \Vdash \psi;\beta} \ (\Vdash K) \qquad \frac{\alpha \Vdash \beta}{\alpha;\varphi \Vdash \beta} \ (K\Vdash)$$

Superscript modalities such as $\alpha^{\triangleleft}$ and $\beta^{\triangleright}$ indicate that for each token ψ in the multiset there is a formula φ such that ψ is $\triangleleft\varphi$ or $\triangleright\varphi$, respectively.

REMARK 5. The axiom is labeled with the identity combinator I. The contraction rules are labeled with W after the binary regular duplicator W, and the thinning rules are labeled with K after the binary regular cancellator K. Although these rules are not combinatory rules in the sense of [21], the analogy between structural rules and combinatory effects is profound. This correlation was observed and noted long ago (see, for example, Curry [17]).

If we keep all the operational rules fixed, then there are still plenty of logics that could be defined.[4] However, the vast majority of those logics would be less than well motivated. We deem a handful of them worthy of interest.

Definition 6. The $L\mathfrak{X}^{*}$ *logics* that we consider are defined by axiom (I) and the connective rules together with the structural rules with checkmarks as indicated in Table 1.[5]

---

[4] A quick approximation suggests that there are 89 logics that can be expected to be distinct.

[5] $\times$ excludes a pair of rules; $\star$ shows that the rules are easily derivable, hence, it is better to omit them—for the sake of economy in proofs.

Table 1. Structural rules in nine logics

Rules	bci	bci$^\nabla$	bci$_\Delta$	bci$^\nabla_\Delta$	bciw	bck	bciw$_\Delta$	bck$^\nabla$	s4
(W⊩), (⊩W)	×	×	×	×	✓	×	✓	×	✓
(▷W⊩), (⊩◁W)	×	✓	×	✓	★	×	★	✓	★
(▷K⊩), (⊩◁K)	×	×	✓	✓	×	★	✓	★	★
(K⊩), (⊩K)	×	×	×	×	×	✓	×	✓	✓

NOTATION 6. The labels for the logics are intended to be somewhat reminiscent of but not identical to common abbreviations for certain logics. For example, the principal simple types of the combinators B, C and I are provable in bci. However, we included not only →, but also ∘, +, ∨ and the modalities ▷ and ◁ (which are not in BCI). Likewise, s4 differs from the logic **S4**.

Definition 7. A *proof* is a tree, in which the vertices are occurrences of sequents; the leaves are instances of (I), and a parent node is justified when that node and its children constitute an instance of a rule. The *root* of the proof tree is the sequent proved.

A formula φ is a *theorem* of an $L\mathfrak{X}^*$ logic iff ⊩ φ has a proof.

Lemma 8. *The logic* s4 *is the* negation-free fragment *of the normal modal logic* **S4**.

Proof (sketch). From Sect. 2, we (will) know that the cut rule is admissible in s4, that is, s4 is a well-formulated sequent calculus. We also assume that we know that **S4** can be formalized as an extension of the propositional part of **LK** from [23]. Namely, the two rules for □ in (1) have to be added, and if ◇ is a primitive too, then two more rules are included for ◇ and the (⊩□) rule is modified by permitting a parametric set $\Delta^\lozenge$ on the right-had side of the ⊩.

The signature of s4 differs from that of usual formulations of **S4**. In other words, we have to explain how to "translate" our formulas. In the presence of (K⊩), (⊩K), (W⊩) and (⊩W), ⊩ $(\varphi \vee \psi) \to (\varphi + \psi)$ and ⊩ $(\psi + \varphi) \to (\psi \vee \varphi)$ are provable. This means that + is a notational variant of ∨. Also, ∘ is idempotent and the following three sequents are provable: ⊩ $(\varphi \circ (\psi \vee \varphi)) \to \varphi$, ⊩ $\psi \to ((\psi \vee \varphi) \circ \psi)$, ⊩ $(\varphi \circ (\psi \vee \chi)) \to ((\varphi \circ \psi) \vee (\varphi \circ \chi))$. Implication is the residual of fusion, that is, → behaves as ⊃ does in **LK**. This means that →, ∘ and ∨/+ are exactly like the positive fragment of classical propositional logic. Setting ▷ to □ and ◁ to ◇, the (▷⊩), (⊩▷), (◁⊩) and (⊩◁) rules are the rules for □ and ◇. There are no other connectives unaccounted for in s4.   ∴

2 Cut Theorems

We formulated our nine $L\mathfrak{X}^*$ logics without the cut rule. However, this does not mean that we would want to neglect the cut rule, rather, the opposite. The cut rule is extremely important for a proof that a sequent calculus defines an algebraizable logic, and that it is equivalent to an axiomatic system.

Definition 9. The *cut rule* is the following.

$$\frac{\alpha \Vdash \psi; \beta \quad \gamma; \psi \Vdash \delta}{\alpha; \gamma \Vdash \beta; \delta} \quad (\text{cut})$$

Later we may refer to this cut rule as the *single cut*—to distinguish this rule from some other versions of cut. It is easy to see that the cut rule is not a derived rule in any $L\mathfrak{X}^*$ logic. However, anything provable with cut is provable without the cut. This is the essence of Theorem 15.

Definition 10. The multiset of formulas in each rule is divided into three categories: principal, subaltern and parametric formulas. The *parametric formulas* are those in $\alpha, \alpha^\triangleright, \beta, \beta^\triangleleft, \gamma$ and δ. In a proof (where the rules are instantiated with concrete sequents), any of these may be $\varnothing$. The *principal formulas* are the newly introduced formulas in the lower sequent of a rule, as well as, the displayed formulas in the lower sequent in the contraction rules. The *subalterns* are the formulas from which the principal formulas result—save in the thinning rules, where there are none. There is a 1–1 correspondence between the elements of multisets of parametric formulas bearing the same letter in a premise and in the conclusion, and we assume that a particular such bijection is fixed when needed.[6]

There is a range of terms and definitions used in the literature in proofs of cut theorems; hence, we briefly state the notions used in the proof of the next theorem.

Definition 11. A formula φ is an *ancestor* of ψ when it is in the transitive closure of the relation emerging from the above analysis through (i) and (ii).

(i) A subaltern is an ancestor of the principal formula in a rule.
(ii) A parametric formula in an upper sequent is an ancestor of its matching token in a lower sequent.[7]

For the next two definitions, we assume that we are given a proof, which may contain applications of the cut rule. We focus on a cut that has no cuts above it in that given proof.

Definition 12. The *left rank* of the cut is the maximal number of consecutive sequents above the left premise of the cut in which ancestors of the cut formula that are the same type as the cut formula occur in the succedent increased by 1. The *right rank* is the number calculated dually. The *rank of the cut* is the sum of the left and right ranks of the cut.

---

[6] This analysis is fairly usual. For the ideas behind it and examples of it, we refer to [17] (and also to [9]).
[7] This notion is an adaptation of a similar notion from Curry [17].

Definition 13. The *contraction measure* of the cut is the number of applications of contraction rules to ancestors of the cut formula that are the same type as the cut formula in the subproof rooted in the lower sequent of the application of the cut rule.

REMARK 7. The previous two definitions depend on the notion of ancestors, and they reflect Curry's insight that the subformula property allows tracking a formula to its origins within a proof. Then, the trace yields a tighter control over the proof itself.

Definition 14. The *degree* of a formula φ is denoted by $\mathfrak{d}(\varphi)$.

(i) If $\varphi \in \mathsf{Prop}$, then $\mathfrak{d}(\varphi) = 0$.
(ii) If φ is $\circ\psi$ (where $\circ$ is a unary connective), then $\mathfrak{d}(\varphi) = \mathfrak{d}(\psi) + 1$.
(iii) If φ is $\psi \curlyvee \varsigma$ (where $\curlyvee$ is a binary connective), then $\mathfrak{d}(\varphi) = \mathfrak{d}(\psi) + \mathfrak{d}(\varsigma) + 1$.

Theorem 15 (Cut theorem). *In any $L\mathfrak{X}^*$ logic, the cut rule is* admissible.

Proof. The structure of the proof is fairly usual. A proof contains finitely many applications of the cut rule. If there is an application of the cut rule, then there is one that is at the top, in the sense that the subtree of the proof tree rooted in the lower sequent of the cut contains no other applications of the cut rule. We show that this subtree can be transformed into a proof tree with the same root but with no applications of the cut rule. Then, finitely many iterations of the argument replace the original proof tree with finitely many cuts with a proof tree (of the same sequent) with no applications of the cut rule.

The main part of the proof is by *triple induction* on the degree of the cut formula, on the contraction measure of the cut and on the rank of the cut. We cannot provide an exhaustive list of cases here; rather, we include two sample steps, and omit the remaining details.[8]

1. If modalities are introduced in the premises of the cut, then one of the cases goes as follows (and it is justified by $\mathfrak{d}(\psi) + 1 = \mathfrak{d}(\lhd\psi)$). (We omit $\vdots$ everywhere; that is, the top sequents are not assumed to be axioms. The symbol "$\rightsquigarrow$" indicates the transformation on the proof tree.)

$$
\begin{array}{c}
(\Vdash\lhd) \dfrac{\alpha \Vdash \psi; \beta}{\alpha \Vdash \lhd\psi; \beta} \qquad (\lhd\Vdash) \dfrac{\gamma^\rhd; \psi \Vdash \delta^\lhd}{\gamma^\rhd; \lhd\psi \Vdash \delta^\lhd} \\[2ex]
(\text{cut}) \dfrac{}{\alpha; \gamma^\rhd \Vdash \beta; \delta^\lhd}
\end{array}
\quad\rightsquigarrow\quad
\begin{array}{c}
\dfrac{\alpha \Vdash \psi; \beta \quad \gamma^\rhd; \psi \Vdash \delta^\lhd}{\alpha; \gamma^\rhd \Vdash \beta; \delta^\lhd} (\text{cut})
\end{array}
$$

2. The next sample step illustrates a reduction in the rank of the cut.

$$
(\text{cut}) \dfrac{\epsilon \Vdash \chi; \eta \qquad (\to\Vdash)\dfrac{\alpha \Vdash \varphi; \beta \quad \gamma; \chi; \psi \Vdash \delta}{\alpha; \gamma; \varphi \to \psi; \chi \Vdash \beta; \delta}}{\alpha; \gamma; \epsilon; \varphi \to \psi \Vdash \beta; \delta; \eta} \quad\rightsquigarrow
$$

---

[8] More details of a triple-inductive proof of the admissibility of the cut rule for a logic with no lattice operators may be found in [8]. Various enhancements of a more usual double-inductive proof of the cut theorem were introduced in [6,7], where a goal was to accommodate constants like Y, y and t.

$$\frac{\epsilon \Vdash \chi; \eta \quad \gamma; \psi; \chi \Vdash \delta}{\frac{\alpha \Vdash \varphi; \beta \quad \gamma; \epsilon; \psi \Vdash \delta; \eta}{\alpha; \gamma; \epsilon; \varphi \to \psi \Vdash \beta; \delta; \eta}} \, \text{(cut)}$$

⸫

•The upshot of the theorem is that the $L\mathfrak{X}^*$ logics are reasonable logics (i.e., they are structural, in algebraic terminology). Also, we may focus on cut-free proofs without a loss of provable sequents.

Lemma 16. *Cut-free proofs in the $L\mathfrak{X}^*$ logics possess the* subformula property. *That is, if φ occurs (as a type) anywhere in a proof of $\alpha \Vdash \beta$, then φ is a subformula of a formula in α or in β.*

Proof. The $L\mathfrak{X}^*$ logics have no special zeroary connectives, hence, the claim follows by a simple inspection of the rules. (Cf. $LE_{\to}^t$ in [7] for a more complicated situation.) We note that the contraction rules may reduce the number of tokens, but they do not omit types. ⸫

3 Decidability

The decidability of a logic may be proved in various ways. This is especially true for propositional modal logics, for which semantic methods have been used widely. Probably, the best-known semantic technique is *filtration* that relies on the relational semantics of normal modal logics, but *algebraic methods* have been successfully applied in some cases. It is not completely straightforward (or easy) to define set-theoretic semantics for the $L\mathfrak{X}^*$ logics. We cannot go into a detailed explanation of the reasons beyond mentioning that in the absence of conjunction, the usual set-theoretic objects—"theories" of some kind or another (or various sorts of filters, algebraically speaking)—are not available. In any case, we are interested here in the sequent calculus formulations of the $L\mathfrak{X}^*$ logics and the properties that we can discover using the sequent calculi.

Sequent calculi are *preeminently suitable* for proofs of decidability (starting with the proof of the decidability of propositional intuitionistic logic). Curry [16] came up with the idea of discarding the (explicit) contraction rules in lieu of repeating the principal formulas of the connective rules in the premises—together with a more relaxed form of the axiom $p \Vdash p$ (or $\varphi \Vdash \varphi$) by allowing other formulas in the axiom as in $\Gamma, \psi \Vdash \psi, \Delta$. Curry proved that the modifications (for the logics he considered) resulted in sequent calculi that proved the same sequents, moreover, the height of the proof tree did not increase. A lemma with a similar claim for a particular logic is often referred to as *Curry's lemma* or as height-preserving admissibility of contraction. A decidability proof then proceeds in a bottom-up fashion, so to speak. In order to determine whether a sequent is provable, a complete proof-search tree is constructed, which is in fact explores all the possibilities as to how the sequent could have been proved. While the search is exhaustive (perhaps, in more than one sense:), its finiteness is guaranteed by the limitations that the cut theorem and Curry's lemma impose (together with an easy use of *Kőnig's lemma*). It is sufficient to look for cut-free proofs, and there is no need to seek proofs that are redundant in a sense stemming from Curry's lemma.

Taking $\Gamma, \psi \Vvdash \psi, \Delta$ as an axiom has the effect of turning thinning into an admissible rule too. This is not acceptable from the point of view of many logics—from the Lambek calculi to relevance logics.[9] Kripke [26] introduced another idea, namely, instead of *requiring* the principal formulas to be parametric in the premises, he *permits* them to be parametric. Of course, this idea is compatible with thinning as a rule, but what is really intriguing about it is that, when thinning is excluded, it still renders contraction admissible.

If thinning is not a rule, then Kripke's invention is an indispensable component of the bottom-up proof search. It reflects the insight that a formula has to be introduced in order to be contracted, hence, a limited amount of contraction in the operational rules is sufficient in place of an explicit contraction rule.

To guarantee the finiteness of the proof-search tree, Kripke introduced a lemma, which, nowadays, is called *Kripke's lemma*. Originally, this lemma is about cognate sequents, and an excellent presentation is in Dunn [19, Sect. 3.6]. In the $L\mathfrak{X}^*$ logics, a pair of sequents are cognate if their antecedent and succedent multisets comprise the same types. However, later on, it was discovered that Kripke's lemma is equivalent to various other lemmas (see [19, 31]). For example, a lemma concerning vectors is stated and proved by induction in Kopylov [25, Lemma 2.2], which also appears to be equipotent to Kripke's lemma.

REMARK 8. Here is a number-theoretic analog of Kripke's lemma that is easy to state; the claim itself is self-evident.[10] Let us consider the positive integers. If we fix P, a finite set of primes, then there are finitely many numbers such that they have no other prime factors (than those in P), and they pairwise do not divide each other. For instance, if we start with $\{3\}$, then we could pick 27, but then 1, 3 and 9 are excluded (because $3 \mid 27$ and $9 \mid 27$). We can add to our collection 81 and 243, but 729 is excluded (because $27 \mid 729$), and so is any higher power of 3. The example is intended to be simple, but the case of one prime factor generalizes to the case of n prime factors without any difficulty.

NOTE 9. Before we embark on proofs of decidability for our $L\mathfrak{X}^*$ logics, it seems prudent to point out that some of our logics (possibly, in a slightly different formulation) and some closely related logics are already known to be decidable. For instance, Meyer [30] proved $LR^\square$ decidable, which is in close proximity to bciw. Linear affine logic was proved decidable in Kopylov [25], which implies the decidability of bck$^\triangledown$. The logic that was proved decidable in Bimbó [8] is orthogonal to bci$^\triangledown_\triangle$, because it has ¬ but lacks ∨. For further relevant results, see [14, 31].

---

[9] See, in chronological order, [28], [1], [22], [11], as well as [7] for motivations and logics that leave out the thinning rules from their sequent calculus formulations.

[10] See Meyer [31] for a discussion of conceptual links that can be created between Dickson's lemma and Kripke's lemma.

Definition 17. We partition the $L\mathfrak{X}^*$ group into *three subgroups:* $L\mathfrak{X}_1^* = \{$ bci, $\text{bci}_\Delta, \text{bck} \}$, $L\mathfrak{X}_2^* = \{$ bciw, $\text{bciw}_\Delta, \text{s4} \}$ and $L\mathfrak{X}_3^* = \{$ $\text{bci}^\triangledown, \text{bci}_\Delta^\triangledown, \text{bck}^\triangledown \}$.

REMARK 10. The rationale behind the division is that we approach the question of decidability similarly for the members of the subgroups, but with some differences between the subgroups. In $L\mathfrak{X}_1^*$, there is no contraction, which means that Curry's bottom-up proof search suffices. The $L\mathfrak{X}_2^*$ logics contain the (W⊩) and (⊩W) rules, and we follow Kripke's approach. For the $L\mathfrak{X}_3^*$ logics, we enhance the Curry–Kripke technique with a new proof search bounded by heap numbers.

We will deal with $L\mathfrak{X}_2^*$ first, where the Curry–Kripke technique is applicable.

Definition 18. The logics (|bciw|), (|bciw$_\Delta$|) and (|s4|) are defined by the axiom (I) and the following connective rules together with the thinning rules from the matching unbracketed logics. (The (K⊩), (⊩K), (▷K⊩) and (⊩◁K) rules are unchanged, that is, they are exactly as in Definition 5. We do not repeat those rules here, though (|bciw$_\Delta$|) and (|s4|) contain some of them.)

$$\frac{\alpha \Vdash \varphi; \beta}{\alpha \Vdash (|\varphi \vee \psi; \beta|)} \,(\Vdash \vee_1) \qquad \frac{\alpha \Vdash \psi; \beta}{\alpha \Vdash (|\varphi \vee \psi; \beta|)} \,(\Vdash \vee_2) \qquad \frac{\alpha; \psi \Vdash \beta \quad \alpha; \varphi \Vdash \beta}{(|\alpha; \varphi \vee \psi|) \Vdash \beta} \,(\vee \Vdash)$$

$$\frac{\alpha \Vdash \varphi; \beta \quad \gamma \Vdash \psi; \delta}{(|\alpha; \gamma|) \Vdash (|\psi \circ \varphi; \beta; \delta|)} \,(\Vdash \circ) \qquad \frac{\alpha; \psi; \varphi \Vdash \beta}{(|\alpha; \varphi \circ \psi|) \Vdash \beta} \,(\circ \Vdash)$$

$$\frac{\alpha; \psi \Vdash \varphi; \beta}{\alpha \Vdash (|\psi \to \varphi; \beta|)} \,(\Vdash \to) \qquad \frac{\alpha \Vdash \psi; \beta \quad \gamma; \varphi \Vdash \delta}{(|\alpha; \gamma; \psi \to \varphi|) \Vdash (|\beta; \delta|)} \,(\to \Vdash)$$

$$\frac{\alpha \Vdash \psi; \varphi; \beta}{\alpha \Vdash (|\varphi + \psi; \beta|)} \,(\Vdash +) \qquad \frac{\alpha; \psi \Vdash \beta \quad \gamma; \varphi \Vdash \delta}{(|\alpha; \gamma; \varphi + \psi|) \Vdash (|\beta; \delta|)} \,(+ \Vdash)$$

$$\frac{\alpha^\triangleright \Vdash \varphi; \beta^\triangleleft}{\alpha^\triangleright \Vdash \triangleright\varphi; \beta^\triangleleft} \,(\Vdash \triangleright) \qquad \frac{\alpha; \varphi \Vdash \beta}{(|\alpha; \triangleright\varphi|) \Vdash \beta} \,(\triangleright \Vdash)$$

$$\frac{\alpha \Vdash \varphi; \beta}{\alpha \Vdash (|\triangleleft\varphi; \beta|)} \,(\Vdash \triangleleft) \qquad \frac{\alpha^\triangleright; \varphi \Vdash \beta^\triangleleft}{\alpha^\triangleright; \triangleleft\varphi \Vdash \beta^\triangleleft} \,(\triangleleft \Vdash)$$

The (|) notation indicates potential contractions to the following extent.

(1) The principal formula ψ occurs in a multiset of parametric formulas α. Then: (|$\psi; \alpha$|) is either $\psi; \alpha$ or α.
(2) A formula ψ occurs is both multisets of parametric formulas α and β. Then: (|$\alpha; \beta$|) is either $\alpha; \beta$ or $\alpha; \beta$ with an occurrence of ψ omitted.
(3) The principal formula ψ occurs in both multisets of parametric formulas α and β. Then: (|$\psi; \alpha; \beta$|) is $\psi; \alpha; \beta$ or $\psi; \alpha; \beta$ with one or two occurrences of ψ omitted; in each case the parametric formulas are dealt with as in (2).

REMARK 11. We should emphasize that no contractions are mandatory within ⦇ ⦈, and whatever contractions are performed, they never lead to a loss of a type from a multiset. Sequents are finite, hence, each application of an operational rule involves finitely many contractions. However, the number of possible contractions depends on the size and shape of the premises to which a rule is applied, not simply on what the rule is.

The operational rules above *do not* introduce vagueness or indeterminacy into the concept of a proof, because in any proof, which comprises concrete sequents, the number of contractions can be determined simply by counting formulas.

REMARK 12. There are no structural rules listed in the previous definition. Contractions are omitted, because the goal is to limit the number of contractions, so that only useful contractions are considered. Thinnings are omitted from the listing, because if the application of a thinning rule would create a sequent where contraction is applicable, then the applications of that thinning rule can be retracted. But we reiterate that if some sort of thinning was in an $L\mathcal{X}_2^*$ logic (as per Definition 6), then the same rule is in the ⦇ ⦈'d version of the logic.

Note also that in the operational rules ($\Vdash\triangleright$) and ($\triangleleft\Vdash$), no contractions are permitted (or possible). The principal formulas of those rules are always distinct from all the types in the multiset of parametric formulas with which they are joined.

We defined three new sequent calculi; therefore, we have to provide a cut theorem for them. (Of course, the labels for the logics express our aim of defining the same logics as before. However, we will *know* that we have reached that goal after the next two theorems.)

Definition 19. The *left rung* of the cut is the length of the longest path in the proof tree starting with the left premise of the cut in which the cut formula occurs in the succedent of each sequent on the path. The *right rung* of the cut is the length of the longest path in the proof tree starting with the right premise of the cut in which the cut formula occurs in the antecedent of each sequent on the path. The *rung of the cut* is the sum of the left and right rungs of the cut.

The notion of a rung (if not the term itself) is a parameter that is often used in proofs of cut theorems.

REMARK 13. In the proof of Theorem 15, we used the single cut rule.[11] However, the admissibility of the single cut is typically proved via a detour through other forms of the cut in calculi that include contraction in some form. This is so in the calculi that are designed to prove decidability using the Curry–Kripke technique.[12]

---

[11] The cut theorem is proved using the single cut in Lambek [28] and in display logics in Belnap [3] and Anderson et al. [2].

[12] The so-called *mix* rule in [23] and the *multicut* rule explicitly stated, for example, in Dunn [18] are versions of the cut that were introduced specifically to facilitate the inductive proof of the cut theorem for the single cut. An early publication that exhibits a suitable version of cut in connection to a decidability proof using the Curry–Kripke method is [4], which is a precursor of the more readily available [5].

The cut rule used in the proof of the next theorem builds in contraction, and it is formulated as

$$\frac{\alpha \Vdash \psi; \beta \quad \gamma; \psi \Vdash \delta}{(\!(\alpha; \gamma)\!) \Vdash (\!(\beta; \delta)\!)} \ (\!(\text{cut})\!).$$

It is obvious that the *single cut rule* is a special instance of this rule.

Theorem 20 (Cut theorem). *The single cut rule is* admissible *in the three logics* $(\!(\mathsf{bciw})\!)$, $(\!(\mathsf{bciw}_\triangle)\!)$ *and* $(\!(\mathsf{s4})\!)$.

Proof. The strategy is once again to eliminate a cut with no cut above it. The proof is by double induction on the degree of the cut formula and on the rung of the application of the cut rule. Once again, we can only include here a couple of steps as illustrations to convey the flavor of the proof.

1. Let us consider a case for $\vee$. The degree of a disjunction is strictly greater than the degree of the disjuncts, that is, $\partial(\psi \vee \varphi) = 1 + \partial(\psi) + \partial(\varphi)$.

$$(\!(\text{cut})\!) \ \frac{(\!(\Vdash\vee)\!) \ \dfrac{\alpha \Vdash \varphi; \beta}{\alpha \Vdash (\!(\psi \vee \varphi; \beta)\!)} \quad (\vee\Vdash)\ \dfrac{\gamma; \psi \Vdash \delta \quad \gamma; \varphi \Vdash \delta}{(\!(\gamma; \psi \vee \varphi)\!) \Vdash \delta}}{(\!(\alpha; \gamma)\!) \Vdash (\!(\beta; \delta)\!)} \quad \rightsquigarrow \quad (\!(\text{cut})\!) \ \frac{\alpha \Vdash \varphi; \beta \quad \gamma; \varphi \Vdash \delta}{(\!(\alpha; \gamma)\!) \Vdash (\!(\beta; \delta)\!)}$$

2. If the cut formula is parametric in the left premise, then that premise might have resulted by $(\!(+\Vdash)\!)$.

$$(\!(\text{cut})\!) \ \frac{(\!(+\Vdash)\!) \ \dfrac{\alpha; \psi \Vdash \beta \quad \gamma; \varphi \Vdash \chi; \delta}{(\!(\alpha; \gamma; \varphi + \psi)\!) \Vdash (\!(\chi; \beta; \delta)\!)} \quad \epsilon; \chi \Vdash \eta}{(\!(\alpha; \gamma; \epsilon; \varphi + \psi)\!) \Vdash (\!(\beta; \delta; \eta)\!)} \quad \rightsquigarrow$$

$$(\!(+\Vdash)\!) \ \frac{\alpha; \psi \Vdash \beta \quad (\!(\text{cut})\!)\ \dfrac{\gamma; \varphi \Vdash \chi; \delta \quad \epsilon; \chi \Vdash \eta}{(\!(\gamma; \epsilon; \varphi)\!) \Vdash (\!(\delta; \eta)\!)}}{(\!(\alpha; \gamma; \epsilon; \varphi + \psi)\!) \Vdash (\!(\beta; \delta; \eta)\!)}$$

⬚∴

Theorem 21 (Curry's lemma). *Let* $\alpha' \Vdash \beta'$ *be a sequent that results in* bciw *from* $\alpha \Vdash \beta$ *by finitely many applications of the* $(\mathsf{W}\Vdash)$ *and* $(\Vdash\mathsf{W})$ *rules. If* $\mathfrak{T}$ *is a proof tree with height* h *of a sequent* $\alpha \Vdash \beta$ *in* $(\!(\mathsf{bciw})\!)$, *then there is proof tree* $\mathfrak{T}'$ *of the sequent* $\alpha' \Vdash \beta'$ *with height* h' *such that* $h' \leq h$. *Similarly, for the two other pairs of logics:* bciw$_\triangle$ *and* $(\!(\mathsf{bciw}_\triangle)\!)$, s4 *and* $(\!(\mathsf{s4})\!)$.

Proof. Both parts of the claim will be important for the decidability proofs later on. The admissibility of the two contraction rules ensures that no provable sequents are lost in moving to the $(\!(\ )\!)$'d logics. Both in the inductive proof of this claim and in the proof search it is crucial that sequents that would result by the $(\mathsf{W}\Vdash)$ and $(\Vdash\mathsf{W})$ rules have shorter proofs than the longer sequents (from which they are obtained) have. The proof is by induction on h, the height of the given proof tree. (Once again, we omit almost all cases due to lack of space.)

1. If $\alpha \Vdash \beta$ is an instance of (1), then $\alpha' \Vdash \beta'$ is $\alpha \Vdash \beta$; hence, the claim is obviously true.

2. We will abbreviate n tokens of φ in a multiset by φ^n (assuming $n \geq 1$). Given n, $n' \leq n$ and $n' \geq 1$. Let us consider the $(\Vdash \circ)$ rule.

$$\cfrac{\cfrac{\alpha; \chi^n \Vdash \varphi; (\varphi \circ \psi)^m; \varsigma^i; \beta \qquad \gamma; \chi^j \Vdash \psi; (\varphi \circ \psi)^k; \varsigma^l; \delta}{\alpha; \gamma; \chi^{(n+j)'} \Vdash (\varphi \circ \psi)^{(m+k)'}; \varsigma^{(i+l)'}; \beta; \delta} \overset{\text{i.h.}}{\rightsquigarrow}}{\cfrac{\alpha; \chi^{n'} \Vdash \varphi; (\varphi \circ \psi)^{m'}; \varsigma^{i'}; \beta \qquad \gamma; \chi^{j'} \Vdash \psi; (\varphi \circ \psi)^{k'}; \varsigma^{l'}; \delta}{\alpha; \gamma; \chi^{(n'+j')'} \Vdash (\varphi \circ \psi)^{(m'+k')'}; \varsigma^{(i'+l')'}; \beta; \delta}}$$

It is easy to see that if we want each of χ and ς to have at least 2 occurrences in the lower sequent, then $n' + j'$ and $i' + l'$ (i.e., applications of the hypothesis of the induction) suffice. Similarly, for 3 occurrences for $\varphi \circ \psi$. However, if $(n + j)' = 1$, $(m + k)' = 1$ or 2, or $(i + l)' = 1$, then we have the upper sequents by the hypothesis of the induction, and the contractions that are part of the $(\Vdash \circ)$ rule yield the desired lower sequent. Here is the most contracted situation, in which the premises are available to us by inductive hypothesis.

$$\cfrac{\alpha; \chi \Vdash \varphi; \varphi \circ \psi; \varsigma; \beta \qquad \gamma; \chi \Vdash \psi; \varphi \circ \psi; \varsigma; \delta}{\alpha; \gamma; \chi \Vdash \varphi \circ \psi; \varsigma; \beta; \delta} \quad (\Vdash \circ)$$

3. Let us consider an extensional rule too, namely, $(\vee \Vdash)$.

$$\cfrac{\cfrac{\alpha; \chi^n; (\psi \vee \varphi)^m; \varphi \Vdash \varsigma^i; \beta \qquad \alpha; \chi^n; (\psi \vee \varphi)^m; \psi \Vdash \varsigma^i; \beta}{\alpha; \chi^{n'}; (\psi \vee \varphi)^{m'} \Vdash \varsigma^{i'}; \beta} \overset{\text{i.h.}}{\rightsquigarrow}}{\cfrac{\alpha; \chi^{n'}; (\psi \vee \varphi)^{m'}; \varphi \Vdash \varsigma^{i'}; \beta \qquad \alpha; \chi^{n'}; (\psi \vee \varphi)^{m'}; \psi \Vdash \varsigma^{i'}; \beta}{\alpha; \chi^{n'}; (\psi \vee \varphi)^{m'} \Vdash \varsigma^{i'}; \beta}} \;\; \therefore$$

Definition 22. A sequence of sequents is *irredundant* when an earlier element of the sequence is not obtainable from a latter one by finitely many applications of the contraction rules. We expand the use of the term "irredundant" to proofs. An *irredundant proof* contains no redundant sequences of sequents.

REMARK 14. The notion of irredundant sequences of sequents is in harmony with Curry's lemma. Looking at a proof tree from its root upward, an irredundant sequence of sequents on a path in the proof tree signals an unnecessary detour in the proof.

Lemma 23 (Kripke's lemma). *An irredundant sequence of cognate sequents is* finite.

As we already mentioned, this lemma is equivalent to various other lemmas in discrete mathematics. For a *direct proof*, we refer to Anderson and Belnap [1, Sect. 13, p. 139].

Lemma 24 (Kőnig's lemma). *A finitely branching tree, in which all branches are finite, is* finite.

This is also a well-known lemma. For a *direct proof*, we refer to Smullyan [32].

Theorem 25. *The logics* $(\!|\mathsf{bciw}|\!)$, $(\!|\mathsf{bciw}_\Delta|\!)$ *and* $(\!|\mathsf{s4}|\!)$ *are decidable.*

Proof. The decision procedure builds a proof-search tree for the given sequent, with the property that if the sequent has a proof, then a subtree of the proof-search tree is a proof. The usual way to do this is to build the tree from its root, which is the sequent that is allegedly provable. A branch may be terminated when it would become redundant. The finiteness of the tree guarantees that an unsuccessful search will not run on indefinitely long.

The finiteness of the tree follows from several factors. Formulas and sequents are finite, with each formula having finitely many subformulas. Each rule has one or two premises, and no sequent can result from infinitely many different potential premises. These features combined with the previous two lemmas exclude infinite trees from consideration.　　∴

Corollary 26. *The logics* bciw, bciw$_\Delta$ *and* s4 *are decidable.*

Proof. The truth of the claim is a consequence of the equivalence of the logics with and without $(\!|\ \ |\!)$.　　∴

NOTE 15. The decidability of s4 is also a consequence of the decidability of **S4** (which is widely known) in view of Lemma 8.

Now we turn to the question of the decidability in the subgroup $L\mathfrak{X}_3^*$.

Definition 27. The logics in $L\mathfrak{X}_2^*$ and $L\mathfrak{X}_3^*$ are paired up with each other as follows: $\langle \mathsf{bciw}, \mathsf{bci}^\triangledown \rangle$, $\langle \mathsf{bciw}_\Delta, \mathsf{bci}_\Delta^\triangledown \rangle$ and $\langle \mathsf{s4}, \mathsf{bck}^\triangledown \rangle$.

Lemma 28. *If* $\alpha \Vdash \beta$ *is provable in an* $L\mathfrak{X}_3^*$ *logic, then* $\alpha \Vdash \beta$ *is provable in its* $L\mathfrak{X}_2^*$ *pair.*

Lemma 29. *If* $\alpha \Vdash \beta$ *is provable in* $\mathsf{bci}^\triangledown$, $\mathsf{bci}_\Delta^\triangledown$ *or* $\mathsf{bck}^\triangledown$, *then it is provable in* $(\!|\mathsf{bciw}|\!)$, $(\!|\mathsf{bciw}_\Delta|\!)$ *or* $(\!|\mathsf{s4}|\!)$, *respectively, by irredundant proofs.*

Proof (of Lemmas 28 and 29). It is sufficient to scrutinize the definitions of the logics together with the proof of Theorem 25.　　∴

REMARK 16. In all the calculi that we consider, the cut rule is admissible. Then, it is enough to look for cut-free proofs, for which the subformula property holds. For a formula to be contracted, it must be introduced by an axiom or rule into the proof. Compound subformulas have more than one subformula, hence, a contraction applied to a compound formula decreases the number of subformulas more than a contraction applied to one of their proper subformulas. Furthermore, a formula to which no contraction is applied remains in the sequent (possibly, as a subformula of a formula), because the subformula property holds. These observations motivate the introduction of the notion of a heap number, which is a cumulation of contractions on subformulas of a formula in a proof.

Definition 30. Let $\alpha \Vdash \beta$ be provable in an $L\mathfrak{X}_2^*$ logic. For any subformula φ of a formula in $\alpha \uplus \beta$, we define the *heap number* of φ, denoted by $\mathsf{h}^\#(\varphi)$ as follows.

(1) If φ is not of the form $\triangleright\psi$ or $\triangleleft\psi$ for some ψ, then $\mathsf{h}^\#(\varphi) = 0$;
(2) otherwise, $\mathsf{h}^\#(\varphi)$ is the maximal number of contractions on φ and the ancestors of φ in any irredundant proof of $\alpha \Vdash \beta$ in the $(\!(\ \,)\!)$'d $L\mathfrak{X}_2^*$ logic in question.

REMARK 17. Given a provable sequent of an $L\mathfrak{X}_2^*$ logic, we may think of all the subformulas having a number attached to them. We know that all the sequents that are provable in their $L\mathfrak{X}_3^*$ pair are among those. However, it is easy to prove that not all sequents provable in an $L\mathfrak{X}_2^*$ logic are provable in their $L\mathfrak{X}_3^*$ pair. Since contractions in the $L\mathfrak{X}_2^*$ logics are possible only on modalized formulas, we transfer all the contractions that might have happened on ancestors of a modalized formula in any irredundant proof to the formula itself.

REMARK 18. We want to emphasize that the definition of a heap number is not recursive. We simply zeroed the heap number for all non-modal formulas, whether they are or are not a subformula of a formula in the provable sequent.

For any provable sequent, there are finitely many irredundant proofs each of which is finite. Hence, the heap number requires the inspection of finitely many finite objects. As we mentioned in Remark 11, in a proof involving applications of the $(\!(\ \,)\!)$ rules, the number of contractions can be simply counted, and there is no ambiguity with respect to which formulas and how many times were contracted. In sum, the notion of a heap number is *well defined*.

Theorem 31. *The logics* $\mathsf{bci}^\triangledown$, $\mathsf{bci}_\triangle^\triangledown$ *and* $\mathsf{bck}^\triangledown$ *are decidable.*

Proof. Let $\alpha \Vdash \beta$ be a given sequent. For any of the $L\mathfrak{X}_3^*$ logics, we can decide, by appeal to Lemma 29, whether the sequent is provable in the $L\mathfrak{X}_2^*$ pair of our $L\mathfrak{X}_3^*$ logic. If the sequent is not provable, then we may conclude that it is not provable in the $L\mathfrak{X}_3^*$ logic either.

If the sequent is provable in the $L\mathfrak{X}_2^*$ pair of our logic, then we start a new proof search using the $L\mathfrak{X}_3^*$ logic itself. The only contraction rules are ($\triangleright\mathsf{W}\Vdash$) and ($\Vdash\triangleleft\mathsf{W}$). We start to build a proof-search tree as usual, and for each modalized formula we limit the number of the applications of the previous two rules by the heap number for the principal formula of the rule.[13]

The proof-search tree is finite. The connective rules—looked at from the lower sequent upward—reduce the number of connectives in the sequent. So do

---

[13] We defined heap numbers in a very liberal manner in order to make sure that all the necessary contractions are permitted. However, even if $\mathsf{h}^\#(\triangleleft\varphi) > 1$, for example, it may happen that in the $L\mathfrak{X}_3^*$ logic no contraction will be applied to the formula, because it occurs on the left-hand side of the $\Vdash$. (Similarly, but dually for $\triangleright\varphi$.) This does not cause any problem in the proof search, because the heap number (like the $(\!(\ \,)\!)$ notation) does not force contractions, rather, it places a limit on the number of potential applications of the contraction rules.

typically the thinning rules. The number of applications of the ($\triangleright$W$\Vdash$) and the ($\Vdash\triangleleft$W) rules is bounded, and there are finitely many modal formulas to start with.

The proof-search tree will contain a proof if there is one. As usual, we assume that the proof-search tree is comprehensive, that is, all the possible upper sequents are added to the tree. This guarantees—as usual—that no potential proof step is missed. We only have to scrutinize whether we have permitted all the needed applications of the ($\triangleright$W$\Vdash$) and ($\Vdash\triangleleft$W) rules. Let us assume that more than heap number-many contractions (i.e., some extra contractions) are required to prove a sequent. The principal formula cannot be by thinning, because the latter could be simply omitted (contradicting the necessity for extra contractions). If the principal formula is by the axiom (1) or a connective rule, then all the atomic subformulas have another occurrence introduced (possibly, on the other side of the $\Vdash$). If those occurrences are contracted, then the extra contractions are not necessary. If they remain in the provable sequent, then the extra contractions must have been applied in some irredundant proof; hence, they must have been counted in the heap number contradicting the starting assumption. ⁖

Lastly, we deal with the subgroup $L\mathfrak{X}_1^*$.

Theorem 32. *The logics* bci, bci$_\triangle$ *and* bck *are decidable.*

Proof. The proof is a simple proof-search. None of the calculi contains a contraction rule, hence, the finiteness of the sequents, of the set of subformulas of a formula and Kőnig's lemma together guarantee the finiteness of the proof-search tree.   ⁖

4 Conclusions

We have selected 9 modal logics, each of which is definable as an extension of a core logic bci that includes disjunction and an implication (with two more intensional connectives), and a pair of modalities $\triangleright$ and $\triangleleft$. We gave a systematic presentation of these logics as sequent calculi. From the point of view of proving their decidability, the $L\mathfrak{X}^*$ logics fall into three groups. Curry's bottom-up approach is applicable to the $L\mathfrak{X}_1^*$ group. Kripke's refinement delivers decidability for the $L\mathfrak{X}_2^*$ group. Finally, the concept of a heap number together with the decidability of the $L\mathfrak{X}_2^*$ logics yields the decidability of the $L\mathfrak{X}_3^*$ logics. To summarize, each of our 9 modal logics turns out to be *decidable*.

Acknowledgments. I am grateful to the organizers of the TABLEAUX, FroCoS and ITP conferences for their invitation for me to speak at those conferences, which triggered the writing of this paper.

I would also like to thank the program committee for helpful comments on the first version of this paper.

References

1. Anderson, A.R., Belnap, N.D.: Entailment: The Logic of Relevance and Necessity, vol. I. Princeton University Press, Princeton (1975)
2. Anderson, A.R., Belnap, N.D., Dunn, J.M.: Entailment: The Logic of Relevance and Necessity, vol. II. Princeton University Press, Princeton (1992)
3. Belnap, N.D.: Display logic. J. Philos. Logic **11**, 375–417 (1982)
4. Belnap, N.D., Wallace, J.R.: A decision procedure for the system $E_{\overline{I}}$ of entailment with negation. Technical report 11, Contract No. SAR/609 (16), Office of Naval Research, New Haven (1961)
5. Belnap, N.D., Wallace, J.R.: A decision procedure for the system $E_{\overline{I}}$ of entailment with negation. Zeitschrift für mathematische Logik und Grundlagen der Mathematik **11**, 277–289 (1965)
6. Bimbó, K.: Admissibility of cut in LC with fixed point combinator. Stud. Logica **81**, 399–423 (2005). doi:10.1007/s11225-005-4651-y
7. Bimbó, K.: $LE_{\rightarrow}^{t}$, $LR_{\wedge}^{\circ}$, LK and cutfree proofs. J. Philos. Logic **36**, 557–570 (2007). doi:10.1007/s10992-007-9048-0
8. Bimbó, K.: The decidability of the intensional fragment of classical linear logic. Theoret. Comput. Sci. **597**, 1–17 (2015). doi:10.1016/j.tcs.2015.06.019
9. Bimbó, K.: Proof Theory: Sequent Calculi and Related Formalisms. Discrete Mathematics and Its Applications. CRC Press, Boca Raton (2015). doi:10.1201/b17294
10. Bimbó, K., Dunn, J.M.: Generalized Galois Logics: Relational Semantics of Nonclassical Logical Calculi. CSLI Lecture Notes, vol. 188. CSLI Publications, Stanford (2008)
11. Bimbó, K., Dunn, J.M.: Calculi for symmetric generalized Galois logics. In: van Benthem, J., Moortgat, M. (eds.) Festschrift for Joachim Lambek. Linguistic Analysis, vol. 36, pp. 307–343. Linguistic Analysis, Vashon (2010)
12. Bimbó, K., Dunn, J.M.: New consecution calculi for $R_{\rightarrow}^{t}$. Notre Dame J. Formal Logic **53**(4), 491–509 (2012). doi:10.1215/00294527-1722719
13. Bimbó, K., Dunn, J.M.: On the decidability of implicational ticket entailment. J. Symb. Logic **78**(1), 214–236 (2013). doi:10.2178/jsl.7801150
14. Bimbó, K., Dunn, J.M.: Modalities in lattice-R (2015). (manuscript, 34 pages)
15. Cresswell, M., Mares, E., Rini, A. (eds.): Logical Modalities from Aristotle to Carnap. The Story of Necessity. Cambridge University Press, Cambridge (2016)
16. Curry, H.B.: A Theory of Formal Deducibility. No. 6 in Notre Dame Mathematical Lectures. University of Notre Dame Press, Notre Dame (1950)
17. Curry, H.B.: Foundations of Mathematical Logic. McGraw-Hill Book Company, New York (1963). (Dover, New York, 1977)
18. Dunn, J.M.: A 'Gentzen system' for positive relevant implication (abstract). J. Symb. Logic **38**, 356–357 (1973)
19. Dunn, J.M.: Relevance logic and entailment. In: Gabbay, D., Guenthner, F. (eds.) Handbook of Philosophical Logic, vol. 3, 1st edn, pp. 117–224. D. Reidel, Dordrecht (1986)
20. Dunn, J.M.: Positive modal logic. Stud. Logica. **55**, 301–317 (1995)
21. Dunn, J.M., Meyer, R.K.: Combinators and structurally free logic. Logic J. IGPL **5**, 505–537 (1997)
22. Dunn, J.M., Restall, G.: Relevance logic. In: Gabbay, D., Guenthner, F. (eds.) Handbook of Philosophical Logic, vol. 6, 2nd edn, pp. 1–128. Kluwer, Amsterdam (2002)

23. Gentzen, G.: Untersuchungen über das logische Schließen. Mathematische Zeitschrift **39**, 176–210 (1935)
24. Gödel, K.: Eine Interpretation des intuitionistischen Aussagenkalküls. In: Feferman, S. (ed.) Collected Works, vol. I, pp. 300–303. Oxford University Press and Clarendon Press, New York and Oxford (1986)
25. Kopylov, A.P.: Decidability of linear affine logic. In: Meyer, A.R. (ed.) Special issue: LICS 1995, Information and Computation, vol. 164, pp. 173–198. IEEE (2001)
26. Kripke, S.A.: The problem of entailment (abstract). J. Symb. Logic **24**, 324 (1959)
27. Kripke, S.A.: Semantical analysis of modal logic I. Normal modal propositional calculi. Zeitschrift für mathematische Logik und Grundlagen der Mathematik, pp. 67–96 (1963)
28. Lambek, J.: The mathematics of sentence structure. Am. Math. Mon. **65**, 154–169 (1958)
29. Lewis, C.I.: A Survey of Symbolic Logic. University of California Press, Berkeley (1918). (Dover Publications, Mineola, 1960)
30. Meyer, R.K.: Topics in modal and many-valued logic. Ph.D. thesis, University of Pittsburgh, Ann Arbor (UMI) (1966)
31. Meyer, R.K.: Improved decision procedures for pure relevant logic. In: Anderson, C.A., Zelëny, M. (eds.) Logic, Meaning and Computation: Essays in Memory of Alonzo Church, pp. 191–217. Kluwer Academic Publishers, Dordrecht (2001)
32. Smullyan, R.M.: First-Order Logic. Springer, New York (1968). doi:10.1007/978-3-642-86718-7. (Dover, New York 1995)

Sequent Systems

Cut-Admissibility as a Corollary
of the Subformula Property

Ori Lahav[1] and Yoni Zohar[2]([⊠])

[1] Max Planck Institute for Software Systems (MPI-SWS), Kaiserslautern, Germany
orilahav@mpi-sws.org
[2] School of Computer Science, Tel Aviv University, Tel Aviv, Israel
yoni.zohar@cs.tau.ac.il

Abstract. We identify two wide families of propositional sequent calculi
for which cut-admissibility is a corollary of the subformula property.
While the subformula property is often a simple consequence of cut-
admissibility, our results shed light on the converse direction, and may be
used to simplify cut-admissibility proofs in various propositional sequent
calculi. In particular, the results of this paper may be used in conjunction
with existing methods that establish the subformula property, to obtain
that cut-admissibility holds as well.

1 Introduction

One of the major consequences of Gentzen's cut-elimination theorem for LK
and LJ [16] is the subformula property: when deriving a sequent s from a set
S of sequents, it suffices to consider the subformulas that occur in $S \cup \{s\}$.
Other formulas may sometimes shorten derivations, but can be safely ignored
when checking whether a derivation exists. Since the introduction of LK and LJ,
various cut-free sequent calculi were found for important non-classical logics –
e.g., modal logics [25,30], many-valued and fuzzy logics [6,22], and paraconsistent
logics [9]. In all these cases, the subformula property (or some generalization of
it) trivially follows from the admissibility of the cut rule.

In this paper we are interested in the converse direction: can cut-admissibility
be obtained as a corollary of the subformula property?

Clearly, one cannot expect an affirmative answer to this question in the general case, as there are well-known calculi admitting the subformula property
but not cut-admissibility. These include, e.g., calculi for the modal logics $S5$
and B [25,30], bi-intuitionistic logic [24], and several calculi for paraconsistent
logics [8].

The main contribution of this paper is an affirmative answer to the question
above for two wide families of sequent calculi. The first is a family of pure
calculi [4] whose derivation rules, like those of LK, do not impose any restrictions
on context formulas. The second is a family of calculi, which we call *intuitionistic
calculi*, in which premises of the form $\Gamma \Rightarrow \Delta$ with $\Gamma \neq \emptyset$ in right introduction
rules forbid context formulas on the right-hand side. This family includes, for
example, the well-known multiple-conclusion calculus for intuitionistic logic [28],

© Springer International Publishing AG 2017
R.A. Schmidt and C. Nalon (Eds.): TABLEAUX 2017, LNAI 10501, pp. 65–80, 2017.
DOI: 10.1007/978-3-319-66902-1_4

as well as the calculi for Nelson's logics N_3 and N_4 [29]. In both families, we further require a certain "directed" structure from their rules (precisely defined below), and show that it suffices to ensure that cut-admissibility follows from the subformula property.

Our result is obtained by providing two different semantics for each given calculus: one for derivations that include only subformulas of the premises and the end sequent, and another for cut-free derivations. The latter provides a sufficient semantic criterion for cut-admissibility. Then, we show that this criterion is met when the calculus enjoys the subformula property.

In order to utilize the full strength of sequent calculi, the subformula property is not enough. For example, various sequent calculi for paraconsistent logics [9] do not enjoy the subformula property, but do admit a simple generalization of it, namely: if a sequent s is derivable, then there exists a derivation of s that uses only subformulas of s and their negations. For this reason, we do not restrict ourselves to the strict subformula property, but consider a more general notion, which is based on an arbitrary "well-behaved" (precisely defined below) ordering of propositional formulas.

Besides its theoretical interest, we believe that our result can be useful in future investigation and development of sequent calculi. Proving the subformula property tends to be an easier task than proving full cut-admissibility, as it typically follows from the admissibility of non-analytic cuts (cuts on formulas that are not subformulas of the end sequent). In addition, our recent paper [20] provides a sufficient criterion for the subformula property for a wide family of pure calculi for sub-classical logics, without relying on cut-admissibility. Using the results of the current paper, we obtain the admissibility of cut in all these calculi.

The rest of this paper is organized as follows. After the definitions of pure calculi and their associated cut-admissibility property in Sect. 2, we introduce our generalized notion of the subformula property in Sect. 3. In Sect. 4, semantic characterizations of the different kinds of derivability in pure sequent calculi are given, and are used in Sect. 5 where our theorem for pure calculi is described. Finally, Sect. 6 provides our result for intuitionistic calculi.

Related Work

Avron and Lev [10] introduced the family of *canonical calculi*, a very restricted sub-family of pure calculi, and proved the equivalence of the subformula property and cut-admissibility in them. The proof was based on the framework of *Nmatrices* (see also [11]), a simple generalization of usual logical matrices. The present paper goes beyond canonical calculi, and Nmatrices do not suffice. Thus, our proof utilizes a more general semantic framework of Lahav and Avron [19]. In this framework, which can be seen as a generalization of Béziau's *bivaluation semantics* [13], sufficient semantic criteria for cut-admissibility and the subformula property were given. The former amounts to the ability to refine three-valued valuations into two-valued ones, while the latter amounts to the ability to extend partial two-valued valuations into full valuations. Later, [21] showed that for pure calculi, the criterion for the subformula property is also necessary. For the present paper, however, the mere ability to extend partial two-valued valuations is not enough, and a constructive extension method is introduced. Finally, in a previous work [20], we studied general conditions for the subformula property in pure calculi, while cut-admissibility was not considered at all.

2 Pure Sequent Calculi

In this section, we define the family of pure sequent calculi [4] and the notion of cut-admissibility. Several examples of well-known calculi that belong to this family are provided as well.

2.1 Preliminaries

Let $At = \{p_1, p_2, \ldots\}$ denote a fixed infinite set of propositional variables. A *propositional language* $\mathcal{L}$ is given by a set $\Diamond_{\mathcal{L}}$ of connectives. $\mathcal{L}$-*formulas* are defined as usual, where *atomic* $\mathcal{L}$-*formulas* are the elements of At. We usually identify a propositional language with its set of formulas (e.g., when writing expressions like $\varphi \in \mathcal{L}$). For a set $\mathcal{F} \subseteq \mathcal{L}$, by $\mathcal{F}$-*formula* we mean a formula φ satisfying $\varphi \in \mathcal{F}$.

An $\mathcal{L}$-*substitution* is a function $\sigma\colon At \to \mathcal{L}$, naturally extended to apply on all $\mathcal{L}$-formulas and on sets of $\mathcal{L}$-formulas.

An $\mathcal{L}$-*sequent* is a pair of finite sets Γ and Δ of $\mathcal{L}$-formulas, denoted $\Gamma \Rightarrow \Delta$. We employ the standard sequent notations, e.g., when writing expressions like $\Gamma, \varphi \Rightarrow \Delta$ or $\Rightarrow \varphi$. The union of two sequents $(\Gamma_1 \Rightarrow \Delta_1) \cup (\Gamma_2 \Rightarrow \Delta_2)$ is the sequent $\Gamma_1, \Gamma_2 \Rightarrow \Delta_1, \Delta_2$. We denote by $frm[\Gamma \Rightarrow \Delta]$ the set $\Gamma \cup \Delta$, and naturally extend this notation to sets of sequents. $\mathcal{L}$-substitutions are extended to apply on $\mathcal{L}$-sequents and sets of $\mathcal{L}$-sequents (by setting $\sigma(\Gamma \Rightarrow \Delta) = \sigma(\Gamma) \Rightarrow \sigma(\Delta)$ and $\sigma(S) = \{\sigma(\Gamma \Rightarrow \Delta) \mid \Gamma \Rightarrow \Delta \in S\}$).

In what follows, $\mathcal{L}$ denotes an arbitrary propositional language. When $\mathcal{L}$ can be inferred from the context, we omit the prefix "$\mathcal{L}-$" from the notions above (as well as from the ones introduced below).

2.2 Pure Sequent Calculi

Following [10], we find it technically convenient to use the object propositional language for specifying derivation rules. (One could use meta-variables and rule schemes instead.)

Definition 1. A *pure $\mathcal{L}$-rule* is a pair $\langle S, s \rangle$, denoted S/s, where S is a finite set of $\mathcal{L}$-sequents and s is an $\mathcal{L}$-sequent. The elements of S are called the *premises* of the rule and s is called the *conclusion* of the rule. We sometimes omit set braces around the premises, and separate them by semi-colons (e.g., when writing expressions like $\Rightarrow p_1; \Rightarrow p_2 / \Rightarrow p_1 \wedge p_2$).

An $\mathcal{L}$-*application* of a pure $\mathcal{L}$-rule $\{s_1, \ldots, s_n\}/s$ is a pair of the form $\langle \{\sigma(s_1) \cup c_1, \ldots, \sigma(s_n) \cup c_n\}, \sigma(s) \cup c_1 \cup \ldots \cup c_n \rangle$ where σ is an $\mathcal{L}$-substitution, and $c_1, \ldots, c_n$ are $\mathcal{L}$-sequents (called the *context sequents* of the application). The sequents $\sigma(s_i) \cup c_i$ are called the *premises* of the application, and the sequent $\sigma(s) \cup c_1 \cup \ldots c_n$ is called the *conclusion* of the application.

For example, the pure rules for introducing implication in classical logic are:

$$p_1 \Rightarrow p_2 \, / \Rightarrow p_1 \supset p_2 \qquad \Rightarrow p_1; \; p_2 \Rightarrow \, / \, p_1 \supset p_2 \Rightarrow$$

Their applications take the form (respectively):

$$\frac{\Gamma, \varphi \Rightarrow \psi, \Delta}{\Gamma \Rightarrow \varphi \supset \psi, \Delta} \qquad \frac{\Gamma_1 \Rightarrow \varphi, \Delta_1 \qquad \Gamma_2, \psi \Rightarrow \Delta_2}{\Gamma_1, \Gamma_2, \varphi \supset \psi \Rightarrow \Delta_1, \Delta_2}$$

Examples for derivation rules that *cannot* be formulated as pure rules include the following rule schemes, that are employed in intuitionistic and modal logic:

$$\frac{\Gamma, \varphi \Rightarrow \psi}{\Gamma \Rightarrow \varphi \supset \psi} \qquad \qquad \frac{\Gamma \Rightarrow \varphi}{\Box \Gamma \Rightarrow \Box \varphi}$$

In turn, pure calculi are simply finite sets of pure rules.

Definition 2. A *pure $\mathcal{L}$-calculus* is a finite set of pure $\mathcal{L}$-rules. A *derivation* of a sequent s from a set S of sequents (a.k.a. "assumptions" or "non-logical axioms") in a pure $\mathcal{L}$-calculus $\mathbf{G}$ is a finite sequence of sequents, where each sequent in the sequence is either one of the following: (*i*) an element of S; (*ii*) the conclusion of an application of a rule of $\mathbf{G}$, all premises of which are preceding elements of the sequence; (*iii*) the conclusion of one of the following standard structural rules,[1] again where all premises are preceding elements of the sequence:

$$(\text{ID}) \qquad\qquad (\text{CUT}) \qquad\qquad\qquad\qquad\qquad (\text{WEAK})$$

$$\frac{}{\varphi \Rightarrow \varphi} \qquad \frac{\Gamma_1 \Rightarrow \varphi, \Delta_1 \qquad \Gamma_2, \varphi \Rightarrow \Delta_2}{\Gamma_1, \Gamma_2 \Rightarrow \Delta_1, \Delta_2} \qquad \frac{\Gamma \Rightarrow \Delta}{\Gamma', \Gamma \Rightarrow \Delta, \Delta'}$$

In (CUT), φ is called the *cut formula*. We write $S \vdash_{\mathbf{G}} s$ if there is a derivation of a sequent s from a set S of sequents in $\mathbf{G}$.

In what follows, unless stated otherwise, we may refer to pure rules and pure calculi simply as *rules* and *calculi*.

The most well-studied property of sequent calculi is the admissibility of the cut rule. When cut is admissible the calculus is generally considered well-behaved, and reasoning about the calculus becomes much easier. Moreover, proof-search algorithms have no need to "guess" the cut formulas. Next, we precisely define cut-admissibility.

---

[1] Note that by defining sequents to be pairs of *sets* we implicitly include other standard structural rules, such as exchange and contraction.

Definition 3. A derivation of s from S in a calculus $\mathbf{G}$ is called *cut-limited* if in every application of (CUT), the cut formula is in $frm[S]$. We write $S \vdash_{\mathbf{G}}^{cf} s$ if such a derivation exists. A calculus $\mathbf{G}$ enjoys *cut-admissibility* if $\vdash_{\mathbf{G}} = \vdash_{\mathbf{G}}^{cf}$.

What we call here cut-admissibility is actually known as *strong* cut-admissibility, in which cuts are allowed, but they are confined to apply only on formulas that appear in the set of assumptions [5]. Usual cut-admissibility only requires that $\vdash_{\mathbf{G}} s$ iff $\vdash_{\mathbf{G}}^{cf} s$ for every sequent s. For pure calculi, however, the two notions are equivalent [5]. Note that this is not the case for intuitionistic calculi, studied in Sect. 6.

Next, we present several examples of pure calculi (they all enjoy cut-admissibility).

Example 1 (Classical Logic). The propositional language $\mathcal{CL}$ consists of three binary connectives $\wedge$, $\vee$, $\supset$, and one unary connective $\neg$. The propositional fragment of Gentzen's fundamental sequent calculus for classical logic [16] can be directly presented as a pure $\mathcal{CL}$-calculus, denoted **LK**, that consists of the following $\mathcal{CL}$-rules:

$$\Rightarrow p_1 \, / \, \neg p_1 \Rightarrow \qquad\qquad p_1 \Rightarrow \, / \Rightarrow \neg p_1$$
$$p_1, p_2 \Rightarrow \, / \, p_1 \wedge p_2 \Rightarrow \qquad\qquad \Rightarrow p_1; \, \Rightarrow p_2 \, / \Rightarrow p_1 \wedge p_2$$
$$p_1 \Rightarrow \, ; p_2 \Rightarrow \, / \, p_1 \vee p_2 \Rightarrow \qquad\qquad \Rightarrow p_1, p_2 \, / \Rightarrow p_1 \vee p_2$$
$$\Rightarrow p_1; p_2 \Rightarrow \, / \, p_1 \supset p_2 \Rightarrow \qquad\qquad p_1 \Rightarrow p_2 \, / \Rightarrow p_1 \supset p_2$$

Example 2 (Paraconsistent Logics). The paper [9] provides sequent calculi for many paraconsistent logics. For example, a pure calculus for da Costa's historical paraconsistent logic C_1, which we call $\mathbf{G}_{C_1}$, consists of the rules of **LK** except for the left-introduction rule of negation, that is replaced by the following pure $\mathcal{CL}$-rules:

$$p_1 \Rightarrow \, / \, \neg\neg p_1 \Rightarrow$$
$$\Rightarrow p_1; \, \Rightarrow \neg p_1 \, / \, \neg(p_1 \wedge \neg p_1) \Rightarrow \qquad \neg p_1 \Rightarrow \, ; \neg p_2 \Rightarrow \, / \, \neg(p_1 \wedge p_2) \Rightarrow$$
$$\neg p_1 \Rightarrow \, ; p_2, \neg p_2 \Rightarrow \, / \, \neg(p_1 \vee p_2) \Rightarrow \qquad p_1, \neg p_1 \Rightarrow \, ; \neg p_2 \Rightarrow \, / \, \neg(p_1 \vee p_2) \Rightarrow$$
$$p_1 \Rightarrow \, ; p_2, \neg p_2 \Rightarrow \, / \, \neg(p_1 \supset p_2) \Rightarrow \qquad p_1, \neg p_1 \Rightarrow \, ; \neg p_2 \Rightarrow \, / \, \neg(p_1 \supset p_2) \Rightarrow$$

Similarly, a pure calculus $\mathbf{G}_{P_1}$ for the *atomic* paraconsistent logic P_1 was given in [3]. It is obtained by replacing the left-introduction rule of negation in **LK** with the following alternative rules:

$$\Rightarrow p_1; \, \Rightarrow p_2 \, / \, \neg(p_1 \wedge p_2) \Rightarrow \qquad\qquad \Rightarrow p_1, p_2 \, / \, \neg(p_1 \vee p_2) \Rightarrow$$
$$p_1 \Rightarrow p_2 \, / \, \neg(p_1 \supset p_2) \Rightarrow \qquad\qquad \Rightarrow \neg p_1 \, / \, \neg\neg p_1 \Rightarrow$$

Example 3 (Many-valued Logics). The paper [6] provides pure sequent calculi for well-known many-valued logics. For example, a calculus for Łukasiewicz three-valued logic, which we call $\mathbf{G}_3$, has the following rules for implication:

$$\neg p_1 \Rightarrow \, ; p_2 \Rightarrow \, ; \, \Rightarrow p_1, \neg p_2 \, / \, p_1 \supset p_2 \Rightarrow \qquad p_1 \Rightarrow p_2; \neg p_2 \Rightarrow \neg p_1 \, / \Rightarrow p_1 \supset p_2$$
$$p_1, \neg p_2 \Rightarrow \, / \, \neg(p_1 \supset p_2) \Rightarrow \qquad\qquad \Rightarrow p_1; \, \Rightarrow \neg p_2 \, / \Rightarrow \neg(p_1 \supset p_2)$$

A pure calculus for the $\mathcal{CL}$-fragment of the logic of bilattices [2] (whose implication-free fragment coincides with the logic of first-degree entailments [1]), which we call $\mathbf{G_4}$, is obtained in a similar manner, by augmenting the positive fragment of $\mathbf{LK}$ with the following rules:

$$p_1, \neg p_2 \Rightarrow \,/\, \neg(p_1 \supset p_2) \Rightarrow \qquad \Rightarrow p_1; \, \Rightarrow \neg p_2 \,/\, \Rightarrow \neg(p_1 \supset p_2)$$

$$\neg p_1 \Rightarrow \,;\, \neg p_2 \Rightarrow \,/\, \neg(p_1 \wedge p_2) \Rightarrow \qquad \Rightarrow \neg p_1, \neg p_2 \,/\, \Rightarrow \neg(p_1 \wedge p_2)$$

$$\neg p_1, \neg p_2 \Rightarrow \,/\, \neg(p_1 \vee p_2) \Rightarrow \qquad \Rightarrow \neg p_1; \, \Rightarrow \neg p_2 \,/\, \Rightarrow \neg(p_1 \vee p_2)$$

$$p_1 \Rightarrow \,/\, \neg\neg p_1 \Rightarrow \qquad \Rightarrow p_1 \,/\, \Rightarrow \neg\neg p_1$$

Example 4 (Logics for access control). Primal infon logic [15] was designed to efficiently reason about access control policies. The quotations-free fragment of its sequent calculus [12] can be presented as a pure calculus, which we denote by $\mathbf{P}$. It is obtained from the positive fragment of $\mathbf{LK}$ by adding the axiomatic rules $\Rightarrow \top$ and $\bot \Rightarrow$, dismissing the left introduction rule of disjunction, and replacing the right introduction rule of implication with the following weaker rule:

$$\Rightarrow p_2 \,/\, \Rightarrow p_1 \supset p_2$$

Another security-oriented formalism that can be described as a pure calculus is the Dolev-Yao intruder deductions model from [14], where it was given as a natural deduction calculus. It is equivalent to the following pure calculus, which we denote by $\mathbf{DY}$. Its language consists of two binary connectives: pairing and encryption. The intended meaning of $\langle p_1, p_2 \rangle$ is the ordered pair of p_1 and p_2. The intended meaning of $[p_1]_{p_2}$ is the encryption of the message p_1 using the key p_2. Accordingly, the following rules correspond to pairing, unpairing, encryption and decryption:

$$\Rightarrow p_1; \, \Rightarrow p_2 \,/\, \Rightarrow \langle p_1, p_2 \rangle \qquad p_1 \Rightarrow \,/\, \langle p_1, p_2 \rangle \Rightarrow \qquad p_2 \Rightarrow \,/\, \langle p_1, p_2 \rangle \Rightarrow$$

$$\Rightarrow p_1; \, \Rightarrow p_2 \,/\, \Rightarrow [p_1]_{p_2} \qquad \Rightarrow p_2; p_1 \Rightarrow \,/\, [p_1]_{p_2} \Rightarrow$$

3   Analyticity: A Generalized Subformula Property

Roughly speaking, analyticity of a propositional calculus provides a computable bound on the formulas that may appear in derivations of a sequent s from a set S of sequents. The special case of the *subformula property* is obtained when the set of subformulas of formulas of $S \cup \{s\}$ provides such a bound. Many useful calculi, however, do not admit this strict property, while still allowing some other effective bound. Here, we generalize the subformula property, by assuming a given ordering of $\mathcal{L}$-formulas, denoted $\prec$, which has to satisfy certain properties, as defined next.

Notation 1. Given a binary relation R on $\mathcal{L}$, we denote by $R[\varphi]$ the set $\{\psi \in \mathcal{L} \mid \langle \psi, \varphi \rangle \in R\}$. This notation is naturally extended to sets ($R[\Gamma] = \bigcup_{\varphi \in \Gamma} R[\varphi]$), sequents ($R[\Gamma \Rightarrow \Delta] = R[\Gamma] \cup R[\Delta]$), and sets of sequents ($R[S] = \bigcup_{s \in S} R[s]$).

Definition 4. An order relation (i.e., irreflexive and transitive relation) $\prec$ is called:

- *safe* if it is prefinite ($\prec[\varphi]$ is finite for every $\varphi \in \mathcal{L}$), and the function $\lambda\varphi \in \mathcal{L}.\prec[\varphi]$ is computable.
- *structural* if $\varphi \prec \psi$ implies $\sigma(\varphi) \prec \sigma(\psi)$ for every substitution σ.

Example 5. The usual subformula relation over $\mathcal{CL}$, which we denote by $\prec_0$, is a structural safe order relation. Another useful structural and safe order relation on $\mathcal{CL}$, denoted $\prec_1$, is given by $\varphi \prec_1 \psi$ iff $\varphi \prec_0 \psi$ or $\varphi \neq \psi$ and $\varphi = \neg\psi'$ for some $\psi' \prec_0 \psi$.

In what follows, $\prec$ denotes an arbitrary safe and structural order relation over $\mathcal{L}$.

The above definition allows us to present a generalization of the subformula property, which we call $\prec$-analyticity.

Definition 5. We call a derivation of a sequent s from a set S of sequents in a calculus $\mathbf{G}$ $\prec$-*analytic* if it consists solely of $\preceq[S \cup \{s\}]$-formulas ($\preceq$ denotes the reflexive closure of $\prec$), and write $S\vdash^{\prec}_{\mathbf{G}}s$ if there exists a $\prec$-analytic derivation of s from S in $\mathbf{G}$. A calculus $\mathbf{G}$ is called $\prec$-*analytic* if $\vdash_{\mathbf{G}}=\vdash^{\prec}_{\mathbf{G}}$.

This generalization of the subformula property inherits its most important consequence, which is decidability. Clearly, if $\prec$ is safe and S is finite, it is decidable whether $S\vdash^{\prec}_{\mathbf{G}}s$. When $\mathbf{G}$ is $\prec$-analytic, the same holds for $\vdash_{\mathbf{G}}$.

Considering the examples above, **LK**, $\mathbf{G}_{P_1}$, **P**, and **DY** are $\prec_0$-analytic; while $\mathbf{G}_{C_1}$, $\mathbf{G}_3$ and $\mathbf{G}_4$ are not $\prec_0$-analytic, but are $\prec_1$-analytic. These facts can be derived from cut-admissibility, and also directly by the method of [20]. The infinite family of calculi for weak double negations from [17], presented in the next example, goes beyond $\prec_0$ and $\prec_1$.

Example 6. In [17], Kamide provides a way of constructing sequent calculi for paraconsistent logics that admit the double negation principle as well as its weaker forms (e.g. $\neg\neg\neg\psi \leftrightarrow \neg\psi$). For this purpose, the paper investigates a hierarchy of weak double negations, by presenting an infinite set $\left\{L2^{n+2} \mid n \in \mathbb{N}\right\}$ of pure calculi, all of which admit cut-admissibility. For example, $L4$ is the calculus $\mathbf{G}_4$ from Example 3, which is $\prec_1$-analytic. Furthermore, for every n, let $\prec_n$ be the transitive closure of the relation $\lhd_n$, defined by: $\varphi \lhd_n \psi$ iff either $\psi = \neg\varphi$, or $\psi = \varphi_1 \sharp \varphi_2$ and $\varphi = \neg^m\varphi_i$ for some $\varphi_1, \varphi_2, \sharp \in \{\wedge, \vee, \supset\}$, $0 \leq m \leq n$, and $i \in \{1, 2\}$. Each $L2^{n+2}$ is $\prec_{n+1}$-analytic. Clearly, the previous definitions of $\prec_0$ and $\prec_1$ coincide with the new ones.

4 Semantics of Pure Sequent Calculi

Cut-admissibility is traditionally proved syntactically, by some form of induction on derivations. In this case, what is actually shown is *cut-elimination*: a method to eliminate cuts from derivations. However, going back at least to [26], semantic methods have also shown to be useful to prove cut-admissibility. We follow the semantic approach, and generalize the framework of bivaluations [13] to obtain semantic counterparts of $\prec$-analytic derivations and cut-limited derivations. The latter allows us to define a semantic sufficient condition for cut-admissibility, that is essential for our result. The soundness and completeness theorems of this section follow from the general result of [19].

We start by defining *trivaluations* – functions that employ three truth values: 1, −1, and 0, that intuitively correspond to "true", "false" and "undetermined", respectively.

Definition 6. An $\mathcal{L}$-*trivaluation* is a function v from $\mathcal{L}$ to $\{-1, 0, 1\}$. We say that v *satisfies a sequent* $\Gamma \Rightarrow \Delta$, denoted $v \models \Gamma \Rightarrow \Delta$, if either $v(\varphi) < 1$ for some $\varphi \in \Gamma$ or $v(\psi) > -1$ for some $\psi \in \Delta$. We say that v *satisfies a set S of sequents*, denoted $v \models S$, if $v \models s$ for every $s \in S$.

In order to associate a set of trivaluations to a given calculus, the following semantic reading of derivation rules is employed:

Definition 7. A trivaluation v *respects* a rule S/s if $v \models \sigma(s)$ whenever $v \models \sigma(S)$ for every substitution σ. v is called **G**-*legal* for a calculus **G** if it respects all rules of **G**.

Depending on **G**, this semantics may not be truth-functional, that is, the value of a compound formula is not always uniquely determined by the values of its immediate subformulas. For this reason trivaluations are defined over the entire language rather than only over atomic formulas.

If one is interested in all possible derivations in a pure calculus (without any restrictions on formulas that may appear in the derivation or serve as cut formulas), the third value 0 is redundant, and an equivalent semantics could be defined using only $\{1, -1\}$. For the cases of $\prec$-analytic and cut-limited derivations, some restrictions apply for when this value can and cannot be used. These restrictions are defined using the following notion of the *support* of trivaluations.

Definition 8. The *support* of a trivaluation v, denoted $\mathrm{supp}(v)$, is the set $\{\varphi \in \mathcal{L} \mid v(\varphi) \neq 0\}$. v is called:

– $\mathcal{F}$-*determined* (for $\mathcal{F} \subseteq \mathcal{L}$) if $\mathcal{F} \subseteq \mathrm{supp}(v)$; and
– *fully determined* if it is $\mathcal{L}$-determined.

The semantic reading of rules as constraints on trivaluations, together with different restrictions on the usage of 0 as a truth value, provide an equivalent semantic view of derivations:

Theorem 1 (Soundness and Completeness)

1. $S \vdash_{\mathbf{G}} s$ *iff* $v \models S$ *implies* $v \models s$ *for every fully determined* **G**-*legal trivaluation* v.

2. $S \vdash_{\mathbf{G}}^{\prec} s$ iff $v \models S$ implies $v \models s$ for every $\preceq [S \cup \{s\}]$-determined $\mathbf{G}$-legal trivaluation v.

3. $S \vdash_{\mathbf{G}}^{cf} s$ iff $v \models S$ implies $v \models s$ for every $frm[S]$-determined $\mathbf{G}$-legal trivaluation v.

Roughly speaking, in the case of $\prec$-analytic derivations, the values -1 and 1 are associated with the formulas that are allowed to be used in derivations. Thus, when semantically describing the existence of a $\prec$-analytic derivation of a sequent s from a set S of sequents in a calculus $\mathbf{G}$, all formulas that are allowed to appear in such a derivation must be assigned either 1 or -1. These are exactly the formulas in $\preceq [S \cup \{s\}]$. Similarly, in the case of cut-limited derivations, cut formulas must be assigned either 1 or -1, and thus cut-limited derivations of s from S are tied to trivaluations in which $frm[S]$-formulas are never assigned 0. Intuitively, if φ cannot serve as a cut formula, we may need a trivaluation v that satisfies $\Rightarrow \varphi$ and $\varphi \Rightarrow$, which is possible iff $v(\varphi) = 0$. Obviously, when allowing all formulas to serve as cut formulas, or when there is no restriction on the formulas that may be used in derivations, all formulas must be assigned either 1 or -1.

Example 7 (Semantics of Classical Logic). It is easy to see that a fully determined $\mathcal{CL}$-trivaluation v is **LK**-legal iff it respects the classical truth tables. For example, the first line of the truth table for conjunction is obtained as follows: Suppose $v(p_1) = v(p_2) = 1$. Then $v \models \{ \Rightarrow p_1, \Rightarrow p_2 \}$, and since v is **LK**-legal, $v \models \Rightarrow p_1 \wedge p_2$, and so $v(p_1 \wedge p_2) = 1$. In addition, the three valued semantics for the cut-limited fragment of **LK** that is obtained from Theorem 1 is equivalent to the Nmatrix semantics in [18].

Example 8 (Alternative Semantics of Łukasiewicz three-valued logic). $\mathbf{G_3}$-legal fully determined trivaluations provide an alternative semantics to Łukasiewicz three-valued logic (Example 3). This semantics is two-valued (as only *fully determined* trivaluations are considered), but not truth-functional. Another two-valued semantics for this logic was presented in [27], and was then used to construct a different calculus for it in [13].

Theorem 1 gives rise to a sufficient semantic criterion for cut-admissibility, which is based on the following notion of *determination*:

Definition 9. We say that a trivaluation v' is a *determination* of a trivaluation v (alternatively, we say that v' *determines* v) if $v(\varphi) = v'(\varphi)$ for every $\varphi \in \mathrm{supp}(v)$. v' is called an *$\mathcal{F}$-determination of v* if, in addition, it is $\mathcal{F}$-determined. If v' is fully determined we call it a *full determination* of v.

It immediately follows from our definitions that:

Proposition 1. *Suppose that v' determines v. Then for every sequent s, if $v' \models s$ then $v \models s$. The converse holds as well when v is $frm[s]$-determined.*

A sufficient semantic criterion for cut-admissibility is given in the following corollary:

Corollary 1. *If every* **G***-legal trivaluation has a* **G***-legal full determination, then* **G** *enjoys cut-admissibility.*

Proof. Suppose $S \nvdash_{\mathbf{G}}^{\mathrm{cf}} s$. By Theorem 1, there exists some $frm[S]$-determined **G**-legal trivaluation v such that $v \models S$ and $v \nvDash s$. Let v' be a **G**-legal full determination of v. By Proposition 1, $v' \models S$ and $v' \nvDash s$, and by Theorem 1, we have $S \nvdash_{\mathbf{G}} s$. □

Remark 1. We note that [19] connects $\prec$-analytic derivations to *partial* two-valued valuations, that are defined over a subset of the language. This subset corresponds to the support of the trivaluations that are used here. For the characterization of cut-limited derivations in [19], three-valued valuations were employed. In the current paper, where the connection between $\prec$-analyticity and cut-admissibility is the main subject, we find it more natural to use a three-valued semantics both for $\prec$-analytic and cut-limited derivations.

5   From Analyticity to Cut-Admissibility

For many calculi, including all calculi presented above, all rules except (CUT) are "$\prec$-ordered": in every application of the rule, every formula φ that appears in the premises satisfies $\varphi \preceq \psi$ for some formula ψ that appears in the conclusion. For such calculi, cut-admissibility immediately entails $\prec$-analyticity, as every cut-limited derivation is $\prec$-analytic. Whether or not the converse holds is the subject of this section.

First, note that (even for "$\prec$-ordered" calculi), $\prec$-analyticity may not imply cut-admissibility:

Example 9. Consider the calculus $\mathbf{LK}_{AX}$, that consists of the following axiomatic rules:

$$\emptyset / p_1, p_2 \Rightarrow p_1 \wedge p_2 \qquad \emptyset / p_1 \wedge p_2 \Rightarrow p_1 \qquad \emptyset / p_1 \wedge p_2 \Rightarrow p_2$$
$$\emptyset / p_1 \vee p_2 \Rightarrow p_1, p_2 \qquad \emptyset / p_1 \Rightarrow p_1 \vee p_2 \qquad \emptyset / p_2 \Rightarrow p_1 \vee p_2$$
$$\emptyset / p_2 \Rightarrow p_1 \supset p_2 \qquad \emptyset / \Rightarrow p_1, p_1 \supset p_2 \qquad \emptyset / p_1, p_1 \supset p_2 \Rightarrow p_2$$
$$\emptyset / \Rightarrow p_1, \neg p_1 \qquad \emptyset / p_1, \neg p_1 \Rightarrow$$

It can be easily shown that $\mathbf{LK}_{AX}$ is $\prec_0$-analytic (since $\mathbf{LK}$ is $\prec_0$-analytic). However, it does not admit cut-admissibility (for instance, the sequent $p_1 \wedge p_2 \Rightarrow p_1 \vee p_2$ has no derivation without cut).

Next, we identify a family of calculi in which analyticity does imply cut-admissibility.

Definition 10. A rule S/s is called $\prec$-*directed* if $frm[S] \subseteq \prec[s]$, and s has the form $\Rightarrow \varphi$ or $\varphi \Rightarrow$ for some formula φ. A calculus **G** is called $\prec$-*directed* if all its rules are $\prec$-directed.

The calculi $\mathbf{LK}$, $\mathbf{G}_{P_1}$, $\mathbf{P}$, and $\mathbf{DY}$ are $\prec_0$-directed, $\mathbf{G}_{C_1}$, $\mathbf{G}_3$ and $\mathbf{G}_4$ are $\prec_1$-directed, and for every n, $L2^{n+2}$ is $\prec_{n+1}$-directed. In contrast, $\mathbf{LK}_{AX}$ (Example 9) is not $\prec$-directed for any $\prec$, as its conclusions include several formulas.

Our first main result is that $\prec$-analyticity guarantees cut-admissibility in the family of $\prec$-directed pure calculi.

Theorem 2. *Every $\prec$-analytic $\prec$-directed pure calculus enjoys cut-admissibility.*

The proof of Theorem 2 goes through Corollary 1: given a pure calculus $\mathbf{G}$ that is $\prec$-analytic and $\prec$-directed, we show that every $\mathbf{G}$-legal trivaluation has a $\mathbf{G}$-legal full determination. This is done by iteratively extending the support of a given $\mathbf{G}$-legal trivaluation v by a single formula φ that is not in $\mathrm{supp}(v)$, but $\prec[\varphi] \subseteq \mathrm{supp}(v)$. The value of φ is determined as follows:

$$v'(\varphi) = \begin{cases} 1 & \nvdash_{\mathbf{G}} \Gamma_v, \varphi \Rightarrow \Delta_v \\ -1 & otherwise \end{cases}$$

where $\Gamma_v = \{\psi \in \prec[\varphi] \mid v(\psi) = 1\}$ and $\Delta_v = \{\psi \in \prec[\varphi] \mid v(\psi) = -1\}$. The correctness of this construction follows from the fact that $\mathbf{G}$ is $\prec$-directed and $\prec$-analytic. By enumerating the formulas while respecting $\prec$, we inductively determine all the formulas that are assigned 0 by v.

For all the calculi mentioned above (except $\mathbf{LK}_{AX}$), this theorem allows one to obtain cut-admissibility as a consequence of $\prec$-analyticity for some (structural and safe) order $\prec$.

6   Intuitionistic Calculi

For various important non-classical logics, there is no known cut-free pure calculus. In particular, Gentzen's original calculus for intuitionistic logic, LJ, is not pure, as it manipulates *single-conclusion sequents*, in which the right-hand side includes at most one formula. An equivalent cut-free sequent calculus, which we call $\mathbf{LJ'}$, was presented in [28]. This calculus employs multiple-conclusion sequents, and restricts only the right introduction rules of implication and negation to apply on single-conclusion sequents. In other words, $\mathbf{LJ'}$ is obtained from $\mathbf{LK}$ by adding the requirement that applications of $p_1 \Rightarrow p_2 / \Rightarrow p_1 \supset p_2$ and $p_1 \Rightarrow / \Rightarrow \neg p_1$ have the forms:

$$\frac{\Gamma, \varphi \Rightarrow \psi}{\Gamma \Rightarrow \varphi \supset \psi} \qquad\qquad \frac{\Gamma, \varphi \Rightarrow}{\Gamma \Rightarrow \neg \varphi}$$

Put differently, $\mathbf{LJ'}$ is obtained from $\mathbf{LK}$ by forbidding right context formulas in all premises of the form $\Gamma \Rightarrow \Delta$ with $\Gamma \neq \emptyset$ of right-introduction rules (rules that introduce some formula on the right-hand side).

Another well-known calculus that follows this pattern, which we call $\mathbf{G}'_4$, is obtained by extending the positive fragment of $\mathbf{LJ}'$ with the rules for negation of $\mathbf{G}_4$ (see Example 3). $\mathbf{G}'_4$, investigated in [7,29], is sound and complete for Nelson's paraconsistent constructive logic $N4$ [23].

Next, we define a general family of calculi, which we call *intuitionistic calculi*, of which $\mathbf{LJ}'$ and $\mathbf{G}'_4$ are particular examples. For them, we show that cut-admissibility is a consequence of $\prec$-analyticity.

Definition 11. A pure rule is called *positive* if its conclusion has the form $\Gamma \Rightarrow \Delta$ for some $\Delta \neq \emptyset$. A derivation in a pure calculus $\mathbf{G}$ is called *intuitionistic* if in every application $\langle \{\sigma(s_1) \cup c_1, \ldots, \sigma(s_n) \cup c_n\}, \sigma(s_0) \cup c_1 \cup \ldots \cup c_n \rangle$ of a positive rule $s_1, \ldots, s_n / s_0$, for every $1 \leq i \leq n$ we have that if s_i has the form $\Gamma_i \Rightarrow \Delta_i$ with $\Gamma_i \neq \emptyset$, then c_i has the form $\Gamma'_i \Rightarrow$.

Derivability, cut-admissibility and $\prec$-analyticity are adopted to intuitionistic derivations in the obvious way:

Definition 12. For a pure calculus $\mathbf{G}$, we write $S \vdash_{\mathbf{G}_{\mathbf{Int}}} s$ if there is an intuitionistic derivation of a sequent s from a set S of sequents in $\mathbf{G}$. We write $S \vdash^{\text{cf}}_{\mathbf{G}_{\mathbf{Int}}} s$ if there is such a derivation which is also cut-limited, and $S \vdash^{\prec}_{\mathbf{G}_{\mathbf{Int}}} s$ if there is such a derivation which is $\prec$-analytic (see Definitions 3 and 5). We say that $\mathbf{G}$ enjoys *Int-cut-admissibility* if $\vdash_{\mathbf{G}_{\mathbf{Int}}} = \vdash^{\text{cf}}_{\mathbf{G}_{\mathbf{Int}}}$, and is *Int-$\prec$-analytic* if $\vdash_{\mathbf{G}_{\mathbf{Int}}} = \vdash^{\prec}_{\mathbf{G}_{\mathbf{Int}}}$.

The difference between pure and intuitionistic calculi is not in the *rules*, but rather in *applications* that are allowed to appear in derivations. Thus, any pure calculus has an intuitionistic counterpart, obtained by considering only intuitionistic derivations. In particular, derivations in $\mathbf{LJ}'$ are exactly intuitionistic derivations of $\mathbf{LK}$. Indeed, for a finite set Γ of formulas and a formula φ, φ follows from Γ in intuitionistic logic iff $\vdash_{\mathbf{LK}_{\mathbf{Int}}} \Gamma \Rightarrow \varphi$. In contrast, φ follows from Γ in classical logic iff $\vdash_{\mathbf{LK}} \Gamma \Rightarrow \varphi$.

Theorem 3. *Every Int-$\prec$-analytic $\prec$-directed pure calculus enjoys Int-cut-admissibility.*

The proof of Theorem 3 has a similar general structure to the proof for pure calculi, but is more challenging, because simple valuation functions do not suffice to characterize the calculi of this family. Instead, a more complex semantic interpretation is employed, which is based on Kripke models. The description of this extended semantics, as well as its role in the proof of Theorem 3, are left for an extended version of this paper.

Theorem 3 allows one to derive the fact that cut is admissible in $\mathbf{LJ}'$ from the fact that $\mathbf{LJ}'$ enjoys the subformula property. More precisely, Int-cut-admissibility of $\mathbf{LK}$ follows from its Int-$\prec_0$-analyticity. Such entailment also holds for the pure calculi presented in the examples above, as well as for the calculi of the next example.

Example 10 (Constructive Negations). The paper [7] includes sequent calculi for logics that replace classical negation with several non-classical negations.

One of the families investigated there consists of calculi that are obtained from the positive fragment of **LJ**$'$ by augmenting it with pure rules for negation. All calculi of this family, except those described in Example 11 below, allow only intuitionistic derivations, and are $\prec_1$-directed and Int-$\prec_1$-analytic. From these facts, Theorem 3 allows us to conclude that cut is admissible in them. These calculi include a calculus for Nelson's constructive logic N_3 [23], as well as the calculus **G**$'_4$ presented above for its paraconsistent variant N_4.

Intuitionistic derivations disallow right context formulas in premises of positive rules (Definition 11), in which the left-hand side is not empty. A natural question that arises regarding Theorem 3 is: Does it still hold if we allow right context formulas for certain premises of a right introduction rule with a non-empty left-hand side, and forbid them in others? The answer is negative as the next example demonstrates.

Example 11 (Beyond Intuitionistic Derivations). Following Example 10, we note that [7,8] investigate also several calculi that include *both* the single-conclusion right-introduction rule of implication and the multiple-conclusion right-introduction rule of negation. The former conforms with the restriction to intuitionistic derivations, as right context formulas are forbidden. The latter allows for non-intuitionistic derivations, as it allows right context formulas in a premise that has a non-empty left side. Such calculi are therefore left out from the scope of Theorems 2 and 3. And indeed, as was shown in [8], all of them are $\prec_1$-analytic, but none of them enjoys cut-admissibility.

7 Conclusion

We identified two general families of propositional sequent calculi, in which a generalized subformula property is equivalent to cut-admissibility. The first is the family of pure calculi that are $\prec$-directed for some safe and structural order $\prec$. The second is the family of "$\prec$-directed intuitionistic calculi", obtained by considering intuitionistic derivations in $\prec$-directed pure calculi.

This result sheds light on the relation between these two fundamental properties. Furthermore, we believe that it may be useful in obtaining simpler cut-admissibility proofs:

1. Theorems 2 and 3 reduce the burden in proving cut-admissibility to establishing only *analytic cut-admissibility*. An application of (CUT) in a derivation of s from S is called a $\prec$-*analytic cut* if the cut formula is in $\prec[S \cup \{s\}]$. In turn, $\prec$-analytic cut-admissibility concerns only the admissibility of non-$\prec$-analytic cuts. Proving this property is often easier than showing full cut-admissibility. For example, when $\prec_0$-analytic cuts are allowed, it is straightforward to prove that **LK** is complete for the classical truth tables. Indeed, assuming $S \nvdash_{\mathbf{LK}} \Gamma \Rightarrow \Delta$, one extends $\Gamma \Rightarrow \Delta$ to a maximal underivable sequent $\Gamma^* \Rightarrow \Delta^*$ that consists solely of $\prec_0 [S \cup \{\Gamma \Rightarrow \Delta\}]$-formulas. Then, a countermodel v can be defined simply by setting $v(\varphi) = 1$ for every $\varphi \in \Gamma^*$

and $v(\psi) = -1$ for every $\psi \in \Delta^*$. Using $\prec_0$-analytic cuts, it immediately follows that $\Gamma^* \cup \Delta^* = \prec_0 [S \cup \{\Gamma \cup \Delta\}]$, which makes it easy to prove that v respects the classical truth tables, and can therefore be extended to a full classical assignment. By Theorem 2, we may conclude that **LK** enjoys (full) cut-admissibility.

2. The results of this paper are useful in combination with our recent paper [20], where we provided a general method for proving $\prec_n$-analyticity (see Example 6 for the definition of $\prec_n$) in a wide family of pure calculi. Concretely, we showed that the $\prec_n$-analyticity of a $\prec_n$-directed calculus **G** is guaranteed if the following property holds:

> For every two rules of **G** of the forms $S_1 / \Rightarrow \varphi_1$ and $S_2 / \varphi_2 \Rightarrow$, and substitutions σ_1, σ_2 such that $\sigma_1(\varphi_1) = \sigma_2(\varphi_2)$, the empty sequent is derivable from $\sigma(S_1) \cup \sigma(S_2)$ using only (CUT).

Then, Theorem 2 ensures that these calculi are not only $\prec_n$-analytic, but they also admit cut-admissibility.

We propose two particular directions for future research. First, our approach should be further developed for more expressible languages, which include quantifiers and modalities. For the former, the three-valued semantics should be elevated to three-valued first-order structures. For the latter, we prospect that the Kripke semantics used here for intuitionistic calculi could be adapted for calculi with modalities. We note, however, that such an approach is expected to have certain limitations, as some analytic calculi for modal logics (e.g., $S5$ and B [25, 30]) do not admit cut-admissibility.

Second, the following questions regarding the relations between derivations and intuitionistic derivations are currently left open: Does $\prec$-analyticity imply Int-$\prec$-analyticity? Does cut-admissibility imply Int-cut-admissibility? Do either of the converses hold?

Acknowledgments. This research was supported by The Israel Science Foundation (grant no. 817-15). We thank Arnon Avron, João Marcos and the TABLEAUX'17 reviewers for their helpful feedback.

References

1. Anderson, A.R., Belnap, N.D.: Entailment: The Logic of Relevance and Necessity, vol. I. Princeton University Press, Princeton (1975)
2. Arieli, O., Avron, A.: The value of the four values. Artif. Intell. **102**(1), 97–141 (1998)
3. Arieli, O., Avron, A.: Three-valued paraconsistent propositional logics. In: Beziau, J.-Y., Chakraborty, M., Dutta, S. (eds.) New Directions in Paraconsistent Logic: 5th WCP. Kolkata, India, pp. 91–129. Springer, New Delhi (2015). doi:10.1007/978-81-322-2719-9_4
4. Avron, A.: Simple consequence relations. Inf. Comput. **92**(1), 105–139 (1991)
5. Avron, A.: Gentzen-type systems, resolution and tableaux. J. Autom. Reason. **10**(2), 265–281 (1993)

6. Avron, A.: Classical Gentzen-type methods in propositional many-valued logics. In: Fitting, M., Orłowska, E. (eds.) Beyond Two: Theory and Applications of Multiple-Valued Logic. STUDFUZZ, vol. 114, pp. 117–155. Physica, Heidelberg (2003). doi:10.1007/978-3-7908-1769-0_5

7. Avron, A.: A non-deterministic view on non-classical negations. Stud. Log.: Int. J. Symb. Log. **80**(2/3), 159–194 (2005)

8. Avron, A.: Non-deterministic semantics for families of paraconsistent logics. Handb. Paraconsist. **9**, 285–320 (2007)

9. Avron, A., Konikowska, B., Zamansky, A.: Modular construction of cut-free sequent calculi for paraconsistent logics. In: Proceedings of the 27th Annual IEEE/ACM Symposium on Logic in Computer Science, LICS 2012, pp. 85–94. IEEE Computer Society (2012)

10. Avron, A., Lev, I.: Non-deterministic multi-valued structures. J. Log. Comput. **15**, 241–261 (2005). Conference version: Avron, A., Lev, I.: Canonical propositional Gentzen-type systems. In: Proceedings of the International Joint Conference on Automated Reasoning, IJCAR 2001. LNAI, vol. 2083, pp. 529–544. Springer, Heidelberg (2001)

11. Avron, A., Zamansky, A.: Non-deterministic semantics for logical systems. In: Gabbay, D., Guenthner, F. (eds.) Handbook of Philosophical Logic. HALO, vol. 16, pp. 227–304. Springer, Dordrecht (2011). doi:10.1007/978-94-007-0479-4_4

12. Beklemishev, L., Gurevich, Y.: Propositional primal logic with disjunction. J. Log. Comput. **24**(1), 257–282 (2014)

13. Béziau, J.-Y.: Sequents and bivaluations. Logique Anal. **44**(176), 373–394 (2001)

14. Comon-Lundh, H., Shmatikov, V.: Intruder deductions, constraint solving and insecurity decision in presence of exclusive or. In: 2003 Proceedings of 18th Annual IEEE Symposium on Logic in Computer Science, pp. 271–280, June 2003

15. Cotrini, C., Gurevich, Y.: Basic primal infon logic. J. Log. Comput. **26**(1), 117–141 (2016)

16. Gentzen, G.: Investigations Into Logical Deduction (1934). (in German). An English translation appears in 'The Collected Works of Gerhard Gentzen', edited by Szabo, M.E., North-Holland (1969)

17. Kamide, N.: A hierarchy of weak double negations. Stud. Log. **101**(6), 1277–1297 (2013)

18. Lahav, O.: Studying sequent systems via non-deterministic multiple-valued matrices. Mult.-Valued Log. Soft Comput. **21**(5–6), 575–595 (2013)

19. Lahav, O., Avron, A.: A unified semantic framework for fully structural propositional sequent systems. ACM Trans. Comput. Log. **14**(4), 271–273 (2013)

20. Lahav, O., Zohar, Y.: On the construction of analytic sequent calculi for subclassical logics. In: Kohlenbach, U., Barceló, P., Queiroz, R. (eds.) WoLLIC 2014. LNCS, vol. 8652, pp. 206–220. Springer, Heidelberg (2014). doi:10.1007/978-3-662-44145-9_15

21. Lahav, O., Zohar, Y.: SAT-based decision procedure for analytic pure sequent calculi. In: Demri, S., Kapur, D., Weidenbach, C. (eds.) IJCAR 2014. LNCS, vol. 8562, pp. 76–90. Springer, Cham (2014). doi:10.1007/978-3-319-08587-6_6

22. Metcalfe, G., Olivetti, N., Gabbay, D.: Proof Theory for Fuzzy Logics. Applied Logic Series, vol. 36. Springer, Netherlands (2009). doi:10.1007/978-1-4020-9409-5

23. Nelson, D.: Constructible falsity. J. Symb. Log. **14**(1), 16–26 (1949)

24. Pinto, L., Uustalu, T.: Proof search and counter-model construction for bi-intuitionistic propositional logic with labelled sequents. In: Giese, M., Waaler, A. (eds.) TABLEAUX 2009. LNCS (LNAI), vol. 5607, pp. 295–309. Springer, Heidelberg (2009). doi:10.1007/978-3-642-02716-1_22

25. Poggiolesi, F.: Gentzen Calculi for Modal Propositional Logic. Trends in Logic, vol. 32. Springer, Netherlands (2011). doi:10.1007/978-90-481-9670-8
26. Schütte, K.: Beweistheorie. Springer, Berlin (1960)
27. Suszko, R.: Remarks on Łukasiewicz's three-valued logic. Bull. Sect. Log. **4**(3), 87–90 (1975)
28. Takeuti, G.: Proof Theory. Studies in Logic and the Foundations of Mathematics. North-Holland Publishing Company, Amsterdam (1975)
29. Wansing, H.: The Logic of Information Structures. LNCS, vol. 681. Springer, Heidelberg (1993). doi:10.1007/3-540-56734-8
30. Wansing, H.: Sequent systems for modal logics. In: Gabbay, D.M., Guenthner, F. (eds.) Handbook of Philosophical Logic. HALO, vol. 8, 2nd edn, pp. 61–145. Springer, Dordrecht (2002). doi:10.1007/978-94-010-0387-2_2

Proof Theory for Indexed Nested Sequents

Sonia Marin$^{(\boxtimes)}$ and Lutz Straßburger

Inria, Saclay, France
sonia.marin@inria.fr

Abstract. Fitting's indexed nested sequents can be used to give deductive systems to modal logics which cannot be captured by pure nested sequents. In this paper we show how the standard cut-elimination procedure for nested sequents can be extended to indexed nested sequents, and we discuss how indexed nested sequents can be used for intuitionistic modal logics.

1 Introduction

Modal logics were originally defined in terms of axioms in a Hilbert system, and later in terms of their semantics in relational structures. Structural proof theory for modal logics, however, was considered a difficult topic as traditional (Gentzen) sequents did not provide fully satisfactory (i.e. analytic and modular) proof systems even for some common modal logics. Nonetheless, the proof theory of modal logics has received more attention in the last decades, and some extensions of traditional sequents were successfully proposed to handle modalities. Two approaches can be distinguished: (1) systems that incorporate relational semantics in the formalism itself like *labelled sequent systems* (e.g., [18,24,27]) which use sequents that explicitly refer to the relational semantics: formulas are labelled with states and relational atoms describe the accessibility relation, and (2) systems that use syntactical devices to handle the modalities like *nested sequents*, which are an extension of ordinary sequents to a structure of tree, first introduced by Kashima [12], and then independently rediscovered by Brünnler [3] and Poggiolesi [21]. They can be translated into a subclass of labelled sequents called in [11] labelled tree sequents, if the relational structure is made explicit. However, compared to labelled deductive systems, the tree structure restricts the expressivity of nested sequents. In particular, it seems that nested sequents cannot give cut-free deductive systems for logics obeying the Scott-Lemmon axioms, which correspond to a "confluence" condition on the relational structure [14].

Fitting recently introduced *indexed nested sequents* [7], an extension of nested sequents which goes beyond the tree structure to give a cut-free system for the classical modal logic K extended with an arbitrary set of Scott-Lemmon axioms. In some sense indexed nested sequents are more similar to labelled systems than pure nested sequents—in fact, the translation between nested sequents and labelled tree sequents mentioned above is naturally extended in [23] to a

---

S. Marin—Supported by ERC Advanced Grant "ProofCert".

R.A. Schmidt and C. Nalon (Eds.): TABLEAUX 2017, LNAI 10501, pp. 81–97, 2017.
DOI: 10.1007/978-3-319-66902-1_5

translation between indexed nested sequents and labelled tree sequents with equality, where some nodes of the underlying tree can be identified.

In this paper we investigate some proof-theoretical properties of indexed nested sequents. The first and foremost one is the cut-elimination theorem. As Fitting's original system does not use a cut rule, this result is actually entailed by his (semantical) completeness theorem. Using the translation mentioned above, one could also use the cut-elimination result for labelled tree sequents with equality, yielding an indirect proof [23]. However, only an internal cut-elimination proof makes a proof formalism a first-class citizen for structural proof theory. For this reason we give in this paper a syntactic proof of cut-elimination carried out within indexed nested sequents. We achieve this by making some subtle but crucial adjustments to the standard cut-elimination proof for pure nested sequents.

One of the main advantages is that this proof can be exported to the intuitionistic framework with basically no effort. We achieve this by using the techniques that had already been successfully used for ordinary nested sequents [8,15,26]. This allows us to present the cut-free indexed nested sequents systems in a uniform manner for classical and intuitionistic modal logic. The deductive systems are almost identical, the main difference being that an intuitionistic sequent has only one "output" formula, in the same way as in ordinary sequent calculus an intuitionistic sequent has only one formula on the right.

As there is no straightforward definition of the extension of intuitionistic modal logic with Scott-Lemmon axioms, the indexed nested sequents system can be seen as one way to define it. This point is examined in the last section with a discussion on the various alternatives that exist in the literature and how they relate to the proposed system.

2   Indexed Nested Sequents and the Scott-Lemmon Axioms

We start by working with formulas in negation normal form, generated by the following grammar, which extends the language of propositional classical logic with the two modalities $\Box$ and $\Diamond$

$$A ::= a \mid \bar{a} \mid A \wedge A \mid A \vee A \mid \Box A \mid \Diamond A \tag{1}$$

where a is taken from a countable set of propositional atoms, $\bar{a}$ is its negation, and $\bar{\bar{a}}$ is equivalent to a. For every formula A, its negation $\bar{A}$, is defined as usual via the De Morgan laws. For now, we use $A \supset B$ as abbreviation for $\bar{A} \vee B$.

Classical modal logic K is obtained from classical propositional logic by adding the axiom k: $\Box(A \supset B) \supset (\Box A \supset \Box B)$ and the *necessitation rule* that allows to derive the formula $\Box A$ from any theorem A.

Stronger modal logics can be obtained by adding to K other axioms. We are interested here specifically in the family of *Scott-Lemmon axioms* of the form

$$\mathsf{g}_{k,l,m,n}: \Diamond^k \Box^l A \supset \Box^m \Diamond^n A \tag{2}$$

for a tuple $\langle k, l, m, n \rangle$ of natural numbers, where $\Box^m$ stands for m boxes and $\Diamond^n$ for n diamonds. Fitting [7] introduced indexed nested sequents exactly to provide a structural proof system for classical modal logic K, that could be extended with rules for the Scott-Lemmon axioms.

A *(pure) nested sequent* is a multiset of formulas and *boxed sequents*, according to the following grammar $\Gamma ::= \emptyset \mid A, \Gamma \mid [\Gamma], \Gamma$ where A is a modal formula. We understand such a nested sequent through its interpretation as a modal formula, written $fm(\cdot)$, given inductively by $fm(\emptyset) = \bot$; $fm(A, \Gamma) = A \vee fm(\Gamma)$; and $fm([\Gamma_1], \Gamma_2) = \Box fm(\Gamma_1) \vee fm(\Gamma_2)$. A nested sequent can therefore be seen as a tree of ordinary *one-sided* sequents, with each node representing the scope of a modal $\Box$. It therefore is of the general form

$$A_1, \ldots, A_k, [\Gamma_1], \ldots, [\Gamma_n] \tag{3}$$

An *indexed nested sequent*, as defined in [7], is a nested sequent where each sequent node (either the root or any interior node) carries an *index*, denoted by lowercase letters like $u, v, w, x, \ldots$, and taken from a countable set (e.g., for simplicity, the set of natural numbers), so we write an indexed sequent by extending (3) in the following way

$$A_1, \ldots, A_k, [^{w_1} \Gamma_1], \ldots, [^{w_n} \Gamma_n] \tag{4}$$

where $\Gamma_1, \ldots, \Gamma_n$ are now indexed sequents, and where the index of the root is not explicitly shown (e.g., we can assume that it is 0). For an indexed nested sequent Σ, we write I_Σ to denote the set of indexes occurring in Σ.

Intuitively, indexed nested sequents are no longer trees, but any kind of *rooted directed graphs*, by identifying nodes carrying the same index.

In nested sequent calculi, a rule can be applied at any depth in the structure, that is, inside a certain nested sequent context. We write $\Gamma^{i_1}\{ \ \} \cdots {}^{i_n}\{ \ \}$ for an n-ary context (i.e. one with n occurrences of the $\{ \ \}$) where $i_1, \ldots, i_n$ are the indexes of the sequent nodes that contain the $\{ \ \}$, in the order of their appearance in the sequent. A hole in a context can be replaced by a formula or sequent. More precisely, we write $\Gamma^{i_1}\{\Delta_1\} \cdots {}^{i_n}\{\Delta_n\}$ for the sequent that is obtained from $\Gamma^{i_1}\{ \ \} \cdots {}^{i_n}\{ \ \}$ by replacing the k-th hole by Δ_k, for each $k \in \{1, \ldots, n\}$ (if $\Delta_k = \emptyset$ it simply amounts to removing the $\{ \ \}$). We might omit the index at the context-braces when this information is clear or not relevant.

Example 2.1. For example, $A, [^1 B, [^2 C, \{ \ \}]], [^3 D, [^1\{ \ \}, A]], [^2 D, \{ \ \}]$ is a ternary context that we can write as $\Gamma^2\{ \ \}^1\{ \ \}^2\{ \ \}$. If we substitute the sequents $\Delta_1 = D, [^4 E]$; $\Delta_2 = F$; and $\Delta_3 = [^5 G]$ into its holes, we get: $\Gamma^2\{\Delta_1\}^1\{\Delta_2\}^2\{\Delta_3\} = A, [^1 B, [^2 C, D, [^4 E]]], [^3 D, [^1 F, A]], [^2 D, [^5 G]]$.

In Fig. 1, the classical system that we call iNK is an adaptation of the system described by Fitting in [7] to our notations and to the one-sided setting. It can also be seen as Brünnler's system [3] extended with indexes.

What is different from the pure nested sequent system is the addition of the two structural rules tp and bc, called *teleportation* and *bracket-copy*, respectively, which are variants of the formula-contraction FC and the sequent-contraction SC of [7]. We need two versions of bc to take care of every possible context where the rule may be applied. Another peculiarity is that in the rules for $\square$ we demand that the index of the new bracket in the premiss does not occur in the conclusion.

$$\text{id} \; \frac{}{\Gamma\{a,\bar{a}\}} \qquad \vee \; \frac{\Gamma\{A,B\}}{\Gamma\{A \vee B\}} \qquad \wedge \; \frac{\Gamma\{A\} \quad \Gamma\{B\}}{\Gamma\{A \wedge B\}} \qquad \diamond \; \frac{\Gamma\{\diamond A, [^u A, \Delta]\}}{\Gamma\{\diamond A, [^u \Delta]\}} \qquad \square \; \frac{\Gamma\{[^v A]\}}{\Gamma\{\square A\}} \; v \text{ is fresh}$$

$$\text{tp} \; \frac{\Gamma^w\{\emptyset\}\,^w\{A\}}{\Gamma^w\{A\}\,^w\{\emptyset\}} \qquad \text{bc}_1 \; \frac{\Gamma^w\{[^u \Delta]\}\,^w\{[^u \emptyset]\}}{\Gamma^w\{[^u \Delta]\}\,^w\{\emptyset\}} \qquad \text{bc}_2 \; \frac{\Gamma^w\{[^u \Delta\,^w\{[^u \emptyset]\}]\}}{\Gamma^w\{[^u \Delta\,^w\{\emptyset\}]\}}$$

Fig. 1. System iNK

$$\text{g}_{k,l,m,n} \; \frac{\Gamma^{u_0}\{[^{u_1}\Delta_1,\ldots[^{u_k}\Delta_k,[^{v_1}\ldots[^{v_l}]\ldots]]\ldots],[^{w_1}\Sigma_1,\ldots[^{w_m}\Sigma_m,[^{x_1}\ldots[^{x_n}]\ldots]]\ldots\}}{\Gamma^{u_0}\{[^{u_1}\Delta_1,\ldots[^{u_k}\Delta_k]\ldots],[^{w_1}\Sigma_1,\ldots[^{w_m}\Sigma_m]\ldots]\}}$$

Fig. 2. Inference rule $\text{g}_{k,l,m,n}$ (where $l + n \neq 0$, $v_1 \ldots v_k$ and $x_1 \ldots x_n$ are fresh, and $v_l = x_n$)

$$\text{g}_{k,0,m,0} \; \frac{\sigma\Gamma^{u_0}\{[^{u_1}\Delta_1,\ldots[^{\sigma(u_k)}\Delta_k],\ldots],[^{w_1}\Sigma_1,\ldots[^{\sigma(w_m)}\Sigma_m],\ldots]\}}{\Gamma^{u_0}\{[^{u_1}\Delta_1,\ldots[^{u_k}\Delta_k],\ldots],[^{w_1}\Sigma_1,\ldots[^{w_m}\Sigma_m],\ldots]\}}$$

Fig. 3. Special case for $\text{g}_{k,0,m,0}$

Finally, for a tuple $\langle k,l,m,n \rangle$ with $l + n \neq 0$, the rule $\text{g}_{k,l,m,n}$ in Fig. 2 is defined as in [7]. It must satisfy that $v_1 \ldots v_k$ and $x_1 \ldots x_n$ are fresh indexes which are pairwise distinct, except for the *confluence condition*: we always have $v_l = x_n$. When one or more elements of the tuple $\langle k,l,m,n \rangle$ are equal to 0, then we have the following special cases:

– if $k = 0$ (or $m = 0$) then u_1 to u_k (resp. w_1 to w_m) all collapse to u_0.
– if $l = 0$ then w_1 to w_l all collapse to u_k, and similarly, if $n = 0$ then x_1 to x_n all collapse to v_m. In particular, if $k = 0$ and $l = 0$, we must have $x_n = u_0$, and similarly, if $m = 0$ and $n = 0$, we demand that $v_l = u_0$.

An example of how this rule can be used to derive an instance of the Scott-Lemmon axioms can be found in the proof of Theorem 4.2.

The case where $l = 0$ and $n = 0$ was not handled by Fitting in [7]; we give a corresponding rule in Fig. 3. In that case, not only do we identify u_k and w_m, but it is also necessary to apply a substitution $\sigma \colon I_\Gamma \to I_\Gamma$ to the indexes in the context $\Gamma^{u_0}\{\ \}$, giving the new context $\sigma\Gamma^{u_0}\{\ \}$, such that $\sigma(u_k) = \sigma(w_m)$ in the whole sequent (and $\sigma(y) = y$ for any other $y \in I_\Gamma$).

For a given set $G \subseteq \mathbb{N}^4$, write iNK + G for the system obtained from iNK by adding the corresponding rules given in Figs. 2 and 3. System iNK + G is sound and complete wrt. the logic corresponding $K + G$ (which is obtained from K by adding the corresponding axioms (2)). Soundness is proven by Fitting [7] wrt. relational frames; and completeness via a translation to *set-prefixed tableaux system* for which in turn he gives a semantic completeness proof.

3   Cut-Elimination

In this section, we present a cut-elimination proof for the indexed nested sequent system iNK + G that relies on a standard double-induction on the height of the derivation above a given cut-rule (left of Fig. 4), and the cut rank.

$$
\mathrm{cut}\ \frac{\Gamma\{A\}\quad \Gamma\{\bar{A}\}}{\Gamma\{\emptyset\}} \qquad\bigg|\qquad \mathrm{w}\ \frac{\Gamma\{\emptyset\}}{\Gamma\{\Delta\}} \qquad \mathrm{c}\ \frac{\Gamma\{\Delta,\Delta\}}{\Gamma\{\Delta\}} \qquad \mathrm{nec}\ \frac{\Gamma}{[\Gamma]} \qquad \mathrm{isub}\ \frac{\Gamma}{\sigma\Gamma}
$$

Fig. 4. Left: the one-sided cut-rule – Right: additional structural rules

Definition 3.1. The *height of a derivation tree* π, denoted by $\mathrm{ht}(\pi)$, is the length of the longest path in the tree from its root to one of its leaves. The *rank* of an instance of cut is the depth of the formula introduced by the cut. We also write cut_r to denote an instance of cut with rank at most r. The *cut-rank* of a derivation π, denoted by $\mathrm{rk}(\pi)$, is the maximal rank of a cut in π.

To facilitate the overall argument, we consider a variant of system iNK, that we call *system* iN̈K, that is obtained from iNK by removing the teleportation rule tp (but keeping the bc-rules), and by replacing the id- and ◇-rules by

$$
\mathrm{\ddot{i}d}\ \frac{}{\Gamma\,{}^u\{a\}\,{}^u\{\bar{a}\}} \qquad\text{and}\qquad \mathrm{\ddot{\diamond}}\ \frac{\Gamma\,{}^u\{\diamond A\}\,{}^u\{[A,\Delta]\}}{\Gamma\,{}^u\{\diamond A\}\,{}^u\{[\Delta]\}} \tag{5}
$$

respectively. The reason behind this is that iNK and iN̈K are equivalent (with and without cut, as shown below in Lemma 3.4), but the tp-rule is admissible in the new system. We will also need some additional structural rules called *weakening*, *contraction*, *necessitation*, and *index substitution* respectively, which are shown on the right in Fig. 4. The rules for weakening and contraction are similar to the standard sequent rules except that they can apply deeply inside a context. The rules nec and isub on the other hand cannot be applied deep inside a context; they always work on the whole sequent. In isub, the sequent $\sigma\Gamma$ is obtained from Γ by applying the substitution $\sigma\colon I_\Gamma \to I_\Gamma$ on the indexes occurring in Γ, where σ can be an arbitrary renaming.

Lemma 3.2. *The rules* nec, w, isub *and* c *are cut-rank and height preserving admissible for* iṄK + G, *and all rules of* iṄK + G *(except for the axiom* ïd*) are cut-rank and height-preserving invertible.*

Proof. This proof is analogous to that for the pure nested sequent systems in [3]. For bc and $g_{k,l,m,n}$, note that their inverses are just weakenings. $\square$

Lemma 3.3. *The rule* tp *is admissible for* iṄK + G *(and for* iṄK + G + cut*).*

Proof. The proof uses an induction on the number of instances of tp in a proof, eliminating topmost instances first, by an induction on the height of the proof above it and a case analysis of the rule r applied just before tp. The only nontrivial case is when r = $\square$:

$$\square\;\cfrac{\Gamma^{u}\{[^{v}A]\}^{u}\{\}}{\cfrac{\Gamma^{u}\{\square A\}^{u}\{\}}{\Gamma^{u}\{\}^{u}\{\square A\}}\;tp}\quad\rightsquigarrow\quad\square\;\cfrac{bc\;\cfrac{tp\;\cfrac{w\;\cfrac{\Gamma^{u}\{[^{v}A]\}^{u}\{\}}{\Gamma^{u}\{[^{v}A]\}^{u}\{[^{v}\;]\}}}{\Gamma^{u}\{[^{v}\;]\}^{u}\{[^{v}A]\}}}{\Gamma^{u}\{\}^{u}\{[^{v}A]\}}}{\Gamma^{u}\{\}^{u}\{\square A\}}$$

we transform the derivation as follows and then use the admissibility of weakening (Lemma 3.2) and the induction hypothesis to conclude. $\square$

Lemma 3.4. *A sequent* Δ *is provable in* iNK + G *(or in* iNK + G + cut*) if and only if it is provable in* iṄK + G *(resp. in* iṄK + G + cut*).*

Proof. Given a proof of Δ in iNK + G, we can observe that the rules id and $\diamond$ are just special cases of the rules ïd and $\ddot{\diamond}$, respectively. Thus, we obtain a proof of Δ in iṄK + G from admissibility of tp (Lemma 3.3). Conversely, if we have a proof of Δ in iṄK + G, we can obtain a proof of Δ in iNK + G by replacing all instance of ïd and $\ddot{\diamond}$ by the following derivations:

$$tp\;\cfrac{id\;\cfrac{}{\Gamma^{u}\{\emptyset\}^{u}\{a,\bar{a}\}}}{\Gamma^{u}\{a\}^{u}\{\bar{a}\}}\qquad\text{and}\qquad tp\;\cfrac{\diamond\;\cfrac{tp\;\cfrac{\Gamma^{u}\{\diamond A\}^{u}\{[A,\Delta]\}}{\Gamma^{u}\{\emptyset\}^{u}\{\diamond A,[A,\Delta]\}}}{\Gamma^{u}\{\emptyset\}^{u}\{\diamond A,[\Delta]\}}}{\Gamma^{u}\{\diamond A\}^{u}\{[\Delta]\}}$$

respectively. The same proof goes for the system with cut. $\square$

Finally we can prove the reduction lemma.

Lemma 3.5 (Reduction Lemma). *If there is a proof π of shape*

$$\mathrm{cut}_{r+1}\;\cfrac{\overset{\pi_1}{\diagdown}\quad\overset{\pi_2}{\diagdown}\;\;\;\;\;\;\;\;\;}{\Gamma\{A\}\qquad\Gamma\{\bar{A}\}}{\Gamma\{\emptyset\}}$$

in iṄK + G *such that* $\mathrm{rk}(\pi_1) \leq r$ *and* $\mathrm{rk}(\pi_2) \leq r$, *then there is proof π' of* $\Gamma\{\emptyset\}$ *in* iṄK + G *such that* $\mathrm{rk}(\pi') \leq r$.

Proof. We proceed by induction on $\mathsf{ht}(\pi_1) + \mathsf{ht}(\pi_2)$, making a case analysis on the bottommost rules in π_1 and π_2. The cases are almost identical to [3]; we only show the ones that are new or different. Details can be found in [16]. As an example of commutative case, we consider when the bottommost rule r of π_1 (or π_2) is $\mathsf{g}_{k,0,m,0}$. Then we have

$$
\mathsf{g}_{k,0,m,0} \dfrac{\dfrac{\pi_1'}{\sigma_{w\to u}\Gamma\{\Gamma_{k-1}\{[^u\Delta]\}, \Gamma_{m-1}\{[^w\Sigma]\}\}\{A\}}}{\Gamma\{\Gamma_{k-1}\{[^u\Delta]\}, \Gamma_{m-1}\{[^w\Sigma]\}\}\{A\}} \qquad \dfrac{\pi_2}{\Gamma\{\Gamma_{k-1}\{[^u\Delta]\}, \Gamma_{m-1}\{[^w\Sigma]\}\}\{\bar{A}\}}
$$
$$
\mathsf{cut} \dfrac{}{\Gamma\{\Gamma_{k-1}\{[^u\Delta]\}, \Gamma_{m-1}\{[^w\Sigma]\}\}\{\emptyset\}}
$$

which can be replaced by

$$
\mathsf{cut} \dfrac{\dfrac{\pi_1'}{\sigma_{w\to u}\Gamma\{\Gamma_{k-1}\{[^u\Delta]\}, \Gamma_{m-1}\{[^w\Sigma]\}\}\{A\}} \qquad \mathsf{isub}\dfrac{\dfrac{\pi_2}{\Gamma\{\Gamma_{k-1}\{[^u\Delta]\}, \Gamma_{m-1}\{[^w\Sigma]\}\}\{\bar{A}\}}}{\sigma_{w\to u}\Gamma\{\Gamma_{k-1}\{[^u\Delta]\}, \Gamma_{m-1}\{[^w\Sigma]\}\}\{\bar{A}\}}}{\mathsf{g}_{k,0,m,0}\dfrac{\sigma_{w\to u}\Gamma\{\Gamma_{k-1}\{[^u\Delta]\}, \Gamma_{m-1}\{[^w\Sigma]\}\}\{\emptyset\}}{\Gamma\{\Gamma_{k-1}\{[^u\Delta]\}, \Gamma_{m-1}\{[^w\Sigma]\}\}\{\emptyset\}}}
$$

where $\Gamma_{k-1}\{\ \}$ and $\Gamma_{m-1}\{\ \}$ correspond to contexts which are of the form $[^{u_1}\Delta_1, \ldots [^{u_{k-1}}\Delta_{k-1}, \{\ \}]]$ and $[^{w_1}\Sigma_1, \ldots [^{w_m}\Sigma_m, \{\ \}]]$ respectively, and we can proceed by induction hypothesis.

The most interesting key case is when the cut-formula $A = \Diamond B$, that is, when when the bottommost rule r of π_1 is $\Diamond$:

$$
\mathsf{cut}_{r+1}\dfrac{\Diamond\dfrac{\dfrac{\pi_1'}{\Gamma\ {}^w\{\Diamond B\}\ {}^w\{[^u B, \Delta]\}}}{\Gamma\ {}^w\{\Diamond B\}\ {}^w\{[^u \Delta]\}} \qquad \Box\dfrac{\dfrac{\pi_2'}{\Gamma\ {}^w\{[^v \bar{B}]\}\ {}^w\{[^u \Delta]\}}}{\Gamma\ {}^w\{\Box\bar{B}\}\ {}^w\{[^u \Delta]\}}}{\Gamma\ {}^w\{\emptyset\}\ {}^w\{[^u \Delta]\}}
$$

which can be reduced to

$$
\mathsf{cut}_r\dfrac{\mathsf{cut}_{r+1}\dfrac{\dfrac{\pi_1'}{\Gamma\ {}^w\{\Diamond B\}\ {}^w\{[^u B, \Delta]\}} \quad \Box\dfrac{\mathsf{w}\dfrac{\dfrac{\pi_2'}{\Gamma\ {}^w\{[^v \bar{B}]\}\ {}^w\{[^u \Delta]\}}}{\Gamma\ {}^w\{[^v \bar{B}]\}\ {}^w\{[^u B, \Delta]\}}}{\Gamma\ {}^w\{\Box\bar{B}\}\ {}^w\{[^u B, \Delta]\}}}{\Gamma\ {}^w\{\emptyset\}\ {}^w\{[^u B, \Delta]\}} \qquad \mathsf{bc}\dfrac{\mathsf{tp}\dfrac{\mathsf{isub}\dfrac{\dfrac{\pi_2'}{\Gamma\ {}^w\{[^v \bar{B}]\}\ {}^w\{[^u \Delta]\}}}{\Gamma\ {}^w\{[^u \bar{B}]\}\ {}^w\{[^u \Delta]\}}}{\Gamma\ {}^w\{[^u\ ]\}\ {}^w\{[^u \bar{B}, \Delta]\}}}{\Gamma\ {}^w\{\emptyset\}\ {}^w\{[^u \bar{B}, \Delta]\}}}{\Gamma\ {}^w\{\emptyset\}\ {}^w\{[^u \Delta]\}}
$$

where on the left branch we use height-preserving admissibility of weakening and proceed by induction hypothesis, and on the right branch we use admissibility of the isub- and tp-rules (Lemmas 3.2 and 3.3). $\qquad\qquad\square$

Theorem 3.6. *If a sequent* Γ *is derivable in* iÑK $+$ G $+$ cut *then it is also derivable in* iÑK $+$ G.

Proof. The proof goes by induction on the cut rank of π; the induction step uses also an induction on the number of occurrences of cut with the maximal rank and Lemma 3.5 to eliminate each time the topmost occurrence in the proof. □

Theorem 3.7. *If a sequent* Γ *is derivable in* iNK $+$ G $+$ cut *then it is also derivable in* iNK $+$ G.

Proof. Following Theorem 3.6 and Lemma 3.4.   □

4   From Classical to Intuitionistic

Starting from the proof system for classical modal logic discussed in the previous section, we will show now how to obtain an intuitionistic variant. This will be done in a similar way as Gentzen did in his original work for the ordinary sequent calculus [9].

The first step is to enrich the language of formulas with implication and disallow negation on atoms, i.e., we no longer restrict formulas to negative normal form:

$$A ::= a \mid \bot \mid A \wedge A \mid A \vee A \mid A \supset A \mid \Box A \mid \Diamond A \qquad (6)$$

We can define $\neg A = A \supset \bot$ and $\top = \neg\bot$. Intuitionistic modal logic IK is obtained from intuitionistic propositional logic by adding the axioms

$$k_1 : \Box(A \supset B) \supset (\Box A \supset \Box B)$$
$$k_2 : \Box(A \supset B) \supset (\Diamond A \supset \Diamond B)$$
$$k_3 : \Diamond(A \vee B) \supset (\Diamond A \vee \Diamond B)$$
$$k_4 : (\Diamond A \supset \Box B) \supset \Box(A \supset B) \qquad (7)$$
$$k_5 : \Diamond\bot \supset \bot$$

and the rule nec, similarly to Sect. 2. The axioms in (7) are logical consequences of k in the classical case but not in the intuitionistic case.[1]

We will consider the following schema as the intuitionistic equivalent to Scott-Lemmon axioms:

$$g_{k,l,m,n} : (\Diamond^k \Box^l A \supset \Box^m \Diamond^n A) \wedge (\Diamond^m \Box^n A \supset \Box^k \Diamond^l A) \qquad (8)$$

The two conjuncts correspond to the classical $g_{k,l,m,n}$ and $g_{m,n,k,l}$ which are equivalent via De Morgan in classical logic, but not in intuitionistic modal logic.

In the following, we will first present a *two-sided* version of the classical one-sided system iNK that was given in Fig. 1. For this, the first step is to include the distinction between input and output formulas into the data structure.

---

[1] This is the variant of IK first mentioned in [5] and [20] and studied in detail in [25]. There are many more variants of intuitionistic modal logic, e.g. [2,6,19,22]. Another popular variant is *constructive modal logic* (e.g. [17]), which rejects axioms k_3-k_5 in (7) and only allows k_1 and k_2. It has a different cut-elimination proof in nested sequents [1]. For this reason we work in this paper with IK which allows all of k_1-k_5.

To that purpose we use here the notion of *polarity*, as studied by Lamarche in [13]. We assign to every formula in the nested sequent a unique polarity: either *input*, denoted by a •-superscript, or *output*, denoted by a ∘-superscript. A two-sided indexed nested sequent therefore is of the following form, denoted by Γ° if it contains at least one input formula and by $\Lambda^\bullet$ otherwise:

$$\begin{aligned}
\Gamma^\circ &::= \Lambda^\bullet \mid \Gamma^\circ, A^\circ \mid \Gamma^\circ, [^w\Gamma^\circ] \\
\Lambda^\bullet &::= \emptyset \mid \Lambda^\bullet, B^\bullet \mid \Lambda^\bullet, [^u\Lambda^\bullet]
\end{aligned} \tag{9}$$

We are now ready to see the inference rules. The two-sided version of $\mathsf{iNK_2}$ is shown in Fig. 5. As expected, the rules for output formulas are the same as in the one-sided case, and the rules for input formulas show dual behavior.

$$\bot^\bullet \frac{}{\Gamma\{\bot^\bullet\}} \qquad \mathsf{id} \frac{}{\Gamma\{a^\bullet, a^\circ\}} \qquad \supset^\bullet_c \frac{\Gamma\{A^\circ\} \quad \Gamma\{B^\bullet\}}{\Gamma\{A \supset B^\bullet\}} \qquad \supset^\circ \frac{\Gamma\{A^\bullet, B^\circ\}}{\Gamma\{A \supset B^\circ\}}$$

$$\wedge^\bullet \frac{\Gamma\{A^\bullet, B^\bullet\}}{\Gamma\{A \wedge B^\bullet\}} \qquad \wedge^\circ \frac{\Gamma\{A^\circ\} \quad \Gamma\{B^\circ\}}{\Gamma\{A \wedge B^\circ\}} \qquad \vee^\bullet \frac{\Gamma\{A^\bullet\} \quad \Gamma\{B^\bullet\}}{\Gamma\{A \vee B^\bullet\}} \qquad \vee^\circ_c \frac{\Gamma\{A^\circ, B^\circ\}}{\Gamma\{A \vee B^\circ\}}$$

$$\Box^\bullet \frac{\Gamma\{\Box A^\bullet, [^w A^\bullet, \Delta]\}}{\Gamma\{\Box A^\bullet, [^w \Delta]\}} \qquad \Box^\circ \frac{\Gamma\{[^v A^\circ]\}}{\Gamma\{\Box A^\circ\}} \qquad \diamond^\bullet \frac{\Gamma\{[^v A^\bullet]\}}{\Gamma\{\diamond A^\bullet\}} \qquad \diamond^\circ_c \frac{\Gamma\{\diamond A^\circ, [^w A^\circ, \Delta]\}}{\Gamma\{\diamond A^\circ, [^w \Delta]\}}$$

$$\mathsf{tp} \frac{\Gamma^w\{\emptyset\}^w\{A\}}{\Gamma^w\{A\}^w\{\emptyset\}} \qquad \mathsf{bc_1} \frac{\Gamma^w\{[^u \Delta]\}^w\{[^u \emptyset]\}}{\Gamma^w\{[^u \Delta]\}^w\{\emptyset\}} \qquad \mathsf{bc_2} \frac{\Gamma^w\{[^u \Delta^w\{[^u \emptyset]\}]\}}{\Gamma^w\{[^u \Delta^w\{\emptyset\}]\}}$$

Fig. 5. Two-sided classical system $\mathsf{iNK_2}$

Finally, the step from classical to intuitionistic simply consists in restricting the number of output formulas in the sequent to one, but it is crucial to observe that we count the whole sequent, and not every bracket separately [26]. So an intuitionistic indexed nested sequent is of the form:

$$\Gamma^\circ ::= \Lambda^\bullet, A^\circ \mid \Lambda^\bullet, [^v\Gamma^\circ] \tag{10}$$

where $\Lambda^\bullet$ is defined as in (9). Moreover, since we do not have an explicit contraction rule, but have it incorporated into inference rules (e.g., $\Box^\bullet$), the inference rules $\vee^\circ$, $\supset^\bullet$ and $\diamond^\circ$ have to adapted, as shown on Fig. 6, in order to maintain the property that each sequent in a proof contains exactly one output formula. In particular, to ensure that both premises of the $\supset^\bullet$-rule are intuitionistic sequents, the notation $\Gamma^{\downarrow}\{\ \}$ stands for the context obtained from $\Gamma\{\ \}$ by removing the output formula. We define $\mathsf{iNIK} = \mathsf{iNK_2} \setminus \{\supset^\bullet, \vee^\circ_c, \diamond^\circ_c\} \cup \{\supset^\bullet_i, \vee^\circ_1, \vee^\circ_2, \diamond^\circ_i\}$. Observe that the structural rules tp, $\mathsf{bc_1}$, and $\mathsf{bc_2}$ are identical for all three systems (one-sided classical, two-sided classical, and two-sided intuitionistic).

$$\supset_i^\bullet \frac{\Gamma^\downarrow\{A \supset B^\bullet, A^\circ\} \quad \Gamma\{B^\bullet\}}{\Gamma\{A \supset B^\bullet\}} \qquad \vee_1^\circ \frac{\Gamma\{A^\circ\}}{\Gamma\{A \vee B^\circ\}} \qquad \vee_2^\circ \frac{\Gamma\{B^\circ\}}{\Gamma\{A \vee B^\circ\}} \qquad \diamond_i^\circ \frac{\Gamma\{[^w A^\circ, \Delta]\}}{\Gamma\{\diamond A^\circ, [^w \Delta]\}}$$

Fig. 6. Intuitionistic variants of some rules for system iNIK

It is also the case that each system can be extended with the rules presented in Figs. 2 and 3. In the classical case, it will give the system $\mathsf{iNK_2 + G}$ equivalent to $\mathsf{iNK + G}$ and basically identical to Fitting's system [7]. In the intuitionistic case, it gives us a system $\mathsf{iNIK + G}$, and the rest of the paper is dedicated to the study of this system. This modular way of adding structural rules for the Scott-Lemmon axioms to the basic deductive system corresponding to K or IK is similar to the way labelled sequent systems handle the Scott-Lemmon axioms.[2]

Finally, the cut-elimination proof conducted in $\mathsf{iNK + G}$ can be reproduced in a similar fashion in $\mathsf{iNK_2 + G}$ and $\mathsf{iNIK + G}$, the two-sided cut-rule being of the form $\mathsf{cut}_c \dfrac{\Gamma\{A^\circ\} \quad \Gamma\{A^\bullet\}}{\Gamma\{\emptyset\}}$ in the classical case, and $\mathsf{cut}_i \dfrac{\Gamma^\downarrow\{A^\circ\} \quad \Gamma\{A^\bullet\}}{\Gamma\{\emptyset\}}$ in the intuitionistic case, where a unique output needs to be maintained in the left branch.

Theorem 4.1. *If a sequent Γ is derivable in $\mathsf{iNK_2 + G + cut}_c$ (resp. $\mathsf{iNIK + G +}$ cut_i) then it is also derivable in $\mathsf{iNK_2 + G}$ (resp. $\mathsf{iNIK + G}$).*

Proof. The proof works similarly to the one of Theorem 3.7. For the intuitionistic system, the cases are similar to [26], except for the specific indexed ones. Details can be found in [16]. □

The cut-elimination theorem can be used to show completeness: every theorem of $\mathsf{K + G}$ (resp. $\mathsf{IK + G}$) is a theorem of $\mathsf{iNK_2 + G}$ (resp. $\mathsf{iNIK + G}$).

Theorem 4.2. *If a formula A is provable in the Hilbert system $\mathsf{IK + G}$, then the sequent A° is provable in the indexed nested sequent system $\mathsf{iNIK + G}$.*

Proof. The axioms of intuitionistic propositional logic as well as the axioms $\mathsf{k_1}$-$\mathsf{k_5}$ can be derived in iNIK, in the same way as in [26]. The inference rule nec can be simulated by the structural rule nec, which is admissible in $\mathsf{iNIK + G}$ (Lemma 3.2), and *modus ponens* mp can be simulated by the cut-rule, which is also admissible

---

[2] Indeed, like $\mathsf{iNK_2}$ and iNIK, Negri's [18] system for classical logic K can be seen as the classical variant of Simpson's system [25] for intuitionistic logic IK. Then the same structural rules can be added to each system to extend it to geometric axioms, so in particular to Scott-Lemmon axioms.

(Theorem 4.1). Thus, it remains to show that any $g_{k,l,m,n}$ axiom can be derived, using the corresponding $g_{k,l,m,n}$-rule (which is the same as $g_{m,n,k,l}$):

$$
\cfrac{
\cfrac{
\cfrac{
\cfrac{
\cfrac{}{
\begin{array}{l}
[^{u_1} \dots [^{u_k} \Box^l p^\bullet, [^{v_1} \Box^{l-1} p^\bullet, \dots [^{v_{l-1}} \Box p^\bullet, [^{v_l}]] \dots]] \dots],\\
\quad [^{w_1} \dots [^{w_m} [^{x_1} \dots [^{x_{n-1}} [^{x_n} p^\bullet, p^\circ]] \dots]] \dots]
\end{array}
} \text{id}
}{
\begin{array}{l}
[^{u_1} \dots [^{u_k} \Box^l p^\bullet, [^{v_1} \Box^{l-1} p^\bullet, \dots [^{v_{l-1}} \Box p^\bullet, [^{v_l} p^\bullet]] \dots]] \dots],\\
\quad [^{w_1} \dots [^{w_m} [^{x_1} \dots [^{x_{n-1}} [^{x_n} p^\circ]] \dots]] \dots]
\end{array}
} \text{tp} \quad c_l = d_n
}{
\begin{array}{l}
[^{u_1} \dots [^{u_k} \Box^l p^\bullet, [^{v_1} \dots [^{v_l}] \dots]] \dots], [^{w_1} \dots [^{w_m} \Diamond^n p^\circ, [^{x_1} \dots [^{x_n}] \dots]] \dots]
\end{array}
} {\scriptstyle l\cdot\Box^\bullet,\, n\cdot\Diamond^\circ}
}{
[^{u_1} \dots [^{u_k} \Box^l p^\bullet] \dots], [^{w_1} \dots [^{w_m} \Diamond^n p^\circ] \dots]
} {\scriptstyle g_{k,l,m,n}}
}{
\Diamond^k \Box^l p^\bullet, \Box^m \Diamond^n p^\circ
} {\scriptstyle k\cdot\Diamond^\bullet,\, m\cdot\Box^\circ}
}{
\Diamond^k \Box^l p \supset \Box^m \Diamond^n p^\circ
} {\scriptstyle \supset^\circ}
$$

And similarly for the other conjunct. □

The same proof can be done in the classical case, and provides an alternative to the completeness of indexed nested sequents wrt. set prefixed tableaux in [7].

However, there are examples of theorems of iNIK + G that are not theorems of IK + G, that is, the indexed nested sequent system is not sound with respect to the Hilbert axiomatisation using what we gave above as the intuitionistic alternative to Scott-Lemmon axioms. There is already a simple counter-example when one considers G to be composed with only the axiom $g_{1,1,1,1} : \Diamond \Box A \supset \Box \Diamond A$. Then

$$F = (\Diamond(\Box(a \vee b) \wedge \Diamond a) \wedge \Diamond(\Box(a \vee b) \wedge \Diamond b)) \supset \Diamond(\Diamond a \wedge \Diamond b) \tag{11}$$

is derivable in iNIK + $g_{1,1,1,1}$, but is not a theorem of IK + $g_{1,1,1,1}$ (as mentioned in [25]). Thus, the logic given by the Hilbert axiomatisation IK + G and the one given by the indexed nested sequent system iNIK + G actually differ in the intuitionistic case. We will address this issue in more detail in the next section.

5 Semantics of the Scott-Lemmon Axioms

In the classical case, the indexed nested sequent system is not only equivalent to the Hilbert axiomatisation using Scott-Lemmon axioms, it is actually sound and complete wrt. the corresponding Kripke semantics. In this section, we investigate the behavior of the indexed nested sequents system iNIK + G with respect to Kripke semantics. For this, we briefly recall the standard Kripke semantics of classical and intuitionistic modal logics. The classical semantics is standard, but the intuitionistic might be less well-known. We use here the birelational models, as they are discussed in [4,20,25].

A *classical frame* $\langle W, R \rangle$ is a non-empty set W of *worlds* and a binary relation $R \subseteq W \times W$, called the *accessibility relation*. An *intuitionistic frame* $\langle W, R, \leq \rangle$ is additionally equipped with a preorder $\leq$ on W, such that:

(F1) For all $u, v, v' \in W$, if uRv and $v \leq v'$, there exists $u' \in W$ such that $u \leq u'$ and $u'Rv'$.

(F2) For all $u', u, v \in W$, if $u \leq u'$ and uRv, there exists $v' \in W$ such that $u'Rv'$ and $v \leq v'$.

A *classical model* $\mathcal{M} = \langle W, R, V \rangle$ is a classical frame together with a *valuation* function $V \colon W \to 2^A$ mapping each world w to the set of propositional variables which are true in w. In an *intuitionistic model* $\langle W, R, \leq, V \rangle$, the function V must be monotone with respect to $\leq$, i.e. $w \leq v$ implies $V(w) \subseteq V(v)$.

We write $w \Vdash a$ if $a \in V(w)$. From there, the relation $\Vdash$ is extended to all formulas in a parallel way in the classical and intuitionistic case, that is, considering a classical model to be a special case of an intuitionistic model, where $w \leq v$ iff $w = v$, we give below the definition for both at the same time:

$w \Vdash A \wedge B$	iff	$w \Vdash A$ and $w \Vdash B$
$w \Vdash A \vee B$	iff	$w \Vdash A$ or $w \Vdash B$
$w \Vdash A \supset B$	iff	for all w' with $w \leq w'$, if $w' \Vdash A$ then also $w' \Vdash B$
$w \Vdash \Box A$	iff	for all w' and u with $w \leq w'$ and $w'Ru$, we have $u \Vdash A$
$w \Vdash \Diamond A$	iff	there is a $u \in W$ such that wRu and $u \Vdash A$

If $w \Vdash A$ we say that w *forces* A. We write $w \nVdash A$ if w does not force A, i.e. it is not the case that $w \Vdash A$. It follows that $\Vdash$ also satisfies monotonicity, i.e. if $w \leq v$ and $w \Vdash A$ then $v \Vdash A$. (In the classical case we also have $w \Vdash \neg A$ iff $w \nVdash A$ which implies the de Morgan dualities, in particular, $w \Vdash \Box(\neg A)$ iff $w \Vdash \neg(\Diamond A)$.) We say that a formula A *is valid in a model* $\mathcal{M}$, if for all $w \in W$ we have $w \Vdash A$. Finally, we say a formula is *classically (or intuitionistically) valid*, if it is valid in all classical (resp. intuitionistic) models.

The Hilbert systems for K and IK, introduced in Sects. 2 and 4 respectively, are sound and complete with respect to arbitrary classical and intuitionistic models respectively. We are now going to adapt the method of Fitting [7] for proving the soundness of the classical system $\mathsf{iNK}_2 + \mathsf{G}$ to study the soundness of our proposed intuitionistic system $\mathsf{iNIK} + \mathsf{G}$ with respect to a subclass of intuitionistic models. The first step is to put intuitionistic indexed nested sequent in correspondence with intuitionistic models in order to define the *validity of a sequent* in a model.

Definition 5.1. Let Σ be an indexed nested sequent. We write I_Σ to denote the set of indexes occurring in Σ, and we write R_Σ for the accessibility relation induced by Σ, that is, the binary relation $R_\Sigma \subseteq I_\Sigma \times I_\Sigma$ defined as: $wR_\Sigma v$ iff $\Sigma = \Gamma^w\{[^v\Delta]\}$ for some $\Gamma\{\ \}$ and Δ, i.e. v is the index of a child of w.

Example 5.2. If we consider the sequent Σ obtained in the Example 2.1, we have that $I_\Sigma = \{0, 1, 2, 3, 4, 5\}$ with 0 being the index of the root, so $R_\Sigma = \{(0,1), (0,2), (0,3), (1,2), (2,4), (2,5), (3,1)\}$.

Definition 5.3. Let Σ be an indexed nested sequent and let $\mathcal{M} = \langle W, R, \leq, V \rangle$ be an intuitionistic Kripke model. A *homomorphism* $h \colon \Sigma \to \mathcal{M}$ is a mapping $h \colon I_\Sigma \to W$, such that $wR_\Sigma v$ implies $h(w)Rh(v)$ for all $w, v \in I_\Sigma$.

A preorder relation between homomorphisms can be obtained from the preorder in an intuitionistic model: For $h, h' \colon \Sigma \to \mathcal{M}$ two homomorphisms, we write $h \leq h'$ if $h(w) \leq h'(w)$ in $\mathcal{M}$ for all $w \in I_\Sigma$. The notion of validity can then be defined by induction on the subsequents of a given sequent.

Definition 5.4. Let Σ and Δ be indexed nested sequents, and $w \in I_\Sigma$. We say that $\langle \Delta, w \rangle$ is an *exhaustive subsequent* of Σ if either $\Delta = \Sigma$ and $w = 0$, or $\Sigma = \Gamma\{[^w \Delta]\}$ for some context $\Gamma\{\ \}$.

Note that for a given index v of Σ, there might be more than one Δ such that $\langle \Delta, v \rangle$ is an exhaustive subsequent of Σ, simply because v occurs more than once in Σ. For this reason we will write $\dot{v}$ to denote a particular occurrence of v in Σ and $\Sigma|_{\dot{v}}$ for the subsequent of Σ rooted at the node $\dot{v}$. $\langle \Sigma|_{\dot{v}}, v \rangle$ stands then for a uniquely defined exhaustive subsequent of Σ.

Definition 5.5. Let $h \colon \Sigma \to \mathcal{M}$ be a homomorphism from a sequent Σ to a model $\mathcal{M}$. Let $w \in I_\Sigma$ and let $\langle \Delta, w \rangle$ be an exhaustive subsequent of Σ. From (9) and (10), Δ has one of the following forms:

- $\Delta = B_1^\bullet, \ldots, B_l^\bullet, [^{v_1} \Lambda_1^\bullet], \ldots, [^{v_n} \Lambda_n^\bullet]$. Then we define $\langle h, w \rangle \Vdash_i \Delta$ if $h(w) \nVdash B_i$ for some $i \leq l$ or $\langle h, v_j \rangle \Vdash_i \Lambda_j^\bullet$ for some $j \leq n$.
- $\Delta = B_1^\bullet, \ldots, B_l^\bullet, [^{v_1} \Lambda_1^\bullet], \ldots, [^{v_n} \Lambda_n^\bullet], A^\circ$. Then we define $\langle h, w \rangle \Vdash_i \Delta$ if either $h(w) \nVdash B_i$ for some $i \leq l$ or $\langle h, v_j \rangle \Vdash_i \Lambda_j^\bullet$ for some $j \leq n$ or $h(w) \Vdash A$.
- $\Delta = B_1^\bullet, \ldots, B_l^\bullet, [^{v_1} \Lambda_1^\bullet], \ldots, [^{v_n} \Lambda_n^\bullet], [^u \Pi^\circ]$. Then we define $\langle h, w \rangle \Vdash_i \Delta$ if either $h(w) \nVdash B_i$ for some $i \leq l$ or $\langle h, v_j \rangle \Vdash_i \Lambda_j^\bullet$ for some $j \leq n$ or for all homomorphisms $h' \geq h$, we have that $\langle h', u \rangle \Vdash_i \Pi^\circ$.

If, for all $h' \geq h$, $\langle h', w \rangle \Vdash_i \Delta$, we say that $\langle \Delta, w \rangle$ *is intuitionistically valid in $\mathcal{M}$ under h*. Then, a sequent Σ is *valid* in a model $\mathcal{M}$, if $\langle \Sigma, 0 \rangle$ is valid in $\mathcal{M}$ under every $h \colon \Sigma \to \mathcal{M}$.

Informally, an indexed nested sequent is valid if it contains anywhere in the sequent tree a valid output formula or an invalid input formula. More formally:

Lemma 5.6. *Let Σ be an indexed nested sequent. Let $\langle \Delta, v \rangle$ be a exhaustive subsequent of Σ. Suppose $\Delta = \Gamma^w\{A\}$ for some context $\Gamma^w\{\ \}$ and some formula A. Let $\mathcal{M}$ be a Kripke model and $h \colon \Sigma \to \mathcal{M}$ a homomorphism.*

- *If $A = A^\circ$ and $h(w) \Vdash A$, then $\langle h, v \rangle \Vdash_i \Delta$.*
- *If $A = A^\bullet$ and $h(w) \nVdash A$, then $\langle h, v \rangle \Vdash_i \Delta$.*

Proof. By induction on the height of the tree rooted at the considered occurrence of v. The base case occurs when A° (or $A^\bullet$) is at the root of that tree. □

We now make explicit the class of model that we are going to consider in order to interpret system iNIK + G. We adapt the notion of graph-consistency introduced by Simpson [25] to the indexed nested sequents framework.

Definition 5.7. A intuitionistic model $\mathcal{M}$ is called *graph-consistent* if for any indexed nested sequent Γ, given any homomorphism $h \colon \Gamma \to \mathcal{M}$, any $w \in I_\Gamma$, and any $w' \geq h(w)$, there exists $h' \geq h$ such that $h'(w) = w'$.[3]

---

[3] One might consider this definition unsatisfactory as it is not a pure frame condition, but we have to leave a detailed study of this issue to future research.

Definition 5.8. Let $\mathcal{M} = \langle W, R, \leq, V \rangle$ be a be an intuitionistic model and let $\langle k, l, m, n \rangle \in \mathbb{N}^4$. We say that $\mathcal{M}$ is a $\mathsf{g}(k, l, m, n)$-*model* if for all $w, u, v \in W$ with $wR^k u$ and $wR^m v$ there is a $z \in W$ such that $uR^l z$ and $vR^n z$.[4] For a set G of $\mathbb{N}^4$-tuples, we say that $\mathcal{M}$ is a G-*model*, if for all $\langle k, l, m, n \rangle \in$ G we have that $\mathcal{M}$ is a $\mathsf{g}(k, l, m, n)$-model.

We finally prove that any theorem of iNIK + G is valid in every graph-consistent G-model by showing that each rule of iNIK + G is sound when interpreted in these models.

Lemma 5.9. *Let* $G \subseteq \mathbb{N}^4$, *and let* $\mathsf{r} \dfrac{\Sigma_1 \quad \cdots \quad \Sigma_n}{\Sigma}$ *be an instance of an inference rule in* iNIK + G *for* $n = 0, 1, 2$. *If all of* $\Sigma_1, \ldots, \Sigma_n$ *are valid in every graph-consistent* G-*model, then so is* Σ.

Proof. First, assume that r is $\mathsf{g}_{k,l,m,n} \dfrac{\Phi}{\Psi}$, for some $\langle k, l, m, n \rangle \in$ G such that $k, l, m, n > 0$ (similar proof when one parameter is 0). By way of contradiction, suppose that Φ is valid in every graph-consistent G-model and that there is a G-model $\mathcal{M} = \langle W, R, \leq, V \rangle$, a homomorphism $h \colon \Psi \to \mathcal{M}$ such that $\langle \Psi, 0 \rangle$ is not valid in $\mathcal{M}$ under h. Recall that Ψ is of form

$$\Psi = \Gamma^{u_0}\{[^{u_1}\Delta_1, \ldots [^{u_k}\Delta_k] \ldots], [^{w_1}\Sigma_1, \ldots [^{w_m}\Sigma_m] \ldots]\}$$

Therefore, there exist $\mathsf{u}_0, \mathsf{u}_k, \mathsf{w}_m$ in W such that $\mathsf{u}_0 = h(u_0)$, $\mathsf{u}_k = h(u_k)$, $\mathsf{w}_m = h(w_m)$, and $\mathsf{u}_0 R^k \mathsf{u}_k$, and $\mathsf{u}_0 R^m \mathsf{w}_m$ (Definitions 5.1 and 5.3). Hence, as $\mathcal{M}$ is in particular a $\mathsf{g}(k, l, m, n)$-model, there exists $\mathsf{y} \in W$ with $\mathsf{u}_k R^l \mathsf{y}$ and $\mathsf{w}_m R^n \mathsf{y}$ (Definition 5.8). Namely, there are worlds $\mathsf{v}_1, \ldots, \mathsf{v}_l, \mathsf{x}_1, \ldots, \mathsf{x}_n$ in W such that $\mathsf{u}_k R \mathsf{v}_1 \ldots \mathsf{v}_{l-1} R \mathsf{v}_l$, $\mathsf{w}_m R \mathsf{x}_1 \ldots \mathsf{x}_{n-1} R \mathsf{x}_n$, and $\mathsf{v}_l = \mathsf{y} = \mathsf{x}_n$. By noting that

$$\Phi = \Gamma^{u_0}\{[^{u_1}\Delta_1, \ldots [^{u_k}\Delta_k, [^{v_1}\ldots[^{v_l}\ ]\ldots]]\ldots], [^{w_1}\Sigma_1, \ldots [^{w_m}\Sigma_m, [^{x_1}\ldots[^{x_n}\ ]\ldots]]\ldots]\}$$

we can define a homomorphism $h' \colon \Phi \to \mathcal{M}$ with $h'(z) = h(z)$ for all $z \in I_\Psi$, $h'(v_i) = \mathsf{v}_i$ for $1 \leq i \leq l$ and $h'(x_j) = \mathsf{x}_j$ for $1 \leq j \leq n$.

We are now going to show that for every $h \colon \Psi \to \mathcal{M}$, and every occurrence $\dot{z}$ of an index $z \in I_\Psi$, we have $\langle h, z \rangle \Vdash_i \Psi|_{\dot{z}}$ iff $\langle h', z \rangle \Vdash_i \Phi|_{\dot{z}}$. We proceed by induction on the height of the tree rooted at $\dot{z}$.

1. The node of $\dot{z}$ is a leaf node of Ψ, and $z \neq u_k$ and $z \neq w_m$. Then we have $\Psi|_{\dot{z}} = \Phi|_{\dot{z}}$ and the claim holds trivially.
2. The node of $\dot{z}$ is an inner node of Ψ, and $z \neq u_k$ and $z \neq w_m$. By the induction hypothesis, for every $t \in I_\Psi$ with $zR_\Psi t$, every occurrence $\dot{t}$ of t in $\Psi|_{\dot{z}}$, and every $h \colon \Psi \to \mathcal{M}$, $\langle h, t \rangle \Vdash_i \Psi|_{\dot{t}}$ iff $\langle h', t \rangle \Vdash_i \Phi|_{\dot{t}}$. The statement follows then by unravelling the definition of $\Vdash_i$ (Definition 5.5).

---

[4] We define the composition of two relations R, S on a set W as usual: $R \circ S = \{(w, v) \mid \exists u. (wRu \wedge uSv)\}$. R^n stands for R composed n times with itself.

3. $z = u_k$. For any occurrence $\dot{z}$ in the context $\Gamma^{z_0}\{\ \}$, the proof is similar to one of the previous cases. Otherwise, we know that $\Psi|_{\dot{z}} = \Delta_k$ and $\Phi|_{\dot{z}} = \Delta_k, [^{v_1}...[^{v_l}\ ]...]$. Furthermore, for all $i \leq l$ and $h'' \geq h$ we have $\langle h'', v_i \rangle \Vdash_i [^{v_{i+1}}...[^{v_l}\ ]...]$, and therefore $\langle h, z \rangle \Vdash_i \Psi|_{\dot{z}}$ iff $\langle h', z \rangle \Vdash_i \Phi|_{\dot{z}}$.

4. $v = w_m$. This case is similar to the previous one.

Since we assumed that $\langle \Psi, 0 \rangle$ is not valid in $\mathcal{M}$ under h, we can conclude that $\langle \Phi, 0 \rangle$ is not valid in $\mathcal{M}$ under h', contradicting the validity of Φ.

The proof for bc, tp, and the other cases of $g_{k,l,m,n}$ is similar.

For the logical rules, we will only consider in detail the case for $\square^\circ$, the others being similar. Suppose that $\Phi = \Gamma^w\{[^v A^\circ]\}$ is valid in every graph-consistent G-model. For $\Psi = \Gamma^w\{\square A^\circ\}$, suppose that there exists a graph-consistent G-model $\mathcal{M} = \langle W, R, \leq, V \rangle$ and a homomorphism $h \colon \Psi \mapsto \mathcal{M}$ such that $\langle \Psi, 0 \rangle$ is not valid in $\mathcal{M}$ under h. Therefore, there exists $h' \geq h$ such that $\langle h', 0 \rangle \Vdash_i \Psi$, in particular by Lemma 5.6, $h'(w) \nVdash \square A$. So there exists w and v such that wRv, $h'(w) \leq w$ and $v \nVdash A$. As $\mathcal{M}$ is graph-consistent, there exists h'' such that $w = h''(w)$. Thus, we can extend h'' by setting $h''(v) = v$ to obtain a homomorphism $h'' \colon \Phi \mapsto \mathcal{M}$, indeed Φ and Ψ have the same set of indexes related by the same underlying structure, but for the fresh index v that does not appear in Ψ. Finally, as $h''(v) \nVdash A$, we have by Lemma 5.6 that $\langle \Phi, 0 \rangle$ is not valid in $\mathcal{M}$ under h'' which contradicts the assumption of validity of Φ. $\square$

Theorem 5.10. *Let* G *be given. If a sequent* Σ *is provable in* iNIK + G *then it is valid in every graph-consistent intuitionistic* G-*model.*

Proof. By induction on the height of the derivation, using Lemma 5.9. $\square$

The soundness result in [7] can be obtained as a corollary of this theorem, as our proof method extends Fitting's technique to the intuitionistic framework.

Corollary 5.11. *Let* G *be given. If a sequent* Σ *is provable in* iNK$_2$ + G *then it is valid in every classical* G-*model.*

6 Discussion

It has long been known that there is a close correspondence between the logic K + G and the Kripke semantics:

Theorem 6.1 (Lemmon and Scott [14]). *Let* G $\subseteq \mathbb{N}^4$. *A formula is derivable in* K + G, *iff it is valid in all classical* G-*models.*

This means that in the classical case, we have a complete triangle between Kripke models, Hilbert axiomatisation and nested sequents systems via Theorems 4.2, 5.11 and 6.1.

In the intuitionistic case, the correspondence is less clear, and a lot of questions are still open. We do have Theorem 4.2 giving that every theorem of IK + G is a theorem of iNIK + G, and Theorem 5.10 giving that every theorem of iNIK + G is valid in all graph-consistent G-models, but there is no proper equivalent to Theorem 6.1 to "link" the two theorems into an actual soundness and completeness result for iNIK + G. As we have seen in Sect. 4, the first inclusion is strict, since the formula in (11) is provable in iNIK + G, but not in IK + G. However, the strictness of the second inclusion is open. The question is: Is there a certain set $G \subseteq \mathbb{N}^4$, such that there exists a formula that is valid in every directed graph-consistent G-models, but that is not a theorem of iNIK + G?

On the other hand, Theorems 6.2.1 and 8.1.4 of [25] entail a parallel result to Theorem 6.1 for a restricted family of the intuitionistic Scott-Lemmon axioms, those for which $l = 1$ and $n = 0$ (or equivalently $l = 0$ and $n = 1$), that is, of the form: $(\lozenge^k \square A \supset \square^m A) \wedge (\lozenge^k A \supset \square^m \lozenge A)$. Therefore, in this restricted case, the inclusions collapse too. The reason why this result holds seems to be that in a derivation of a theorem of such a logic, the steps referring to non-tree graphs can be eliminated via appealing to the closure of the accessibility relation (see [25]). This is similar to what happens when going from indexed to pure nested sequents calculi, and suggests that a pure nested sequent calculus could be provided for these logics in the intuitionistic case too. Indeed, these axioms are the intuitionistic variants of some of the *path axioms* of [10], for which a pure nested sequent calculus is given; but for the general case, [10] only provides a display calculus.

To conclude, we can say that for intuitionistic modal logics the accurate definition might actually come from structural proof-theoretical studies rather than Hilbert axiomatisations or semantical considerations. For Simpson [25] there are two different (but equivalent) ways to define intuitionistic modal logics, either the natural deduction systems he proposes, or the extension of the standard translation for intuitionistic modal logics into first-order intuitionistic logic. Equivalence between the natural deduction systems and the Hilbert axiomatisations, or direct interpretation of the natural deduction systems in intuitionistic (birelational) structures are just side-results. He therefore sees their failure for the majority of logics not as a problem, but rather as another justification of the validity of the proof-theoretic approach.

References

1. Arisaka, R., Das, A., Straßburger, L.: On nested sequents for constructive modal logic. LMCS **11**(3:7), 1–33 (2015)
2. Bierman, G., de Paiva, V.: On an intuitionistic modal logic. Stud. Log. **65**(3), 383–416 (2000)
3. Brünnler, K.: Deep sequent systems for modal logic. Arch. Math. Log. **48**(6), 551–577 (2009)
4. Fischer Servi, G.: Semantics for a class of intuitionistic modal calculi. In: Dalla Chiara, M.L. (ed.) Italian Studies in the Philosophy of Science. Boston Studies in the Philosophy of Science, vol. 47, pp. 59–72. Springer, Dordrecht (1980). doi:10.1007/978-94-009-8937-5_5
5. Fischer Servi, G.: Axiomatizations for some intuitionistic modal logics. Rend. Sem. Mat. Univers. Politecn. Torino **42**(3) (1984)

6. Fitch, F.B.: Intuitionistic modal logic with quantifiers. Port. Math. **7**(2), 113–118 (1948)
7. Fitting, M.: Cut-free proof systems for Geach logics. IfCoLog J. Log. Their Appl. **2**(2), 17–64 (2015)
8. Galmiche, D., Salhi, Y.: Label-free natural deduction systems for intuitionistic and classical modal logics. J. Appl. Non-Class. Log. **20**(4), 373–421 (2010)
9. Gentzen, G.: Untersuchungen über das logische Schließen. I. Mathematische Zeitschrift **39** (1934)
10. Goré, R., Postniece, L., Tiu, A.: On the correspondence between display postulates and deep inference in nested sequent calculi for tense logics. LMCS **7**(2:8), 1–38 (2011)
11. Goré, R., Ramanayake, R.: Labelled tree sequents, tree hypersequents and nested (deep) sequents. AIML **9**, 279–299 (2012)
12. Kashima, R.: Cut-free sequent calculi for some tense logics. Stud. Log. **53**(1), 119–135 (1994)
13. Lamarche, F.: On the algebra of structural contexts. Math. Struct. Comput. Sci. (2001, accepted)
14. Lemmon, E.J., Scott, D.S.: An Introduction to Modal Logic. Blackwell, Oxford (1977)
15. Marin, S., Straßburger, L.: Label-free modular systems for classical and intuitionistic modal logics. AIML **10**, 387–406 (2014)
16. Marin, S., Straßburger, L.: On the proof theory of indexed nested sequents for classical and intuitionistic modal logics. Research Report RR-9061, Inria Saclay (2017). https://hal.inria.fr/hal-01515797
17. Mendler, M., Scheele, S.: Cut-free Gentzen calculus for multimodal CK. Inf. Comput. **209**(12), 1465–1490 (2011)
18. Negri, S.: Proof analysis in modal logics. J. Phil. Log. **34**, 507–544 (2005)
19. Pfenning, F., Davies, R.: A judgmental reconstruction of modal logic. Math. Struct. Comput. Sci. **11**(4), 511–540 (2001)
20. Plotkin, G., Stirling, C.: A framework for intuitionistic modal logic. In: Theoretical Aspects of Reasoning About Knowledge (1986)
21. Poggiolesi, F.: The method of tree-hypersequents for modal propositional logic. In: Makinson, D., Malinowski, J., Wansing, H. (eds.) Towards Mathematical Philosophy. Trends in Logic, vol. 28. Springer, Dordrecht (2009). doi:10.1007/978-1-4020-9084-4_3
22. Prawitz, D.: Natural Deduction, A Proof-Theoretical Study. Almqvist & Wiksell, Stockholm (1965)
23. Ramanayake, R.: Inducing syntactic cut-elimination for indexed nested sequents. In: Olivetti, N., Tiwari, A. (eds.) IJCAR 2016. LNCS (LNAI), vol. 9706, pp. 416–432. Springer, Cham (2016). doi:10.1007/978-3-319-40229-1_29
24. Russo, A.: Generalising propositional modal logic using labelled deductive systems. In: Baader, F., Schulz, K.U. (eds.) Frontiers of Combining Systems. Applied Logic Series, vol. 3. Springer, Dordrecht (1996). doi:10.1007/978-94-009-0349-4_2
25. Simpson, A.: The proof theory and semantics of intuitionistic modal logic. Ph.D. thesis, University of Edinburgh (1994)
26. Straßburger, L.: Cut elimination in nested sequents for intuitionistic modal logics. In: Pfenning, F. (ed.) FoSSaCS 2013. LNCS, vol. 7794, pp. 209–224. Springer, Heidelberg (2013). doi:10.1007/978-3-642-37075-5_14
27. Viganò, L.: Labelled Non-classical Logic. Kluwer Academic Publisher, Dordrecht (2000)

Interpreting Sequent Calculi as Client-Server Games

Christian G. Fermüller[✉] and Timo Lang[✉]

TU Vienna, Vienna, Austria
{chrisf,timo}@logic.at

Abstract. Motivated by the interpretation of substructural logics as resource-conscious reasoning, we introduce a client-server game characterizing provability in single-conclusion sequent calculi. The set up is modular and allows to capture multiple logics, including intuitionistic and (affine) linear intuitionistic logic. We also provide a straightforward interpretation of subexponentials, and moreover introduce a game where the information provided by the server is organized as a stack, rather than as a multiset or list.

Keywords: Game semantics · Resource interpretation · Linear logic

1 Introduction

Resource consciousness is routinely cited as a motivation for considering substructural logics (see, e.g., [10]). But usually the reference to resources is kept informal, like in Girard's well-known example of being able to buy a pack of Camels and/or a pack of Marlboros [5] with a single dollar, illustrating linear implication as well as the ambiguity of conjunction between the "multiplicative" and "additive" reading. The invitation to distinguish, e.g., between a "causal", action-oriented interpretation of implication and a more traditional understanding of implication as a timeless, abstract relation between propositions is certainly inspiring and motivating. However, the specific shape and properties of proof systems for usual substructural logics owe more to a deep analysis of Gentzen's sequent system than to action-oriented models of handling scarce resources of a specific kind.

Various semantics, in particular so-called game semantics for (fragments of) linear logics [1,3] offer additional leverage points for a logical analysis of resource consciousness. But these semantics hardly support a straightforward reading of sequent derivations as action plans devised by resource conscious agents. Moreover, the inherent level of abstraction often does not match the appeal of (e.g.) Girard's very concrete and simple picture of action-oriented inference.

We introduce a two-player game based on the idea that a proof is an *action-plan*, i.e. a *strategy* for one of the players (the "Client") to reduce particular *structured information* to information provided by the other player (the "Server"). As we will show, the interpretation of game states as single conclusion sequents leads

Funded by FWF projects W1255-N23 and FWF P25417-G15 LOGFRADIG.

R.A. Schmidt and C. Nalon (Eds.): TABLEAUX 2017, LNAI 10501, pp. 98–113, 2017.
DOI: 10.1007/978-3-319-66902-1_6

to variations of the basic game, that match (affine) intuitionistic linear logic, but also other substructural logics. To emphasize the indicated shift of perspective, relative to traditional interpretations of formulas as sentences, propositions, or types, we introduce the notion of an *information package*, which emphasizes the interpretation of formulas as (in general) compound information, that is built up from atomic pieces of information using constructors that indicate possible ways of accessing the information.

Obviously our Client-Server games constitute a variant of *game semantics*; therefore a few words on the relation to other forms of game semantics are appropriate. Already in the late 1950s Lorenzen [9] proposed to *justify* intuitionistic logic in terms of a dialogue game, where a proponent defends a statement against systematic attacks by an opponent. Logical validity is identified with the existence of a winning strategy for the proponent. This setup has later been generalized to other logics; see, e.g., [7,11]. While there are some obvious similarities between Lorenzen-style dialogue games and our Client-Server games there are differences at the structural level. In particular, Lorenzen and his followers argue that the two players should have 'equal rights': both the specific rules for the logical connectives and the so-called frame rules, that regulate the overall progression of a dialogue, should be as symmetric as possible. In contrast, we deliberately break this symmetry and view the Client as the active 'scheduler' of the interaction with a largely passive or at least dis-interested Server. Similar remarks hold for game semantics developed for (fragments of) linear logic in the wake of [1,3,8]. The idea there is to view propositions as games and connectives as operators on games. Again, the symmetry between the two players is important, as witnessed by the prominence of the copy-cat strategy, which has no counterpart in our Client-Server games. Finally, Japaridze's Computability Logic [6] deserves to be mentioned, where formulas are interpreted as computational problems. The underlying model of interactive computation is a game between a machine and the environment. While somewhat related in spirit to our (much simpler and more specific) game model, the corresponding logics and inference mechanisms are again quite different. Probably the most important feature of our approach is that we aim at a *direct interpretation* of sequent rules as rules for systematically reducing information packages to its components.

The paper is structured as follows: in Sect. 2, we introduce our client-server game in its basic form. In Sect. 3, we show that this game captures provability in intuitionistic logic. Section 4 describes a resource-aware version of the game, which is shown to capture affine logic, and, with a small modification, intuitionistic linear logic. In Sect. 5, we make some remarks on the interpretation of (sub)exponentials. The final Sect. 6 discusses a variant of the game where information packages are arranged in a stack.

2   A Client-Server Game for Intuitionistic Logic

In our $\mathbf{C}/\mathbf{S}(\mathbf{I})$-game, a *client* $\mathbf{C}$ maintains that the information packaged as G can be obtained from the information represented by the packages $F_1, \ldots, F_n$, provided by a *server* $\mathbf{S}$, via stepwise reduction of complex information packages (henceforth short *ips*, singular *ip*) into simpler ones. At any state of the game, the *bunch of information provided by* **S** is a (possibly empty) multiset of ips. The ip G which **C** currently claims to be obtainable from that information is called **C**'s *current ip*. The corresponding state is denoted by

$$F_1, \ldots, F_n \rhd G.$$

The game proceeds in rounds that are always initiated by **C** and, in general, solicit some action from **S**. We look at the game from the client's point of view.[1] There are two different types of requests that **C** may submit to **S**: (1) UNPACK an ip provided by the server, and (2) CHECK my (i.e. the clients) current ip. We call the ip chosen by **C** for either the UNPACK- or CHECK-request the *active ip*. Thus in a CHECK-request the active ip is always **C**'s current ip. Both UNPACK- and CHECK-requests depend on the *structure* of the active ip. For now, we will consider the following types of ips:

– *atomic* ips, which admit no further reduction
– among those, a special ip $\bot$, denoting an elementary *inconsistency*
– *complex* ips which are build from simpler ips by means of the constructors $\wedge$, $\vee$, and $\rightarrow$ (called *any of, some of* and *given* respectively).

We use lowercase letters a, b, c for atomic ips and uppercase letters F, G, H, K for ips which may be either complex or atomic. Multisets of ips are denoted by Γ or Δ. The rules for reducing complex ips are given in Table 1. One may easily introduce other constructors for complex ips into the game by specifying their UNPACK- and CHECK-rules, and we will see some examples of that later.

At the beginning of each round of the game **C** is free to choose whether she wants to continue with a request of type UNPACK (if possible) or of type CHECK; moreover in the first case **C** can freely choose any occurrence of a non-atomic ip or an occurrence of $\bot$ in the bunch of information provided by **S**. Formally, each initial state $F_1, \ldots, F_n \rhd G$ induces an extensive two-players win/lose (zero sum) game of perfect information in the usual game theoretic sense.

The corresponding game tree is finitely branching, but may be infinite since **C** may request to unpack the same ip repeatedly. Intuitively, a *strategy for* **C** is a function telling **C** how to move in (some initial part of) the game when it is her turn. We require strategies to be finite objects. A strategy τ for **C** can therefore be identified with a finite subtree of the game tree satisfying

1. the root of τ is the initial state of the relevant instance of the **C/S**(I)-game in question
2. at each state S, if the strategy τ tells **C** to continue with a round of type (UNPACK $F_1 \vee F_2$), (UNPACK $F_1 \rightarrow F_2$) or (CHECK $F_1 \wedge F_2$), then τ branches at S into two successor states according to the possible choices available to **S** as specified by the rules. On the other hand, no branching occurs at states where τ tells **C** to continue according to any other rule, since those rules do not involve a choice of **S**.

---

[1] Since we only care about winning strategies for **C**, the server **S** may be viewed as acting nondeterministically or probabilistically, if preferred.

Table 1. Atoms, constructors and rules for $\mathbf{C}/\mathbf{S}(\mathrm{I})$

a	Atomic ip
	UNPACK: Not possible unless $a = \bot$. In the latter case, the game ends and $\mathbf{C}$ wins
	CHECK: The game ends and $\mathbf{C}$ wins iff a is contained in the bunch of information provided by $\mathbf{S}$
$F_1 \wedge F_2$	Any of F_1, F_2
	UNPACK: $\mathbf{C}$ chooses an ip out of $\{F_1, F_2\}$ which $\mathbf{S}$ then has to add to the bunch of provided information
	CHECK: $\mathbf{S}$ chooses an ip out of $\{F_1, F_2\}$ and sets it as $\mathbf{C}$'s new current ip
$F_1 \vee F_2$	Some of F_1, F_2
	UNPACK: $\mathbf{S}$ chooses an ip out of $\{F_1, F_2\}$ and adds it to the bunch of provided information
	CHECK: $\mathbf{C}$ chooses an ip out of $\{F_1, F_2\}$ and sets it as the new current ip
$(F_1 \to F_2)$	F_2 given F_1
	UNPACK: $\mathbf{S}$ chooses whether to add F_2 to the bunch of provided information, or to force $\mathbf{C}$ to replace its current ip by F_1
	CHECK: F_1 is added to the bunch of provided information and $\mathbf{C}$'s current ip is replaced by F_2

A strategy τ is called a *winning strategy* if additionally all leaves are winning states for $\mathbf{C}$ according to either rule (CHECK a) or (UNPACK $\bot$).

The game rules are *local*: the validity of a move of $\mathbf{C}$ only depends on the presence of a certain ip in the current game state, but not on the complete bunch of provided information. Furthermore, $\mathbf{S}$'s moves are restricted to ips previously chosen by $\mathbf{C}$, and ips different from the active one are never touched at all in a move. It follows that we can regard a strategy τ for $\mathbf{C}$ in a game state $\Gamma \rhd F$ also as a strategy in $\Delta, \Gamma \rhd F$ for any multiset of ips Δ. Indeed, viewed as a subtree of the full game tree for $\Gamma \rhd F$, τ is isomorphic to a subtree τ^Δ of the full game tree for $\Delta, \Gamma \rhd F$ obtained by adding the multiset Δ to all the nodes in τ. By abuse of notation, we will not distinguish between τ and τ^Δ.

The following proposition sums up these observations and some easy consequences for further reference:

Proposition 1. *Let $\Gamma \rhd F$ be a game state and Δ a multiset of ips.*

1. *If τ is a strategy for $\mathbf{C}$ in $\Gamma \rhd F$, then τ is also a strategy for $\mathbf{C}$ in $\Delta, \Gamma \rhd F$.*
2. *Furthermore, if a sequence of moves in the game $\Gamma \rhd F$ according to τ leads to a state $\Gamma' \rhd F'$, then the same sequence of moves leads to the state $\Delta, \Gamma' \rhd F'$ in the game $\Delta, \Gamma \rhd F$.*

3. If τ is winning strategy for C in $\Gamma \triangleright F$, then τ is also a winning strategy for C in $\Delta, \Gamma \triangleright F$.

Proof. (1) and (2) are immediate from the discussion preceeding the proposition. For (3), let τ be a winning strategy for C in $\Gamma \triangleright F$. Then by (2), moving according to τ in $\Delta, \Gamma \triangleright F$ leads to states of the form $\Delta, \Gamma' \triangleright F'$ where $\Gamma' \triangleright F'$ is a winning state. But if $\Gamma' \triangleright F'$ is a winning state for C, then so is $\Delta, \Gamma' \triangleright F'$, since the winning conditions for C are local. Hence τ is also a winning strategy for C in $\Delta, \Gamma \triangleright F$. □

3   The Adequateness of C/S(I) for Intuitionistic Logic

Let us now identify atomic ips with propositional variables and complex ips with their corresponding propositional formulas. It is well-known that we may read winning strategies for C as proofs in a sequent calculus, where the turnstile $\Rightarrow$ stands for $\triangleright$ and the initial sequents correspond to winning states. In our case, the initial sequents are thus

$$\overline{\Gamma, a \Rightarrow a} \qquad \text{and} \qquad \overline{\Gamma, \perp \Rightarrow F}$$

corresponding to the states $\Gamma, a \triangleright a$ (where C wins by sending a (CHECK a)-request) and $\Gamma, \perp \triangleright F$ (where C wins by sending an (UNPACK $\perp$)-request). The UNPACK-rule for $\vee$ translates to the sequent rule

$$\frac{\Gamma, F_1 \vee F_2, F_1 \Rightarrow H \qquad \Gamma, F_1 \vee F_2, F_2 \Rightarrow H}{\Gamma, F_1 \vee F_2 \Rightarrow H}$$

where the two premises correspond to the two possible choices of S. The CHECK-rule for $\vee$ translates to the pair of rules

$$\frac{\Gamma \Rightarrow F_1}{\Gamma \Rightarrow F_1 \vee F_2} \qquad \text{and} \qquad \frac{\Gamma \Rightarrow F_2}{\Gamma \Rightarrow F_1 \vee F_2}$$

corresponding to the two possible choices of C. Similarly, one writes down the sequent rules for the remaining connectives $\wedge, \rightarrow$. Using this translation, the rules and initial sequents exactly match the sequent calculus **LIk** for intuitionistic logic (cf. [12]). We obtain:

Theorem 2. *The following are equivalent:*

1. C *has a winning strategy in the $C/S(I)$-game $(\Gamma \triangleright H)$*
2. $(\mathbf{LIk} \vdash \Gamma \Rightarrow H)$
3. $(\bigwedge \Gamma \Rightarrow H)$ *is intuitionistically valid.*[2]

---

[2] $\bigwedge \Gamma$ denotes the conjunction of all formulas in Γ.

Proof. The equivalence of (2) and (3) are the soundness and completeness theorem for **LIk**. For the equivalence of (1) and (2), recall that we can view a winning strategy in a **C/S**(I)-game $\Gamma \rhd F$ as subtrees of the full game tree, where a branching occurs iff **S** choses the next move. Using the translation given above, such a subtree can be read as a proof in **LIk** of the sequent $\Gamma \Rightarrow F$, and conversely, every **LIk**-proof with end-sequent $\Gamma \Rightarrow F$ can be read as a winning strategy in the **C/S**(I)-game $\Gamma \rhd F$. $\qquad\qquad\square$

Example: Consider the **LIk**-proof

$$\frac{\dfrac{F,\Gamma \Rightarrow F \qquad H,F,\Gamma \Rightarrow H}{F,\Gamma \Rightarrow H}\ (F \to H) \qquad \dfrac{G,\Gamma \Rightarrow G \qquad H,G,\Gamma \Rightarrow H}{G,\Gamma \Rightarrow H}\ (G \to H)}{\underbrace{F \vee G, F \to H, G \to H \Rightarrow H}_{=:\Gamma}}\ (F \vee G)$$

where we have labelled the inference steps with the principal formula of the applied **LIk**-rule. The corresponding winning strategy for the game state $F \vee G, F \to H, G \to H \rhd H$ can be described as follows: First, **C** sends an (UNPACK $F \vee G$)-request, forcing **S** to add either F or G to the bunch of provided information. Then **C** sends either an (UNPACK $F \to H$) or an (UNPACK $G \to H$)-request, depending on which ip out of F, G has chosen by **S** in the previous move. **S** can now either add H to the bunch of provided information; in this case **C** wins with a subsequent CHECK-request, since H is her current ip. Otherwise, **S** can replace **C**'s current ip by F or G respectively, but this is exactly the ip that **S** has added to the bunch of provided information in a previous move. Hence, **C** wins also in this situation by sending a CHECK-request.

LIk arises from the traditional sequent calculus **LI** for intuitionistic logic by eliminating contraction by building into the logical rules and eliminating weakening by generalizing the initial sequents (axioms) correspondingly.[3]

We get a game directly matching the rules for **LI** by making the following modifications to the **C/S**(I)-game: First, we change the UNPACK-rules such that the active ip is *removed* from the bunch of provided information after use; second, we add two types of request called DISMISS and COPY, which allow **C** to either remove or duplicate ips from the bunch of provided information: and finally we allow only

$$a \rhd a \qquad \text{and} \qquad \bot \rhd F$$

as winning states for **C**. Let us call the modified game **C/S**(I)*.

Via Theorem 2, results from the structural proof theory of **LIk** or **LI** turn into statements about winning strategies in **C/S**(I) or **C/S**(I)*. As a simple example (which works for either variant of the calculus/game), the *soundness* of the rule

$$\frac{\Gamma \Rightarrow F \qquad \Gamma \Rightarrow G}{\Gamma \Rightarrow F \wedge G}\ (\wedge \mathrm{R})$$

---

[3] We assume that **LI** is already formulated using multisets - otherwise, this would be another difference between the calculi.

says that if $\mathbf{C}$ has a winning strategy τ for $\Gamma \rhd F$ and σ for $\Gamma \rhd G$, then she has a winning strategy in $\Gamma \rhd F \wedge G$. The winning strategy, of course, is this: In her first move, $\mathbf{C}$ sends a (CHECK $F \wedge G$) request. If now $\mathbf{S}$ chooses F, the game is in a state $\Gamma \rhd F$ where she can move according to τ to win; otherwise, if $\mathbf{S}$ picks G, she moves according to σ.

More interestingly, the *invertibility* of the ($\wedge$R) rule – the fact that the validity of its conclusion implies the validity of its premises – says that if $\mathbf{C}$ has a winning strategy in $\Gamma \rhd F \wedge G$, then she has such a winning strategy where her first move is (CHECK $F \wedge G$).

The correspondence of Theorem 2 goes both ways; for example, Proposition 1 is nothing but a game theoretic proof of the admissibility of the weakening rule in **LIk**. As yet another example, The cut-elimination theorem for the calculus **LIk** tells us that if $\mathbf{C}$ has winning strategies in $\Gamma \rhd G$ and $G, \Delta \rhd H$ then she has also a winning strategy in $\Gamma, \Delta \rhd H$. Below, we give a proof of cut-admissibility for the $\rightarrow$-free fragment of **LI** by using the game semantics of $\mathbf{C}/\mathbf{S}(I)^*$. In this fragment, we can give a particularly simple and intuitive description of the winning strategy obtained from combining the winning strategies for $\Gamma \rhd G$ and $G, \Delta \rhd H$.

Proposition 3. *Assume that $\rightarrow$ does not appear in Γ, Δ, G, H. If $\mathbf{C}$ has winning strategies in the $\mathbf{C}/\mathbf{S}(I)^*$-games $\Gamma \rhd G$ and $G, \Delta \rhd H$ then she also has a winning strategy in $\Gamma, \Delta \rhd H$.*

Proof. Let τ be a winning strategy for $\Gamma \rhd G$ and σ a winning strategy for $G, \Delta \rhd H$. We prove by induction on the structure of G that $\mathbf{C}$ wins in $\Gamma, \Delta \rhd H$.

1. $G \equiv a$ for atomic a: Since the game ends when atomic ips are checked, all but the last move in τ must be UNPACK-requests. Since τ is winning, a play on $\Gamma \rhd a$ according to τ always ends in a state of the form $\perp \rhd a$ or $a \rhd a$. $\mathbf{C}$ can thus move according to τ in the game $\Gamma, \Delta \rhd H$ to arrive at a state $\perp, \Delta \rhd H$ or $a, \Delta \rhd H$. In the first case she wins by sending DISMISS-requests repeatedly until she is in the winning state $\perp \rhd H$. In the second case, she can move according to σ to win.

2. $G \equiv F_1 \wedge F_2$: $\mathbf{C}$ starts moving according to τ in the game $\Gamma, \Delta \rhd H$ until a (CHECK $F_1 \wedge F_2$)-request appears (if that does not happen, the game must arrive eventually at a state $\Gamma', \perp, \Delta \rhd H$ where $\mathbf{C}$ can easily win). The game is now in a state $\Gamma', \Delta \rhd H$. Note that $\mathbf{C}$ must have winning strategies in $\Gamma' \rhd F_1$ and $\Gamma' \rhd F_2$, since by moving according to τ in the game $\Gamma \rhd F_1 \wedge F_2$ she ends up in a state $\Gamma' \rhd F_1 \wedge F_2$ and now, since the next step in τ is (CHECK $F_1 \wedge F_2$), $\mathbf{C}$ must be prepared for any choice of F_1, F_2 by $\mathbf{S}$.
   Back to the game state $\Gamma', \Delta \rhd H$. Here, $\mathbf{C}$ now switches to the strategy σ and moves until an (UNPACK $F_1 \wedge F_2$)-request appears (again, if this does not happen, the game must arrive at a state where $\mathbf{C}$ obviously wins). The game is then in a state $\Gamma', \Delta' \rhd H'$. Without loss of generality, let us assume that σ tells $\mathbf{C}$ to pick F_1 in the rule for $\wedge$. Then $\mathbf{C}$ has a winning strategy

$\Delta', F_1 \triangleright H'$, because this state arises by starting in $F_1 \wedge F_2, \Delta \triangleright H$ and moving according to the winning strategy σ.

Applying the induction hypothesis to the states $\Gamma' \triangleright F_1$ and $\Delta', F_1 \triangleright H'$ (and their respective winning strategies), we thus know that $\mathbf{C}$ has a winning strategy in $\Gamma', \Delta' \triangleright H'$, which is exactly the current game state.

3. $G = F_1 \vee F_2$: similar to the previous case.   □

Remark 4. *Note that the number of moves in the winning strategy constructed in the above proof is polynomially bounded in the number of moves in the winning strategies for $\Gamma \triangleright G$ and $G, \Delta \triangleright H$. This cannot be the case if we include $\rightarrow$, since it is known that cut reduction in the full fragment of intuitionistic logic increases proof size exponentially.*

4 Resource Consciousness

Probably the most important step in turning the $\mathbf{C}/\mathbf{S}(I)$-game into a 'resource conscious' one, regards rules that entail a choice by $\mathbf{S}$ and thus require $\mathbf{C}$ to be prepared to act in more than just one possible successor state to the current state. The $\mathbf{C}/\mathbf{S}(I)$-rules allow $\mathbf{C}$ to use all the information provided by $\mathbf{S}$ in each of the possible successor states. If, instead, we require $\mathbf{C}$ to declare which ips she intends to use for which of those options – taking care that she is using each occurrence of an ip exactly once – then we arrive at rules that match multiplicative instead of additive connectives.

Following the tradition of linear logic, we do not discard the previously defined rules, but rather extend the game by new ip constructors and their corresponding resource concious rules. We also introduce a unary 'safety' constructor ! (called *exponential* in the literature on linear logic). Ips prefixed by ! are meant to be exempt from resource consciousness and thus behave like ips in the $\mathbf{C}/\mathbf{S}(I)$-game. Ips not prefixed by ! are called *unsecured*. Table 2 lists all new constructors and their corresponding rules.[4] Let us denote by $\mathbf{C}/\mathbf{S}(IAL)$ the following modification of game $\mathbf{C}/\mathbf{S}(I)$:

1. Constructors and rules for $\otimes$, $\multimap$ and ! are added as in Table 2
2. The UNPACK-rules for $\wedge$, $\vee$ and $\rightarrow$ are changed so that the active ip is *removed* at the end of the request.

We claim that the logic captured by $\mathbf{C}/\mathbf{S}(IAL)$ is *intuitionistic affine logic* **IAL**, i.e. intuitionistic linear logic with weakening [5]. A standard sequent calculus for **IAL** is presented in Table 3. We need the following preliminary result analogous to Proposition 1:

Proposition 5. *If C has a winning strategy in the $\mathbf{C}/\mathbf{S}(IAL)$-game $\Gamma \triangleright F$ and Δ is any multiset of ips, then C also has a winning strategy in $\Delta, \Gamma \triangleright F$.*

---

[4] In these rules, the operations of *replacing* and *removing* an ip in a multiset are meant to affect only the active *instance* of the ip, rather than all instances of the ip in the multiset.

Table 2. Resource conscious rules in **C**/**S**(IAL)

$\otimes(F_1,\ldots,F_n)$	Each of $F_1,\ldots,F_n$
	UNPACK: $\otimes(F_1,\ldots,F_n)$ is replaced by $F_1,\ldots,F_n$
	CHECK: **C** marks every unsecured ip in the bunch of provided information with one of $F_1,\ldots F_n$. Next, **S** chooses one F_i out of $F_1,\ldots F_n$. Then **C**'s current ip is changed to F_i and all unsecured ips not marked with F_i are removed
$(F_1 \multimap F_2)$	F_2 from F_1
	UNPACK: **C** marks every unsecured ip in the bunch of provided information (except the instance of $(F_1 \multimap F_2)$) with either F_1 or F_2. **S** then chooses between the premise F_1 and the conclusion F_2. If **S**'s choice was F_1, **C**'s current ip is changed to F_1 and all ips marked with F_2 are removed. If **S**'s choice was F_2, F_2 is added to the bunch of provided ips and all ips marked with F_1 are removed. In any case, the instance of $F_1 \multimap F_2$ is removed as well
	CHECK: F_1 is added to the bunch of provided information and **C**'s current ip is replaced by F_2
$!F$	Safe F
	UNPACK: A copy of F is added to the bunch of provided information, and then an UNPACK-request is performed on this copy
	CHECK: All unsecured ips are removed, and **C**'s current ip is changed to F

Proof. By induction on the number of steps in a winning strategy for $\Gamma \rhd F$. We only consider the case that $F \equiv !G$ and the first step in the winning strategy is to send a (CHECK $!G$)-request. Let us write the state as $!\Gamma_1, \Gamma_2 \rhd !G$, where we assume that all ips in Γ_2 are unsecured ($!\Gamma$ denotes $\{!F \mid F \in \Gamma\}$). The request results in the state $!\Gamma_1 \rhd G$, for which **C** therefore has a winning strategy. It follows that **C** wins in $\Delta, !\Gamma_1, \Gamma_2 \rhd !G$: She starts by sending a (CHECK $!G$)-request, resulting in the state $\Delta_1, !\Gamma_1 \rhd G$, where Δ_1 denotes the set of all safe formulas in Δ. Since **C** has a winning strategy for $!\Gamma_1 \rhd G$, the induction hypothesis implies that she also wins in $\Delta_1, !\Gamma_1 \rhd G$. □

Theorem 6. *The following are equivalent:*

*1. **C** has a winning strategy in the **C**/**S***(IAL)-game $\Gamma \rhd H$
*2. **IAL** $\vdash \Gamma \Rightarrow H$*

Proof (Sketch). Again, we use the correspondence between winning strategies and proofs described in Sect. 3. However, the game rules do not directly match the rules of **IAL** in all cases, thus we have to provide some further arguments.

Table 3. The sequent calculus **IAL**

$$\frac{}{a \Rightarrow a}\ (\text{id}) \qquad \frac{}{\bot \Rightarrow A}\ (\bot) \qquad \frac{\Gamma \Rightarrow A}{B, \Gamma \Rightarrow A}\ (\text{W})$$

$$\frac{\Gamma, A_i \Rightarrow C}{\Gamma, A_1 \wedge A_2 \Rightarrow C}\ (\wedge \text{L}i)\ i = 1, 2 \qquad \frac{\Gamma \Rightarrow A \quad \Gamma \Rightarrow B}{\Gamma \Rightarrow A \wedge B}\ (\wedge \text{R})$$

$$\frac{\Gamma, A \Rightarrow C \quad \Gamma, B \Rightarrow C}{\Gamma, A \vee B \Rightarrow C}\ (\vee \text{L}) \qquad \frac{\Gamma \Rightarrow A_i}{\Gamma \Rightarrow A_1 \vee A_2}\ (\vee \text{R}i)\ i = 1, 2$$

$$\frac{\Gamma, A, B \Rightarrow C}{\Gamma, A \otimes B \Rightarrow C}\ (\otimes \text{L}) \qquad \frac{\Gamma \Rightarrow A \quad \Delta \Rightarrow B}{\Gamma, \Delta \Rightarrow A \otimes B}\ (\otimes \text{R})$$

$$\frac{\Gamma \Rightarrow A \quad \Delta, B \Rightarrow C}{\Gamma, \Delta, A \multimap B \Rightarrow C}\ (\multimap \text{L}) \qquad \frac{\Gamma, A \Rightarrow B}{\Gamma \Rightarrow A \multimap B}\ (\multimap \text{R})$$

$$\frac{\Gamma, !A, !A \Rightarrow B}{\Gamma, !A \Rightarrow B}\ (!\text{C}) \qquad \frac{\Gamma, A \Rightarrow B}{\Gamma, !A \Rightarrow B}\ (!\text{dR}) \qquad \frac{!\Gamma \Rightarrow A}{!\Gamma \Rightarrow !A}\ (!\text{R})$$

First, there is no game rule corresponding to weakening (W). This is not a problem, because weakening is admissible in the game theoretic version of the rules by Proposition 5.[5]

Second, there is no game rule corresponding to (!C). Rather, the splitting in multiplicative rules is changed so that safe formulas never need to be split, making the duplication of safe formulas obsolete. The equivalence of the thus obtained calculus is known in the literature (see for example the *dyadic* calculus of [2]).

Finally, the (UNPACK $!F$)-rule in our game semantics forces us to immediately unpack the copy of F after it has been created. There is no such requirement in **IAL**: here we may create a copy of a safe formula by a combination of (!C) and (!dR), which might be used only later in a proof (if at all). It is however not hard to check that such a detour is never necessary. This can also be seen as a special case of Andreoli's results on *Focusing* [2]. □

Before closing this section, let us remark that we also obtain a game adequate for **ILL** (full intuitionistic linear logic) by allowing only

$$a \rhd a \qquad \text{and} \qquad \bot \rhd F$$

---

[5] We remark that (W) is *not* admissible in **IAL**, even if one relaxes the axioms, because of the (!R)-rule. Our corresponding (CHECK $!F$)-rule is different: It could be written as

$$\frac{!\Gamma \Rightarrow F}{\Delta, !\Gamma \Rightarrow !F}$$

which has a built-in weakening.

as winning states for **C** and introducing atomic ips $0, 1, \top$ with their corresponding rules. This amounts to an interpretation of sequents as **C/S**-game states, where **C** announces that she needs *precisely* the information provided by **S** to obtain her current ip.

5   Interpreting Exponentials and Subexponentials

The UNPACK-rule for $!$ (together with the CHECK-rule for $\otimes$ and the UNPACK-rule for $\multimap$) shows that safe ips are exempt from resource consciousness: operations are performed on copies of the safe ip rather than on the ip itself. The UNPACK-rule for $!$ says that the safety predicate is *hereditary*: If F can be demonstrated from a bunch of safe ips, then F is also safe.

C can send (UNPACK $!F$)-requests to the same ip $!F$ as often as she wishes. Furthermore, if **C** has a winning strategy for $\Gamma \rhd !F$ then she also has winning strategies for $\Gamma \rhd F^{\otimes n}$ for any n, where $F^{\otimes n}$ denotes $\underbrace{F \otimes \ldots \otimes F}_{n}$. This is most easily seen by first checking that **C** has a winning strategy in $!F \rhd F^{\otimes n}$ and then using the fact that the cut rule is admissible in **IAL**.

The meaning of $!F$ is often paraphrased as 'arbitrarily many F'. But this intuition is not without pitfalls, as the observation demonstrates.

Lemma 7. *Assume $a, b \neq \bot$. **C** has a winning strategy in $a, !(a \multimap a \otimes b) \rhd b^{\otimes n}$ for any n, but she has no winning strategy in $a, !(a \multimap a \otimes b) \rhd !b$.*

Formulated proof-theoretically, Lemma 7 entails that the infinitary rule

$$\frac{\Gamma \Rightarrow F^{\otimes n} \text{ for all } n}{\Gamma \Rightarrow !F} \; (!\mathrm{R}^{\omega})$$

is not admissible in IAL. The interpretation of $!$ is improved by thinking of $!F$ not as arbitrarily many F's, but as a *single* container containing (potentially) arbitrarily many F's. The problem is that this does not tell us much about what we should require from a proof of $!F$.

Instead, we invite the reader to think of the rules for the safety predicate as (partially) specifying a concept of safety, where being exempt from consumption through unpacking (i.e., resource consciousness) is the essential minimal requirement. This also aligns with the observation that when adding another unary constructor $!'$ with the same rules as $!$ to **IAL**, one cannot[6] prove the equivalence of $!$ and $!'$. Variants of the standard exponential introduced in this way are usually called *subexponentials*. In the 'arbitrarily many'-interpretation of the exponential, the existence of subexponentials seems to be mysterious – how can there be two *different* concepts of 'arbitrarily many'?

---

[6] We remark that the combination of the rules $(!\mathrm{C})$, $(!\mathrm{dR})$ and $(!\mathrm{R}^{\omega})$ *does* define an exponential $!$ uniquely. However, cut is not admissible in the resulting system.

In the safety interpretation, we may think of different subexponentials !'s as corresponding to different *levels of safety*. In fact, we can add constructors $!_1, !_2, \ldots, !_n$, where greater indices denote greater safety. A natural generalization of the !-rule is then the following:

$!_i F$ safety level i for F

> UNPACK: A copy of F is added to the bunch of provided information, and then an UNPACK request on this copy is invoked
>
> CHECK: All ips of safety level *less than i* (including the unsecured ones) are removed, and **C**'s current ip is changed to F.

One may go further and arrange the safety levels in a *partial order* rather than a linear order, with the obvious modification of the (CHECK)-rule. At some point, one loses cut-admissibility of the logic – we refer the reader to [4, Chap. 5].

6   The Server as Stack

In the games considered so far, **C**'s choice of the active ip at the beginning of each round was completely free. We now consider a variant of the game where the bunch of provided information is a list rather than a multiset, and **C** can only access the last element in the list. In other words, we think of the server as a *stack*. We include this new game in the discussion as an example of a variant which arises naturally in the context of Client/Server-interactions, but not in the proof-theoretic context.

The game rules are as given in Table 4. Note that in UNPACK-requests, the active ip is now always the topmost element of the stack.

Let us call the resulting game **C/S(STACK)**. Again, we translate game states to sequents (which are now *lists* of ips) and game rules to sequent rules. We write stacks from left to right, so that the rightmost element of a list of ips corresponds to the topmost element of the stack. Let us call the resulting system **LSTACK**. The initial sequents are thus

$$\overline{\Gamma, a \Rightarrow a} \qquad \text{and} \qquad \overline{\Gamma, \bot \Rightarrow F} \; .$$

Of the rules, we only mention those for $\to$ and $(;)$ explicitly. They are

$$\frac{\Gamma, G \Rightarrow H \qquad \Gamma \Rightarrow F}{\Gamma, F \to G \Rightarrow H} \; (\to L) \qquad \frac{\Gamma_1, F, \Gamma_2 \Rightarrow G}{\Gamma_1, \Gamma_2 \Rightarrow F \to G} \; (\to R)$$

and

$$\frac{\Gamma, G, F \Rightarrow H}{\Gamma, (F; G) \Rightarrow H} \; (;L) \qquad \frac{\Gamma_2 \Rightarrow F \qquad \Gamma_1 \Rightarrow G}{\Gamma_1, \Gamma_2 \Rightarrow (F; G)} \; (;R)$$

where Γ_1 and Γ_2 correspond to the lower and the upper part of the stack in the rule (CHECK $(F; G)$) respectively.

Table 4. Constructors and rules for **C/S(STACK)**

a	Atomic ip
	UNPACK: Not possible unless $a = \perp$. In the latter case, the game ends and **C** wins
	CHECK: The game ends and **C** wins iff a is the topmost item on the stack.
$F_1 \wedge F_2$	Any of F_1, F_2
	UNPACK: **C** chooses an ip F_i out of $\{F_1, F_2\}$. **S** then has to replace $F_1 \wedge F_2$ by F_i
	CHECK: **S** chooses an ip out of $\{F_1, F_2\}$ and sets it as **C**'s new current ip.
$F_1 \vee F_2$	some of F_1, F_2
	UNPACK: **S** replaces $F_1 \vee F_2$ by one ip out of $\{F_1, F_2\}$
	CHECK: **C** chooses an ip out of $\{F_1, F_2\}$ and sets it as the new current ip.
$(F_1 \rightarrow F_2)$	F_2 given F_1
	UNPACK: **S** removes $(F_1 \rightarrow F_2)$ and chooses whether to add F_2 on top of the stack, or to force **C** to replace its current ip by F_1
	CHECK: **C** choses a position in the stack at which **S** has to insert F_1, and changes her current ip to F_2
$(F_1; F_2)$	F_2 after F_1
	UNPACK: **S** replaces $(F_1; F_2)$ by the two ips F_2, F_1 (so that F_1 becomes the topmost element of the stack)
	CHECK: **C** chooses a splitting of the stack into an upper and a lower part (both parts may be empty). **S** then decides whether to change **C**'s current ip to F_1 and continue the game with the upper part of the stack, or to change **C**'s current ip to F_2 and continue the game with the lower part of the stack

Analogously to Theorems 2 and 6, we have

Theorem 8. *The following are equivalent:*

1. C has a winning strategy in the **C/S(STACK)***-game* $\Gamma \triangleright H$*.*
2. **LSTACK** $\vdash \Gamma \Rightarrow H$*.*

The rules for the connective (;) resemble those of the $\otimes$ of linear logic, only that in the right rule, the premises are split in an ordered way. (;) internalizes the linear order of the stack. It has the following properties, which are straightforward to check:

Proposition 9

1. *(non-commutativity)* C *has no winning strategy in* $(F; G) \rhd (G; F)$.
2. *(associativity 1)* C *has a winning strategy in* $(F; (G; H)) \rhd ((F; G); H)$.
3. *(associativity 2)* C *has a winning strategy in* $((F; G); H) \rhd (F; (G; H))$.

Proposition 10

1. C *has a winning strategy in* $\Gamma, F \rhd F$.
2. C *has a winning strategy in* $\Gamma, F, F \to G \rhd G$.

Proof. The proof of (1) proceeds by induction on F. If F is atomic, $\Gamma, F \rhd F$ is already a winning state for C. If $F \equiv G \to H$, the **LSTACK**-derivation

$$\dfrac{\dfrac{\Gamma, G, H \Rightarrow H \qquad \Gamma, G \Rightarrow G}{\Gamma, G, G \to H \Rightarrow H} (\to\text{L})}{\Gamma, G \to H \Rightarrow G \to H} (\to\text{R})$$

demonstrates that C can always move to a state $\Gamma, G, H \rhd H$ or $\Gamma, G \rhd G$, for both of which she has winning strategies by the induction hypothesis. If $F \equiv (G; H)$, the **LSTACK**-derivation

$$\dfrac{\dfrac{G \Rightarrow G \qquad \Gamma, H \Rightarrow H}{\Gamma, H, G \Rightarrow (G; H)} (;\text{R})}{\Gamma, (G; H) \Rightarrow (G; H)} (;\text{L})$$

demonstrates that C can always move to a state $G \rhd G$ or $\Gamma, H \rhd C$, and again she has winning strategies for both states by the induction hypothesis. The other cases are similar.

For (2), C starts the game $\Gamma, F, F \to G \rhd G$ by sending an (UNPACK $F \to G$)-request. Depending on the subsequent choice of S, the game is then either in the state $\Gamma, F, G \rhd G$ or $\Gamma, F \rhd F$. For both of these states, C has a winning strategy by (1). □

Proposition 11. *If C has a winning strategy in* $\Gamma, (F; G), \Delta \Rightarrow H$, *then she also has a winning strategy in* $\Gamma, G, F, \Delta \Rightarrow H$.

Proof. Let τ be a winning strategy for C in $\Gamma, (F; G), \Delta \Rightarrow H$. C can use essentially the same strategy τ in $\Gamma, G, F, \Delta \Rightarrow H$. If during the game, the indicated occurence of G, F is on top of the stack and τ tells her to (CHECK $(F; G)$), C simply skips this step. □

The converse to Proposition 11 fails: For example, C has a winning strategy in

$$K, F \to G, G \to H \rhd F \to H$$

as the following **LSTACK**-derivation shows:

$$\dfrac{\dfrac{K, F, F \to G, H \Rightarrow H \qquad \dfrac{K, F, G \Rightarrow G \qquad K, F \Rightarrow F}{K, F, F \to G \Rightarrow G} (\to\text{L})}{K, F, F \to G, G \to H \Rightarrow H}}{K, F \to G, G \to H \Rightarrow F \to H} (\to\text{R})$$

In contrast, $\mathbf{C}$ has no winning strategy in $((F \to G); K), G \to H \rhd F \to H$. This is because $(;)$ prevents $\mathbf{C}$ from inserting the premise F below $F \to G$ in the stack as her first step in the winning strategy. One easily checks that no other proof exists, assuming that F, G, H, K are pairwise distinct atoms.

The discussed properties allow one to wrap up whole game states in single information packages: For any game state $S \equiv F_1, \ldots, F_n \rhd G$ let $IP(S) :=$ $((\ldots (F_n; F_{n-1}); F_{n-2}); \ldots); F_1) \to G$.

Proposition 12. *$\mathbf{C}$ has a winning strategy in a game state S iff $\mathbf{C}$ has a winning strategy in the state $\rhd IP(S)$.*

Proof. For the direction from left to right, $\mathbf{C}$ starts the game for $\rhd IP(S)$ by sending a (CHECK $\to$)-request, followed by $(n-1)$-many UNPACK(;)-requests. The game is then in the state S, for which $\mathbf{C}$ has a winning strategy by assumption. For the other direction, it is clear (by lack of other choices) that a winning strategy for $IP(S)$ must start with a (CHECK $\to$)-request, and hence $\mathbf{C}$ has a winning strategy for the subsequent state $((\ldots (F_n; F_{n-1}); F_{n-2}); \ldots); F_1) \rhd G$. By applying Proposition 11 $(n-1)$-times, we see that $\mathbf{C}$ has a winning strategy in $F_1, \ldots, F_n \rhd G$.   □

Formulated proof-theoretically, Proposition 12 says that **LSTACK** is an *internal calculus*: There is a uniform way of mapping sequents S to formulas $IP(S)$ such that S is provable iff its formula interpretation $IP(S)$ is provable.

Finally observe that combining winning strategies for different game states in **C/S(STACK)** would require to merge stacks. Hence the following observation should not come as a surprise.

Proposition 13. *The cut rule is not admissible in* **LSTACK**.

Proof. Let a, b, c be pairwise distinct atoms and $a \neq \bot$. The sequents $a, b \to c \Rightarrow b \to c$ and $b, b \to c \Rightarrow c$ are provable. Applying the cut rule (with cut formula $b \to c$) yields the sequent $b, a, b \to c \Rightarrow c$, which is not provable:

$$\frac{b, a, c \Rightarrow c \qquad \overline{b, a \Rightarrow b}^{\ ??}}{b, a, b \to c \Rightarrow c} (\to\text{L})$$

□

7   Conclusion

We have introduced an interpretation of single-conclusioned sequent calculi as means of information extraction: formulas are seen as information packages and a derivation of $\Gamma \Rightarrow F$ corresponds to a winning strategy of a Client $\mathbf{C}$ that seeks to reduce the information F to the information Γ provided by the Server $\mathbf{S}$. In this manner we obtain an interpretation of a standard sequent calculus for intuitionistic logic that naturally extends to (affine) intuitionistic linear logic **IAL**. In particular exponentials and subexponentials receive a robust interpretation in terms of safeness from destruction through consumption. To demonstrate that our game semantics does not only fit already known calculi, we also applied it to a new concept: sequents where the left hand side represents a stack, rather than a set, multiset, or list of information packages.

We view the presented ideas and results as just a starting point for a more thorough analysis of deduction in analytic calculi in terms of reducing structured information to atomic information and plan to address, e.g., the following questions in future research: Which further operators for packaging information should be considered? Which alternative forms of storing information on a server lead to sequent calculi? Can the approach be lifted to quantifiers? Does the new interpretation of rule-admissibility lead to further insights into the underlying logics? How can the Client/Server view assist in organizing efficient proof search?

References

1. Abramsky, S., Jagadeesan, R.: Games and full completeness for multiplicative linear logic. J. Symb. Log. **59**(02), 543–574 (1994)
2. Andreoli, J.-M.: Logic programming with focusing proofs in linear logic. J. Log. Comput. **2**(3), 297–347 (1992)
3. Blass, A.: A game semantics for linear logic. Ann. Pure Appl. Log. **56**(1), 183–220 (1992)
4. Danos, V., Joinet, J.-B., Schellinx, H.: The structure of exponentials: uncovering the dynamics of linear logic proofs. In: Gottlob, G., Leitsch, A., Mundici, D. (eds.) KGC 1993. LNCS, vol. 713, pp. 159–171. Springer, Heidelberg (1993). doi:10.1007/BFb0022564
5. Girard, J.-Y.: Linear logic: its syntax and semantics. In: Advances in linear logic (Ithaca, NY, 1993). London Mathematical Society Lecture Note Series, vol. 222, pp. 1–42. Cambridge University Press, Cambridge (1995)
6. Japaridze, G.: The intuitionistic fragment of computability logic at the propositional level. Ann. Pure Appl. Log. **147**(3), 187–227 (2007)
7. Keiff, L.: Dialogical logic. In: Zalta, E.N. (ed.) The Stanford Encyclopedia of Philosophy. Metaphysics Research Lab, Stanford University, summer 2011 edition (2011)
8. Lafont,Y., Streicher, T.: Games semantics for linear logic. In: Proceedings of Sixth Annual IEEE Symposium on Logic in Computer Science, LICS 1991, pp. 43–50. IEEE (1991)
9. Lorenzen, P.: Logik und Agon. In: Atti del XII Congresso Internazionale di Filosofia, vol. 4, pp. 187–194 (1960)
10. Paoli, F.: Substructural Logics: A Primer. Springer, Heidelberg (2013)
11. Rahman, S., Rückert, H.: Dialogical connexive logic. Synthese **127**(1), 105–139 (2001)
12. Troelstra, A.S., Schwichtenberg, H.: Basic proof theory. Cambridge Tracts in Theoretical Computer Science, vol. 43, 2nd edn. Cambridge University Press, Cambridge (2000)

A Forward Unprovability Calculus
for Intuitionistic Propositional Logic

Camillo Fiorentini[1]([✉]) and Mauro Ferrari[2]

[1] DI, Univ. degli Studi di Milano, Via Comelico, 39, 20135 Milano, Italy
fiorentini@di.unimi.it
[2] DiSTA, Univ. degli Studi dell'Insubria, Via Mazzini, 5, 21100 Varese, Italy

Abstract. The inverse method is a saturation based theorem proving technique; it relies on a forward proof-search strategy and can be applied to cut-free calculi enjoying the subformula property. This method has been successfully applied to a variety of logics. Here we apply this method to derive the unprovability of a goal formula G in Intuitionistic Propositional Logic. To this aim we design a forward calculus $\mathbf{FRJ}(G)$ for Intuitionistic unprovability. From a derivation of G in $\mathbf{FRJ}(G)$ we can extract a Kripke countermodel for G. Since in forward methods sequents are not duplicated, the generated countermodels do not contain redundant worlds and are in general very concise.

1   Introduction

The inverse method, introduced by Maslov [15], is a saturation based theorem proving technique closely related to (hyper)resolution [6]; it relies on a forward proof-search strategy and can be applied to cut-free calculi enjoying the subformula property. Given a goal, a set of instances of the rules of the calculus at hand is selected; such specialized rules are repeatedly applied in the forward direction, starting from the axioms (i.e., the rules without premises). Proof-search terminates if either the goal is obtained or the database of proved facts saturates (no new fact can be added). The inverse method has been originally applied to Classical Logic and successively extended to some non-classical logics, see, e.g., [2,6,7,14]. A significant investigation is presented in [4,5], where focused calculi and polarization of formulas are exploited to reduce the search spaces in forward proof-search. These techniques are at the heart of the design of the prover Imogen [16].

In all the mentioned papers, the inverse method has been exploited to prove the validity of a goal in a specific logic. Here we follow the dual approach, namely: we design a forward calculus to derive the unprovability of a goal formula in Intuitionistic Propositional Logic (IPL). This different perspectives requires a deep adjustment of the method itself. Sequents $\Gamma \vdash A$ of standard forward calculi encode the fact that the rhs (right-hand side) formula A is provable from the set of lhs (left-hand side) formulas Γ in the understood logic. In our viewpoint, a sequent $\Gamma \Rightarrow A$ signifies the unprovability of A from Γ in IPL. From a semantic viewpoint, this means that, in some world of a Kripke model, all the formulas

© Springer International Publishing AG 2017
R.A. Schmidt and C. Nalon (Eds.): TABLEAUX 2017, LNAI 10501, pp. 114–130, 2017.
DOI: 10.1007/978-3-319-66902-1_7

in Γ are forced and A is not forced. In standard forward reasoning, axioms have the form $p \vdash p$, where p is a proper atomic subformula of the goal. In our approach, axioms have the form $\Gamma^{\mathrm{At}} \Rightarrow p$, where p is an atomic subformula of the goal formula G and Γ^{At} is a "maximal" subset of atomic subformulas of G such that $p \notin \Gamma^{\mathrm{At}}$. A tricky task is how to cope with rules having more than one premise. In standard calculi, the lhs formulas must be gathered; e.g., a forward application of the rule $R\wedge$ to the sequents $\Gamma_1 \vdash A_1$ and $\Gamma_2 \vdash A_2$ yields the sequent $\Gamma_1 \cup \Gamma_2 \vdash A_1 \wedge A_2$. In our approach, since we have to preserve unprovability, we must intersect the lhs formulas. Apparently, the rule for $R\vee$ applied to $\Gamma_1 \Rightarrow A_1$ and $\Gamma_2 \Rightarrow A_2$ should generate $\Gamma_1 \cap \Gamma_2 \Rightarrow A_1 \vee A_2$, but such a rule is not sound. For instance, let $H = p \supset q_1 \vee q_2$, and let us take the unprovable sequents $q_2, p, H \Rightarrow q_1$ and $q_1, p, H \Rightarrow q_2$; the alleged $R\vee$ rule yields $p, H \Rightarrow q_1 \vee q_2$, which is provable. The drawback is that we cannot retain both p and H in the conclusion; thus, we need a more clever strategy to join sequents. To formalize this, beside sequents $\Gamma \Rightarrow A$, we call *regular*, we introduce sequents $\Sigma; \Theta \rightarrow A$, we call *irregular*, where the formulas in the lhs are partitioned in two sets Σ and Θ; in forward proof-search, formulas in the sets Σ must be kept as much as possible. We can only join irregular sequents, provided that some side conditions are matched, and the outcome is a regular sequent. The rules of the calculus (see Fig. 1) depend on the goal formula G, hence we call the obtained calculus **FRJ**(G) (Forward Refutation calculus parametrized by G). Differently from standard sequent calculi, lhs of sequents only host propositional variables and implicative formulas $A \supset B$; moreover **FRJ**(G) only supplies right rules.

The rules of **FRJ**(G) are inspired by Kripke semantics. In Sect. 4 we show that, from a derivation of G, we can extract a countermodel for G, namely a Kripke model such that, at its root, the formula G is not forced, hence G is not valid in IPL [3]. Actually, there is a close correspondence between a derivation and the related Kripke model. Thus, our forward proof-search procedure can be understood as a top-down method to build a countermodel for G, starting from the final worlds down to the root. Our approach is dual to the standard one, where countermodels are built bottom-up, mimicking the backward application of rules, see [1,8,9,11,17,18]. This different viewpoint has a significant impact in the outcome. Indeed, the countermodels generated by a backward procedure are always trees, which might contain some redundancies. Instead, forward methods are prone to re-use sequents and to not replicate them; thus the generated models do not contain duplications and are in general very concise (see the models in Figs. 5 and 8). In Sect. 4 we also show that, given a countermodel for G, we can build a derivation of G; this proves the completeness of **FRJ**(G). We point out that **FRJ**(G) can be viewed as a forward presentation of the calculus **Rbu** presented in [10].

As remarked in [16], the saturated database generated as a consequence of a failed proof-search in forward calculi for IPL "may be considered a kind of countermodel for the goal sequent". However, as far as we know, no method has been proposed to effectively extract it. Actually, the main problem comes from the high level of non-determinism involved in the construction of countermodels.

Here we study the dual problem of intuitionistic unprovability and we conjecture that the saturated database generated by a failed proof-search can be considered as *a kind of derivation of the goal*.

To evaluate the potential of our approach we have implemented `frj`, a Java prototype of our proof-search procedure based on the JTabWb framework [12][1]. `frj` implements term-indexing, forward and backward subsumption and it allows the user to generate the rendering of proofs and of the extracted countermodels.

2   Preliminaries

We consider the propositional language $\mathcal{L}$ based on a denumerable set of propositional variables $\mathcal{V}$, the connectives $\wedge$, $\vee$, $\supset$ (as usual, $\wedge$ and $\vee$ bind stronger than $\supset$) and the logical constant $\bot$; $\neg A$ is a shorthand for $A \supset \bot$. By $\mathcal{V}^{\bot}$ we denote the set $\mathcal{V} \cup \{\bot\}$ and by $\mathcal{L}^{\supset}$ the set of the implicative formulas $A \supset B$ of $\mathcal{L}$. Capital Greek letters Γ, Σ, ... denote sets of formulas; we use notations like Γ^{At} and $\Gamma^{\supset}$ to mean that $\Gamma^{\text{At}} \subseteq \mathcal{V}$ and $\Gamma^{\supset} \subseteq \mathcal{L}^{\supset}$. Given a formula G, $\text{Sf}(G)$ is the set of all subformulas of G (including G itself) and $\text{Sf}^{-}(G) = \text{Sf}(G) \backslash \{G\}$. By $\text{S}_{\text{L}}(G)$ and $\text{S}_{\text{R}}(G)$ we denote the smallest subsets of $\text{Sf}(G)$ such that $G \in \text{S}_{\text{R}}(G)$ and, given $\text{Sx} \in \{\text{S}_{\text{L}}, \text{S}_{\text{R}}\}$ ($\overline{\text{S}_{\text{L}}} = \text{S}_{\text{R}}$ and $\overline{\text{S}_{\text{R}}} = \text{S}_{\text{L}}$):

- $A \odot B \in \text{Sx}(G)$ implies $\{A, B\} \subseteq \text{Sx}(G)$, where $\odot \in \{\wedge, \vee\}$;
- $A \supset B \in \text{Sx}(G)$ implies $B \in \text{Sx}(G)$ and $A \in \overline{\text{Sx}}(G)$

(see the examples in Figs. 2, 4 and 6). By $|A|$ we denote the *size* of A, namely the number of symbols in A. A *Kripke model* is a structure $\mathcal{K} = \langle P, \leq, \rho, V \rangle$, where $\langle P, \leq \rangle$ is a finite poset with minimum ρ and $V : P \to 2^{\mathcal{V}}$ is a function such that $\alpha \leq \beta$ implies $V(\alpha) \subseteq V(\beta)$. The *forcing relation* $\Vdash \subseteq P \times \mathcal{L}$ is defined as follows:

- $\mathcal{K}, \alpha \not\Vdash \bot$ and, for every $p \in \mathcal{V}$, $\mathcal{K}, \alpha \Vdash p$ iff $p \in V(\alpha)$;
- $\mathcal{K}, \alpha \Vdash A \wedge B$ iff $\mathcal{K}, \alpha \Vdash A$ and $\mathcal{K}, \alpha \Vdash B$;
- $\mathcal{K}, \alpha \Vdash A \vee B$ iff $\mathcal{K}, \alpha \Vdash A$ or $\mathcal{K}, \alpha \Vdash B$;
- $\mathcal{K}, \alpha \Vdash A \supset B$ iff, for every $\beta \in P$ such that $\alpha \leq \beta$, $\mathcal{K}, \beta \not\Vdash A$ or $\mathcal{K}, \beta \Vdash B$.

Monotonicity property holds for arbitrary formulas, i.e.: $\mathcal{K}, \alpha \Vdash A$ and $\alpha \leq \beta$ imply $\mathcal{K}, \beta \Vdash A$. A formula A is *valid* in $\mathcal{K}$ iff $\mathcal{K}, \rho \Vdash A$. Intuitionistic Propositional Logic IPL coincides with the set of the formulas valid in all Kripke models [3]. If $\mathcal{K}, \rho \not\Vdash A$, we say that $\mathcal{K}$ is a *countermodel* for A and that A is *refutable*. A *final world* γ of $\mathcal{K}$ is a maximal world in $\langle P, \leq \rangle$; for every classically valid formula A, we have $\mathcal{K}, \gamma \Vdash A$. Let Γ be a set of formulas. By $\mathcal{K}, \alpha \Vdash \Gamma$ we mean that $\mathcal{K}, \alpha \Vdash A$ for every $A \in \Gamma$. Using the above notation we avoid to mention the model $\mathcal{K}$ whenever it is understood (e.g., we write $\alpha \Vdash A$ instead of $\mathcal{K}, \alpha \Vdash A$). The *closure* of Γ, denoted by $\mathcal{C}l(\Gamma)$, is the smallest set containing the formulas X defined by the following grammar:

$$X ::= C \mid X \wedge X \mid A \vee X \mid X \vee A \mid A \supset X \qquad C \in \Gamma, \ A \text{ any formula}$$

---

[1] `frj` is available at http://github.com/ferram/jtabwb_provers/.

The following properties of closures can be easily proved:

(*Cl*1) $\mathcal{K}, \alpha \Vdash \Gamma$ implies $\mathcal{K}, \alpha \Vdash Cl(\Gamma)$.
(*Cl*2) $A \in Cl(\Gamma)$ implies $A \in Cl(\Gamma \cap \mathrm{Sf}(A))$.
(*Cl*3) $\Gamma \subseteq Cl(\Gamma)$ and $Cl(Cl(\Gamma)) = Cl(\Gamma)$.
(*Cl*4) $\Gamma_1 \subseteq \Gamma_2$ implies $Cl(\Gamma_1) \subseteq Cl(\Gamma_2)$.
(*Cl*5) $Cl(\Gamma) \cap \mathcal{V} = \Gamma \cap \mathcal{V}$.
(*Cl*6) $\Gamma_1 \subseteq Cl(\Gamma_2)$ implies $Cl(\Gamma_1) \subseteq Cl(\Gamma_2)$ (this follows from (*Cl*3) and (*Cl*4)).

3   The Calculus FRJ(G)

The Forward Refutation calculus **FRJ**(G) is a forward calculus to infer the unprovability of a goal formula G in IPL. We design **FRJ**(G) so that it enjoys the *finite rule property* [6]. To deal with multi-premise rules, we use two types of sequents. Let $\overline{\Gamma}^{\mathrm{At}} = \mathrm{SL}(G) \cap \mathcal{V}$, $\overline{\Gamma}^{\supset} = \mathrm{SL}(G) \cap \mathcal{L}^{\supset}$ and $\overline{\Gamma} = \overline{\Gamma}^{\mathrm{At}} \cup \overline{\Gamma}^{\supset}$; sequents σ of **FRJ**(G) have the form:

- $\Gamma \Rightarrow C$, where $\Gamma \subseteq \overline{\Gamma}$ and $C \in \mathrm{SR}(G)$ (*regular sequents*);
- $\Sigma ; \Theta \to C$, where $\Sigma \cup \Theta \subseteq \overline{\Gamma}$ and $C \in \mathrm{SR}(G)$ (*irregular sequents*).

We set $\mathrm{Lhs}(\sigma) = \Gamma$ if σ is regular and $\mathrm{Lhs}(\sigma) = \Sigma \cup \Theta$ if σ is irregular; $\mathrm{Rhs}(\sigma) = C$. Left formulas of irregular sequents σ are partitioned in the sets Σ, the *stable set* of σ, and Θ. In forward proof-search, formulas in Σ are preserved as much as possible, while some of the formulas in Θ can be lost. We give the reader an insight into **FRJ**(G) rules, focusing on the semantic aspects. The crucial point (see Sect. 4) is that **FRJ**(G) satisfies the following soundness property:

(S1) if $\sigma = \Gamma \Rightarrow C$ is provable in **FRJ**(G), then there exists a world α of a model $\mathcal{K}$ such that $\alpha \Vdash \Gamma$ and $\alpha \nVdash C$.
(S2) if $\sigma = \Sigma ; \Theta \to C$ is provable in **FRJ**(G) and σ can be used to (directly or indirectly) prove a regular sequent in **FRJ**(G), then there exist a world α of a model $\mathcal{K}$ and a set Γ such that $\Sigma \subseteq \Gamma \subseteq \Sigma \cup \Theta$ and $\alpha \Vdash \Gamma$ and $\alpha \nVdash C$.

In both cases, it follows that C is not provable from Γ in IPL.

Rules of **FRJ**(G) are displayed in Fig. 1; below σ refers to the conclusion of a rule and $\sigma_1, \sigma_2, \ldots$ to its premises. In forward calculi, proof-search starts from axiom sequents. We have two rules to introduce axioms: $\mathrm{Ax}_{\Rightarrow}$ (regular axioms) and $\mathrm{Ax}_{\to}$ (irregular axioms). In irregular axioms the set Σ is empty; moreover, irregular axioms are the only irregular sequents σ' such that $\mathrm{Rhs}(\sigma') \in \mathcal{V}^{\perp}$.

There are no left rules, but only rules to introduce the connectives $\wedge, \vee, \supset$ in the right and the rules $\bowtie^{\mathrm{At}}$ and $\bowtie^{\vee}$ to join sequents. In rule $\vee$, the stable sets Σ_1 and Σ_2 of the premises are maintained in the conclusion, while the sets Θ_1 and Θ_2 are intersected; by the side conditions, $\mathrm{Lhs}(\sigma) \subseteq \mathrm{Lhs}(\sigma_1) \cap \mathrm{Lhs}(\sigma_2)$. We have two rules to introduce a formula $A \supset B$ in the right: $\supset_{\in}$ and $\supset_{\notin}$. In both rules, in the premise σ_1 we have $\mathrm{Rhs}(\sigma_1) = B$. In standard refutation calculi, to make $A \supset B$ unprovable it is assumed that $A \in \mathrm{Lhs}(\sigma_1)$. Here we relax this

$\overline{\Gamma}^{\mathrm{At}} = \mathrm{SL}(G) \cap \mathcal{V}, \ \overline{\Gamma}^{\supset} = \mathrm{SL}(G) \cap \mathcal{L}^{\supset}, \overline{\Gamma} = \overline{\Gamma}^{\mathrm{At}} \cup \overline{\Gamma}^{\supset}.$

In the conclusion σ of each rule, $\mathrm{Rhs}(\sigma) \in \mathrm{SR}(G)$

$$\frac{}{\overline{\Gamma}^{\mathrm{At}} \setminus \{F\} \Rightarrow F} \mathrm{Ax}_{\Rightarrow} \qquad \frac{}{\cdot \, ; \, \overline{\Gamma}^{\mathrm{At}} \setminus \{F\}, \overline{\Gamma}^{\supset} \to F} \mathrm{Ax}_{\to} \qquad F \in \mathcal{V}^{\perp}$$

$$\frac{\Gamma \Rightarrow A_k}{\Gamma \Rightarrow A_1 \wedge A_2} \wedge \qquad \frac{\Sigma \, ; \, \Theta \to A_k}{\Sigma \, ; \, \Theta \to A_1 \wedge A_2} \wedge \quad k \in \{1,2\}$$

$$\frac{\Sigma_1 \, ; \, \Theta_1 \to C_1 \qquad \Sigma_2 \, ; \, \Theta_2 \to C_2}{\Sigma_1, \Sigma_2 \, ; \, \Theta_1 \cap \Theta_2 \to C_1 \vee C_2} \vee \quad \begin{array}{l} \Sigma_1 \subseteq \Sigma_2 \cup \Theta_2 \\ \Sigma_2 \subseteq \Sigma_1 \cup \Theta_1 \end{array}$$

$$\frac{\Gamma \Rightarrow B}{\Gamma \Rightarrow A \supset B} \supset_{\in} \quad A \in Cl(\Gamma) \qquad \frac{\Sigma \, ; \, \Theta, \Lambda \to B}{\Sigma, \Lambda \, ; \, \Theta \to A \supset B} \supset_{\in} \quad A \in Cl(\Sigma \cup \Lambda)$$

$$\frac{\Gamma \Rightarrow B}{\cdot \, ; \, \Theta \to A \supset B} \supset_{\notin} \quad \begin{array}{l} \Theta \subseteq Cl(\Gamma) \cap \overline{\Gamma} \\ A \in Cl(\Gamma) \setminus Cl(\Theta) \end{array}$$

Let $\Upsilon = \{A_1, \ldots, A_n\}$ and $\sigma_j = \underbrace{\Sigma_j^{\mathrm{At}}, \Sigma_j^{\supset}}_{\Sigma_j} \, ; \, \underbrace{\Theta_j^{\mathrm{At}}, \Theta_j^{\supset}}_{\Theta_j} \to A_j$ for every $1 \leq j \leq n$

$$\Sigma^{\mathrm{At}} = \bigcup_{1 \leq j \leq n} \Sigma_j^{\mathrm{At}} \quad \Theta^{\mathrm{At}} = \bigcap_{1 \leq j \leq n} \Theta_j^{\mathrm{At}} \quad \Sigma^{\supset} = \bigcup_{1 \leq j \leq n} \Sigma_j^{\supset} \quad \Theta^{\supset} = (\bigcap_{1 \leq j \leq n} \Theta_j^{\supset})/\Upsilon$$

$$\frac{\sigma_1 \quad \cdots \quad \sigma_n}{\Sigma^{\mathrm{At}}, \Theta^{\mathrm{At}} \setminus \{F\}, \Sigma^{\supset}, \Theta^{\supset} \Rightarrow F} \bowtie^{\mathrm{At}} \quad \begin{array}{l} \Sigma_i \subseteq \Sigma_j \cup \Theta_j, \text{ for every } i \neq j \\ Y \supset Z \in \Sigma^{\supset} \text{ implies } Y \in \Upsilon \\ F \in \mathcal{V}^{\perp} \setminus \Sigma^{\mathrm{At}} \end{array}$$

$$\frac{\sigma_1 \quad \cdots \quad \sigma_n}{\Sigma^{\mathrm{At}}, \Theta^{\mathrm{At}}, \Sigma^{\supset}, \Theta^{\supset} \Rightarrow C_1 \vee C_2} \bowtie^{\vee} \quad \begin{array}{l} \Sigma_i \subseteq \Sigma_j \cup \Theta_j, \text{ for every } i \neq j \\ Y \supset Z \in \Sigma^{\supset} \text{ implies } Y \in \Upsilon \\ \{C_1, C_2\} \subseteq \Upsilon \end{array}$$

Fig. 1. The calculus **FRJ**(G).

condition and we require that $A \in Cl(\mathrm{Lhs}(\sigma_1))$; this compensates the lack of left rules. In rule $\supset_{\in}$ the conclusion σ satisfies $A \in Cl(\mathrm{Lhs}(\sigma))$, while in $\supset_{\notin}$ we have $A \notin Cl(\mathrm{Lhs}(\sigma))$ (whence the subscripts $\in$ and $\notin$ in the rule names). In $\supset_{\in}$, σ_1 and σ have the same type. If $\sigma_1 = \Sigma \, ; \, \Theta_1 \to B$, we have to partition Θ_1 as $\Theta \cup \Lambda$ so that $A \in Cl(\Sigma \cup \Lambda)$; since $A \in Cl(\mathrm{Lhs}(\sigma_1))$, at least a set Λ can be selected. Formulas in Λ are shifted to the left of semicolon since they must be preserved as much as possible. Instead, $\supset_{\notin}$ is the only rule that turns a regular sequent $\sigma_1 = \Gamma \Rightarrow B$ into an irregular one. In the conclusion, the set Σ is empty and Θ is any (possibly empty) subset of $Cl(\Gamma) \cap \overline{\Gamma}$ such that $A \notin Cl(\Theta)$; the latter condition allows us to introduce a decreasing weight function on sequents.

The *join* rules $\bowtie^{\mathrm{At}}$ and $\bowtie^{\vee}$ apply to $n \geq 1$ irregular sequents $\sigma_1, \ldots, \sigma_n$ and yield a regular sequent σ; these are the only rules that convert irregular sequents to a regular one (note that rule $\bowtie^{\vee}$ is similar to the rule r_n presented in [19]). These two rules have a similar structure and only differ in $\mathrm{Rhs}(\sigma)$. The first side condition is a generalization of the conditions in rule $\vee$. In the construction of the countermodel, we use join rules to downward expand it by a new world α.

We wish that, for every $A \supset B$ in $\mathrm{Lhs}(\sigma)$, A is not forced in α and, to guarantee this, we need a premise σ_j such that $\mathrm{Rhs}(\sigma_j) = A$; if this happens, we say that $A \supset B$ is *supported* (by σ_j). For every premise σ_j, the stable set $\Sigma_j^\supset$ must be kept in the conclusion; accordingly, the premises $\sigma_1, \ldots, \sigma_n$ must be chosen so that every $A \supset B$ occurring in some $\Sigma_j^\supset$ is supported; this is formalized by the second side condition. In the conclusion, $\Theta^\supset$ only keeps the implications $A \supset B$ in the intersection of the $\Theta_j^\supset$ which are supported. In the definition of $\Theta^\supset$, the notation $\Gamma^\supset/\Upsilon$ defines the set of $Y \supset Z \in \Gamma^\supset$ such that $Y \in \Upsilon$ (the *restriction* of $\Gamma^\supset$ to Υ). We point out the following special case of application of $\bowtie^{\mathrm{At}}$ having only one premise:

$$\frac{\Sigma^{\mathrm{At}}, \Sigma^\supset \, ; \, \Theta^{\mathrm{At}}, \Theta^\supset \to A}{\Sigma^{\mathrm{At}}, \Sigma^\supset, \Theta^{\mathrm{At}} \setminus \{F\}, \Theta^\supset/\{A\} \Rightarrow F} \bowtie^{\mathrm{At}} \qquad \begin{array}{l} Y \supset Z \in \Sigma^\supset \text{ implies } Y = A \\ F \in \mathcal{V}^\perp \setminus \Sigma^{\mathrm{At}} \end{array}$$

Note that the unsound application of $R\vee$ mentioned in the Introduction is prevented. Indeed, let $\sigma_1 = \cdot \, ; q_2, p, H \to q_1$ and $\sigma_2 = \cdot \, ; q_1, p, H \to q_2$, with $H = p \supset q_1 \vee q_2$. If we apply rule $\bowtie^\vee$ to σ_1 and σ_2 we get the unprovable sequent $p \Rightarrow q_1 \vee q_2$; the formula H is lost since it is not supported (no premise has p in the right). We stress that provable irregular sequents might have a valid formula C in the right. For instance, let $C = \neg(p \wedge \neg p)$ and $\Delta = \{p, \neg p\}$. Then $\sigma_1 = \cdot \, ; \Delta \to \perp$ is an axiom of $\mathbf{FRJ}(C)$. Since $p \wedge \neg p \in Cl(\Delta)$, we can apply $\supset_\in$ to σ_1 and get $\sigma = \Delta \, ; \cdot \to C$. Note that $\alpha \Vdash C$, for every world α; by (S2) it follows that σ cannot be used to derive a regular sequent.

We say that $\mathcal{D}$ is an $\mathbf{FRJ}(G)$-*derivation of* G if the root sequent of $\mathcal{D}$ has the form $\Gamma \Rightarrow G$; G *is provable in* $\mathbf{FRJ}(G)$ iff there exists an $\mathbf{FRJ}(G)$-derivation of G. Soundness and completeness of $\mathbf{FRJ}(G)$ are stated as follows:

Theorem 1. *G is refutable iff G is provable in* $\mathbf{FRJ}(G)$.   □

Soundness (if side) immediately follows by (S1). Note that completeness (only if side) hides subsumption, which is typical of forward reasoning. Indeed, an $\mathbf{FRJ}(G)$-derivation $\mathcal{D}$ of G has root $\Gamma \Rightarrow G$, thus $\mathcal{D}$ actually shows that the formula $(\wedge \Gamma) \supset G$ is refutable (equivalently, G is not provable from assumptions Γ). By the proof of completeness (Lemma 4 of Sect. 4), we can introduce the following proof-search restrictions:

(PS1) In rule $\supset_\in$, Λ is a *minimal* set satisfying the side condition, namely: $\Lambda' \subsetneq \Lambda$ implies $A \notin Cl(\Sigma \cup \Lambda')$.
(PS2) In rule $\supset_\notin$, Θ is a *maximal* set satisfying the side condition, namely: $\Theta \subsetneq \Theta' \subseteq Cl(\Gamma) \cap \overline{\Gamma}$ implies $A \in Cl(\Theta')$.
(PS3) In $\bowtie^{\mathrm{At}}$, for every $Y \in \Upsilon$ there is $Y \supset Z \in \mathrm{SL}(G)$.
(PS4) In $\bowtie^\vee$, for every $Y \in \Upsilon$, either there is $Y \supset Z \in \mathrm{SL}(G)$ or there is $Y \vee Z \in \mathrm{SR}(G)$ or there is $Z \vee Y \in \mathrm{SR}(G)$.

For instance, let $\sigma = \cdot \, ; p, q \to B$ be an $\mathbf{FRJ}(G)$-sequent and $p \vee q \in \mathrm{SL}(G)$. The application of $\supset_\in$ to σ admits three conclusions, which differ in the choice of Λ:

$$\sigma_1 = p \, ; q \to C \qquad \sigma_2 = q \, ; p \to C \qquad \sigma_3 = p, q \, ; \cdot \to C \qquad C = p \vee q \supset B$$

In the first two applications the shifted set Λ is minimal. In the latter application the chosen Λ is not minimal, hence this application is ruled out. Henceforth, we assume that $\mathbf{FRJ}(G)$-derivations comply with (PS1)–(PS4).

$S = H \supset \neg\neg p \vee \neg p \qquad H = (\neg\neg p \supset p) \supset \neg p \vee p$

$\mathrm{SL}(S) = \{ H, \neg p \vee p, \neg\neg p, \neg p, p \} \quad \mathrm{SR}(S) = \{ S, \neg\neg p \vee \neg p, \neg\neg p \supset p, \neg\neg p, \neg p, p, \bot \}$

(1)	$\cdot\, ;\, p,\, H,\, \neg\neg p,\, \neg p \to \bot$	$\mathrm{Ax}_\to$	// Start
(2)	$\cdot\, ;\, H,\, \neg\neg p,\, \neg p \to p$	$\mathrm{Ax}_\to$	
(3)	$p\, ;\, H,\, \neg\neg p,\, \neg p \to \neg p$	$\supset_\in$ (1)	// Iteration 1
(4)	$\neg\neg p\, ;\, H,\, \neg p \to \neg\neg p \supset p$	$\supset_\in$ (2)	
(5)	$\neg p \Rightarrow \bot$	$\bowtie^{\mathrm{At}}$ (2)	
(6)	$p,\, \neg\neg p \Rightarrow \bot$	$\bowtie^{\mathrm{At}}$ (3)	// Iteration 2
(7)	$\cdot\, ;\, H \to \neg\neg p$	$\supset_{\not\in}$ (5)	
(8)	$\cdot\, ;\, H, \neg\neg p \to \neg p$	$\supset_{\not\in}$ (6)	// Iteration 3
(9)	$H,\, \neg\neg p \Rightarrow p$	$\bowtie^{\mathrm{At}}$ (4) (8)	// Iteration 4
(10)	$\cdot\, ;\, H \to \neg\neg p \supset p$	$\supset_{\not\in}$ (9)	// Iteration 5
(11)	$H \Rightarrow \neg\neg p \vee \neg p$	$\bowtie^{\vee}$ (7) (8) (10)	// Iteration 6
(12)	$H \Rightarrow S$	$\supset_\in$ (11)	// Iteration 7

Fig. 2. $\mathbf{FRJ}(S)$-derivation $\mathcal{D}_S$ of S.

Example 1. Let us consider the following instances S and T of *Scott* and *Anti-Scott* principles, which are equivalent to Nishimura formulas N_{10} and N_9 respectively [3] (the schema generating N_i is given in Sect. 5):

$$S = ((\neg\neg p \supset p) \supset \neg p \vee p) \supset \neg\neg p \vee \neg p \qquad T = S \supset (\neg\neg p \supset p) \vee \neg\neg p$$

Both formulas are valid in Classical Logic but not in IPL. Figures 2 and 4 show an $\mathbf{FRJ}(S)$-derivation $\mathcal{D}_S$ of S and an $\mathbf{FRJ}(T)$-derivation $\mathcal{D}_T$ of T respectively, in linear representation. We populate the database of proved sequents according with the naïve recipe of [6]: we start by inserting the axioms; then we enter a loop where, at each iteration, we apply the rules to the sequents collected in previous steps. We only show the sequents needed to get the goal. The tree-like structure of the derivations is displayed in Figs. 3 and 5. $\Diamond$

Given two sequents σ_1 and σ_2 of $\mathbf{FRJ}(G)$, $\sigma_1 \mapsto_0 \sigma_2$ iff σ_2 is the conclusion of a rule of $\mathbf{FRJ}(G)$ having σ_1 among the premises; thus, in forward computation, σ_2 is obtained from σ_1. By $\mapsto$ we denote the transitive closure of $\mapsto_0$, while $\mapsto_*$ is the reflexive closure of $\mapsto$. By inspecting the rules of the calculus and using the properties of closures, one can easily prove that[2]:

Lemma 1. $\sigma' \mapsto \sigma$ *implies* $\mathrm{Lhs}(\sigma) \subseteq \mathcal{C}l(\mathrm{Lhs}(\sigma'))$. $\square$

---

[2] An appendix with some of the omitted proofs is available at authors' homepage.

$$\cfrac{\cfrac{\sigma_{(2)}}{\sigma_{(5)}*}\ \bowtie^{At}}{\sigma_{(7)}} \qquad \cfrac{\cfrac{\sigma_{(1)}}{\cfrac{\sigma_{(3)}}{\sigma_{(6)}*}}\ \bowtie^{At}}{\sigma_{(8)}} \qquad \cfrac{\cfrac{\sigma_{(2)}}{\sigma_{(4)}}\quad\cfrac{\cfrac{\sigma_{(1)}}{\cfrac{\sigma_{(3)}}{\sigma_{(6)}*}}\ \bowtie^{At}}{\sigma_{(8)}}}{\sigma_{(9)}*}\ \bowtie^{At} \\ \cfrac{\qquad\qquad\qquad\qquad\qquad\qquad\qquad\cfrac{\sigma_{(9)}*}{\sigma_{(10)}}\ \bowtie^{\vee}}{} $$

$$\cfrac{\sigma_{(7)} \qquad\qquad \sigma_{(8)} \qquad\qquad \sigma_{(10)}}{\cfrac{\sigma_{(11)}*}{\sigma_{(12)}}}\ \bowtie^{\vee}$$

*: p-sequents

$\boxed{\sigma_{(6)}: p}$

$\boxed{\sigma_{(5)}:}\qquad\boxed{\sigma_{(9)}:}$

$\boxed{\sigma_{(11)}:}$

$\sigma_{(k)}$ refers to the sequent at line (k) in Fig. 2

$\phi(\sigma) = \sigma$, for every p-sequent σ

$\phi(\sigma_{(12)}) = \sigma_{(11)}$

Fig. 3. The model $\mathrm{Mod}(\mathcal{D}_S)$ (see Fig. 2).

$T = S \supset (\neg\neg p \supset p) \vee \neg\neg p \qquad S = H \supset \neg\neg p \vee \neg p \qquad H = (\neg\neg p \supset p) \supset \neg p \vee p$

$\mathrm{SL}(T) = \{\, S,\ \neg\neg p \supset p,\ \neg\neg p \vee \neg p,\ \neg\neg p,\ \neg p,\ p \,\}$

$\mathrm{SR}(T) = \{\, T,\ H,\ (\neg\neg p \supset p) \vee \neg\neg p,\ \neg\neg p \supset p,\ \neg\neg p,\ \neg p \vee p,\ \neg p,\ p,\ \bot \,\}$

(1)	$\cdot\,;\ p,\ S,\ \neg\neg p \supset p,\ \neg\neg p,\ \neg p \to \bot$	$\mathrm{Ax}_{\to}$
(2)	$\cdot\,;\ S,\ \neg\neg p \supset p,\ \neg\neg p,\ \neg p \to p$	$\mathrm{Ax}_{\to}$
(3)	$p\,;\ S,\ \neg\neg p \supset p,\ \neg\neg p,\ \neg p \to \neg p$	$\supset_{\in}$ (1)
(4)	$\neg p\,;\ p,\ S,\ \neg\neg p \supset p,\ \neg\neg p \to \neg\neg p$	$\supset_{\in}$ (1)
(5)	$\neg p,\ \neg\neg p \supset p \Rightarrow \bot$	$\bowtie^{At}$ (2) (4)
(6)	$p,\ \neg\neg p \Rightarrow \bot$	$\bowtie^{At}$ (3)
(7)	$\cdot\,;\ S,\ \neg\neg p \supset p \to \neg\neg p$	$\supset_{\notin}$ (5)
(8)	$\cdot\,;\ S,\ \neg\neg p \supset p,\ \neg\neg p \to \neg p$	$\supset_{\notin}$ (6)
(9)	$\cdot\,;\ S,\ \neg\neg p \supset p,\ \neg\neg p \to \neg p \vee p$	$\vee$ (2) (8)
(10)	$\neg\neg p \Rightarrow p$	$\bowtie^{At}$ (8)
(11)	$\neg\neg p \supset p\,;\ S,\ \neg\neg p \to H$	$\supset_{\in}$ (9)
(12)	$\cdot\,;\ S \to \neg\neg p \supset p$	$\supset_{\notin}$ (10)
(13)	$\neg\neg p \supset p,\ S \Rightarrow \neg p \vee p$	$\bowtie^{\vee}$ (2) (7) (8) (11)
(14)	$\cdot\,;\ S \to H$	$\supset_{\notin}$ (13)
(15)	$S \Rightarrow (\neg\neg p \supset p) \vee \neg\neg p$	$\bowtie^{\vee}$ (7) (12) (14)
(16)	$S \Rightarrow T$	$\supset_{\in}$ (15)

Fig. 4. $\mathbf{FRJ}(T)$-derivation $\mathcal{D}_T$ of T.

$$
\begin{array}{c}
\cfrac{\cfrac{\sigma(1)}{\sigma(2)\quad\sigma(4)}\ \bowtie^{At}}{\cfrac{\sigma(5)*}{\sigma(7)}}\qquad
\cfrac{\cfrac{\cfrac{\cfrac{\sigma(1)}{\sigma(3)}}{\sigma(6)*}\ \bowtie^{At}}{\sigma(8)}\qquad}{\cfrac{\sigma(10)*}{\sigma(12)}}\ \bowtie^{At}\qquad
\cfrac{\cfrac{\vdots\quad\vdots\quad\cfrac{\cfrac{\vdots}{\sigma(2)\ \sigma(8)}}{\sigma(9)}}{\sigma(2)\ \sigma(7)\ \sigma(8)\quad\sigma(11)}\ \bowtie^{\vee}}{\cfrac{\sigma(13)*}{\sigma(14)}}\ \bowtie^{\vee}
}{\cfrac{\sigma(15)*}{\sigma(16)}}
\end{array}
$$

*: p-sequents

$\sigma_{(k)}$ refers to the sequent at line (k) in Fig. 4

$\phi(\sigma) = \sigma$, for every p-sequent σ

$\phi(\sigma_{(16)}) = \sigma_{(15)}$

$\sigma_{(6)}: p$ $\sigma_{(5)}:$ $\sigma_{(10)}:$ $\sigma_{(13)}:$ $\sigma_{(15)}:$

Fig. 5. The model $\mathrm{Mod}(\mathcal{D}_T)$ (see Fig. 4).

Let $\mathcal{D}$ be an **FRJ**(G)-derivation of G. We show that we can extract from $\mathcal{D}$ a countermodel $\mathrm{Mod}(\mathcal{D})$ for G. We call *p-sequent* (*prime sequent*) any regular sequent occurring in $\mathcal{D}$ which is either an axiom or the conclusion of a join rule. Let $\mathrm{P}(\mathcal{D})$ be the set of p-sequents occurring in $\mathcal{D}$. Then, $\mathrm{Mod}(\mathcal{D})$ is the model $\langle \mathrm{P}(\mathcal{D}), \leq, \rho, V\rangle$ where:

$$\sigma_1 \leq \sigma_2 \text{ iff } \sigma_2 \mapsto_* \sigma_1 \qquad \rho \text{ is the minimum of } \mathrm{P}(\mathcal{D}) \qquad V(\sigma) = \mathrm{Lhs}(\sigma) \cap \mathcal{V}$$

We remark that ρ is well-defined. Indeed, since the root sequent of $\mathcal{D}$ is regular, there is $\rho \in \mathrm{P}(\mathcal{D})$ such that $\sigma_p \mapsto_* \rho$, for every $\sigma_p \in \mathrm{P}(\mathcal{D})$, hence ρ is the minimum. Moreover, by Lemma 1 and $(Cl5)$, $\sigma_1 \leq \sigma_2$ implies $V(\sigma_1) \subseteq V(\sigma_2)$, hence the definition of V is sound. For every regular sequent σ occurring in $\mathcal{D}$, let $\phi(\sigma)$ be the p-sequent immediately above σ, namely:

$$\phi(\sigma) = \sigma_p \quad \text{iff } \sigma_p \in \mathrm{P}(\mathcal{D}) \text{ and } \sigma_p \mapsto_* \sigma \text{ and}$$
$$\text{for every } \sigma'_p \in \mathrm{P}(\mathcal{D}), \sigma_p \mapsto_* \sigma'_p \mapsto_* \sigma \text{ implies } \sigma'_p = \sigma_p.$$

Note that, for $\sigma_p \in \mathrm{P}(\mathcal{D})$, we have $\phi(\sigma_p) = \sigma_p$. One can easily check that ϕ is a surjective map from the set of regular sequents of $\mathcal{D}$ onto $\mathrm{Mod}(\mathcal{D})$; moreover, if σ_1 and σ_2 are regular and $\sigma_1 \mapsto_* \sigma_2$, then $\phi(\sigma_2) \leq \phi(\sigma_1)$. In the next section we show that $\phi(\sigma) \Vdash \mathrm{Lhs}(\sigma)$ and $\phi(\sigma) \nVdash \mathrm{Rhs}(\sigma)$, and this proves the above property (S1).

Example 2. The models $\mathrm{Mod}(\mathcal{D}_S)$ and $\mathrm{Mod}(\mathcal{D}_T)$ and the related maps ϕ are shown in Figs. 3 and 5 respectively. The bottom world is the root and $\sigma < \sigma'$ iff the world σ is drawn below σ'. For each σ, we display the set $V(\sigma)$. As another example, in Fig. 6 we show the **FRJ**(K)-derivation and the related countermodel of the Kreisel-Putnam principle $K = (\neg a \supset b \vee c) \supset (\neg a \supset b) \vee (\neg a \supset c)$ [3]. $\Diamond$

By the above examples, it is clear that, whenever we search for an $\mathbf{FRJ}(G)$-derivation of G, we are also trying to build a countermodel for G in a backward style, starting from the final worlds down to the root.

We conclude the section by exhibiting a *weight* function wg on sequents of $\mathbf{FRJ}(G)$ such that, after a rule application, the weight of sequents decreases; accordingly, the naïve proof-search procedure always terminates, even if we do not implement any redundancy check. Let $\sigma_1 \mapsto_0 \sigma_2$ and, for $k \in \{1,2\}$, let

$$\Gamma_k = \mathrm{Lhs}(\sigma_k) \qquad C_k = \mathrm{Rhs}(\sigma_k) \qquad \overline{Cl}(\Gamma_k) = Cl(\Gamma_k) \cap \mathrm{SL}(G)$$

Let $\mathcal{R}$ be the rule applied to get σ_2 from σ_1. If $\mathcal{R}$ is not a join, then $|C_2| > |C_1|$, which implies $|G| - |C_2| < |G| - |C_1|$. By Lemma 1 and $(Cl6)$, $Cl(\Gamma_2) \subseteq Cl(\Gamma_1)$ hence $||\overline{Cl}(\Gamma_2)|| \leq ||\overline{Cl}(\Gamma_1)||$, where $||\_||$ is the cardinality function. If $\mathcal{R} = \supset_{\not\in}$ and $C_2 = A \supset B$, then $A \in \mathrm{SL}(G)$ and $A \in Cl(\Gamma_1) \setminus Cl(\Gamma_2)$, hence $||\overline{Cl}(\Gamma_2)|| < ||\overline{Cl}(\Gamma_1)||$. This suggests that we can define wg(σ) as the triple of non-negative integers:

$$\mathrm{wg}(\sigma) = \langle ||Cl(\Gamma) \cap \mathrm{SL}(G)||, \mathrm{tp}(\sigma), |G| - |C| \rangle$$

where tp$(\sigma) = 0$ if σ is a regular sequent, 1 otherwise. The component tp(σ) accommodates the case where σ is the conclusion of a join rule. By the previous remarks we get ($\prec$ is the standard lexicographic order on triples of integers):

Lemma 2. $\sigma_1 \mapsto \sigma_2$ *implies* $\langle 0,0,0 \rangle \preceq \mathrm{wg}(\sigma_2) \prec \mathrm{wg}(\sigma_1)$. $\qquad\square$

We can exploit wg to show that the depth of $\mathrm{Mod}(\mathcal{D})$ is $N = ||\mathrm{SL}(G)||$ at most. Indeed, let σ_1 and σ_2 be two p-sequents such that $\sigma_1 \mapsto \sigma_2$. Then, there is an irregular sequent σ' such that $\sigma_1 \mapsto \sigma' \mapsto \sigma_2$ and σ' is the conclusion of $\supset_{\not\in}$. Accordingly, if $\mathrm{wg}(\sigma_1) = \langle k_1, 0, \_ \rangle$ and $\mathrm{wg}(\sigma_2) = \langle k_2, 0, \_ \rangle$, we have $k_2 < k_1 \leq N$. Thus, at most N distinct p-sequents can occur along a branch of $\mathcal{D}$, and this settles a bound on the depth of $\mathrm{Mod}(\mathcal{D})$.

4 Soundness and Completeness

We prove that, given an $\mathbf{FRJ}(G)$-derivation $\mathcal{D}$ of G, $\mathrm{Mod}(\mathcal{D})$ is a countermodel for G. The *height* of a sequent σ in $\mathcal{D}$, denoted by $\mathrm{h}(\sigma)$, is the maximum length of a path from σ to an axiom sequent of $\mathcal{D}$.

Lemma 3. *Let* $\mathcal{D}$ *be an* $\mathbf{FRJ}(G)$-*derivation and* σ *a sequent occurring in* $\mathcal{D}$.

(i) *If* $\sigma = \Gamma \Rightarrow C$, *then* $\phi(\sigma) \Vdash \Gamma$ *and* $\phi(\sigma) \not\Vdash C$.
(ii) *If* $\sigma = \Sigma; \Theta \to C$, *let* $\sigma_p \in \mathrm{P}(\mathcal{D})$ *such that* $\sigma \mapsto \sigma_p$ *and* $\sigma_p \Vdash \Sigma \cap \mathrm{Sf}^-(C)$; *then* $\sigma_p \not\Vdash C$.

Proof. We prove the assertions by a main induction (IH1) on the height $\mathrm{h}(\sigma)$ of σ in $\mathcal{D}$. Let $\mathcal{R}$ be the rule applied to get σ; we proceed by a case analysis on $\mathcal{R}$, only detailing some representative cases.

$$K = K_0 \supset K_1 \qquad K_0 = \neg a \supset b \vee c \qquad K_1 = (\neg a \supset b) \vee (\neg a \supset c)$$
$$\text{SL}(K) = \{K_0, \neg a, a, b, c\} \qquad \text{SR}(K) = \{K, K_1, \neg a \supset b, \neg a \supset c, a, b, c, \bot\}$$

(1)	$\cdot\,; a, b, c, K_0, \neg a \to \bot$	$\text{Ax}_\to$
(2)	$\cdot\,; b, c, K_0, \neg a \to a$	$\text{Ax}_\to$
(3)	$a\,; b, c, K_0, \neg a \to \neg a$	$\supset_\in$ (1)
(4)	$c, \neg a \Rightarrow b$	$\bowtie^{\text{At}}$ (2)
(5)	$b, \neg a \Rightarrow c$	$\bowtie^{\text{At}}$ (2)
(6)	$a, b, c, K_0 \Rightarrow \bot$	$\bowtie^{\text{At}}$ (3)
(7)	$\cdot\,; c, K_0 \to \neg a \supset b$	$\supset_{\notin}$ (4)
(8)	$\cdot\,; b, K_0 \to \neg a \supset c$	$\supset_{\notin}$ (5)
(9)	$\cdot\,; b, c, K_0 \to \neg a$	$\supset_{\notin}$ (6)
(10)	$K_0 \Rightarrow K_1$	$\bowtie^\vee$ (7) (8) (9)
(11)	$K_0 \Rightarrow K$	$\supset_\in$ (10)

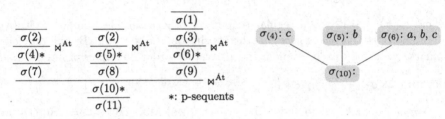

Fig. 6. The $\mathbf{FRJ}(K)$-derivation $\mathcal{D}_K$ of K and the model $\text{Mod}(\mathcal{D}_K)$.

Let $\mathcal{R} = \text{Ax}_\to$. Then (see Fig. 1) $\sigma = \cdot\,; \overline{\Gamma}^{\text{At}} \setminus \{C\}, \overline{\Gamma}^\supset \to C$ and $C \in \mathcal{V}^\perp$. Let $\Gamma^{\text{At}} = V(\sigma_p)$. Since $\sigma \mapsto \sigma_p$, by Lemma 1 and ($Cl5$) we get $\Gamma^{\text{At}} \subseteq \text{Lhs}(\sigma)$. This implies $C \notin \Gamma^{\text{At}}$, hence $\sigma_p \not\Vdash C$, and this proves (ii).

Let $\mathcal{R} = \vee$:

$$\dfrac{\sigma_1 = \Sigma_1\,; \Theta_1 \to C_1 \qquad \sigma_2 = \Sigma_2\,; \Theta_2 \to C_2}{\sigma = \Sigma_1, \Sigma_2\,; \Theta_1 \cap \Theta_2 \to C_1 \vee C_2} \vee \qquad \begin{array}{l} \Sigma_1 \subseteq \Sigma_2 \cup \Theta_2 \\ \Sigma_2 \subseteq \Sigma_1 \cup \Theta_1 \end{array}$$

By hypothesis $\sigma_p \Vdash (\Sigma_1 \cup \Sigma_2) \cap \text{Sf}^-(C_1 \vee C_2)$. Let $k \in \{1, 2\}$. Since $\sigma_k \mapsto \sigma_p$ (indeed, $\sigma_k \mapsto_0 \sigma$ and $\sigma \mapsto \sigma_p$) and $\sigma_p \Vdash \Sigma_k \cap \text{Sf}^-(C_k)$, by (IH1) applied to σ_k we get $\sigma_p \not\Vdash C_k$. Thus, $\sigma_p \not\Vdash C_1 \vee C_2$, which proves (ii).

Let $\mathcal{R}$ be the rule $\bowtie^{\text{At}}$ ($\Sigma^{\text{At}}, \Sigma^\supset, \Theta^{\text{At}}, \Theta^\supset$ are defined as in Fig. 1):

$$\dfrac{\ldots \; \sigma_j = \Sigma_j^{\text{At}}, \Sigma_j^\supset\,; \Theta_j^{\text{At}}, \Theta_j^\supset \to A_j \; \ldots}{\begin{array}{l}\sigma = \Sigma^{\text{At}}, \Theta^{\text{At}} \setminus \{C\}, \Sigma^\supset, \Theta^\supset \Rightarrow C \\ \Gamma^{\text{At}} = \Sigma^{\text{At}} \cup (\Theta^{\text{At}} \setminus \{C\}) \qquad \Gamma^\supset = \Sigma^\supset \cup \Theta^\supset \qquad \Gamma = \Gamma^{\text{At}} \cup \Gamma^\supset\end{array}} \bowtie^{\text{At}} \quad \begin{array}{l} j = 1 \ldots n \\ C \in \mathcal{V}^\perp \setminus \Sigma^{\text{At}} \end{array}$$

Note that $\sigma \in \text{P}(\mathcal{D})$, $\phi(\sigma) = \sigma$ and $V(\sigma) = \Gamma^{\text{At}}$. Since $C \notin \Gamma^{\text{At}}$, we get:

(P1) $\sigma \Vdash \Gamma^{\text{At}}$ and $\sigma \not\Vdash C$.

To complete the proof of (i), it remains to show that $\sigma \Vdash \Gamma^{\supset}$. To this aim, by a secondary induction hypothesis (IH2) on $|H|$ and $|A_j|$ we prove that:

(P2) $H \in \Gamma^{\supset}$ implies $\sigma \Vdash H$.
(P3) $\sigma \nVdash A_j$, for every $1 \leq j \leq n$.

Let $H \in \Gamma^{\supset}$. Then, there is $k \in \{1, \ldots, n\}$ such that $H = A_k \supset B$. Let $\sigma_p \in \mathrm{P}(\mathcal{D})$ be such that $\sigma \leq \sigma_p$ and $\sigma_p \Vdash A_k$; we show that $\sigma_p \Vdash B$. Let $\Gamma_p = \mathrm{Lhs}(\sigma_p)$; since $\sigma_p \mapsto_* \sigma$, by Lemma 1, $H \in \mathcal{C}l(\Gamma_p)$. Since $|A_k| < |H|$, we can apply (IH2) on (P3) and claim that $\sigma \nVdash A_k$, hence $\sigma_p \neq \sigma$ and $\mathrm{h}(\sigma_p) < \mathrm{h}(\sigma)$. By (IH1) applied to σ_p, we have $\sigma_p \Vdash \Gamma_p$ and, by ($\mathcal{C}l1$), $\sigma_p \Vdash H$, namely $\sigma_p \Vdash A_k \supset B$. Since $\sigma_p \Vdash A_k$, we conclude $\sigma_p \Vdash B$, and this proves (P2). Let $j \in \{1, \ldots, n\}$. Note that $\mathrm{h}(\sigma_j) < \mathrm{h}(\sigma)$, $\sigma_j \mapsto \sigma$ and $\sigma \in \mathrm{P}(\mathcal{D})$; thus, we can prove $\sigma \nVdash A_j$ by applying (IH1) on σ_j, provided that (†) $\sigma \Vdash (\Sigma_j^{\mathrm{At}} \cup \Sigma_j^{\supset}) \cap \mathrm{Sf}^-(A_j)$. Since $\Sigma_j^{\mathrm{At}} \subseteq V(\sigma)$, we get $\sigma \Vdash \Sigma_j^{\mathrm{At}}$. Let $H \in \Sigma_j^{\supset} \cap \mathrm{Sf}^-(A_j)$. Since $H \in \Gamma^{\supset}$ and $|H| < |A_j|$, by (IH2) on (P2) we get $\sigma \Vdash H$. Thus (†) holds and this concludes the proof of (P3). By (P1) and (P2), Point (i) follows $\qquad\square$

Let $\mathcal{D}$ be an $\mathbf{FRJ}(G)$-derivation of $\sigma = \Gamma \Rightarrow G$. By Lemma 3 (i), $\phi(\sigma) \Vdash \Gamma$ and $\phi(\sigma) \nVdash G$; this proves property (S1) (Sect. 3), from which the soundness of $\mathbf{FRJ}(G)$ follows. We prove Property (S2). If σ matches the hypothesis of (S2), then σ occurs in an $\mathbf{FRJ}(G)$-derivation $\mathcal{D}$ of a regular sequent. Let $\sigma_p \in \mathrm{P}(\mathcal{D})$ such that $\sigma \mapsto \sigma_p$ and, for every $\sigma_p' \in \mathrm{P}(\mathcal{D})$, $\sigma \mapsto \sigma_p' \mapsto_* \sigma_p$ implies $\sigma_p' = \sigma_p$; let $\Gamma_p = \mathrm{Lhs}(\sigma_p)$. By definition of $\mathbf{FRJ}(G)$, one can easily check that $\Sigma \subseteq \Gamma_p \subseteq \Sigma \cup \Theta$. By Lemma 3 (i) $\sigma_p \Vdash \Gamma_p$, which implies $\sigma_p \Vdash \Sigma$, hence $\sigma_p \Vdash \Sigma \cap \mathrm{Sf}^-(C)$; by Lemma 3 (ii), it follows that $\sigma_p \nVdash C$.

   To conclude this section, we sketch a semantic proof of completeness, which allows us to devise a complete proof-search strategy where redundancies are cut by exploiting subsumption. Let $\mathcal{K}$ be a countermodel for G. We write:

- $\mathcal{K}, \alpha \Vdash^* H$ iff $\mathcal{K}, \alpha \Vdash H$ and either $H \in \mathcal{V}$ or $H = A \supset B$ and $\mathcal{K}, \alpha \nVdash A$.
- $\mathcal{K}, \alpha \Vdash^* \Gamma$ iff $\mathcal{K}, \alpha \Vdash^* H$ for every $H \in \Gamma$.
- $\Lambda_\alpha = \{A \in \mathrm{SL}(G) \text{ s.t. } \mathcal{K}, \alpha \Vdash A\}$ and $\Lambda_\alpha^* = \{A \in \mathrm{SL}(G) \text{ s.t. } \mathcal{K}, \alpha \Vdash^* A\}$.
- $\Omega_\alpha = \{C \in \mathrm{SR}(G) \text{ s.t. } \mathcal{K}, \alpha \nVdash C\}$.

Note that $\Lambda_\alpha^* \subseteq \mathcal{V} \cup \mathcal{L}^{\supset}$; moreover, $\alpha \leq \beta$ implies $\Lambda_\alpha^* \subseteq \Lambda_\beta$, whereas $\Lambda_\alpha^* \subseteq \Lambda_\beta^*$ might not hold. One can easily prove that $\Lambda_\alpha = \mathcal{C}l(\Lambda_\alpha^*)$. We state the main lemma to prove the completeness of $\mathbf{FRJ}(G)$; by $\vdash_{\mathbf{FRJ}(G)} \sigma$ we mean that there exists an $\mathbf{FRJ}(G)$-derivation of σ.

Lemma 4. *Let $\mathcal{K} = \langle P, \leq, \rho, V \rangle$ be a countermodel for G and $\alpha \in P$. For every $C \in \Omega_\alpha$, we can choose Γ, Σ and Θ such that:*

(i) $\vdash_{\mathbf{FRJ}(G)} \sigma$, *where* $\sigma = \Gamma \Rightarrow C$.
(ii) *there is* $\beta \in P$ *such that* $\alpha \leq \beta$ *and* $\Lambda_\beta^* \subseteq \Gamma$.
(iii) $\vdash_{\mathbf{FRJ}(G)} \sigma$, *where* $\sigma = \Sigma; \Theta \to C$.
(iv) $\Sigma \subseteq \Lambda_\alpha^* \subseteq \Sigma \cup \Theta$.

Let S_α be the set of sequents selected in (i) and (iii) and S_α^* the union of S_β such that $\alpha \leq \beta$. Then, to prove $\sigma \in S_\alpha$ we only need to use sequents in S_α^*. □

The proof of the lemma hints the strategy one can follow to prove the goal G. For every $\alpha \in P$ and $C \in \Omega_\alpha$, let $\sigma_\alpha^{\Rightarrow}(C) = \Gamma \Rightarrow C$ and $\sigma_\alpha^{\rightarrow}(C) = \Sigma; \Theta \to C$ be the sequents of S_α matching Lemma 4. The derivations of $\sigma_\alpha^{\Rightarrow}(C)$ and $\sigma_\alpha^{\rightarrow}(C)$ can be built by visiting the model $\mathcal{K}$ downward. For each world α, we firstly consider the sequents $\sigma_\alpha^{\rightarrow}(C)$ and then the sequents $\sigma_\alpha^{\Rightarrow}(C)$, ordering the right formulas C in increasing order w.r.t. $|C|$. When we reach the root ρ, we get a derivation of $\sigma_\rho^{\Rightarrow}(G)$, and this proves the goal.

Example 3. In Fig. 7 we show a countermodel $\mathcal{K}$ for S (see Example 1) and an **FRJ**(S)-derivation of S built from $\mathcal{K}$. We start from the final worlds α and β of $\mathcal{K}$ and then we move downward. Since $\gamma < \alpha$, we can choose $\sigma_\gamma^{\Rightarrow}(\bot) = \sigma_\alpha^{\Rightarrow}(\bot)$ and $\sigma_\gamma^{\Rightarrow}(\neg p) = \sigma_\alpha^{\Rightarrow}(\neg p)$; however, since $p \notin \Lambda_\gamma^*$, we cannot set $\sigma_\gamma^{\rightarrow}(\neg p) = \sigma_\alpha^{\rightarrow}(\neg p)$, but we have to provide a different definition.   ◇

The plain proof-search procedure outlined in Example 1 suffers from the plethora of redundant sequents generated at each step. To reduce the size of the database DB of proved sequents, we introduce the following notions of subsumption:

$$\Gamma, \Gamma' \Rightarrow C \text{ subsumes } \Gamma \Rightarrow C \qquad \Sigma; \Theta, \Theta' \to C \text{ subsumes } \Sigma; \Theta \to C$$

Let us assume that DB contains two distinct sequents σ_1 and σ_2 such that σ_1 subsumes σ_2. If σ_2 matches point (ii) of Lemma 4, then σ_1 matches (ii) as well. Thus, if σ_2 corresponds to some $\sigma_\alpha^{\Rightarrow}(C)$, we can replace σ_2 with σ_1 and set $\sigma_\alpha^{\Rightarrow}(C) = \sigma_1$. By Lemma 4, there is no use in keeping both σ_1 and σ_2 in DB, but we can safely remove σ_2. A similar argument applies if σ_2 satisfies (iv). Accordingly, whenever in proof-search we derive a new sequent σ:

- If σ is subsumed by a sequent in DB, then σ is discarded (*forward subsumption*).
- We add σ to DB and we delete from DB all the sequents σ' which are subsumed by σ and all the sequents σ'' such that $\sigma' \mapsto \sigma''$ (*backward subsumption*).

Note that the DB's in Figs. 2, 4, 6 and 7 do not contain redundancies of this kind. We ascertained that, even with the formulas S and T of Example 1, subsumption tests considerably shrink the size of the corresponding DB's.

To evaluate the potential of our approach, we are developing `frj`, a Java implementation of our proof-search procedure based on the JTabWb framework [12]. So far we have implemented the plain forward strategy and the redundancy checks based on forward and backward subsumption. At each iteration of the main loop, `frj` applies all the possible instances of rules $\wedge$, $\vee$, $\supset_\in$ and $\supset_\notin$ involving at least a premise proved in the last step. To manage jump rules, `frj` maintains a list of *j-compatible* (jump-compatible) sets $\mathcal{J}_k$, namely $\mathcal{J}_k$ is a set of irregular sequents matching the first two side conditions of jump rules. At each iteration the list is updated resting on the set $\mathcal{I}$ of irregular sequents proved in the last iteration. In particular, each j-compatible set $\mathcal{J}_k$ is possibly extended

$$\begin{array}{l}
\alpha{:}\ p \\
\qquad \beta{:} \qquad \gamma{:} \\
\qquad\qquad \rho{:}
\end{array}$$

$$S = H \supset \neg\neg p \vee \neg p \qquad H = (\neg\neg p \supset p) \supset \neg p \vee p$$
$$\mathrm{S_L}(S) = \{\, H,\ \neg p \vee p,\ \neg\neg p,\ \neg p,\ p \,\}$$
$$\mathrm{S_R}(S) = \{\, S,\ \neg\neg p \vee \neg p,\ \neg\neg p \supset p,\ \neg\neg p,\ \neg p,\ p,\ \bot \,\}$$

$$\Lambda_\alpha^* = \{\, p,\ \neg\neg p \,\} \qquad \Lambda_\alpha = \Lambda_\alpha^* \cup \{\, \neg p \vee p,\ H \,\} \qquad \Omega_\alpha = \{\, \bot,\ \neg p \,\}$$
$$\Lambda_\beta^* = \{\, \neg p \,\} \qquad \Lambda_\beta = \Lambda_\beta^* \cup \{\, \neg p \vee p,\ H \,\} \qquad \Omega_\beta = \{\, \bot,\ p,\ \neg\neg p \,\}$$
$$\Lambda_\gamma^* = \Lambda_\gamma = \{\, H,\ \neg\neg p \,\} \qquad \Omega_\gamma = \{\, \bot,\ p,\ \neg p,\ \neg\neg p \supset p \,\} \qquad \Lambda_\rho^* = \Lambda_\rho = \{ H \} \qquad \Omega_\rho = \mathrm{S_R}(S)$$

(1)	$\cdot\,;\ p,\ H,\ \neg\neg p,\ \neg p \to \bot$	$\mathrm{Ax}_\to$	$\overrightarrow{\sigma_\alpha}(\bot)\ \bullet$
(2)	$p\,;\ H,\ \neg\neg p,\ \neg p \to \neg p$	$\supset_\in$ (1)	$\overrightarrow{\sigma_\alpha}(\neg p)\ \bullet$
(3)	$p,\ \neg\neg p \Rightarrow \bot$	$\bowtie^{\mathrm{At}}$ (2)	$\overrightarrow{\sigma_\alpha}(\bot)\ \bullet$
(4)	$p,\ \neg\neg p \Rightarrow \neg p$	$\supset_\in$ (3)	$\overrightarrow{\sigma_\alpha}(\neg p)$
(5)	$\cdot\,;\ H,\ \neg\neg p,\ \neg p \to p$	$\mathrm{Ax}_\to$	$\overrightarrow{\sigma_\beta}(p)\ \bullet$
(6)	$\neg p\,;\ p,\ H,\ \neg\neg p \to \neg\neg p$	$\supset_\in$ (1)	$\overrightarrow{\sigma_\beta}(\neg\neg p)$
(7)	$\neg p \Rightarrow \bot$	$\bowtie^{\mathrm{At}}$ (5)	$\overrightarrow{\sigma_\beta}(\bot)\ \bullet$
(8)	$\neg p \Rightarrow p$	$\bowtie^{\mathrm{At}}$ (5)	$\overrightarrow{\sigma_\beta}(p)$
(9)	$\neg p \Rightarrow \neg\neg p$	$\supset_\in$ (7)	$\overrightarrow{\sigma_\beta}(\neg\neg p)$
(10)	$\cdot\,;\ H,\ \neg\neg p \to \neg p$	$\supset_\notin$ (3)	$\overrightarrow{\sigma_\gamma}(\neg p)\ \bullet$
(11)	$\neg\neg p\,;\ H,\ \neg p \to \neg\neg p \supset p$	$\supset_\in$ (5)	$\overrightarrow{\sigma_\gamma}(\neg\neg p \supset p)\ \bullet$
(12)	$H,\ \neg\neg p \Rightarrow p$	$\bowtie^{\mathrm{At}}$ (10) (11)	$\overrightarrow{\sigma_\gamma}(p)\ \bullet$
(13)	$H,\ \neg\neg p \Rightarrow \neg\neg p \supset p$	$\supset_\in$ (12)	$\overrightarrow{\sigma_\gamma}(\neg\neg p \supset p)$
(14)	$\cdot\,;\ H \to \neg\neg p$	$\supset_\notin$ (7)	$\overrightarrow{\sigma_\rho}(\neg\neg p)\ \bullet$
(15)	$\cdot\,;\ H \to \neg\neg p \supset p$	$\supset_\notin$ (12)	$\overrightarrow{\sigma_\rho}(\neg\neg p \supset p)\ \bullet$
(16)	$\cdot\,;\ H \to \neg\neg p \vee \neg p$	$\vee$ (10) (14)	$\overrightarrow{\sigma_\rho}(\neg\neg p \vee \neg p)$
(17)	$H\,;\ \cdot \to S$	$\supset_\in$ (16)	$\overrightarrow{\sigma_\rho}(S)$
(18)	$H \Rightarrow \neg\neg p \vee \neg p$	$\bowtie^{\vee}$ (10) (14) (15)	$\overrightarrow{\sigma_\rho}(\neg\neg p \vee \neg p)\ \bullet$
(19)	$H \Rightarrow S$	$\supset_\in$ (18)	$\overrightarrow{\sigma_\rho}(S)$ **goal**

$$\overrightarrow{\sigma_\beta}(\bot) = \overrightarrow{\sigma_\gamma}(\bot) = \overrightarrow{\sigma_\rho}(\bot) = \overrightarrow{\sigma_\alpha}(\bot) \qquad \overrightarrow{\sigma_\gamma}(p) = \overrightarrow{\sigma_\rho}(p) = \overrightarrow{\sigma_\beta}(p)$$
$$\overset{\Rightarrow}{\sigma_\gamma}(\bot) = \overset{\Rightarrow}{\sigma_\rho}(\bot) = \overset{\Rightarrow}{\sigma_\alpha}(\bot) \qquad \overset{\Rightarrow}{\sigma_\gamma}(\neg p) = \overset{\Rightarrow}{\sigma_\rho}(\neg p) = \overset{\Rightarrow}{\sigma_\alpha}(\neg p) \qquad \overrightarrow{\sigma_\rho}(\neg p) = \overrightarrow{\sigma_\gamma}(\neg p)$$
$$\overset{\Rightarrow}{\sigma_\rho}(p) = \overset{\Rightarrow}{\sigma_\beta}(p) \qquad \overset{\Rightarrow}{\sigma_\rho}(\neg\neg p) = \overset{\Rightarrow}{\sigma_\beta}(\neg\neg p) \qquad \overset{\Rightarrow}{\sigma_\rho}(\neg\neg p \supset p) = \overset{\Rightarrow}{\sigma_\gamma}(\neg\neg p \supset p)$$

$\bullet$: needed to prove the goal

Fig. 7. $\mathbf{FRJ}(S)$-derivation of S built from a contermodel for S.

with elements of $\mathcal{I}$ and the new j-compatible sets issued from $\mathcal{I}$ are added. For every j-compatible set $\mathcal{J}_k$, every possible jump rule having premises $\mathcal{J}_k$ is applied. We also exploit backward subsumption to optimize the implementation of jump rules: whenever backward subsumption is detected, every subsumed irregular sequent occurring in a j-compatible set is replaced by the subsuming one (one can easily check that such a replacement does not affect completeness).

5   Related and Future Work

We have introduced a forward calculus to derive the unprovability of a goal formula G in IPL. As discussed in Sect. 3, whenever we search for an $\mathbf{FRJ}(G)$-derivation of G, we are also trying to build a countermodel for G top-down, starting from the final worlds down to the root. One of the advantages of forward vs. backward reasoning is that, provided one implements suitable redundancy checks, derivations are more concise since sequents are reused and not duplicated. As a consequence, the obtained models are in general compact and do not contain redundant worlds. For instance, the models in Figs. 3, 5 and 6 are the minimal countermodels for the formulas S, T and K respectively. The model in Fig. 5 is particularly significant since it is not a tree, hence it cannot be obtained by the standard proof-search procedures (see, e.g., [1,8,9,11,13,17,18]), which only generate tree-shaped models. We can prove that, as in the case of the calculus **LSJ** [9], the generated models have minimal depth. Moreover, a comparison between frj and the prover lsj for **LSJ**, performed on 1000 random generated formulas, shows that the former generates smaller countermodels than the latter. As a significant example, let us consider the one-variable formulas N_i of the Nishimura family [3], which are not valid in IPL:

$$N_1 = p \qquad N_{2n+3} = N_{2n+1} \vee N_{2n+2}$$
$$N_2 = \neg p \qquad N_{2n+4} = N_{2n+3} \supset N_{2n+1}$$

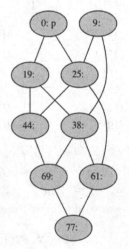

For such formulas frj generates the standard "tower-like" minimum countermodel [3] (for N_{17} see the outcome in Fig. 8) while lsj generates tree-like models with several redundancies.

While a success in proof-search in $\mathbf{FRJ}(G)$ yields a countermodel for G, when proof-search fails we get a saturated database DB, which can be understood as a "proof-certificate" of the validity of G in IPL (a dual remark for a forward calculus for IPL has been issued in [16]). An interesting matter is the analysis of the information content of such a DB; in particular, we are investigating how to exploit the information in DB to build a derivation of G.

As for frj, the main source of inefficiency is the application of join rules. Indeed, the prover must exhaustively check the side conditions of join rules application for every subset of the set of proved irregular sequents. So far, to reduce the search-space we have exploited conditions (PS3) and (PS4) of Sect. 3. We aim at devising more clever strategies to cut down the sets of premises. Finally, we plan to investigate the applicability of the method to other logics.

Fig. 8. Countermodel for N_{17}

References

1. Avellone, A., Fiorentini, C., Momigliano, A.: A semantical analysis of focusing and contraction in intuitionistic logic. Fundam. Inform. **140**(3–4), 247–262 (2015)
2. Brock-Nannestad, T., Chaudhuri, K.: Disproving using the inverse method by iterative refinement of finite approximations. In: Nivelle, H. (ed.) TABLEAUX 2015. LNCS, vol. 9323, pp. 153–168. Springer, Cham (2015). doi:10.1007/978-3-319-24312-2_11
3. Chagrov, A., Zakharyaschev, M.: Modal Logic. Oxford University Press, Oxford (1997)
4. Chaudhuri, K., Pfenning, F.: A focusing inverse method theorem prover for first-order linear logic. In: Nieuwenhuis, R. (ed.) CADE 2005. LNCS, vol. 3632, pp. 69–83. Springer, Heidelberg (2005). doi:10.1007/11532231_6
5. Chaudhuri, K., Pfenning, F., Price, G.: A logical characterization of forward and backward chaining in the inverse method. In: Furbach, U., Shankar, N. (eds.) IJCAR 2006. LNCS, vol. 4130, pp. 97–111. Springer, Heidelberg (2006). doi:10.1007/11814771_9
6. Degtyarev, A., Voronkov, A.: The inverse method. In: Robinson, J.A., et al. (eds.) Handbook of Automated Reasoning, pp. 179–272. Elsevier and MIT Press (2001)
7. Donnelly, K., Gibson, T., Krishnaswami, N., Magill, S., Park, S.: The inverse method for the logic of bunched implications. In: Baader, F., Voronkov, A. (eds.) LPAR 2005. LNCS (LNAI), vol. 3452, pp. 466–480. Springer, Heidelberg (2005). doi:10.1007/978-3-540-32275-7_31
8. Ferrari, M., Fiorentini, C., Fiorino, G.: FCUBE: an efficient prover for intuitionistic propositional logic. In: Fermüller, C.G., Voronkov, A. (eds.) LPAR 2010. LNCS, vol. 6397, pp. 294–301. Springer, Heidelberg (2010). doi:10.1007/978-3-642-16242-8_21
9. Ferrari, M., Fiorentini, C., Fiorino, G.: Contraction-free linear depth sequent calculi for intuitionistic propositional logic with the subformula property and minimal depth counter-models. J. Autom. Reason. **51**(2), 129–149 (2013)
10. Ferrari, M., Fiorentini, C., Fiorino, G.: A terminating evaluation-driven variant of G3i. In: Galmiche, D., Larchey-Wendling, D. (eds.) TABLEAUX 2013. LNCS (LNAI), vol. 8123, pp. 104–118. Springer, Heidelberg (2013). doi:10.1007/978-3-642-40537-2_11
11. Ferrari, M., Fiorentini, C., Fiorino, G.: An evaluation-driven decision procedure for G3i. ACM Trans. Comput. Log. (TOCL) **16**(1), 8:1–8:37 (2015)
12. Ferrari, M., Fiorentini, C., Fiorino, G.: JTabWb: a Java framework for implementing terminating sequent and tableau calculi. Fundam. Inform. **150**, 119–142 (2017)
13. Goré, R., Postniece, L.: Combining derivations and refutations for cut-free completeness in bi-intuitionistic logic. J. Log. Comput. **20**(1), 233–260 (2010)
14. Kovács, L., Mantsivoda, A., Voronkov, A.: The inverse method for many-valued logics. In: Castro, F., Gelbukh, A., González, M. (eds.) MICAI 2013. LNCS, vol. 8265, pp. 12–23. Springer, Heidelberg (2013). doi:10.1007/978-3-642-45114-0_2
15. Maslov, S.J.: An invertible sequential version of the constructive predicate calculus. Zap. Naučn. Sem. Leningrad. Otdel. Mat. Inst. Steklov. (LOMI), **4**, 96–111 (1967)
16. McLaughlin, S., Pfenning, F.: Imogen: focusing the polarized inverse method for intuitionistic propositional logic. In: Cervesato, I., Veith, H., Voronkov, A. (eds.) LPAR 2008. LNCS (LNAI), vol. 5330, pp. 174–181. Springer, Heidelberg (2008). doi:10.1007/978-3-540-89439-1_12

17. Negri, S.: Proofs and countermodels in non-classical logics. Log. Univers. **8**(1), 25–60 (2014)
18. Pinto, L., Dyckhoff, R.: Loop-free construction of counter-models for intuitionistic propositional logic. In: Behara, et al. (eds.) Symposia Gaussiana, Conference A, pp. 225–232. Walter de Gruyter, Berlin (1995)
19. Skura, T.: A complete syntactical characterization of the intuitionistic logic. Reports Math. Log. **75**(8), 75–80 (1989)

Hypersequent Calculi for Lewis' Conditional Logics with Uniformity and Reflexivity

Marianna Girlando[1], Björn Lellmann[2]([⊠]), Nicola Olivetti[1], and Gian Luca Pozzato[3]

[1] Aix Marseille Université, CNRS, ENSAM, Université de Toulon, LSIS UMR 7296, 13397 Marseille, France
{marianna.girlando,nicola.olivetti}@univ-amu.fr
[2] Technische Universität Wien, Vienna, Austria
lellmann@logic.at
[3] Dip. di Informatica, Universitá di Torino, Turin, Italy
gianluca.pozzato@unito.it

Abstract. We present the first internal calculi for Lewis' conditional logics characterized by uniformity and reflexivity, including non-standard internal hypersequent calculi for a number of extensions of the logic VTU. These calculi allow for syntactic proofs of cut elimination and known connections to S5. We then introduce standard internal hypersequent calculi for all these logics, in which sequents are enriched by additional structures to encode plausibility formulas as well as diamond formulas. These calculi provide both a decision procedure for the respective logics and constructive countermodel extraction from a failed proof search attempt.

1 Introduction

Conditional logics have a long history going back, e.g., to the works of Stalnaker, Lewis, Nute, Chellas, Burgess, Pollock in the 60's–70's [3,4,13,14,18]. In his seminal works Lewis proposed a formalization of conditional logics to capture counterfactual and other hypothetical conditionals that cannot be accommodated by the material implication of classical logic [13]. Conditional logics have since found an interest in several fields of knowledge representation, from reasoning about prototypical properties and nonmonotonic reasoning [9] to modeling belief change. A successful attempt to relate conditional logic and belief update (as opposite to belief revision) was carried out by Grahne [8], who established a precise mapping between belief update operators and Lewis' logic VCU. The relation is expressed by the so-called *Ramsey's Rule*:

$A \circ B \to C$ holds if and only if $A \to (B \mathrel{\Box\!\!\to} C)$ holds

Supported by the Project TICAMORE ANR-16-CE91-0002-01, by the EU under Marie Skłodowska-Curie Grant Agreement No. [660047], and by the project "ExceptionOWL", Università di Torino and Compagnia di San Paolo, call 2014 "Excellent (young) PI".

R.A. Schmidt and C. Nalon (Eds.): TABLEAUX 2017, LNAI 10501, pp. 131–148, 2017.
DOI: 10.1007/978-3-319-66902-1_8

where the operator $\circ$ is any *update* operator satisfying Katsuno and Mendelzon's postulates. The relation means that C is entailed by "A updated by B" if and only if the conditional $B \mathbin{\square\!\!\rightarrow} C$ is entailed by A. In this sense it can be said that the conditional $B \mathbin{\square\!\!\rightarrow} C$ expresses an hypothetical update of a piece of information A.

The family of logics studied by Lewis in [13] is semantically characterized by *sphere models*, where each world x is equipped with a set of nested sets of worlds $\mathsf{SP}(x)$. Each set in $\mathsf{SP}(x)$ is called a *sphere*: the intuition is that concerning x, worlds in inner spheres are more plausible than worlds belonging only to outer spheres. Lewis takes as primitive the *comparative plausibility* connective $\preccurlyeq$, with a formula $A \preccurlyeq B$ meaning "A is at least as plausible as B". The conditional $A \mathbin{\square\!\!\rightarrow} B$ is then defined as "A is impossible or $A \wedge \neg B$ is less plausible than A". Vice versa, $\preccurlyeq$ can be defined in terms of $\mathbin{\square\!\!\rightarrow}$.

In this paper we continue our proof-theoretic investigation of the family of Lewis' logics, concentrating on the logics characterized by two properties: (i) *Uniformity*: all worlds have the same set of accessible worlds, where the worlds accessible from a world x are those belonging to any sphere $\alpha \in \mathsf{SP}(x)$; (ii) *Total reflexivity*: every world x belongs to some sphere $\alpha \in \mathsf{SP}(x)$. The basic logic is $\mathbb{VTU}$; we will then consider some of its extensions, including the above mentioned $\mathbb{VCU}$. It is worth mentioning that equivalent logics are those of Comparative Concept Similarity studied in the context of ontologies [17]. These logics contain a connective $\rightleftharpoons$, which allows to express, e.g.,

$$PicassoPainting \sqsubseteq BraquePainting \rightleftharpoons GiottoPainting$$

asserting that "Picasso's paintings are more similar to Braque's paintings than to Giotto's ones". The semantics is provided in terms of Distance Space Models, defined as a set of worlds equipped with a distance function. It turns out that the basic logic of Comparative Concept Similarity coincides with Lewis' logic $\mathbb{VWU}$ and the one defined by "minspace" Distance Models coincides with $\mathbb{VCU}$, so that Distance Space Models provide an alternative simple and natural semantics for conditional logics with uniformity [1,17].

Here we investigate *internal calculi* for logics extending $\mathbb{VTU}$, i.e., calculi where each configuration of a derivation corresponds to a formula of the corresponding logic, in contrast to external calculi which make use of extra-logical elements (such as labels, terms and relations on them). Ideally, we seek calculi with the following features: (i) they should be *standard*, i.e., each connective is handled by a finite set of rules with a finte and fixed set of premises; (ii) they should be *modular*, i.e., it should be possible to obtain calculi for stronger logics by adding independent rules to a base calculus; (iii) they should have good proof-theoretical properties, such as a syntactic proof of cut admissibility; finally (iv) they should provide a decision procedure for the respective logics. In our opinion requirement (i) is particularly important: a standard calculus provides a self-explanatory presentation of the logic, thus a kind of proof-theoretic semantics.

In previous work [7], we defined calculi with many of these properties for weaker logics of the Lewis' family. For the logics with *uniformity* to the best of our knowledge no internal calculi are known; the only known external calculi for these adopt a hybrid language and a relational semantics [6]. We also consider logics with *absoluteness*, a property stronger than uniformity stating that all worlds have the same system of spheres. It is unlikely that sequents, even extended as in [7], are sufficient to capture logics with uniformity: Since modal logic S5 can be embedded into $\mathbb{VTU}$, a sequent calculus for the latter would most probably also yield a sequent calculus for S5. The existence of such a calculus, however, would be very surprising. We therefore adopt the framework of *hypersequents* [2], where the basic objects are multisets of sequents.

We first provide a non-standard hypersequent calculus for $\mathbb{VTU}$ and its extensions and syntactically prove cut-elimination and hence completeness. We then show that by translating $\Box A$ as $\bot \preccurlyeq \neg A$ the calculi - restricted to such formulas - correspond to known hypersequent calculi for S5. Further, we construct standard calculi for all the logics by enriching the hypersequents with additional structural connectives encoding plausibility and "possible" formulas respectively. The obtained standard calculi provide decision procedures for the respective logics. Finally, we give a direct semantic completeness proof for the logics without absoluteness, by considering the invertible version of the rules and constructing a countermodel from a failed attempt at proof search. Thus, the calculi can also be used for countermodel generation, a task of independent interest.

2   Preliminaries

We consider the *conditional logics* of [13]. The set of *conditional formulae* is given by $A :: = p \mid \bot \mid A \rightarrow A \mid A \preccurlyeq A$, where $p \in \mathcal{V}$ is a propositional variable. We define the boolean connectives $\land, \lor, \top$ in terms of $\bot$ and $\rightarrow$ as usual. Intuitively, a formula $A \preccurlyeq B$ is interpreted as "A is at least as plausible as B". Lewis' *counterfactual implication* $\Box\!\!\rightarrow$ is defined by $A \mathbin{\Box\!\!\rightarrow} B \equiv (\bot \preccurlyeq A) \lor \neg((A \land \neg B) \preccurlyeq A)$, whereas the *outer modality* $\Box$ is defined by $\Box A \equiv (\bot \preccurlyeq \neg A)$. The logics we consider are defined as follows:

Definition 1. *A* universal sphere model *(or* model*) is a triple* $\langle W, \mathsf{SP}, [\![.]\!]\rangle$, *consisting of a non-empty set* W *of elements, called* worlds, *a mapping* $\mathsf{SP} : W \rightarrow 2^{2^W}$, *and a propositional valuation* $[\![.]\!] : \mathcal{V} \rightarrow 2^W$. *Elements of* $\mathsf{SP}(x)$ *are called* spheres. *We assume the following conditions:*

- *for every* $\alpha \in \mathsf{SP}(w)$ *we have* $\alpha \neq \emptyset$ *(non-emptiness)*
- *for every* $\alpha, \beta \in \mathsf{SP}(w)$ *we have* $\alpha \subseteq \beta$ *or* $\beta \subseteq \alpha$ *(sphere nesting)*
- *for all* $w \in W$ *we have* $\mathsf{SP}(w) \neq \emptyset$ *(normality)*
- *for all* $w \in W$ *we have* $w \in \bigcup \mathsf{SP}(w)$ *(total reflexivity)*
- *for all* $w, v \in W$ *we have* $\bigcup \mathsf{SP}(w) = \bigcup \mathsf{SP}(v)$ *(uniformity)*

The valuation $[\![.]\!]$ *is extended to all formulae by:* $[\![\bot]\!] = \emptyset$; $[\![A \rightarrow B]\!] = (W - [\![A]\!]) \cup [\![B]\!]$; $[\![A \preccurlyeq B]\!] = \{w \in W \mid \text{for all } \alpha \in \mathsf{SP}(w). \text{ if } [\![B]\!] \cap \alpha \neq \emptyset, \text{ then } [\![A]\!] \cap \alpha \neq \emptyset\}$. *We also write* $w \Vdash A$ *instead of* $w \in [\![A]\!]$ *as well as* $\alpha \Vdash^\forall A$ *for* $\forall x \in \alpha. \, x \Vdash A$ *and* $\alpha \Vdash^\exists A$ *for* $\exists x \in \alpha. \, x \Vdash A$[1]. *Validity and satisfiability of formulae in a class of models are defined as usual. Conditional logic* $\mathbb{VTU}$ *is the set of formulae valid in all universal sphere models.*

---

[1] Using this notation we thus have: $x \Vdash A \preccurlyeq B$ iff for all $\alpha \in \mathsf{SP}(x). \; \alpha \Vdash^\forall \neg B$ or $\alpha \Vdash^\exists A$.

Table 1. Lewis' logics and axioms.

$(CPR) \dfrac{\vdash B \to A}{\vdash A \preccurlyeq B}$	$(CPA) (A \preccurlyeq A \vee B) \vee (B \preccurlyeq A \vee B)$
$(TR) (A \preccurlyeq B) \wedge (B \preccurlyeq C) \to (A \preccurlyeq C)$	$(CO) (A \preccurlyeq B) \vee (B \preccurlyeq A)$
$(N) \neg(\perp \preccurlyeq \top)$	$(T) (\perp \preccurlyeq \neg A) \to A$
$(U1) \neg(\perp \preccurlyeq A) \to (\perp \preccurlyeq (\perp \preccurlyeq A))$	$(U2) (\perp \preccurlyeq \neg A) \to (\perp \preccurlyeq \neg(\perp \preccurlyeq \neg A))$
$(W) A \to (A \preccurlyeq \top)$	$(C) (A \preccurlyeq \top) \to A$
$(A1) (A \preccurlyeq B) \to (\perp \preccurlyeq \neg(A \preccurlyeq B))$	$(A2) \neg(A \preccurlyeq B) \to (\perp \preccurlyeq (A \preccurlyeq B))$

$$\mathcal{A}_{\mathbf{VTU}} := \{(CPR), (CPA), (TR), (CO), (N), (T), (U1), (U2)\}$$

$$\mathcal{A}_{\mathbf{VWU}} := \mathcal{A}_{\mathbf{VTU}} \cup \{(W)\} \qquad \mathcal{A}_{\mathbf{VCU}} := \mathcal{A}_{\mathbf{VTU}} \cup \{(W), (C)\} \qquad \mathcal{A}_{\mathbf{VTA}} := \mathcal{A}_{\mathbf{VTU}} \cup \{(A1), (A2)\}$$

$$\mathcal{A}_{\mathbf{VWA}} := \mathcal{A}_{\mathbf{VTU}} \cup \{(W), (A1), (A2)\} \qquad \mathcal{A}_{\mathbf{VCA}} := \mathcal{A}_{\mathbf{VTU}} \cup \{(W), (C), (A1), (A2)\}$$

Extensions of $\mathbf{VTU}$ are defined by additional conditions on the class of models, namely:

- *weak centering*: for all $\alpha \in \mathsf{SP}(w)$ we have $w \in \alpha$;
- *centering*: for all $w \in W$ we have $\{w\} \in \mathsf{SP}(w)$;
- *absoluteness*: for all $w, v \in W$ we have $\mathsf{SP}(w) = \mathsf{SP}(v)$.

Extensions of $\mathbf{VTU}$ are denoted by concatenating letters for these properties: $\mathbb{W}$ for weak centering, $\mathbb{C}$ for centering, and $\mathbb{A}$ for absoluteness. We consider the following systems[2]:

$\mathbf{VTU}$	$\mathbf{VTA}$: $\mathbf{VTU}$ + *absoluteness*
$\mathbf{VWU}$: $\mathbf{VTU}$ + *weak centering*	$\mathbf{VWA}$: $\mathbf{VTA}$ + *weak centering*
$\mathbf{VCU}$: $\mathbf{VTU}$ + *centering*	$\mathbf{VCA}$: $\mathbf{VTA}$ + *centering*

These logics can be characterized by axioms in a Hilbert-style system [13, Chap. 6]. The modal axioms in the language with only the comparative plausibility operator are given in Table 1 ($\vee$ and $\wedge$ bind stronger than $\preccurlyeq$). Propositional axioms and rules are standard.

3   Hypersequent Calculi

In this section we introduce calculi for $\mathbf{VTU}$ and extensions. We call a calculus *standard* if (a) it has a finite number of rules and (b) each rule has a finite and fixed number of premises. With respect to this definition, the calculi introduced in this section are *non-standard*, whereas the calculi we introduce in Sect. 6 are standard.

Our calculi are based on hypersequents, where as usual a *sequent* is a pair consisting of two multisets of formulae, written as $\Gamma \Rightarrow \Delta$.

---

[2] Observe that $\mathbf{VTA}$+*weak centering* collapses to S5, since in any model over a set of worlds W it must be for all $w \in W$, $\mathsf{SP}(w) = \{W\}$. Furthermore, $\mathbf{VTA}$ + *centering* collapses to Classical Logic, as in any model the set of worlds must be a singleton $\{w\}$ and $\mathsf{SP}(w) = \{\{w\}\}$, so that $A \preccurlyeq B$ is equivalent to the material implication $B \to A$. See also Proposition 16 below..

$$\frac{}{\mathcal{G} \mid \Gamma, p \Rightarrow p, \Delta} \text{ init} \qquad \frac{}{\mathcal{G} \mid \Gamma, \bot \Rightarrow \Delta} \bot_L \qquad \frac{\mathcal{G} \mid \Gamma, A, A \Rightarrow \Delta}{\mathcal{G} \mid \Gamma, A \Rightarrow \Delta} \text{ ICL} \qquad \frac{\mathcal{G} \mid \Gamma \Rightarrow A, A, \Delta}{\mathcal{G} \mid \Gamma \Rightarrow A, \Delta} \text{ ICR}$$

$$\frac{\mathcal{G} \mid \Gamma, B \Rightarrow \Delta \quad \mathcal{G} \mid \Gamma \Rightarrow A, \Delta}{\mathcal{G} \mid \Gamma, A \to B \Rightarrow \Delta} \to_L \qquad \frac{\mathcal{G} \mid \Gamma, A \Rightarrow B, \Delta}{\mathcal{G} \mid \Gamma \Rightarrow A \to B, \Delta} \to_R$$

$$\frac{\{\mathcal{G} \mid \Sigma \Rightarrow \Pi \mid C_k \Rightarrow [D]_1^{k-1}, [A]_1^n : k \leq m\} \quad \cup \quad \{\mathcal{G} \mid \Sigma \Rightarrow \Pi \mid B_k \Rightarrow [D]_1^m, [A]_1^n : k \leq n\}}{\mathcal{G} \mid \Sigma, [C \preccurlyeq D]_1^m \Rightarrow [A \preccurlyeq B]_1^n, \Pi} R_{m,n}$$

$$\frac{\{\mathcal{G} \mid \Sigma \Rightarrow \Pi \mid \Omega \Rightarrow \Theta \mid C_k \Rightarrow [D]_1^{k-1} : k \leq m\} \quad \cup \quad \{\mathcal{G} \mid \Sigma \Rightarrow \Pi \mid \Omega \Rightarrow [D]_1^m, \Theta\}}{\mathcal{G} \mid \Sigma, [C \preccurlyeq D]_1^m \Rightarrow \Pi \mid \Omega \Rightarrow \Theta} \text{trf}_m$$

$$\frac{\{\mathcal{G} \mid \Sigma \Rightarrow \Pi \mid C_k \Rightarrow [D]_1^{k-1} : k \leq m\} \quad \cup \quad \{\mathcal{G} \mid \Sigma \Rightarrow [D]_1^m, \Pi\}}{\mathcal{G} \mid \Sigma, [C \preccurlyeq D]_1^m \Rightarrow \Pi} T_m$$

$$\frac{\{\mathcal{G} \mid \Sigma \Rightarrow \Pi \mid C_k \Rightarrow [D]_1^{k-1}, [A]_1^n : k \leq m\} \quad \cup \quad \{\mathcal{G} \mid \Sigma \Rightarrow [D]_1^m, [A]_1^n, \Pi\}}{\mathcal{G} \mid \Sigma, [C \preccurlyeq D]_1^m \Rightarrow [A \preccurlyeq B]_1^n, \Pi} W_{m,n}$$

$$\frac{\mathcal{G} \mid \Sigma, C \Rightarrow \Pi \quad \mathcal{G} \mid \Sigma \Rightarrow D, \Pi}{\mathcal{G} \mid \Sigma, C \preccurlyeq D \Rightarrow \Pi} R_C \qquad \frac{\mathcal{G} \mid \Sigma \Rightarrow A, \Pi}{\mathcal{G} \mid \Sigma \Rightarrow A \preccurlyeq B, \Pi} R_W \qquad \frac{\mathcal{G} \mid \Sigma, \Gamma \Rightarrow \Pi, \Delta \mid \Omega \Rightarrow \Theta}{\mathcal{G} \mid \Sigma \Rightarrow \Pi \mid \Omega, \Gamma \Rightarrow \Theta, \Delta} \text{spl}$$

$$\frac{\mathcal{G} \mid \Sigma \Rightarrow \Pi \mid \Omega, C \preccurlyeq D \Rightarrow \Theta}{\mathcal{G} \mid \Sigma, C \preccurlyeq D \Rightarrow \Pi \mid \Omega \Rightarrow \Theta} \text{abs}_L \qquad \frac{\mathcal{G} \mid \Sigma \Rightarrow \Pi \mid \Omega \Rightarrow A \preccurlyeq B, \Theta}{\mathcal{G} \mid \Sigma \Rightarrow A \preccurlyeq B, \Pi \mid \Omega \Rightarrow \Theta} \text{abs}_R$$

$$\mathsf{H}_{\text{VTU}} : \{\text{init}, \bot_L, \text{ICL}, \text{ICR}, \to_L, \to_R\} \cup \{R_{m,n} : m \geq 0, n \geq 1\} \cup \{\text{trf}_m : m \geq 1\} \cup \{T_m : m \geq 1\}$$

$$\mathsf{H}_{\text{VWU}} : \mathsf{H}_{\text{VTU}} \cup \{W_{m,n} : m + n \geq 1\} \qquad \mathsf{H}_{\text{VCU}} : \mathsf{H}_{\text{VTU}} \cup \{R_C, R_W\}$$

$$\mathsf{H}_{\text{VTA}} : \mathsf{H}_{\text{VTU}} \cup \{\text{abs}_L, \text{abs}_R\} \quad \mathsf{H}_{\text{VWA}} : \mathsf{H}_{\text{VWU}} \cup \{\text{abs}_L, \text{abs}_R\} \quad \mathsf{H}_{\text{VCA}} : \mathsf{H}_{\text{VCU}} \cup \{\text{abs}_L, \text{abs}_R, \text{spl}\}$$

Fig. 1. The hypersequent calculi for VTU and extensions.

Definition 2. *A* hypersequent *is a non-empty multiset of sequents, written* $\Gamma_1 \Rightarrow \Delta_1 \mid \ldots \mid \Gamma_n \Rightarrow \Delta_n$, *where* $n \geq 1$ *is the cardinality of the multiset. The* conditional formula interpretation *of a hypersequent is*

$$\iota_{\preccurlyeq}(\Gamma_1 \Rightarrow \Delta_1 \mid \ldots \mid \Gamma_n \Rightarrow \Delta_n) := \square(\bigwedge \Gamma_1 \to \bigvee \Delta_1) \vee \ldots \vee \square(\bigwedge \Gamma_n \to \bigvee \Delta_n)$$

where $\square$ *is the* outer modality *defined by* $\square A \equiv (\bot \preccurlyeq \neg A)$.

The rules of the calculi $\mathsf{H}_{\mathcal{L}}$ extend the calculi from [12] to the hypersequent setting and are given in Fig. 1. These calculi are *non-standard*, meaning that the rules have an unbounded number of premises. We abbreviate multisets of formulae $A_k, \ldots, A_n$ to $[A]_k^n$, and $C_k \preccurlyeq D_k, \ldots, C_n \preccurlyeq D_n$ to $[C \preccurlyeq D]_k^n$ with the convention that $[A]_k^n$ is empty if $k > n$. The crucial rule for uniformity is the rule trf_m. Intuitively it unpacks a number of comparative plausibility formulae behaving like boxed formulae on the left hand side of a component in the conclusion into a different component in the rightmost premise, most clearly seen in the case of $n = 1$. The leftmost set of premises ensures that the comparative plausibility formulae indeed behave like boxed formulae. The rule T_m is the local version of trf_m, and essentially captures total reflexivity.

Lemma 3. *For $\mathcal{L}$ any of the considered logics, the calculus $\mathsf{H}_{\mathcal{L}}$ is sound for $\mathcal{L}$.*

Proof. This follows from validity of $\Box A \to A$ in all the logics and the fact that the rules preserve soundness with respect to ι. The latter is shown for each rule by constructing a countermodel for one of the premises from a countermodel for the conclusion, using that the sphere system is universal. For all the rules apart from trf, $\mathsf{abs}_L, \mathsf{abs}_R, \mathsf{spl}$ this follows as in [12], using that $\Box A \to \Box\Box A$ is valid. For $\mathsf{abs}_L, \mathsf{abs}_R$ this follows straightforwardly from absoluteness, and for spl this follows from the fact that frames for $\mathbb{VCA}$ are degenerate in the sense that $\mathsf{SP}(w) = \{\{w\}\}$ for every world w (see footnote 2).

For the rule trf, let $\mathfrak{M} = \langle W, \mathsf{SP}, [\![.]\!] \rangle$ be a $\mathbb{VTU}$ model, let $w \in W$, and suppose that

$$\mathfrak{M}, w \models \neg\iota(\mathcal{G}) \wedge \Diamond (\bigwedge \Sigma \wedge \bigwedge_{i=1}^{m}(C_i \preccurlyeq D_i) \wedge \neg\bigvee \Delta) \wedge \Diamond (\bigwedge \Omega \wedge \neg\bigvee \Theta). \quad (1)$$

Then in particular $\mathfrak{M}, w \models \neg(\iota(\mathcal{G}) \vee \Box(\bigwedge \Sigma \to \Pi) \vee \Box(\bigwedge\Omega \to \Theta))$. Furthermore, suppose that for every $k \leq m$ we have

$$\mathfrak{M}, w \models \iota(\mathcal{G}) \vee \Box(\bigwedge \Sigma \to \bigvee \Pi) \vee \Box(\bigwedge \Omega \to \bigvee \Theta) \vee \Box\left(C_k \to \bigvee_{i=1}^{k-1} D_i\right). \quad (2)$$

Then from the case $k = 1$ of (2) we obtain $\mathfrak{M}, w \models \Box\neg C_1$. From this together with (1) and the fact that for every $v \in \bigcup \mathsf{SP}(w)$ we have $\bigcup \mathsf{SP}(v) = \bigcup \mathsf{SP}(w)$ we then obtain $\mathfrak{M}, w \models \Box\neg D_1$. Similarly, using the case $k = 2$ of (2) we get $\mathfrak{M}, w \models \Box\neg D_2$ and continuing like this we get $\mathfrak{M}, w \models \Box\neg D_1 \wedge \ldots \wedge \Box\neg D_m$. Together with (1) this gives $\mathfrak{M}, w \models \neg\iota(\mathcal{G}) \wedge \Diamond(\bigwedge \Sigma \wedge \neg\bigvee \Pi) \wedge \Diamond(\bigwedge\Omega \wedge \neg(D_1 \vee \ldots \vee D_m \vee \bigvee \Theta))$ and hence we have a countermodel for the remaining premise. $\qquad \Box$

By induction on the formula complexity we straightforwardly obtain:

Lemma 4. *For every formula A we have $\mathsf{H}_{\mathcal{L}} \vdash \mathcal{G} \mid \Gamma, A \Rightarrow A, \Delta$.*

As usual, a rule is *admissible* in $\mathsf{H}_{\mathcal{L}}$ if whenever the premises are derivable in $\mathsf{H}_{\mathcal{L}}$, then so is its conclusion. It is *depth-preserving admissible*, if the depth of the derivation of its conclusion is at most the maximal depth of the derivations of its premises.

Lemma 5. *The rules $\mathsf{IW}, \mathsf{EW}, \mathsf{mrg}$ from Fig. 2 are depth-preserving admissible in $\mathsf{H}_{\mathcal{L}}$.*

Proof. By induction on the depth of the derivation in all cases. For mrg, if the last applied rule was trf_m, we might need to replace it with T_m. $\qquad \Box$

$$\frac{\mathcal{G} \mid \Gamma \Rightarrow \Delta}{\mathcal{G} \mid \Gamma, \Sigma \Rightarrow \Delta, \Pi} \; \mathsf{IW} \qquad \frac{\mathcal{G}}{\mathcal{G} \mid \Rightarrow} \; \mathsf{EW} \qquad \frac{\mathcal{G} \mid \Gamma \Rightarrow \Delta \mid \Sigma \Rightarrow \Pi}{\mathcal{G} \mid \Gamma, \Sigma \Rightarrow \Delta, \Pi} \; \mathsf{mrg}$$

Fig. 2. The structural rules of internal and external weakening and merge.

Observe that from admissibility of mrg using the internal contraction rules we also immediately obtain admissibility of the external contraction rules, i.e., contraction on hypersequent components. We first show completeness of the systems with the *cut rule*:

$$\frac{\mathcal{G} \mid \Gamma \Rightarrow \Delta, A \quad \mathcal{H} \mid A, \Sigma \Rightarrow \Pi}{\mathcal{G} \mid \mathcal{H} \mid \Gamma, \Sigma \Rightarrow \Delta, \Pi} \text{ cut}$$

Cut-free completeness then will follow from cut elimination. In the following we write $\mathsf{H}_{\mathcal{L}}\mathsf{cut}$ for the system $\mathsf{H}_{\mathcal{L}}$ with the cut rule.

Lemma 6 (Completeness with cut). *For $\mathcal{L}$ one of the considered logics the calculus $\mathsf{H}_{\mathcal{L}}\mathsf{cut}$ is complete for $\mathcal{L}$, i.e., whenever $A \in \mathcal{L}$, then $\mathsf{H}_{\mathcal{L}}\mathsf{cut} \vdash \Rightarrow A$.*

Proof. By deriving the axioms and using cut to simulate modus ponens and the rule (CPR). The interesting cases are the axioms (U1), (U2) for uniformity and (A1), (A2) for absoluteness. The derivation for (U1) is as follows:

$$\cfrac{\cfrac{\cfrac{\cfrac{\Rightarrow \mid A \Rightarrow \bot \mid \Rightarrow \bot \mid \bot \Rightarrow}{} \bot_L \quad \cfrac{\Rightarrow \mid A \Rightarrow A, \bot \mid \Rightarrow \bot}{} \text{Lem. 4}}{\Rightarrow \mid A \Rightarrow \bot \mid \bot \preccurlyeq A \Rightarrow \bot} \text{trf}_1}{\Rightarrow \bot \preccurlyeq A \mid \bot \preccurlyeq A \Rightarrow \bot} R_{0,1}}{\cfrac{\Rightarrow \bot \preccurlyeq A, \bot \preccurlyeq (\bot \preccurlyeq A)}{\Rightarrow \neg(\bot \preccurlyeq A) \rightarrow (\bot \preccurlyeq (\bot \preccurlyeq A))} \neg_L, \rightarrow_R} R_{0,1}}$$

The derivations of the remaining axioms are similar, using the rules $\mathsf{abs}_L, \mathsf{abs}_R$ in the case of absoluteness.   □

4   Cut Elimination

To obtain cut-free completeness for all systems we now give a syntactic proof of cut elimination. For this, in the presence of absoluteness we consider slightly extended calculi containing also versions of the rules $W_{m,n}, R_C, R_W$ where absoluteness is built in:

$$\cfrac{\{\, \mathcal{G} \mid \Sigma \Rightarrow \Pi \mid \Omega \Rightarrow \Theta \mid C_k \Rightarrow [\boldsymbol{D}]_1^{k-1}, [\boldsymbol{A}]_1^n : k \leq m \,\} \\ \cup \; \{\, \mathcal{G} \mid \Sigma \Rightarrow \Pi \mid \Omega \Rightarrow [\boldsymbol{D}]_1^m, [\boldsymbol{A}]_1^n, \Theta \,\}}{\mathcal{G} \mid \Sigma, [\boldsymbol{C} \preccurlyeq \boldsymbol{D}]_1^m \Rightarrow [\boldsymbol{A} \preccurlyeq \boldsymbol{B}]_1^n, \Pi \mid \Omega \Rightarrow \Theta} W_{m,n}^{\mathsf{abs}}$$

$$\frac{\mathcal{G} \mid \Sigma \Rightarrow \Pi \mid \Omega, C \Rightarrow \Theta \quad \mathcal{G} \mid \Sigma \Rightarrow \Pi \mid \Omega \Rightarrow D, \Theta}{\mathcal{G} \mid \Sigma, C \preccurlyeq D \Rightarrow \Pi \mid \Omega \Rightarrow \Theta} R_C^{\mathsf{abs}} \qquad \frac{\mathcal{G} \mid \Sigma \Rightarrow \Pi \mid \Omega \Rightarrow A, \Theta}{\mathcal{G} \mid \Sigma \Rightarrow A \preccurlyeq B, \Pi \mid \Omega \Rightarrow \Theta} R_W^{\mathsf{abs}}$$

Since these are derivable using the original version of the rule followed by applications of $\mathsf{abs}_L, \mathsf{abs}_R$, cut elimination in the extended system entails cut elimination in the original system. As can be expected, due to the presence of contraction cut elimination in a hypersequent system is rather more involved than in the sequent case of [12]. Moreover, due to the form of the absoluteness rules we cannot simply apply the general results of [11], although the strategy for the cut elimination proof is the same: Intuitively, an application of the cut rule (shown before Lemma 6) with cut formula of maximal complexity is permuted up in the derivation of the left premiss, where applications of contraction are swallowed up in a more general induction hypothesis, until an occurrence of the cut formula is principal (Lemma 10). Then essentially the fact that contractions can be permuted above logical rules is used to obtain a single occurrence of the cut formula in the left premiss of the cut, and the cut is permuted up in the right premiss. Again, contractions are swallowed up by a generalised induction hypothesis, and once the cut formula becomes principal in the last applied rule, its complexity is reduced (Lemma 9). For technical reasons we also include the rule mrg in the calculus when proving çut elimination. By Lemma 5 it is clear that all applications of this rule can then be eliminated in the cut-free system. In the following we write $\mathsf{H}_{\mathcal{L}}^{*}$ for the system $\mathsf{H}_{\mathcal{L}}$ with cut, mrg and with the rules $W_{m,n}^{\mathsf{abs}}, R_{C}^{\mathsf{abs}}, R_{W}^{\mathsf{abs}}$ where applicable, and abbreviate $\underbrace{A, \ldots, A}_{n\text{-times}}$ to A^{n}.

Definition 7. *The* cut rank *of a $\mathsf{H}_{\mathcal{L}}^{*}$-derivation $\mathcal{D}$ is the maximal complexity of a cut formula occurring in $\mathcal{D}$, written $\rho(\mathcal{D})$. A rule is* cut-rank preserving admissible *in $\mathsf{H}_{\mathcal{L}}^{*}$ if whenever its premiss(es) are derivable in $\mathsf{H}_{\mathcal{L}}^{*}$ with cut-rank n, then so is its conclusion.*

Lemma 8. *The rules* EW, IW *are depth- and cut-rank preserving admissible in $\mathsf{H}_{\mathcal{L}}^{*}$.*

Proof. Standard induction on the depth of the derivation.　　□

Lemma 9 (Shift Right). *Suppose that for $k > 0$ and $n_1, \ldots, n_k > 0$ there are $\mathsf{H}_{\mathcal{L}}^{*}$-derivations $\mathcal{D}_1$ and $\mathcal{D}_2$ of $\mathcal{G} \mid \Omega \Rightarrow \Theta, A$ and $\mathcal{H} \mid A^{n_1}, \Xi_1 \Rightarrow \Upsilon_1 \mid \ldots \mid A^{n_k}, \Xi_k \Rightarrow \Upsilon_k$ with $\rho(\mathcal{D}_1) < |A| > \rho(\mathcal{D}_2)$ and such that the displayed occurrence of A is principal in the last rule application in $\mathcal{D}_1$. Then there is a $\mathsf{H}_{\mathcal{L}}^{*}$-derivation $\mathcal{D}$ with endhypersequent $\mathcal{G} \mid \mathcal{H} \mid \Omega, \Xi_1 \Rightarrow \Theta, \Upsilon_1 \mid \ldots \mid \Omega, \Xi_k \Rightarrow \Theta, \Upsilon_k$ and $\rho(\mathcal{D}) < |A|$.*

Proof. By induction on the depth of $\mathcal{D}_2$. If none of the displayed occurrences of A is principal in the last rule in $\mathcal{D}_2$, we apply the induction hypothesis on the premiss(es) of that rule, followed by the same rule (and possibly structural rules). If at least one of the displayed occurrences is principal in the last rule in $\mathcal{D}_2$, we distinguish cases according to the last applied rule in $\mathcal{D}_1$, with subcases according to the last rule in $\mathcal{D}_2$. For space reasons we only consider an exemplary case, the remaining cases are similar. Suppose the last rules in $\mathcal{D}_1$ and $\mathcal{D}_2$ are $R_{m,n+1}$ and trf_s respectively, that A is the formula $E \preccurlyeq F$ and that $\mathcal{D}_1$ ends in:

$$\frac{\left\{ \mathcal{G} \mid \Omega \Rightarrow \Theta \mid C_j \Rightarrow [D]_1^{j-1}, [A]_1^n, E : 1 \leq j \leq m \right\} \cup \left\{ \mathcal{G} \mid \Omega \Rightarrow \Theta \mid B_j \Rightarrow [D]_1^m, [A]_1^n, E : 1 \leq j \leq n \right\} \cup \left\{ \mathcal{G} \mid \Omega \Rightarrow \Theta \mid F \Rightarrow [D]_1^m, [A]_1^n, E \right\}}{\mathcal{G} \mid \Omega, [C \preccurlyeq D]_1^m \Rightarrow [A \preccurlyeq B]_1^n, E \preccurlyeq F, \Theta} R_{m,n+1}$$

First we apply the induction hypothesis to the conclusion of this and the premisses of trf_s to eliminate all the occurrences of $E \preccurlyeq F$ from the context.

Hence we assume that the only occurrences of $E \preccurlyeq F$ in the conclusion of trf_s are principal and that $\mathcal{D}_2$ ends in:

$$\frac{\begin{array}{l}\{\mathcal{H} \mid \Xi \Rightarrow \Upsilon \mid \Sigma \Rightarrow \Pi \mid G_j \Rightarrow [\boldsymbol{H}]_1^{j-1} : 1 \leq j \leq r\} \cup \{\mathcal{H} \mid \Xi \Rightarrow \Upsilon \mid \Sigma \Rightarrow \Pi \mid E \Rightarrow [\boldsymbol{H}]_1^{r}\} \\ \cup \{\mathcal{H} \mid \Xi \Rightarrow \Upsilon \mid \Sigma \Rightarrow \Pi \mid G_j \Rightarrow [H]_1^{j-1}, F : r < j \leq s\} \cup \{\mathcal{H} \mid \Xi \Rightarrow \Upsilon \mid \Sigma \Rightarrow \Pi, [\boldsymbol{H}]_1^{s}, F\}\end{array}}{\mathcal{H} \mid \Xi, [\boldsymbol{G} \preccurlyeq \boldsymbol{H}]_1^{r}, E \preccurlyeq F, [\boldsymbol{G} \preccurlyeq \boldsymbol{H}]_{r+1}^{s} \Rightarrow \Upsilon \mid \Sigma \Rightarrow \Pi} \ \mathsf{trf}_s$$

with $E \preccurlyeq F$ not occurring in $[\boldsymbol{G} \preccurlyeq \boldsymbol{H}]_1^{r}$. Cuts on the formulae E and F then yield:

$$\begin{array}{l}\{\mathcal{H} \mid \Xi \Rightarrow \Upsilon \mid \Sigma \Rightarrow \Pi \mid G_j \Rightarrow [\boldsymbol{H}]_1^{j-1} : 1 \leq j \leq r\} \\ \cup \ \{\mathcal{G} \mid \mathcal{H} \mid \Omega \Rightarrow \Theta \mid \Xi \Rightarrow \Upsilon \mid \Sigma \Rightarrow \Pi \mid C_j \Rightarrow [\boldsymbol{D}]_1^{j-1}, [\boldsymbol{A}]_1^{n}, [\boldsymbol{H}]_1^{r} : 1 \leq j \leq m\} \\ \cup \ \{\mathcal{G} \mid \mathcal{H} \mid \Omega \Rightarrow \Theta \mid \Xi \Rightarrow \Upsilon \mid \Sigma \Rightarrow \Pi \mid B_j \Rightarrow [\boldsymbol{D}]_1^{m}, [\boldsymbol{A}]_1^{n}, [\boldsymbol{H}]_1^{r} : 1 \leq j \leq n\} \\ \cup \ \{\mathcal{G} \mid \mathcal{H} \mid \Omega \Rightarrow \Theta \mid \Xi \Rightarrow \Upsilon \mid \Sigma \Rightarrow \Pi \mid G_j \Rightarrow [H]_1^{j-1}, [\boldsymbol{D}]_1^{m}, [\boldsymbol{A}]_1^{n}, [\boldsymbol{H}]_1^{r} : r < j \leq s\}\end{array}$$

Admissibility of internal weakening (Lemma 8) and an application of $R_{m+s,n+t}$ then gives:

$$\mathcal{G} \mid \mathcal{H} \mid \Omega, [\boldsymbol{G} \preccurlyeq \boldsymbol{H}]_1^{r}, [\boldsymbol{C} \preccurlyeq \boldsymbol{D}]_1^{m}, [\boldsymbol{G} \preccurlyeq \boldsymbol{H}]_{r+1}^{s} \Rightarrow [\boldsymbol{A} \preccurlyeq \boldsymbol{B}]_1^{n}, [\boldsymbol{I} \preccurlyeq \boldsymbol{J}]_1^{t}, \Theta \mid \Xi \Rightarrow \Upsilon$$

Iterating this process to eliminate the remaining occurrences of $E \preccurlyeq F$ from $[\boldsymbol{G} \preccurlyeq \boldsymbol{H}]_{r+1}^{s}$, followed by mrg and applications of contraction then yields the desired sequent. $\qquad \square$

Lemma 10 (Shift Left). *Suppose that for $k > 0$ and $n_1, \ldots, n_k > 0$ there are $\mathsf{H}_{\mathcal{L}}^{*}$-derivations $\mathcal{D}_1$ and $\mathcal{D}_2$ of the hypersequents $\mathcal{G} \mid \Omega_1 \Rightarrow \Theta_1, A^{n_1} \mid \ldots \mid \Omega_k \Rightarrow \Theta_k, A^{n_k}$ and $\mathcal{H} \mid A, \Xi \Rightarrow \Upsilon$ with $\rho(\mathcal{D}_1) < |A| > \rho(\mathcal{D}_2)$. Then there is a $\mathsf{H}_{\mathcal{L}}^{*}$-derivation $\mathcal{D}$ with endsequent $\mathcal{G} \mid \mathcal{H} \mid \Omega_1, \Xi \Rightarrow \Theta_1, \Upsilon \mid \ldots \mid \Omega_k, \Xi \Rightarrow \Theta_k, \Upsilon$ and $\rho(\mathcal{D}) < |A|$.*

Proof. By induction on the depth of $\mathcal{D}_1$. If none of the displayed occurrences of A is principal in the last rule in $\mathcal{D}_1$ or the active formula of abs_R, we apply the induction hypothesis on the premiss(es) of the last rule in $\mathcal{D}_1$ followed by the same rule and possibly admissibility of weakening and contraction. If one of the occurrences of A is active in abs_R, we use admissibility of EW (Lemma 8) and abs_L on $\mathcal{D}_2$ to obtain $\mathcal{H} \mid \Xi \Rightarrow \Upsilon \mid A \Rightarrow$. Then the induction hypothesis on this and the premiss of abs_R followed by mrg and IW yields the result. If an occurrence of A is principal in the last rule in $\mathcal{D}_1$, we use the induction hypothesis to remove all the occurrences of A in the context of that rule. Then, in case this rule is $R_{m,n}, W_{m,n}, W_{m,n}^{\mathsf{abs}}$, we apply contraction in the premisses and apply the same rule, so that only one occurrence of A is principal. Now Lemma 9 yields the result. $\qquad \square$

Theorem 11 (Cut Elimination). *Let $\mathcal{L} \in \{\mathsf{VTU}, \mathsf{VWU}, \mathsf{VCU}, \mathsf{VTA}, \mathsf{VWA}, \mathsf{VCA}\}$. If a hypersequent is derivable in $\mathsf{H}_{\mathcal{L}}^{*}$, then it is derivable in $\mathsf{H}_{\mathcal{L}}$.*

Proof. First we eliminate all applications of cut by induction on the tuples $\langle \rho(\mathcal{D}), \sharp(\mathcal{D}) \rangle$ under the lexicographic ordering, where $\sharp(\mathcal{D})$ is the number of applications of cut in $\mathcal{D}$ with cut formula of complexity $\rho(\mathcal{D})$. Then applications of

$W_{m,n}^{\mathrm{abs}}, R_C^{\mathrm{abs}}, R_W^{\mathrm{abs}}$ are replaced with the $W_{m,n}, R_C, R_W$ and $\mathrm{abs}_L, \mathrm{abs}_R$, and mrg is eliminated using Lemma 5. It is straightforward to check that applications of $W_{m,n}^{\mathrm{abs}}, R_C^{\mathrm{abs}}, R_W^{\mathrm{abs}}$ are only introduced in systems including the absoluteness rules. □

Corollary 12 (Cut-free completeness). *If $A \in \mathcal{L}$, then $\mathsf{H}_{\mathcal{L}} \vdash \Rightarrow A$.*

5 Connections to Modal Logic

The constructed hypersequent calculi provide purely syntactical proofs of results from [13] connecting the conditional logics to, e.g., modal logic S5. We write $\mathcal{L}^{\square}$ for the *modal fragment* of a conditional logic $\mathcal{L}$, i.e., the fragment where comparative plausibility formulae are restricted to the shape $(\bot \preccurlyeq \neg A)$, and we write $A^{\square}$ for the result of replacing every subformula $\bot \preccurlyeq \neg B$ of A with $\square B$. The proofs use the fact that the hypersequent calculus H_{S5} with the propositional rules of Fig. 1, the structural rules and the rules

$$\frac{\mathcal{G} \mid \Gamma \Rightarrow \square A, \Delta \mid \Rightarrow A}{\mathcal{G} \mid \Gamma \Rightarrow \square A, \Delta} \, \square_R \qquad \frac{\mathcal{G} \mid \Gamma, \square A \Rightarrow \Delta \mid \Sigma, A \Rightarrow \Pi}{\mathcal{G} \mid \Gamma, \square A \Rightarrow \Delta \mid \Sigma \Rightarrow \Pi} \, \square_L \qquad \frac{\mathcal{G} \mid \Gamma, \square A, A \Rightarrow \Delta}{\mathcal{G} \mid \Gamma, \square A \Rightarrow \Delta} \, \mathsf{T}$$

is cut-free complete for S5 [16], see also [11].

Lemma 13. *If $A^{\square} \in \mathsf{S5}$, then $A \in \mathcal{L}^{\square}$ for each of the logics $\mathcal{L}$ considered here.*

Proof. By translating H_{S5}-derivations into $\mathsf{H}_{\mathcal{L}}$-derivations. E.g., $\square_L$ is translated into:

$$\frac{\dfrac{\mathcal{G} \mid \Gamma, \bot \preccurlyeq \neg A \Rightarrow \Delta \mid \Sigma \Rightarrow \Pi \mid \neg \Rightarrow}{} \bot_L \quad \dfrac{\dfrac{\mathcal{G} \mid \Gamma, \bot \preccurlyeq \neg A \Rightarrow \Delta \mid \Sigma, A \Rightarrow \Pi}{\mathcal{G} \mid \Gamma, \bot \preccurlyeq \neg A \Rightarrow \Delta \mid \Sigma \Rightarrow \neg A, \Pi} \neg_L}{} \mathsf{trf}_1}{\dfrac{\dfrac{\mathcal{G} \mid \Gamma, \bot \preccurlyeq \neg A, \bot \preccurlyeq \neg A \Rightarrow \Delta \mid \Sigma \Rightarrow \Pi}{\mathcal{G} \mid \Gamma, \bot \preccurlyeq \neg A \Rightarrow \Delta \mid \Sigma \Rightarrow \Pi}}{} \mathsf{ICL}}$$

The translations of $\square_R, \mathsf{T}$ are similar, using $R_{0,1}$ and T_1 respectively. □

The backwards direction is similar, but translates into the calculus H_{S5} above with a form of Avron's *modal splitting rule* from [2]:

$$\frac{\mathcal{G} \mid \Gamma \Rightarrow \Delta \mid \Sigma, \square \Omega \Rightarrow \square \Theta, \Pi}{\mathcal{G} \mid \Gamma, \square \Omega \Rightarrow \square \Theta, \Delta \mid \Sigma \Rightarrow \Pi} \, MS$$

It is straightforward to check that the resulting calculus is sound for S5.

Lemma 14. *If $\mathcal{L} \neq \mathbb{VCA}$ and $A \in \mathcal{L}^{\square}$, then $A^{\square} \in \mathsf{S5}$.*

Proof. By translating derivations in $\mathsf{H}_{\mathcal{L}}$ into derivations in $\mathsf{H}_{\mathsf{S5}}\mathsf{cut}$ and applying cut elimination. In particular, an application of the rule $R_{m,n}$

$$\frac{\{\mathcal{G} \mid \Gamma \Rightarrow \Delta \mid \bot \Rightarrow \neg D_1, \ldots, \neg D_{j-1}, \bot^n : 1 \leq j \leq m\}}{\cup \ \{\mathcal{G} \mid \Gamma \Rightarrow \Delta \mid \neg B_j \Rightarrow \neg D_1, \ldots, \neg D_m, \bot^n : 1 \leq j \leq n\}}{\mathcal{G} \mid \Gamma, \bot \preccurlyeq \neg D_1, \ldots, \bot \preccurlyeq \neg D_m \Rightarrow \bot \preccurlyeq \neg B_1, \ldots, \bot \preccurlyeq \neg B_n, \Delta} \, R_{m,n}$$

is translated into

$$\cfrac{\cfrac{\cfrac{\cfrac{\mathcal{G} \mid \Gamma \Rightarrow \Delta \mid \neg B_1 \Rightarrow \neg D_1, \ldots, \neg D_m, \bot^n}{\mathcal{G} \mid \Gamma, \Box D_1, \ldots, \Box D_m \Rightarrow \Box B_1, \Delta \mid \neg B_1 \Rightarrow \neg D_1, \ldots, \neg D_m, \bot^n} \text{ IW}}{\mathcal{G} \mid \Gamma, \Box D_1, \ldots, \Box D_m \Rightarrow \Box B_1, \Delta \mid D_1, \ldots, D_m \Rightarrow B_1} \text{ prop}}{\mathcal{G} \mid \Gamma, \Box D_1, \ldots, \Box D_m \Rightarrow \Box B_1, \Delta} \Box_L, \Box_R}{\mathcal{G} \mid \Gamma, \Box D_1, \ldots, \Box D_m \Rightarrow \Box B_1, \ldots, \Box B_n, \Delta} \text{ IW}$$

Here prop uses derivability of the inversions of the propositional rules using cut. Similarly, applications of T_m and trf_m are translated using m applications of $\Box_L$ and T respectively. Applications of $W_{m,n}$ and R_C are translated by T, and R_W is replaced with weakening, using that whenever $\mathcal{G} \mid \Gamma \Rightarrow \Delta, \bot$ is derivable in the system for S5, then so is $\mathcal{G} \mid \Gamma \Rightarrow \Delta$. Finally, $\mathsf{abs}_L, \mathsf{abs}_R$ are replaced with the modalised splitting rule MS.   □

Theorem 15 [13, Sect. 6.3]. *Let* $\mathcal{L} \neq \mathbb{VCA}$. *Then* $A \in \mathcal{L}^\Box$ *iff* $A^\Box \in$ S5.

The proof of the previous theorem is immediate from the preceeding lemmas. It is then also straightforward to derive the known collapses of the counterfactual implication $\Box\!\rightarrow$ in $\mathbb{VWA}$ and $\mathbb{VCA}$. Recall that $A \mathrel{\Box\!\rightarrow} B \equiv (\bot \preccurlyeq A) \vee \neg((A \wedge \neg B) \preccurlyeq A)$.

Proposition 16. *1.* $\mathsf{H}_{\mathbb{VWA}} \vdash \Rightarrow (A \mathrel{\Box\!\rightarrow} B) \leftrightarrow \Box(A \rightarrow B)$
2. $\mathsf{H}_{\mathbb{VCA}} \vdash \Rightarrow A \leftrightarrow \Box A$
3. $\mathsf{H}_{\mathbb{VCA}} \vdash \Rightarrow (A \mathrel{\Box\!\rightarrow} B) \leftrightarrow (A \rightarrow B)$ *and* $\mathsf{H}_{\mathbb{VCA}} \vdash \Rightarrow (A \preccurlyeq B) \leftrightarrow (B \rightarrow A)$.

6 Standard Calculi

To convert the non-standard calculi $\mathsf{H}_\mathcal{L}$ into standard calculi, we consider an extended notion of sequents, where the succedent contains additional structural connectives. These sequents extend those of [7,15] with a connective $\langle . \rangle$ interpreting possible formulae.

Definition 17. *A* conditional block *is a tuple* $[\Sigma \lhd C]$ *containing a multiset* Σ *of formulae and a single formula* C. *A* transfer block *is a multiset of formulae, written* $\langle \Theta \rangle$. *An* extended sequent *is a tuple* $\Gamma \Rightarrow \Delta$ *consisting of a multiset* Γ *of formulae and a multiset* Δ *containing formulae, conditional blocks, and transfer blocks. An* extended hypersequent *is a multiset containing extended sequents, written* $\Gamma_1 \Rightarrow \Delta_1 \mid \ldots \mid \Gamma_n \Rightarrow \Delta_n$.

The *formula interpretation* of an extended sequent is (all blocks shown explicitly):

$$\iota_e(\Gamma \Rightarrow \Delta, [\Sigma_1 \lhd C_1], \ldots, [\Sigma_n \lhd C_n], \langle \Theta_1 \rangle, \ldots, \langle \Theta_m \rangle)$$
$$:= \bigwedge \Gamma \rightarrow \bigvee \Delta \vee \bigvee_{i=1}^n \bigvee_{B \in \Sigma_i} (B \preccurlyeq C_i) \vee \bigvee_{j=1}^m \Diamond(\bigvee \Theta_j)$$

The *formula interpretation* of an extended hypersequent is given by

$$\iota_e(\Gamma_1 \Rightarrow \Delta_1 \mid \ldots \mid \Gamma_n \Rightarrow \Delta_n) := \Box \iota_e(\Gamma_1 \Rightarrow \Delta_1) \vee \ldots \vee \Box \iota_e(\Gamma_n \Rightarrow \Delta_n)$$

The rules of the non-invertible calculi for $\mathbb{VTU}$ and extensions are given in Fig. 3.

$$\dfrac{\mathcal{G} \mid \Gamma \Rightarrow \Delta, [A \triangleleft B]}{\mathcal{G} \mid \Gamma \Rightarrow \Delta, A \preccurlyeq B} \; \preccurlyeq_R \qquad \dfrac{\mathcal{G} \mid \Gamma \Rightarrow \Delta, [B, \Sigma \triangleleft C] \quad \mathcal{G} \mid \Gamma \Rightarrow \Delta, [\Sigma \triangleleft A]}{\mathcal{G} \mid \Gamma, A \preccurlyeq B \Rightarrow \Delta, [\Sigma \triangleleft C]} \; \preccurlyeq_L$$

$$\dfrac{\mathcal{G} \mid \Gamma \Rightarrow \Delta, [\Sigma_1, \Sigma_2 \triangleleft A] \quad \mathcal{G} \mid \Gamma \Rightarrow \Delta, [\Sigma_1, \Sigma_2 \triangleleft B]}{\mathcal{G} \mid \Gamma \Rightarrow \Delta, [\Sigma_1 \triangleleft A], [\Sigma_2 \triangleleft B]} \; com \qquad \dfrac{\mathcal{G} \mid \Gamma \Rightarrow \Delta \mid A \Rightarrow \Sigma}{\mathcal{G} \mid \Gamma \Rightarrow \Delta, [\Sigma \triangleleft A]} \; jump$$

$$\dfrac{\mathcal{G} \mid \Gamma \Rightarrow \Delta \mid A \Rightarrow \Theta \quad \mathcal{G} \mid \Gamma \Rightarrow \Delta, \langle \Theta, B \rangle}{\mathcal{G} \mid \Gamma, A \preccurlyeq B \Rightarrow \Delta, \langle \Theta \rangle} \; T$$

$$\dfrac{\mathcal{G} \mid \Gamma \Rightarrow \Delta, \langle \bot \rangle}{\mathcal{G} \mid \Gamma \Rightarrow \Delta} \; in_{trf} \qquad \dfrac{\mathcal{G} \mid \Gamma \Rightarrow \Delta \mid \Sigma \Rightarrow \Theta, \Pi}{\mathcal{G} \mid \Gamma \Rightarrow \Delta, \langle \Theta \rangle \mid \Sigma \Rightarrow \Pi} \; jump_U \qquad \dfrac{\mathcal{G} \mid \Gamma \Rightarrow \Delta, \Theta}{\mathcal{G} \mid \Gamma \Rightarrow \Delta, \langle \Theta \rangle} \; jump_T$$

$$\dfrac{}{\mathcal{G} \mid \Gamma, \bot \Rightarrow \Delta} \; \bot_L \qquad \dfrac{}{\mathcal{G} \mid \Gamma, p \Rightarrow \Delta, p} \; init \qquad \dfrac{\mathcal{G} \mid \Gamma, A, A \Rightarrow \Delta}{\mathcal{G} \mid \Gamma, A \Rightarrow \Delta} \; ICL \qquad \dfrac{\mathcal{G} \mid \Gamma \Rightarrow \Delta, A, A}{\mathcal{G} \mid \Gamma \Rightarrow \Delta, A} \; ICR$$

$$\dfrac{\mathcal{G} \mid \Gamma, B \Rightarrow \Delta \quad \mathcal{G} \mid \Gamma \Rightarrow \Delta, A}{\mathcal{G} \mid \Gamma, A \to B \Rightarrow \Delta} \; \to_L \qquad \dfrac{\mathcal{G} \mid \Gamma, A \Rightarrow \Delta, B}{\mathcal{G} \mid \Gamma \Rightarrow \Delta, A \to B} \; \to_R$$

$$\dfrac{\mathcal{G} \mid \Gamma \Rightarrow \Delta, [\Sigma \triangleleft A], [\Sigma \triangleleft A]}{\mathcal{G} \mid \Gamma \Rightarrow \Delta, [\Sigma \triangleleft A]} \; Con_S \qquad \dfrac{\mathcal{G} \mid \Gamma \Rightarrow \Delta, [\Sigma, A, A \triangleleft B]}{\mathcal{G} \mid \Gamma \Rightarrow \Delta, [\Sigma, A \triangleleft B]} \; Con_B$$

$$\dfrac{\mathcal{G} \mid \Gamma \Rightarrow \Delta, \Sigma}{\mathcal{G} \mid \Gamma \Rightarrow \Delta, [\Sigma \triangleleft A]} \; W \qquad \dfrac{\mathcal{G} \mid \Gamma, A \Rightarrow \Delta \quad \mathcal{G} \mid \Gamma \Rightarrow B, \Delta}{\mathcal{G} \mid \Gamma, A \preccurlyeq B \Rightarrow \Delta} \; C \qquad \dfrac{\mathcal{G} \mid \Sigma, \Gamma \Rightarrow \Pi, \Delta \mid \Omega \Rightarrow \Theta}{\mathcal{G} \mid \Sigma \Rightarrow \Pi \mid \Omega, \Gamma \Rightarrow \Theta, \Delta} \; spl$$

$$\dfrac{\mathcal{G} \mid \Gamma \Rightarrow \Delta \mid \Sigma, A \preccurlyeq B \Rightarrow \Pi}{\mathcal{G} \mid \Gamma, A \preccurlyeq B \Rightarrow \Delta \mid \Sigma \Rightarrow \Pi} \; abs_L \qquad \dfrac{\mathcal{G} \mid \Gamma \Rightarrow \Delta \mid \Sigma \Rightarrow A \preccurlyeq B, \Pi}{\mathcal{G} \mid \Gamma \Rightarrow A \preccurlyeq B, \Delta \mid \Sigma \Rightarrow \Pi} \; abs_R$$

$SH_{VTU} = \{\bot_L, init, \to_L, \to_R, ICL, ICR, Con_S, Con_B\} \cup \{\preccurlyeq_R, \preccurlyeq_L, com, jump, T, in_{trf}, jump_U, jump_T\}$

$SH_{VWU} = SH_{VTU} \cup \{W\} \qquad SH_{VCU} = SH_{VWU} \cup \{C\} \qquad SH_{VTA} = SH_{VTU} \cup \{abs_L, abs_R\}$

$SH_{VWA} = SH_{VWU} \cup \{abs_L, abs_R\} \qquad SH_{VCA} = SH_{VCU} \cup \{abs_L, abs_R, spl\}$

Fig. 3. The non-invertible standard calculi for extensions of VTU

Theorem 18 (Soundness). *If* $SH_{\mathcal{L}} \vdash \mathcal{G}$, *then* $\vdash_{\mathcal{L}} \iota_e(\mathcal{G})$, *and if* $SH_{\mathcal{L}} \vdash \; \Rightarrow A$, *then* $A \in \mathcal{L}$.

Proof. As for Lemma 3, by showing that the rules preserve validity under ι_e and using validity of $\Box A \to A$. For the rules $\preccurlyeq_L, \preccurlyeq_R, , , jump, W, C$ this is similar as in [7]. For rule T, if the interpretation of the conclusion is falsified in $\mathfrak{M}, w$, then there is a world $v \in SP(w)$ with $\mathfrak{M}, v \Vdash \bigwedge \Gamma \wedge (A \preccurlyeq B) \wedge \neg \bigvee \Delta \wedge \Box \neg \bigvee \Theta$. If $[\![B]\!] = \emptyset$, then in particular $\mathfrak{M}, v \Vdash \Box \neg (\bigvee \Theta \vee B)$, and the formula interpretation of the second premiss is falsified in $\mathfrak{M}, w$. Otherwise, from $\mathfrak{M}, v \Vdash A \preccurlyeq B$ we obtain a world $x \in \bigcup SP(v) = \bigcup SP(w)$ with $\mathfrak{M}, x \Vdash A$, and from $\mathfrak{M}, v \Vdash \Box \neg \bigvee \Theta$ we also get that $\mathfrak{M}, x \Vdash \neg \bigvee \Theta$. Hence the formula interpretation of the first premiss is falsified at $\mathfrak{M}, w$. The remaining cases are similar. □

Theorem 19 (Completeness). *If* $A \in \mathcal{L}$ *then* $SH_{\mathcal{L}} \vdash \; \Rightarrow A$.

Proof. By simulating derivations in $H_{\mathcal{L}}$. Most of the rules are simulated as in [7], except for the rules trf_m, T_m. For T_m the derivation is given in Fig. 4. The derivation of trf_m only replaces $jump_T$ with $jump_U$. □

$$\frac{\mathcal{G} \mid \Gamma \Rightarrow \Delta \mid C_m \Rightarrow [D]_1^{m-1}}{\mathcal{G} \mid \Gamma \Rightarrow \Delta \mid C_m \Rightarrow [D]_1^{m-1}, \bot} \; \text{IW}$$

$$\frac{\dfrac{\dfrac{\mathcal{G} \mid \Gamma \Rightarrow [D]_1^m, \Delta}{\mathcal{G} \mid \Gamma \Rightarrow [D]_1^m, \bot, \Delta} \; \text{IW}}{\mathcal{G} \mid \Gamma \Rightarrow \Delta, \langle [D]_1^m, \bot \rangle} \; \text{jump}_T}{\mathcal{G} \mid \Gamma, C_m \preccurlyeq D_m \Rightarrow \Delta, \langle [D]_1^{m-1}, \bot \rangle} \; \text{T}$$

$$\frac{\mathcal{G} \mid \Gamma, [C \preccurlyeq D]_2^m \Rightarrow \Delta \mid C_1 \Rightarrow}{\mathcal{G} \mid \Gamma, [C \preccurlyeq D]_2^m \Rightarrow \Delta \mid C_1 \Rightarrow \bot} \; \text{IW}$$

$$\vdots$$

$$\mathcal{G} \mid \Gamma, [C \preccurlyeq D]_2^m \Rightarrow \Delta, \langle D_1, \bot \rangle \; \text{T}$$

$$\frac{\mathcal{G} \mid \Gamma, [C \preccurlyeq D]_1^m \Rightarrow \Delta, \langle \bot \rangle}{\mathcal{G} \mid \Gamma, [C \preccurlyeq D]_1^m \Rightarrow \Delta} \; \text{in}_{\text{trf}}$$

Fig. 4. The derivation of T_m in $\mathsf{SH}_{\mathbb{VTU}}$.

7   Semantic Completeness via Invertible Calculi

An alternative completeness proof for the logics without absoluteness is given semantically by constructing a countermodel from a failed proof search. For this we consider the invertible versions $\mathsf{SH}_{\mathcal{L}}^i$ of the calculi from Sect. 6, given in Fig. 5. Equivalence with the non-invertible calculi follows from admissibility of the structural rules, including the ones below, the proofs of which are standard by induction on the depth of the derivation:

$$\frac{\mathcal{G} \mid \Gamma \Rightarrow \Delta}{\mathcal{G} \mid \Gamma \Rightarrow \Delta, [\Sigma \lhd C]} \; \text{CW} \qquad \frac{\mathcal{G} \mid \Gamma \Rightarrow \Delta, [\Sigma \lhd C]}{\mathcal{G} \mid \Gamma \Rightarrow \Delta, [\Sigma, A \lhd C]} \; \text{CIW} \qquad \frac{\mathcal{G} \mid \Gamma \Rightarrow \Delta}{\mathcal{G} \mid \Gamma \Rightarrow \Delta, \langle \Theta \rangle} \; \text{TW}$$

Lemma 20. *The rules* $\text{IW}, \text{EW}, \text{CW}, \text{CIW}, \text{TW}$ *are admissible in* $\mathsf{SH}_{\mathcal{L}}$.

Lemma 21. *The rules* $\text{ICL}, \text{ICR}, \text{Con}_B, \text{Con}_S, \text{mrg}$ *are admissible in* $\mathsf{SH}_{\mathcal{L}}^i$.

From Lemmas 20 and 21 it immediately follows that:

Proposition 22. *The invertible and non-invertible calculi are equivalent.*

Definition 23. *An extended hypersequent* $\mathcal{G}$ *is* $\mathbb{VTU}$-*saturated if it satisfies all of the following conditions:*

1. $(\preccurlyeq_R)$ *if* $\Gamma \Rightarrow \Delta, A \preccurlyeq B \in \mathcal{G}$, *then* $[\Sigma, A \lhd B] \in \Delta$ *for some* Σ;
2. $(\preccurlyeq_L)$ *if* $\Gamma, C \preccurlyeq D \Rightarrow \Delta, [\Sigma \lhd A] \in \mathcal{G}$, *then* $D \in \Sigma$ *or* $[\Sigma \lhd C] \in \Delta$;
3. (com) *if* $\Gamma \Rightarrow \Delta, [\Sigma \lhd A], [\Pi \lhd B] \in \mathcal{G}$, *then* $\Sigma \subseteq \Pi$ *or* $\Pi \subseteq \Sigma$;
4. $(jump)$ *if* $\Gamma \Rightarrow \Delta, [\Sigma \lhd A] \in \mathcal{G}$, *then* $A, \Theta \Rightarrow \Sigma, \Pi \in \mathcal{G}$ *for some* Θ, Π;
5. (T) *if* $\Gamma, C \preccurlyeq D \Rightarrow \Delta, \langle \Theta \rangle \in \mathcal{G}$, *then* $D \in \Theta$ *or* $C, \Sigma \Rightarrow \Theta, \Pi \in \mathcal{G}$ *for some* Σ, Π;
6. (in_{trf}) *if* $\Gamma \Rightarrow \Delta \in \mathcal{G}$, *then* $\langle \Theta \rangle \in \Delta$ *for some* Θ;
7. $(\text{jump}_U, \text{jump}_T)$ *if* $\Gamma \Rightarrow \Delta, \langle \Theta \rangle \in \mathcal{G}$ *and* $\Sigma \Rightarrow \Pi \in \mathcal{G}$, *then* $\Theta \subseteq \Pi$;
8. $(\rightarrow_L)$ *if* $\Gamma, A \rightarrow B \Rightarrow \Delta \in \mathcal{G}$, *then* $B \in \Gamma$ *or* $A \in \Delta$;
9. $(\rightarrow_R)$ *if* $\Gamma \Rightarrow A \rightarrow B, \Delta \in \mathcal{G}$, *then* $A \in \Gamma$ *and* $B \in \Delta$;

$$\dfrac{\mathcal{G} \mid \Sigma \Rightarrow \Pi, A \preccurlyeq B, [A \lhd B]}{\mathcal{G} \mid \Sigma \Rightarrow \Pi, A \preccurlyeq B} \preccurlyeq_R^i \qquad \dfrac{\mathcal{G} \mid \Omega \Rightarrow \Theta, [\Sigma \lhd A] \mid A \Rightarrow \Sigma}{\mathcal{G} \mid \Omega \Rightarrow \Theta, [\Sigma \lhd A]} \text{ jump}^i$$

$$\dfrac{\mathcal{G} \mid \Omega, C \preccurlyeq D \Rightarrow \Theta, [D, \Sigma \lhd A] \quad \mathcal{G} \mid \Omega, C \preccurlyeq D \Rightarrow \Theta, [\Sigma \lhd A], [\Sigma \lhd C]}{\mathcal{G} \mid \Omega, C \preccurlyeq D \Rightarrow \Theta, [\Sigma \lhd A]} \preccurlyeq_L^i$$

$$\dfrac{\mathcal{G} \mid \Omega \Rightarrow \Theta, [\Sigma_1, \Sigma_2 \lhd A], [\Sigma_2 \lhd B] \quad \mathcal{G} \mid \Omega \Rightarrow \Theta, [\Sigma_1 \lhd A], [\Sigma_1, \Sigma_2 \lhd B]}{\mathcal{G} \mid \Omega \Rightarrow \Theta, [\Sigma_1 \lhd A], [\Sigma_2 \lhd B]} \text{ com}^i$$

$$\dfrac{\mathcal{G} \mid \Sigma, A \preccurlyeq B \Rightarrow \Pi, \langle \Theta \rangle \mid A \Rightarrow \Theta \quad \mathcal{G} \mid \Sigma, A \preccurlyeq B \Rightarrow \Pi, \langle \Theta, B \rangle}{\mathcal{G} \mid \Sigma, A \preccurlyeq B \Rightarrow \Pi, \langle \Theta \rangle} \text{ T}^i$$

$$\dfrac{\mathcal{G} \mid \Gamma \Rightarrow \Delta, \langle \bot \rangle}{\mathcal{G} \mid \Gamma \Rightarrow \Delta} \text{ in}_{\text{trf}}^i \qquad \dfrac{\mathcal{G} \mid \Gamma \Rightarrow \Delta, \langle \Theta \rangle \mid \Sigma \Rightarrow \Theta, \Pi}{\mathcal{G} \mid \Gamma \Rightarrow \Delta, \langle \Theta \rangle \mid \Sigma \Rightarrow \Pi} \text{ jump}_U^i \qquad \dfrac{\mathcal{G} \mid \Gamma \Rightarrow \Delta, \langle \Theta \rangle, \Theta}{\mathcal{G} \mid \Gamma \Rightarrow \Delta, \langle \Theta \rangle} \text{ jump}_T^i$$

$$\dfrac{}{\mathcal{G} \mid \Omega, \bot \Rightarrow \Theta} \bot_L \qquad \dfrac{}{\mathcal{G} \mid \Omega, p \Rightarrow \Theta, p} \text{ init}$$

$$\dfrac{\mathcal{G} \mid \Omega, A \to B, B \Rightarrow \Theta \quad \mathcal{G} \mid \Omega, A \to B \Rightarrow \Theta, A}{\mathcal{G} \mid \Omega, A \to B \Rightarrow \Theta} \to_L^i \qquad \dfrac{\mathcal{G} \mid \Omega, A \Rightarrow \Theta, A \to B, B}{\mathcal{G} \mid \Omega \Rightarrow \Theta, A \to B} \to_R^i$$

$$\dfrac{\mathcal{G} \mid \Gamma \Rightarrow \Delta, [\Sigma \lhd A], \Sigma}{\mathcal{G} \mid \Gamma \Rightarrow \Delta, [\Sigma \lhd A]} \text{ W}^i \qquad \dfrac{\mathcal{G} \mid \Gamma, C \preccurlyeq D, C \Rightarrow \Delta \quad \mathcal{G} \mid \Gamma, C \preccurlyeq D \Rightarrow D, \Delta}{\mathcal{G} \mid \Gamma, C \preccurlyeq D \Rightarrow \Delta} \text{ C}^i$$

$$\dfrac{\mathcal{G} \mid \Gamma, A \preccurlyeq B \Rightarrow \Delta \mid \Sigma, A \preccurlyeq B \Rightarrow \Pi}{\mathcal{G} \mid \Gamma, A \preccurlyeq B \Rightarrow \Delta \mid \Sigma \Rightarrow \Pi} \text{ abs}_L^i \qquad \dfrac{\mathcal{G} \mid \Gamma \Rightarrow A \preccurlyeq B, \Delta \mid \Sigma \Rightarrow A \preccurlyeq B, \Pi}{\mathcal{G} \mid \Gamma \Rightarrow A \preccurlyeq B, \Delta \mid \Sigma \Rightarrow \Pi} \text{ abs}_R^i$$

$$\text{SH}_{\text{VTU}}^i = \{\bot_L^i, \text{init}^i, \to_L^i, \to_R^i\} \cup \{\preccurlyeq_R^i, \preccurlyeq_L^i, \text{com}^i, \text{jump}^i, \text{T}^i, \text{in}_{\text{trf}}^i, \text{jump}_U^i, \text{jump}_T^i\}$$

$$\text{SH}_{\text{VWU}}^i = \text{SH}_{\text{VTU}}^i \cup \{\text{W}^i\} \qquad \text{SH}_{\text{VCU}}^i = \text{SH}_{\text{VWU}}^i \cup \{\text{C}^i\} \qquad \text{SH}_{\text{VTA}}^i = \text{SH}_{\text{VTU}}^i \cup \{\text{abs}_L^i, \text{abs}_R^i\}$$

$$\text{SH}_{\text{VWA}}^i = \text{SH}_{\text{VWU}}^i \cup \{\text{abs}_L^i, \text{abs}_R^i\} \qquad \text{SH}_{\text{VCA}}^i = \text{SH}_{\text{VCU}}^i \cup \{\text{abs}_L^i, \text{abs}_R^i\}$$

Fig. 5. The invertible standard calculi for extensions of VTU

It is VWU-saturated *(resp. VCU-saturated) if it also satisfies (W) (resp. (C))* below:

1. (W) if $\Gamma \Rightarrow \Delta, [\Sigma \lhd A] \in \mathcal{G}$, then $\Sigma \subseteq \Delta$;
2. (C) if $\Gamma, C \preccurlyeq D \Rightarrow \Delta \in \mathcal{G}$, then $C \in \Gamma$ or $D \in \Delta$;

A VTU-saturated extended hypersequent $\mathcal{G}$ is called *unprovable* if it is not an instance of (init) or ($\bot_L$). We construct a countermodel from an unprovable VTU-saturated extended hypersequent $\mathcal{G} = \Gamma_1 \Rightarrow \Delta_1 \mid \ldots \mid \Gamma_n \Rightarrow \Delta_n$ as follows:

- $W := \{1, \ldots, n\}$
- $[\![p]\!] := \{i \leq n : p \in \Gamma_i\}$

The sphere systems $\text{SP}(i)$ for $i \leq n$ are then defined as follows: Assume that $\Gamma_i \Rightarrow \Delta_i$ is

$$\Gamma_i \Rightarrow \Delta_i', [\Sigma_1 \lhd A_1], \ldots, [\Sigma_k \lhd A_k]$$

where Δ_i' contains no conditional blocks. First observe that due to saturation condition 3 we may assume w.l.o.g. that $\Sigma_1 \subseteq \Sigma_2 \subseteq \ldots \subseteq \Sigma_k$. Moreover, by condition 4 for every $j \leq k$ there is a component $\Gamma_{m_j} \Rightarrow \Delta_{m_j} \in \mathcal{G}$ with $A_j \in \Gamma_{m_j}$ and $\Sigma_j \subseteq \Delta_{m_j}$. Hence we set

$$\text{SP}(i) := \{\{m_k\}, \{m_k, m_{k-1}\}, \ldots, \{m_k, \ldots, m_1\}, W\}$$

Call the resulting structure $\mathfrak{M}_{\mathcal{G}}$.

Lemma 24. *For a* VTU-*saturated hypersequent* $\mathcal{G}$ *the structure* $\mathfrak{M}_\mathcal{G}$ *is a* VTU-*model.*

Proof. Nesting of spheres is obvious from the fact that $\{m_k\} \subseteq \{m_k, m_{k-1}\} \subseteq \ldots \subseteq \{m_k, \ldots, m_1\} \subseteq W$; reflexivity and uniformity follow from the fact that $W \in \mathsf{SP}(i)$. $\square$

Lemma 25. *Let* $\mathcal{G} = \Gamma_1 \Rightarrow \Delta_1 \mid \ldots \mid \Gamma_n \Rightarrow \Delta_n$ *be a* VTU-*saturated hypersequent and let* $\mathfrak{M}_\mathcal{G}$ *be define as above with world* i *associated to component* $\Gamma_i \Rightarrow \Delta_i$. *Then:*

1. *given a formula* A, *if* $A \in \Gamma_i$ *then* $\mathfrak{M}_\mathcal{G}, i \Vdash A$
2. *given a formula* A, *if* $A \in \Delta_i$ *then* $\mathfrak{M}_\mathcal{G}, i \nVdash A$
3. *given a block* $[\Sigma \lhd C]$, *if* $[\Sigma \lhd C] \in \Delta_i$, *then* $\mathfrak{M}_\mathcal{G}, i \nVdash \bigvee_{B \in \Sigma}(B \preccurlyeq C)$
4. *given a formula* B, *if* $\langle \Theta, B \rangle \in \Delta_i$ *for some* Θ, *then* $\mathfrak{M}_\mathcal{G}, i \nVdash \lozenge B$

Proof. We prove statements 1 and 2 by mutual induction on the complexity of A. The base case and the propositional case are straightforward, hence we consider $A = E \preccurlyeq F$. Let $i \in W$ be associated to $\Gamma_i \Rightarrow \Delta_i$ with $\Delta_i = \Delta_i', [\Sigma_1 \lhd D_1], \ldots, [\Sigma_k \lhd D_k], \langle \Theta \rangle$, where Δ_i' contains no conditional block and $\Sigma_1 \subseteq \Sigma_2 \subseteq \ldots \subseteq \Sigma_k$.

- Suppose $E \preccurlyeq F \in \Gamma_i$. For $\alpha \in \mathsf{SP}(i)$, we have to show that $\alpha \Vdash^\forall \neg F$ or $\alpha \Vdash^\exists E$.

  In case $\alpha \neq W$ we have $\alpha = \{m_k, \ldots, m_j\}$ for some $j \le k$ and each $m_\ell \in \alpha$ comes from a block $[\Sigma_\ell \lhd D_\ell]$ and is associated to a component $D_\ell, \Lambda_\ell \Rightarrow \Pi_\ell, \Sigma_\ell$ of $\mathcal{G}$. By saturation condition $(\preccurlyeq_L)$, either $F \in \Sigma_j$ or $E = D_j$. In the former case with $\Sigma_j \subseteq \Sigma_{j+1} \subseteq \ldots \Sigma_k$ and the induction hypothesis we have $\mathfrak{M}_\mathcal{G}, m_\ell \nVdash F$, for $\ell = j, \ldots, k$, showing that $\alpha \Vdash^\forall \neg F$. If $E = D_j$, by induction hypothesis on the component $E, \Lambda_j \Rightarrow \Pi_j, \Sigma_j$, we get $\mathfrak{M}_\mathcal{G}, m_j \Vdash E$, showing $\alpha \Vdash^\exists E$.

  In case $\alpha = W$, by saturation condition (T) either $F \in \langle \Theta \rangle$, or $E, \Lambda \Rightarrow \Pi, \Theta \in \mathcal{G}$ for some Λ, Π. In the latter case for the world j associated to the component $E, \Lambda \Rightarrow \Pi, \Theta$ by induction hypothesis on E we get $\mathfrak{M}_\mathcal{G}, j \Vdash E$, whence $W \Vdash^\exists E$. In the former case we have $F \in \langle \Theta \rangle$. Any $k \in W$ (including k=i) is associated to a component $\Gamma_k \Rightarrow \Delta_k$, but by saturation condition (jump$_T$, jump$_U$) we have $\Theta \subseteq \Delta_k$, whence $F \in \Delta_k$; by induction hypothesis on F we have $\mathfrak{M}_\mathcal{G}, k \nVdash F$, showing $W \Vdash^\forall \neg F$.

- Suppose $E \preccurlyeq F \in \Delta_i$. Recall that $\mathsf{SP}(i) = \{\{m_k\}, \{m_k, m_{k-1}\}, \ldots, \{m_k, \ldots, m_1\}, W\}$ with each m_ℓ associated to a sequent $D_\ell, \Lambda_\ell \Rightarrow \Pi_\ell, \Sigma_\ell \in \mathcal{G}$ coming from a block $[\Sigma_\ell \lhd D_\ell] \in \Delta_i$, for $\ell = j, \ldots, k$. By saturation, there is $j \le k$ with $D_j = F$ and $E \in \Sigma_j$. Consider m_j associated to the component $F, \Lambda_j \Rightarrow \Sigma_j, \Pi$. By induction hypothesis we get $\mathfrak{M}_\mathcal{G}, m_j \Vdash F$. Since $\Sigma_j \subseteq \Sigma_{j+1} \subseteq \ldots \subseteq \Sigma_k$, we also get $\mathfrak{M}_\mathcal{G}, m_\ell \nVdash E$, for $\ell = j, \ldots, k$. Thus for $\alpha = \{m_k, \ldots, m_j\} \in \mathsf{SP}(i)$ we get $\alpha \nVdash^\forall \neg F$ and $\alpha \nVdash^\exists E$, showing $\mathfrak{M}_\mathcal{G}, i \nVdash E \preccurlyeq F$.

The proof of 3 uses 2, recalling that a block is a disjunction of $\preccurlyeq$-formulas. The proof of 4 uses 2 with an argument as in the proof of 1 for the case of $\alpha = W$ with $B \in \langle \Theta \rangle$. $\square$

The countermodel construction described above can be extended to $\mathbb{VWU}$ and $\mathbb{VCU}$ by modifying the definition of the model as follows. For $\mathbb{VWU}$, let $\mathsf{SP}(i) := \{\{m_k, i\}, \{m_k, m_{k-1}, i\}, \ldots, \{m_k, \ldots, m_1, i\}, W\}$. For $\mathbb{VCU}$, we add $\{i\}$ to $\mathsf{SP}(i)$ for any i. The proof of Lemma 25 can be easily extended to both cases (statements 1 and 2), using the specific saturation conditions for these systems. We leave the details to the reader; the case of Absoluteness will be handled in future work. From Lemma 25 we obtain:

Lemma 26. *For* $\mathcal{L} \in \{\mathbb{VTU}, \mathbb{VWU}, \mathbb{VCU}\}$ *let* $\mathcal{G} = \Gamma_1 \Rightarrow \Delta_1 \mid \ldots \mid \Gamma_n \Rightarrow \Delta_n$ *be a $\mathcal{L}$-saturated hypersequent and let* $\mathfrak{M}_\mathcal{G}$ *be defined as above, then*

- *for any* $i \in W$ *associated to sequent* $\Gamma_i \Rightarrow \Delta_i$ *we have* $\mathfrak{M}_\mathcal{G}, i \not\Vdash \iota_e(\Gamma_i \Rightarrow \Delta_i)$
- *for any* $i \in W$ *we have* $\mathfrak{M}_\mathcal{G}, i \not\Vdash \iota_e(\mathcal{G})$

To use these results in a decision procedure, we consider *local loop checking*: rules are not applied if there is a premiss from which the conclusion is derivable using structural rules. Since these are all admissible in $\mathsf{SH}^i_\mathcal{L}$, this does not jeopardise completeness.

Proposition 27. *Backwards proof search with local loop checking terminates and every leaf of the resulting derivation is an axiom or a saturated sequent.*

Proof. By Lemmas 20 and 21, we may assume that the proof search only considers *duplication-free* sequents, i.e., sequents containing duplicates neither of formulae nor of blocks. By the subformula property, the number of duplication-free sequents possibly relevant to a derivation of a sequent is bounded in the number of subformulae of that sequent, and hence backwards proof search for $\mathcal{G}$ terminates. Furthermore, every leaf is either an axiom or a saturated sequent, since otherwise another rule could be applied. $\square$

Theorem 28 (Completeness). *If* $\iota_e(\mathcal{G}) \in \mathcal{L}$, *then* $\mathsf{SH}_\mathcal{L} \vdash \mathcal{G}$ *for* $\mathcal{L} \in \{\mathbb{VTU}, \mathbb{VWU}, \mathbb{VCU}\}$.

Proof. By Proposition 27 backwards proof search with root $\mathcal{G}$ terminates and every leaf of it is an axiom or a saturated sequent. By invertibility of the rules each sequent $\mathcal{G}'$ occurring as a leaf is valid. But then $\mathcal{G}'$ must an axiom, since otherwise, by Lemma 26 we can bulid a countermodel $\mathfrak{M}_{\mathcal{G}'}$ falsifying $\iota_e(\mathcal{G}')$ and hence by monotonicity also $\iota_e(\mathcal{G})$. $\square$

We note that Proposition 27 gives rise to a (non-optimal) CO-NEXPTIME-decision procedure for validity: Since applying backwards proof search with local loop checking to an input sequent $\Rightarrow G$ terminates and every leaf of the resulting derivation is an instance of init or $\perp_L$ or a saturated sequent, in order to check whether $\Rightarrow G$ is derivable is suffices to non-determinstically choose a duplication-free $\mathcal{L}$-saturated extended hypersequent containing only subformulas of G and containing a component $\Gamma \Rightarrow \Delta, G$. If this is not possible, then backwards proof search will produce a proof of $\Rightarrow G$. But if it is possible, then by Lemma 26 this hypersequent gives rise to a countermodel for G. Since the size of duplication-free extended hypersequents consisting of subformulae of G is bounded exponentially in the number of subformulae of G, this gives the CO-NEXPTIME complexity bound. Of course it is known that the logics of this section are EXPTIME-complete [5].

8   Conclusion

In this work we have introduced to our knowledge the first internal hypersequent calculi for Lewis' conditional logics with uniformity and reflexivity, both in nonstandard and in standard form. While the former lend themselves to syntactic cut elimination, the latter are amenable to a semantic completeness proof via countermodel construction from a failed proof search and give rise to decision procedures for the considered logics.

While the treatment of these logics is an important step towards a comprehensive proof-theoretic treatment of the whole family of Lewis' logics, many interesting questions are still open. In particular, we plan to extend the semantic completeness proof also to the logics with absoluteness. Further, by moving to the framework of *grafted hypersequents* [10] we expect to be able to extend our results to the logics VU and VNU. Concerning Lewis' conditional logics, this would leave only the logics satisfying *Stalnaker's assumption* [13] lacking a satisfactory internal proof system. Their proof-theoretic investigation will be subject of future research. Finally, we aim at providing complexity-optimal proof methods for the logics under consideration. In particular, for logics with absoluteness, one could make the blocks "global" to the whole hypersequent. We conjecture that such calculi could yield complexity-optimal decision procedures.

References

1. Alenda, R., Olivetti, N.: Preferential semantics for the logic of comparative similarity over triangular and metric models. In: Cerro, L.F., Herzig, A., Mengin, J. (eds.) JELIA 2012. LNCS (LNAI), vol. 7519, pp. 1–13. Springer, Heidelberg (2012). doi:10.1007/978-3-642-33353-8_1
2. Avron, A.: The method of hypersequents in the proof theory of propositional nonclassical logics. In: Hodges, W., Hyland, M., Steinhorn, C., Truss, J. (eds.) Logic: From Foundations to Applications. Clarendon Press, New York (1996)
3. Burgess, J.P.: Quick completeness proofs for some logics of conditionals. Notre Dame J. Formal Log. **22**, 76–84 (1981)
4. Chellas, B.F.: Basic conditional logics. J. Philos. Log. **4**, 133–153 (1975)
5. Friedman, N., Halpern, J.Y.: On the complexity of conditional logics. In: Doyle, J., Sandewall, E., Torasso, P. (eds.) KR 1994, pp. 202–213. Morgan Kaufmann (1994)
6. Giordano, L., Gliozzi, V., Olivetti, N., Schwind, C.: Tableau calculus for preference-based conditional logics: PCL and its extensions. ACM TOCL **10**(3), 21:1–21:50 (2009)

7. Girlando, M., Lellmann, B., Olivetti, N., Pozzato, G.L.: Standard sequent calculi for Lewis' logics of counterfactuals. In: Michael, L., Kakas, A. (eds.) JELIA 2016. LNCS, vol. 10021, pp. 272–287. Springer, Cham (2016). doi:10.1007/978-3-319-48758-8_18

8. Grahne, G.: Updates and counterfactuals. J. Log. Comput. **8**(1), 87–117 (1998)

9. Kraus, S., Lehmann, D., Magidor, M.: Nonmonotonic reasoning, preferential models and cumulative logics. Artif. Intell. **44**(1–2), 167–207 (1990)

10. Kuznets, R., Lellmann, B.: Grafting hypersequents onto nested sequents. Log. J. IGPL **24**, 375–423 (2016)

11. Lellmann, B.: Hypersequent rules with restricted contexts for propositional modal logics. Theoret. Comput. Sci. **656**, 76–105 (2016)

12. Lellmann, B., Pattinson, D.: Sequent systems for Lewis' conditional logics. In: Cerro, L.F., Herzig, A., Mengin, J. (eds.) JELIA 2012. LNCS, vol. 7519, pp. 320–332. Springer, Heidelberg (2012). doi:10.1007/978-3-642-33353-8_25

13. Lewis, D.: Counterfactuals. Blackwell, London (1973)

14. Nute, D.: Topics in Conditional Logic. Reidel, Dordrecht (1980)

15. Olivetti, N., Pozzato, G.L.: A standard internal calculus for Lewis' counterfactual logics. In: Nivelle, H. (ed.) TABLEAUX 2015. LNCS, vol. 9323, pp. 270–286. Springer, Cham (2015). doi:10.1007/978-3-319-24312-2_19

16. Restall, G.: Proofnets for S5: sequents and circuits for modal logic. In: Logic Colloquium 2005. Lecture Notes in Logic, vol. 28, pp. 151–172. Cambridge University Press (2007)

17. Sheremet, M., Tishkovsky, D., Wolter, F., Zakharyaschev, M.: A logic for concepts and similarity. J. Log. Comput. **17**(3), 415–452 (2007)

18. Stalnaker, R.: A theory of conditionals. In: Rescher, N. (ed.) Studies in Logical Theory, pp. 98–112. Blackwell (1968)

VINTE: An Implementation of Internal Calculi for Lewis' Logics of Counterfactual Reasoning

Marianna Girlando[1]([⊠]), Björn Lellmann[2], Nicola Olivetti[1], Gian Luca Pozzato[3], and Quentin Vitalis[4]

[1] Aix Marseille Université, CNRS, ENSAM, Université de Toulon, LSIS UMR 7296, 13397 Marseille, France
{marianna.girlando,nicola.olivetti}@univ-amu.fr
[2] Technische Universität Wien, Vienna, Austria
lellmann@logic.at
[3] Dipartimento di Informatica, Universitá di Torino, Turin, Italy
gianluca.pozzato@unito.it
[4] Département Informatique, École Spéciale Militaire de Saint-Cyr, Guer, France
quentin.vitalis@protonmail.com

Abstract. We present VINTE, a theorem prover for conditional logics for counterfactual reasoning introduced by Lewis in the seventies. VINTE implements some internal calculi recently introduced for the basic system $\mathbb{V}$ and some of its significant extensions with axioms $\mathbb{N}$, $\mathbb{T}$, $\mathbb{C}$, $\mathbb{W}$ and $\mathbb{A}$. VINTE is inspired by the methodology of lean $T^A P$ and it is implemented in Prolog. The paper shows some experimental results, witnessing that the performances of VINTE are promising.

1 Introduction

Conditional logics are extensions of classical logic by a *conditional* operator $\Box\!\!\rightarrow$. They have a long history [11], and recently they have found an interest in several fields of AI and knowledge representation. Just to mention a few (see [1] for a complete bibliography), they have been used to reason about prototypical properties, to model belief change [8], to reason about access control policies [5], to formalize epistemic change in a multi-agent setting [2,4]. Conditional logics can also provide an axiomatic foundation of nonmonotonic reasoning [9]: here a conditional $A \Box\!\!\rightarrow B$ is read "normally, if A then B".

In early seventies, Lewis proposed a formalization of conditional logics in order to represent a kind of hypothetical reasoning that cannot be captured by the material implication of classical logic [10]. His original motivation was to formalize counterfactuals, that is to say, conditionals of the form "if A were the case then B would be the case", where A is false. The family of logics studied by Lewis is semantically characterized by sphere models, a particular kind of

Supported by the Project TICAMORE ANR-16-CE91-0002-01, by the EU under Marie Skłodowska-Curie Grant Agreement No. [660047], and by the Project "ExceptionOWL", Università di Torino and Compagnia di San Paolo, call 2014.

R.A. Schmidt and C. Nalon (Eds.): TABLEAUX 2017, LNAI 10501, pp. 149–159, 2017.
DOI: 10.1007/978-3-319-66902-1_9

neighbourhood models introduced by Lewis himself. In Lewis' terminology, a *sphere* denotes a set of worlds; in sphere models, each world is equipped with a nested system of such spheres. From the viewpoint of the given world, inner sets represent the "most plausible worlds", while worlds belonging only to outer sets are considered as less plausible. In order to treat the conditional operator, Lewis takes as primitive the comparative plausibility connective $\preccurlyeq$: a formula $A \preccurlyeq B$ means "A is at least as plausible as B". The conditional $A \,\square\!\!\rightarrow B$ can be then defined as "A is impossible" or "$A \wedge \neg B$ is less plausible than $A \wedge B$". However, the latter assertion is equivalent to the simpler one "$A \wedge \neg B$ is less plausible than A"[1].

In previous works [6,16] we have introduced internal, standard, cut-free calculi for most logics of the Lewis family, namely logics $\mathbb{V}$, $\mathbb{VN}$, $\mathbb{VT}$, $\mathbb{VW}$, $\mathbb{VC}$, $\mathbb{VA}$ and $\mathbb{VNA}$. Here we describe a Prolog implementation of the invertible calculi $\mathcal{I}_{\mathcal{L}}^i$ introduced in [6]. The program, called VINTE, gives a decision procedure for the respective logics, and it is inspired by the methodology of lean $T^A P$ [3]. The idea is that each axiom or rule of the sequent calculi is implemented by a Prolog clause of the program. The resulting code is therefore simple and compact: the implementation of VINTE for $\mathbb{V}$ consists of only 3 predicates, 21 clauses and 57 lines of code. We provide experimental results by comparing VINTE with the following theorem provers for conditional logics: CondLean [12], GOALD$\mathcal{U}$CK [13] and NESCOND [14,15], and we show that the performances of VINTE are quite promising. The program VINTE, as well as all the Prolog source files, are available for free usage and download at http://193.51.60.97:8000/vinte/.

2   Lewis' Conditional Logics

We consider the *conditional logics* defined by Lewis in [10]. The set of *conditional formulae* is given by $\mathcal{F} :: = p \mid \bot \mid \mathcal{F} \rightarrow \mathcal{F} \mid \mathcal{F} \preccurlyeq \mathcal{F}$, where $p \in \mathcal{V}$ is a propositional variable. The other boolean connectives are defined in terms of $\bot, \rightarrow$ as usual. Intuitively, a formula $A \preccurlyeq B$ is interpreted as "A is at least as plausible as B".

As mentioned above, Lewis' counterfactual implication $\square\!\!\rightarrow$ can be defined in terms of comparative plausibility $\preccurlyeq$ as

$$A \,\square\!\!\rightarrow B \equiv (\bot \preccurlyeq A) \vee \neg((A \wedge \neg B) \preccurlyeq A).$$

The semantics of this logic is defined by Lewis in terms of *sphere semantics*:

Definition 1. *A* sphere model *(or* model*) is a triple* $\langle W, \mathsf{SP}, [\![.]\!] \rangle$*, consisting of a non-empty set W of elements, called* worlds*, a mapping* $\mathsf{SP} : W \rightarrow \mathcal{P}(\mathcal{P}(W))$*, and a propositional valuation* $[\![.]\!] : \mathcal{V} \rightarrow \mathcal{P}(W)$*. Elements of* $\mathsf{SP}(x)$ *are called* spheres*. We assume the following conditions: for every* $\alpha \in \mathsf{SP}(w)$ *we have* $\alpha \neq \emptyset$*, and for every* $\alpha, \beta \in \mathsf{SP}(w)$ *we have* $\alpha \subseteq \beta$ *or* $\beta \subseteq \alpha$*. The latter condition is called* sphere nesting*.*

---

[1] It is worth noticing that in turn the connective $\preccurlyeq$ can be defined in terms of $\square\!\!\rightarrow$.

Table 1. Lewis' logics and axioms.

CPR $\dfrac{\vdash B \to A}{\vdash A \preccurlyeq B}$

TR $(A \preccurlyeq B) \wedge (B \preccurlyeq C) \to (A \preccurlyeq C)$

N $\neg(\bot \preccurlyeq \top)$

T $(\bot \preccurlyeq \neg A) \to A$

C $(A \preccurlyeq \top) \to A$

CPA $(A \preccurlyeq A \vee B) \vee (B \preccurlyeq A \vee B)$

CO $(A \preccurlyeq B) \vee (B \preccurlyeq A)$

W $A \to (A \preccurlyeq \top)$

A1 $(A \preccurlyeq B) \to \left(\bot \preccurlyeq \neg(A \preccurlyeq B)\right)$

A2 $\neg(A \preccurlyeq B) \to \left(\bot \preccurlyeq (A \preccurlyeq B)\right)$

$$\mathcal{A}_{\mathbb{V}} := \{\mathsf{CPR}, \mathsf{CPA}, \mathsf{TR}, \mathsf{CO}\}$$

$\mathcal{A}_{\mathbb{VN}} := \mathcal{A}_{\mathbb{V}} \cup \{\mathsf{N}\}$ $\qquad$ $\mathcal{A}_{\mathbb{VT}} := \mathcal{A}_{\mathbb{V}} \cup \{\mathsf{N}, \mathsf{T}\}$ $\qquad$ $\mathcal{A}_{\mathbb{VW}} := \mathcal{A}_{\mathbb{V}} \cup \{\mathsf{N}, \mathsf{T}, \mathsf{W}\}$

$\mathcal{A}_{\mathbb{VC}} := \mathcal{A}_{\mathbb{V}} \cup \{\mathsf{N}, \mathsf{T}, \mathsf{W}, \mathsf{C}\}$ $\quad$ $\mathcal{A}_{\mathbb{VA}} := \mathcal{A}_{\mathbb{V}} \cup \{\mathsf{A1}, \mathsf{A2}\}$ $\quad$ $\mathcal{A}_{\mathbb{VNA}} := \mathcal{A}_{\mathbb{V}} \cup \{\mathsf{N}, \mathsf{A1}, \mathsf{A2}\}$

The valuation $[\![.]\!]$ is extended to all formulae by: $[\![\bot]\!] = \emptyset$; $[\![A \to B]\!] = (W - [\![A]\!]) \cup [\![B]\!]$; $[\![A \preccurlyeq B]\!] = \{w \in W \mid \text{for all } \alpha \in \mathsf{SP}(w). \text{ if } [\![B]\!] \cap \alpha \neq \emptyset, \text{ then } [\![A]\!] \cap \alpha \neq \emptyset\}$. For $w \in W$ we also write $w \Vdash A$ instead of $w \in [\![A]\!]$. As for spheres, we write $\alpha \Vdash^\forall A$ meaning $\forall x \in \alpha. x \Vdash A$ and $\alpha \Vdash^\exists A$ meaning $\exists x \in \alpha. x \Vdash A$[2]. Validity and satisfiability of formulae in a class of models are defined as usual. Conditional logic $\mathbb{V}$ is the set of formulae valid in all sphere models.

Extensions of $\mathbb{V}$ are semantically given by specifying additional conditions on the class of sphere models, namely:

- *normality*: for all $w \in W$ we have $\mathsf{SP}(w) \neq \emptyset$;
- *total reflexivity*: for all $w \in W$ we have $w \in \bigcup \mathsf{SP}(w)$;
- *weak centering*: normality holds and for all $\alpha \in \mathsf{SP}(w)$ we have $w \in \alpha$;
- *centering*: for all $w \in W$ we have $\{w\} \in \mathsf{SP}(w)$;
- *absoluteness*: for all $w, v \in W$ we have $\mathsf{SP}(w) = \mathsf{SP}(v)$[3].

Extensions of $\mathbb{V}$ are denoted by concatenating the letters for these properties: $\mathbb{N}$ for normality, $\mathbb{T}$ for total reflexivity, $\mathbb{W}$ for weak centering, $\mathbb{C}$ for centering, and $\mathbb{A}$ for absoluteness. All the above logics can be characterized by axioms in a Hilbert-style system [10, Chap. 6]. The modal axioms formulated in the language with only the comparative plausibility operator are presented in Table 1 (where $\vee$ and $\wedge$ bind stronger than $\preccurlyeq$). The propositional axioms and rules are the standard ones.

3 Internal Calculi for Conditional Logics

Table 2 presents calculi $\mathcal{I}^i_{\mathcal{L}}$, where $\mathcal{L}$ ranges over the logics $\mathbb{V}, \mathbb{VN}, \mathbb{VT}, \mathbb{VW}$, $\mathbb{VC}, \mathbb{VA}, \mathbb{VNA}$, introduced in [6]. The basic constituent of sequents are *blocks*

---

[2] Employing this notation, satisfiability of a $\preccurlyeq$-formula in a model becomes the following: $x \Vdash A \preccurlyeq B$ iff for all $\alpha \in \mathsf{SP}(x)$. $\alpha \Vdash^\forall \neg B$ or $\alpha \Vdash^\exists A$.

[3] It is worth noticing that absoluteness can be equally stated as *local absoluteness*: $\forall w \in W, \forall v \in \bigcup \mathsf{SP}(w)$ it holds $\mathsf{SP}(w) = \mathsf{SP}(v)$.

Table 2. The calculus $\mathcal{I}_V^i$ and its extensions.

$$\frac{}{\Gamma, \bot \Rightarrow \Delta} \perp_L \qquad \frac{}{\Gamma, p \Rightarrow \Delta, p} \text{ init} \qquad \frac{\Gamma, B \Rightarrow \Delta \quad \Gamma \Rightarrow \Delta, A}{\Gamma, A \to B \Rightarrow \Delta} \to_L \qquad \frac{\Gamma, A \Rightarrow \Delta, B}{\Gamma \Rightarrow \Delta, A \to B} \to_R$$

$$\frac{\Gamma \Rightarrow \Delta, [A \lhd B]}{\Gamma \Rightarrow \Delta, A \preccurlyeq B} \preccurlyeq_R \qquad \frac{\Gamma, A \preccurlyeq B \Rightarrow \Delta, [B, \Sigma \lhd C] \quad \Gamma, A \preccurlyeq B \Rightarrow \Delta, [\Sigma \lhd A], [\Sigma \lhd C]}{\Gamma, A \preccurlyeq B \Rightarrow \Delta, [\Sigma \lhd C]} \preccurlyeq_L^i$$

$$\frac{}{\Gamma \Rightarrow \Delta, \top} \top_R \qquad \frac{\Gamma \Rightarrow \Delta, [\Sigma_1, \Sigma_2 \lhd A], [\Sigma_2 \lhd B] \quad \Gamma \Rightarrow \Delta, [\Sigma_1 \lhd A], [\Sigma_1, \Sigma_2 \lhd B]}{\Gamma \Rightarrow \Delta, [\Sigma_1 \lhd A], [\Sigma_2 \lhd B]} \text{ com}^i$$

$$\frac{\bot \preccurlyeq A, \Gamma \Rightarrow \Delta \quad \Gamma \Rightarrow \Delta, [A \wedge \neg B \lhd A]}{A \mathbin{\square\!\!\rightarrow} B, \Gamma \Rightarrow \Delta} \square\!\!\rightarrow_L \qquad \frac{(A \preccurlyeq \neg B) \preccurlyeq A, \Gamma \Rightarrow \Delta, [\bot \lhd A]}{\Gamma \Rightarrow \Delta, A \mathbin{\square\!\!\rightarrow} B} \square\!\!\rightarrow_R$$

$$\frac{A \Rightarrow \Sigma}{\Gamma \Rightarrow \Delta, [\Sigma \lhd A]} \text{ jump} \qquad \frac{\Gamma \Rightarrow \Delta, [\bot \lhd \top]}{\Gamma \Rightarrow \Delta} \text{ N}$$

$$\frac{\Gamma, A \preccurlyeq B \Rightarrow \Delta, B \quad \Gamma, A \preccurlyeq B \Rightarrow \Delta, [\bot \lhd A]}{\Gamma, A \preccurlyeq B \Rightarrow \Delta} \text{ T}^i \qquad \frac{\Gamma \Rightarrow \Delta, [\Sigma \lhd A], \Sigma}{\Gamma \Rightarrow \Delta, [\Sigma \lhd A]} \text{ W}^i$$

$$\frac{\Gamma, A \preccurlyeq B \Rightarrow \Delta, B \quad \Gamma, A \preccurlyeq B, A \Rightarrow \Delta}{\Gamma, A \preccurlyeq B \Rightarrow \Delta} \text{ C}^i \qquad \frac{\Gamma^{\preccurlyeq}, B \Rightarrow \Delta^{\preccurlyeq}, [\Sigma \lhd B], \Sigma}{\Gamma \Rightarrow \Delta, [\Sigma \lhd B]} \text{ A}^i$$

Here $\Gamma^{\preccurlyeq} \Rightarrow \Delta^{\preccurlyeq}$ is $\Gamma \Rightarrow \Delta$ restricted to formulae of the form $C \preccurlyeq D$ and blocks.

$$\mathcal{I}_V^i := \{\bot_L, \top_R, \text{init}, \to_L, \to_R, \square\!\!\rightarrow_L, \square\!\!\rightarrow_R, \preccurlyeq_R, \preccurlyeq_L^i, \text{com}^i, \text{jump}\}$$

$$\mathcal{I}_{VN}^i := \mathcal{I}_V^i \cup \{N\} \qquad \mathcal{I}_{VW}^i := \mathcal{I}_V^i \cup \{N, T^i, W^i\} \qquad \mathcal{I}_{VA}^i := \mathcal{I}_V^i \cup \{A^i\}$$
$$\mathcal{I}_{VT}^i := \mathcal{I}_V^i \cup \{N, T^i\} \qquad \mathcal{I}_{VC}^i := \mathcal{I}_V^i \cup \{N, T^i, W^i, C^i\} \qquad \mathcal{I}_{VNA}^i := \mathcal{I}_V^i \cup \{N, A^i\}$$

of the form $[A_1, \ldots, A_m \lhd A]$, with $A_1, \ldots, A_m, A$ formulas, representing disjunctions of $\preccurlyeq$-formulas. A *sequent* is a tuple $\Gamma \Rightarrow \Delta$, where Γ is a multiset of conditional formulae, and Δ is a multiset of conditional formulae and blocks. The *formula interpretation* of a sequent is given by:

$$\iota(\Gamma \Rightarrow \Delta', [\Sigma_1 \lhd A_1], \ldots, [\Sigma_n \lhd A_n]) := \bigwedge \Gamma \to \bigvee \Delta' \vee \bigvee_{1 \le i \le n} \bigvee_{B \in \Sigma_i} (B \preccurlyeq A_i)$$

As usual, given a formula $G \in \mathcal{L}$, in order to check whether G is valid we look for a derivation of $\Rightarrow G$. Given a sequent $\Gamma \Rightarrow \Delta$, we say that it is derivable if it admits a *derivation*, namely a tree whose root is $\Gamma \Rightarrow \Delta$, every leaf is an instance of init or $\bot_L$ or $\top_R$, and every non-leaf node is (an instance of) the conclusion of a rule having (an instance of) the premises of the rule as children.

In [6] it is shown that:

Theorem 1. *The calculi $\mathcal{I}_{\mathcal{L}}^i$ are sound and complete for the respective logics.*

In [6] it has been also shown that the calculi $\mathcal{I}_{\mathcal{L}}^i$ can be used in a decision procedure for the logic $\mathcal{L}$ as follows. Since contractions and weakenings are admissible we may assume that a derivation of a duplication-free sequent (containing duplicates neither of formulae nor of blocks) only contains duplication-free sequents: whenever a (backwards) application of a rule introduces a duplicate of a formula already in the sequent, it is immediately deleted in the next step using a backwards application of weakening. While officially our calculi do not contain the weakening rules, the proof of admissibility of weakening yields a procedure to transform a derivation with these rules into one without. Since all rules have the subformula property, the number of duplication-free sequents possibly relevant to a derivation of a sequent is bounded in the number of subformulae of that sequent, and hence enumerating all possible loop-free derivations of the above form yields a decision procedure for the logic.

Theorem 2. *Proof search with the blocking technique above for a sequent $\Gamma \Rightarrow \Delta$ in calculus $\mathcal{I}_{\mathcal{L}}^i$ always comes to an end in a finite number of steps.*

As usual, in order to implement such a decision procedure, we have to control the application of the rules to avoid the introduction of duplicated sequents. Concerning the rule $\preccurlyeq_L^i$, the principal formula $A \preccurlyeq B$ is copied into the premises, then we have to avoid that, in a backward application of the rule, such formula is redundantly applied by using the same block $[\Sigma \lhd C]$. Since no rule, with the exception of jump, remove formulas from blocks, we allow a backward application of $\preccurlyeq_L^i$ to a sequent $\Gamma, A \preccurlyeq B \Rightarrow \Delta, [\Sigma \lhd C]$ if neither $[B, \Sigma \lhd C]$ nor $[\Sigma' \lhd C]$, where $B, \Sigma \subset \Sigma'$ belong to Δ, and neither $[\Sigma \lhd A]$ nor $[\Sigma' \lhd A]$, where $\Sigma \subset \Sigma'$ belong to Δ. Similarly for the com^i rule, which can be applied backward to blocks $[\Sigma_1 \lhd A]$ and $[\Sigma_2 \lhd B]$ if neither $[\Sigma_1, \Sigma_2 \lhd A]$ nor $[\Sigma_1, \Sigma_2 \lhd B]$ are introduced redundantly in the premises. For rules like W^i, whose premises contain the principal formula, we just need to check whether the formulas introduced in the premises by a backward application of the rule already belong to such premises or not. In the first case, the application of the rule is blocked. As an example, if W^i is applied to $\Rightarrow [A \lor B \lhd C]$, then the premiss is $\Rightarrow [A \lor B \lhd C], A \lor B$, that becomes $(*) \Rightarrow [A \lor B \lhd C], A, B$ after an application of the rule $\lor_R$. The rule W^i can be further applied to $(*)$, since $A \lor B$ does not belong to the right-hand side of the sequent, then obtaining the premiss $\Rightarrow [A \lor B \lhd C], A, B, A \lor B$, and at this point neither W^i nor $\lor_R$ can be further applied.

4   Design of VINTE

In this section we present a Prolog implementation of the internal calculi $\mathcal{I}_{\mathcal{L}}^i$ recalled in Sect. 3. The program, called VINTE (V: INTernal calculi and Extensions), is inspired by the "lean" methodology of leanT^AP, even if it does not follow its style in a rigorous manner. The program comprises a set of clauses, each one of them implements a sequent rule or axiom of $\mathcal{I}_{\mathcal{L}}^i$. The proof search is provided for free by the mere depth-first search mechanism of Prolog, without any additional ad hoc mechanism.

VINTE represents a sequent with a pair of Prolog lists [Gamma,Delta], where Gamma and Delta represent the left-hand side and the right-hand side of the sequent, respectively. Elements of Gamma are formulas, whereas elements of Delta can be either formulas or pairs [Sigma,A], where Sigma is a Prolog list, representing a block $[\Sigma \lhd A]$. Symbols $\top$ and $\bot$ are represented by constants true and false, respectively, whereas connectives $\neg$, $\wedge$, $\vee$, $\rightarrow$, $\preccurlyeq$, and $\Box\!\!\rightarrow$ are represented by $-,\hat{} , ?, ->, <,$ and $=>$. Propositional variables are represented by Prolog atoms. As an example, the Prolog pair

```
[ [-(p?q), p, p -> q, p < r], [q, p => (q^r), [ [true, p, q], r] ] ]
```

is used to represent the sequent

$$\neg(P \vee Q), P, P \rightarrow Q, P \preccurlyeq R \Rightarrow Q, P \Box\!\!\rightarrow (Q \wedge R), [\top, P, Q \lhd R].$$

The calculi $\mathcal{I}_{\mathcal{L}}^{i}$ are implemented by the predicate

```
prove([Gamma,Delta],ProofTree).
```

This predicate succeeds if and only if the sequent $\Gamma \Rightarrow \Delta$ represented by the pair of lists [Gamma,Delta] is derivable. When it succeeds, the output term ProofTree matches with a representation of the derivation found by the prover. For instance, in order to prove that the formula $(A \preccurlyeq B) \vee (B \preccurlyeq A)$ is valid in $\mathbb{V}$, one queries VINTE with the goal: prove([[],[(a<b)?(b<a)]],ProofTree). Each clause of prove implements an axiom or rule of $\mathcal{I}_{\mathcal{L}}^{i}$. To search a derivation of a sequent $\Gamma \Rightarrow \Delta$, VINTE proceeds as follows. First of all, if $\Gamma \Rightarrow \Delta$ is an instance of either $\bot_L$ or $\top_R$ or init, the goal will succeed immediately by using one of the following clauses for the axioms:

```
prove([Gamma,Delta],tree(axb):-member(false,Gamma),!.
prove([Gamma,Delta],tree(axt)):-member(true,Delta),!.
prove([Gamma,Delta],tree(init)):-member(P,Gamma),member(P,Delta),!.
```

If $\Gamma \Rightarrow \Delta$ is not an instance of the ending rules, then the first applicable rule will be chosen, e.g. if Δ contains a formula A < B, then the clause implementing the $\preccurlyeq_R$ rule will be chosen, and VINTE will be recursively invoked on the unique premise of such a rule. VINTE proceeds in a similar way for the other rules. The ordering of the clauses is such that the application of the branching rules is postponed as much as possible, with the exception of the rule jump which is the last rule to be applied. As an example, the clause implementing $\preccurlyeq_L^i$ is as follows:

```
1.  prove([Gamma,Delta],tree(precL,Sub1,Sub2)):-
2.      member(A < B,Gamma),
3.      select([Sigma,C],Delta,NewDelta),
4.      remove_duplicates([B|Sigma],NewSigma),
5.      \+memberOrdSet([NewSigma,C],Delta),
6.      \+memberOrdSet([Sigma,A],Delta), !,
7.      prove([Gamma,[[NewSigma,C]|NewDelta]],Sub1),
8.      prove([Gamma,[[Sigma,A]|Delta]],Sub2).
```

In line 4, the auxiliary predicate remove_duplicates is invoked in order to remove duplicated formulas in the multiset of formulas B, Σ. This is equivalent to apply weakening if the formula B already belongs to Γ. Another auxiliary predicate, memberOrdSet, is then invoked in lines 5 and 6 in order to implement the decision procedure described at the end of Sect. 3: Prolog ordsets are used in order to deal with the equivalence of lists where formulas occur in different orders. Since the rule is invertibile, Prolog cut ! is used in line 6 to eventually block backtracking. The jump rule is implemented as follows:

```
1.   prove([Gamma,Delta],tree(jump,SubTree)):-
2.       member([Sigma,A],Delta),
3.       prove([[A],Sigma],SubTree).
```

This is the only non invertible rule, and a backtracking point is introduced by the choice of the block $[\Sigma \lhd A]$ in Δ to which apply the rule.

The implementation of the calculi for extensions of $\mathbb{V}$ is very similar. The only significant difference is in the more sophisticated mechanism needed to ensure termination. As an example, in system implementing the calculus for $\mathbb{VC}$, the predicate prove is equipped by a further parameter, called AppliedC, containing the list of formulas of the form $A \preccurlyeq B$ to which the rule C^i has been already applied in the current branch. The code implementing the rule C^i is as follows:

```
1.  prove([Gamma,Delta],tree(c,Sub1,Sub2),AppliedC):-
2.  member(A < B,Gamma),
3.  \+member(A < B,AppliedC),
4.  (\+member(B,Delta);\+member(A,Gamma)), !,
5.  prove([Gamma,[B|Delta]],Sub1,[A<B|AppliedC]),
6.  prove([[A|Gamma],Delta],Sub2,[A<B|AppliedC]).
```

Line 3 shows how this parameter is used in order to avoid multiple application of C^i to the same formula $A \preccurlyeq B$ in a given branch, then the consequent loop in the proof search: if $A \preccurlyeq B$ belongs to AppliedC, then the rule C^i has been already applied to it in the current branch and it is no longer applied; otherwise, the predicate prove is recursively invoked on the premisses of the rule, and $A \preccurlyeq B$ is added to the list of formulas already employed for applications of C^i.

VINTE can be used by means of a simple web interface, implemented in php and allowing the user to check whether a conditional formula is valid by using his computer as well as his mobile device. The web interface also allows the user to choose the conditional system to adopt, namely $\mathbb{V}$ or one of the extensions mentioned in Sect. 2. When a formula is valid, VINTE builds a pdf file showing a derivation in the invertible calculi recalled in Sect. 3 as well as the LaTeX source file. Prolog source codes and experimental results are also available. Some pictures of VINTE are shown in Figs. 1 and 2.

Fig. 1. Home page of VINTE.

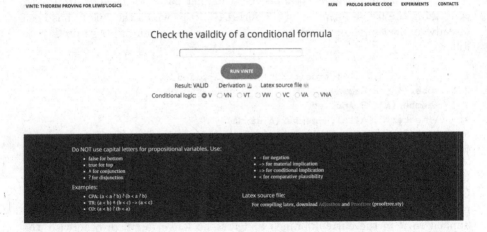

Fig. 2. When the user wants to check whether a formula F is valid, then (i) he selects the conditional logic to use, (ii) he types F in the form and (iii) clicks the button in order to execute the calculi presented in Sect. 3.

5   Performance of VINTE

The performance of VINTE seems to be promising. We have tested it by running SICStus Prolog 4.0.2 on an Apple MacBook Pro, 2.7 GHz Intel Core i7, 8 GB RAM machine. In absence of theorem provers specifically tailored for Lewis' logics, we have compared the performances of VINTE with those of the following theorem provers for conditional logics:

– CondLean 3.1, implementing labelled sequent calculi [12];
– GOALD$\mathcal{U}$CK, implemented a goal-directed proof procedure [13];
– NESCOND, implementing nested sequent calculi [14,15].

All the above mentioned theorem provers take into account conditional logics based on the *selection function semantics* [11], namely conditional logic CK and extensions with axioms ID, MP, CEM, CSO, that are weaker than the ones considered by VINTE, then the experimental results are only partially significant and only aim at conjecturing that the performance of VINTE is promising.

We have performed two kinds of experiments: 1. we have tested the four provers on randomly generated formulas, fixing different time limits; 2. we have tested VINTE for system VN and NESCOND over a set of valid formulas in the logic CK, therefore also valid in VN [10].

Concerning 1 (Table 3), we have tested the four provers over 2000 random sequents with 20 formulas built from 7 different atomic variables and with a high level of nesting (10): both VINTE and NESCOND are able to answer in all cases within 1 s, whereas CondLean 3.1 is not able to conclude anything in 55 cases over 1000. Performance of GOALD$\mathcal{U}$CK is even worse, since it fails to answer in 174 cases. The differences seem much more significant when considering sequents with more formulas (100) and with a higher level of nesting (20): with a time limit of 5 ms, GOALD$\mathcal{U}$CK is faster than CondLean 3.1 and NESCOND, since it is not able to answer only in 136 cases over 1000, against 173 timeouts of CondLean 3.1 and 479 timeouts of NESCOND. VINTE is able to answer again in all cases, and only NESCOND is also able to complete all the tests, when the time limit is extended to 1 s. We have repeated the above experiments by considering implementations of VINTE for extensions of V, obtaining the results summarized in Table 4.

As mentioned, since the four provers take into account different logics, in general they give a different answer over the same - randomly generated - sequent. Then, this kind of tests over CK formulas could be considered not very significant. Instead, we should test VINTE over a set of significant formulas for the specific Lewis' logics that it is designed for: to this aim, we are currently developing a set of benchmarks for VINTE drawn by valid instances of Lewis' axioms.

Table 3. Number of timeouts over 1000 random sequents using VINTE for V.

Seq. with 20 formulas (nesting lev.10)		
Prover	Limit **5 ms**	Limit **1 s**
VINTE	3	0
CondLean 3.1	55	14
GOALD$\mathcal{U}$CK	249	174
NESCOND	35	0

Seq. with 100 formulas (nesting lev.20)		
Prover	Limit **5 ms**	Limit **1 s**
VINTE	45	0
CondLean 3.1	173	141
GOALD$\mathcal{U}$CK	136	133
NESCOND	479	0

Table 4. Number of timeouts of VINTE for extensions of $\mathbb{V}$ (average of different systems) over 1000 random sequents.

Seq. with 20 formulas (nesting lev.10)			Seq. with 100 formulas (nesting lev.20)		
Prover	Limit **5 ms**	Limit **1 s**	Prover	Limit **5 ms**	Limit **1 s**
VINTE	8	2	VINTE	1	0
CondLean 3.1	65	17	CondLean 3.1	180	80
GOALD$\mathcal{U}$CK	276	198	GOALD$\mathcal{U}$CK	327	18
NESCOND	46	5	NESCOND	19	6

Concerning 2, we have considered 76 valid formulas obtained by translating K valid formulas provided by Heuerding in conditional formulas: $\Box A$ is replaced by $\top \mathrel{\Box\!\!\rightarrow} A^4$, whereas $\Diamond A$ is replaced by $\neg(\top \mathrel{\Box\!\!\rightarrow} \neg A)$. We have compared the performance of VINTE, implementation for $\mathbb{VN}$, with those of NESCOND, the best prover among those taken into account for conditional logics based on the selection function semantics [15]. As expected, the performance of NESCOND is still significantly better than those of VINTE: fixing a time limit of 1ms, NESCOND is able to check the validity of the considered formula in the 86 % of cases, whereas VINTE is able to answer only in the 11 % of cases. However, VINTE is able to reach a percentage of successes of 37 % by extending the time limit to 1 s, and over 60% in 3 s (even if, in this last case, NESCOND is not able to answer only in 2 cases over 76). Obviously, this result is justified by the fact that VINTE supports stronger systems of conditional logics with respect to NESCOND, which is specifically tailored for CK and all the proposed results are restricted to such weaker system supported by both provers.

6   Conclusions and Future Issues

We have presented VINTE, a theorem prover implementing internal calculi for Lewis' conditional logics introduced in [6]. Our long term project is to develop both calculi and theorem provers for the whole family of Lewis' logics. One further step in this direction is represented by the hypersequent calculi for containing both uniformity (all worlds have the same set of accessible worlds) and total reflexivity presented in [7]. Notice that an implementation of *hypersequent* calculi is an interesting task in itself.

We also aim at improving the performances of VINTE by implementing standard refinements and heuristics. We also intend to extend VINTE to handle countermodel generation for unprovable formulas. Last, as mentioned in the previous section, we are currently developing a set of benchmarks for VINTE for a more detailed analysis of the performances of the theorem prover.

---

[4] It is worth noticing that this translation introduces an exponential blowup.

References

1. Alenda, R., Olivetti, N., Pozzato, G.L.: Nested sequent calculi for normal conditional logics. J. Log. Comput. **26**(1), 7–50 (2016)
2. Baltag, A., Smets, S.: The logic of conditional doxastic actions. Texts Log. Games **4**, 9–31 (2008). Special Issue on New Perspectives on Games and Interaction
3. Beckert, B., Posegga, J.: leanTAP: lean tableau-based deduction. J. Autom. Reason. **15**(3), 339–358 (1995)
4. Board, O.: Dynamic interactive epistemology. Games Econ. Behav. **49**(1), 49–80 (2004)
5. Genovese, V., Giordano, L., Gliozzi, V., Pozzato, G.L.: Logics in access control: a conditional approach. J. Log. Comput. **24**(4), 705–762 (2014)
6. Girlando, M., Lellmann, B., Olivetti, N., Pozzato, G.L.: Standard sequent calculi for Lewis' logics of counterfactuals. In: Michael, L., Kakas, A. (eds.) JELIA 2016. LNCS, vol. 10021, pp. 272–287. Springer, Cham (2016). doi:10.1007/978-3-319-48758-8_18
7. Girlando, M., Lellmann, B., Olivetti, N., Pozzato, G.L.: Hypersequent calculi for Lewis' conditional logics with uniformity and reflexivity. In: Nalon, C., Schmidt, R.A. (eds.) TABLEAUX 2017. LNCS (LNAI), vol. 10501, pp. 131–148. Springer, Cham (2017)
8. Grahne, G.: Updates and counterfactuals. J. Log. Comput. **8**(1), 87–117 (1998)
9. Kraus, S., Lehmann, D., Magidor, M.: Nonmonotonic reasoning, preferential models and cumulative logics. Artif. Intell. **44**(1–2), 167–207 (1990)
10. Lewis, D.: Counterfactuals. Blackwell, Hoboken (1973)
11. Nute, D.: Topics in Conditional Logic. Reidel, Dordrecht (1980)
12. Olivetti, N., Pozzato, G.L.: CondLean 3.0: improving condlean for stronger conditional logics. In: Beckert, B. (ed.) TABLEAUX 2005. LNCS (LNAI), vol. 3702, pp. 328–332. Springer, Heidelberg (2005). doi:10.1007/11554554_27
13. Olivetti, N., Pozzato, G.L.: Theorem proving for conditional logics: condlean and goalduck. J. Appl. Non-Class. Log. **18**(4), 427–473 (2008)
14. Olivetti, N., Pozzato, G.L.: NESCOND: an implementation of nested sequent calculi for conditional logics. In: Demri, S., Kapur, D., Weidenbach, C. (eds.) IJCAR 2014. LNCS (LNAI), vol. 8562, pp. 511–518. Springer, Cham (2014). doi:10.1007/978-3-319-08587-6_39
15. Olivetti, N., Pozzato, G.L.: Nested sequent calculi and theorem proving for normal conditional logics: the theorem prover NESCOND. Intelligenza Artificiale **9**(2), 109–125 (2015)
16. Olivetti, N., Pozzato, G.L.: A standard internal calculus for Lewis' counterfactual logics. In: Nivelle, H. (ed.) TABLEAUX 2015. LNCS, vol. 9323, pp. 270–286. Springer, Cham (2015). doi:10.1007/978-3-319-24312-2_19

Tableaux

Goal-Sensitive Reasoning with Disconnection Tableaux

Lee A. Barnett[✉]

The University of North Carolina at Chapel Hill, Chapel Hill, NC 27599, USA
lbarnett@cs.unc.edu

Abstract. One of the challenges that has been outlined for instantiation-based theorem proving methods is their application in reasoning over theories with many axioms, as in tasks involving large ontologies or mathematical libraries. Goal-sensitive methods, which restrict inferences to those related to the goal to be refuted, tend to outperform other methods on large axiom sets especially. This paper presents a goal-sensitive adaptation of the disconnection tableau calculus, leveraging the advantages of goal-sensitivity in an instantiation-based, tableau-guided proof method. A proof of the method's completeness follows its description, as well as a discussion of planned future work in this area.

Keywords: Theorem proving · Instance-based methods · Goal-sensitivity

1 Introduction

Instantiation-based automated reasoning methods combine the expressive power of first-order logic with existing propositional theorem-proving technology to solve difficult problems efficiently. These methods apply Herbrand's theorem to show the unsatisfiability of a set of first-order clauses by reducing to ground instances of clauses. One of the application domains of such methods is reasoning over very large axiom sets, in which their performance is promising [5,11]. Growing interest in this area suggests that more work should be done to improve the strength and efficiency of these methods.

Goal-sensitive methods, which restrict inferences to those related to a particular goal to be refuted, tend to perform better especially over large theories because of their ability to ignore potentially very large parts of the axiom set known to be satisfiable [14]. In methods without goal-sensitivity, to prove a theorem φ from an axiom set T, it is possible that most inferences do not involve φ at all. It is desirable to have methods which are first-order and goal-sensitive [12].

The disconnection calculus was developed in [2], and its tableau format was elaborated on and presented more rigorously in [8] as the disconnection tableau calculus. Instead of interleaving instance generation with a separate propositional procedure, the disconnection tableau calculus uses a tableau as a data structure for guiding its search so that unsatisfiability detection is integrated into the

© Springer International Publishing AG 2017
R.A. Schmidt and C. Nalon (Eds.): TABLEAUX 2017, LNAI 10501, pp. 163–174, 2017.
DOI: 10.1007/978-3-319-66902-1_10

instance generation procedure. In this paper, the disconnection tableau calculus is shown to be incapable of goal-sensitive reasoning as-is, and an adapted form of the calculus, referred to as the goal-sensitive disconnection tableau calculus or GSDC, is introduced which makes this kind of reasoning possible.

In Sect. 2 an explanation of terminology and background information is provided, along with an overview of the disconnection tableau calculus. In Sect. 3 the goal-sensitive adaptation to the calculus is presented, and Sect. 4 provides a proof of this adaptation's completeness. Section 5 concludes and provides a description of future work.

2   Preliminaries and Background

Definitions of terms and basic notions used in this paper are explained here for clarification. An overview of the basic disconnection tableau method follows.

2.1   Terminology

A first-order language $\mathcal{L}$ with function symbols is assumed. As usual, a *literal* is an atom or a negated atom. Literals L and $\neg L$ are *complementary*. The set of ground atoms over $\mathcal{L}$ is the *Herbrand base* of $\mathcal{L}$; the set of ground terms over $\mathcal{L}$ is its *Herbrand universe*. A *Herbrand interpretation* is a set of literals containing exactly one of A or $\neg A$, for each atom A in the Herbrand base.

A *clause* is a disjunction of literals, often written as a set containing those literals. In this paper, the clauses in a clause set S are assumed to be pairwise variable-disjoint.

A *substitution* σ is a finite set $\{t_1/x_1, t_2/x_2, \ldots, t_n/x_n\}$, where the x_i are distinct variables and the t_i are terms such that $t_i \neq x_i$ for any $i = 1, \ldots, n$. Applying σ to an expression E means to simultaneously replace each occurrence of x_i in E with the corresponding t_i for each $i = 1, \ldots, n$. The expression resulting from applying σ to E is written as $E\sigma$ and is called an *instance* of E. Given a clause set S, its *Herbrand set* S^* consists of all ground instances of clauses in S with terms from the Herbrand universe.

For substitutions σ and τ, their *composition* $\sigma\tau$ is a substitution which, when applied to an expression E, has the same result as first applying σ to E, and then applying τ. This is expressed by the identity $E(\sigma\tau) = (E\sigma)\tau$. If there exists a substitution τ' such that $\tau = \sigma\tau'$, then σ is said to be *more general* than τ. The substitution σ is a *unifier* of expressions E_1 and E_2 if $E_1\sigma = E_2\sigma$. If such a substitution exists, E_1 and E_2 are said to be *unifiable*. A *most general unifier* or *mgu* is a unifier which is more general than any other unifier.

The definitions and notions more specific to the disconnection tableau calculus itself are provided below. A description of the method follows these definitions.

A *literal occurrence* is a pair $\langle L, C \rangle$ such that L is a literal and C is a clause in which it appears. When convenient, $\langle L, C \rangle$ may be written as L_C. For a substitution σ, let $\langle L, C \rangle \sigma$ (and $L_C\sigma$) denote the literal occurrence $\langle L\sigma, C\sigma \rangle$.

A *connection* or *link* is a pair of literal occurrences $\ell = \{L_C, K_D\}$ such that C and D are variable-disjoint and there exists a mgu σ of L and $\neg K$. A clause $C\sigma$ is called a *linking instance* of C with respect to ℓ.

A *path* through a clause set S is a function π mapping each clause $C \in S$ to a single literal $L \in C$. A path may be represented by the set of literal occurrences $P = \{L_C \mid L = \pi(C)\}$. The *set of clauses* of P, written $\mathrm{Cl}(P)$, is the domain of the function π; the *set of literals* of P, written $\mathrm{Lit}(P)$, is the image of π. A path is *complementary* if there exist literal occurrences $L_C, \neg L_D \in P$. A path which is not complementary is *open* or *consistent*. The following proposition from [9] emphasizes the use of this notion of path.

Proposition 1. *If S is a clause set and P is an open path through the Herbrand set S^*, then the set of literals of P is a model for S.*

A *tableau* is a downward tree in which every non-root node N is labeled with a literal occurrence. Specifically, for a clause set S, a tableau for S is a tree in which the children $N_1, \ldots, N_m$ of each node N are labeled with $\langle L_1, C\rangle, \langle L_2, C\rangle, \ldots,$ $\langle L_m, C\rangle$, respectively, for $C = L_1 \vee L_2 \vee \cdots \vee L_m$ an instance of a clause in S. A *branch* of a tableau is a maximal sequence $\{N_1, N_2, \ldots\}$ of nodes in T such that N_1 is a child of the root node, and N_{i+1} is a child of N_i for all $i \geq 1$. A branch B has an associated path P_B, which can be represented by the set of literal occurrences labeling the nodes on B.

2.2 Disconnection Tableau Calculus

Here the basic calculus of the disconnection tableau method is described. Construction of a tableau for a clause set S begins with respect to an input path P_S through S called the *initial path*. The initial path remains fixed during construction of the tableau for S. The calculus consists of the following *linking rule*: given P_S and a tableau branch B such that $P_S \cup P_B$ contains a pair of literal occurrences L_C and K_D forming a link ℓ with mgu σ,

1. expand B with a variable-disjoint renaming of a linking instance of one of the clauses with respect to ℓ, say $C\sigma$, and
2. below the node labeled $L\sigma$, expand the branch with a variable-disjoint renaming of a linking instance of $D\sigma$ with respect to ℓ.

That is, a clause linking step is performed and the coupled linking instances are attached below the leaf node N of the current tableau branch B. For each branch B, the links which can be used to expand B by the linking rule are those belonging to $P_S \cup P_B$; in this way the initial path acts as a prefix shared by all branches in the tableau. Requiring that the attached linking instances be variable-disjoint maintains that all clauses on the tableau are pairwise variable-disjoint. After being used to expand B, a link need not be used any more on B below the node N, "disconnecting" the connected literals. Additionally, disconnection tableaux are generally required to be *variant-free*; that is, links which would expand the tableau with a clause which could be obtained by a renaming of a clause already on the tableau are not considered. A branch is *saturated* if there exist no links to expand it in a variant-free manner.

The normal tableau closure condition of requiring two complementary literals on the same branch is not sufficient, so a modified notion of closure is typically used. A branch B is *closed with respect to a term* t, or *t-closed*, if its associated path P_B becomes complementary when all variables occurring in the literals on B are replaced with t. A branch is $\forall$-*closed* if it is t-closed for any term t. In other words, a branch is $\forall$-closed if it contains literals $L, \neg K$ such that $L\theta = K\theta$ for a substitution θ identifying all variables. Both closure conditions can be used for disconnection tableaux, but as in [8] the weaker notion of $\forall$-closure is used here, since then the results in this paper will hold automatically for t-closure as well. As a result a tableau is said to be *closed* if all its branches are $\forall$-closed; a tableau is saturated if it is closed or if it contains a saturated branch. An example closed disconnection tableau is shown in Fig. 1.

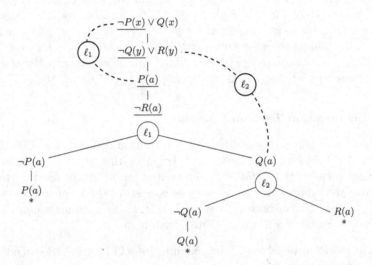

Fig. 1. Example closed disconnection tableau. The literals contained in the initial path are underlined.

Disconnection tableaux for a clause set S, with chosen initial path P_S, are defined as the elements of any sequence $T_0, T_1, \ldots$, where T_0 is the tableau consisting of only the root node, and any T_i, for $i > 0$, can be obtained from T_{i-1} by an application of the linking rule. The disconnection tableau calculus is sound and complete for any choice of initial path: a clause set S is unsatisfiable if and only if for any initial path P_S, there is a finite closed disconnection tableau for S with P_S.

As described, the disconnection tableau calculus is non-deterministic and requires an *inference strategy* for guiding tableau construction by making choices concerning the initial path, the next branch chosen for expansion, and the next linking step to be performed on that branch. An inference strategy which always results in a saturated tableau is called *systematic* or *fair*. A more thorough description of the disconnection tableau calculus and inference strategies can be found in [9].

3   Goal-Sensitivity

The notion of goal-sensitivity in theorem proving originated from resolution with set of support [15], a strategy appearing as a feature of contemporary theorem provers which use the given-clause loop [10]. Goal-sensitivity has been used in the context of equational reasoning [3] and as part of a set of criteria for analyzing theorem proving methods [13]. A recent formulation of goal-sensitivity was given in [4], which is used here and summarized below.

The clause set S is assumed to comprise a collection of assumptions, known to be consistent among themselves, and a collection of clauses generated from the negation $\neg\varphi$ of a conjectured formula φ. As such the clause set is taken to be $S = T \cup G$, where $T \cap G = \emptyset$. The set G consists of clauses generated from $\neg\varphi$, referred to as *goal clauses*, while the set T is the collection of assumptions.

The central notion of goal-sensitivity is *relevance*. Initially, only clauses in G are considered relevant. An inference is considered relevant if at least one of its hypotheses is relevant; clauses that result from the application of a relevant inference are relevant as well. A theorem proving strategy is *goal-sensitive* if it only performs relevant inferences. In other words, a method is goal-sensitive if all inferences involve clauses in, or deduced from, the clauses generated from the negated conjecture $\neg\varphi$.

Define a literal to be relevant if it belongs to a relevant clause, a literal occurrence to be relevant if its clause is relevant, and a link to be relevant if it contains a relevant literal occurrence.

3.1   Disconnection Tableau Calculus Is Not Goal-Sensitive

Even inference strategies for the disconnection tableau calculus that prioritize the selection of relevant links will require in some cases non-relevant links to be expanded. As an immediate example, if the initial path does not include any literals complementary to the specified goal literal, there will be no relevant links for selection. However, making sure that relevant links exist on the initial path is not enough to ensure goal-sensitivity.

Example 1. Consider the input clause set given in Fig. 2, with the single goal clause $G = \{\neg R(a)\}$. Let the initial path P be the one selecting the leftmost literal in each clause, indicated by the underlined literals. Then there are two links on this path: $\ell_1 = \{\underline{R(x)} \vee \neg Q(x), \neg R(a)\}$, and $\ell_2 = \{\underline{\neg P(x)} \vee Q(x), P(a)\}$.

Again, the goal clause here is $\neg R(a)$, indicated by the boxed clause. Only ℓ_1 is relevant initially, so we select it to expand the tableau. After this step, the left branch is closed, leaving only the right branch open. The only link on $P_S \cup P_B$ is ℓ_2, which is not relevant. However, expansion of ℓ_2 closes the tableau, showing the unsatisfiability of the clause set.

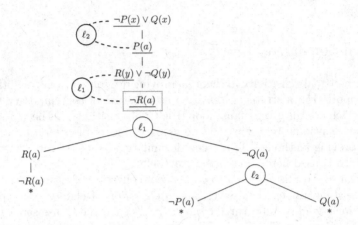

Fig. 2. Example in which non-relevant links must be expanded to close the tableau. The goal clause is indicated by the box.

Notice that in Example 1 above, had the initial path included $Q(x)$ then a relevant link $\ell_3 = \{\neg P(x) \vee Q(x), \neg Q(a)\}$ would have been present on B, and goal-sensitive construction of the tableau would have been possible. To reason with disconnection tableaux in a goal-sensitive manner, particular literal occurrences in $T = S \setminus G$ must be available for linking. The next section describes a method for finding these literal occurrences during tableau construction.

4   Goal-Sensitive Disconnection Tableau Calculus

The typical input to the disconnection tableau calculus is a clause set S and an initial path P_S through S. In the previous section it is shown that P_S can be chosen so that non-relevant linking steps must be performed to close the tableau. As a result, the *goal-sensitive disconnection tableau calculus* or *GSDC* requires a new notion of path.

Definition 1 (Multipath). *A* multipath *over a clause set S is a relation $\pi \subseteq S \times \bigcup S$ such that $\pi(C, L)$ implies $L \in C$.*

Here, $\bigcup S$ refers to the set of all literals occurring in clauses in S; that is,

$$\bigcup S := \bigcup_{C \in S} \{L \mid L \in C\}.$$

Similar to paths, a multipath π over S may be represented by a set of literal occurrences $P = \{L_C \mid \pi(C, L)\}$. The terms *set of literals* and *set of clauses* for paths are defined similarly for multipaths. Whereas a path is defined as a function from S to $\bigcup S$, a multipath is simply a relation. As a result, multipaths differ from paths in two ways: first, there may be multiple literal occurrences from the same clause on a multipath, and second, not every clause in S need have a specified literal occurrence.

The GSDC takes as input a clause set $S = T \cup G$, where T is known to be consistent and G is the set of goal clauses as before. Instead of starting with an input, fixed initial path, a multipath is dynamically constructed over the consistent set of assumptions during tableau construction. The GSDC consists of two rules, the first of which is usual linking rule from the disconnection tableau calculus, where the initial path P_S over S has been replaced with a multipath P over T. The second is the following rule to add new literal occurrences to the multipath P over T to expand a branch B:

Definition 2 (Multipath-add rule). *If no relevant links exist on $P \cup P_B$, then for each $L_C \in P_B$, do the following:*

- *for each $D \in T$, if there exists $K \in D$ such that $\{L_C, K_D\}$ is a link which has not been used on B, add K_D to P.*

The multipath P over T takes the place of the initial path in the usual disconnection calculus in that it acts as a common prefix of all branches. Each open branch B is expanded by application of the linking rule to a relevant link. If none exist for an open branch B, the multipath-add rule is applied to find links which have not yet been used on B, if they exist.

At the beginning of tableau construction, P consists of only the literal occurrences in T which form a link with some clause in G; this is referred to as the *initial multipath*. As a result, the literal occurrences added to P by the multipath-add rule for a branch B are those which form new relevant links, making these available for expanding B by applying the linking rule.

Tableaux for the GSDC are defined in a similar manner to disconnection tableaux, except that the fixed initial path P_S over S has been replaced with a dynamically constructed multipath.

Definition 3 (Goal-sensitive disconnection tableau sequence). *A goal-sensitive disconnection tableau sequence is defined as any sequence*

$$(\mathcal{T}_0, P_0), (\mathcal{T}_1, P_1), (\mathcal{T}_2, P_2), \ldots$$

such that $\mathcal{T}_0$ is the tableau which consists of only the root node, P_0 is the initial multipath, and for $i > 0$, either

- *$\mathcal{T}_i$ is obtained from $(\mathcal{T}_{i-1}, P_{i-1})$ by an application of the linking rule and $P_i = P_{i-1}$, or*
- *$\mathcal{T}_i = \mathcal{T}_{i-1}$ and P_i is obtained from P_{i-1} by an application of the multipath-add rule.*

Any tableau $\mathcal{T}_i$ in the sequence above is called a goal-sensitive disconnection tableau *for S.*

The branch and tableau closure condition used here for the GSDC is $\forall$-closure, as for the usual disconnection tableau calculus. However, an altered definition of saturation is used. The GSDC expand a branches in a tableau until it closes, or until there are no links to expand it further, even after applying the multipath-add rule.

Definition 4 (Relevance-saturation). *A branch B is relevance-saturated if it cannot be expanded in a variant-free manner by an application of the multipath-add rule followed by an application of the linking rule. A tableau is relevance-saturated if it is closed, or if one of its branches is relevance-saturated.*

Like the usual disconnection tableau calculus, an inference strategy is needed for branch and link selection.

Definition 5 (Revelance-fairness). *An inference strategy is relevance-fair if it always results in a relevance-saturated tableau.*

This method is sound and complete when guided by a relevance-fair inference strategy. Its soundness follows from the soundness of the usual disconnection tableau calculus, as any closed tableau constructed by the GSDC is simply a closed disconnection tableau. Its completeness is shown in the following section. The remainder of this section provides examples of tableaux constructed with the GSDC.

Example 2. Consider the clause set from Example 1, with initial satisfiable set $T = \{\neg P(x) \vee Q(x), R(y) \vee \neg Q(y), P(a)\}$ and goal clause $G = \neg R(a)$. There are two links ℓ_1 and ℓ_2 as defined in Example 1. The multipath P initially contains just the literal occurrence $\langle R(y), R(y) \vee \neg Q(y) \rangle$.

The linking rule expands the tableau with ℓ_1, the only relevant link. As before, the left branch closes, leaving the right branch B open. Since there are no relevant links on $P \cup P_B$, and B is open, the multipath-add rule is applied, setting $P = \{R(y) \vee \neg Q(y), \neg P(x) \vee Q(x)\}$. The updated branch B now contains the unused, relevant link $\ell = \{\neg P(x) \vee Q(x), \neg Q(a)\}$. Expanding ℓ closes the tableau.

The following example illustrates the importance of the multipath definition allowing multiple literals from a single clause to be present on P.

Example 3. Let the $S = T \cup G$ be given as in Fig. 2. Since two links are possible between the top clause and the goal, but only one will lead to a tableau closure, it is important to include multiple literal occurrences for this clause in the multipath.

The following example shows the advantage of goal-sensitivity; that links between clauses not related to the goal need not be considered.

Example 4. Let $S = T \cup G$ be given as in Fig. 3. After expanding the only relevant link, the multipath-add rule searches for other literals to link with $\neg Q(a)$. However, since none are present in T, the branch becomes relevance-saturated, and tableau construction ends, showing satisfiability of the clause set S (Fig. 4).

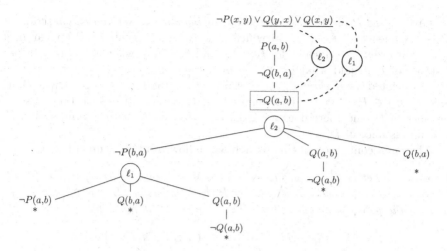

Fig. 3. Example tableau in which multiple literals from a single clause must be added to the multipath.

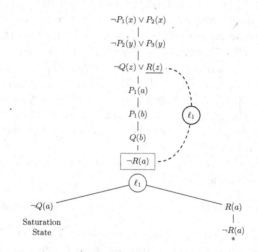

Fig. 4. Example in which tableau construction terminates early on a satisfiable clause set S because no relevant links can be made.

4.1 Completeness

The aim of this section is to show the completeness of the GSDC; that is, that whenever $S = T \cup G$ is unsatisfiable, for a consistent clause set T, the GSDC constructs a closed tableau. The main idea is that when a branch in a goal-sensitive disconnection tableau for S is relevance-saturated, an instance-preserving enumeration [8] of that branch can be combined with a model for T to construct a model for S.

Given a set P of literal occurrences, an *instance-preserving enumeration* of P is a sequence $\ell_1, \ell_2, \ell_3, \ldots$ in which exactly the elements of P appear in a particular order. Specifically, for $\ell_i = L_C$ and $\ell_j = K_D$, whenever C is a proper instance of D it holds that $i > j$. To any instance-preserving enumeration E of P is associated its *Herbrand path* P^* through S^*, the Herbrand set of $\mathrm{Cl}(P)$, as follows: $L_C \in P^*$ if and only if there exists $\ell_m = K_D$ in E such that C is an instance of D, and there does not exist $\ell_n = K'_{D'}$ in E, with $n > m$, such that C is an instance of D'.

The main conclusion of this section will follow from the lemma below.

Lemma 1. *Let B be a relevance-saturated branch in a tableau for $S = T \cup G$, where T is a satisfiable clause set. Let P' be a consistent Herbrand path for T, and P_B the path associated with B. Then the set of literals I of*

$$P = P_B^* \cup \{L_C \in P' \mid C \in (Cl(S) \setminus Cl(P_B))\}$$

is a partial Herbrand model for S.

Proof. We show that P is a consistent Herbrand path through S^*. Suppose not; that is, that there exist complementary literal occurrences L_C and $\neg L_D$ in P. Because B is open, the path P_B is consistent, so it must be that not both L_C and $\neg L_D$ belong to P_B^*. Because P' is consistent and $(P \setminus P_B^*) \subseteq P'$, it must be that not both L_C and $\neg L_D$ belong to $P \setminus P_B^*$ either. Without loss of generality, then, assume $L_C \in P_B^*$ and $\neg L_D \in P \setminus P_B^*$. Then in the tableau L_C is a node on branch B, so L_C is relevant. Since B is open, the multipath-add rule would have added $\neg L_D$ to the multipath over T, and then $\ell = \{L_C, \neg L_D\}$ would have been a relevant link on B. This contradicts the assumption that $\neg L_D \in P \setminus P_B^*$; that is, that $D \notin \mathrm{Cl}(P_B)$.

Since P is a consistent Herbrand path through S^*, then by proposition 1, P is a partial Herbrand model for S.

The main result of this section follows as a result of this lemma.

Proposition 2. *If $S = T \cup G$ is an unsatisfiable clause set, T is a satisfiable clause set, and f is a relevance-fair strategy, then the tableau for S and f is a $\forall$-closed disconnection tableau for S.*

Proof. Let $\mathcal{T}$ be the tableau for S and f and suppose that $\mathcal{T}$ had an open branch B. Since f is a fair strategy, then B would be relevance-saturated. Therefore by Lemma 1, S would be satisfiable.

5   Discussion and Conclusion

In this paper the GSDC was presented, an adaptation of the disconnection tableau calculus that allows for goal-sensitive reasoning. A proof of completeness was given along with examples of the method in use. The GSDC is an automated reasoning method that is both instantiation-based and goal-sensitive, a combination which could have practical use in areas such as formal software verification that handle very large axiom sets.

The usual disconnection tableau calculus benefits from well-chosen initial paths in that they can lead to significantly shorter proofs, but the GSDC as presented simply initializes the multipath using the set of literal occurrences which form links with the goal. However, the multipath-add rule ensures that relevant links are found, and the method is complete, regardless of the way the initial multipath is specified. In other words, a well-chosen multipath for initializing tableau construction can lead to shorter proofs in the GSDC as well, while remaining goal-sensitive.

The mechanics and notions employed by the GSDC as described are similar to those of previous methods, including hyper tableaux [1], and as such the first planned follow-up to this work is a detailed qualitative comparison. In addition, an experimental evaluation of the GSDC is needed. An implementation of the disconnection tableau calculus was developed as the disconnection calculus theorem prover or DCTP [7], and so an initial planned follow-up to this work is to implement the GSDC as an extension of the DCTP and evaluate its performance. As a future research direction, we are interested in adapting other instantiation-based methods to be goal-sensitive as well, including the Inst-Gen method [6].

References

1. Baumgartner, P.: Hyper tableau — the next generation. In: Swart, H. (ed.) TABLEAUX 1998. LNCS, vol. 1397, pp. 60–76. Springer, Heidelberg (1998). doi:10.1007/3-540-69778-0_14

2. Billon, J.-P.: The disconnection method. In: Miglioli, P., Moscato, U., Mundici, D., Ornaghi, M. (eds.) TABLEAUX 1996. LNCS, vol. 1071, pp. 110–126. Springer, Heidelberg (1996). doi:10.1007/3-540-61208-4_8

3. Bonacina, M.P., Hsiang, J.: On fairness of completion-based theorem proving strategies. In: Book, R.V. (ed.) RTA 1991. LNCS, vol. 488, pp. 348–360. Springer, Heidelberg (1991). doi:10.1007/3-540-53904-2_109

4. Bonacina, M.P., Plaisted, D.A.: Semantically-guided goal-sensitive reasoning: inference system and completeness. J. Autom. Reason. 1–54 (2017, in press). Published online 6 August 2016 with doi:10.1007/s10817-016-9384-2

5. Korovin, K.: Instantiation-based automated reasoning: from theory to practice. In: Schmidt, R.A. (ed.) CADE 2009. LNCS, vol. 5663, pp. 163–166. Springer, Heidelberg (2009). doi:10.1007/978-3-642-02959-2_14

6. Korovin, K.: Inst-Gen – a modular approach to instantiation-based automated reasoning. In: Voronkov, A., Weidenbach, C. (eds.) Programming Logics. LNCS, vol. 7797, pp. 239–270. Springer, Heidelberg (2013). doi:10.1007/978-3-642-37651-1_10

7. Letz, R., Stenz, G.: DCTP - a disconnection calculus theorem prover - system abstract. In: Goré, R., Leitsch, A., Nipkow, T. (eds.) IJCAR 2001. LNCS, vol. 2083, pp. 381–385. Springer, Heidelberg (2001). doi:10.1007/3-540-45744-5_30

8. Letz, R., Stenz, G.: Proof and model generation with disconnection tableaux. In: Nieuwenhuis, R., Voronkov, A. (eds.) LPAR 2001. LNCS, vol. 2250, pp. 142–156. Springer, Heidelberg (2001). doi:10.1007/3-540-45653-8_10

9. Letz, R., Stenz, G.: The disconnection tableau calculus. J. Autom. Reason. **38**(1), 79–126 (2007)

10. McCune, W.: Otter 3.3 reference manual. Technical report ANL/MCS-TM-263, MCS Division, Argonne National Laboratory, Argonne, IL (2003)

11. Pease, A., Sutcliffe, G., Siegel, N., Trac, S.: The annual SUMO reasoning prizes at CASC. In: Proceedings of the IJCAR Workshop on Practical Aspects of Automated Reasoning. CEUR Workshop Proceedings, vol. 373, pp. 66–70 (2008)

12. Plaisted, D.A.: History and prospects for first-order automated deduction. In: Felty, A.P., Middeldorp, A. (eds.) CADE 2015. LNCS, vol. 9195, pp. 3–28. Springer, Cham (2015). doi:10.1007/978-3-319-21401-6_1

13. Plaisted, D.A., Zhu, Y.: The Efficiency of Theorem Proving Strategies. Vieweg, Berlin (1997)

14. Reif, W., Schellhorn, G.: Theorem proving in large theories. In: Bibel, W., Schmitt, P.H. (eds.) Automated Deduction- A Basis for Applications: Volume III Applications. Applied Logic Series, pp. 225–241. Springer, Dordrecht (1998). doi:10.1007/978-94-017-0437-3_9

15. Wos, L., Robinson, G.A., Carson, D.F.: Efficiency and completeness of the set of support strategy in theorem proving. J. ACM **12**(4), 536–541 (1965)

Tableaux for Policy Synthesis for MDPs with PCTL* Constraints

Peter Baumgartner[✉], Sylvie Thiébaux, and Felipe Trevizan

Data61/CSIRO and Research School of Computer Science, ANU,
Canberra, Australia
{peter.baumgartner,sylvie.thiebaux,felipe.trevizan}@anu.edu.au

Abstract. Markov decision processes (MDPs) are the standard formalism for modelling sequential decision making in stochastic environments. Policy synthesis addresses the problem of how to control or limit the decisions an agent makes so that a given specification is met. In this paper we consider PCTL*, the probabilistic counterpart of CTL*, as the specification language. Because in general the policy synthesis problem for PCTL* is undecidable, we restrict to policies whose execution history memory is finitely bounded a priori. Surprisingly, no algorithm for policy synthesis for this natural and expressive framework has been developed so far. We close this gap and describe a tableau-based algorithm that, given an MDP and a PCTL* specification, derives in a non-deterministic way a system of (possibly nonlinear) equalities and inequalities. The solutions of this system, if any, describe the desired (stochastic) policies. Our main result in this paper is the correctness of our method, i.e., soundness, completeness and termination.

1 Introduction

Markov decision processes (MDPs) are the standard formalism for modelling sequential decision making in stochastic environments, where the effects of an agent's actions are only probabilistically known. The core problem is to synthesize a policy prescribing or restricting the actions that the agent may undertake, so as to guarantee that a given specification is met. Popular specification languages for this purpose include CTL, LTL, and their probabilistic counterparts PCTL and probabilistic LTL (pLTL). Traditional algorithms for policy synthesis and probabilistic temporal logic model-checking [9,17] are based on bottom-up formula analysis [15,16] or Rabin automata [2,11,21].

We deviate from this mainstream research in two ways. The first significant deviation is that we consider PCTL* as a specification language, whereas previous synthesis approaches have been limited to pLTL and PCTL. PCTL* is the probabilistic counterpart of CTL* and subsumes both PCTL and pLTL. For example, the PCTL* formula $\mathbf{P}_{\geq 0.8}\, \mathbf{G}\, ((T > 30^\circ) \rightarrow \mathbf{P}_{\geq 0.5}\, \mathbf{F}\, \mathbf{G}\, (T < 24^\circ))$ says *"with probability at least 0.8, whenever the temperature exceeds 30° it will eventually stay below 24° with probability at least 0.5"*. Because of the nested

© Springer International Publishing AG 2017
R.A. Schmidt and C. Nalon (Eds.): TABLEAUX 2017, LNAI 10501, pp. 175–192, 2017.
DOI: 10.1007/978-3-319-66902-1_11

probability operator **P** the formula is not in pLTL, and because of the nested temporal operators **FG** it is not in PCTL either.

Because in its full generality the policy synthesis problem for PCTL* is highly undecidable [5], one has to make concessions to obtain a decidable fragment. In this paper we chose to restrict to policies whose execution history memory is finitely bounded a priori. (For example, policies that choose actions in the current state dependent on the last ten preceding states.) However, we do target synthesizing stochastic policies, i.e., the actions are chosen according to a probability distribution (which generalizes the deterministic case and is known to be needed to satisfy certain formulas [2]). Surprisingly, no algorithm for policy synthesis in this somewhat restricted yet natural and expressive framework has been developed so far, and this paper closes this gap.

The second significant deviation from the mainstream is that we pursue a different approach based on analytic tableau and mathematical programming. Our tableau calculus is goal-oriented by focusing on the given PCTL* formula, which leads to analysing runs only on a by-need basis. This restricts the search space to partial policies that only cover the states reachable from the initial state under the policy and for which the formula imposes constraints on the actions that can be selected. In contrast, traditional automata based approaches require a full-blown state space exploration. (However, we do not have an implementation yet that allows us to evaluate the practical impact of this.) We also believe that our approach, although using somewhat non-standard tableau features, is conceptually simpler and easier to comprehend. Of course, this is rather subjective.

On a high level, the algorithm works as follows. The input is an MDP, the finite-history component of the policy to be synthesized, and a PCTL* formula to be satisfied. Starting from the MDP's initial state, the tableau calculus symbolically executes the transition system given by the MDP by analysing the syntactic structure of the given PCTL* formula, as usual with tableau calculi. Temporal formulas (e.g., **FG**-formulas) are expanded repeatedly using usual expansion laws and trigger state transitions. The process stops at trivial cases or when a certain loop condition is met. The underlying loop checking technique was developed only recently, by Mark Reynolds, in the context of tableau for satisfiability checking of LTL formulas [18]. It is an essential ingredient of our approach and we adapted it to our probabilistic setting.

Our tableaux have two kinds of branching. One kind is traditional or-branching, which represents non-deterministic choice by going down exactly one child node. It is used, e.g., in conjunction with recursively calling the tableau procedure itself. Such calls are necessary to deal with nested **P**-operators, since at the time of analyzing a **P**-formula it is, roughly speaking, unknown if the formula will hold true under the policy computed only later, as a result of the algorithm. The other kind of branching represents a union of alternatives. It is used for disjunctive formulas and for branching out from a state into successor states. Intuitively, computing the probability of a disjunctive formula $\phi_1 \vee \phi_2$ is a function of the probabilities of *both* ϕ_1 and ϕ_2, so both need to be computed.

Also, the probability of an **X**-formula **X**ϕ at a given state is a function of the probability of ϕ at *all* successor states, and so, again, all successor states need to be considered.

The tableau construction always terminates and derives a system of (possibly nonlinear) equalities and inequalities over the reals. The solutions of this system, if any, describe the desired stochastic, finite-history policies. The idea of representing policies as the solutions of a set of mathematical constraints is inspired by the abundant work in operations research, artificial intelligence, and robotics that optimally solves MDPs with simpler constraints using linear programming [1,10,12,22].

Our main result in this paper is the correctness of our algorithm, i.e., soundness, completeness and termination. To our knowledge, it is the first and only policy synthesis algorithm for PCTL* that doesn't restrict the language (but only slightly the policies).

Related Work. Methods for solving the PCTL* *model checking* problem over Markov Chains are well established. The (general) policy synthesis however is harder than the model checking problem; it is known to be undecidable for even PCTL. The main procedure works bottom-up from the syntax tree of the given formula, akin to the standard CTL/CTL* model checking procedure. Embedded **P**-formulas are recursively abstracted into boolean variables representing the sets of states satisfying these formulas, which are computed by LTL model checking techniques using Rabin automata. Our *synthesis* approach is rather different. While there is a rough correspondence in terms of recursive calls to treat **P** formulas, we do not need Rabin (or any other) automata; they are supplanted by the loop-check technique mentioned above.

The work the most closely related to ours is that of Brázdil *et al.* [6–8]. Using Büchi automata, they obtain complexity results depending on the variant of the synthesis problem studied. However, they consider only *qualitative* fragments. For the case of interest in this paper, PCTL*, they obtain results for the fragment qPCTL*. The logic qPCTL* limits the use of the path quantifier **P** to formulas of the form $\mathbf{P}_{=1}\,\psi$ or $\mathbf{P}_{=0}\,\psi$, where ψ is a path formula. On the other hand, we cover the full logic PCTL* which has arbitrary formulas of the form $\mathbf{P}_{\sim z}\,\psi$ where $\sim\ \in \{<,\leq,>,\geq\}$ and $z \in [0,1]$. In contrast to the works mentioned, we have to restrict to memory-dependent policies with an *a priori* limited finite memory. Otherwise the logic becomes highly undecidable [5].

2   Preliminaries

We assume the reader is familiar with basic concepts of Markov Decision Processes (MDPs), probabilistic model checking, and policy synthesis. See [3,13,17] for introductions and overviews. In the following we summarize the notions relevant to us and we introduce our notation.

Given a fixed finite vocabulary AP of *atomic propositions* $a, b, c, \ldots$, a *(propositional) interpretation* I is any subset of AP. It represents the assignment of each element in I to *true* and each other atomic proposition in $AP \setminus I$ to *false*. A *distribution on a countable set* X is a function $\mu\colon X \mapsto [0,1]$ such that $\sum_{x \in X} \mu(x) = 1$, and $Dist(X)$ is the set of all distributions on X.

A *Markov Decision Process (MDP)* is a tuple $\mathcal{M} = (S, s_{\text{init}}, A, P, L)$ where: S is a finite set of states; $s_{\text{init}} \in S$ is the *initial state*; A is a finite set of *actions* and we denote by $A(s) \subseteq A$ the *set of actions enabled* in $s \in S$; $P(t|s, \alpha)$ is the probability of transitioning to $t \in S$ after applying $\alpha \in A(s)$ in state s; and $L\colon S \mapsto 2^{AP}$ labels each state in S with an interpretation. We assume that every state has at least one enabled action, i.e., $A(s) \neq \emptyset$ for all $s \in S$, and that P is a distribution on enabled actions, i.e., $P(\cdot|s, \alpha) \in Dist(S)$ iff $\alpha \in A(s)$. For any s and $\alpha \in A(s)$ let $Succ(s, \alpha) = \{t \mid P(t|s, \alpha) > 0\}$ be the states reachable from s with non-zero probability after applying α.

Given a state $s \in S$ of $\mathcal{M}$, a *run from s (of $\mathcal{M}$)* is an infinite sequence $r = (s = s_1) \xrightarrow{\alpha_1} s_2 \xrightarrow{\alpha_2} s_3 \cdots$ of states $s_i \in S$ and actions $\alpha_i \in A(s_i)$ such that $P(s_{i+1}|s_i, \alpha_i) > 0$, for all $i \geq 1$. We denote by $Runs(s)$ the set of all runs from $s \in S$ and $Runs = \cup_{s \in S} Runs(s)$. A *path from $s \in S$ (of $\mathcal{M}$)* is a finite prefix of a run from s and we define $Paths(s)$ and $Paths$ in analogy to $Runs(s)$ and $Runs$. We often write runs and paths in abbreviated form as state sequences $s_1 s_2 \cdots$ and leave the actions implicit. Given a path $p = s_1 s_2 \cdots s_n$ let $first(p) = s_1$ and $last(p) = s_n$. Similarly, for a run $r = s_1 s_2 \cdots$, $first(r) = s_1$.

A policy π represents a decision rule on how to choose an action given some information about the environment. In its most general form, a *history-dependent (stochastic) policy (for $\mathcal{M}$)* is a function $\pi\colon Paths \mapsto Dist(A)$ such that, for all $p \in Paths$, $\pi(p)(\alpha) > 0$ only if $\alpha \in A(last(p))$. Technically, the MDP $\mathcal{M}$ together with π induces an infinite-state Markov chain $\mathcal{M}_\pi$ over $Paths$ and this way provides a probability measure for runs of $\mathcal{M}$ under π [3,14]. However, since $Paths$ is an infinite set, a history-dependent policy might not be representable; moreover, the problem of finding such a policy that satisfies PCTL* constraints is undecidable [5]. To address these issues we limit ourselves to finite-memory policies. Such policies provide a distribution on actions for a current state from S and a current *mode*, and are more expressive than Markovian policies.

Formally, a *finite-memory policy (for $\mathcal{M}$)* is a DFA $\pi_{\text{fin}} = (M, \text{start}, \Delta, \text{act})$ where M is a finite set of *modes*, $\text{start}\colon S \mapsto M$ returns an initial mode to pair with a state $s \in S$, $\Delta\colon M \times S \mapsto M$ is the *(mode) transition function*, and $\text{act}\colon M \times S \mapsto Dist(A)$ is a function such that, for all $\langle m, s \rangle \in M \times S$, $\text{act}(m, s)(\alpha) > 0$ only if $\alpha \in A(s)$. We abbreviate $\text{act}(m, s)(\alpha)$ as $\text{act}(m, s, \alpha)$.

Any finite-memory policy can be identified with a history-dependent policy, see again [3] for details. Essentially, an MDP $\mathcal{M}$ together with π_{fin} again induces a Markov chain $\mathcal{M}_{\pi_{\text{fin}}}$, this time over the finite state space $M \times S$, labelling function $L_{\pi_{\text{fin}}}(\langle m, s \rangle) := L(s)$, and transition probability function $P^{\mathcal{M}_{\pi_{\text{fin}}}}(\langle m', s' \rangle | \langle m, s \rangle) := \Sigma_{\alpha \in A(s)} \text{act}(m, s, \alpha) \cdot P(s'|s, \alpha)$ if $m' = \Delta(m, s)$ and 0 otherwise. A *path from $\langle m_1, s_1 \rangle$ (of $\mathcal{M}_{\pi_{\text{fin}}}$)* is a sequence of the form $\langle m_1, s_1 \rangle \cdots \langle m_n, s_n \rangle$ such that $m_{i+1} = \Delta(m_i, s_i)$ and $P^{\mathcal{M}_{\pi_{\text{fin}}}}(\langle m_{i+1}, s_{i+1} \rangle | \langle m_i, s_i \rangle) > 0$, for all $1 \leq i < n$. If $m_1 = \text{start}(s_1)$ we get a *path from s_1 (of $\mathcal{M}_{\pi_{\text{fin}}}$)*, similarly for runs. The definition of the satisfaction relation "$\models$" below applies to such runs $\langle \text{start}(s_1), s_1 \rangle \cdots$ from s_1 of $\mathcal{M}_{\pi_{\text{fin}}}$ if π is a finite-memory policy π_{fin}.

The definition of finite-memory policies π_{fin} can be made more sophisticated, e.g., by letting Δ depend also on actions, or by making modes dependent on a given PCTL* specification. In its current form, the Δ-component of π_{fin} can be setup already, e.g., to encode in $\langle m, s \rangle$ "the last ten states preceding s".

Policy Synthesis for PCTL*. *(PCTL*) formulas* follow the following grammar:

$$\phi \quad := \quad \textit{true} \mid a \in AP \mid \phi \wedge \phi \mid \neg\phi \mid \mathbf{P}_{\sim z}\, \psi \qquad \text{(State formula)}$$
$$\psi \quad := \quad \phi \mid \psi \wedge \psi \mid \neg\psi \mid \mathbf{X}\,\psi \mid \psi\mathbf{U}\psi \qquad \text{(Path formula)}$$

In the definition of state formulas, $\sim\, \in \{<, \leq, >, \geq\}$ and $0 \leq z \leq 1$. A *proper path formula* is a path formula that is not a state formula. A formula is *classical* iff it is made from atomic propositions and the Boolean connectives $\neg$ and $\wedge$ only (no occurrences of $\mathbf{P}$, $\mathbf{X}$ or $\mathbf{U}$). We write *false* as a shorthand for $\neg\textit{true}$.

Given an MDP $\mathcal{M}$, a history-dependent policy π, state $s \in S$ and state formula ϕ, define a satisfaction relation $\mathcal{M}, \pi, s \models \phi$, briefly $s \models \phi$, as follows:

$$s \models \textit{true} \qquad\qquad s \models \phi_1 \wedge \phi_2 \text{ iff } s \models \phi_1 \text{ and } s \models \phi_2$$
$$s \models a \text{ iff } a \in L(s) \qquad s \models \neg\phi \text{ iff } s \not\models \phi$$
$$s \models \mathbf{P}_{\sim z}\, \psi \text{ iff } \text{Pr}^{\mathcal{M}_\pi}(\{r \in \textit{Runs}^{\mathcal{M}_\pi}(s) \mid \mathcal{M}, \pi, r \models \psi\}) \sim z$$

In the preceding line, $\textit{Runs}^{\mathcal{M}_\pi}(s)$ denotes the set of all runs from s of $\mathcal{M}_\pi$, and $\text{Pr}^{\mathcal{M}_\pi}(R)$ denotes the probability of a (measurable) set $R \subseteq \textit{Runs}^{\mathcal{M}_\pi}$. That is, the probability measure for $\mathcal{M}$ and π is defined via the probability measure of the Markov chain $\mathcal{M}_\pi$.

We need to define the satisfaction relation $\mathcal{M}, \pi, r \models \psi$, briefly $r \models \psi$, for path formulas ψ. Let $r = s_1 s_2 \cdots$ be a run of $\mathcal{M}$ and $r[n] := s_n s_{n+1} \cdots$, for any $n \geq 1$. Then:

$$r \models \phi \text{ iff } \text{first}(r) \models \phi \qquad r \models \psi_1 \wedge \psi_2 \text{ iff } r \models \psi_1 \text{ and } r \models \psi_2$$
$$r \models \neg\psi \text{ iff } r \not\models \psi \qquad\qquad r \models \mathbf{X}\psi \text{ iff } r[2] \models \psi$$
$$r \models \psi_1\mathbf{U}\psi_2 \text{ iff } \text{exists } n \geq 1 \, s.t. \, r[n] \models \psi_2 \text{ and } r[m] \models \psi_1 \text{ for all } 1 \leq m < n$$

In this paper we focus on the problem of synthesizing only the act-component of an otherwise fully specified finite memory policy. More formally:

Definition 2.1 (Policy Synthesis Problem). *Let* $\mathcal{M} = (S, s_{\text{init}}, A, P, L)$ *be an MDP, and* $\pi_{\text{fin}} = (M, \text{start}, \Delta, \cdot)$ *be a partially specified finite-memory policy with* act *unspecified. Given state formula* ϕ*, find* act *s.th.* $\mathcal{M}, \pi_{\text{fin}}, s_{\text{init}} \models \phi$ *if it exists, otherwise report failure.*

Useful Facts About PCTL* Operators. Next we summarize some well-known or easy-to-prove facts about PCTL* operators. By the *expansion laws* for the $\mathbf{U}$-operator we mean the following equivalences:

$$\psi_1 \mathbf{U} \psi_2 \equiv \psi_2 \vee (\psi_1 \wedge \mathbf{X}(\psi_1 \mathbf{U} \psi_2)) \quad \neg(\psi_1 \mathbf{U} \psi_2) \equiv \neg\psi_2 \wedge (\neg\psi_1 \vee \mathbf{X}\neg(\psi_1 \mathbf{U} \psi_2)) \quad \text{(E)}$$

For $\sim\; \in \{<, \leq, >, \geq\}$ define the operators $\widetilde{\sim}$ and $[\sim]$ as follows:

$$\widetilde{<} = \geq \quad \widetilde{\leq} = > \quad \widetilde{>} = \leq \quad \widetilde{\geq} = < \quad [<] = > \quad [\leq] = \geq \quad [>] = < \quad [\geq] = \leq$$

Some of the following equivalences cannot be used for "model checking" PCTL* (the left (P1) equivalence, to be specific) which involves reasoning over *all* policies. In the context of Markov Chains, which we implicitly have, there is no problem:

$$\neg\mathbf{P}_{\sim z}\,\psi \equiv \mathbf{P}_{\widetilde{\sim} z}\,\psi \qquad\qquad \mathbf{P}_{\sim z}\,\neg\psi \equiv \mathbf{P}_{[\sim]\,1-z}\,\psi \qquad\qquad \text{(P1)}$$

$$\mathbf{P}_{\geq 0}\,\psi \equiv \textit{true} \qquad\qquad \mathbf{P}_{>1}\,\psi \equiv \textit{false} \qquad\qquad \text{(P2)}$$

$$\mathbf{P}_{\leq 1}\,\psi \equiv \textit{true} \qquad\qquad \mathbf{P}_{<0}\,\psi \equiv \textit{false} \qquad\qquad \text{(P3)}$$

$$\mathbf{P}_{\geq u}\,\mathbf{P}_{\sim z}\,\psi \equiv \mathbf{P}_{\sim z}\,\psi \quad \text{if } u \neq 0 \qquad \mathbf{P}_{>u}\,\mathbf{P}_{\sim z}\,\psi \equiv \mathbf{P}_{\sim z}\,\psi \quad \text{if } u \neq 1 \qquad \text{(P4)}$$

$$\mathbf{P}_{\leq u}\,\mathbf{P}_{\sim z}\,\psi \equiv \mathbf{P}_{\geq 1-u}\,\mathbf{P}_{\widetilde{\sim} z}\,\psi \qquad \mathbf{P}_{<u}\,\mathbf{P}_{\sim z}\,\psi \equiv \mathbf{P}_{>1-u}\,\mathbf{P}_{\widetilde{\sim} z}\,\psi \qquad \text{(P5)}$$

Nonlinear Programs. Finally, a *(nonlinear) program* is a set Γ of constraints of the form $e_1 \bowtie e_2$ where $\bowtie\; \in \{<, \leq, >, \geq, \doteq\}$ and e_1 and e_2 are arithmetic expressions comprised of numeric real constants and variables. The numeric operators are $\{+, -, \cdot, /\}$, all with their expected meaning (the symbol $\doteq$ is equality). All variables are implicitly bounded over the range $[0, 1]$. A solver (for nonlinear programs) is a decision procedure that returns a satisfying variable assignment (a solution) for a given Γ, and reports unsatisfiability if no solution exists. We do not further discuss solvers in the rest of this paper, we just assume one as given. Examples of open source solvers include Ipopt and Couenne.[1]

3   Tableau Calculus

Introduction and Overview. We describe a tableau based algorithm for the policy synthesis problem in Definition 2.1. Hence assume as given an MDP $\mathcal{M} = (S, s_{\text{init}}, A, P, L)$ and a partially specified finite-memory policy $\pi_{\text{fin}} = (M, \text{start}, \Delta, \cdot)$ with act unspecified.

A *labelled formula* $\mathcal{F}$ is of the form $\langle m, s \rangle : \Psi$ where $\langle m, s \rangle \in M \times S$ and Ψ is a possibly empty set of path formulas, interpreted conjunctively. When we speak of the *probability* of $\langle m, s \rangle : \Psi$ we mean the value of $\Pr^{\mathcal{M}\pi_{\text{fin}}}(\{r \in Runs(\langle m, s \rangle) \mid \mathcal{M}, \pi_{\text{fin}}, r \models \bigwedge \Psi\})$ for the completed π_{fin}. For simplicity we also call Ψ a "formula" and call $\langle m, s \rangle$ a *policy state*. A *sequent* is an expression of the form $\Gamma \vdash \mathcal{F}$ where Γ is a program.

Our algorithm consists of three steps, the first one of which is a tableau construction. A *tableau for* $\Gamma \vdash \mathcal{F}$ is a finite tree whose root is labelled with $\Gamma \vdash \mathcal{F}$ and such that every inner node is labelled with the premise of an inference

---

[1] http://projects.coin-or.org/.

rule and its children are labelled with the conclusions, in order. If $\Gamma \vdash \mathcal{F}$ is the label of an inner node we call $\mathcal{F}$ the *pivot of the node/sequent/inference*. By a *derivation from* $\Gamma \vdash \mathcal{F}$, denoted by $\text{TABLEAU}(\Gamma \vdash \mathcal{F})$, we mean any tableau for $\Gamma \vdash \mathcal{F}$ obtained by stepwise construction, starting from a root-node only tree and applying an inference rule to (the leaf of) every branch as long as possible. There is one inference rule, the *P*-rule, which recursively calls the algorithm itself. A branch is terminated when no inference rule is applicable, which is exactly the case when its leaf is labelled by a pseudo-sequent, detailed below. The inference rules can be applied in any way, subject to only preference constraints.

Given a state formula ϕ, the algorithm starts with a derivation from $\Gamma_{\text{init}} \vdash$ $\mathcal{F}_{\text{init}} := \{x_{\langle \text{start}(s_{\text{init}}), s_{\text{init}}\rangle}^{\{\phi\}} \doteq 1\} \vdash \langle \text{start}(s_{\text{init}}), s_{\text{init}}\rangle : \{\phi\}$. (The constraint Γ_{init} forces ϕ to be "true".) The derivation represents the obligation to derive a satisfiable extension $\Gamma_{\text{final}} \supseteq \Gamma_{\text{init}}$. A (any) solution σ then determines the act-component act_σ of π_{fin} such that $\mathcal{M}, \pi_{\text{fin}}, s_{\text{init}} \models \phi$. In more detail, Γ_{final} will contain constraints of the form $x_{\langle m,s\rangle}^\alpha \doteq 0$ or $x_{\langle m,s\rangle}^\alpha > 0$ for the probability of applying action α in policy state $\langle m, s\rangle$. Let the *policy domain of a program* Γ be the set of all policy states $\langle m, s\rangle \in M \times S$ such that $x_{\langle m,s\rangle}^\alpha$ occurs in Γ, for some α. This lets us initially define $\text{act}_\sigma(m, s, \alpha) := \sigma(x_{\langle m,s\rangle}^\alpha)$ for every $\langle m, s\rangle$ in the policy domain of Γ_{final}. Only for the purpose of satisfying the definition of finite memory policies, we then make act_σ trivially total by choosing an *arbitrary* distribution for $\text{act}_\sigma(m, s)$ for all remaining $\langle m, s\rangle \in M \times S$. (The latter are not reachable and hence do not matter.) We call $\pi_{\text{fin}}(\sigma) := (M, \text{start}, \Delta, \text{act}_\sigma)$ the *policy completed by* σ.

Similarly, Γ_{final} contains variables of the form $x_{\langle m,s\rangle}^\Psi$, and $\sigma(x_{\langle m,s\rangle}^\Psi)$ is the probability of $\langle m, s\rangle : \Psi$ under the policy $\pi_{\text{fin}}(\sigma)$. (We actually need these variable indexed by tableau nodes, see below.) If Ψ is a state formula its value will be 0 or 1, encoding truth values.

Contrary to traditional tableau calculi, the result of the computation – the extension Γ_{final} – cannot always be obtained in a branch-local way. To explain, there are two kinds of branching in our tableaux: *don't-know (non-deterministic) branching* and *union branching*. The former is always used for exhaustive case analysis, e.g., whether $x_{\langle m,s\rangle}^\alpha \doteq 0$ or $x_{\langle m,s\rangle}^\alpha > 0$, and the algorithm guesses which alternative to take (cf. step 2 below). The latter analyzes the Boolean structure of the pivot. Unlike as with traditional tableaux, *all* children need to be expanded, and each fully expanded branch contributes to Γ_{final}.

More precisely, we formalize the synthesis algorithm as a three-step procedure. *Step one* consists in deriving $\text{TABLEAU}(\Gamma_{\text{init}} \vdash \mathcal{F}_{\text{init}})$. *Step two* consists in removing from the step one tableau every don't-know branching by retaining exactly one child of the parent node of the don't-know branching, and deleting all other children and the subtrees below them. This itself is a don't-know non-deterministic process; it corresponds to going down one branch in traditional tableau. The result is denoted by $\text{CHOOSE}(T_1)$, where T_1 is the step one tableau. *Step three* consists in first building a combined program by taking the union of the Γ's in the leaves of the branches of the step two tableau. This program then is extended with a set of constraints by the FORCE operator.

More precisely, FORCEing captures the situation when a run reaches a bottom strongly connected component (BSCC). Any formula is satisfied in a BSCC with probability 0 or 1, which can be determined solely by qualitative formula evaluation in the BSCC. Details are below. For now let us just define $\text{GAMMA}(T_2) = \bigcup \{\Gamma \mid \Gamma \vdash \cdot \text{ is the leaf of a branch in } T_2\} \cup \text{FORCE}(T_2)$ where $T_2 = \text{CHOOSE}(T_1)$.

We can formulate our main results now. Proofs are in the long version [4].

Theorem 3.1 (Soundness). *Let $\mathcal{M} = (S, s_{\text{init}}, A, P, L)$ be an MDP, $\pi_{\text{fin}} = (M, \text{start}, \Delta, \cdot)$ be a partially specified finite-memory policy with act unspecified, and ϕ a state formula. Suppose there is a program $\Gamma_{\text{final}} := \text{GAMMA}(\text{CHOOSE}(\text{TABLEAU}(\{x_{\langle \text{start}(s_{\text{init}}), s_{\text{init}}\rangle}^{\{\phi\}} \doteq 1\} \vdash \langle \text{start}(s_{\text{init}}), s_{\text{init}}\rangle : \{\phi\})))$ such that Γ_{final} is satisfiable. Let σ be any solution of Γ_{final} and $\pi_{\text{fin}}(\sigma)$ be the policy completed by σ. Then it holds $\mathcal{M}, \pi_{\text{fin}}(\sigma), s_{\text{init}} \models \phi$.*

Theorem 3.2 (Completeness). *Let $\mathcal{M} = (S, s_{\text{init}}, A, P, L)$ be an MDP, $\pi_{\text{fin}} = (M, \text{start}, \Delta, \text{act})$ a finite-memory policy, and ϕ a state formula. Suppose $\mathcal{M}, \pi_{\text{fin}}, s_{\text{init}} \models \phi$. Then there is a satisfiable program $\Gamma_{\text{final}} := \text{GAMMA}(\text{CHOOSE}(\text{TABLEAU}(\{x_{\langle \text{start}(s_{\text{init}}), s_{\text{init}}\rangle}^{\{\phi\}} \doteq 1\} \vdash \langle \text{start}(s_{\text{init}}), s_{\text{init}}\rangle : \{\phi\})))$ and a solution σ of Γ_{final} such that $\text{act}_\sigma(m, s, \alpha) = \text{act}(m, s, \alpha)$ for every pair $\langle m, s\rangle$ in the policy domain of Γ_{final}. Moreover $\mathcal{M}, \pi_{\text{fin}}(\sigma), s_{\text{init}} \models \phi$.*

Inference Rules. There are two kinds of inference rules, giving two kinds of branching:

$$\textit{Name} \quad \frac{\Gamma \vdash \langle m, s\rangle : \Psi}{\Gamma_{left} \vdash \langle m, s\rangle : \Psi \qquad \Gamma_{right} \vdash \langle m, s\rangle : \Psi} \quad \text{if } condition$$

(Don't-know branching)

The pivot in the premise is always carried over into both conclusions. Only the constraint Γ is modified into $\Gamma_{left} \supseteq \Gamma$ and $\Gamma_{right} \supseteq \Gamma$, respectively, for an exhaustive case analysis.

$$\textit{Name} \quad \frac{\Gamma \vdash \langle m, s\rangle : \Psi}{\Gamma_1 \vdash \langle m_1, s_1\rangle : \Psi_1 \quad \cup \quad \cdots \quad \cup \quad \Gamma_n \vdash \langle m_n, s_n\rangle : \Psi_n} \quad \text{if } condition \ (n \geq 1)$$

(Union branching)

All union branching rules satisfy $\Gamma_i \supseteq \Gamma$, and $\langle m_i, s_i\rangle = \langle m, s\rangle$ or $\langle m_i, s_i\rangle = \langle \Delta(m, s), t\rangle$ for some state t. The $\cup$-symbol is decoration for distinguishing the two kinds of branching but has no meaning beyond that. Union branching stands for the union of the runs from $\langle m_i, s_i\rangle$ satisfying Ψ_i, and computing its probability requires developing *all* n children.

We need to clarify a technical add-on. Let u be the tableau node with the premise pivot $\langle m, s\rangle : \Psi$. A union branching inference extends u with children nodes, say, $u_1, \ldots, u_n$, with conclusion pivots $\langle m_i, s_i\rangle : \Psi_i$. The program Γ_n will contain a constraint that makes a variable $(x_u)_{\langle m, s\rangle}^{\Psi}$ for the premise dependent on all variables $(x_{u_i})_{\langle m_i, s_i \rangle}^{\Psi_i}$ for the respective conclusions. *This is a key invariant and is preserved by all inference rules.* In order to lighten the notation, however, we usually drop the variable's index, leaving the node implicit. For instance, we write $x_{\langle m, s \rangle}^{\Psi}$ instead of $(x_u)_{\langle m, s \rangle}^{\Psi}$. The index u is needed for not inadvertently identifying the same pivot at different points in the symbolic execution of a run. Fresh names $x, y, z, \ldots$ for the variables would do as well.

Most unary union branching rules have a premise $\Gamma \vdash \langle m, s \rangle : \{\psi\} \uplus \Psi$ and the conclusion is $\Gamma, \gamma_{one} \vdash \langle m, s \rangle : \Psi'$, for some Ψ'. The pivot is specified by pattern matching, where $\uplus$ is disjoint union, and γ_{one} is a macro that expands to $x_{\langle m, s \rangle}^{\{\psi\} \uplus \Psi} \doteq x_{\langle m, s \rangle}^{\Psi'}$.

Other inference rules derive pseudo-sequents of the form $\Gamma \vdash \boldsymbol{X}$, $\Gamma \vdash \boldsymbol{\checkmark}$, $\Gamma \vdash$ Yes-Loop and $\Gamma \vdash$ No-Loop. They indicate that the probability of the pivot is 0, 1, or that a loop situation arises that may need further analysis. Pseudo-sequents are always leaves.

Now we turn to the concrete rules. They are listed in decreasing order of preference.

$$\top \quad \frac{\Gamma \vdash \langle m, s \rangle : \{\psi\} \uplus \Psi}{\Gamma, \gamma_{one} \vdash \langle m, s \rangle : \Psi} \left\{ \begin{array}{l} \text{if } \psi \text{ is clas-} \\ \text{sical and} \\ L(s) \models \psi \end{array} \right. \qquad \boldsymbol{X} \quad \frac{\Gamma \vdash \langle m, s \rangle : \{\psi\} \uplus \Psi}{\Gamma, x_{\langle m, s \rangle}^{\{\psi\} \uplus \Psi} \doteq 0 \vdash \boldsymbol{X}} \left\{ \begin{array}{l} \text{if } \psi \text{ is clas-} \\ \text{sical and} \\ L(s) \not\models \psi \end{array} \right.$$

$$\boldsymbol{\checkmark} \quad \frac{\Gamma \vdash \langle m, s \rangle : \emptyset}{\Gamma, x_{\langle m, s \rangle}^{\emptyset} \doteq 1 \vdash \boldsymbol{\checkmark}} \qquad \neg\neg \quad \frac{\Gamma \vdash \langle m, s \rangle : \{\neg\neg\psi\} \uplus \Psi}{\Gamma, \gamma_{one} \vdash \langle m, s \rangle : \{\psi\} \cup \Psi}$$

$$\neg\mathsf{P} \quad \frac{\Gamma \vdash \langle m, s \rangle : \{\neg\mathsf{P}_{\sim z}\,\psi\} \uplus \Psi}{\Gamma, \gamma_{one} \vdash \langle m, s \rangle : \{\mathsf{P}_{\not\approx z}\,\psi\} \cup \Psi} \qquad \mathsf{P}\neg \quad \frac{\Gamma \vdash \langle m, s \rangle : \{\mathsf{P}_{\sim z}\,\neg\psi\} \uplus \Psi}{\Gamma, \gamma_{one} \vdash \langle m, s \rangle : \{\mathsf{P}_{[\sim]\,1 - z}\,\psi\} \cup \Psi}$$

These are rules for evaluating classical formulas and for negation. The $\boldsymbol{X}$ rule terminates the branch and assigns a probability of 0 to the premise pivot, as no run from $\langle m, s \rangle$ satisfies (the conjunction of) $\{\psi\} \uplus \Psi$, as ψ is false in s. A similar reasoning applies to the $\top$ and $\boldsymbol{\checkmark}$ rules. The $\neg\mathsf{P}$ and $\mathsf{P}\neg$ rules are justified by law (P1). The $\mathsf{P}\neg$ rule is needed for removing negation between P-formulas as in $\mathsf{P}_{\sim z}\,\neg\mathsf{P}_{\sim v}\,\psi$.

$$\wedge \quad \frac{\Gamma \vdash \langle m, s \rangle : \{\psi_1 \wedge \psi_2\} \uplus \Psi}{\Gamma, \gamma_{one} \vdash \langle m, s \rangle : \{\psi_1, \psi_2\} \cup \Psi}$$

$$\neg\wedge \quad \frac{\Gamma \vdash \langle m, s \rangle : \{\neg(\psi_1 \wedge \psi_2)\} \uplus \Psi}{\Gamma \vdash \langle m, s \rangle : \{\neg\psi_1\} \cup \Psi \quad \cup \quad \Gamma, \gamma \vdash \langle m, s \rangle : \{\psi_1, \neg\psi_2\} \cup \Psi}$$

$$\text{where } \gamma = x_{\langle m, s \rangle}^{\{\neg(\psi_1 \wedge \psi_2)\} \uplus \Psi} \doteq x_{\langle m, s \rangle}^{\{\neg\psi_1\} \cup \Psi} + x_{\langle m, s \rangle}^{\{\psi_1, \neg\psi_2\} \cup \Psi}$$

These are rules for conjunction. Not both ψ_1 and ψ_2 can be classical by preference of the $\top$ and $\boldsymbol{X}$ rules. The $\wedge$ rule is obvious with the conjunctive reading of formula sets. The $\neg\wedge$ rule deals, essentially, with the disjunction $\neg\psi_1 \vee \neg\psi_2$, which requires splitting. However, unlike to the classical logic case, $\neg\psi_1 \vee \neg\psi_2$ represents the union of the runs from s satisfying $\neg\psi_1$ and the runs from s satisfying $\neg\psi_2$. As these sets may overlap the rule works with a *disjoint* union by taking $\neg\psi_1$ on the one side, and $\psi_1 \wedge \neg\psi_2$ on the other side so that it is correct to add their probabilities up in γ.

$$\textbf{P1} \quad \frac{\Gamma \vdash \langle m,s \rangle : \{\textbf{P}_{\sim z}\,\psi\} \uplus \Psi}{\Gamma, \gamma_{\text{one}} \vdash \langle m,s \rangle : \{\psi'\} \cup \Psi} \quad \begin{cases} \text{if } \textbf{P}_{\sim z}\,\psi \text{ is the left hand side of an equivalence} \\ \text{(P2)-(P5) and } \psi' \text{ is its right hand side} \end{cases}$$

$$\textbf{P2} \quad \frac{\Gamma \vdash \langle m,s \rangle : \{\textbf{P}_{\sim z}\,\psi\} \uplus \Psi}{\Gamma, \gamma_{\text{one}} \vdash \langle m,s \rangle : \{\psi\} \cup \Psi} \quad \text{if see text} \qquad \textbf{P3} \quad \frac{\Gamma \vdash \langle m,s \rangle : \{\textbf{P}_{\sim z}\,\psi\} \uplus \Psi}{\Gamma, \gamma_{\text{one}} \vdash \langle m,s \rangle : \{\neg\psi\} \cup \Psi} \quad \text{if see text}$$

These are rules for simplifying **P**-formulas. The condition in **P2** is "$\sim \in \{>, \geq\}$ and ψ is a state formula", and in **P3** it is "$\sim \in \{<, \leq\}$ and ψ is a state formula". In the rules **P2** and **P3** trivial cases for z are excluded by preference of **P1**. Indeed, this preference is even needed for soundness. The rule **P2** can be explained as follows: suppose we want to know if $\mathcal{M}, \pi, \langle m,s \rangle \models \textbf{P}_{\sim z}\,\psi$. For that we need the probability of the set of runs from $\langle m,s \rangle$ that satisfy ψ and compare it with z. Because ψ is a *state* formula this set is comprised of all runs from s if $\mathcal{M}, \pi, \langle m,s \rangle \models \psi$, or the empty set otherwise, giving it probability 1 or 0, respectively. With $\sim \in \{>, \geq\}$ conclude $\mathcal{M}, \pi, s \models \textbf{P}_{\sim z}\,\psi$, or its negation, respectively. The rule **P3** is justified analogously. The only difference is that $\sim \in \{<, \leq\}$ and so the $\textbf{P}_{\sim z}$ quantifier acts as a negation operator instead of idempotency.

At this stage, when all rules above have been applied exhaustively to a given branch, the leaf of that branch must be of the form $\Gamma \vdash \langle m,s \rangle :$ $\{\textbf{P}_{\sim z_1}\,\psi_1, \ldots, \textbf{P}_{\sim z_n}\,\psi_n\}$, for some $n \geq 0$, where each ψ_i is a non-negated proper path formula.

$$\textbf{P} \quad \frac{\Gamma \vdash \langle m,s \rangle : \Psi}{\Gamma, \Gamma', \gamma_{\text{left}} \vdash \langle m,s \rangle : \Psi \qquad \Gamma, \Gamma', \gamma_{\text{right}} \vdash \langle m,s \rangle : \Psi} \quad \begin{cases} \text{if } \textbf{P}_{\sim z}\,\psi \in \Psi, \text{ and} \\ \gamma_{\text{left}} \notin \Gamma \text{ and } \gamma_{\text{right}} \notin \Gamma \end{cases}$$

$$\textbf{PT} \quad \frac{\Gamma \vdash \langle m,s \rangle : \{\textbf{P}_{\sim z}\,\psi\} \uplus \Psi}{\Gamma, \gamma_{\text{one}} \vdash \langle m,s \rangle : \Psi} \quad \text{if } \gamma_{\text{left}} \in \Gamma$$

$$\textbf{PX} \quad \frac{\Gamma \vdash \langle m,s \rangle : \{\textbf{P}_{\sim z}\,\psi\} \uplus \Psi}{\Gamma, x_{\langle m,s \rangle}^{\{\textbf{P}_{\sim z}\,\psi\} \uplus \Psi} \doteq 0 \vdash \textbf{X}} \quad \text{if } \gamma_{\text{right}} \in \Gamma \ .$$

where $\Gamma' = \textsc{Gamma}(\textsc{Choose}(\textsc{Tableau}(\emptyset \vdash \langle \text{start}(s), s \rangle : \{\psi\})))$,

$\gamma_{\text{left}} = x_{\langle \text{start}(s),s \rangle}^{\{\psi\}} \sim z$, and $\gamma_{\text{right}} = x_{\langle \text{start}(s),s \rangle}^{\{\psi\}} \,\overline{\sim}\, z$

These are rules for **P**-formulas. Unlike classical formulas, **P**-formulas cannot be evaluated in a state, because their truth value depends on the solution of the program Γ_{final}. The **P** rule analyzes $\textbf{P}_{\sim z}\,\psi$ in a deferred way by first getting a constraint $x_{\langle \text{start}(s),s \rangle}^{\{\psi\}} \doteq e$, for some expression e, for the probability of $\langle \text{start}(s), s \rangle : \{\psi\}$ by a recursive call.[2] This call is not needed if Γ already determines a truth value for $\textbf{P}_{\sim z}\,\psi$ because of $\gamma_{\text{left}} \in \Gamma$ or $\gamma_{\text{right}} \in \Gamma$. These tests are done modulo node labels of variables, i.e., $(x_u)_{\langle \text{start}(s),s \rangle}^{\{\psi\}}$ and $(x_v)_{\langle \text{start}(s),s \rangle}^{\{\psi\}}$ are

---

[2] By the semantics of the **P**-operator, the sub-derivation has to start from $\langle \text{start}(s), s \rangle$, not $\langle m,s \rangle$.

considered equal for any u, v. Because the value of e is not known at the time of the inference, the **P** rule don't-know non-deterministically branches out into whether $x^{\{\psi\}}_{\langle \mathrm{start}(s), s \rangle} \sim z$ holds or not, as per the constraints γ_{left} and γ_{right}. The **PT** and **PX** rules then lift the corresponding case to the evaluation of $\mathbf{P}_{\sim z}\, \psi$, which is possible now thanks to γ_{left} or γ_{right}.

Observe the analogy between these rules and their counterparts T and X for classical formulas. Note that the rules **P**, **PT** and **PX** cannot be combined into one, because γ_{left} or γ_{right} could have been added earlier, further above in the branch, or in a recursive call. In this case only **PT**/**PX** can applied.

At this stage, in a leaf $\Gamma \vdash \langle m, s \rangle : \Psi$ the set Ψ cannot contain any state formulas, as they would all be eliminated by the inference rules above; all formulas in Ψ now are possibly negated **X**-formulas or **U**-formulas.

$$\mathbf{U} \quad \frac{\Gamma \vdash \langle m, s \rangle : \{\psi_1 \mathbf{U} \psi_2\} \uplus \Psi}{\Gamma \vdash \langle m, s \rangle : \{\psi_2\} \cup \Psi \quad \cup \quad \Gamma, \gamma \vdash \langle m, s \rangle : \{\psi_1, \neg \psi_2, \mathbf{X}\,(\psi_1 \mathbf{U} \psi_2)\} \cup \Psi}$$

$$\text{where } \gamma \;=\; x^{\{\psi_1 \mathbf{U} \psi_2\} \uplus \Psi}_{\langle m, s \rangle} \doteq x^{\{\psi_2\} \cup \Psi}_{\langle m, s \rangle} + x^{\{\psi_1, \neg \psi_2, \mathbf{X}(\psi_1 \mathbf{U} \psi_2)\} \cup \Psi}_{\langle m, s \rangle}$$

$$\neg \mathbf{U} \quad \frac{\Gamma \vdash \langle m, s \rangle : \{\neg(\psi_1 \mathbf{U} \psi_2)\} \uplus \Psi}{\Gamma \vdash \langle m, s \rangle : \{\neg \psi_1, \neg \psi_2\} \cup \Psi \quad \cup \quad \Gamma, \gamma \vdash \langle m, s \rangle : \{\psi_1, \neg \psi_2, \mathbf{X}\neg(\psi_1 \mathbf{U} \psi_2)\} \cup \Psi}$$

$$\text{where } \gamma \;=\; x^{\{\neg(\psi_1 \mathbf{U} \psi_2)\} \uplus \Psi}_{\langle m, s \rangle} \doteq x^{\{\neg \psi_1, \neg \psi_2\} \cup \Psi}_{\langle m, s \rangle} + x^{\{\psi_1, \neg \psi_2, \mathbf{X}\neg(\psi_1 \mathbf{U} \psi_2)\} \cup \Psi}_{\langle m, s \rangle}$$

These are expansion rules for **U**-formulas. The standard expansion law is $\psi_1 \mathbf{U} \psi_2 \equiv \psi_2 \vee (\psi_1 \wedge \mathbf{X}\,(\psi_1 \mathbf{U} \psi_2))$. As with the $\neg \wedge$ rule, the disjunction in the expanded formula needs to be disjoint by taking $\psi_2 \vee (\psi_1 \wedge \neg \psi_2 \wedge \mathbf{X}\,(\psi_1 \mathbf{U} \psi_2))$ instead. Similarly for $\neg \mathbf{U}$.

$$\neg \mathbf{X} \quad \frac{\Gamma \vdash \langle m, s \rangle : \{\neg \mathbf{X}\, \psi\} \uplus \Psi}{\Gamma, \gamma_{\mathrm{one}} \vdash \langle m, s \rangle : \{\mathbf{X}\,\neg \psi\} \cup \Psi}$$

The $\neg \mathbf{X}$ rule is obvious.

At this stage, if $\Gamma \vdash \langle m, s \rangle : \Psi$ is a leaf sequent then Ψ is of the form $\{\mathbf{X}\,\psi_1, \ldots, \mathbf{X}\,\psi_n\}$, for some $n \geq 1$. This is an important configuration that justifies a name: we say that a labelled formula $\langle m, s \rangle : \Psi$, a sequent $\Gamma \vdash \langle m, s \rangle : \Psi$ or a node labelled with $\Gamma \vdash \langle m, s \rangle : \Psi$ is *poised* if Ψ is of the form $\{\mathbf{X}\,\psi_1, \ldots, \mathbf{X}\,\psi_n\}$ where $n \geq 1$. (The notion "poised" is taken from [18].) A poised $\langle m, s \rangle : \{\mathbf{X}\,\psi_1, \ldots, \mathbf{X}\,\psi_n\}$ will be expanded by transition into the successor states of s by using enabled actions $\alpha \in A(s)$. That some α is enabled does not, however, preclude a policy with $\mathrm{act}_\sigma(m, s, \alpha) = 0$. The rule A makes a guess whether this is the case or not:

$$\mathbf{A} \quad \frac{\Gamma \vdash \langle m, s \rangle : \Psi}{\Gamma, \gamma_{\mathrm{left}} \vdash \langle m, s \rangle : \Psi \quad \Gamma, \gamma_{\mathrm{right}} \vdash \langle m, s \rangle : \Psi} \quad \begin{cases} \text{if } \Gamma \vdash \langle m, s \rangle : \Psi \text{ is poised,} \\ \alpha \in A(s), \gamma_{\mathrm{left}} \notin \Gamma \text{ and } \gamma_{\mathrm{right}} \notin \Gamma \end{cases}$$

$$\text{where } \gamma_{\mathrm{left}} \;=\; x^\alpha_{\langle m, s \rangle} \doteq 0 \text{ and } \gamma_{\mathrm{right}} \;=\; x^\alpha_{\langle m, s \rangle} > 0$$

With a minor modification we get a calculus for *deterministic* policies. It only requires to re-define γ_{right} as $\gamma_{\mathrm{right}} = x^\alpha_{\langle m, s \rangle} \doteq 1$. As a benefit the program Γ_{final} will be linear.

After the A rule has been applied exhaustively, for each $\alpha \in A(s)$ either $x^{\alpha}_{\langle m,s \rangle} > 0 \in \Gamma$ or $x^{\alpha}_{\langle m,s \rangle} \doteq 0 \in \Gamma$. If $x^{\alpha}_{\langle m,s \rangle} > 0 \in \Gamma$ we say that α *is prescribed in* $\langle m,s \rangle$ *by* Γ and define $Prescribed(\langle m,s \rangle, \Gamma) = \{\alpha \mid x^{\alpha}_{\langle m,s \rangle} > 0 \in \Gamma\}$.

The set of prescribed actions in a policy state determines the *Succ*-relation of the Markov chain under construction. To get the required distribution over enabled actions, it suffices to enforce a distribution over prescribed actions, with this inference rule:

$$Prescribed \quad \frac{\Gamma \vdash \langle m,s \rangle : \Psi}{\Gamma, \gamma^{\alpha}_{\langle m,s \rangle} \vdash \langle m,s \rangle : \Psi} \quad \begin{cases} \text{if } \Gamma \vdash \langle m,s \rangle : \Psi \text{ is poised,} \\ \alpha \in A(s) \text{ and } \gamma^{\alpha}_{\langle m,s \rangle} \notin \Gamma \end{cases}$$

$$\text{where } \gamma^{\alpha}_{\langle m,s \rangle} = \Sigma_{\alpha \in Prescribed(\langle m,s \rangle, \Gamma)} \, x^{\alpha}_{\langle m,s \rangle} \doteq 1$$

If the CHOOSE operator in step two selects the leftmost branch among the A-inferences then Γ_{final} contains $x^{\alpha}_{\langle m,s \rangle} \doteq 0$, for all $\alpha \in A(s)$. This is inconsistent with the constraint introduced by the *Prescribed*-inference, corresponding to the fact that runs containing $\langle m,s \rangle$ in this case do not exist.

We are now turning to a "loop check" which is essential for termination, by, essentially, blocking the expansion of certain states into successor states that do not mark progress. For that, we need some more concepts. For two nodes u and v in a branch we say that u *is an ancestor of* v and write $u \leq v$ if $u = v$ or u is closer to the root than v. An ancestor is *proper*, written as $u < v$, if $u \leq v$ but $u \neq v$. We say that two sequents $\Gamma_1 \vdash \mathcal{F}_1$ and $\Gamma_2 \vdash \mathcal{F}_2$ are *indistinguishable* iff $\mathcal{F}_1 = \mathcal{F}_2$, i.e., they differ only in their Γ-components. Two nodes u and v are *indistinguishable* iff their sequents are. We write Ψ_u to denote the formula component of u's label, i.e., to say that the label is of the form $\Gamma \vdash \langle m,s \rangle : \Psi_u$; similarly for $\mathcal{F}_u$ to denote u's labelled formula.

Definition 3.3 (Blocking). *Let w be a poised leaf and $v < w$ an ancestor node. If (i) v and w are indistinguishable, and (ii) for every $\mathbf{X}$-eventuality $\mathbf{X}(\psi_1 \mathbf{U} \psi_2)$ in Ψ_v there is a node x with $v < x \leq w$ such that $\psi_2 \in \Psi_x$ then w is* yes-blocked *by v. If there is an ancestor node $u < v$ such that (i) u is indistinguishable from v and v is indistinguishable from w (and hence u is indistinguishable from w), and (ii) for every $\mathbf{X}$-eventuality $\mathbf{X}(\psi_1 \mathbf{U} \psi_2)$ in Ψ_u, if there is a node x with $\psi_2 \in \Psi_x$ and $v < x \leq w$ then there is a node y with $\psi_2 \in \Psi_y$ and $u < y \leq v$, then w is* no-blocked *by u.*

When we say that a sequent is yes/no-blocked we mean that its node is yes/no-blocked.

In the yes-blocking case all $\mathbf{X}$-eventualities in Ψ_v become satisfied along the way from v to w. This is why w represents a success case. In the no-blocking case some $\mathbf{X}$-eventualities in Ψ_v may have been satisfied along the way from u to v, but not all, as this would be a yes-blocking instead. Moreover, no progress has been made along the way from v to w for satisfying the missing $\mathbf{X}$-eventualities. This is why w represents a failure case. The blocking scheme is adapted from [18] for LTL satisfiability to our probabilistic case. See [18,19] for more explanations and examples, which are instructive also for its usage in our framework.

Blocking is used in the following inference rules, collectively called the Loop rules. In these rules, the node v is an ancestor node of the leaf the rule is applied to.

$$\text{Yes-Loop} \quad \frac{\Gamma \vdash \langle m, s \rangle : \Psi}{\Gamma, x^{\Psi}_{\langle m,s\rangle} \doteq (x_v)^{\Psi}_{\langle m,s\rangle} \vdash \text{Yes-Loop}} \quad \text{if } \Gamma \vdash \langle m, s \rangle : \Psi \text{ is yes-blocked by } v$$

$$\text{No-Loop} \quad \frac{\Gamma \vdash \langle m, s \rangle : \Psi}{\Gamma, x^{\Psi}_{\langle m,s\rangle} \doteq (x_v)^{\Psi}_{\langle m,s\rangle} \vdash \text{No-Loop}} \quad \text{if } \Gamma \vdash \langle m, s \rangle : \Psi \text{ is no-blocked by } v$$

In either case, if v is indistinguishable from w then the probability of $\mathcal{F}_v$ and $\mathcal{F}_w$ are exactly the same, just because $\mathcal{F}_v = \mathcal{F}_w$. This justifies adding $x^{\Psi}_{\langle m,s\rangle} \doteq (x_v)^{\Psi}_{\langle m,s\rangle}$.

The Loop rules have a side-effect that we do not formalize: they add a link from the conclusion node (the new leaf node) to the blocking node v, called the *backlink*. It turns the tableau into a graph that is no longer a tree. The backlinks are used only for reachability analysis in step three of the algorithm. Figure 1 has a graphical depiction.

By preference of inference rules, the **X** rule introduced next can be applied only if a Loop rule does not apply. The Loop rules are at the core of the termination argument.[3]

For economy of notation, when $\Psi = \{\psi_1, \ldots, \psi_n\}$, for some $\psi_1, \ldots, \psi_n$ and $n > 0$, let **X** Ψ denote the set $\{\mathbf{X}\,\psi_1, \ldots, \mathbf{X}\,\psi_n\}$.

$$\mathbf{X} \quad \frac{\Gamma \vdash \langle m, s \rangle : \mathbf{X}\,\Psi}{\Gamma \vdash \langle m', t_1 \rangle : \Psi \;\cup\; \cdots \;\cup\; \Gamma \vdash \langle m', t_{k-1} \rangle : \Psi \;\cup\; \Gamma, \gamma_1 \vdash \langle m', t_k \rangle : \Psi}$$

where
$$m' = \Delta(m, s) \quad,$$
$$\{t_1, \ldots, t_k\} = \bigcup_{\alpha \in Prescribed(\langle m,s\rangle, \Gamma)} Succ(s, \alpha) \text{ , for some } k \geq 0$$
$$\gamma_1 = x^{\mathbf{X}\,\Psi}_{\langle m,s\rangle} \doteq \Sigma_{\alpha \in Prescribed(\langle m,s\rangle, \Gamma)} [x^{\alpha}_{\langle m,s\rangle} \cdot (\Sigma_{t \in Succ(s,\alpha)} P(t|s, \alpha) \cdot x^{\Psi}_{\langle m',t\rangle})]$$

This is the (only) rule for expansion into successor states. If u is the node the **X** rule is applied to and $u_1, \ldots, u_k$ are its children then each u_i is called an **X**-*successor (of u)*.

The **X** rule follows the set of actions prescribed in $\langle m, s \rangle$ by Γ through to successor states. This requires summing up the probabilities of carrying out α, as represented by $x^{\alpha}_{\langle m,s\rangle}$, multiplied by the sums of the successor probabilities weighted by the respective transition probabilities. This is expressed in the constraint γ_1. Only these k successors need to be summed up, as all other, non-prescribed successors, have probability 0.

---

[3] The argument is standard for calculi based on formula expansion, as embodied in the **U** and ¬**U** rules: the sets of formulas obtainable by these rules is a subset of an a priori determined *finite* set of formulas. This set consists of all subformulas of the given formula closed under negation and other operators. Any infinite branch hence would have to repeat one of these sets infinitely often, which is impossible with the loop rules. Moreover, the state set S and the mode set M are finite and so the other rules do not cause problems either.

Forcing Probabilities. We are now turning to the FORCE operator which we left open in step three of the algorithm. It forces a probability 0 or 1 for certain labelled formulas occurring in a bottom strongly connected component in a tree from step two. The tree in the figure to the right helps to illustrate the concepts introduced in the following.

We need some basic notions from graph theory. A subset M of the nodes N of a given graph is *strongly connected* if, for each pair of nodes u and v in M, v is reachable from u passing only through states in M. A *strongly connected component (SCC)* is a maximally strongly connected set of nodes (i.e., no superset of it is also strongly connected). A *bottom strongly connected component (BSCC)* is a SCC M from which no state outside M is reachable from M.

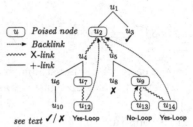

Fig. 1. An example tableau T from step 2. The subgraph below u_2 is a strongly connected component if u_{10} is X-ed.

Let $T = \text{CHOOSE}(\text{TABLEAU}(\Gamma \vdash \mathcal{F}))$ be a tree without don't-know branching obtained in step 2. We wish to take T together with its backlinks as the graph under consideration and analyse its BSCCs. However, for doing so we cannot take T as it is. On the one hand, our tableaux describe state transitions introduced by X rule applications. Intuitively, these are amenable to BSCC analysis as one would do for state transition systems. On the other hand, T has interspersed rule applications for analysing Boolean structure, which distort the state transition structure. These rule applications have to be taken into account prior to the BSCC analysis proper.

For this, we distinguish between X-links and +-links in T. An X-link is an edge between a node and its child if the X rule was applied to the node, making its child an X-successor, otherwise it is a +-link. ("+-link" because probabilities are summed up.)

Let u be a node in T and $Subtree_T(u)$, or just $Subtree(u)$, the subtree of T rooted at u without the backlinks. We say that u is a *0-deadend (in T)* if $Subtree_T(u)$ has no X-links and every leaf in $Subtree_T(u)$ is X-ed. In a 0-deadend the probabilities all add up to a zero probability for the pivot of u. This is shown by an easy inductive argument.

Definition 3.4 (Ambiguous node). *Let u be a node in T. We say that u is ambiguous (in T) iff (i) $Subtree_T(u)$ contains no ✓-ed leaf, and (ii) $Subtree_T(u)$ contains no X-successor 0-deadend node. We say that u is unambiguous iff u is not ambiguous.*

The main application of Definition 3.4 is when the node u is the root of a BSCCs, defined below. The probability of u's pivot $\langle m, s \rangle : \Psi$ then is not uniquely determined. This is because expanding u always leads to a cycle, a node with the same pivot, and there is no escape from that according to conditions (i) or (ii) in Definition 3.4. In other words, the probability of $\langle m, s \rangle : \Psi$ is defined only in terms of itself.[4]

In the figure above, the node u_1 is unambiguous because of case (i) in Definition 3.4. Assuming u_{10} is ✓-ed, the node u_2 is unambiguous by case (i). The pivot in u_{10}, then, has probability 1 which is propagated upwards to u_4 (and enforces probability 0 for the pivot of u_7). It contributes a non-zero probability to the transition from u_2 to u_4 and this way escapes a cycle. If u_{10} is ✗-ed, the node u_2 is ambiguous.

If case (ii) in Definition 3.4 is violated there is an ✗-successor node whose pivot has probability 0. Because every ✗-link has a non-zero transition probability, the probabilities obtained through the other ✗-successor nodes add up to a value strictly less than 1. This also escapes the cycle leading to underspecified programs (not illustrated above).

Let $0(T) = \{w \mid w \text{ is a node in some 0-deadend of } T\}$ be all nodes in all 0-deadends in T. In the example, $0(T) = \{u_6, u_{10}, u_8\}$ if u_{10} is ✗-ed and $0(T) = \{u_8\}$ if u_{10} is ✓-ed.

Let u be a node in T and $M(u) = \{w \mid w \text{ is a node in s Subtree}(u)\} \setminus 0(T)$. That is, $M(u)$ consists of the nodes in the subtree rooted at u after ignoring the nodes from the 0-deadend subtrees. In the example $M(u_2) = \{u_2, u_4, u_5, u_7, u_9, u_{12}, u_{13}, u_{14}\}$ if u_{10} is ✗-ed. If u_{10} is ✓-ed then u_6 and u_{10} have to be added.

We say that u *is the root of a BSCC (in T)* iff u is poised, ambiguous and $M(u)$ is a BSCC in T (together with the backlinks). In the example, assume that u_{10} is ✗-ed. Then u_2 is poised, ambiguous and the root of a BSCC. In the example, that $M(u_2)$ is a BSCC in T is easy to verify.

Now suppose that u is the root of a BSCC with pivot $\langle m, s \rangle : \mathbf{X} \Psi$. This means that the probability of $\langle m, s \rangle : \mathbf{X} \Psi$ is not uniquely determined. This situation then is fixed by means of the FORCE operation, generally defined as follows:

$\text{Bscc}(T) := \{u \mid u \text{ is the root of a BSCC in } T\}$

$\text{FORCE}(T) := \{(x_u)_{\langle m,s \rangle}^{\mathbf{X} \Psi} \doteq \chi \mid u \in \text{Bscc}(T), \text{ and}$
$\qquad\qquad\qquad \text{if some leaf of the subtree rooted at } u \text{ is a Yes-Loop}$
$\qquad\qquad\qquad \text{then } \chi = 1 \text{ else } \chi = 0\}$

That is, FORCEing removes the ambiguity for the probability of the pivot $\langle m, s \rangle : \mathbf{X} \Psi$ at the root u of a BSCC by setting it to 1 or to 0. If FORCEing adds $(x_u)_{\langle m,s \rangle}^{\mathbf{X} \Psi} \doteq 1$ then there is a run that satisfies every ✗-eventuality in $\mathbf{X} \Psi$, by following the branch to a Yes-Loop. Because we are looking at a BSCC, for fairness reasons, *every* run will do this, and infinitely often so, this way giving $\mathbf{X} \Psi$ probability 1. Otherwise, if there is no Yes-Loop, there is some ✗-eventuality in $\mathbf{X} \Psi$ that cannot be satisfied, forcing probability 0.

---

[4] In terms of the resulting program, $(x_u)_{\langle m,s \rangle}^{\psi}$ is not constrained to any specific value in $[0..1]$. This can be shown by "substituting in" the equalities in Γ_{final} for the probabilities of the pivots in the subtree below u and arithmetic simplifications.

4 Example

The following is only a brief summary of an example spelled out in detail in the long version [4] of this paper. Consider the MDP on the right. The initial state is s_1. Action β leads non-deterministically to states s_2 and s_3, each with probability 0.5. The actions α_i for $i \in \{1,2,3\}$ are self-loops with probability one (not shown). The label set of s_2 is $\{a\}$ in all other states it is empty. The partially specified finite-memory policy 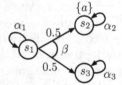 $\pi_{\mathrm{fin}} = (\{\mathrm{m}\}, \mathrm{start}, \Delta, \cdot)$ has a single mode m, making π_{fin} Markovian. The functions start and Δ hence always return m, allowing us to abbreviate $\langle m, s_i \rangle$ as just s_i. Let the state formula of interest be $\phi = \mathbf{P}_{\geq 0.3} \, \mathbf{F} \, \mathbf{G} \, a$. We wish to obtain a Γ_{final} such that any solution σ synthesizes a suitable act_σ, i.e., the policy $\pi_{\mathrm{fin}}(\sigma)$ completed by σ satisfies $\mathcal{M}, \pi_{\mathrm{fin}}(\sigma), s_1 \models \phi$.

The BSCCs depend on whether $\mathrm{act}_\sigma(\mathrm{m}, s_1, \beta) > 0$ holds, i.e., if β can be executed at s_1. (This is why the calculus needs to make a corresponding guess, with its A-rule.) If not, then s_2 and s_3 are unreachable, and the self-loop at s_1 is the only BSCC, which does not satisfy $\mathbf{G} \, a$. If yes, then there are two BSCCs, the self-loop at s_2 and the self-loop at s_3, and the BSCC at s_2 satisfies $\mathbf{G} \, a$. By fairness of execution, with probability one some BSCC will be reached, and the BSCC at s_2 is reached with probability 0.5, hence, if $\mathrm{act}_\sigma(\mathrm{m}, s_1, \beta) > 0$. In other words, devising *any* policy that reaches s_2 will hence suffice to satisfy ϕ. The expected result thus is just a constraint on σ saying $\mathrm{act}_\sigma(\mathrm{m}, s_1, \beta) > 0$. Indeed, the derivation will show that.

In brief, the derivation starts with the initial sequent $\{x_{s_1}^\phi \doteq 1\} \vdash s_1 : \{\phi\}$. The first inference is a P-inference, branching out on $x_{s_1}^{\mathbf{F}\,\mathbf{G}\,a} \geq 0.3$ and its negation. (The latter case quickly leads to an unsatisfiable program.) The P-inference triggers a recursive call with the start sequent $\emptyset \vdash x_{s_1}^{\mathbf{F}\,\mathbf{G}\,a}$. This tableau leads to an open branch with sequent $\emptyset \vdash x_{s_1}^{\mathbf{X}\,\mathbf{F}\,\mathbf{G}\,a}$ and all other branches X-ed, inducing a constraint $x_{s_1}^{\mathbf{F}\,\mathbf{G}\,a} \doteq x_{s_1}^{\mathbf{X}\,\mathbf{F}\,\mathbf{G}\,a}$. This is plausible, as s_1 falsifies $\mathbf{G} \, a$, and hence exactly the successor states of s_1 need to be considered.

As said, the interesting case is if β can be executed at s_1, so let us assume that. The tableau derivation continues the open branch and arrives at s_3. Further expansion leads to No-Loop leaves only. This gives a trivial constraint $x_{s_3}^{\mathbf{F}\,\mathbf{G}\,a} \doteq x_{s_3}^{\mathbf{F}\,\mathbf{G}\,a}$ only, but FORCEing adds $x_{s_3}^{\mathbf{F}\,\mathbf{G}\,a} \doteq 0$. The tableau derivation also arrives at s_2, this time with a BSCC with Yes-Loop leaf, contributing $x_{s_2}^{\mathbf{F}\,\mathbf{G}\,a} \doteq 1$.

If desired, the resulting program Γ_{final} can be simplified so that it becomes obvious that only the constraint $x_{s_1}^\beta > 0$ is essential for satisfiability.

5 Conclusions and Future Work

In this paper we presented a first-of-its kind algorithm for the controller synthesis problem for Markov Decision Processes whose intended behavior is described by PCTL* formulas. The only restriction we had to make – to get decidability – is to require policies with finite history. We like to propose that the description of the algorithm is material enough for one paper, and so we leave many interesting questions for future work.

The most pressing theoretical question concerns the exact worst-case complexity of the algorithm. Related to that, it will be interesting to specialize and analyze our framework for fragments of PCTL*, such as probabilistic LTL and CTL or simpler fragments and restricted classes of policies that might lead to *linear* programs (and ideally to solving only a polynomial number of such programs). For instance, we already mentioned that computing deterministic policies leads to linear programs in our tableau (see the description of the A inference rule how this is done.) Moreover, it is well-known that cost-optimal stochastic policies for classes of MDPs with simple constraints bounding the probability of reaching a goal state can be synthesized in linear time in the size of the MDP by solving a *single* linear program [1,12]. An interesting question is how far these simple constraints can be generalised towards PCTL* whilst remaining in the linear programming framework (see e.g. [20]).

On implementation, a naïve implementation of the algorithm as presented above would perform poorly in practice. However, it is easy to exploit some straightforward observations for better performance. For instance, steps one (tableau construction) and two (committing to a don't-know non-deterministic choice) should be combined into one. Then, if a don't know non-deterministic inference rule is carried out the first time, every subsequent inference with the same rule and pivot can be forced to the same conclusion, at the time the rule is applied. Otherwise an inconsistent program would result, which never needs to be searched for. Regarding space, although all children of a union branching inference rule need to be expanded, this does not imply they always all need to be kept in memory simultaneously. Nodes can be expanded in a one-branch-at-a-time fashion and using a global variable for Γ_{final} for collecting the programs in the leaves of the branches *if they do not belong to a bottom strongly connected component*. Otherwise, the situation is less obvious and we leave it to future work. Another good source of efficiency improvements comes from more traditional tableau. It will be mandatory to exploit techniques such as dependency-directed backtracking, lemma learning, and early failure checking for search space pruning.

Acknowledgements. This research was funded by AFOSR grant FA2386-15-1-4015. We would also like to thank the anonymous reviewers for their constructive and helpful comments.

References

1. Altman, E.: Constrained Markov Decision Processes, vol. 7. CRC Press, Boca Raton (1999)
2. Baier, C., Größer, M., Leucker, M., Bollig, B., Ciesinski, F.: Controller synthesis for probabilistic systems. In: TCS 2004 (2004)
3. Baier, C., Katoen, J.: Principles of Model Checking. MIT Press, Cambridge (2008)
4. Baumgartner, P., Thiébaux, S., Trevizan, F.: Tableaux for policy synthesis for MDPS with PCTL* constraints. CoRR, abs/1706.10102 (2017)

5. Brázdil, T., Brozek, V., Forejt, V., Kucera, A.: Stochastic games with branching-time winning objectives. In: 21th IEEE Symposium on Logic in Computer Science LICS (2006)
6. Brázdil, T., Forejt, V.: Strategy synthesis for Markov decision processes and branching-time logics. In: Caires, L., Vasconcelos, V.T. (eds.) CONCUR 2007. LNCS, vol. 4703, pp. 428–444. Springer, Heidelberg (2007). doi:10.1007/978-3-540-74407-8_29
7. Brázdil, T., Forejt, V., Kučera, A.: Controller synthesis and verification for Markov decision processes with qualitative branching time objectives. In: Aceto, L., Damgård, I., Goldberg, L.A., Halldórsson, M.M., Ingólfsdóttir, A., Walukiewicz, I. (eds.) ICALP 2008. LNCS, vol. 5126, pp. 148–159. Springer, Heidelberg (2008). doi:10.1007/978-3-540-70583-3_13
8. Brázdil, T., Kučera, A., Stražovský, O.: On the decidability of temporal properties of probabilistic pushdown automata. In: Diekert, V., Durand, B. (eds.) STACS 2005. LNCS, vol. 3404, pp. 145–157. Springer, Heidelberg (2005). doi:10.1007/978-3-540-31856-9_12
9. Courcoubetis, C., Yannakakis, M.: The complexity of probabilistic verification. J. ACM **42**(4), 857–907 (1995)
10. Ding, X.C., Pinto, A., Surana, A.: Strategic planning under uncertainties via constrained Markov decision processes. In: IEEE International Conference on Robotics and Automation ICRA (2013)
11. Ding, X.C., Smith, S., Belta, C., Rus, D.: Optimal control of Markov decision processes with linear temporal logic constraints. IEEE Trans. Automat. Contr. **59**(5), 1244–1257 (2014)
12. Dolgov, D., Durfee, E.: Stationary deterministic policies for constrained MDPs with multiple rewards, costs, and discount factors. In: IJCAI (2005)
13. Forejt, V., Kwiatkowska, M., Norman, G., Parker, D.: Automated verification techniques for probabilistic systems. In: Bernardo, M., Issarny, V. (eds.) SFM 2011. LNCS, vol. 6659, pp. 53–113. Springer, Heidelberg (2011). doi:10.1007/978-3-642-21455-4_3
14. Kemeny, J., Snell, J., Knapp, A.: Denumerable Markov Chains: With a Chapter of Markov Random Fields by David Griffeath, vol. 40. Springer, Heidelberg (2012)
15. Kučera, A., Stražovský, O.: On the controller synthesis for finite-state Markov decision processes. In: Sarukkai, S., Sen, S. (eds.) FSTTCS 2005. LNCS, vol. 3821, pp. 541–552. Springer, Heidelberg (2005). doi:10.1007/11590156_44
16. Kwiatkowska, M., Norman, G., Parker, D.: Stochastic model checking. In: Bernardo, M., Hillston, J. (eds.) SFM 2007. LNCS, vol. 4486, pp. 220–270. Springer, Heidelberg (2007). doi:10.1007/978-3-540-72522-0_6
17. Kwiatkowska, M., Parker, D.: Automated verification and strategy synthesis for probabilistic systems. In: Hung, D., Ogawa, M. (eds.) ATVA 2013. LNCS, vol. 8172, pp. 5–22. Springer, Cham (2013). doi:10.1007/978-3-319-02444-8_2
18. Reynolds, M.: A new rule for LTL tableaux. In: GandALF (2016)
19. Reynolds, M.: A traditional tree-style tableau for LTL. CoRR, abs/1604.03962 (2016)
20. Sprauel, J., Kolobov, A., Teichteil-Königsbuch, F.: Saturated path-constrained MDP: planning under uncertainty and deterministic model-checking constraints. In: AAAI (2014)
21. Svorenová, M., Cerna, I., Belta, C.: Optimal control of MDPs with temporal logic constraints. In: CDC (2013)
22. Trevizan, F., Thiébaux, S., Santana, P., Williams, B.: Heuristic search in dual space for constrained stochastic shortest path problems. In: ICAPS (2016)

Minimisation of ATL* Models

Serenella Cerrito[1]([⊠]) and Amélie David[2]

[1] IBISC, Université Evry Val d'Essonne, Évry, France
serena.cerrito@ibisc.univ-evry.fr
[2] Université Paris-Descartes, Paris, France
amelie.david@parisdescartes.fr

Abstract. The aim of this work is to provide a general method to minimize the size (number of states) of a model $\mathcal{M}$ of an ATL* formula. Our approach is founded on the notion of alternating bisimulation: given a model $\mathcal{M}$, it is transformed in a stepwise manner into a new model $\mathcal{M}'$ minimal with respect to bisimulation. The method has been implemented and will be integrated into the prover TATL, that constructively decides satifiability of an ATL* formula by building a tableau from which, when open, models of the input formula can be extracted.

Keywords: Alternating-time temporal logic · Bisimulation · Model minimization · Tableaux

1 Introduction

The Alternating-time temporal logic ATL* has been introduced in [AHK02] and proposed as a logical framework for the specification and the verification of properties of open systems, that is systems interacting with an environment whose behaviour is unknown or only partially known. The logic ATL* can be seen as a multi-agent extension of the branching time temporal logic CTL* where the path quantifiers are generalized to "strategic quantifiers", indexed with coalitions of agents A, ranging existentially over collective strategies of A and then universally over all paths (computations) coherent with the selected collective strategy. The language of ATL* allows the expression of statements of the type *"Coalition A has a collective strategy to guarantee the satisfaction of the objective Ψ no matter what its opponents do"*, and can therefore model the interaction of an open system with an environment by setting the environment to be the system opponent.

The semantics of ATL* is based on the notion of concurrent game models (CGMs), a generalisation of labelled transition systems to the multi-agent framework where an edge connecting two states is labelled by a vector describing the synchronous actions of all the agents, rather than by the action of a single agent. The aim of this work is to provide a general method to minimize the size (number of states) of a model $\mathcal{M}$ of an ATL* formula.

Independently from the specific logic of interest, to get minimal models is useful for several tasks: hardware and software verification, fault analysis, and

© Springer International Publishing AG 2017
R.A. Schmidt and C. Nalon (Eds.): TABLEAUX 2017, LNAI 10501, pp. 193–208, 2017.
DOI: 10.1007/978-3-319-66902-1_12

common sense reasoning. Several different criteria of minimality have been studied in the literature. In the case of first order classical logic, some works minimize the domain (see for instance [Hin88, Lor94]), while others minimize the interpretation either of a certain set of predicates (see for instance [McC87]) or of all the predicates (see for instance [BY00, Nie96, GHS01, HFK00]).

These minimality criteria can be applied to modal logics, too. Minimal model generation where certain predicates are minimal has been mostly studied in the context of non-monotonic operators and non-monotonic semantics (see for instance [GGOP08, GH09, BLW09]). In the case of modal logics, however, it is quite natural to adopt minimality criteria founded on the notion of bisimulation. The work [PS14] presents terminating procedures for the generation of models that are minimal for a given notion of *subset-simulation* for the propositional modal logic K and all combinations of its extensions with the axioms T, B, D, 4 and 5. Roughly, what is minimized there is not the number of worlds, but the number of propositions holding at worlds.

In the specific case of temporal logics the emphasis is rather on the reduction of the size of the state space. This is crucial if the considered temporal logic has to be used to model systems whose properties need to be model-checked. In the case of CTL and CTL*, having as semantics (labelled) transition systems ((L)TS), models are minimized with respect to bisimulation by using coarsest partition algorithms refining step by step an initial partition of the set of states of a given LTS [LIS12, KS90, PT87].

Our work is inspired by the above mentioned partition-refinement approach for LTS but treats the more complex case of ATL* models, namely CGMs. We rewrite a CGM $\mathcal{M}$ into a bisimilar smaller model by using the definition of alternating bisimulation, that is specific to ATL* [DGL16, ÅGJ07].

The intended application is the synthesis of ATL* models from formal specifications by means of the software TATL, available on line via a dynamic web page [Dav]. Up to our knowledge, TATL is the only existing running system that decides the satisfiability of an ATL* formula (and by means of a trivial preliminary rewriting also of CTL* formulae). TATL constructively decides the satisfiability of a given ATL* formula ϕ by exhibiting a tableau for ϕ [CDG14, Dav15]. A tableau for ϕ is built by analysing the formula and producing states of the candidate models, so as to obtain a finite graph. When the final tableau is open, it is a non-empty labelled graph representing a graph of CGMs satisfying ϕ at some initial state. The completeness proof (with respect to unsatisfiability), being constructive, provides a procedure to build a model of ϕ from an open tableau [CDG14, Dav15]. Such a procedure, however, can generate a model that has an unnecessarily large number of states, because eventualities are sequentially treated to assure their realizability: eventualities that might be simultaneously realized are systematically realized one after the other. To reduce the size of such a model is important, for instance, for the purpose of model synthesis from a formal specification written in ATL*: CGMs that contain an unnecessary great number of states are difficult to grasp and expensive to treat (for instance to model check additional properties).

The aim of this work is to provide a procedure that, when applied to a (finite) ATL* model $\mathcal{M}$ of a formula ϕ, outputs a model $\mathcal{M}'$ of ϕ that is bisimilar to $\mathcal{M}$, and that is *minimal with respect to alternating bisimulation*. It is worthwhile observing that this does not mean that $\mathcal{M}'$ will be a model of ϕ having the minimum number of states necessary to satisfy ϕ. We will illustrate this point in Sect. 3 by means of Example 1.

The outline of our presentation is the following. In Sect. 2 we recall some background definitions. Section 3 is the core of the paper and provides our minimisation algorithm and its foundations. Section 4 briefly discusses the implementation (ongoing work). Finally, we conclude and we sketch some lines of future work.

2   Preliminaries

We recall here some standard definitions about ATL*.

Definition 1 (Concurrent Game Model). *Given a set of atomic propositions P, a CGM (Concurrent Game Model) is a 5-tuple*

$$\mathcal{M} = \langle \mathbb{A}, \mathbb{S}, \{\mathsf{Act}_a\}_{a \in \mathbb{A}}, \{\mathsf{act}_a\}_{a \in \mathbb{A}}, \mathsf{out}, \mathsf{L} \rangle$$

such that:
- $\mathbb{A} = \{1, \ldots, k\}$ *is a finite non-empty set of agents;*
- $\mathbb{S}$ *is a non-empty set of states;*
- *For each $a \in \mathbb{A}$, Act_a is a non-empty set of actions. If $A \subseteq \mathbb{A}$, then A is a coalition of agents. Given a coalition A, an A-move is a k-ple $\langle \alpha_1, \ldots, \alpha_k \rangle$ where, for any $i, 1 \leq i \leq k$, if $i \in A$ then $\alpha_i \in \mathsf{Act}_a$, else $\alpha_i = *$ (* being a place-holder symbol distinct from each action). A move of the coalition $\mathbb{A}$ will also be called global move. The set of all the A-moves is denoted by Act_A. The notation σ_A denotes an element of Act_A, and if $a \in A$, $\sigma_A(a)$ means the action of the agent a in the A-move σ_A;*
- act_a *is a function mapping a state s to a non-empty subset of Act_a; $\mathsf{act}_a(s)$ denotes the set of actions of the agent a that are available at state s. Given a coalition A, a mapping act_A associating to a state a set of A-moves is naturally induced by the function act_a; $\mathsf{act}_A(s)$ is the set of all the A-moves available to coalition A at state s;*
- out *is a transition function, associating to each $s \in \mathbb{S}$ and each $\sigma_{\mathbb{A}} \in \mathsf{act}_{\mathbb{A}}(s)$ a state $\mathsf{out}(s, \sigma_{\mathbb{A}}) \in \mathbb{S}$: the state reached when each $a \in \mathbb{A}$ does the action σ_a at s;*
- L *is a labelling function $\mathsf{L} : \mathbb{S} \to \mathcal{P}(P)$, associating to each state s the set of propositions holding at s.*

It is worthwhile observing that the above definition does not require the set $\mathbb{S}$ to be finite. In our intended application, however, where models are constructed out of open finite tableaux, it will always be finite.[1]

---

[1] Indeed, the existence of sound, complete and terminating tableaux for ATL * is a proof of the finite model property for ATL*.

Below, $p \in P$ and A is a *coalition* of agents.

Definition 2 (ATL*syntax).

State formulae: $\psi := p \mid (\neg\psi) \mid (\psi \wedge \psi) \mid (\langle\!\langle A \rangle\!\rangle \Phi)$
Path formulae: $\Phi := \psi \mid (\neg\Phi) \mid (\Phi \wedge \Phi) \mid (\bigcirc\Phi) \mid (\square\Phi) \mid (\Phi U \Phi)$

It is worthwhile observing that any ATL* state formula is also an ATL* path formula, while the converse is false. State formulae will always be noted by lower case Greek letters, and path formulae by upper case Greek letters. Unless explicitly stated otherwise, in the sequel by ATL* formula we mean an ATL* state formula.

ATL is the syntactical fragment of ATL* obeying to the constraint that any temporal operator in a formula is prefixed by a quantifier $\langle\!\langle A \rangle\!\rangle$ and that no quantifier can have a boolean operator in its immediate scope, analogously to CTL w.r.t. CTL*. Hence any ATL formula is a state formula.

The semantics for ATL* is based on the notions of concurrent game model, *play* and *strategy*.

A play λ in a CGM $\mathcal{M}$ is an infinite sequence of elements of $\mathbb{S}$: $s_0, s_1, s_2, \ldots$ such that for every $i \geq 0$, there is a global move $\sigma_{\mathbb{A}} \in \text{act}_{\mathbb{A}}(s_i)$ such that $\text{out}(s_i, \sigma_{\mathbb{A}}) = s_{i+1}$. Given a play λ, we denote by λ_0 its initial state, by λ_i its $(i+1)$th state, by $\lambda_{\leq i}$ the prefix $\lambda_0 \ldots \lambda_i$ of λ and by $\lambda_{\geq i}$ the suffix $\lambda_i \lambda_{i+1} \ldots$ of λ. Given a prefix $\lambda_{\leq i} : \lambda_0 \ldots \lambda_i$, we say that it has length $i + 1$ and write $|\lambda_{\leq i}| = i + 1$. An empty prefix has length 0. A (non-empty) *history* at state s is a finite prefix of a play ending with s. We denote by $\text{Plays}_{\mathcal{M}}$ and $\text{Hist}_{\mathcal{M}}$ respectively the set of plays and set of histories in a CGM $\mathcal{M}$.

Given a coalition $A \subseteq \mathbb{A}$ of agents, a *perfect recall strategy* F_A is a function which maps each element $\lambda = \lambda_0 \ldots \lambda_\ell$ of $\text{Hist}_{\mathcal{M}}$ to an A-move σ_A belonging to $\text{act}_A(\lambda_\ell)$ (the set of actions available to A at state λ_ℓ). Whenever F_A depends only on the state λ_ℓ the strategy is said to be *positional*. In the rest of the paper we always consider perfect recall strategies.

For any coalition A, a global move $\sigma_{\mathbb{A}}$ *extends* an A-move σ_A whenever for each agent $a \in A$, $\sigma_A(a) = \sigma_{\mathbb{A}}(a)$. Let σ_A be an A-move; the notation $\text{Out}(s, \sigma_A)$ denotes the set of states $\text{out}(s, \sigma_{\mathbb{A}})$ where $\sigma_{\mathbb{A}}$ is any global move extending σ_A. Intuitively, $\text{Out}(s, \sigma_A)$ denotes the set of the states that are successors of s when the coalitions A plays at s the A-move σ_A and the other agents play no matter which move.

A play $\lambda = \lambda_0, \lambda_1, \ldots$ is said to be *coherent with a strategy* F_A if and only if for each $j \geq 0$, $\lambda_{j+1} \in \text{Out}(\lambda_j, \sigma_A)$, where σ_A is the A-move chosen by F_A at state λ_i.

The notion $\mathcal{M}$ *satisfies the formula* Φ *at state* s, noted $\mathcal{M}, s \models \Phi$, is defined by induction on ϕ as follows (omitting the obvious boolean cases):

- $\mathcal{M}, s \models p$ iff $p \in L(s)$, for any proposition $p \in \mathbb{P}$;
- $\mathcal{M}, s \models \langle\!\langle A \rangle\!\rangle \Phi$ iff there exists an A-strategy F_A such that, for all plays λ starting at s and coherent with the strategy F_A, $\mathcal{M}, \lambda \models \Phi$;
- $\mathcal{M}, \lambda \models \varphi$ iff $\mathcal{M}, \lambda_0 \models \varphi$;

- $\mathcal{M}, \lambda \models \bigcirc \Phi$ iff $\mathcal{M}, \lambda_{\geq 1} \models \Phi$;
- $\mathcal{M}, \lambda \models \square \Phi$ iff $\mathcal{M}, \lambda_{\geq i} \models \Phi$ for all $i \geq 0$;
- $\mathcal{M}, \lambda \models \Phi \mathsf{U} \Psi$ iff there exists an $i \geq 0$ where $\mathcal{M}, \lambda_{\geq i} \models \Psi$ and for all $0 \leq j < i$, $\mathcal{M}, \lambda_{\geq j} \models \Phi$.

Given a CGM $\mathcal{M}$ and a formula ϕ, we say that $\mathcal{M}$ *satisfies* ϕ whenever there is a state s such that $\mathcal{M}, s \models \phi$; then we also say that $\mathcal{M}$ *satisfies* ϕ *at* s and that $\mathcal{M}$ *is a model of* ϕ.

The works [ÅGJ07, DGL16] define a notion of bisimulation appropriate to CGMs and analogous to the notion of bisimulation for transition systems (see, for instance, [LIS12]).

Definition 3 (Alternating Bisimulation [ÅGJ07, DGL16]). *Let* $\mathcal{M}_1 = \langle \mathbb{A}, \mathbb{S}, \{\mathsf{Act}_a\}_{a \in \mathbb{A}}, \mathsf{out}, \mathsf{L} \rangle$ *and* $\mathcal{M}_2 = \langle \mathbb{A}, \mathbb{S}', \{\mathsf{Act}'_a\}_{a \in \mathbb{A}}, \mathsf{out}', \mathsf{L}' \rangle$ *be two CGMs over the same set of atomic propositions and over the same set of agents.*

- *Let* A *be a coalition. A relation* $\beta \subseteq \mathbb{S} \times \mathbb{S}'$ *is an alternating* A-*bisimulation between* $\mathcal{M}_1$ *and* $\mathcal{M}_2$ *iff for all* $s_1 \in \mathbb{S}$ *and* $s_2 \in \mathbb{S}'$, $s_1 \beta s_2$ *implies that the following hold:*
  1. ***Local Harmony.*** $\mathsf{L}(s_1) = \mathsf{L}'(s_2)$;
  2. ***Forth.*** *For any* $\alpha_A \in \mathsf{act}_A(s_1)$ *there is an* $\alpha'_A \in \mathsf{act}'_A(s_2)$ *such that for any* $t_2 \in \mathsf{Out}(s_2, \alpha'_A)$ *there exists* $t_1 \in \mathsf{Out}(s_1, \alpha_A)$ *such that* $t_1 \beta t_2$;
  3. ***Back.*** *For any* $\alpha_A \in \mathsf{act}_A(s_2)$ *there is an* $\alpha'_A \in \mathsf{act}'_A(s_1)$ *such that for any* $t_3 \in \mathsf{Out}(s_1, \alpha'_A)$ *there exists* $t_4 \in \mathsf{Out}(s_2, \alpha_A)$ *such that* $t_3 \beta t_4$.
- *When* β *is an alternating* A-*bisimulation between* $\mathcal{M}_1$ *and* $\mathcal{M}_2$, *we note* $\mathcal{M}_1 \overset{\beta}{\rightleftarrows}_A \mathcal{M}_2$;
- *If* β *is an alternating* A-*bisimulation between* $\mathcal{M}_1$ *and* $\mathcal{M}_2$ *for every coalition* $A \subseteq \mathbb{A}$, *then* β *is a full alternating bisimulation and we note:* $\mathcal{M}_1 \overset{\beta}{\rightleftarrows} \mathcal{M}_2$;
- *When* β *is a full bisimulation between* $\mathcal{M}_1$ *and* $\mathcal{M}_2$, β *is total on* $\mathbb{S}$ *and its inverse is total on* $\mathbb{S}'$, *then it is a global alternating bisimulation between* $\mathcal{M}_1$ *and* $\mathcal{M}_2$. *The models* $\mathcal{M}_1$ *and* $\mathcal{M}_2$ *are said to be bisimilar when such a relation* β *exists.*

Figure 1, borrowed from [DGL16], illustrates the above definition.

Remark 1. A full alternating bisimulation β is a fixpoint solution of the equation $X = E(X)$ where a value of X is a subset of $\mathbb{S} \times \mathbb{S}'$ such that if $\langle q, q'_2 \rangle \in X$ then $\mathsf{L}(q) = \mathsf{L}'(q')$ and, for any relation $r \subseteq \mathbb{S} \times \mathbb{S}'$, $\langle s_1, s_2 \rangle \in E(r)$ if and only if: $\langle s_1, s_2 \rangle \in r$, $\mathsf{L}(s_1) = \mathsf{L}'(s_2)$, and for every coalition A, the following two conditions hold: (i) for any $\alpha_A \in \mathsf{act}_A(s_1)$ there is an $\alpha'_A \in \mathsf{act}'_A(s_2)$ such that for any $t_2 \in \mathsf{Out}(s_2, \alpha'_A)$ there exists $t_1 \in \mathsf{Out}(s_1, \alpha_A)$ such that $t_1 r t_2$, and (ii) for any $\alpha_A \in \mathsf{act}_A(s_2)$ there is an $\alpha'_A \in \mathsf{act}'_A(s_1)$ such that for any $t_3 \in \mathsf{Out}(s_1, \alpha'_A)$ there exists $t_4 \in \mathsf{Out}(s_2, \alpha_A)$ such that $t_3 r t_4$.

Observe also that, given a CGM having set of states $\mathbb{S}$, X may be a subset of $\mathbb{S} \times \mathbb{S}$ (*i.e* we can have $\mathbb{S} = \mathbb{S}'$).

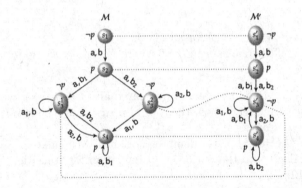

Fig. 1. An alternating bisimulation between two CGMs

Remark 1 will be useful in the following, to understand how our approach to minimization of a model constructs a maximal fixed point of the above equation in a stepwise manner.

It is also worthwhile observing that bisimilarity between CGMs is reflexive, symmetric and transitive, i.e. is an equivalence relation.

The following theorem extends to the case of ATL* and perfect recall strategies a result presented in [ÅGJ07, DGL16] for ATL and positional strategies.

Theorem 1. *Let $\mathcal{M}$ and $\mathcal{M}'$ be two CGMs.*

1. *If $\mathcal{M} \overset{\beta}{\rightleftarrows}_A \mathcal{M}'$ and $s_1 \beta s_2$, then, for any ATL* (state) formula ϕ such that A is the only coalition occurring in ϕ, $\mathcal{M}, s_1 \models \phi$ iff $\mathcal{M}', s_2 \models \phi$.*

2. *If $\mathcal{M} \overset{\beta}{\rightleftarrows} \mathcal{M}'$ and $s_1 \beta s_2$, then, for any ATL* formula ϕ, $\mathcal{M}, s_1 \models \phi$ iff $\mathcal{M}', s_2 \models \phi$.*

The detailed proof of Theorem 1 is given in the last section of [CD], the long draft of this work available on line. The key idea is that if β is a full alternating bisimulation between $\mathcal{M}$ and $\mathcal{M}'$ and F_A is a strategy for a coalition A in $\mathcal{M}$ then F_A can be simulated in $\mathcal{M}'$ by exploiting the existence of β. As a consequence of Theorem 1, if $\mathcal{M}$ and $\mathcal{M}'$ are bisimilar then, for any (state) formula ϕ, $\mathcal{M}$ is a model of ϕ if and only if $\mathcal{M}'$ is a model of ϕ.

3   Model Minimization

Before describing our approach to model minimization, let us consider a simple intuitive example showing that to rewrite a given model $\mathcal{M}$ of a formula ϕ into a model $\mathcal{M}'$ that is minimal with respect to alternating bisimulation does not necessarily mean to get a model of ϕ having the minimum number of states.

Example 1. Let ϕ be $\langle\langle 1 \rangle\rangle \bigcirc p$, stating that agent 1 can assure that p holds at a successor state. Let's assume that this agent can perform only one action at each state. Take $\mathcal{M}_1$ to have two states, 1 and 2, where 2 is the only successor of 1, 1 is the only successor of 2, and p is false at 1 but true at 2. Clearly $\mathcal{M}_1$ satisfies ϕ at state 1. Now, take $\mathcal{M}_2$ to be a model having 3 states, A, B and C, where B is the only successor of A, C is the only successor of B, A is the only successor of C and the only state not satisfying p is A. Obviously ϕ keeps true at state A. The application of our minimisation procedure to $\mathcal{M}_2$ will output $\mathcal{M}_2$ itself, not $\mathcal{M}_1$. The reason is that, by Theorem 1, any state s' of the output model must satisfy exactly the same formulae as s, where s is a bisimilar state of the input model. In $\mathcal{M}_1$, state 1 satisfies $\neg p \wedge \langle\!\langle 1 \rangle\!\rangle (\bigcirc p \wedge \bigcirc \bigcirc \neg p)$ while in $\mathcal{M}_2$ state A satisfies $\neg p \wedge \langle\!\langle 1 \rangle\!\rangle (\bigcirc p \wedge \bigcirc \bigcirc p)$, thus 1 and A cannot be bisimilar. It is worthwhile noticing, however, that such an unnatural model of ϕ as $\mathcal{M}_2$ would not be generated by the tableau procedure for ATL* having input $\phi = \langle\!\langle 1 \rangle\!\rangle \bigcirc p$. In general, tableau construction analyses the input formula and produces tableau states (states of a candidate model) only when they are needed.

Our approach to the minimization of a model $\mathcal{M}$ satisfying a given formula Φ consists in rewriting it into the smallest bisimilar model in a stepwise manner. The definitions and results that follow are the foundations of our procedure.

3.1 Quotient Models

Given a partition $P = \{C_1, \ldots, C_k\}$ of the set of the states of a CGM, we will say that each set C_i is a *cluster* of the partition P.

Definition 4 (Harmonious partition). *A harmonious partition P of a CGM $\mathcal{M}$ is a partition of the set of states of $\mathcal{M}$ such that for each cluster C of P, if $s, s' \in C$ then $\mathsf{L}(s) = \mathsf{L}(s')$.*

Given a CGM, a state s, a coalition A and a move σ_A available for A at s, we say that a state t is *reachable* from s via σ_A if $t \in \mathsf{Out}(s, \sigma_A)$, i.e. there is a global move $\sigma_{\mathbb{A}}$ extending σ_A such that $t = \mathsf{out}(s, \sigma_{\mathbb{A}})$.

Definition 5 (Behavioural equivalence of states w.r.t. a partition). *Let P be a harmonious partition of a CGM and let s and t be two states such that $\mathsf{L}(s) = \mathsf{L}(t)$.*

- *Let A be a coalition. We say that s and t are (behaviourally) A-equivalent w.r.t. P, and we note $s \equiv_{PA} t$, when:*
  - *Given any action $\sigma_A \in \mathsf{act}_A(s)$, there is an action $\sigma'_A \in \mathsf{act}_A(t)$ such that the set of clusters of states that are reachable from t via σ'_A is a subset of the set of clusters of states that are reachable from s via σ_A.*
  - *Given any action $\sigma_A \in \mathsf{act}_A(t)$, there is an action $\sigma'_A \in \mathsf{act}_A(s)$ such that the set of clusters of states that are reachable from s via σ'_A is a subset of the set of clusters of states that are reachable from t via σ_A.*
- *We say that s and t are (behaviourally) equivalent w.r.t. P, and we note $s \equiv_P t$, when $s \equiv_{PA} t$ for each coalition A.*

It is worthwhile observing that $\equiv_{PA}$ (resp. $\equiv_P$) is an equivalence relation.

Remark 2. It is important to observe that given a harmonious partition P of the set of states of a CGM, the behavioural equivalence w.r.t. P of two states for a coalition does not imply their behavioural equivalence for another coalition. To see this, let us consider Example 2.

Example 2. Let $\mathcal{M}_1$ be a CGM having four states: s_1, s_2, s_3 and s_4, and three agents, 1, 2 and 3. Let p be the only boolean variable and let: $L(s_1) = L(s_2) = \{p\}$, $L(s_3) = L(s_4) = \emptyset$. Each agent can play either action 0 or action 1 at states s_1 and s_2, and only action 3 at s_3 and s_4. The transitions are: $\mathsf{out}(s_1, \langle 0,0,0\rangle) = \mathsf{out}(s_1, \langle 1,1,1\rangle) = s_3$, $\mathsf{out}(s_1, \alpha_1)) = s_1$ for any other global move α_1 available at s_1, $\mathsf{out}(s_2, \langle 0,0,0\rangle) = \mathsf{out}(s_2, \langle 0,0,1\rangle) = s_4$, $\mathsf{out}(s_2, \alpha_2)) = s_2$ for any other global move α_2 available at s_2, $\mathsf{out}(s_3, \langle 3,3,3\rangle) = s_3$ and $\mathsf{out}(s_4, \langle 3,3,3\rangle) = s_4$.

Let P be the harmonious partition of the set of states where s_1 and s_2 are in the cluster C_1, while s_3 and s_4 are in the cluster C_2. For $A = \{1\}$ it is easy to see that $s_1 \equiv_{PA} s_2$. In fact, action 0 available at s_1 is simulated by action 0 available at s_2 and also action 1 available at s_1 is simulated by action 0 available at s_2. Conversely, action 0 at s_2 is simulated by action 0 (or 1) at s_1. However, for $A' = \{1,2\}$, $s_1 \not\equiv_{PA'} s_2$. Indeed, at state s_1 the formula $\langle\!\langle 1,2\rangle\!\rangle \bigcirc \neg p$ is false, while at state s_2 it is true (it suffices to play $\langle 0,0,*\rangle$). This shows that the equivalence of states for a coalition A does not imply the equivalence for each coalition A' such that $A \subset A'$.

The same example shows that the equivalence of states for a coalition A'' does not imply the equivalence for each coalition A''' such that $A''' \subset A''$. In fact, take $A'' = \{1,2,3\}$. If the coalition plays the global move $\langle 0,0,0\rangle$ at s_1, which leads to the cluster C_2, then it can play the same move at s_2 to get the same effect; if it plays $\langle 1,1,1\rangle$ at s_1 then it can play either $\langle 0,0,0\rangle$ or $\langle 0,0,1\rangle$ at s_2 to get the same effect; finally, if it plays any move different form $\langle 0,0,0\rangle$ and $\langle 1,1,1\rangle$ at s_1, then it can play any move different form $\langle 0,0,0\rangle$ and $\langle 0,0,1\rangle$ at s_2 to get the same effect. A symmetrical reasoning on the actions that the coalition A'' can play at s_2 allow us to conclude that $s_1 \equiv_{PA''} s_2$. However taking the subset coalition A''' to be $\{1,2\}$ we get, as already seen, that $s_1 \not\equiv_{PA'''} s_2$.

Below we always assume that $\mathbb{S}$ is finite.

Definition 6 (Stability). *Given a partition $P = \{C_1, \ldots, C_n\}$ of the set of states $\mathbb{S}$ of a CGM and a relation $r \subseteq \mathbb{S} \times \mathbb{S}$, P is stable w.r.t. r when, for any $1 \le i \le n$, $s, t \in C_i$ implies $s \, r \, t$.*

If P is stable w.r.t. $\equiv_P$, then obviously it is stable w.r.t. $\equiv_{PA}$ for each coalition A.

Our minimization procedure builds step by step the coarsest harmonious partition P of the set of states of the model $\mathcal{M}$ to be minimized that is stable w.r.t. $\equiv_P$. Then it builds out of P a minimal model bisimilar to $\mathcal{M}$ as a quotient of $\mathbb{S}$ with respect the equivalence $\equiv_P$.

Definition 7 (Quotient model). *Let $\mathcal{M}$ be a CGM*

$$\langle \mathbb{A}, \mathbb{S}, \{Act_a\}_{a \in \mathbb{A}}, \{act_a\}_{a \in \mathbb{A}}, \mathsf{out}, L\rangle$$

Let $P = \{C_1, \ldots, C_n\}$ be a harmonious partition of $\mathbb{S}$ that is stable w.r.t. $\equiv_P$. Let ρ be a function associating to each cluster C_i of P an element of C_i as representative element of C_i.

A quotient-model $\mathcal{M}'$ of $\mathcal{M}$ w.r.t. $\equiv_P$ and ρ is defined as a

$$\mathcal{M}' = \langle \mathbb{A}, \mathbb{S}', \{\mathsf{Act}_a\}_{a \in \mathbb{A}}, \{\mathsf{act}'_a\}_{a \in \mathbb{A}}, \mathsf{out}', \mathsf{L}' \rangle$$

where:

- *$\mathbb{S}'$ is the set of clusters in P: $\mathbb{S}' = \{C_1, \ldots, C_n\}$;*
- *For any $C \in \mathbb{S}'$, $a \in \mathbb{A}$, $\alpha \in \mathsf{Act}_a$, we set $\alpha \in \mathsf{act}'_a(C)$ if and only if $\alpha \in \mathsf{act}_a(\rho(C))$;*
- *The set $\{\mathsf{Act}'_a\}_{a \in \mathbb{A}}$ is constructed accordingly;*
- *C_i is connected to C_j via $\sigma_{\mathbb{A}}$ if and only if in the model $\mathcal{M}$ we have $\mathsf{out}(\rho(C_i), \sigma_{\mathbb{A}}) \in C_j$. This defines the transition function out'.*
  More precisely:
  for any $C_i, C_j \in \mathbb{S}'$, for any global move $\sigma_{\mathbb{A}}$ such that, for any $a \in \mathbb{A}$, $\sigma_{\mathbb{A}}(a) \in \mathsf{act}'_a(C_i)$, we set: $\mathsf{out}'(C_i, \sigma_{\mathbb{A}}) = C_j$ if and only if there is some $t \in C_j$ such that $t \in \mathsf{out}(\rho(C_i), \sigma_{\mathbb{A}})$;
- *For any C_i, $\mathsf{L}'(C_i) = \mathsf{L}(s)$, for any $s \in C_i$.*

Let us observe that, formally, the construction of a quotient model $\mathcal{M}'$ of $\mathcal{M}$ depends not only on the partition P, but also on the choice ρ of a representative state r_i of C_i. However, given a partition P that is stable with respect to the relation $\equiv_P$, the choice of ρ can have an effect only on labels of connecting edges in $\mathcal{M}'$ but not on the existence of a connection between two states of $\mathcal{M}'$ (that is, clusters of P). In fact, let C_i be a cluster, r_i be a state in $\mathcal{M}$ such that $\rho(C_i) = r_i$ and s be any other element of C_i. Then $s \equiv_P r_i$ by construction, therefore:

- If $\sigma_{\mathbb{A}}$ leads from r_i to a $t \in C_j$ in $\mathcal{M}$ then by definition there is some global action leading from s to some state (possibly another than t) that belongs to the same cluster C_j;
- If no global action leads from r_i to C_j in $\mathcal{M}$ then no global action leads from s to C_j in $\mathcal{M}$. In fact if some global action $\sigma_{\mathbb{A}}$ leads from s to some state in C_j then some global action $\sigma'_{\mathbb{A}}$ leads from r_i to some state in C_j, since $s \equiv_P r_i$.

Therefore a quotient model of $\mathcal{M}$ w.r.t. a harmonious partition P of $\mathcal{M}$'s states is unique modulo renaming of edge labels.

The following result states that a quotient model of $\mathcal{M}$, as defined above, is indeed bisimilar to $\mathcal{M}$.

Theorem 2. *Let $\mathcal{M}$ be a CGM $\langle \mathbb{A}, \mathbb{S}, \{\mathsf{Act}_a\}_{a \in \mathbb{A}}, \{\mathsf{act}_a\}_{a \in \mathbb{A}}, \mathsf{out}, \mathsf{L} \rangle$. Let $P = \{C_1, \ldots, C_n\}$ be a harmonious partition of its states that is stable w.r.t. $\equiv_P$ and let ρ be a function choosing representative elements from clusters. Let $\mathcal{M}' = \langle \mathbb{A}, \mathbb{S}', \{\mathsf{Act}_a\}_{a \in \mathbb{A}}, \{\mathsf{act}'_a\}_{a \in \mathbb{A}}, \mathsf{out}', \mathsf{L}' \rangle$ be a quotient-model of $\mathcal{M}$ w.r.t. $\equiv_P$ and ρ. Then the relation $\beta \subseteq \mathbb{S} \times \mathbb{S}'$ defined by: $s\beta C_i$ iff $s \in C_i$ is a global alternating bisimulation between $\mathcal{M}$ and $\mathcal{M}'$.*

The proof of Theorem 2 is given in the last section of [CD].

As a consequence of Theorem 2 and Theorem 1 we get that if $\mathcal{M}$ is a model, P a partition of its states that is stable w.r.t. $\equiv_P$, $\mathcal{M}'$ a corresponding quotient model, and finally, ϕ is any ATL* formula (over the given sets of propositions and agents), then $\mathcal{M}$ is a model of ϕ if and only if $\mathcal{M}'$ is a model of ϕ.

3.2   Minimization Algorithm

When the model $\mathcal{M}$ to be minimized has a finite number of states, as it is in our intended application to model minimization in TATL, a maximal bisimulation relation $\beta \subseteq \mathbb{S} \times \mathbb{S}$, hence a corresponding minimal partition P of $\mathbb{S}$ stable w.r.t. $\equiv_P$ inducing a minimal quotient model of a CGM $\mathcal{M}$, can be given a stepwise characterization and effectively constructed, analogously to the case of labelled partition systems. More precisely:

Definition 8 (Stratified bisimilarity relations). *Given a CGM* $\langle \mathbb{A}, \mathbb{S},$ $\{\mathsf{Act}_a\}_{a \in \mathbb{A}}, \{\mathsf{act}_a\}_{a \in \mathbb{A}}, \mathsf{out}, \mathsf{L}\rangle$, *the stratified alternating bisimulation relations* $\beta_k \subseteq \mathbb{S} \times \mathbb{S}$ *for* $k \in \mathbb{N}$ *are defined as follows:*

- $s_1 \beta_0 s_2$ *iff* $s_1, s_2 \in \mathbb{S}$ *and* $\mathsf{L}(s_1) = \mathsf{L}'(s_2)$;
- $s_1 \beta_{k+1} s_2$ *iff* $s_1 \beta_k s_2$, $\mathsf{L}(s_1) = \mathsf{L}'(s_2)$ *and for each coalition* $A \subseteq \mathbb{A}$:
    1. **Forth.** *For any* $\alpha_A \in \mathsf{act}_A(s_1)$ *there is an* $\alpha'_A \in \mathsf{act}'_A(s_2)$ *such that for any* $t_2 \in \mathsf{Out}(s_2, \alpha'_A)$ *there exists* $t_1 \in \mathsf{Out}(s_1, \alpha_A)$ *such that* $t_1 \beta_k t_2$.
    2. **Back.** *For any* $\alpha_A \in \mathsf{act}_A(s_2)$ *there is an* $\alpha'_A \in \mathsf{act}'_A(s_1)$ *such that for any* $t_3 \in \mathsf{Out}(s_1, \alpha'_A)$ *there exists* $t_4 \in \mathsf{Out}(s_2, \alpha_A)$ *such that* $t_3 \beta_k t_4$.
- *By construction, for any* k *we have* $\beta_{k+1} \subseteq \beta_k$. *Set the relation* β^* *to be* $\bigcap_{k \in \mathbb{N}} \beta_k$.

When $\mid \mathbb{S} \mid$ is finite, the relation β^* can be obviously be computed in finite time since there is a j, $0 \leq j \leq \mid \mathbb{S} \mid$ such that $\beta^* = \beta_j$. By Remark 1 any full alternating bisimulation relation that is a subset of $\mathbb{S} \times \mathbb{S}$ is a fixpoint solution of the equation $X = E(X)$, where X is a subset of $S \times S$ having the property that if $\langle q, q' \rangle \in X$ then $\mathsf{L}(q) = \mathsf{L}'(q')$. We have:

Theorem 3. *The relation* β^* *is the maximal fixpoint solution of the equation* $X = E(X)$.

This can be shown by arguments similar to those proving an analogous claim for labelled transition systems [HM85]. The detailed proof can be found in the last section of the longer version of this work [CD].

Remark 3. We can observe that if P_k is the harmonious partition of $\mathbb{S}$ corresponding to a given stratified alternating bisimulation relation β_k then $s_1 \equiv_{P_k} s_2$ (as in Definition 5) if and only if $s_1 \beta_{k+1} s_2$. The two formalizations capture the same concept, but behavioural equivalence directly corresponds to the implementation of our minimization algorithm (see Sect. 4). Moreover, any harmonious partition P of the set of states of a model $\mathcal{M}$ is stable w.r.t. the relation $\equiv_P$

(as in Definition 6) if and only if $\equiv_P$ is a solution of the equation $X = E(X)$, although not necessarily the maximal one, corresponding to the minimal, *i.e* coarsest, partition. The partition of $\mathbb{S}$ induced by β^* is the minimal partition that is stable with respect $\equiv_P$.

Let P^* be the partition of the states $\mathbb{S}$ of a CGM $\mathcal{M}$ induced by β^*. The quotient model of $\mathcal{M}$ with respect to $\equiv_{P^*}$ is the minimization of $\mathcal{M}$ with respect to alternating bisimilarity. This yields an algorithm that minimizes $\mathcal{M}$ by computing, step by step, the partition P^* starting from an initial partition; its underlying general principle is:

Let P_0, the initial partition, be such that $s_1, s_2 \in \mathbb{S}$ belong to the same cluster if and only if $\mathsf{L}(s_1) = \mathsf{L}'(s_2)$. For each $i > 0$, refine the partition P_{i-1} until $P_{i-1} = P_i$. Output P_i as the value of P^*.

4   Implementation and Application to TATL

We have implemented (in OCaml, the same language used for TATL) our minimization algorithm in order to add to TATL a new functionality: the minimization of the model extracted from an open tableau for an input formula ϕ by executing the procedure given by the completeness proof for ATL* tableaux in [Dav15]. So far, TATL does not show any model, but only the tableau. The forthcoming version of TATL will allow the user to visualize the model generated by the completeness proof procedure and also its minimization. In this section we give the pseudo-code of our implementation.

Obviously the algorithm terminates, because the number of iterations of the main loop is upper bounded by the size of the set of states, which is finite.

The core function is SPLIT that splits a cluster of the current partition P_i in two clusters whenever two states s and t in it are not behaviourally equivalent with respect to P_i; to do so it calls the function EQUIVALENCE. In the pseudo-code of this function, clusterS is the set of all the clusters of the current partition containing some successor of the state s, according to the transition function; the meaning of clusterT is analogous. EQUIVALENCE checks the behavioural equivalence of states w.r.t. the current partition for each coalition A (as in Definition 5), by means of the function EQUIVALENCE_BY_COALITIONS. For space reason, the pseudo code of this last function is not given here. This function checks if two states in a given cluster of the current partition P are behaviourally equivalent with respect to P for all coalitions or not, which inevitably makes the program to have an exponential complexity. It is necessary to check each coalition because behavioural equivalence of two states w.r.t. the current partition for a given coalition does not imply equivalence for another coalition (see Remark 2 and Example 2).

The following result states the correction of our procedure with respect to the specification of minimizing the input model relatively to alternating bisimulation. Below, by "application of *REFINE* to $\mathcal{M}$" we mean the execution of *REFINE* where the initial partition is such that two states of $\mathcal{M}$ are in the same cluster if and only if they have the same labels.

Algorithm 1. *REFINE*

Function Main()
    $P \leftarrow$ initial partition
    change $\leftarrow$ true
    while change **do**
        change $\leftarrow$ false
        for all cluster $B \in P$ **do**
            if SPLIT$(B, P) = \{B_1, B_2\} \neq \{B\}$ **then**
                Refine P by replacing B by B_1 and B_2
                change $\leftarrow$ true
            end if
        end for
    end while

Function SPLIT(B, P)
    choose a state $s \in B$
    $B_1, B_2 \leftarrow \emptyset$
    for all $t \in B$ **do**
        if EQUIVALENCE(s, t, P) **then**
            $B_1 \leftarrow B_1 \cup \{t\}$
        else
            $B_2 \leftarrow B_2 \cup \{t\}$
        end if
    end for
    if $B_2 = \emptyset$ **then**
        return $\{B_1\}$
    else
        return $\{B_1, B_2\}$
    end if

Function EQUIVALENCE(s, t, P)
    if $s = t$ **then**
        true
    else
        if $\mathsf{L}(s) = \mathsf{L}(t)$ **then**
            clusterS $\leftarrow$ set of successor clusters of s
            clusterT $\leftarrow$ set of successor clusters of t
            if clusterS $=$ clusterT **then**
                EQUIVALENCE_BY_COALITIONS(s, t, P)
            else
                false
            end if
        else
            false
        end if
    end if

Theorem 4. *Let $\mathcal{M}$ be an* ATL* *model. The procedure that applies REFINE to $\mathcal{M}$, computing the partition P^* of $\mathcal{M}$'s states, and outputs the model $\mathcal{M}$' that is the quotient model of $\mathcal{M}$ with respect to P^*, is such that $\mathcal{M}$' is minimal among the models that are bisimilar to $\mathcal{M}$.*

Proof of Theorem 4. First, we show that the output of *REFINE* is the partition P^* associated to β^*, where $\beta*$ is as in Definition 8. Let P_0 denote the initial partition of the procedure, P_1, $P_2 \ldots P_m$ the partitions computed in the main loop until stability, $r_0, r_1, r_2 \ldots r_m$ the corresponding equivalence relations, and $r = r_m$ the relation corresponding to the final result P. An easy induction on $i \in \mathbb{N}$ proves that $\beta^* \subseteq \beta_i \subseteq r_i$. Hence $\beta^* \subseteq r$. For the converse inclusion, let us observe that if P is the result of the main procedure, then P is stable w.r.t. $\equiv_P$ (see the definition of the function SPLIT). By Remark 3, r is a solution of the fixed point equation $X = E(X)$. Hence $r \subseteq \beta^*$, because, by Theorem 3, β^* is the maximal solution of such an equation. Thus $\beta^* = r$.

Then, the result follows as a consequence of the previous theorems.   □

Also the model extraction function from a tableau (via the procedure of the completeness proof) has been implemented and partial tests of our implementation of the minimization algorithm applied to the model extracted by the tableau have been done, but a complete and representative set of test cases still needs to be constructed.

The last figure illustrates the minimization procedure via a simple example, with one agent, chosen among the tests so far done. The input formula ϕ of the tableau, as provided to the software TATL, is exhibited on the top: it is $\langle\langle 1 \rangle\rangle((\langle\langle 1 \rangle\rangle \square \langle\langle \emptyset \rangle\rangle \bigcirc \Diamond \square a) \wedge (\bigcirc(\neg b \wedge \neg a)))$, where a and b are propositional letters and $\emptyset$ is the empty coalition. The graph on the left, having eight states, is the model of the formula produced by the completeness procedure: it satisfies ϕ at state $n1$. At the right, the minimized model, having three states and satisfying ϕ at state $n1$. The literals holding at each state are indicated inside each state ellipse (Fig. 2).

5   Conclusions

Up to our knowledge, the algorithm proposed in this work is the first procedure that minimizes ATL* models with respect to alternating bisimulation.

This algorithm has a time complexity that is exponential in the size of $\mathbb{A}$, since, as observed, all the coalitions – that is all the subsets of $\mathbb{A}$– need to be checked in order to conclude that a given cluster of the current partition does not need to be split. It is interesting to compare it with the classical partition-refinement minimization algorithms for labelled transition systems, whose complexity depend only on the number n of states of the system and the number m of transitions: the algorithm in [KS90] has time complexity $O(nm)$ while the optimized algorithm in [PT87] has time complexity $m \log n$.

In [KS90,LIS12], that have inspired our work, the minimization procedure acts on structures that are independent of any syntax and any logic: labelled transition systems where only edges are labelled; these structure are not Kripke

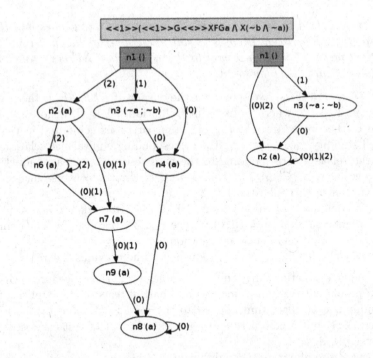

Fig. 2. Input (left) and output (right) of the minimization algorithm

models of any logic. However, it is immediate to extend that approach to minimize CTL* models with respect to bisimulation.[2] The global structure of that procedure is the same as for *REFINE*. The crucial difference is at the level of the very notion of bisimulation (alternating bisimulation, for ATL*), which is both conceptually and algorithmically more complex for ATL* than for CTL*. This is obviously tied to the different semantics: labelled transition systems can be seen as concurrent game structures with exactly one agent. This difference is reflected by the different behaviour of the function SPLIT for the two logics.

Although the problem of minimizing an ATL* model is intrinsically exponential, it would be interesting to face issues of optimisation of our algorithm with the view of making it more efficient for practical use.

As we said, we implemented and tested our algorithm, but a large, complete and representative set of test cases is still ongoing work. When this will be finished we will add to the prover TATL the functionality of exhibiting minimized models of the input formula.

In this work we have considered only ATL* with perfect information. Recently a definition of bisimilarity of models coping with imperfect information has been proposed [BCD+17] and it might be interesting to explore the possibility of extending our study to the minimization of models of ATL* with imperfect information.

---

[2] A similar approach might be used also for models of the μ-calculus.

Aknowledgements. The authors would like to thank Damien Regnault and Marta Cialdea Mayer for their careful reading of first drafts of this work and for their useful remarks. The very first ideas underlying this work rose in the context of the direction of a project of two fourth year university students at the university of Evry Val d'Essonne: Lylia Bellabiod and Théo Chelim.

References

[ÅGJ07] Ågotnes, T., Goranko, V., Jamroga, W.: Alternating-time temporal logics with irrevocable strategies. In: Proceedings of the 11th Conference on Theoretical Aspects of Rationality and Knowledge (TARK-2007), Brussels, Belgium 25–27 June 2007, pp. 15–24 (2007)

[AHK02] Alur, R., Henzinger, T.A., Kupferman, O.: Alternating-time temporal logic. J. ACM **49**(5), 672–713 (2002)

[BCD+17] Belardinelli, F., Condurache, R., Dima, C., Jamroga, W., Jones, A.V.: Bisimulations for verifying strategic abilities applied to voting protocols. In: Proceedings of AAMAS 2017. IFAAMAS (2017)

[BLW09] Bonatti, P.A., Lutz, C., Wolter, F.: The complexity of circumscription in DLs. J. Artif. Intell. Res. **35**, 717–773 (2009)

[BY00] Bry, F., Yahya, A.: Positive unit hyperresolution tableaux and their application to minimal model generation. J. Autom. Reason. **25**(1), 35–82 (2000)

[CD] Cerrito, S., David, A.: Minimisation of ATL* models: extended draft. https://www.ibisc.univ-evry.fr/~serena/MiniDraft.pdf

[CDG14] Cerrito, S., David, A., Goranko, V.: Optimal tableaux-based decision procedure for testing satisfiability in the alternating-time temporal logic ATL+. In: Demri, S., Kapur, D., Weidenbach, C. (eds.) IJCAR 2014. LNCS, vol. 8562, pp. 277–291. Springer, Cham (2014). doi:10.1007/978-3-319-08587-6_21

[Dav] David, A.: TATL: tableaux for ATL*. http://atila.ibisc.univ-evry.fr/tableau_ATL_star/index.php

[Dav15] David, A.: Deciding ATL* satisfiability by tableaux. In: Felty, A.P., Middeldorp, A. (eds.) CADE 2015. LNCS, vol. 9195, pp. 214–228. Springer, Cham (2015). doi:10.1007/978-3-319-21401-6_14

[DGL16] Demri, S., Goranko, V., Lange, M.: Temporal Logics in Computer Science. Cambridge Tracts in Theoretical Computer Science. Cambridge University Press, Cambridge (2016)

[GGOP08] Giordano, L., Gliozzi, V., Olivetti, N., Pozzato, G.L.: Reasoning about typicality in preferential description logics. In: Hölldobler, S., Lutz, C., Wansing, H. (eds.) JELIA 2008. LNCS, vol. 5293, pp. 192–205. Springer, Heidelberg (2008). doi:10.1007/978-3-540-87803-2_17

[GH09] Grimm, S., Hitzler, P.: A preferential tableaux calculus for circumscriptive ALCO. In: Polleres, A., Swift, T. (eds.) RR 2009. LNCS, vol. 5837, pp. 40–54. Springer, Heidelberg (2009). doi:10.1007/978-3-642-05082-4_4

[GHS01] Georgieva, L., Hustadt, U., Schmidt, R.A.: Computational space efficiency and minimal model generation for guarded formulae. In: Nieuwenhuis, R., Voronkov, A. (eds.) LPAR 2001. LNCS (LNAI), vol. 2250, pp. 85–99. Springer, Heidelberg (2001). doi:10.1007/3-540-45653-8_6

[HFK00] Hasegawa, R., Fujita, H., Koshimura, M.: Efficient minimal model generation using branching lemmas. In: McAllester, D. (ed.) CADE 2000. LNCS, vol. 1831, pp. 184–199. Springer, Heidelberg (2000). doi:10.1007/10721959_15

[Hin88] Hintikka, J.: Model minimization - an alternative to circumscription. J. Autom. Reason. **4**(1), 1–13 (1988)

[HM85] Hennessy, M., Milner, R.: Algebraic laws for nondeterminism and concurrency. J. ACM **32**(1), 137–161 (1985)

[KS90] Kanellakis, P.C., Smolka, S.A.: CCS expressions, finite state processes, and three problems of equivalence. Inf. Comput. **86**(1), 43–68 (1990)

[LIS12] Aceto, L., Ingolfsdottir, A., Jiri, S.: The algorithmics of bisimilarity. In: Sangiorgi, D., Rutten, J. (eds.) Advanced Topics in Bisimulation and Coinduction, pp. 100–171. Cambridge University Press, Cambridge (2012)

[Lor94] Lorenz, S.: A tableau prover for domain minimization. J. Autom. Reason. **13**(3), 375–390 (1994)

[McC87] McCarthy, J.: Circumscription: a form of non-monotonic reasoning. In: Ginsberg, M.L. (ed.) Readings in Nonmonotonic Reasoning, pp. 145–151. Kaufmann, Los Altos (1987)

[Nie96] Niemelä, I.: A tableau calculus for minimal model reasoning. In: Miglioli, P., Moscato, U., Mundici, D., Ornaghi, M. (eds.) TABLEAUX 1996. LNCS, vol. 1071, pp. 278–294. Springer, Heidelberg (1996). doi:10.1007/3-540-61208-4_18

[PS14] Papacchini, F., Schmidt, R.A.: Terminating minimal model generation procedures for propositional modal logics. In: Demri, S., Kapur, D., Weidenbach, C. (eds.) IJCAR 2014. LNCS, vol. 8562, pp. 381–395. Springer, Cham (2014). doi:10.1007/978-3-319-08587-6_30

[PT87] Paige, R., Tarjan, R.E.: Three partition refinement algorithms. SIAM J. Comput. **16**(6), 973–989 (1987)

Non-clausal Connection Calculi
for Non-classical Logics

Jens Otten[(✉)]

Department of Informatics, University of Oslo,
PO Box 1080, Blindern, 0316 Oslo, Norway
jeotten@ifi.uio.no

Abstract. The paper introduces non-clausal connection calculi for first-order intuitionistic and several first-order modal logics. The notion of a non-clausal matrix together with the non-clausal connection calculus for classical logic are extended to intuitionistic and modal logics by adding prefixes that encode the Kripke semantics of these logics. Details of the required prefix unification and some optimization techniques are described. Furthermore, compact Prolog implementations of the introduced non-classical calculi are presented. An experimental evaluation shows that non-clausal connection calculi are a solid basis for proof search in these logics, in terms of time complexity and proof size.

1 Introduction

Intuitionistic and modal logics are among the most popular *non-classical logics*. *Intuitionistic logic* is used, e.g., within interactive proof assistants, such as NuPRL [4] and Coq [2]. *Modal logics* have applications in, e.g., planning, natural language processing, and program verification. Hence, *(fully) automated reasoning* in these logics is an important task and many applications would benefit from more powerful reasoning tools. Unfortunately, *automated theorem proving (ATP)*, i.e., deciding whether a formula is *valid* in these non-classical logics is even harder than for classical logic. For the propositional fragment, intuitionistic and (most) modal logics are *PSPACE-complete* whereas classical logic is "only" *NP*-complete. Adapting complex ATP systems for classical first-order logic to these non-classical logics is in general not easily possible.

A popular approach for dealing with intuitionistic and modal logics is to encode their *Kripke semantics* with so-called labels or *prefixes* [22,23]. Two of the most powerful ATP systems for these logics, ileanCoP [11] and MleanCoP [14], use prefixes and are based on *clausal* connection calculi [10]. While the use of a clausal form technically simplifies the proof calculus, the standard translation as well as the definitional translation into clausal form introduce a significant overhead into the proof search [12]. Furthermore, both translations modify the original structure of the formula.

This paper introduces prefixed *non-clausal* connection calculi for first-order intuitionistic and several first-order modal logics. Syntax, semantics, prefixes

© Springer International Publishing AG 2017
R.A. Schmidt and C. Nalon (Eds.): TABLEAUX 2017, LNAI 10501, pp. 209–227, 2017.
DOI: 10.1007/978-3-319-66902-1_13

and the underlying matrix characterizations are described (Sect. 2). Afterwards, non-clausal calculi are presented together with prefixed non-clausal matrices and the required prefix unifications for intuitionistic logic (Sect. 3) and modal logic (Sect. 4). After the description of some optimization techniques (Sect. 5), compact implementations of these non-clausal calculi are presented (Sect. 6) and evaluated (Sect. 7). The paper concludes with a short summary and an outlook on future work (Sect. 8).

2   Preliminaries

The standard notation for first-order formulae is used. Terms (denoted by t) are built up from functions (denoted by f), constants and (term) variables (denoted by x). An atomic formula (denoted by A) is built up from predicate symbols and terms. A *(first-order) formula* (denoted by F, G, H) is built up from atomic formulae, the connectives $\neg, \wedge, \vee, \Rightarrow$, and the standard first-order quantifiers $\forall$ and $\exists$. A *literal* L has the form A or $\neg A$. Its *complement* $\overline{L}$ is A if L is of the form $\neg A$; otherwise $\overline{L}$ is $\neg L$. A *connection* is a set $\{A, \neg A\}$ of literals with the same predicate symbol but different polarity. A *quantifier* or *term substitution* σ_Q is a mapping from the set of term variables to the set of terms. In $\sigma_Q(L)$ all term variables x in L are substituted by their image $\sigma_Q(x)$.

2.1   Intuitionistic Logic

Intuitionistic logic and classical logic share the same *syntax*, but their *semantics* is different. For example, the formula $A \vee \neg A$ is valid in classical logic but not in intuitionistic logic. The semantics of intuitionistic logic requires a proof for A or for $\neg A$. As this property neither holds for A nor for $\neg A$, the formula is not valid in intuitionistic logic. Formally, the semantics of intuitionistic logic is specified by a Kripke semantics [23].

Hence, the following three rules of the (multi-succedent) *sequent calculus for intuitionistic logic* [6,23] differ from the ones for classical logic:

$$\frac{\Gamma, G \vdash}{\Gamma \vdash \neg G, \Delta} \; \neg\text{-right} \; , \qquad \frac{\Gamma, G \vdash H}{\Gamma \vdash G \Rightarrow H, \Delta} \; \Rightarrow\text{-right} \; , \qquad \frac{\Gamma \vdash G[x \backslash a]}{\Gamma \vdash \forall x \, G, \Delta} \; \forall\text{-right} \; .$$

In all three rules the set of formulae Δ does not occur in the sequent of the premises anymore. As these formulae might be necessary within a bottom-up search in order to complete a proof, the application of these rules need to be controlled. To this end, a prefix is assigned to each subformula G of a given formula F.

Definition 1 (Intuitionistic prefix). *A prefix (denoted by p, q) is a string (sequence of characters) over an alphabet $\Phi \cup \Psi$, in which Φ is a set of prefix variables $(V_1, \dots)$ and Ψ is a set of prefix constants $(a_1, \dots)$. For every $\neg / \Rightarrow / \forall$ or atomic formula A preceding a subformula G of a formula F, an element of Φ or Ψ is added to the prefix p of G depending on the "polarity" of $\neg / \Rightarrow / \forall / A$ (see [23] or Sect. 3 for details).*

Semantically, a prefix encodes a sequence of worlds in a Kripke model. Proof-theoretically, prefix constants and variables represent applications of the rules $\neg$-*right*, $\Rightarrow$-*right*, $\forall$-*right*, and $\neg$-*left*, $\Rightarrow$-*left*, $\forall$-*left* in the sequent calculus, in the sequent calculus, respectively. The prefix p of a subformula G, denoted by $pre(G)$ or $G\!:\!p$, specifies the sequence of these rules that have to be applied (bottom-up) to obtain G in the sequent. In order to preserve the atomic formulae that form an axiom in the intuitionistic sequent calculus, their prefixes need to unify under an intuitionistic substitution σ_J. An additional *domain condition* ensures that σ_Q and σ_J are mutually consistent [23].

Definition 2 (Intuitionistic substitution; σ-complementary). *An intuitionistic substitution $\sigma_J : \Phi \rightarrow (\Phi \cup \Psi)^*$ maps elements of Φ to strings over $\Phi \cup \Psi$. In $\sigma_J(p)$ prefix variables are replaced according to σ_J. A connection $\{L_1\!:\!p_1, L_2\!:\!p_2\}$ is σ-complementary for a combined substitution $\sigma{=}(\sigma_Q, \sigma_J)$ iff $\sigma_Q(L_1) = \sigma_Q(\overline{L_2})$ and $\sigma_J(p_1) = \sigma_J(p_2)$. σ is admissible iff the cumulative domain condition holds (see Sect. 2.2).*

2.2 Modal Logics

Modal logics extend the *syntax* of classical logic with the unary modal operators $\Box$ and $\Diamond$. They are used to represent the modalities "it is necessarily true that" and "it is possibly true that", respectively. The *Kripke semantics* of the standard modal logics are defined by a set of worlds W and a binary *accessibility relation* $R_i \subseteq W \times W$ between these worlds. In each single world $w \in W$ the classical semantics applies to the standard connectives and quantifiers, whereas the modal operators are interpreted with respect to accessible worlds: $\Box F$ or $\Diamond F$ are true in a world w, if F is true in *all* worlds w' or *some* world w' with $(w, w'){\in}R$, respectively. The properties of the accessibility relation R determine the specific modal logic. In this paper the modal logics D, T, S4, and S5 are considered. Their accessibility relation is serial (D)[1], reflexive (T), reflexive and transitive (S4), or an equivalence relation (S5). The standard semantics is considered with rigid term designation, i.e. every term denotes the same object in every world, and terms are local, i.e. any ground term denotes an existing object in every world.

The *sequent calculus for the (cumulative) modal logics D, T, and S4* consists of the axiom and rules of the classical sequent calculus and four additional modal rules:

$$\frac{\Gamma^+, F \vdash \Delta^+}{\Gamma, \Box F \vdash \Delta}\ \Box\text{-}left \qquad \frac{\Gamma^* \vdash F, \Delta^*}{\Gamma \vdash \Box F, \Delta}\ \Box\text{-}right$$

$$\frac{\Gamma^+ \vdash F, \Delta^+}{\Gamma \vdash \Diamond F, \Delta}\ \Diamond\text{-}right \qquad \frac{\Gamma^*, F \vdash \Delta^*}{\Gamma, \Diamond F \vdash \Delta}\ \Diamond\text{-}left$$

logic	Γ^+	Δ^+	Γ^*	Δ^*
D	$\Gamma_{(\Box)}$	$\Delta_{(\Diamond)}$	$\Gamma_{(\Box)}$	$\Delta_{(\Diamond)}$
T	Γ	Δ	$\Gamma_{(\Box)}$	$\Delta_{(\Diamond)}$
S4	Γ	Δ	$\Gamma_{\Box}$	$\Delta_{\Diamond}$

---

[1] A relation $R \subseteq W \times W$ is *serial* iff for all $w_1 \in W$ there is some $w_2 \in W$ with $(w_1, w_2) \in R$.

with $\Gamma_\square := \{\square G \,|\, \square G \in \Gamma\}$, $\Delta_\lozenge := \{\lozenge G \,|\, \lozenge G \in \Delta\}$, $\Gamma_{(\square)} := \{G \,|\, \square G \in \Gamma\}$, and $\Delta_{(\lozenge)} := \{G \,|\, \lozenge G \in \Delta\}$. To avoid deleting formulae in the sets Γ^*, Δ^*, Γ^+ and Δ^+ that are required for a proof, the (bottom-up) application of the modal rules need to be controlled. Again, a prefix is used to name sequences of accessible worlds and assigned to each subformula G of a given formula F.

Definition 3 (Modal prefix). *A prefix (denoted by p, q) is a string (sequence of characters) over an alphabet $\nu \cup \Pi$, in which ν is a set of prefix variables $(V_1, \dots)$ and Π is a set of prefix constants $(a_1, \dots)$. For every $\square / \lozenge$ preceding a subformula G of a formula F, an element of ν or Π is added to the prefix p of G depending on the "polarity" of $\square / \lozenge$ (see [23] or Sect. 4 for details).*

Semantically, a prefix denotes a sequence of worlds in a model. Proof-theoretically, prefix variables and constants represent applications of the rules $\square$-*left*/$\lozenge$-*right* and $\square$-*right*/$\lozenge$-*left*, respectively. A prefix of a formula F captures the modal context of F and specifies the sequence of modal rules that have to be applied (bottom-up) in order to obtain F in the sequent. In order to preserve the atomic formulae that form an axiom in the modal sequent calculus, their prefixes need to unify under a modal substitution σ_M.

Definition 4 (Modal substitution). *A modal substitution $\sigma_M : \nu \to (\nu \cup \Pi)^*$ maps elements of ν to strings over $\nu \cup \Pi$. In $\sigma_M(p)$ prefix variables are replaced according to σ_M. A connection $\{L_1 : p_1, L_2 : p_2\}$ is σ-complementary for a substitution $\sigma = (\sigma_Q, \sigma_M)$ iff $\sigma_Q(L_1) = \sigma_Q(\overline{L_2})$ and $\sigma_M(p_1) = \sigma_M(p_2)$. σ is admissible iff the accessibility condition and the domain condition hold. For S5 only the last prefix character is considered.*

The accessibility and the domain condition ensure that the modal substitution respects the accessibility relation and domain variant of the considered modal logic.

Definition 5 (Accessibility condition; domain condition). *For the modal logics D and T the accessibility condition $|\sigma_M(V)| = 1$ or $|\sigma_M(V)| \leq 1$, respectively, has to hold for all $V \in \nu$. The domain condition ensures that all "eigenvariables" $\bar{x}$ in a term t assigned to a variable x exist in the same world as x. In case of the varying domain variants, objects may only exist in the world in which they are introduced, hence, $\sigma_M(\mathrm{pre}(\bar{x})) = \sigma_M(\mathrm{pre}(x))$ has to hold.[2] For the cumulative domain variants, $\bar{x}$ has to be introduced before x, hence, $\sigma_M(\mathrm{pre}(\bar{x})) \preceq \sigma_M(\mathrm{pre}(x))$.[3] For the constant domain variants there is no restriction on the substitutions as every object exists in every world. Furthermore, the reduction ordering induced by σ has to be irreflexive (see [23] for details).*

---

[2] $pre(x)$ for a variable x is the prefix $pre(QxG)$ of the corresponding subformula QxG, $Q \in \{\forall, \exists\}$.

[3] $u \preceq w$ holds iff u is an initial substring of w or $u = w$. This condition, as well as the fact that there is no accessibility condition for S5, are slightly corrected conditions of [23].

2.3   Matrix Characterizations

For the matrix characterization of validity in non-classical logics, the notion
of matrices is generalized to arbitrary first-order formulae as already done for
classical logic [13].

Definition 6 (Matrix). *A (non-clausal) matrix $M(F)$, representing a formula
F, is a set of clauses, in which a clause is a set of literals and matrices (see [13]
for details).*

Whereas the definition of paths needs to be generalized to non-clausal
matrices[4], all other concepts used for clausal matrices, e.g. the definitions of
connections and term substitutions remain unchanged.

Definition 7 (Path). *A path through a matrix M (or a clause C) is inductively defined as follows. The (only) path through a literal L is $\{L\}$. If $p_1, \ldots, p_n$
are paths through the clauses $C_1, \ldots, C_n$, respectively, then $p_1 \cup \ldots \cup p_n$ is a
path through the matrix $M = \{C_1, \ldots, C_n\}$. If $p_1, \ldots, p_n$ are paths through the
matrices/literals $M_1, \ldots, M_n$, respectively, then $p_1, \ldots, p_n$ are also paths through
the clause $C = \{M_1, \ldots, M_n\}$.*

The notion of *multiplicity* is used to encode the number of clause copies used
in a proof. It is a function $\mu : M_C \to I\!N$ from the set of clauses M_C in M that
assigns a natural number to each clause in M specifying how many copies of
this clause are considered in a proof. In the *copy of a clause C* every (term and
prefix) variable in C is replaced by a unique new variable. M^μ denotes the matrix
that includes these clause copies. Clause copies correspond to applications of the
contraction rule in the sequent calculus.

Theorem 1 (Matrix characterization for non-classical logic [23]). *A
formula F is valid in intuitionistic / modal logic iff there is (1) a multiplicity
μ, (2) an admissible substitution $\sigma = (\sigma_Q, \sigma_J)/\sigma = (\sigma_Q, \sigma_M)$, and (3) a set of
σ-complementary connections, such that every path through $M^\mu(F)$ contains a
connection from this set.*

Any proof method that is based on the matrix characterization and operates
in a connection-oriented way is called a *connection method* [3,17]. The specific
calculus of a connection method is called a *connection calculus*.

3   Intuitionistic Logic

The connection calculus for intuitionistic logic to be introduced now is based
on the matrix characterization of logical validity presented in Sect. 2.3. It uses
a *connection-driven* search strategy in order to calculate an appropriate set of
connections. The prefixed non-clausal matrix is the main concept used in the
intuitionistic connection calculus. Furthermore, the use of prefixes requires an
additional prefix unification algorithm.

---

[4] The original characterization [23] uses a "tableau-like" definition and not non-clausal
matrices.

3.1   Prefixed Non-clausal Matrices

An intuitionistic non-clausal matrix is a set of prefixed clauses, which consist of prefixed literals and prefixed (sub)matrices. The *polarity* 0 or 1 is used to represent negation in a matrix, i.e. literals of the form A and $\neg A$ are represented by A^0 and A^1, respectively.

The *irreflexivity test* of the *reduction ordering* is realized by the *occurs check* during the term and prefix unifications. To this end, the *skolemization* technique, originally used to eliminate *eigenvariables* in classical logic, is extended and also used for prefix constants, a technique that is already used in the intuitionistic clausal calculus [10].

In the following, ε denotes the empty string, $u \circ w$ (shortly uw) denotes the concatenation of the strings u and w, and $G[x\backslash t]$ denotes the formula G in which all free occurrences of the variable x are replaced by the term t.

Definition 8 (Intuitionistic non-clausal matrix). *Let F be a formula, pol be a polarity, and p be a prefix. The* intuitionistic (non-clausal) matrix $M(F^{pol}{:}p)$ *of a prefixed formula $F^{pol}{:}p$ is a set of prefixed clauses, in which a prefixed clause is a set of prefixed literals and prefixed (non-clausal) matrices, and defined inductively according to Table 1. x^* is a new term variable, t^* is the Skolem term $f^*(x_1,\ldots,x_n)$ in which f^* is a new function symbol and $x_1,\ldots,x_n$ are all free term and prefix variables in $(\forall xG)^0 : p$ or $(\exists xG)^1 : p$. V^* is a new prefix variable, a^* is a prefix constant of the form $f^*(x_1,\ldots,x_n)$ in which f^* is a new function symbol and $x_1,\ldots,x_n$ are all free term and prefix variables in $A^0 : p$, $(\neg G)^0 : p$, $(G{\Rightarrow}H)^0 : p$, or $(\forall xG)^0 : p$. The* intuitionistic (non-clausal) matrix $M(F)$ *of F is the intuitionistic matrix $M(F^0 : \varepsilon)$.*

In the *graphical representation* of a non-clausal matrix, its clauses are arranged horizontally, while the literals and (sub-)matrices of each clause are arranged vertically.

For example, the formula $(P(a) \wedge \forall x(P(x){\Rightarrow}P(f(x))) \Rightarrow P(f(f(a)))) \wedge (Q{\Rightarrow}Q)$ has the simplified (redundant brackets are omitted) intuitionistic non-clausal matrix

$$\{\{ \{\{P(a)^1{:}a_1V_1\}, \{P(x)^0{:}a_1V_2V_3a_2(V_2,x,V_3), P(f(x))^1{:}a_1V_2V_3V_4\},$$
$$\{P(f(f(a)))^0{:}a_1a_3\}\}, \{\{Q^1{:}a_4V_5\},\{Q^0{:}a_4a_5\}\} \}\}$$

Table 1. The definition of the prefixed non-clausal matrix for intuitionistic logic

type	$F^{pol}:p$	$M(F^{pol}:p)$	type	$F^{pol}:p$	$M(F^{pol}:p)$
atomic	$A^0:p$	$\{\{A^0:pa^*\}\}$	atomic	$A^1:p$	$\{\{A^1:pV^*\}\}$
α	$(G{\wedge}H)^1:p$	$\{\{M(G^1:p)\}\},\{\{M(H^1:p)\}\}$	α	$(\neg G)^0:p$	$M(G^1:pa^*)$
	$(G{\vee}H)^0:p$	$\{\{M(G^0:p)\}\},\{\{M(H^0:p)\}\}$		$(\neg G)^1:p$	$M(G^0:pV^*)$
	$(G{\Rightarrow}H)^0{:}p$	$\{\{M(G^1:pa^*)\}\},\{\{M(H^0:pa^*)\}\}$	γ	$(\forall xG)^1:p$	$M(G[x\backslash x^*]^1:pV^*)$
β	$(G{\wedge}H)^0:p$	$\{\{M(G^0:p),M(H^0:p)\}\}$		$(\exists xG)^0:p$	$M(G[x\backslash x^*]^0:p)$
	$(G{\vee}H)^1:p$	$\{\{M(G^1:p),M(H^1:p)\}\}$	δ	$(\forall xG)^0:p$	$M(G[x\backslash t^*]^0:pa^*)$
	$(G{\Rightarrow}H)^1{:}p$	$\{\{M(G^0:pV^*),M(H^1:pV^*)\}\}$		$(\exists xG)^1:p$	$M(G[x\backslash t^*]^1:p)$

and the graphical representation (where $a_2(V_2, x, V_3)$ is a (skolemized) prefix constant):

$$\left[\left[\left[\,[P(a)^1{:}a_1V_1]\,\begin{bmatrix}P(x)^0{:}a_1V_2V_3a_2(V_2,x,V_3)\\P(f(x))^1{:}a_1V_2V_3V_4\end{bmatrix}\,[P(f(f(a)))^0{:}a_1a_3]\,\right]\right.\right.$$
$$\left.\left.\quad[\,[Q^1{:}a_4V_5]\,[Q^0{:}a_4a_5]\,]\,\right]\right]\,.$$

3.2 Prefix Unification

The intuitionistic substitution σ_J is calculated by a *prefix unification algorithm* [10]. For a given set of prefix equations $\bar{E} = \{p_1 = q_1, \ldots, p_n = q_n\}$, an appropriate substitution σ_J is a unifier such that $\sigma_J(p_i) = \sigma_J(q_i)$ for all $1 \leq i \leq n$. A set of unifiers Σ is a set of *most general unifiers (mgu)* for $\bar{E}$ if and only if every unifier τ is an instance of some $\sigma \in \Sigma$ (completeness) and no unifier $\sigma \in \Sigma$ is an instance of another unifier $\tau \in \Sigma$ (minimality). General algorithms for string unification[5] exist, but the number of most general unifiers might not be finite. The following unification algorithm is more efficient, as it takes the *prefix property* into account: for prefixes $p_i = u_1 X w_1$ and $p_j = u_2 X w_2$ (also in case $i = j$) with $X \in \Phi \cup \Psi$ the property $u_1 = u_2$ holds. This reflects the fact that prefixes correspond to sequences of connectives and quantifiers within the same formula.

Definition 9 (Intuitionistic prefix unification). *The unification for the prefix equation $\{p = q\}$ is carried out by applying the rewriting rules R1 to R10 in Fig. 1. It is $V, \bar{V}, V' \in \Phi$ with $V \neq \bar{V}$, V' is a new prefix variable, $a, b \in \Psi$, $X \in \Phi \cup \Psi$, and $u, w, z \in (\Phi \cup \Psi)^*$. For rule 10 the restriction $(*)$ $u = \varepsilon$ or $w \neq \varepsilon$ or $X \in \Psi$ applies. $\sigma_J(V) = u$ is written $\{V \backslash u\}$. The unification starts with the tuple $(\{p = \varepsilon | q\}, \{\})$. The application of a rewriting rule $E \to E', \tau$ replaces the tuple (E, σ_J) by the tuple $(E', \tau(\sigma_J))$. E and E' are prefix equations, σ_J and τ are (intuitionistic) substitutions. The unification terminates when the tuple $(\{\}, \sigma_J)$ is derived. In this case, σ_J represents a most general unifier. Rules can be applied non-deterministically and lead to a set of mgu [10].*

In the worst-case, the number of mgu grows exponentially with respect to the length of the prefixes p and q. To solve a *set* of prefix equations

R1. $\{\varepsilon = \varepsilon | \varepsilon\}$	$\to \{\}, \{\}$	R6. $\{Vu = \varepsilon | aw\}$	$\to \{u = \varepsilon | aw\}, \{V \backslash \varepsilon\}$
R2. $\{\varepsilon = \varepsilon | Xu\}$	$\to \{Xu = | \varepsilon\}, \{\}$	R7. $\{Vu = z | abw\}$	$\to \{u = \varepsilon | bw\}, \{V \backslash za\}$
R3. $\{Xu = \varepsilon | Xw\}$	$\to \{u = | w\}, \{\}$	R8. $\{Vau = \varepsilon | \bar{V}w\}$	$\to \{\bar{V}w = V | au\}, \{\}$
R4. $\{au = \varepsilon | Vw\}$	$\to \{Vw = | au\}, \{\}$	R9. $\{Vau = Xz | \bar{V}w\}$	$\to \{\bar{V}w = V' | au\}, \{V \backslash XzV'\}$
R5. $\{Vu = z | \varepsilon\}$	$\to \{u = | \varepsilon\}, \{V \backslash z\}$	R10. $\{Vu = z | Xw\}$	$\to \{Vu = zX | w\}, \{\}$ $(*)$

Fig. 1. The prefix unification for intuitionistic logic and modal logic S4

---

[5] This is also called the *monoid* problem; it is the equation theory in which there is a neutral element ε and the associativity of the string concatenation operator $\circ$ holds.

$\bar{E} = \{p_1 = p_1, \ldots, q_n = t_q\}$, the equations in $\bar{E}$ are solved one after the other and each calculated unifier is applied to the remaining prefix equations in $\bar{E}$.

For example, for the prefix equation $\{a_1 V_2 V_3 = a_1 a_3\}$ there are the two derivations:

$\{a_1 V_2 V_3 = \dot{\varepsilon}|a_1 a_3\}, \{\} \xrightarrow{\text{R3}} \{V_2 V_3 = \varepsilon|a_3\}, \{\} \xrightarrow{\text{R6}} \{V_3 = \varepsilon|a_3\}, \{V_2\backslash\varepsilon\} \xrightarrow{\text{R10}}$

$\{V_3 = a_3|\varepsilon\}, \{V_2\backslash\varepsilon\} \xrightarrow{\text{R5}} \{\varepsilon = \varepsilon|\varepsilon\}, \{V_2\backslash\varepsilon, V_3\backslash a_3\}$ and $\{a_1 V_2 V_3 = \varepsilon|a_1 a_3\}, \{\} \xrightarrow{\text{R3}}$

$\{V_2 V_3 = \varepsilon|a_3\}, \{\} \xrightarrow{\text{R10}} \{V_2 V_3 = a_3|\varepsilon\}, \{\} \xrightarrow{\text{R5}} \{V_3 = \varepsilon|\varepsilon\}, \{V_2\backslash a_3\} \xrightarrow{\text{R5}} \{\varepsilon = \varepsilon|\varepsilon\},$ $\{V_2\backslash a_3, V_3\backslash\varepsilon\},$

which yield the most general unifiers $\sigma_J^1 = \{V_2\backslash\varepsilon, V_3\backslash a_3\}$ and $\sigma_J^2 = \{V_2\backslash a_3, V_3\backslash\varepsilon\}$.

3.3   An Intuitionistic Non-clausal Connection Calculus

The non-clausal connection calculus for intuitionistic logic is an extension of the non-clausal connection calculus for classical logic [13], in which a prefix is added to each literal and an additional prefix unification is used to identify σ-complementary connections. According to the matrix characterization in Sect. 2.3, a formula F is valid, iff all paths through its matrix $M^\mu(F)$ (with added clause copies) contain a σ-complementary connection. The calculus uses a *connection-driven* search strategy in order check this property. In each (reduction and extension) step of a derivation in the calculus, a σ-complementary connection is identified and only paths that do not contain this connection are investigated afterwards. If every path contains a σ-complementary connection, the proof search succeeds and the given formula is valid. A *non-clausal connection proof* can be illustrated within the graphical matrix representation.

For example, the proof of the matrix from Sect. 3.1 consists of four connections, marked by an arc in the graphical matrix representation, that are σ-complementary with $\sigma_Q = \{x\backslash a, x'\backslash fa\}$, $\sigma_J = \{V_1\backslash a_2(\varepsilon, a, \varepsilon), V_2\backslash\varepsilon, V_3\backslash\varepsilon, V_4\backslash a_2(\varepsilon, fa, \varepsilon), V_2'\backslash\varepsilon, V_3'\backslash\varepsilon, V_4'\backslash a_3\}$:

copy

$$\left[\left[\left[\,[P^1 a{:}a_1 V_1]\,\right]\left[\begin{array}{c}P^0 x{:}a_1 V_2 V_3 a_2(V_2, x, V_3)\\ P^1 fx{:}a_1 V_2 V_3 V_4\end{array}\right]\overbrace{\left[\begin{array}{c}P^0 x'{:}a_1 V_2' V_3' a_2(V_2', x', V_3')\\ P^1 fx'{:}a_1 V_2' V_3' V_4'\end{array}\right]}\,[P^0 ffa{:}a_1 a_3]\,\right]\right.$$
$$\left.\left[\,[Q^1{:}a_4 V_5]\,[Q^0{:}a_4 a_5]\,\right]\,\right]\right]$$

But, e.g., for the formula $P \vee \neg P$ there is no intuitionistic connection proof of its matrix $\{\{P^0{:}a_1\}, \{P^1{:}a_2 A_1\}\}$, as the two prefixes of the only connection cannot be unified.

A few additional concepts are required as follows in order to specify which clauses can be used within the generalized non-clausal extension rule. The term α-related is used to express that a clause occurs besides a literal in a matrix. The definitions of free variables and clause copies have to be generalized to cover non-clausal matrices.

Definition 10 (α-related; parent clause; clause copy). *A clause C is α-related to a literal L iff it occurs besides L in the graphical matrix representation;*

more precisely, C is α-related to a literal L iff $\{C', C''\} \subseteq M'$ for some matrix M', such that C' contains L and C'' contains C (or $C=C''$). C' is a parent clause of C iff $M' \in C'$ and $C \in M'$ for some M'. In the copy *of a clause C all free variables in C are replaced by fresh variables. $M[C_1 \backslash C_2]$ denotes the matrix M, in which the clause C_1 is replaced by the clause C_2.*

Definition 11 (Extension clause; β-clause). *C is an* extension clause (e-clause) *of the matrix M with respect to a set of literals $Path$ iff either (a) C contains a literal of $Path$, or (b) C is α-related to all literals of $Path$ occurring in M and if C has a parent clause, it contains a literal of $Path$. In the β-clause of C_2 with respect to L_2, denoted by β-clause$_{L_2}(C_2)$, L_2 and all clauses that are α-related to L_2 are deleted from C_2.*

In the example, the literal $Q^1{:}a_4V_5$ is only α-related to the literal $Q^0{:}a_4a_5$. The parent clause of $\{Q^1{:}a_4V_5\}$ is the clause C' in the whole matrix $\{C'\}$ of the example. Furthermore, the clause $\{Q^0{:}a_4a_5\}$ is an extension clause with respect to $\{Q^1{:}a_4V_5\}$.

The non-clausal connection calculus for intuitionistic logic adds prefixes and an intuitionistic substitution σ_J to the non-clausal connection calculus for classical logic.

Definition 12 (Intuitionistic non-clausal connection calculus). *The axiom and the rules of the* intuitionistic (non-clausal) connection calculus *are given in Fig. 2. It works on tuples "$C, M, Path$", where M is a prefixed non-clausal matrix, C is a prefixed (subgoal) clause or ε and (the active) $Path$ is a set of prefixed literals or ε. $\sigma = (\sigma_Q, \sigma_J)$ is a combined term and intuitionistic substitution. An* intuitionistic (non-clausal) connection proof *of a prefixed matrix M is an intuitionistic connection proof of $\varepsilon, M, \varepsilon$.*

Proof search in the non-clausal connection calculus is carried out by applying the rules of the calculus in an analytic *way (i.e. bottom-up) starting with*

Axiom (A) $\dfrac{}{\{\},M,Path}$	*Start (S)* $\dfrac{C_2,M,\{\}}{\varepsilon,M,\varepsilon}$ and C_2 is copy of $C_1{\in}M$

Reduction (R) $\dfrac{C,M,Path\cup\{L_2:p_2\}}{C\cup\{L_1:p_1\},M,Path\cup\{L_2:p_2\}}$ and $\{L_1:p_1,L_2:p_2\}$ is σ-complementary

Extension (E) $\dfrac{C_3,M[C_1\backslash C_2],Path\cup\{L_1:p_1\} \quad C,M,Path}{C\cup\{L_1:p_1\},M,Path}$

and $C_3:=\beta\text{-}clause_{L_2}(C_2)$, C_2 is copy of C_1, C_1 is e-clause of M wrt. $Path\cup\{L_1:p_1\}$, C_2 contains $L_2:p_2$, $\{L_1:p_1,L_2:p_2\}$ is σ-complementary

Decomposition (D) $\dfrac{C\cup C_1,M,Path}{C\cup\{M_1\},M,Path}$ and $C_1{\in}M_1$

Fig. 2. The non-clausal connection calculus for intuitionistic and modal logic

$\varepsilon, M, \varepsilon$, in which M is the matrix of the given formula. At first, a start clause is selected. Afterwards, connections are successively identified by applying reduction and extension rules. This process is guided by the *active path*, a subset of a path through M. During the proof search, backtracking might be required, i.e. alternative rules or rule instances have to be considered if the chosen rule or rule instance does not lead to a proof. This might happen when choosing the clause C_1 in the start and extension rules, the literal L_2 in the reduction and extension rules or the clause C_1 in the decomposition rule. The multiplicity μ is increased *dynamically* whenever an extension rule is applied.

The substitutions σ_Q and σ_J are *rigid*, i.e. applied to the whole derivation, and calculated whenever a reduction or extension rule is applied. The term substitution σ_Q is calculated by one of the well-known algorithms for term unification. The intuitionistic substitution is calculated by a prefix unification algorithm (Sect. 3.2).

Theorem 2 (Correctness and completeness). *A first-order formula F is valid in intuitionistic logic iff there is a proof in the non-clausal connection calculus for $M(F)$.*

The proof is based on the matrix characterization for modal logic (Theorem 1), the correctness and completeness of the non-clausal connection calculus for classical logic [13] and the correctness of the prefix unification [7]. It is crucial to use a "general" non-clausal approach [13] without optimizations that work only for classical logic.

4   Modal Logic

The non-clausal connection calculus for modal logic is similar to the one for intuitionistic logic; only the prefixed non-clausal matrix and the prefix unification is adapted.

4.1   Prefixed Non-clausal Matrices

In the modal non-clausal matrix, prefixes are determined by the modal operators. All other concepts, including the extended skolemization technique, are used in the same way as for the non-clausal matrix for intuitionistic logic (see Sect. 3.1). See [14] and the references therein for a motivation and examples for the usage of modal prefixes.

Definition 13 (Modal non-clausal matrix). *Let F be a formula, pol be a polarity, and p be a prefix. The modal (non-clausal) matrix $M(F^{pol}{:}p)$ of a prefixed formula $F^{pol}{:}p$ is defined inductively according to Table 2. x^* is a new term variable, t^* is the Skolem term $f^*(x_1, \ldots, x_n)$ in which f^* is a new function symbol and $x_1, \ldots, x_n$ are all free term and prefix variables in $(\forall x G)^0 : p$ or $(\exists x G)^1 : p$. V^* is a new prefix variable, a^* is a prefix constant of the form $f^*(x_1, \ldots, x_n)$ in which f^* is a new function symbol and $x_1, \ldots, x_n$ are all free term and prefix variables in $(\square G)^0 : p$ or $(\lozenge G)^1 : p$. The modal (non-clausal) matrix $M(F)$ of F is the modal matrix $M(F^0 : \varepsilon)$.*

Table 2. The definition of the prefixed non-clausal matrix for modal logic

type	$F^{pol}:p$	$M(F^{pol}:p)$	type	$F^{pol}:p$	$M(F^{pol}:p)$
atomic	$A^0:p$	$\{\{A^0:p\}\}$	atomic	$A^1:p$	$\{\{A^1:p\}\}$
α	$(G \wedge H)^1:p$	$\{\{M(G^1:p)\}\},\{\{M(H^1:p)\}\}$	α	$(\neg G)^0:p$	$M(G^1:p)$
	$(G \vee H)^0:p$	$\{\{M(G^0:p)\}\},\{\{M(H^0:p)\}\}$		$(\neg G)^1:p$	$M(G^0:p)$
	$(G \Rightarrow H)^0:p$	$\{\{M(G^1:p)\}\},\{\{M(H^0:p)\}\}$	γ	$(\forall x G)^1:p$	$M(G[x\backslash x^*]^1:p)$
β	$(G \wedge H)^0:p$	$\{\{M(G^0:p),M(H^0:p)\}\}$		$(\exists x G)^0:p$	$M(G[x\backslash x^*]^0:p)$
	$(G \vee H)^1:p$	$\{\{M(G^1:p),M(H^1:p)\}\}$	δ	$(\forall x G)^0:p$	$M(G[x\backslash t^*]^0:p)$
	$(G \Rightarrow H)^1:p$	$\{\{M(G^0:p),M(H^1:p)\}\}$		$(\exists x G)^1:p$	$M(G[x\backslash t^*]^1:p)$
ν	$(\Box G)^1:p$	$M(G^1:pV^*)$	π	$(\Box G)^0:p$	$M(G^0:pa^*)$
	$(\Diamond G)^0:p$	$M(G^0:pV^*)$		$(\Diamond G)^1:p$	$M(G^1:pa^*)$

4.2 Prefix Unification

Again, a prefix unification algorithm is used to calculate the modal substitution σ_M. Depending on the modal logic, the accessibility condition (see Sect. 2.2) has to be respected when calculating this substitution, i.e. for all $V \in \nu$: $|\sigma_M(V)| = 1$ for the modal logic D and $|\sigma_M(V)| \leq 1$ for the modal logic T; there is no restriction for the modal logics S4 and S5. The prefix unification for D is a simple pattern matching, i.e. the standard term unification can be used. For S4 the (general) prefix unification for intuitionistic logic can be used (see Sect. 3.2). For S5 only the last character of each prefix (or ε if the prefix is ε) has to be unified. By structural induction it can be shown that the following procedure computes a set of mgu for the modal logic T (that contains fewer mgu than the unification procedure presented in [7]).

Definition 14 (Modal T prefix unification). *The unification for the prefix equation $\{p = q\}$ is carried out by applying the rewriting rules in Fig. 3. It is $V, \bar{V} \in \nu$ with $V \neq \bar{V}$, $a \in \Pi$, $X \in \nu \cup \Pi$, $u, w \in (\nu \cup \Pi)^*$. The rules are applied in the same way as those for intuitionistic logic (see Sect. 3.2), but the tuple has the form (E, σ_M) and terminates with the tuple $(\{\}, \sigma_M)$, in which case σ_M represents a most general unifier.*

R1.	$\{\varepsilon = \varepsilon\|\varepsilon\}$	$\rightarrow \{\}\{\}$	R6.	$\{au = \varepsilon\|Vw\} \rightarrow \{Vw = a\|u\}, \{\}$
R2.	$\{\varepsilon = \varepsilon\|Xw\}$	$\rightarrow \{Xw = \varepsilon\|\varepsilon\}, \{\}$	R7.	$\{Vu = \varepsilon\|\bar{V}w\} \rightarrow \{w = V\|u\}, \{\bar{V}\backslash\varepsilon\}$
R3.	$\{Vu = \varepsilon\|\varepsilon\}$	$\rightarrow \{u = \varepsilon\|\varepsilon\}, \{V\backslash\varepsilon\}$	R8.	$\{Vu = X\|w\} \rightarrow \{u = X\|w\}, \{V\backslash\varepsilon\}$
R4.	$\{Xu = \varepsilon\|Xw\} \rightarrow \{u = \varepsilon\|w\}, \{\}$		R9.	$\{Vu = X\|w\} \rightarrow \{u = \varepsilon\|w\}, \{V\backslash X\}$
R5.	$\{\bar{V}u = \varepsilon\|Xw\} \rightarrow \{\bar{V}u = X\|w\}, \{\}$		R10.	$\{au = V\|w\} \rightarrow \{u = \varepsilon\|w\}, \{V\backslash a\}$

Fig. 3. The prefix unification for the modal logic T

4.3 A Modal Non-clausal Connection Calculus

The non-clausal connection calculus for modal logic uses the same concepts as the one for intuitionistic logic. The intuitionistic substitution σ_J is replaced by the one for modal logic σ_M, and the definition of σ-complementary is adapted (see Sect. 2.2). Proof search is carried out in the same way as for intuitionistic logic (see Sect. 3.3).

Definition 15 (Modal non-clausal connection calculus). *The axiom and the rules of the* modal (non-clausal) connection calculus *are given in Fig. 2. It works on tuples "$C, M, Path$", where M is a prefixed non-clausal matrix, C is a prefixed (subgoal) clause or ε and (the active) $Path$ is a set of prefixed literals or ε. $\sigma = (\sigma_Q, \sigma_M)$ is a combined (rigid) term and modal substitution. A modal (non-clausal) connection proof of a prefixed matrix M is a modal connection proof of $\varepsilon, M, \varepsilon$.*

Theorem 3 (Correctness and completeness). *A modal first-order formula F is valid in modal logic iff there is a proof in the non-clausal connection calculus for $M(F)$.*

The proof is based on the matrix characterization for modal logic (Theorem 1), the correctness and completeness of the non-clausal connection calculus for classical logic [13] and the correctness of the prefix unifications. Again, the "general" non-clausal calculus [13] without any optimizations for classical logic has to be used.

5   Optimizations

Optimization techniques, such as positive start clauses, regularity, lemmata and restricted backtracking, can be employed in a similar way as in the non-clausal connection calculus for classical logic [13] if the prefixes are additionally taken into account.

Positive Start Clause. Like for the clausal connection calculus, the start clause of the non-clausal connection calculus can be restricted to positive clauses. A clause is positive iff all of its elements (matrices and literals) are positive; a matrix is positive iff it contains at least one positive clause; a literal is positive iff its polarity is 0. If there is no positive clause in a matrix M of F, then there exists a path through M that contains no positive literal, hence, according to the matrix characterization F cannot be valid. The *positive clause C_1 of a clause C*, consists only of the clauses of C that are positive.

Regularity. Regularity is an effective technique for pruning the search space in clausal connection calculi [8]. The *regularity condition* ensures that no literal occurs more than once in the active path. It is integrated into the non-classical non-clausal connection calculus in Fig. 2 by adding the following restriction to the reduction and the extension rule: $\forall\ L':p' \in C \cup \{L_1:p_1\}:\ \sigma(L':p') \notin \sigma(Path)$, in which the combined substitution σ is applied to term/prefix variables. Additional backtracking can be avoided if the combined substitution σ is not modified in order to satisfy the regularity condition.

Lemmata. The idea of *lemmata* (or *factorization*) is to reuse subproofs during the proof search [8]. To this end an additional set of lemmata (i.e. literals) and a lemma rule [12] is added to the non-clausal connection calculus. Again, a lemma literal $L:p$ has to unify under a *combined* substitution σ, in order to apply the lemma rule.

Restricted Backtracking. Proof search in the non-clausal connection calculus is *not* confluent. In order to achieve completeness, *backtracking* (see remarks in Sect. 3.3) is necessary. The idea of *restricted backtracking* is to cut off any alternative connections once a literal from the subgoal clause has been solved [12]. A literal L is called *solved* if it is the literal L_1 of a reduction or extension rule application (see Fig. 2) and in the case of the extension rule, there is also a proof for the left premise. Restricted backtracking is correct (as the search space is only pruned), but incomplete [12]. It can be applied in the intuitionistic or modal non-clausal connection calculus as well.

6   Implementation

The implementations of the intuitionistic and modal non-clausal connection calculi of Fig. 2 follow the *lean methodology* [1], which is already used for the clausal connection provers leanCoP [11,16], ileanCoP [11] and MleanCoP [14]. It uses very compact Prolog code to implement the basic calculus and adds a few essential optimization techniques in order to prune the search space. The resulting *na*tural *n*onclausal *c*onnection provers for *i*ntuitionistic logic nanoCoP-i and *m*odal logics nanoCoP-M are available at http://www.leancop.de/nanocop-i/ and http://www.leancop.de/nanocop-m/.

Modal and Intuitionistic Non-clausal Matrices. In the first step the input formula F is translated into its intuitionistic/modal non-clausal matrix $M := M(F)$ according to Tables 1 or 2; redundant brackets of the form "$\{\{\ldots\}\}$" are removed. Additionally, every (sub-)clause $(I,V,FV):C$ and (sub-)matrix $J:M$ are marked with unique *indices* I and J; clauses C are also marked with a set V of (free) term and prefix variables and a set FV of (free) term variables of the form $x:pre(x)$ that are newly introduced in C. Atomic formulae and term/prefix constants are represented by Prolog atoms, term/prefix variables by Prolog variables; literals with polarity 1 are marked with "-". Sets, e.g. clauses and matrices, are represented by Prolog lists (representing multisets); prefixes are represented by Prolog lists and marked with the polarity of the corresponding literal. For example, the non-clausal matrix from Sect. 3.1 is represented by the Prolog term

```
[(2^K)^[]^[]: [16^K:[(17^K)^[]^[]: [-(q): -([15^[]])], (19^K)^[]^[]:[q:[15^[]]]],
   5^K: [(6^K)^[]^[]: [-(p(a)): -([3^[]])],
      (8^K)^[W,X,V]^[X:[3^[],V]]: [p(X):[3^[],V,W], -(p(f(X))): -([3^[],V,W])],
      (14^K)^[]^[]: [p(f(f(a))):[3^[]]]] ] ]
```

in which the Prolog variable K is instantiated later on in order to enumerate clause copies (as an optimization for intuitionistic logic, prefix characters introduced by atomic formulae are *only* considered during the unification). In a second step, the matrix M is written into Prolog's database. For every literal Lit in M the fact lit(Lit,ClaB,ClaC,Grnd) is asserted into the database where ClaC $\in M$ is the (largest) clause in which Lit occurs and ClaB is the β-clause of ClaC with respect to Lit. Grnd is set either to g or n depending if the smallest clause in which Lit occurs is ground or not. No other modifications of the original formula (structure) are done during these two preprocessing steps.

Non-classical Non-clausal Proof Search. The nanoCoP-i/M source code is shown in Fig. 4. The underlined text was added to the nanoCoP code for classical logic [15]: (1) prefixes are added to all literals, (2) the sets PreS and VarS are added, which contain prefix equations and free (prefixed) term variables, respectively, and (3) a prefix unification is added. First, nanoCoP-i/M performs a classical proof search, in which the prefixes of each connection are stored in PreS. If the search succeeds, the domain condition is checked and the prefixes in PreS are unified (line 4), using the predicates domain_cond and prefix_unify (which need 18 and between 7 to 22 lines of code).

The predicate prove(Mat,PathLim,Set,Proof) implements the start rule (lines 1–4) and iterative deepening on the size of the active path (lines 5–9). Mat is the matrix generated in the preprocessing step, PathLim is the size limit for Path, and Proof contains the returned (non-clausal) connection proof. Set $\subseteq \{$cut, comp$(I)\}$, for $I \in I\!N$, is used to control restricted backtracking [12]. The predicate positiveC(Cla,Cla1) returns the positive clause Cla1 of Cla (needs 7 additional lines of code). The predicate prove(Cla,Mat,Path,PathI, PathLim,Lem,PreS,VarS,Set,Proof) implements the axiom (line 10), the decomposition rule (lines 11–16), the reduction rule (lines 17–20, 24–26, 37–38), and the extension rule (lines 17–20, 28–49) of the calculus in Fig. 2. Cla, Mat, and Path represent the subgoal clause C, the prefixed matrix M and the (active) *Path*. The *indexed path* PathI contains the indices of all clauses and matrices that contain literals of Path; it is used for calculating extension clauses. The substitution σ is stored implicitly by Prolog. The predicate prove_ec(ClaB,Cla1,Mat,ClaB1,Mat1) calculates extension clauses (lines 39–49). Additional optimization techniques (see Sect. 5) are regularity (line 19), lemmata (line 21), and restricted backtracking (line 36).

7   Evaluation

The following tests were conducted on a Xeon system with 4 GB of RAM running Linux and ECLiPSe Prolog 5.10. The CPU time limit was set to 100 s.

ILTP Library. Table 3 shows the number of solutions on all 2550 first-order problems of the ILTP library v1.1.2 [19] for the intuitionistic theorem provers

```
      % start rule
(1)   prove(Mat,PathLim,Set,[(I^0)^V:Cla1|Proof]) :-
(2)       member((I^0)^V^VS:Cla,Mat), positiveC(Cla,Cla1),
(3)       prove(Cla1,Mat,[],[I^0],PathLim,[],PreS,VarS,Set,Proof),
(4)       append(VarS,VS,VarS1), domain_cond(VarS1), prefix_unify(PreS).

(5)   prove(Mat,PathLim,Set,Proof) :-
(6)       retract(pathlim) ->
(7)       ( member(comp(PathLim),Set) -> prove(Mat,1,[],Proof) ;
(8)         PathLim1 is PathLim+1, prove(Mat,PathLim1,Set,Proof) ) ;
(9)       member(comp(_),Set) -> prove(Mat,1,[],Proof).

      % axiom
(10)  prove([],_,_,_,_,_,[],[],_,[]).

      % decomposition rule
(11)  prove([J^K:Mat1|Cla],MI,Path,PI,PathLim,Lem,PreS,VarS,Set,Proof) :- !,
(12)      member(I^_^FV:Cla1,Mat1),
(13)  ·   prove(Cla1,MI,Path,[I,J^K|PI],PathLim,Lem,PreS1,VarS1,Set,Proof1),
(14)      prove(Cla,MI,Path,PI,PathLim,Lem,PreS2,VarS2,Set,Proof2),
(15)      append(PreS2,PreS1,PreS), append(FV,VarS1,VarS3),
(16)      append(VarS2,VarS3,VarS), append(Proof1,Proof2,Proof).

      % reduction and extension rules
(17)  prove([Lit:Pre|Cla],MI,Path,PI,PathLim,Lem,PreS,VarS,Set,Proof) :-
(18)      Proof=[[I^V:[NegLit|ClaB1]|Proof1]|Proof2],
(19)      \+ (member(LitC,[Lit:Pre|Cla]), member(LitP,Path), LitC==LitP),
(20)      (-NegLit=Lit;-Lit=NegLit) ->
(21)      ( member(LitL,Lem), Lit:Pre==LitL, ClaB1=[], Proof1=[],
(22)        PreS3=[], VarS3=[]
(23)        ;
(24)        member(NegL:PreN,Path), unify_with_occurs_check(NegL,NegLit),
(25)        ClaB1=[], Proof1=[],
(26)        \+ \+ prefix_unify([Pre=PreN]), PreS3=[Pre=PreN], VarS3=[]
(27)        ;
(28)        lit(NegLit:PreN,ClaB,Cla1,Grnd1),
(29)        ( Grnd1=g -> true ; length(Path,K), K<PathLim -> true ;
(30)          \+ pathlim -> assert(pathlim), fail ),
(31)        \+ \+ prefix_unify([Pre=PreN]),
(32)        prove_ec(ClaB,Cla1,MI,PI,I^V^FV:ClaB1,MI1),
(33)        prove(ClaB1,MI1,[Lit:Pre|Path],[I|PI],PathLim,Lem,PreS1,VarS1,
(34)              Set,Proof1), PreS3=[Pre=PreN|PreS1], append(VarS1,FV,VarS3)
(35)      ),
(36)      ( member(cut,Set) -> ! ; true ),
(37)      prove(Cla,MI,Path,PI,PathLim,[Lit:Pre|Lem],PreS2,VarS2,Set,Proof2),
(38)      append(PreS3,PreS2,PreS), append(VarS2,VarS3,VarS).

      % extension clause (e-clause)
(39)  prove_ec((I^K)^V:ClaB,IV:Cla,MI,PI,ClaB1,MI1) :-
(40)      append(MIA,[(I^K1)^V1:Cla1|MIB],MI), length(PI,K),
(41)      ( ClaB=[J^K:[ClaB2]|_], member(J^K1,PI),
(42)        unify_with_occurs_check(V,V1), Cla=[_:[Cla2|_]|_],
(43)        append(ClaD,[J^K1:MI2|ClaE],Cla1),
(44)        prove_ec(ClaB2,Cla2,MI2,PI,ClaB1,MI3),
(45)        append(ClaD,[J^K1:MI3|ClaE],Cla3),
(46)      . append(MIA,[(I^K1)^V1:Cla3|MIB],MI1)
(47)        ;
(48)        (\+member(I^K1,PI);V\==V1) ->
(49)        ClaB1=(I^K)^V:ClaB, append(MIA,[IV:Cla|MIB],MI1) ).
```

Fig. 4. Source code of the nanoCoP-i and nanoCoP-M core provers

JProver, ileanTAP, ft, ileanCoP, and nanoCoP-i. JProver [21] is based on a simple prefixed non-clausal connection calculus [7]; ileanTAP [9] uses a prefixed free-variable tableau calculus; ft [20] is a C implementation of an analytic tableau calculus; ileanCoP [10,11] implements a prefixed *clausal* connection calculus. In order to make the results comparable, the *core prover* of ileanCoP was used with the standard ("[nodef]") and the definitional ("[def]") translation into clausal form. nanoCoP-i was tested without and with restricted backtracking, i.e. Set=[] and Set=[cut,comp(6)], respectively. The "full" version of ileanCoP 1.2, which additionally uses a fixed strategy scheduling, proves 787 problems. Compared to ileanCoP "[nodef]", 39% of the proofs of nanoCoP-i "[ ]" are on average 36% shorter (in terms of number of connections); 60% have the same size. Compared to ileanCoP "[def]", 51% of the proofs are on average 38% shorter; 48% have the same size. There is a significant performance improvement of nanoCoP-i compared to ileanCoP, even though most of the tested problems have a "clausal-like" structure, which also explains that about half of the proofs have the same size.

Table 3. Results on the first-order problems of the ILTP library

	JProver	ileanTAP	ft (C)	ileanCoP 1.2		nanoCoP-i 1.0	
	11-2005	1.17	1.23	[nodef]	[def]	[]	[cut,comp(6)]
Proved	258	308	334	601	640	**704**	764
Refuted	4	4	30	82	78	89	89

QMLTP Library. Table 4 shows the number of solutions on all 580 unimodal problems of the QMLTP library v1.1 [18] (for the varying, cumulative, and constant domain variants) for the modal theorem provers MleanTAP, MleanCoP, and nanoCoP-M. MleanTAP implements a prefixed tableau calculus; MleanCoP [14] uses a prefixed *clausal* connection calculus. Again, the *core prover* of MleanCoP was tested with the (better performing) definitional translation ("[def]") into clausal form. nanoCoP-M was tested without and with restricted backtracking, i.e. Set=[] and Set=[cut,comp(6)], respectively; both versions refute the same number of (invalid) formulae. Compared to MleanCoP "[def]", between 33% and 48% of the proofs of nanoCoP-M "[ ]" are on average between 38% and 41% shorter (in terms of number of connections) depending on the specific modal logic; at most 3% of the proofs are larger (due to a different proof search order of MleanCoP and nanoCoP-M). There is a significant performance improvement; nanoCoP-M proves or refutes up to 10% more problems than MleanCoP. Again, most of the tested problems have a "clausal-like" structure, hence, for about half of the proved problems, the proofs of MleanCoP and nanoCoP-M have the same size.

Table 4. Results on the unimodal problems (varying/cumul./constant) of the QMLTP library

Logic	MleanTAP 1.3	MleanCoP 1.3		nanoCoP-M 1.0		
		[def]	[def]	[]	[]	[cut.comp(6)]
	(proved)	(proved)	(refuted)	(proved)	(refuted)	(proved)
D	100/120/135	152/170/187	246/226/209	**158/177/194**	266/246/230	167/187/204
T	138/162/175	188/212/229	148/126/112	**211/231/248**	153/133/119	222/244/263
S4	169/205/220	236/282/296	121/95/82	**261/306/320**	124/98/85	271/321/336
S5	219/272/272	313/372/372	90/41/41	**329/392/392**	92/44/44	343/414/414

8   Conclusion

This paper introduced non-clausal connection calculi for some popular non-classical logics. Combining the notion of prefixes with an efficient non-clausal calculus provides the foundation for an efficient proof search in these logics. The resulting *prefixed non-clausal* connection calculi can either be seen as *non-clausal* versions of prefixed *clausal* connection calculi for non-classical logics [10,14], or as extensions of the non-clausal connection calculus for classical logic [13], to which prefixes have been added.

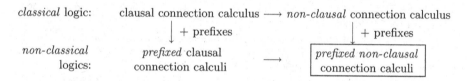

Using prefixed non-clausal matrices, the proof search works directly on the original structure of the input formula; no translation steps to any clausal or normal form are required. Hence, the presented calculi for intuitionistic and several modal logics combine the advantages of more *natural* non-clausal tableau or sequent calculi with the goal-oriented *efficiency* of a connection-based proof search.

An experimental evaluation of two compact implementations of the introduced calculi shows that the non-clausal approach does not only speed up the proof search, but that the resulting non-clausal proofs are also significantly shorter. nanoCoP-i also has a significantly higher performance than JProver [21], which uses a non-clausal connection calculus [7] that does not add clause copies dynamically during the proof search.

Future work includes the adaption of the non-clausal calculus to other non-classical logics, e.g. to those modal logics for which a (prefixed) matrix characterization exists [23] and to description logics [5], as well as the integration of additional proof search techniques, e.g. strategy scheduling and learning.

Acknowledgements. The author would like to thank Arild Waaler for his support through the Sirius Center at the University of Oslo funded by the Research Council of Norway. Furthermore, he would like to thank Wolfgang Bibel for his comments.

References

1. Beckert, B., Posegga, J.: leanTAP: lean tableau-based deduction. J. Autom. Reason. **15**(3), 339–358 (1995)
2. Bertot, Y., Castéran, P.: Interactive Theorem Proving and Program Development Coq'Art: The Calculus of Inductive Constructions. EATCS Series. Springer, Heidelberg (2004). doi:10.1007/978-3-662-07964-5
3. Bibel, W.: Automated Theorem Proving Artificial Intelligence, 2nd edn. F. Vieweg und Sohn, Wiesbaden (1987). doi:10.1007/978-3-322-90102-6
4. Constable, R.L., et al.: Implementing Mathematics with the NuPRL Proof Development System. Prentice-Hall, Englewood Cliffs (1986)
5. Freitas, F., Otten, J.: A connection calculus for the description logic $\mathcal{ALC}$. In: Khoury, R., Drummond, C. (eds.) AI 2016. LNCS, vol. 9673, pp. 243–256. Springer, Cham (2016). doi:10.1007/978-3-319-34111-8_30
6. Gentzen, G.: Untersuchungen über das Logische Schließen. Mathematische Zeitschrift **39**(176–210), 405–431 (1935)
7. Kreitz, C., Otten, J.: Connection-based theorem proving in classical and non-classical logics. J. Univ. Comput. Sci. **5**(3), 88–112 (1999)
8. Letz, R., Stenz, G.: Model elimination and connection tableau procedures. In: Robinson, A., Voronkov, A. (eds.) Handbook of Automated Reasoning, pp. 2015–2112. Elsevier Science, Amsterdam (2001)
9. Otten, J.: ileanTAP: an intuitionistic theorem prover. In: Galmiche, D. (ed.) TABLEAUX 1997. LNCS, vol. 1227, pp. 307–312. Springer, Heidelberg (1997). doi:10.1007/BFb0027422
10. Otten, J.: Clausal connection-based theorem proving in intuitionistic first-order logic. In: Beckert, B. (ed.) TABLEAUX 2005. LNCS (LNAI), vol. 3702, pp. 245–261. Springer, Heidelberg (2005). doi:10.1007/11554554_19
11. Otten, J.: leanCoP 2.0 and ileanCoP 1.2: high performance lean theorem proving in classical and intuitionistic logic (system descriptions). In: Armando, A., Baumgartner, P., Dowek, G. (eds.) IJCAR 2008. LNCS, vol. 5195, pp. 283–291. Springer, Heidelberg (2008). doi:10.1007/978-3-540-71070-7_23
12. Otten, J.: Restricting backtracking in connection calculi. AI Commun. **23**(2–3), 159–182 (2010)
13. Otten, J.: A non-clausal connection calculus. In: Brünnler, K., Metcalfe, G. (eds.) TABLEAUX 2011. LNCS (LNAI), vol. 6793, pp. 226–241. Springer, Heidelberg (2011). doi:10.1007/978-3-642-22119-4_18
14. Otten, J.: MleanCoP: a connection prover for first-order modal logic. In: Demri, S., Kapur, D., Weidenbach, C. (eds.) IJCAR 2014. LNCS (LNAI), vol. 8562, pp. 269–276. Springer, Cham (2014). doi:10.1007/978-3-319-08587-6_20
15. Otten, J.: nanoCoP: a non-clausal connection prover. In: Olivetti, N., Tiwari, A. (eds.) IJCAR 2016. LNCS (LNAI), vol. 9706, pp. 302–312. Springer, Cham (2016). doi:10.1007/978-3-319-40229-1_21
16. Otten, J., Bibel, W.: leanCoP: lean connection-based theorem proving. J. Symb. Comput. **36**(1–2), 139–161 (2003)
17. Otten, J., Bibel, W.: Advances in connection-based automated theorem proving. In: Hinchey, M.G., Bowen, J.P., Olderog, E.-R. (eds.) Provably Correct Systems. NMSSE, pp. 211–241. Springer, Cham (2017). doi:10.1007/978-3-319-48628-4_9
18. Raths, T., Otten, J.: The QMLTP problem library for first-order modal logics. In: Gramlich, B., Miller, D., Sattler, U. (eds.) IJCAR 2012. LNCS (LNAI), vol. 7364, pp. 454–461. Springer, Heidelberg (2012). doi:10.1007/978-3-642-31365-3_35

19. Raths, T., Otten, J., Kreitz, C.: The ILTP problem library for intuitionistic logic. J. Autom. Reason. **38**, 261–271 (2007)
20. Sahlin, D., Franzen, T., Haridi, S.: An intuitionistic predicate logic theorem prover. J. Logic Comput. **2**(5), 619–656 (1992)
21. Schmitt, S., Lorigo, L., Kreitz, C., Nogin, A.: JProver: integrating connection-based theorem proving into interactive proof assistants. In: Goré, R., Leitsch, A., Nipkow, T. (eds.) IJCAR 2001. LNCS, vol. 2083, pp. 421–426. Springer, Heidelberg (2001). doi:10.1007/3-540-45744-5_34
22. Waaler, A.: Connections in nonclassical logics. In: Robinson, A., Voronkov, A. (eds.) Handbook of Automated Reasoning, pp. 1487–1578. Elsevier Science, Amsterdam (2001)
23. Wallen, L.A.: Automated Deduction in Non-Classical Logics. MIT Press, Cambridge (1990)

Rule Refinement for Semantic Tableau Calculi

Dmitry Tishkovsky and Renate A. Schmidt$^{(\boxtimes)}$

School of Computer Science, The University of Manchester, Manchester, UK
Renate.Schmidt@manchester.ac.uk

Abstract. This paper investigates refinement techniques for semantic tableau calculi. The focus is on techniques to reduce branching in inference rules and thus allow more effective ways of carrying out deductions. We introduce an easy to apply, general principle of atomic rule refinement, which depends on a purely syntactic condition that can be easily verified. The refinement has a wide scope, for example, it is immediately applicable to inference rules associated with frame conditions of modal logics, or declarations of role properties in description logics, and it allows for routine development of hypertableau-like calculi for logics with disjunction and negation. The techniques are illustrated on Humberstone's modal logic $K_m(\neg)$ with modal operators defined with respect to both accessibility and inaccessibility, for which two refined calculi are given.

1 Introduction

The tableau method is a popular deduction method in automated reasoning. Tableau methods in various forms are successfully used and applied for many non-classical logics and are especially apt for new application domains to develop new deduction systems. Of all the different forms, semantic tableau calculi in the styles of Smullyan and Fitting [8,22] are widely used and widely taught in logic courses, because the rules of inference are easily explained and understood, and deductions are carried out in a completely goal-directed way. In explicit semantic tableau approaches the application of the inference rules is order independent (because these approaches are proof confluent), which avoids the overhead and complication associated with handling don't know non-determinism of non-invertible rules in direct methods [1] (see also the discussion in [13]). Because semantic tableau approaches construct and return models, they are suitable for fault diagnosis and debugging, which is useful in areas such as ontology development, theory creation and multi-agent systems.

We are interested in refinements of semantic tableau calculi that lead to improvements in carrying out deductions. When carrying out deductions by hand a natural inclination is to delay the application of branching rules as much as possible because these are cumbersome. When it can no longer be delayed, we tend to apply rules creating fewer branches earlier than those creating more branches, unless looking ahead allows us to see that several branches created

This research was supported by UK EPSRC research grant EP/H043748/1.

R.A. Schmidt and C. Nalon (Eds.): TABLEAUX 2017, LNAI 10501, pp. 228–244, 2017.
DOI: 10.1007/978-3-319-66902-1_14

by an inference step can be closed quickly. In a prover, where everything is automated, the overhead of branching is high as well, so that similar strategies are useful and have been shown to give significant speed-ups, as we found for example in the evaluations undertaken in [14,23]. Similar considerations and better performance have motivated the development and use of hypertableau, hyperresolution or selection-based resolution methods [3,4,7,16].

It is therefore natural to ask whether there are general principles, which achieve these kinds of refinements in semantic tableau calculi. In [19] we described a general condition for reducing the branching in inference rules without loosing completeness of calculi devised in the tableau synthesis framework. Because this condition is inductive, at present it needs to be checked manually and it is open whether it can be checked automatically.

In this paper we extend the possibilities of refining inference rules, thereby making progress toward the aim of automating rule refinement in the tableau synthesis framework. We describe two new approaches to satisfy the general rule refinement condition of the tableau synthesis framework. For the first approach we introduce *atomic rule refinement* as a specialisation of the general rule refinement technique with the advantage that it is syntactic and therefore automatic. This guarantees that atomic rule refinement preserves constructive completeness of a tableau calculus. In the second approach we show how to extend a set of non-refinable rules by altering the semantic specification of the logic and obtain a modified set of rules which can be refined. The approaches are illustrated on first-order frame conditions of modal logics, and a tableau calculus for the modal logic $K_m(\neg)$ of 'some', 'all' and 'only' [12]. This logic is an extension of basic multi-modal logic K_m allowing negation on accessibility relations.

The paper is structured as follows. In the next two sections we sketch the main ideas of the tableau synthesis framework [19] and two existing refinements: general rule refinement and internalisation refinement. In Sect. 4 we introduce and investigate *atomic rule refinement*, which we show preserves constructive completeness and illustrate its usefulness in several examples. In Sect. 5 we show how atomic rule refinement can be used to construct hypertableau-like calculi. In the final section we apply the presented techniques to the extended modal logic $K_m(\neg)$. The proofs may be found in the long version [24].

2   The Tableau Synthesis Framework

The tableau synthesis framework provides a method for systematically deriving a tableau calculus for a propositional logic L [19]. In the following we give a minimal description of the main ingredients, the tableau language and tableau formulae in the calculi obtained using the method.

As the generated calculi are designed to construct models, the formulae in them are expressed in a *meta-language* FO(L) that extends the *object language* $\mathcal{L}$ of the logic with extra symbols sufficient to define models and truth valuations of formulas. Consider, for example, the basic modal logic K_m with multiple modalities. The *object language* is a two-sorted language in which the formulae

$$\frac{\nu_f(\neg p, x)}{\neg \nu_f(p, x)} \quad \frac{\neg \nu_f(\neg p, x)}{\nu_f(p, x)} \quad \frac{\nu_f(p \vee q, x)}{\nu_f(p, x) \mid \nu_f(q, x)} \quad \frac{\neg \nu_f(p \vee q, x)}{\neg \nu_f(p, x), \ \neg \nu_f(q, x)} \quad \frac{\nu_f([r]p, x)}{\neg \nu_r(r, x, y) \mid \nu_f(p, y)}$$

$$\frac{\neg \nu_f([r]p, x)}{\nu_r(r, x, f(r, p, x)), \ \neg \nu_f(p, f(r, p, x))} \qquad \frac{\nu_f(p, x), \ \neg \nu_f(p, x)}{\bot} \quad \frac{\nu_r(r, x, y), \ \neg \nu_r(r, x, y)}{\bot}$$

Fig. 1. Generated tableau calculus T_{K_m} for K_m

are defined by the BNF $\phi \overset{\text{def}}{=} p \mid \neg\phi \mid \phi \vee \phi \mid [r]\phi$ in sort f, where r is a variable or constant over the second sort r. The *meta-language* extends the object language with a domain sort D (for the domain of interpretation), and two designated predicate symbols ν_f and ν_r (the holds predicates) plus the connectives of first-order logic and the equality predicate $\approx$. The language is expressive enough to define the semantics of basic modal logic K_m as follows.

$$\forall x \ (\nu_f(\neg p, x) \leftrightarrow \neg \nu_f(p, x)) \qquad \forall x \ (\nu_f(p \vee q, x) \leftrightarrow \nu_f(p, x) \vee \nu_f(q, x))$$

(1) $\forall x \ (\nu_f([r]p, x) \leftrightarrow \forall y \ (\nu_r(r, x, y) \rightarrow \nu_f(p, y)))$

Intuitively, $\nu_f(p, x)$ can be read as 'p is true in the world x' (or formally $x \in p^{\mathcal{I}}$), and $\nu_r(r, x, y)$ as 'y is an r-successor of x' (or $(x, y) \in r^{\mathcal{I}}$). Thus we can read (1) as saying: $[r]p$ is true in x iff for any r-successor y of x, p is true in y.

The stages in the tableau synthesis method are *synthesis*, *refinement* and *blocking*. The synthesis stage will transform the semantic specification of a logic such as the above into a tableau calculus T_L. The tableau calculus T_{K_m} produced for modal logic K_m is given in Fig. 1. This calculus allows reasoning in the semantics of the logic and we can use it for testing the (un)satisfiability of K_m-formulae, and for model building.

The actual creation of the tableau calculus is not important for this paper, only that we have a sound and complete semantic tableau calculus at hand. When certain well-definedness conditions are true for the semantic definition of a logic the generated tableau calculus T_L is sound and constructively complete [19]. A tableau calculus is *sound* when for a satisfiable set of tableau formulae any fully expanded tableau derivation has an open branch. A tableau calculus is *constructively complete*, if from every open fully expanded branch an interpretation can be constructed that validates all formulae on the branch. This interpretation is the *canonical interpretation* denoted by $\mathcal{I}(\mathcal{B})$.

Because the rule language and the initial calculus is heavily laden with meta-language notation, a crucial second stage in the method is the *refinement* stage. This is described in the next section. The paper is a contribution to this stage.

The third stage involves adding some form of *blocking* or *loop checking* mechanism to ensure termination or find models for finitely satisfiable input. For different modal and description logics various standard blocking mechanisms have been developed. In the tableau synthesis framework, blocking is realised by the use of equality-based blocking, which can be incorporated through additional inference rules, and is independent of the tableau calculus or the logic.

Refinements of equality reasoning and equality-based blocking in semantic tableau-like approaches have been studied in [4,14,18,21].

3 Refinement Techniques

The refinement stage of the tableau synthesis method involves two refinements: *rule refinement* and *internalisation*.

Rule refinement addresses the problem of reducing branching in inference rules by turning conclusions into premises [19]. Suppose T_L is a sound and constructively complete tableau calculus for a logic L and suppose ρ is a tableau rule in T_L. Suppose ρ has the form $\rho \stackrel{\text{def}}{=} X_0/X_1 \mid \cdots \mid X_m$, where each X_i is a set $\{\psi_1, \ldots, \psi_k\}$ of formulae. For simplicity and without loss of generality, we assume the aim is to refine away the first denominator X_1.

Let the rules ρ_j with $j = 1, \ldots, k$ be defined by

$$\rho_j \stackrel{\text{def}}{=} \frac{X_0 \cup \{\sim\psi_j\}}{X_2 \mid \cdots \mid X_m},$$

where $\sim$ denotes complementation, i.e., $\sim\phi = \psi$, if $\phi = \neg\psi$, and $\sim\phi = \neg\psi$, otherwise. Each rule ρ_j is obtained from the rule ρ by removing the first denominator X_1 and adding the complement of one of the formulae in X_1 as a premise. Intuitively, we may think of the refined rules as incorporating a look-ahead and branch closure, since when $\sim\psi_j$ is on the branch then the branch X_1 can be immediately closed. Note that there is however no guarantee that the formulae $\sim\psi_j$ are actually on the branch, even though there may be enough information so that $\mathcal{I}(\mathcal{B}) \not\models \psi_j$ and thus $\mathcal{I}(\mathcal{B}) \not\models X_1$ for particular instances, where $\mathcal{I}(\mathcal{B})$ is the canonical interpretation associated with the current (partial) branch $\mathcal{B}$. We say a branch $\mathcal{B}$ is *reflected* in the canonical interpretation $\mathcal{I}(\mathcal{B})$, if $\mathcal{I}(\mathcal{B})$ validates all formulae occurring on the branch $\mathcal{B}$.

Let $\text{Ref}(\rho, T_L)$ denote the *refined tableau calculus* obtained from T_L by replacing the rule ρ with the rules $\rho_1, \ldots, \rho_k$. We say that $\text{Ref}(\rho, T_L)$ is the *(ρ-)rule refinement* of T_L. One can show that each rule ρ_j is derivable [10] in T_L and this implies that the calculus $\text{Ref}(\rho, T_L)$ is sound. In general, $\text{Ref}(\rho, T_L)$ is neither constructively complete nor complete. Nevertheless, the following theorem holds [19].

Theorem 1. *Let T_L be a tableau calculus which is sound and constructively complete for the logic L. Let ρ be the rule $X_0/X_1 \mid \cdots \mid X_m$ in T_L and suppose $\text{Ref}(\rho, T_L)$ is the rule refinement of T_L. Further, suppose $\mathcal{B}$ is an open branch in a $\text{Ref}(\rho, T_L)$-tableau derivation and for every set Y of $\mathcal{L}$-formulae from $\mathcal{B}$ the following holds. Then, $\mathcal{B}$ is reflected in the interpretation $\mathcal{I}(\mathcal{B})$ induced by $\mathcal{B}$.*

General Rule Refinement Condition: *If all formulae in Y are reflected in $\mathcal{I}(\mathcal{B})$ then for any $E_1, \ldots, E_l \in Y$ and any domain terms $t_1, \ldots, t_n$,*

$$\text{if } X_0(\overline{E}, t_1, \ldots, t_n) \subseteq \mathcal{B} \text{ and } \mathcal{I}(\mathcal{B}) \not\models X_1(\overline{E}, \|t_1\|, \ldots, \|t_n\|)$$
$$\text{then } X_i(\overline{E}, t_1, \ldots, t_n) \subseteq \mathcal{B} \text{ for some } i = 2, \ldots, m.$$

$X_i(\overline{E}, t_1, \ldots, t_n)$ denotes the set of instances of the formulae in X_i under uniform substitution of $E_1, \ldots, E_l$ and $t_1, \ldots, t_n$ for $p_1, \ldots, p_l$ and $x_1, \ldots, x_n$, respectively, where $p_1, \ldots, p_l$ and $x_1, \ldots, x_n$ are respectively all the $\mathcal{L}$-variables and all the domain variables occurring in the rule ρ. The notation $\|t_i\|$ denotes the equivalence classes of terms modulo the equational theory defined by the term equalities encountered on the branch.

The general rule refinement condition states that if there is information in the branch $\mathcal{B}$ to exclude $X_1(\overline{E}, t_1, \ldots, t_n)$ from holding in the model $\mathcal{I}(\mathcal{B})$ constructed from $\mathcal{B}$ then all the formulae of at least one of the other denominators of the rule are on the branch $\mathcal{B}$. In [19] a weaker condition for rule refinement is given,[1] but the condition of Theorem 1 is sufficient for the results of this paper. A consequence of the theorem is the following.

Corollary 1. *If the general rule refinement condition of Theorem 1 holds for every open branch $\mathcal{B}$ of any fully expanded $\mathsf{Ref}(\rho, T_L)$-tableau then the refined calculus $\mathsf{Ref}(\rho, T_L)$ is constructively complete for the logic L.*

The generalisation of this refinement which turns more than one denominator of a rule into premises is not difficult.

As an example of rule refinement let us consider the (box) rule obtained from (1) in the tableau synthesis framework. Rule refinement gives (something close to) the usual box rule ($\Box$).

$$(\mathsf{box})\ \frac{\nu_f([r]p, x)}{\neg\nu_r(r, x, y)\ |\ \nu_f(p, y)} \qquad (\Box)\ \frac{\nu_f([r]p, x),\ \nu_r(r, x, y)}{\nu_f(p, y)}$$

It can be proved directly that the general rule refinement condition is true in any branch of the refined calculus $\mathsf{Ref}((\mathsf{box}), T_{K_m})$ of the generated calculus T_{K_m} of basic modal logic K_m. By Corollary 1 the refined calculus is therefore constructively complete.

Theorem 2. *The tableau calculus $\mathsf{Ref}((\mathsf{box}), T_{K_m})$ is sound and constructively complete for basic multi-modal logic K_m.*

In Sect. 6 we give an example where this rule refinement is not possible in an extension of the logic K_m. In fact, the general rule refinement condition is too strong to hold generally, because tableau calculi do not include introduction rules (just elimination rules), but we give examples in Sects. 4 and 6 where the refinement condition does hold.

Internalisation refinement in the tableau synthesis process involves eliminating some of the extra-logical notation, by expressing the rules in a tableau language as close as possible to the language of the logic. In particular, the internalisation involves reduction of the calculus to one where the holds predicates ν_s have been eliminated and the domain sort symbols are expressed in the language of the logic, provided this is possible. The idea is that each atomic

---

[1]   The general rule refinement condition given here corresponds to condition ($\ddagger$) in [19].

$$\frac{@_i p, \ @_i \neg p}{\bot} \qquad \frac{@_i \neg\neg p}{@_i p} \qquad \frac{@_i(p \lor q)}{@_i p \mid @_i q} \qquad \frac{@_i \neg(p \lor q)}{@_i \neg p, \ @_i \neg q}$$

$$\frac{@_i[r]p, \ @_i \neg[r]\neg j}{@_j p} \qquad \frac{@_i \neg[r]p}{@_i \neg[r]\neg f(r,p,i), \ @_{f(r,p,i)} \neg p}$$

Fig. 2. Refined tableau calculus $T_{K_m}^{\mathrm{ref}}$.

formula $\nu_s(E, \bar{a})$ in the tableau calculus is replaced by a suitable formula of the logic, and all syntactically redundant rules are removed from the calculus.

For example, if the logic L contains nominals and the @ connective of hybrid logic [5] then the elements of the domain sort D can be identified with nominals and the formulae $\nu_f(\phi, v)$ and $\nu_r(\alpha, v, w)$ can be internalised as the formulae $@_v \phi$ and $@_v \neg[\alpha] \neg w$ respectively, where v and w have become nominals. The refined and internalised calculus for basic modal logic K_m is given in Fig. 2.

If the logic is not expressive enough then an option is to simplify the notation of the rules by reformulating them using labels and the ':' connective (of varying arity), to rephrase the rules in notation more familiar from the literature (alternative notations also exist).

The internalisation refinement simplifies the tableau language and, in many cases, reduces the number of the rules in the tableau calculus. In our experience it is easiest and produces better results, if rule refinement is performed first, followed by the internalisation refinement.

4   Atomic Rule Refinement

In this section we introduce the technique of *atomic rule refinement*. Under this refinement, formulae in the conclusions are only moved upwards to premise positions if *the formulae are negated $\mathcal{L}$-atomic formulae* in the language FO(L).

By definition, a FO(L)-formula ϕ is $\mathcal{L}$-*atomic* if it is an atomic formula of FO(L) and all occurrences of $\mathcal{L}$-formulae in ϕ are also atomic. Thus, $\nu_s(E, \bar{t})$ is $\mathcal{L}$-atomic only if E is an atomic formula of $\mathcal{L}^s$. For example, the formulae $\nu_f(p, x)$ and $\nu_r(r, f(r, p, x), x)$ are $\mathcal{L}(K_m)$-atomic, but the formulae $\neg \nu_f(p, x)$, $\nu_f(\neg p, x)$ and $\nu_f(p \lor q, x)$ are not. The respective reasons are that $\neg \nu_f(p, x)$ is a negated $\mathcal{L}(K_m)$-atomic formula and $\nu_f(\neg p, x)$ and $\nu_f(p \lor q, x)$ are not $\mathcal{L}$-atomic in FO(K_m).

Using the notation and assumptions of Theorem 1, we can prove:

Theorem 3. *Assume that for an open branch $\mathcal{B}$ of the refined tableau calculus* Ref(ρ, T_L) *and for every set Y of $\mathcal{L}$-formulae from $\mathcal{B}$ the following holds. Then, $\mathcal{B}$ is reflected in $\mathcal{I}(\mathcal{B})$.*

Atomic Rule Refinement Condition: *If all formulae in Y are reflected in $\mathcal{I}(\mathcal{B})$ then for any $E_1, \ldots, E_l \in Y$ and any domain terms $t_1, \ldots, t_n$,*

$$X_0(\overline{E}, t_1, \ldots, t_n) \subseteq \mathcal{B} \text{ implies that}$$
$$X_1(\overline{E}, t_1, \ldots, t_n) = \{\neg \xi_1, \ldots, \neg \xi_k\} \text{ and all } \xi_1, \ldots, \xi_k \text{ are } \mathcal{L}\text{-atomic.}$$

Unlike the general rule refinement condition, the atomic rule refinement condition is purely syntactic and, thus, can be automatically checked against each given open branch $\mathcal{B}$. However, even if all the formulae from X_1 are negated $\mathcal{L}$-atomic formulae, their instantiation within a branch of a tableau derivation can, in general, produce a formula which is not a negated $\mathcal{L}$-atom. Therefore, similar to Corollary 1, by Theorem 3, in order to preserve constructive completeness we need to make sure that the atomic rule refinement condition holds for every branch of any derivation in the refined calculus.

Corollary 2. *If the assumptions and condition of Theorem 3 holds for every open branch $\mathcal{B}$ of any fully expanded $\mathsf{Ref}(\rho, T_L)$-tableau then the refined calculus $\mathsf{Ref}(\rho, T_L)$ is constructively complete for the logic L.*

In the following we give several examples of atomic rule refinement.

Example 1. The refinement ($\Box$) of the rule (box) mentioned in the previous section is an example of an atomic rule refinement. Because any instantiation of $\nu_r(r, x, y)$ in the language of K_m is an $\mathcal{L}(K_m)$-atomic formula, constructive completeness of the refined calculus $\mathsf{Ref}((\mathsf{box}), T_{K_m})$ follows from Corollary 2.

Example 2. Suppose we wish to impose that *one* accessibility relation r of our modal logic is irreflexive, i.e., we specify that $\forall x \,\neg\nu_r(r, x, x)$. This generates the rule $/\neg\nu_r(r, x, x)$.[2] Using atomic rule refinement the rule can be refined to the following closure rule

$$(\mathsf{irr}) \; \frac{\nu_r(r, x, x)}{\bot}, \qquad \text{or in internalised form the rule} \qquad \frac{@_i\neg[r]\neg i}{\bot} \; .$$

Example 3. If we wish to specify that *all* relations are irreflexive, atomic rule refinement allows us to use the rule $\nu_r(r, x, x)/\bot$. Because the language of K_m contains only atomic relations $r_1, \ldots, r_m$ and no relational connectives, any instantiation of r and variable x in $\nu_r(r, x, x)$ produces only $\mathcal{L}(K_m)$-atomic formulae of the form $\nu_r(r_i, t, t)$ (where t is a term of the domain sort). Therefore, the atomic rule refinement condition is true for any branch of any tableau derivation in the calculus $\mathsf{Ref}((\mathsf{box}), T_{K_m})$ extended with the (irr) rule. Thus, by Corollary 2, the calculus $\mathsf{Ref}((\mathsf{box}), T_{K_m})$ extended with the (irr) rule is sound and constructively complete for the logic K_m with irreflexive relations.

Applying the internalisation refinement we obtain the following theorem for the labelled tableau calculus.

Theorem 4. *$T_{K_m}^{ref}$ extended with the rule $@_i\neg[r]\neg i/\bot$ for each irreflexive relation r in K_m is sound and constructively complete (or, where r denotes a variable, for the case that each relation in the logic is irreflexive).*

---

[2] In the framework the rule would have a premise involving domain predication, but in this paper we silently assume domain predication without making it explicit in the interest of simplicity of presentation, see [19] for details.

Example 4. The following frame condition from [2] states the *existence of an immediate predecessor* for every element in a model.

$$\forall x \exists y \forall z \Big(\nu_r(r,y,x) \wedge x \not\approx y \wedge \big((\nu_r(r,y,z) \wedge \nu_r(r,z,x)) \rightarrow (z \approx x \vee z \approx y) \big) \Big)$$

We first reduce the formula to a form acceptable in the tableau synthesis framework. Let g be a new Skolem function which depends on two arguments, one of the sort r and one from the domain sort. The existential quantifier is eliminated from the frame conditions and decomposed to give three formulae (see [19]):

$$\forall x \; \nu_r(r, g(r,x), x), \qquad \forall x \; (x \not\approx g(r,x)),$$

$$\forall x \forall z \; \big((\nu_r(r, g(r,x), z) \wedge \nu_r(r, z, x)) \rightarrow (g(r,x) \approx z \vee z \approx x) \big).$$

From these formulae three rules are generated:

$$\frac{}{\nu_r(r, g(r,x), x)}, \qquad \frac{}{x \not\approx g(r,x)},$$

$$\frac{}{\neg \nu_r(r, g(r,x), z) \mid \neg \nu_r(r, z, x) \mid g(r,x) \approx z \mid z \approx x}.$$

Atomic rule refinement is not applicable to the first rule since the conclusion is not negated. Consider the second and third rules. Applying the same argument as in Example 3 above we find that no instantiation of $x \approx g(r,x)$, $\nu_r(r, g(r,x), z)$, and $\nu_r(r, z, x)$ within the language $\mathsf{FO}(\mathrm{K}_m)$ produces a formula which is not $\mathcal{L}(\mathrm{K}_m)$-atomic. This means the atomic rule refinement condition holds for these rules. Refining the second rule once and the third rule twice, the rules

$$\frac{x \approx g(r,x)}{\bot} \qquad \text{and} \qquad \frac{\nu_r(r, g(r,x), z), \; \nu_r(r, z, x)}{g(r,x) \approx z \mid z \approx x}$$

are obtained. By Corollary 2, constructive completeness of any tableau calculus in the language $\mathsf{FO}(\mathrm{K}_m)$ is preserved under these refinements. Internalising $\mathsf{FO}(\mathrm{K}_m)$ in the hybrid logic extension of K_m we obtain the following theorem.

Theorem 5. $T^{ref}_{\mathrm{K}_m}$ *extended with the rules*

$$\frac{}{@_{g(r,i)} \neg[r]\neg i}, \qquad \frac{@_i g(r,i)}{\bot} \qquad \text{and} \qquad \frac{@_{g(r,i)} \neg[r]\neg j, \; @_j \neg[r]\neg i}{@_{g(r,i)} j \mid @_j i}$$

is sound and constructively complete for K_m over the class of models satisfying the frame condition of existence of an immediate predecessor.

The use of Skolem terms is not in agreement with common, present practice in the area, but they provide a useful technical device to enhance the scope of semantic tableau approaches by accommodating properties and specifications with negative occurrences of existential quantification, which produce rules where these occurrences appear in premise positions, cf. Example 4. This easily accommodates non-geometric theories. Skolem terms also allow for effective implementation of blocking and equality reasoning, since, e.g., no inference steps need to be recomputed when blocking occurs (cf. the comments in [14]).

Examples 3 and 4 are important because they show that atomic rule refinement allows *automatic refinement of tableau rules generated from frame conditions of modal logics.* Furthermore, the case of the last rule in Example 4 is a particularly clear illustration of the benefits of rule refinement. In that case the unrefined rule is applicable for every pair of domain elements and creates four branches on application, whereas the refined rule replacing it, is only applied to formulae matching two premises, and then creates only two branches. This *constraining effect on the search space* is an important benefit of rule refinement. In general, using the fairness requirements for tableau derivations, it is possible to map each refined derivation to its unrefined counterpart where each rule application is either mapped to itself or to the application of the corresponding unrefined rule. Since more premises need to be satisfied, the refined rule will be applied less often and each of its applications produces fewer branches than the corresponding point of the unrefined tableau. Thus, each refined derivation (in other words, the search space) is smaller than its unrefined counterpart.

Another important point is the *incrementality* of the technique: the rules can be refined one by one without affecting the refinability of other rules. It is therefore *more flexible, robust* and *useful* than general rule refinement, of which it is a special case.

Because of these attractive features we have used atomic rule refinement in other recent work. In [23] we applied the tableau synthesis framework and atomic rule refinement in the creation of terminating tableau calculi for a bi-intuitionistic logic with interacting modal operators, called BISKT. This logic can be equivalently embedded into a tense logic $Kt(H, R)$ with several interacting modalities [18] via an extension of the standard embedding of intuitionistic propositional logic into modal logic S4. $Kt(H, R)$ was subject to an investigation of the numerous possibilities of defining tableau calculi for modal logics, and their relative efficiency [18]. Interestingly, we found that the tableau calculi of BISKT [23] exhibited better performance than those of $Kt(H, R)$ [18], which we attribute to the greater constraining power of atomic rule refinement in the style of calculus used for BISKT.

In [14] we used atomic rule refinement to obtain a tableau calculus with dynamically generated hypertableau-like inference rules for description logic ontologies. In particular, the standard inference rule $/@_i\alpha$ for TBox statements α, which hold universally, is replaced by a set of refined rules for each statement in the TBox. E.g., for the statement $A_1 \sqcap A_2 \sqsubseteq B$ the specifically generated rule is $@_i A_1, @_i A_2/@_i B$, where A_1, A_2, B are atomic concepts. For satisfiable and unsatisfiable inputs, the evaluation results showed improved performance for this refinement. The speed-up was particularly marked for unsatisfiable inputs (2.5–6 times faster on average), which was found to be mainly due to the presence of additional closure rules such as $@_i A, @_i B/\bot$ generated from the disjointness statement $A \sqcap B \sqsubseteq \bot$, where A and B are atomic concepts. The results also showed a 22% (and 74%) drop in memory use for satisfiable (and unsatisfiable) inputs when using refined rules. The essential idea in this work is generalised in the next section.

5 Hypertableau

Let the given logic $\tilde{L}$ have disjunction-like connectives $\vee$ and negation-like connectives $\neg$ for some sort s of the logic. Assume T_L is a tableau calculus sound and constructively complete for L and contains the rules

$$\frac{\nu_s(p \vee q, \overline{x})}{\nu_s(p, \overline{x}) \mid \nu_s(q, \overline{x})} \quad \text{and} \quad \frac{\nu_s(\neg p, \overline{x})}{\neg \nu_s(p, \overline{x})},$$

which are the usual rules for disjunction and negation. We transform the synthesised calculus T_L into a new calculus T_L^{hyp} in three steps. For simplicity we assume that disjunction in L is associative and commutative with respect to satisfiability, that is, the following statements are entailed by the semantic specification of L.

$$\nu_s(p \vee q, \overline{x}) \leftrightarrow \nu_s(q \vee p, \overline{x}) \qquad \nu_s((p \vee q) \vee r, \overline{x}) \leftrightarrow \nu_s(p \vee (q \vee r), \overline{x})$$

This assumption is not essential for the transformation but allows us to flatten disjunctions and avoid a combinatorial blow-up.

In the first step of the transformation, the usual disjunction rule $\nu_s(p \vee q, \overline{x}) / \nu_s(p, \overline{x}) \mid \nu_s(q, \overline{x})$ is replaced by the set of the rules (for $k > 1$):

$$(\mathsf{split}_k) \quad \frac{\nu_s(p_1 \vee \cdots \vee p_k, \overline{x})}{\nu_s(p_1, \overline{x}) \mid \cdots \mid \nu_s(p_k, \overline{x})} \quad.$$

We denote by T_L^{sp} a tableau calculus obtained from T_L by replacing the usual disjunction rule by the rules (split_k). The (split_k) rules and the usual disjunction rule are derivable from each other. Therefore, the transformed calculus T_L^{sp} is sound and constructively complete.

For the second step consider the following rules (for $m + n > 1$)

$$(\mathsf{split}_{mn}^+) \quad \frac{\nu_s(\neg p_1 \vee \cdots \vee \neg p_m \vee q_1 \vee \cdots \vee q_n, \overline{x})}{\neg \nu_s(p_1, \overline{x}) \mid \cdots \mid \neg \nu_s(p_m, \overline{x}) \mid \nu_s(q_1, \overline{x}) \mid \cdots \mid \nu_s(q_n, \overline{x})}$$

with the side-condition that only atomic substitutions are allowed for $p_1, \ldots, p_m$. Note, m is the maximal number of negated atoms in the disjunction which match the premise. That is, the rules are applicable only to formulae of the shape $\nu_s(\neg E_1 \vee \cdots \vee \neg E_m \vee F_1 \vee \cdots \vee F_n, \overline{x})$, where all $E_1, \ldots, E_m$ are $atomic$ formulae of the logic L and no $F_1, \ldots, F_n$ is a negated atomic formula of L.

Let $T_L^{\mathsf{sp}+}$ be a tableau calculus obtained from T_L^{sp} by replacing the rules (split_k) by the rules (split_{mn}^+). The rules (split_k) and (split_{mn}^+) are derivable from each other and, thus, the following theorem holds.

Theorem 6. $T_L^{\mathsf{sp}+}$ *is sound and constructively complete for the logic* L.

Now we are in a position to use atomic rule refinement to refine the rules (split_{mn}^+) to the rules ($m + n > 1$)

$$(\text{hyp}_{mn}) \quad \frac{\nu_{\mathsf{s}}(\neg p_1 \vee \cdots \vee \neg p_m \vee q_1 \vee \cdots \vee q_n, \overline{x}), \ \nu_{\mathsf{s}}(p_1, \overline{x}), \ \cdots, \ \nu_{\mathsf{s}}(p_m, \overline{x})}{\nu_{\mathsf{s}}(q_1, \overline{x}) \mid \cdots \mid \nu_{\mathsf{s}}(q_n, \overline{x})}$$

with the restriction that only atomic substitutions are allowed for $p_1, \ldots, p_m$. These are hypertableau-like rules. Similarly to the rules in the previous step, an application of the rule (hyp_{mn}) is allowed only to formulae of the shape $\nu_{\mathsf{s}}(\neg E_1 \vee \cdots \vee \neg E_m \vee F_1 \vee \cdots \vee F_n)$, where all $E_1, \ldots, E_m$ are atomic formulae and no $F_1, \ldots, F_n$ are negated atomic formulae of the logic L. Notice that in the case of $n = 0$ the rules (hyp_{mn}) are atomic closure rules.

Let T_L^{hyp} be the calculus obtained from T_L^{sp} by adding the (hyp_{mn}) rules. By Corollary 2 and Theorem 6 we obtain constructive completeness of T_L^{hyp}.

Theorem 7. *T_L^{hyp} is sound and constructively complete for the logic L.*

Thus, for any (propositional) logic L with disjunction and negation connectives and any sound and constructive complete calculus for L with the usual disjunction and negation rules, it is possible to devise a hypertableau-like calculus that is sound and constructively complete for the logic L.

Derivations in T_L^{hyp} can be done more efficiently if the logic L has additional properties. We already assume associativity and commutativity of disjunction. Suppose now that the satisfiability of formulae in a subset of the language $\mathcal{L}$ is reducible to the satisfiability of formulae in conjunctive normal form:

$$\nu_{\mathsf{s}}(E, \overline{x}) \leftrightarrow \bigwedge_{i=1}^{I} \nu_{\mathsf{s}_{ij}} \left(\bigvee_{j=1}^{J_i} E_{ij}, \overline{x} \right) \qquad \text{where } \mathsf{s} \text{ and } \mathsf{s}_{ij} \text{ are sorts of the logic.}$$

Thus, every formula E has an equi-satisfiable clausal representation as a set of clauses $C_1, \ldots, C_I$, where $C_i = E_{i1} \vee \cdots \vee E_{iJ_i}$ for each $i = 1, \ldots, I$. Since disjunction is associative and commutative, we can assume that, in every clause, all negated atomic formulae (negative literals) of the logic appear before all other formulae. Let $\mathcal{A}$ be a reduction algorithm which transforms any formula E into such equi-satisfiable clausal normal form.

Cases of logics become interesting when there are many clauses with negated atomic formulae, because then the (hyp_{mn}) rules with $m > 0$ are applied more frequently in derivations in T_L^{hyp}. Since the (hyp_{mn}) rules with $m > 0$ create fewer branching points in derivations than the (hyp_{mn}) rules with $m = 0$, derivations in T_L^{hyp} will have fewer branches and therefore performance is enhanced.

The conclusions of the (hyp_{mn}) rules are allowed to contain non-atomic $\mathcal{L}$-formulae which have to be decomposed further by other rules of the calculus. For the conclusions of other rules, we have two alternatives. One is to use the rules of the tableau calculus to decompose their formulae up to atomic components. The other alternative is to apply the reduction algorithm $\mathcal{A}$ to every new conclusion of any rule different from the (hyp_{mn}) rules. The first alternative uses the decomposition rules of the tableau calculus (assuming it includes rules for conjunction and disjunction) and the second one uses the algorithm $\mathcal{A}$. In the implementation of a prover these two alternatives have to be carefully balanced, depending on the complexity of the algorithm $\mathcal{A}$ and how efficiently it is implemented. There is an efficient clausification algorithm for Boolean parts which runs in polynomial time on the length of the input [17]. Thus, we can assume that every conclusion of a rule is immediately transformed into a set of clauses. This allows to omit all the rules for Boolean connectives except the hypertableau rules. We give an example of a hypertableau-style calculus in the next section.

6   Case Study: The Modal Logic of 'Some', 'All' and 'Only'

As an illustration of the usefulness and generality of the refinement techniques investigated in this paper, we apply them to the modal logic $K_m(\neg)$ of 'some', 'all' and 'only' [12]. $K_m(\neg)$ is the extension of the basic multi-modal logic K_m with the relational negation.

Following the tableau synthesis framework [19] the language $\mathcal{L}$ has two sorts: a sort f for formulae and a sort r for relations. Assuming the sort r is formed over a set of relational constants $\{a_1, \ldots, a_m\}$, in $\mathcal{L}$ every *relation* α is defined by the BNF $\alpha \stackrel{\text{def}}{=} a_1 \mid \cdots \mid a_m \mid \neg\alpha$, where $\neg$ is a relational connective. The sort f is formed over a set of propositional variables $\{p, q, \ldots\}$ and every *formula* ϕ is defined by the BNF $\phi \stackrel{\text{def}}{=} p \mid \neg\phi \mid \phi \vee \phi \mid [\alpha]\phi$, where α ranges over all relations in the language.

The semantic specification language $FO(K_m(\neg))$ for $K_m(\neg)$ is a first-order language over the sorts f and r and an additional *domain sort* D. Formulae of $\mathcal{L}$ are encoded in the obvious way as terms of the appropriate sorts in $FO(K_m(\neg))$. That is, every logical connective of $\mathcal{L}$ is represented by a function in $FO(K_m(\neg))$. Every propositional variable of $\mathcal{L}$ is an individual variable of the sort f in $FO(K_m(\neg))$. Besides the individual constants $a_1, \ldots, a_m$ for relations, the language $FO(K_m(\neg))$ has a countable set of relation variables $r, r', \ldots$. The additional sort D has a countable set of individual variables $x, y, z, \ldots$. Furthermore, the semantic specification language has two predicate symbols ν_f and ν_r of sort (f, D) and (r, D, D), respectively, to encode satisfiability. The meaning of these symbols can be understood from the definitions given next. The semantic specification consists of the following formulae, one for each of the logical connectives of $K_m(\neg)$.

$$\forall x \, (\nu_f(\neg p, x) \leftrightarrow \neg\nu_f(p, x)) \qquad \forall x \, (\nu_f(p \vee q, x) \leftrightarrow \nu_f(p, x) \vee \nu_f(q, x))$$
$$\forall x \forall y \, (\nu_r(\neg r, x, y) \leftrightarrow \neg\nu_r(r, x, y)) \qquad \forall x \, (\nu_f([r]p, x) \leftrightarrow \forall y \, (\nu_r(r, x, y) \rightarrow \nu_f(p, y)))$$

Compared to the specification of K_m, the specification of $K_m(\neg)$ is extended with the second clause in the left column, which defines relational negation.

The logic $K_m(\neg)$ is interesting because of the presence of three quantifier operators. These are the necessity operator $[\alpha]$, the possibility operator $\neg[\alpha]\neg$ and a third operator, the sufficiency operator $[\neg\alpha]\neg$, sometimes referred to as the window operator. $\nu_f([\alpha]\phi, v)$ can be read as saying 'ϕ is true in *all* α-successors',

$$\frac{\nu_f(\neg p, x)}{\neg \nu_f(p, x)} \qquad \frac{\neg \nu_f(\neg p, x)}{\nu_f(p, x)} \qquad \frac{\nu_f(p \vee q, x)}{\nu_f(p, x) \mid \nu_f(q, x)} \qquad \frac{\neg \nu_f(p \vee q, x)}{\neg \nu_f(p, x), \ \neg \nu_f(q, x)}$$

$$\frac{\nu_f([r]p, x)}{\neg \nu_r(r, x, y) \mid \nu_f(p, y)} \qquad \frac{\neg \nu_f([r]p, x)}{\nu_r(r, x, f(r, p, x)), \ \neg \nu_f(p, f(r, p, x))}$$

$$\frac{\nu_f(p, x), \ \neg \nu_f(p, x)}{\bot} \qquad \frac{\nu_r(r, x, y), \ \neg \nu_r(r, x, y)}{\bot} \qquad \frac{\nu_r(\neg r, x, y)}{\neg \nu_r(r, x, y)} \qquad \frac{\neg \nu_r(\neg r, x, y)}{\nu_r(r, x, y)}$$

Fig. 3. Generated tableau calculus $T_{K_m(\neg)}$ for $K_m(\neg)$

$\nu_f(\neg[\alpha]\neg\phi, v)$ as 'ϕ is true in *some* α-successor', and $\nu_f([\neg\alpha]\neg\phi, v)$ as 'ϕ is true in *only* α-successors of v'. $K_m(\neg)$ is a sublogic of Boolean modal logic [9] and the description logics $\mathcal{ALBO}$ and $\mathcal{ALBO}^{id}$ [20]. $K_m(\neg)$ has the finite model property [9] but the tree model property fails for the logic (e.g. [15]). The results of [15] imply that the satisfiability problem in $K_m(\neg)$ is ExpTime-complete.

The tableau calculus $T_{K_m(\neg)}$ obtained from the semantic specification of $K_m(\neg)$ in the tableau synthesis framework is given in Fig. 3. New compared to the generated tableau calculus for the basic modal logic K_m in Fig. 1 are the last two rules for relational negation. Because the semantic specification of $K_m(\neg)$ is well-defined in the sense of [19], from Theorems 5.1 and 5.6 in that work, we immediately obtain the following result.

Theorem 8 (Soundness and constructive completeness). *The calculus* $T_{K_m(\neg)}$ *is sound and constructively complete for the logic* $K_m(\neg)$.

However, none of the rules of the tableau calculus for $K_m(\neg)$ from Fig. 3 are refinable. In particular, the (box) rule cannot be refined to the ($\square$) rule (as discussed in Sect. 4) without loosing constructive completeness. Take for instance the set of formulae $\{\nu_f([\neg\neg r]p, a), \nu_r(r, a, b), \neg\nu_f(p, b)\}$. The set is not $K_m(\neg)$-satisfiable but none of the rules of the refined calculus $\mathsf{Ref}((\mathsf{box}), T_{K_m(\neg)})$ are applicable to the set.

A possibility for refinement is the atomic refinement of *instances* of rules. Atomic rule refinement would allow us to use the rule ($\square$) on formulae $[r]\phi$, where r is bound to a relational constant. We would still need to use the rule (box) when r is bound to a complex relational formula (in this case a negated relational formula). This kind of refinement is generally possible, and will be useful in practice, but leads to an uneven treatment of box formulae. Better would be if all instances of a rule can be refined.

In fact, by a small amendment of the semantic specification it *is* possible to refine the (box) rule generally, for *all* instances. Observe that the semantic specification of $K_m(\neg)$ entails the following formula.

$$\forall x \, (\nu_f([\neg r]p, x) \rightarrow \forall y \, (\neg \nu_r(r, x, y) \rightarrow \nu_f(p, y)))$$

This means the formula can be added to the semantic specification of $K_m(\neg)$ without changing the class of models of the logic. We use the notation $T^+_{K_m(\neg)}$ to

$$\frac{@_ip,\ @_i\neg p}{\bot} \qquad \frac{@_i\neg\neg p}{@_ip} \qquad \frac{@_i(p \vee q)}{@_ip \mid @_iq} \qquad \frac{@_i\neg(p \vee q)}{@_i\neg p,\ @_i\neg q} \qquad \frac{@_i[r]p,\ @_i\neg[r]\neg j}{@_jp}$$

$$\frac{@_i\neg[r]p}{@_i\neg[r]\neg f(r,p,i),\ @_{f(r,p,i)}\neg p} \qquad \frac{@_i\neg[\neg r]\neg j}{@_i[r]\neg j} \qquad \frac{@_i[\neg r]\neg j}{@_i\neg[r]\neg j} \qquad \frac{@_i[\neg r]p}{@_i\neg[r]\neg j \mid @_jp}$$

Fig. 4. Refined tableau calculus $T_{K_m(\neg)}^{\text{ref}}$.

refer to the tableau calculus generated from the semantic specification extended with this formula. $T_{K_m(\neg)}^{+}$ consists of the rules listed in Fig. 3 and the rule:

$$([\neg]) \quad \frac{\nu_f([\neg r]p, x)}{\nu_r(r, x, y) \mid \nu_f(p, y)} \ .$$

We can check that the well-definedness conditions from [19] are satisfied for the extended semantic specification of $K_m(\neg)$. Therefore, by the results of the tableau synthesis framework, the extended calculus $T_{K_m(\neg)}^{+}$ is sound and constructively complete for $K_m(\neg)$. Note, the rule $([\neg])$ is a derived rule in the calculus $T_{K_m(\neg)}$.

While the rule $([\neg])$ neither satisfies the atomic nor the general rule refinement condition, the *general* rule refinement condition is now satisfied for the (box) rule, and, thus, as a consequence of Corollary 1 we get:

Theorem 9. *The tableau calculus* $\text{Ref}((\text{box}), T_{K_m(\neg)}^{+})$ *using the* $(\square)$ *rule instead of the* (box) *rule is sound and constructively complete for the logic* $K_m(\neg)$.

The internalisation refinement is possible for the new calculus if nominals and the @ operator of hybrid logic [5] are introduced to the tableau language of $K_m(\neg)$. This significantly strengthens the tableau language and allows all formulae $\nu_f(\phi, a)$ and $\neg\nu_f(\phi, a)$ to be replaced by the formulae $@_a\phi$ and $@_a\neg\phi$, respectively, and the formulae $\nu_r(\alpha, a, b)$ and $\neg\nu_r(\alpha, a, b)$ can be replaced respectively by the formulae $@_a\neg[\alpha]\neg b$ and $@_a[\alpha]\neg b$ (the latter is equivalent to $@_a\neg\langle\alpha\rangle b$). In this case the result of the refinement is a significantly simplified calculus, reminiscent of standard labelled tableau calculi. The obtained rules are listed in Fig. 4. We denote this calculus by $T_{K_m(\neg)}^{\text{ref}}$. By the results of this paper and [19] it is sound and constructively complete for $K_m(\neg)$.

Because disjunction and negation in $K_m(\neg)$ are Boolean, it is possible to devise a hypertableau calculus for $K_m(\neg)$, see Fig. 5. By Theorem 7, this calculus is sound and constructively complete for $K_m(\neg)$. In summary, we have:

Theorem 10. *The refined tableau calculi* $T_{K_m(\neg)}^{\text{ref}}$ *and* $T_{K_m(\neg)}^{\text{hyp}}$ *(of Figs. 4 and 5) are sound and constructively complete for the logic* $K_m(\neg)$.

A further example of systematic rule refinement using the ideas of this paper is the description logic $\mathcal{ALBO}^{\text{id}}$, for which we presented a tableau calculus in [20]. $\mathcal{ALBO}^{\text{id}}$ is an extension of the description logic $\mathcal{ALC}$ with individuals, the inverse

$$\dfrac{@_i\neg p_1 \vee \cdots \vee \neg p_m \vee q_1 \vee \cdots \vee q_n, \ @_i p_1, \ \ldots, \ @_i p_m}{@_i q_1 \ | \ \cdots \ | \ @_i q_n} \left(\begin{array}{c} m+n > 1 \\ p_1, \ldots, p_m \text{ are atomic} \end{array} \right)$$

$$\dfrac{@_i p, \ @_i \neg p}{\bot} \qquad \dfrac{@_i [r]p, \ @_i \neg[r]\neg j}{@_j p} \qquad \dfrac{@_i \neg[r]p}{@_i \neg[r]\neg f(r,p,i), \ @_{f(r,p,i)} \neg p}$$

$$\dfrac{@_i \neg[\neg r]\neg j}{@_i [r]\neg j} \qquad \dfrac{@_i [\neg r]\neg j}{@_i \neg[r]\neg j} \qquad \dfrac{@_i [\neg r]p}{@_i \neg[r]\neg j \ | \ @_j p}$$

Fig. 5. Hybrid hypertableau calculus $T^{\text{hyp}}_{K_m(\neg)}$ for $K_m(\neg)$

role (relation) connective, Boolean connectives on roles and the identity role. Although that work predates the work in [19] and the present work, the tableau calculus in [20] of $\mathcal{ALBO}^{\text{id}}$ can be in fact synthesised by altering the semantic specification similar as described for $K_m(\neg)$ in this section. Using the results of the previous section a hypertableau calculus can be defined for $\mathcal{ALBO}^{\text{id}}$.

7   Concluding Remarks

The paper has investigated refinement of inference rules for semantic tableau calculi in the setting of the tableau synthesis framework. We introduced atomic rule refinement as a general principle to reduce branching and simplify the way deductions are carried out with disjunctive formulae. A distinctive feature of the refinement is that it is syntactic and can be automated. As we have shown the approach covers two important cases: refinement of inference rules generated from frame conditions and systematically developing hypertableau-like calculi. In both cases, properties of the language of the logic are exploited. In the first case, because frame conditions are properties on atomic relations, the condition for atomic rule refinement trivially holds. In the second case, formulae of the logic were transformed into a normal form and the hypertableau rule was defined by constraining disjunctive splitting rules with atomic premises.

In the case study of $K_m(\neg)$ we showed that even if none of the rules of the initially generated calculus are refinable (without loss of completeness) there may be ways to modify the semantic specification for the logic and extend the calculus by additional rules in order to achieve refinability. In this case the addition of derivable rule enabled the refinement of other rules in the calculus.

Adding analytic cut rules [6] to the calculus is another approach to make rule refinement possible. This allows KE tableau calculi to be systematically derived in the framework. Due to space limitation we do not elaborate on this case.

We have considered rule refinement in the tableau synthesis framework. Since its rule language gives full freedom to generate sets of inference rules for any logic, where the semantics can be expressed in a first-order language, the results of the paper apply to all calculi that can be described in the framework. The refinements and essential ideas are however more general and can be applied to other types of deduction calculi, which deserves to be investigated. Further work will include the investigation of other refinements and reduction of the search space, such as ordering restrictions [11].

References

1. Abate, P., Goré, R.: The tableau workbench. Electr. Notes Theoret. Comput. Sci. **231**, 55–67 (2009)
2. Babenyshev, S., Rybakov, V., Schmidt, R.A., Tishkovsky, D.: A tableau method for checking rule admissibility in S4. Electr. Notes Theoret. Comput. Sci. **262**, 17–32 (2010)
3. Baumgartner, P., Furbach, U., Niemelä, I.: Hyper tableaux. In: Alferes, J.J., Pereira, L.M., Orlowska, E. (eds.) JELIA 1996. LNCS, vol. 1126, pp. 1–17. Springer, Heidelberg (1996). doi:10.1007/3-540-61630-6_1
4. Baumgartner, P., Schmidt, R.A.: Blocking and other enhancements for bottom-up model generation methods (2016). arXiv e-Print arXiv:1611.09014 [cs.AI]
5. Blackburn, P., Seligman, J.: What are hybrid languages? In: AiML-1, pp. 41–62. CSLI Publ. (1998)
6. D'Agostino, M., Mondadori, M.: The taming of the cut. Classical refutations with analytic cut. J. Log. Comput. **4**(3), 285–319 (1994)
7. De Nivelle, H., Schmidt, R.A., Hustadt, U.: Resolution-based methods for modal logics. Logic J. IGPL **8**(3), 265–292 (2000)
8. Fitting, M.: Proof Methods for Modal and Intuitionistic Logics. Reidel, Kufstein (1983)
9. Gargov, G., Passy, S., Tinchev, T.: Modal environment for Boolean speculations. In: Proceedings of the 1986 Gödel Conference, pp. 253–263. Plenum (1987)
10. Goré, R.: Tableau methods for modal and temporal logics. In: D'Agostino, M., Gabbay, D.M., Hähnle, R., Posegga, J. (eds.) Handbook of Tableau Methods, pp. 297–396. Springer, Dordrecht (1999). doi:10.1007/978-94-017-1754-0_6
11. Hähnle, R., Klingenbeck, S.: A-ordered tableaux. J. Log. Comput. **6**(6), 819–833 (1996)
12. Humberstone, I.L.: The modal logic of 'all and only'. Notre Dame J. Formal Log. **28**(2), 177–188 (1987)
13. Hustadt, U., Schmidt, R.A.: Simplification and backjumping in modal tableau. In: Swart, H. (ed.) TABLEAUX 1998. LNCS (LNAI), vol. 1397, pp. 187–201. Springer, Heidelberg (1998). doi:10.1007/3-540-69778-0_22
14. Khodadadi, M., Schmidt, R.A., Tishkovsky, D.: A refined tableau calculus with controlled blocking for the description logic $\mathcal{SHOI}$. In: Galmiche, D., Larchey-Wendling, D. (eds.) TABLEAUX 2013. LNCS, vol. 8123, pp. 188–202. Springer, Heidelberg (2013). doi:10.1007/978-3-642-40537-2_17
15. Lutz, C., Sattler, U.: The complexity of reasoning with Boolean modal logics. In: AiML-3, pp. 329–348. CSLI Publ. (2002)
16. Motik, B., Shearer, R., Horrocks, I.: Hypertableau reasoning for description logics. J. Artif. Intell. Res. **36**, 165–228 (2009)
17. Nonnengart, A., Weidenbach, C.: Computing small clause normal forms. In: Handbook of Automated Reasoning, pp. 335–367. Elsevier (2001)
18. Schmidt, R.A., Stell, J.G., Rydeheard, D.: Axiomatic and tableau-based reasoning for Kt(H, R). In: AiML-10, pp. 478–497. College Publ. (2014)

19. Schmidt, R.A., Tishkovsky, D.: Automated synthesis of tableau calculi. Log. Methods Comput. Sci. **7**(2:6), 1–32 (2011)
20. Schmidt, R.A., Tishkovsky, D.: Using tableau to decide description logics with full role negation and identity. ACM Trans. Comput. Log. **15**(1), 7:1–7:31 (2014)
21. Schmidt, R.A., Waldmann, U.: Modal tableau systems with blocking and congruence closure. In: Nivelle, H. (ed.) TABLEAUX 2015. LNCS (LNAI), vol. 9323, pp. 38–53. Springer, Cham (2015). doi:10.1007/978-3-319-24312-2_4
22. Smullyan, R.M.: First Order Logic. Springer, Heidelberg (1971)
23. Stell, J.G., Schmidt, R.A., Rydeheard, D.: A bi-intuitionistic modal logic: foundations and automation. J. Log. Algebr. Methods Program. **85**(4), 500–519 (2016)
24. Tishkovsky, D., Schmidt, R.A.: Rule refinement for semantic tableau calculi (2017). http://www.cs.man.ac.uk/~schmidt/publications/ruleref_long.pdf

Transitive Closure and Cyclic Proofs

Completeness for Ancestral Logic
via a Computationally-Meaningful Semantics

Liron Cohen[(✉)]

Cornell University, Ithaca, USA
lironcohen@cornell.edu

Abstract. First-order logic (FOL) is evidently insufficient for the many applications of logic in computer science, mainly due to its inability to provide inductive definitions. Therefore, only an extension of FOL which allows finitary inductive definitions can be used as a framework for automated reasoning. The minimal logic that is suitable for this goal is Ancestral Logic (AL), which is an extension of FOL by a transitive closure operator. In order for AL to be able to serve as a reasonable (and better) substitute to the use of FOL in computer science, it is crucial to develop adequate, user-friendly proof systems for it. While the expressiveness of AL renders any effective proof system for it incomplete with respect to the standard semantics, there are useful approximations. In this paper we show that such a Gentzen-style approximation is both sound and complete with respect to a natural, computationally-meaningful Henkin-style semantics for AL.

1 Introduction

In [8] it was forcefully argued that logic plays a central role in computer science. Evidence for this claim was provided by listing a variety of applications of logic in different areas in computer science, such as descriptive complexity, database query languages, program verification and more. However, when examining this list of applications, it turns out that first-order logic (FOL), which is the logic usually associated with 'logic', does not actually suffice for any of the mentioned applications.[1] Evidently, extensions of FOL are needed in almost all of the examples given in [8]:

- The characterization of complexity classes which is done in descriptive complexity always uses logics that are more expressive than FOL, such as second-order logic (SOL), or logics which are intermediate between FOL and SOL.
- Verification of programs involve *inductive arguments* which are not a part of the logical machinery of FOL.

---

[1] Actually, at this point we are only referring to the formal *languages* used in the applications, ignoring (for the time being) other essential components of the notion of a 'logic', like the corresponding consequence relation.

© Springer International Publishing AG 2017
R.A. Schmidt and C. Nalon (Eds.): TABLEAUX 2017, LNAI 10501, pp. 247–260, 2017.
DOI: 10.1007/978-3-319-66902-1_15

- [8] only mentioned query languages which are directly based on FOL, like SQL. However, its poor expressive power is the reason that the SQL 3 (1999) standard added a WITH RECURSIVE construct which allows transitive closures to be computed inside the query processor, and by now such a construct is implemented also in IBM DB2, Microsoft SQL Server, and PostgreSQL. Datalog too implements transitive closure computations.
- Not only do type theories obviously go beyond FOL, but even their presentation and description cannot be done in FOL, since their introduction makes a massive use of *inductive definitions* of typing judgments.
- Most applications of model-checking rely on the notion of *reachability*, which is not first-order definable. It is noted in [18] that "In all interesting applications of model-checking, reachability properties have to be checked, which are not expressible in the FOL-signature of labeled graphs (transition systems)".
- A crucial notion for reasoning about knowledge is that of *common knowledge*. This notion is *inductively defined* in terms of the basic knowledge operators. However, this definition is not expressible in FOL and so is usually introduced by brute force.

All these examples (as well as many others) reveal that what FOL is lacking is the ability to provide inductive definitions. More particularly, the notion of the transitive closure of a given binary relation seems to be the key necessary component which is not expressible in FOL. In fact, because of this inability, FOL cannot even serve as its own meta-logic, since all its basic syntactic categories (such as terms, formulas, and formal derivations of formulas) are introduced via inductive definitions. Hence, only some extension of FOL which allows finitary inductive definitions ([5]) can be used as a framework for automated reasoning. While SOL clearly enjoys this property, it does not seem satisfactory that dealing with basic inductive definitions requires using the strong notions involved in SOL, such as quantifying over all subsets of infinite sets. Full SOL also has many disadvantages, among which are its doubtful semantics (as it is based on debatable ontological commitments), and what is more, the fact that it is difficult to deal with from a proof-theoretical point of view.

In [1,2] it was shown that the *minimal* framework that can be used for the above mentioned goal is Ancestral Logic, AL (which is also known in the literature as TC-logic). This is the logic obtained from FOL by the addition of a transitive closure operator. Although several other logics which are intermediate between FOL and SOL have been suggested in the literature (such as: weak second-order logic, ω-logic, logics with a "cardinality quantifier", logics with Henkin quantifiers, etc.), we strongly believe that AL should be taken as the basic logic which underlies most applications of logic in computer science. Its advantages include: being useful in the finite cases[2], having intuitive formal

---

[2] A great deal of attention has been given to AL in the area of finite model theory, and in related areas of computer science, like complexity classes (see, e.g., [4]). However, not much has been done so far about it in the context of *arbitrary* structures, or from a proof theoretical point-of-view.

proof systems, and entering very naturally in computer science applications[3]. Another important advantage of AL is the simplicity of the transitive closure notion. Anyone, even with no mathematical background whatsoever, can easily grasp the concept of the ancestor of a given person (or, in other words, the idea of the transitive closure of a certain binary relation).

In order for AL to be used as the foundational logic in computer science applications, its theory must first be developed to the point it can serve as a reasonable (and in many cases, better) substitute for the use of FOL (or higher-order logics). Since our goal is to explore the use of this logic in such applications, the emphasis should be on the construction of adequate, user-friendly formal systems for AL. Due to the expressiveness of AL, there can be no sound and complete effective proof system for it (see, e.g., [15]). Instead, one should look for useful approximations (like in the case of SOL). In [1,2] a Gentzen-style proof system for AL was presented and its proof-theoretical properties were explored.[4] It was shown to be natural and effective, as well as sound with respect to the intended semantics. In this paper we provide further evidence for the usefulness of the system by proving that it is both sound and complete with respect to a generalized Henkin-style semantics.[5] This semantics for AL is based on the one used for the completeness proof for SOL given in [9].

The rest of this paper is organized as follows: In Sect. 2 the formal definition of the reflexive transitive closure operator and ancestral logic are given. Then, some of the most important model-theoretic properties of ancestral logic are presented. Section 3 provides a natural Gentzen-style system which is adequate for ancestral logic in the sense that it is sound with respect to the standard semantics, and captures the properties that govern the transitive closure operator. Section 4 contains the main result of the paper: a completeness theorem for the proof system for AL with respect to a natural Henkin-style semantics. Finally, in Sect. 5 we conclude with some remarks and ideas for further research.

2   The Language and its Semantics

The essential idea in embedding the general concept of the transitive closure operator
into a logical framework is that one may treat a formula with two (distinct) free variables as a definition of a binary relation. Below is the formal definition of first-order logic augmented by a transitive closure operator, and its semantics. In this paper (following suggestions made in, e.g., [12–14]) we take the reflexive form of the transitive closure operator as the primitive notion. In [2] it was

---

[3] To demonstrate one such application of AL in computer science, in [3] a constructive version of AL was shown to subsume Kleene algebra with tests [11] (as the reflexive transitive closure operator is essentially Kleene's star operator), while offering much more expressive power. This demonstrates that AL can serve as a natural programming logic for specifying, developing and reasoning about programs.

[4] In fact, [2] presented several proof systems for different variations of AL, and the connection between them was investigated.

[5] To be precise, we take here an equivalent variant of a system presented in [2].

shown that the two forms of the operator, the reflexive one and the non-reflexive one, are equivalent in the presence of equality.

Throughout the paper we use the following standard notations:

- $Fv(\varphi)$ for the set of free variable in the formula φ.
- $v[x := a]$ for the x-variant of the assignment v which assigns a to x.
- $\varphi\left\{\frac{t_1}{x_1}, \ldots, \frac{t_n}{x_n}\right\}$ for the result of simultaneously substituting t_i for the free occurrences of x_i in φ $(i = 1, \ldots, n)$.

Definition 1. *Let σ be some first-order signature, and let $\mathcal{L}$ be the corresponding first-order language. The language $\mathcal{L}_{RTC}$ is obtained from $\mathcal{L}$ by the addition of the reflexive transitive closure operator (RTC), together with the following clause concerning the definition of a formula:*

- *$(RTC_{x,y}\varphi)(s,t)$ is a formula in $\mathcal{L}_{RTC}$ for any formula φ in $\mathcal{L}_{RTC}$, distinct variables x, y, and terms s, t.*

The free occurrences of x and y in φ become bound in this formula.

Note that φ in the above definition can be *any* formula in $\mathcal{L}_{RTC}$. That is, it may contain free variables other than x, y (treated as parameters), or it may not contain x, y at all. Also, φ can have a RTC-subformula, i.e. nesting of the RTC operator are allowed.

The intended meaning of a formula of the form $(RTC_{x,y}\varphi)(s,t)$ is the "infinite disjunction":

$$s = t \vee \varphi\{\tfrac{s}{x}, \tfrac{t}{y}\} \vee \exists w_1(\varphi\{\tfrac{s}{x}, \tfrac{w_1}{y}\}) \wedge \varphi\{\tfrac{w_1}{x}, \tfrac{t}{y}\}) \vee$$
$$\exists w_1 \exists w_2(\varphi\{\tfrac{s}{x}, \tfrac{w_1}{y}\} \wedge \varphi\{\tfrac{w_1}{x}, \tfrac{w_2}{y}\} \wedge \varphi\{\tfrac{w_2}{x}, \tfrac{t}{y}\}) \vee \ldots$$

where $w_1, w_2, \ldots$ are all fresh variables.

Definition 2. *Let M be a structure for $\mathcal{L}_{RTC}$, and v an assignment in M. Ancestral logic (AL) is semantically defined as classical first-order logic, with the following additional clause concerning the satisfaction relation:*

- *The pair $\langle M, v \rangle$ is said to satisfy the formula $(RTC_{x,y}\varphi)(s,t)$ (denoted by $M, v \models (RTC_{x,y}\varphi)(s,t))$ if $v(s) = v(t)$, or there exist $a_0, \ldots, a_n \in D$ $(n > 0)$ such that $v(s) = a_0$, $v(t) = a_n$, and $M, v[x := a_i, y := a_{i+1}] \models \varphi$ for $0 \leq i \leq n - 1$.*

A simple compactness argument shows that the reflexive transitive closure operator is in general not first-order definable. However, it is definable in second-order logic by the formula: $\forall X((Xs \wedge \forall x \forall y (\varphi(x, y) \wedge Xx \rightarrow Xy)) \rightarrow Xt)$. Therefore, ancestral logic is intermediate between first- and second-order logics. An important indication that the expressive power of ancestral logic captures a very significant and natural fragment of SOL is provided by the fact that AL is equivalent in its expressive power to several other logics between FOL and SOL that have been suggested and investigated in the literature (such as those mentioned in the introduction).

The natural numbers can be categorically characterized in AL using only equality, zero and the successor function (see [2]). This implies that the upward Löwenheim-Skolem theorem fails for AL, as well as the compactness theorem (see [15]). Moreover, if addition is added to the language, all recursive functions and relations are definable in AL (see [1]), and thus the set of valid formulas of AL in this language is not even arithmetical. Hence AL is inherently incomplete, i.e., any formal deductive system which is sound for AL is incomplete. Nevertheless, as we shall demonstrate, there are very natural formal approximations which are sound, and seem to encompass all forms of reasoning for this logic that are used in practice.

3   Formal Proof System for AL

As in the case of SOL, since there can be no sound and complete formal system for AL, one should instead look for useful approximations. Such approximations should be:

- natural and effective,
- sound with respect to the intended semantics,
- both sound and complete with respect to some natural generalization of the intended semantics.

Such equivalent Hilbert-style approximations were suggested already in [12–14]. Nevertheless, the use of Hilbert-type systems is impractical, since they are not suitable for mechanization. A better, computationally-oriented approach would be to explore Gentzen-style systems for AL. This was done in [2], and we here review the system and its main properties.

Definition 3. *Let G be a Gentzen-style system (see, e.g., [6]).*

- *A sequent s is said to be provable from a set of sequents S in G, denoted by $S \vdash_G s$, if there exists a derivation in G of s from S.*
- *A formula φ is said to be provable from a set of formulas T in G, denoted by $T \vdash_G \varphi$, if there is a derivation in G of $\Rightarrow \varphi$ from the set $\{\Rightarrow \psi \mid \psi \in T\}$.*

In what follows the letters Γ, Δ represent finite (possibly empty) multisets of formulas, φ, ψ arbitrary formulas, x, y, z, u, v variables, and r, s, t terms.

Let $\mathcal{LK}$ be the Gentzen-style system for classical first-order logic [6,17], including the substitution rule (though it was not a part of the original system).

Definition 4. *The system AL_G for $\mathcal{L}_{RTC}$ is defined by adding to $\mathcal{LK}$ the following axiom:*

$$\Gamma \Rightarrow \Delta, (RTC_{x,y}\varphi)(s,s) \tag{1}$$

and the following inference rules:

$$\frac{\Gamma \Rightarrow \Delta, (RTC_{x,y}\varphi)(s,r) \quad \Gamma \Rightarrow \Delta, \varphi\left\{\frac{r}{x}, \frac{t}{y}\right\}}{\Gamma \Rightarrow \Delta, (RTC_{x,y}\varphi)(s,t)} \tag{2}$$

$$\frac{\Gamma, \psi\left(x\right), \varphi\left(x, y\right) \Rightarrow \Delta, \psi\left\{\frac{y}{x}\right\}}{\Gamma, \psi\left\{\frac{s}{x}\right\}, \left(RTC_{x,y}\varphi\right)\left(s, t\right) \Rightarrow \Delta, \psi\left\{\frac{t}{x}\right\}} \tag{3}$$

In all the rules we assume that the terms which are substituted are free for substitution, and that no forbidden capturing occurs. In Rule (3) x should not occur free in Γ and Δ, and y should not occur free in Γ, Δ and ψ.

For languages with equality, the system $AL_G^=$ is obtained from AL_G by the addition of standard equality axioms (see, e.g., [17]).

Rule (3) is a generalized induction principle. It states that if t is a φ-descendant of s or equal to it, then if s has some hereditary property which is passed down from one object to another if they are φ-related, then t also has that property. In the case of arithmetic this rule captures the induction rule of Peano's Arithmetics PA (see [2]).[6]

The system AL_G is adequate for handling the RTC operator, in the sense that it is sound and it gives the RTC operator the intended meaning of the reflexive transitive closure operator. Furthermore, all fundamental rules concerning the RTC operator that have been suggested in the literature (as far as we know) are derivable in it. The Lemma below provides some examples.

Lemma 5. *The following rules are derivable in AL_G:*

$$\frac{\Gamma \Rightarrow \Delta, \left(RTC_{x,y}\varphi\right)\left(s, r\right) \quad \Gamma \Rightarrow \Delta, \left(RTC_{x,y}\varphi\right)\left(r, t\right)}{\Gamma \Rightarrow \Delta, \left(RTC_{x,y}\varphi\right)\left(s, t\right)} \tag{4}$$

$$\frac{\Gamma, \varphi \Rightarrow \Delta, \psi}{\Gamma, \left(RTC_{x,y}\varphi\right)\left(s, t\right) \Rightarrow \Delta, \left(RTC_{x,y}\psi\right)\left(s, t\right)} \tag{5}$$

$$\frac{\left(RTC_{x,y}\varphi\right)\left(s, t\right), \Gamma \Rightarrow \Delta}{\left(RTC_{u,v}\left(RTC_{x,y}\varphi\right)\left(u, v\right)\right)\left(s, t\right), \Gamma \Rightarrow \Delta} \tag{6}$$

$$\frac{\Gamma \Rightarrow \Delta, \left(RTC_{x,y}\varphi\right)\left(s, t\right)}{\Gamma \Rightarrow \Delta, \left(RTC_{y,x}\varphi\right)\left(t, s\right)} \quad \frac{\left(RTC_{x,y}\varphi\right)\left(s, t\right), \Gamma \Rightarrow \Delta}{\left(RTC_{y,x}\varphi\right)\left(t, s\right), \Gamma \Rightarrow \Delta} \tag{7}$$

In (5) x, y should not occur free in Γ and Δ, and in (6) u, v should not occur free in φ.

4 Henkin-Style Completeness

Though AL_G cannot be complete for its intended semantics, it can be shown to be complete for a more liberal yet natural semantics, in the spirit of the Henkin semantics used for the completeness of SOL (see, e.g. [9,15]). Thus, in this section we introduce a similar Henkin-style semantic characterizations for $\mathcal{L}_{RTC}$, and prove the completeness of AL_G with respect to it. This will establish that AL_G indeed meets also the third criterion of a useful approximation for AL given at the beginning of Sect. 3.

---

[6] In fact, it was shown in [2] that in the case of arithmetics the ordinal number of AL_G is ε_0, like in the case of PA.

First we recall the concepts of Henkin structures. A σ-Henkin structure is a standard structure together with a subset of the power-set of its domain (called its set of admissible subsets) which is closed under parametric definability.

Definition 6. *Let σ be a first-order signature. A σ-Henkin structure M is a triple $\langle D, I, D' \rangle$, such that:*

- *$\langle D, I \rangle$ is a standard structure for σ (i.e., D is a non-empty domain and I is an interpretation function on σ in D)*
- *$D' \subseteq P(D)$ such that for each formula φ in σ, and assignment v in M[7]:*

$$\{a \in D \mid M, v\, [x := a] \models \varphi\} \in D'$$

In case $D' = P(D)$, the σ-Henkin structure is called a standard structure.

Notice that in finite structures every subset of the domain is parametrically definable, hence non-standard σ-Henkin structures are necessarily infinite.

It should be noted that the notion of "non-standard" structures is commonly used in mathematical logic, but in a different sense. There are two ways in which a σ-Henkin structure can be non-standard. The "standard way" for it to be non-standard is by having a non-standard first-order part $\langle D, I \rangle$ (in which case D' must necessarily be non-standard). However, a σ-Henkin structure can be non-standard even in case its first-order part is standard, simply by having $D' \subsetneq P(D)$. The latter is what we here mean by a non-standard σ-Henkin structure.

Definition 7. *Let $\mathcal{L}_{RTC}$ be the language based on the signature σ. $\mathcal{L}_{RTC}$ formulas are interpreted in σ-Henkin structures as in standard structures, except for the following clause:*

- *$M, v \models (RTC_{x,y}\varphi)(s, t)$ if for every $A \in D'$, if $v(s) \in A$ and for every $a, b \in D$: $(a \in A \wedge M, v\, [x := a, y := b] \models \varphi) \rightarrow b \in A$, then $v(t) \in A$.*

Example 8. To give an example of a non-standard σ-Henkin structure, consider the relational language of arithmetic $\sigma = \{0, S, =\}$, where S stands for the successor relation (note that we here use equality in the signature). Let M be the structure whose first-order part is the standard structure of the natural numbers, and let D' be the collection of subsets of the natural numbers that are definable without parameters in the language of AL (i.e. definable by a formula with only one free variable). A set that is definable relative to definable parameters is definable without parameters, so D' is closed under definability. Thus, M is a σ-Henkin structure which is clearly non-standard as $D' \subsetneq P(D)$. Now, AL has a categorical characterization of the natural numbers (see, e.g., [1, 2, 15]), and it is straightforward to verify that M indeed satisfies all the characterizing axioms.

The next proposition shows that the generalized Henkin-style semantics coincides with the standard semantics on standard structures.

---

[7] An assignment v in M is defined as in the standard semantics.

Proposition 9. *Let M be a standard structure and v an assignment in M. Then, the followings are equivalent:*

1. $v(s) = v(t)$ or there exist $a_0, \ldots, a_n \in D$ $(n > 0)$ such that $v(s) = a_0$, $v(t) = a_n$, and $M, v[x := a_i, y := a_{i+1}] \models \varphi$ for $0 \le i \le n - 1$.
2. for every $A \subseteq D$, if $v(s) \in A$ and for every $a, b \in D$: $M, v[x := a, y := b] \models \varphi$ and $a \in A$ implies $b \in A$, then $v(t) \in A$.

Proof. Suppose (1). Let $A \subseteq D$ be a set that is closed under φ, and v an assignment such that $v(s) = a_0 \in A$. If $v(s) = v(t)$ we are done. Otherwise, by induction on the sequence $a_0, \ldots, a_n$ it is straightforward to prove that $v(t) = a_n \in A$. For the converse, assume by contradiction that (1) does not hold. Take A to be that set which includes $v(s)$ as well as all $a_n \in D$ such that there exist $a_0, \ldots, a_{n-1} \in D$ $(n > 0)$ where $v(s) = a_0$, and $M, v[x := a_i, y := a_{i+1}] \models \varphi$ for $0 \le i \le n - 1$. By assumption, $v(t) \notin A$, which contradicts (2), since A is obviously φ-closed. □

Before proceeding, a discussion of the value of this type of generalized Henkin semantics for AL is in order. This semantics originated in the completeness result for SOL [9]. There, in order to achieve completeness, the semantics of the non first-order part of the language (the second-order variables) had to weakened. Similarly, we here form a relaxation of the intended semantics for AL by taking a more liberal condition for the non first-order part of the language, the RTC operator. On standard structures, this semantics gives to an RTC-formula its intended top-down meaning (as in Proposition 9(2)). That is, $(RTC_{x,y}\varphi)(s,t)$ holds when *any* property (represented by A) which is closed under φ and contains the interpretation of s also contains the interpretation of t. This corresponds to the standard mathematical definition of the operator as the union of the identity relation with the intersection over *all* transitive binary relations that contain the interpretation of φ (to see this, notice that $a \in A \to b \in A$ may be considered as a transitive binary relation). Now, this is a strong requirement which also renders this definition non-constructive (apart from in trivial cases). The Henkin-style semantics given above relaxes this definition by referring not to all $A \subseteq D$, but only to certain ones. The closure condition on Henkin structures entails that those A's on which the property should be verified are those which are definable (with parameters) in the language. This is a definitional approach to the transitive closure operator which is very much computationally-oriented. The meaning of the transitive closure is what gives AL its inductive power, which is required for many applications in computer science (as surveyed in the Introduction). But the inductive power actually needed and used in such applications is not over arbitrary elements, but over elements which can be defined.

This generalization of the semantics is what entails the completeness result for AL_G in the sequel. This is because in the induction rule of the formal system AL_G there is an implicit condition that the hereditary property can be defined by a formula, there denoted by ψ. Actually, this condition holds in any formal system, and thus is a critical property in any computational framework. In light of that, the completeness result also suggests that those "standard truths" of AL which are not provable in ALG hold due to inductive reasoning on some non-definable (non-computable) set.

Any classical structure $M = \langle D, I \rangle$ for σ induces a set of σ-Henkin structures $H(M) = \{M_H = \langle D, I, D' \rangle \mid M_H \text{ is a } \sigma\text{-Henkin structure}\}$. Conversely, each σ-Henkin structure M corresponds to the classical structure obtained by the forgetfulness of D'.

Definition 10. *Let $T \cup \{\varphi\}$ be a set of formulas in a language based on the signature σ. We say that $T \models_H \varphi$ if every σ-Henkin model of T is a model of φ. We say that $T \models_S \varphi$ if every standard model of T is a model of φ.*

Proposition 11. *Let $T \cup \{\varphi\}$ be a set of formulas. If $T \models_H \varphi$ then $T \models_S \varphi$.*

Proof. Follows from the fact that every standard model for T may be viewed as a Henkin model. □

We start by showing the completeness of ALG. Therefore in what follows, unless mentioned otherwise, we assume $\mathcal{L}_{RTC}$ does not contain equality.

Theorem 12 (Soundness). *Let $T \cup \{\varphi\}$ be a set of sentences in $\mathcal{L}_{RTC}$. Then, $T \vdash_{ALG} \varphi$ implies $T \models_H \varphi$.*

Proof. It is straightforward to verify that Axiom (1) and Rule (2) of ALG are sound with respect to the Henkin-style semantics. For Rule (3) simply take $A := \{a \in D \mid M, v\,[x := a] \models \psi\}$. Now, $A \in D'$ since σ-Henkin structures are closed under parametric definability. By the assumptions we have that A is φ-closed and $v(s) \in A$, which by the semantics of the RTC formula entails $v(t) \in A$. □

The main result of this section is Theorem 13 below, which we shall prove using several lemmas and definitions.

Theorem 13 (Completeness). *Let $T \cup \{\varphi\}$ be a set of sentences in $\mathcal{L}_{RTC}$. Then, $T \models_H \varphi$ implies $T \vdash_{ALG} \varphi$.*

We prove the completeness theorem using the standard method, showing that if $T \nvdash_{ALG} \varphi$, then $T \nvDash_H \varphi$. First, we extend the language $\mathcal{L}_{RTC}$ to a language $\mathcal{L}'_{RTC}$ by adding to it countably many new constant symbols, $c_1, c_2, \ldots$, and countably many new monadic predicates, $P_1, P_2, \ldots$. It is easy to see that $T \nvdash_{ALG} \varphi$ in the extended language as well.

Definition 14. *We say that a set of $\mathcal{L}'_{RTC}$ sentences Γ contains Henkin witnesses if the followings hold:*

1. *if $\exists x \varphi \in \Gamma$, then $\varphi\{\frac{c}{x}\} \in \Gamma$ for some constant c.*
2. *if $\neg(RTC_{x,y}\varphi)(s,t) \in \Gamma$, then $P(s)$, $\forall x, y\,(P(x) \wedge \varphi(x,y) \to P(y))$, $\neg P(t) \in \Gamma$ for some monadic predicate P.*
3. *if φ is a formula of $\mathcal{L}'_{RTC}$ with $Fv(\varphi) = \{x\}$, then $\forall x\,(P(x) \leftrightarrow \varphi) \in \Gamma$ for some monadic predicate P.*

The next Lemma established that the standard method of relational extension by definitions is conservative.

Lemma 15. *Let T be a set of sentences in $\mathcal{L}'_{RTC}$ such that $T \nvdash_{ALG} \varphi$, and let θ be a sentence of the form $\forall x\, (P\,(x) \leftrightarrow \psi)$, where P is a fresh monadic predicate (i.e. does not occur in $T \cup \{\varphi, \psi\}$). Then, $T, \theta \nvdash_{ALG} \varphi$.*

Proof. Suppose by contradiction that there is a proof from $T \cup \{\forall x\, (P\,(x) \leftrightarrow \psi)\}$ of φ in ALG, where P is a fresh monadic predicate. First rename all bound variables in the proof (apart from x in the formula $\forall x\, (P\,(x) \leftrightarrow \psi)$) with new variables not occurring in the proof or in $\forall x\, (P\,(x) \leftrightarrow \psi)$. Now, replace all the occurrences of formulas of the form $P\,(t)$ in the proof by $\psi \{\frac{t}{x}\}$. Then, every occurrence of $\forall x\, (P\,(x) \leftrightarrow \psi)$ in the proof becomes an occurrence of $\forall x\, (\psi \leftrightarrow \psi)$, which of course is provable in ALG. It is straightforward to show that if the replacement is done on an axiom, then the result is still an axiom of ALG. It is also easy to verify that all the inference rules apply equally to the formulas after the replacement. Also notice that since P does not occur in $T \cup \{\varphi\}$, the replacement procedure applied to a formula in $T \cup \{\varphi\}$ results in the same formula. Hence, the replacement procedure indeed produces a proof of φ from T in ALG. This shows that $T \vdash_{ALG} \varphi$, which is a contradiction.   □

Lemma 16. *Let P be a monadic predicate and θ a formula of $\mathcal{L}'_{RTC}$. Then:*

$$P\,(s), \forall x, y\, (P\,(x) \wedge \theta\,(x, y) \to P\,(y)), \neg P\,(t) \vdash_{ALG} \neg \,(RTC_{x,y}\theta)\,(s, t)$$

Proof. The claim immediately follows from Rule (3), taking $\varphi\,(x, y) := \theta\,(x, y)$ and $\psi\,(x) := P\,(x)$.   □

Lemma 17. *There exists an extension of T to a set of sentences T' in the language $\mathcal{L}'_{RTC}$ such that:*

1. *T' is a maximal theory in $\mathcal{L}'_{RTC}$ such that $T' \nvdash_{ALG} \varphi$.*
2. *T' contains Henkin witnesses.*

Proof. Fix two enumerations: one of all sentences of $\mathcal{L}'_{RTC}$: $\psi_1, \psi_2, \ldots$; and one of all the formulas of $\mathcal{L}'_{RTC}$ with one free variable x: $\theta_1, \theta_2, \ldots$. Define a sequence of theories $T_0, T_1, \ldots$ inductively in the following way: $T_0 = T$, and for $i > 0$ T_i is constructed from T_{i-1} as follows:

1. If $i = 2n - 1$ for some $n \in \mathbb{N}$, then:
   (a) If $T_{i-1} \cup \{\psi_n\} \vdash_{ALG} \varphi$, then $T_i = T_{i-1}$.
   (b) If $T_{i-1} \cup \{\psi_n\} \nvdash_{ALG} \varphi$, then:
      i. If ψ_n is not of the form $\exists x\psi$ or $\neg\,(RTC_{x,y}\psi)\,(s, t)$, $T_i = T_{i-1} \cup \{\psi_n\}$.
      ii. If $\psi_n = \exists x\psi$, then $T_i = T_{i-1} \cup \{\psi_n, \psi\{\frac{c_j}{x}\}\}$, for c_j a fresh constant symbol not in T_{i-1}.
      iii. If $\psi_n = \neg\,(RTC_{x,y}\psi)\,(s, t)$, then $T_i = T_{i-1} \cup \{\psi_n, P_j\,(s), \neg P_j\,(t), \forall x, y\, (P_j\,(x) \wedge \psi\,(x, y) \to P_j\,(y))\}$, for P_j a fresh monadic predicate not in T_{i-1}.

2. If $i = 2n$ for some $n \in \mathbb{N}$, then $T_i = T_{i-1} \cup \{\forall x \, (P_j(x) \leftrightarrow \theta_n)\}$, for P_j a fresh monadic predicate not in T_{i-1}.

We show by induction that for every $i \in \mathbb{N}$, $T_i \nvdash_{ALG} \varphi$. Lemma 15 entails that if $T_{2n-1} \nvdash_{ALG} \varphi$, then $T_{2n} \nvdash_{ALG} \varphi$. For $i = 2n - 1$: Cases (a) and (b i) are trivial, and Case (b ii) is provable just as in the standard completeness proof for FOL. Thus, we here prove Case (b iii). Assume by contradiction that $T_{i-1}, \neg (RTC_{x,y}\psi)(s,t), P_j(s), \forall x, y.P_j(x) \wedge \psi(x,y) \rightarrow P_j(y), \neg P_j(t) \vdash_{ALG} \varphi$. Since $P_j(s), \forall x, y.P_j(x) \wedge \psi(x,y) \rightarrow P_j(y), \neg P_j(t) \vdash_{ALG} \neg(RTC_{x,y}\psi)(s,t)$, by Lemma 16 we have $T_{i-1}, P_j(s), \forall x, y.P_j(x) \wedge \psi(x,y) \rightarrow P_j(y), \neg P_j(t) \vdash_{ALG} \varphi$. Now, P_j is a fresh monadic predicate which does not appear in $T_{i-1} \cup \{\varphi\}$. Therefore, it is straightforward to verify that replacing all occurrences of formulas of the form $P_j(r)$ in the above proof with $(RTC_{x,y}\psi)(s,r)$ results in a proof in ALG of φ from the set $T_{i-1} \cup \{(RTC_{x,y}\psi)(s,s), \neg(RTC_{x,y}\psi)(s,t), \forall x, y. (RTC_{x,y}\psi)(s,x) \wedge \psi(x,y) \rightarrow (RTC_{x,y}\psi)(s,y)\}$. Now, $(RTC_{x,y}\psi)(s,s)$ is an axiom of ALG, and $\forall x, y \, ((RTC_{x,y}\psi)(s,x) \wedge \psi(x,y) \rightarrow (RTC_{x,y}\psi)(s,y))$ is provable in ALG using Rule (2). Hence, we get that $T_{i-1}, \neg(RTC_{x,y}\psi)(s,t) \vdash_{ALG} \varphi$, which contradicts the original assumption that $T_{i-1} \cup \{\psi_i\} \nvdash_{ALG} \varphi$. Therefore, $T_i \nvdash_{ALG} \varphi$.

Now, take $T' = \bigcup_{i=0}^{\infty} T_i$. The construction of T' entails that it satisfies the two requirements of the claim.   □

Next we construct a Henkin model for T', which does not satisfy φ.

Definition 18. *Define M by:*

- $D = \{t \mid t \text{ is a closed term}\}$
- $D' = \{\{t \mid P(t) \in T'\} \mid P \text{ is a monadic predicate}\}$
- $\langle t_1, \ldots, t_n \rangle \in I(P)$ iff $P(t_1, \ldots, t_n) \in T'$
- $I(c) = c$ for a constant symbol c
- $I(f)(t_1, \ldots, t_n) = f(t_1, \ldots, t_n)$ for a n-ary function symbol f

Notice that $D' = \{I(P) \mid P \text{ is a monadic predicate}\}$.

Lemma 19. *Let ψ be a formula in $\mathcal{L}'_{RTC}$. The following holds:*

- $M, v \models \psi$ iff $M \models \psi \left\{ \frac{v(x_1)}{x_1}, \ldots, \frac{v(x_n)}{x_n} \right\}$, where $Fv(\psi) = \{x_1, \ldots, x_n\}$.
- $T' \models_H \forall x \psi$ iff $T' \models_H \psi \left\{ \frac{t}{x} \right\}$ for every closed term t.

Lemma 20. *M is a σ-Henkin structure.*

Proof. The claim follows from the fact that T' contains Henkin witnesses of the third type in Definition 14, i.e., a monadic predicate was introduced for each parametrically definable subset (using the new constant symbols instead of the parameters). To see this, let v be an assignment in M, and let ψ be a formula with $Fv(\psi) = \{x_1, \ldots, x_n\}$. Then, $\{a \in D \mid M, v[x_1 := a] \models \psi\} = \left\{a \in D \mid M, v[x_1 := a] \models \psi \left\{ \frac{v(x_2)}{x_2}, \ldots, \frac{v(x_n)}{x_n} \right\} \right\}$. In T' there exists a monadic predicate which forms a Henkin witness for $\psi \left\{ \frac{v(x_2)}{x_2}, \ldots, \frac{v(x_n)}{x_n} \right\}$, denote it by $P_k(x_1)$. This entails that $\left\{ a \in D \mid M, v[x_1 := a] \models \psi \left\{ \frac{v(x_2)}{x_2}, \ldots, \frac{v(x_n)}{x_n} \right\} \right\} = I(P_k) \in D'$.   □

Lemma 21. *For every sentence θ in $\mathcal{L}'_{RTC}$: $M \models \theta$ iff $\theta \in T'$.*

Proof. By induction on θ. The base case follows immediately from the definition of M. For the connectives and quantifiers the proof is similar to the standard proof for FOL (using Henkin witnesses for existential formulas). We next prove the case for $\theta = (RTC_{x,y}\psi)(s,t)$.

($\Rightarrow$) : Assume $M \models (RTC_{x,y}\psi)(s,t)$. Hence, for every monadic predicate P, if for every $a,b \in D$:$(a \in I(P) \wedge M, v[x := a, y := b] \models \psi) \rightarrow b \in I(P)$ and $I(s) \in I(P)$, then $I(t) \in I(P)$. Using the induction hypothesis and the base case we get that for any monadic predicate P, if $P(s) \in T'$ and for any two closed terms a,b, if $P(a) \in T'$ and $\psi(a,b) \in T'$ then $P(b) \in T'$, then $P(t) \in T'$. From this we deduce (using Lemma 19) that for any monadic predicate P, if $P(s) \in T'$ and $\forall x, y (P(x) \wedge \psi(x,y) \rightarrow P(y)) \in T'$, then $P(t) \in T'$. Assume by contradiction that $(RTC_{x,y}\psi)(s,t) \notin T'$. By the maximality of T', we get that $\neg(RTC_{x,y}\psi)(s,t) \in T'$. Therefore, T' contains Henkin witnesses of the type $P(s)$, $\forall x, y (P(x) \wedge \psi(x,y) \rightarrow P(y))$ and $\neg P(t)$ for some monadic predicate P. But this contradicts the consistency of T', since we showed that for any monadic predicate P, if $P(s) \in T'$ and $\forall x, y (P(x) \wedge \psi(x,y) \rightarrow P(y)) \in T'$, then $P(t) \in T'$. Hence we conclude that $(RTC_{x,y}\psi)(s,t) \in T'$.

($\Leftarrow$) : Assume $M \nvDash (RTC_{x,y}\psi)(s,t)$. So, $M \models \neg(RTC_{x,y}\psi)(s,t)$ and there exists a monadic predicate P such that $I(s) \in I(P)$, $I(t) \notin I(P)$, and for every $a,b \in D$: $(a \in I(P) \wedge M, v[x := a, y := b] \models \psi) \rightarrow b \in I(P)$. By the induction hypothesis and the base case we get that there exists a monadic predicate P such that $P(s) \in T'$, $P(t) \notin T'$, and for any two closed terms a,b, if $P(a) \in T'$ and $\psi(a,b) \in T'$ then $P(b) \in T'$. Therefore, by the maximality of T', $P(s) \in T'$, $\neg P(t) \in T'$ and $\forall x, y (P(x) \wedge \psi(x,y) \rightarrow P(y)) \in T'$ (the latter holds since assuming otherwise leads to a contradiction using a Henkin witness for an existential formulas). This entails, by Lemma 16, $T' \vdash_{ALG} \neg(RTC_{x,y}\psi)(s,t)$. Assuming $(RTC_{x,y}\psi)(s,t) \in T'$ contradicts the consistency of T', therefore $(RTC_{x,y}\psi)(s,t) \notin T'$.   □

From the above series of definitions and lemmas we can finally prove Theorem 13. Since the original theory T is contained in T' and $\varphi \notin T'$, Lemma 21 entails that the model M constructed in Definition 18 satisfies T, but not φ. Hence, we get that $T \nvDash_H \varphi$, which concludes the proof of the Completeness Theorem for ALG.

The completeness of $AL_G^=$ is obtained similarly. Soundness of the additional equality rules is straightforward. The main modification needed in the completeness proof for languages with equality is in the construction of the structure M (Definition 18). In this case M is obtained by taking the domain D to be the quotient set on terms under the equivalence relation: $t_1 \equiv t_2$ iff $t_1 = t_2 \in T'$. The other components of the definition are then altered straightforwardly, taking the equivalence class of closed terms instead of the terms themselves (just as in the standard completeness proof for first-order languages with equality).

It should be noted that in [2] a Gentzen-style proof system for the non-reflexive transitive closure operator was presented, and it was shown that there exist provability preserving interpretations between the two logics. Using similar methods to the ones used here, it is straightforward to provide a generalized Henkin-style semantics for the non-reflexive transitive closure operator and to prove that its corresponding proof system is complete with respect to it.

5   Conclusions and Further Research

In this paper we took another step in the development of the theory of AL as a foundational logical framework for computer science applications. A Henkin-style semantics for AL was introduced and a natural formal system for AL was proven to be sound and complete with respect to it. This leads to various open questions and possible research directions in the exploration of the theory of AL.

One important research task is establishing some form of cut-elimination theorem for AL_G. A non-constructive result might be obtainable using methods similar to the ones used for SOL in [7,16]. To achieve constructive cut-elimination result a plausible option is to search for a suitable definition of the notion "subformula" under which some form of analytical cut-elimination can be obtained. It is clear that the usual definition of a subformula should be revised, exactly as the straightforward notion of subformula used in propositional languages is changed on the first-order level, where for example a formula of the form $\psi\{\frac{t}{x}\}$ is considered to be a subformula of $\forall x \psi$, even though it might be much longer than the latter. Thus the induction rule of AL_G satisfies the subformula property only if we take a formula to be a subformula of every substitution instance of it.

The system AL_G is not complete with respect to the intended semantics. It is not difficult to express its consistency in the language $\{=, 0, S, +\}$ as a logically valid (under the standard semantics) sentence $Con_{AL_G^=}$ of AL. By Gödel's theorem on consistency proofs, $Con_{AL_G^=}$ is not a theorem of $AL_G^=$. It would be interesting to find what valid principles of AL (not available in AL_G) can be used to derive it. The completeness result of this paper suggests that those principles are connected with inductive reasoning over arbitrary (undefinable) sets.

Another interesting task is to determine and explore fragments of AL that are more convenient to work with, but are still sufficient for at least some concrete applications. An example of such a fragment may be the one which corresponds to the use of the *deterministic* transitive closure operator (see, e.g., [10]). Another option worth investigating is to restrict the induction rule by allowing only φ's of the form $y = t$, where $Fv(t) = \{x\}$. Implicitly, this is the fragment of AL used in Peano's Arithmetics.

In [15] it is noted that Craig interpolation theorem and Beth definability theorem fail for logics in which the notion of finiteness can be expressed. Thus, a future research task is to find appropriate AL counterparts (whenever such exist) to central model-theoretic properties of FOL such as these.

Acknowledgments. This research was supported by: Ministry of Science, Technology and Space, Israel; Fulbright Post-doctoral Scholar program; Weizmann Institute of Science – National Postdoctoral Award Program for Advancing Women in Science; Eric and Wendy Schmidt Postdoctoral Award program for Women in Mathematical and Computing Sciences; and Cornell University PRL Group.

The author is indebt to A. Avron for his invaluable comments and expertise that greatly assisted this research.

References

1. Avron, A.: Transitive closure and the mechanization of mathematics. In: Kamareddine, F.D. (ed.) Thirty Five Years of Automating Mathematics. Applied Logic Series, vol. 28, pp. 149–171. Springer, Netherlands (2003). doi:10.1007/978-94-017-0253-9_7

2. Cohen, L., Avron, A.: The middle ground-ancestral logic. Synthese, 1–23 (2015)

3. Cohen, L., Constable, R.L.: Intuitionistic ancestral logic. J. Logic Comput. (2015)

4. Ebbinghaus, H.D., Flum, J.: Finite Model Theory. Springer Science & Business Media, New York (2005)

5. Feferman, S.: Finitary inductively presented logics. Stud. Logic Found. Math. **127**, 191–220 (1989)

6. Gentzen, G.: Investigations into Logical Deduction (1934). (in German). An English translation appears in 'The Collected Works of Gerhard Gentzen', edited by M.E. Szabo. North-Holland (1969)

7. Girard, J.Y.: Proof Theory and Logical Complexity, vol. 1. Humanities Press, London (1987)

8. Halpern, J.Y., Harper, R., Immerman, N., Kolaitis, P.G., Vardi, M.Y., Vianu, V.: On the unusual effectiveness of logic in computer science. Bull. Symb. Logic **7**(02), 213–236 (2001)

9. Henkin, L.: Completeness in the theory of types. J. Symb. Logic **15**(2), 81–91 (1950)

10. Immerman, N.: Languages that capture complexity classes. SIAM J. Comput. **16**(4), 760–778 (1987)

11. Kozen, D.: Kleene algebra with tests. ACM Trans. Program. Lang. Syst. (TOPLAS) **19**(3), 427–443 (1997)

12. Martin, R.M.: A homogeneous system for formal logic. J. Symb. Logic **8**(1), 1–23 (1943)

13. Martin, R.M.: A note on nominalism and recursive functions. J. Symb. Logic **14**(1), 27–31 (1949)

14. Myhill, J.: A derivation of number theory from ancestral theory. J. Symb. Logic **17**(3), 192–197 (1952)

15. Shapiro, S.: Foundations Without Foundationalism: A Case for Second-Order Logic. Oxford University Press, Oxford (1991)

16. Tait, W.W.: A nonconstructive proof of gentzen's hauptsatz for second order predicate logic. Bull. Am. Math. Soc. **72**(6), 980–983 (1966)

17. Takeuti, G.: Proof Theory. Courier Dover Publications, Mineola (1987)

18. Wohrle, S., Thomas, W.: Model checking synchronized products of infinite transition systems. In: Logic in Computer Science, pp. 2–11 (2004)

A Cut-Free Cyclic Proof System
for Kleene Algebra

Anupam Das and Damien Pous[(⊠)]

Univ. Lyon, CNRS, ENS de Lyon, UCB Lyon 1, LIP, Lyon, France
Damien.Pous@ens-lyon.fr

Abstract. We introduce a sound non-wellfounded proof system whose regular (or 'cyclic') proofs are complete for (in)equations between regular expressions. We achieve regularity by using *hypersequents* rather than usual sequents, with more structure in the succedent, and relying on the discreteness of *rational languages* to drive proof search. By inspection of the proof search space we extract a PSPACE bound for the system, which is optimal for deciding such (in)equations.

1 Introduction

Kleene algebra is a finite quasi-equational theory over regular expressions [11], which admits *formal languages* and *binary relations* as free models. Indeed, Krob and Kozen independently proved its completeness: every equation which is universally valid in one of those models, or equivalently, whose members denote the same rational language, is provable from the axioms of Kleene algebra [21,28]. This theorem is important in practice since it shows that the equational theory of Kleene algebra is decidable, and actually PSPACE-complete: it reduces to the problem of comparing rational languages. Thanks to the model of binary relations, Kleene algebra and its extensions have been used to reason abstractly about program correctness [1,2,17,24,25]. The aforementioned decidability result actually made it possible to automate reasoning steps in proof assistants [5,26,31].

Following work in substructural logics about residuated lattices [29], Jipsen proposed a sequent system for Kleene algebra and asked whether the cut-rule is admissible in this system [19]—Buszkowski proved it is not [10]. Wurm recently proposed a different sequent system [34], but his cut-admissibility theorem does not hold [12, Appendix A]. Proofs in these two systems are finite and well-founded.

An extended version of this abstract is available on HAL [12]. This work was supported by the European Research Council (ERC) under the Horizon 2020 programme (CoVeCe, grant agreement No. 678157) and the LABEX MILYON (ANR-10-LABX-0070) of Université de Lyon, within the program "Investissements d'Avenir" (ANR-11-IDEX-0007).

R.A. Schmidt and C. Nalon (Eds.): TABLEAUX 2017, LNAI 10501, pp. 261–277, 2017.
DOI: 10.1007/978-3-319-66902-1_16

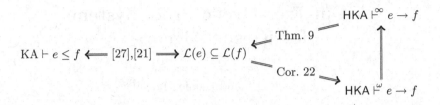

Fig. 1. Algebraic and proof-theoretic views on rational language equivalence.

Palka proposed a sequent system for *star-continuous action lattices* [30], and thus in particular for Kleene algebra. She proved completeness and cut-elimination. Her system is wellfounded but relies on an 'ω-rule' for Kleene star with infinitely many premises, in the traditional school of infinitary proof theory [33]. Doing so has the advantage of being simple, but it does not admit any reasonable notion of 'finiteness': every proof is necessarily infinite. As a consequence, such a system cannot be used for proof search.

In similar lines of work, the ω-rule can often be restricted to only finitely many cases by some finite model property of the logic [7,8]. This indeed could be done for Palka's system, requiring an exponential number of cases, leading to rather large proofs and inefficient proof search. Such systems do not obey the subformula property and are only *weakly* sound, preserving validity rather than truth, making metalogical properties, such as interpolation, difficult to prove.

We introduce in this paper a calculus HKA for Kleene algebra whose non-wellfounded proofs we prove sound and complete (Sects. 5 and 6). This calculus is cut-free and admits the subformula property. We actually prove that its regular fragment—those proofs with potentially cyclic but finite dependency graphs—is complete. Our approach is related to other works on cyclic systems for logics, e.g. [13,15], but is more fine-grained proof theoretically. We give a diagrammatic summary of our contributions in Fig. 1, where we use the symbols $\vdash^\omega$ and $\vdash^\infty$ to distinguish between regular proofs and arbitrary, potentially infinite proofs resp.

Starting from Palka's system, a natural idea when looking for a regular system consists in replacing her infinitary rules for Kleene star by finitary ones, and allowing non-wellfounded proofs. Doing so, we obtain the calculus LKA described in Sect. 3: proofs that are well-founded but of infinite width in Palka's system become finitely branching but infinitely deep in LKA. These non-wellfounded proofs of LKA admit an elegant proof theory, but we show that its regular fragment is not complete: there are valid inequalities which require arbitrarily large sequents to appear in their proofs. We solve this problem by allowing slightly more structure in the succedents of sequents, moving to *hypersequents* to design the calculus HKA (Sect. 4). After showing completeness, inspection of the regular proofs of HKA yields an alternative proof that the equational theory of rational languages is in PSPACE, without relying on automata-theoretic arguments (Sect. 7). We conclude this paper with some further comments and directions for future work (Sect. 8).

2   Kleene Algebra

We consider *regular expressions* over a finite *alphabet* A:

$$e, f ::= e \cdot e \mid e + e \mid e^* \mid 1 \mid 0 \mid a \in A$$

Sometimes we simply write ef for $e \cdot f$. Each expression e denotes a rational language $\mathcal{L}(e) \subseteq A^*$, defined in the usual way [20]. A *Kleene algebra* is a tuple $(K, 0, 1, +, \cdot, *)$ where $(K, 0, 1, +, \cdot)$ is an idempotent semiring and:[1]

(a) $1 + xx^* \leq x^*$;
(b) if $xy \leq y$ then $x^*y \leq y$;
(c) if $yx \leq y$ then $yx^* \leq y$.

There are several equivalent variants of this definition [11]. Intuitively we have that x^*y (resp. yx^*) is the least fixpoint of $z \mapsto y + xz$ (resp. $z \mapsto y + zx$).

We write $\mathrm{KA} \vdash e \leq f$ if $e \leq f$ is provable from the axioms of Kleene Algebra, i.e. is true in all Kleene algebras (by completeness of first-order logic). We have the following completeness result, independently due to Kozen and Krob:

Theorem 1 [21,28]. $\mathrm{KA} \vdash e \leq f$ *if and only if* $\mathcal{L}(e) \subseteq \mathcal{L}(f)$.

Formal languages, i.e. subsets of A^*, form a Kleene algebra, so the left-right implication is straightforward. The converse, completeness, is much harder.

3   An Intrinsically Non-regular System: LKA

A sequent is an expression $\Gamma \to e$, where Γ is a (possibly empty) list of regular expressions and e is a regular expression. For such a sequent we refer to Γ as the *antecedent* and e as the *succedent*. We say a sequent $e_1, \ldots, e_n \to e$ is *valid* if $\mathcal{L}(e_1 \cdots e_n) \subseteq \mathcal{L}(e)$, i.e. the comma is interpreted as sequential composition, and the sequent arrow as inclusion. We refer to expressions as 'formulae' when it is more natural proof theoretically, e.g. 'subformula' or 'principal formula'.

$$id \frac{}{e \to e} \qquad 0\text{-}l \frac{}{\Gamma, 0, \Delta \to e} \qquad 1\text{-}l \frac{\Gamma, \Delta \to e}{\Gamma, 1, \Delta \to e} \qquad 1\text{-}r \frac{}{\to 1}$$

$$\cdot\text{-}l \frac{\Gamma, e, f, \Delta \to g}{\Gamma, e \cdot f, \Delta \to g} \qquad +\text{-}l \frac{\Gamma, e, \Delta \to g \quad \Gamma, f, \Delta \to g}{\Gamma, e + f, \Delta \to g} \qquad *\text{-}l \frac{\Gamma, \Delta \to f \quad \Gamma, e, e^*, \Delta \to f}{\Gamma, e^*, \Delta \to f}$$

$$\cdot\text{-}r \frac{\Gamma \to e \quad \Delta \to f}{\Gamma, \Delta \to e \cdot f} \qquad +\text{-}r_i \frac{\Gamma \to e_i}{\Gamma \to e_1 + e_2} i \in \{1, 2\} \qquad *\text{-}r_1 \frac{}{\to e^*} \qquad *\text{-}r_2 \frac{\Gamma \to e \quad \Delta \to e^*}{\Gamma, \Delta \to e^*}$$

Fig. 2. The rules of LKA.

---

[1] Here we write $x \leq y$ as a shorthand for $x + y = y$.

The rules of LKA are given in Fig. 2. Aside from the ∗-rules, these form a fragment of non-commutative intuitionistic linear logic [16],[2] or alternatively the Lambek calculus [29], restricted to the following connectives: multiplicative conjunction $(\cdot)$, multiplicative truth (1), additive disjunction (+) and additive falsity (0) (for which there is no right rule). The rules for Kleene star arise from the characterisation of e^* as a fixed point: $e^* = \mu x.(1 + ex)$. In contrast, Palka [30] interprets Kleene star as an infinite sum $e^* = \Sigma_i e^i$, corresponding to ∗-*continuity* in a Kleene algebra, whence her left rule for Kleene star with infinitely many premises and the infinitely many corresponding right rules.

The rules of LKA are *sound*: if each premiss of a rule is true in a Kleene algebra then so is its conclusion. LKA also has the *subformula property*: any expression in the premiss of a rule instance is a subformula of an expression in its conclusion. On the other hand, the usual finite well-founded proof system arising from these rules is not complete: there are valid sequents which conclude no finite proof tree of LKA rules, cf. Example 4 below. To obtain completeness, we consider *non-wellfounded* proofs. Intuitively, these are infinite trees built from the rules of LKA. More formally:

Definition 2. *A (binary, possibly infinite) tree is a prefix-closed subset of* $\{0,1\}^*$. *An* LKA-*preproof is a labelling* π *of a tree by sequents such that, for every node* v *with children* $v_1, \ldots v_n$ $(n = 0, 1, 2)$, *the expression* $\frac{\pi(v_1) \ \cdots \ \pi(v_n)}{\pi(v)}$ *is an instance of an* LKA *rule. A preproof is* regular *if it has only finitely many distinct subtrees, i.e. it can be expressed as the infinite unfolding of a finite graph.*

Preproofs are not always sound (hence the terminology). Consider, for instance, the preproof on the right deriving a non-valid sequent, where we use the symbol • to indicate a circularity (i.e. to identify steps whose conclusions root the same subtree). Fortunately, we may rule out such behaviours by a simple fairness criterion:

$$1\text{-}r\,\frac{}{\to 1} \quad *\text{-}r_2\,\frac{\vdots}{a \to 1^*}\bullet$$
$$*\text{-}r_2\,\frac{}{a \to 1^*}\bullet$$

Definition 3. *A proof is a preproof that is fair for* ∗-*l, i.e. where every infinite branch contains infinitely many occurrences of* ∗-*l. We write* LKA $\vdash^\infty \Gamma \to e$ *if there is an* LKA *proof of* $\Gamma \to e$.

This criterion is somewhat simpler than the ones from other works, e.g. [13, 15], which require a finer analysis of formula occurrences in infinite branches. However, for our purposes, the condition above suffices and, indeed, leads to a simpler correctness checking procedure for a preproof, cf. Sect. 7.

Example 4. Here is an (infinite but regular) proof of $a^*(b+c)^* \le a^*(c+b)^*$ in LKA. The fairness criterion is satisfied since the only circularity goes through a ∗-*l* rule.

---

[2] This logic is non-commutative because there is no exchange rule, and intuitionistic since there is exactly one formula on the right-hand side.

$$
\dfrac{
\dfrac{id}{a^*\to a^*}
\quad
\dfrac{
\dfrac{*\text{-}r_1}{\to (c+b)^*}
\quad
\dfrac{
\dfrac{
\dfrac{\dfrac{id}{b\to b}}{b\to c+b}{\scriptstyle +\text{-}r_2}
\quad
\dfrac{\dfrac{id}{c\to c}}{c\to c+b}{\scriptstyle +\text{-}r_1}
}{b+c\to c+b}{\scriptstyle +\text{-}l}
\quad
\dfrac{\vdots}{(b+c)^*\to (c+b)^*}\!\bullet{\scriptstyle \ *\text{-}l}
}{b+c,(b+c)^*\to (c+b)^*}{\scriptstyle *\text{-}r_2}
}{(b+c)^*\to (c+b)^*}\!\bullet{\scriptstyle \ *\text{-}l}
}{a^*,(b+c)^*\to a^*(c+b)^*}{\scriptstyle \cdot\cdot\text{-}r}
}{a^*(b+c)^*\to a^*(c+b)^*}{\scriptstyle \cdot\cdot\text{-}l}
$$

Note that this sequent has no finite wellfounded proof in LKA.

Theorem 5. (Soundness). *If* LKA $\vdash^\infty e_1,\dots,e_n \to e$ *then* $\mathcal{L}(e_1\cdots\cdot e_n)\subseteq\mathcal{L}(e)$.

Proof (idea). Similar to the proof we give in Sect. 5 for the system HKA. □

While LKA satisfies the subformula property, the size and number of sequents occurring in a proof are not *a priori* bounded, due to the *-l rule. In fact, this system does not admit regular proofs for all valid sequents. An example is the inequality $aa^* \leq a^*a$, whose only proof in LKA is the following:

$$
\dfrac{
\dfrac{
\dfrac{
\dfrac{\dfrac{*\text{-}r_1}{\to a^*}\quad\dfrac{id}{a\to a}}{a\to a^*a}{\scriptstyle \cdot\cdot\text{-}r}
}{a\to a^*a}{\scriptstyle *\text{-}l}
\quad
\dfrac{
\dfrac{\dfrac{id}{a\to a}\quad\dfrac{*\text{-}r_1}{\to a^*}}{a\to a^*}{\scriptstyle *\text{-}r_2}
\quad \dfrac{id}{a\to a}
}{a,a\to a^*a}{\scriptstyle \cdot\cdot\text{-}r}
\quad
\dfrac{\dfrac{id}{a,a,a,a^*\to a^*a}\quad\vdots}{a,a,a^*\to a^*a}{\scriptstyle *\text{-}l}
}{a,a^*\to a^*a}{\scriptstyle *\text{-}l}
}{aa^*\to a^*a}{\scriptstyle \cdot\cdot\text{-}l}
\qquad (1)
$$

This proof necessarily contains all sequents of the form $a,\dots,a,a^* \to a^*a$. Even though it could arguably be 'described' in a finite way, this would require an external specification, contrary to the notion of regularity which simply allows cycles in the dependency graph of a proof. Indeed, only finitely many sequents occur in a regular proof, and so they are somewhat easier to reason about.

Many cases of non-regularity can be avoided by adding *symmetric* versions of the $*$ rules in LKA:

$$
{}_{*\text{-}l'}\dfrac{\Gamma,\Delta \to f \quad \Gamma,e^*,e,\Delta \to f}{\Gamma,e^*,\Delta \to f}
\qquad
{}_{*\text{-}r'_2}\dfrac{\Gamma \to e^* \quad \Delta \to e}{\Gamma,\Delta \to e^*}
\qquad (2)
$$

For instance, using these rules, it is not hard to see that the situation (1) above can be handled by a well-founded finite proof (see [12, Appendix B]).

However, adding the rules from (2) above does not always suffice for regularity. Consider the valid sequent $a^* \to (aa)^* + a(aa)^*$. It is not hard to see that any proof must contain a path of just *-l steps, since we are never able to apply a +-r step while there remains an a^* on the left. Thus it admits no regular proof in LKA, even with the rules from (2).

Similarly, consider the valid sequent $(a + b)^* \to a^*(ba^*)^*$. Any proof of this sequent, even with symmetric rules, must contain some path of sequents whose antecedents denote languages containing $a^m(a+b)^*a^n$, for sufficiently large m, n. Along such a path a $\cdot$-r step is never valid and so one is forced to apply $*$-l and $+$-l rules forever, again yielding a non-regular proof.

The next section presents a system where we can avoid these issues by reasoning *underneath* $\cdot$ and $+$ in the succedent, and thus arrive at a general completeness theorem for regular proofs. We come back to the problem cases discussed above at the end of the next section, in Example 23.

4 A Calculus Whose Regular Proofs Are Complete: HKA

We denote lists of formulae by Γ, Δ etc. as before. We will use X, Y, Z to vary over multisets of lists. A *hypersequent* is an expression $\Gamma \to X$, where Γ is a list and X is a multiset of lists. Henceforth we may simply say 'sequent' instead of 'hypersequent' when it is not ambiguous. We use the comma, ',', for both delimiting lists and denoting union of multisets, using angled brackets $\langle \cdot \rangle$ to distinguish lists in a multiset. Here is the general form of a hypersequent:

$$e_1, \ldots, e_l \to \langle f_{11}, \ldots, f_{1n_1} \rangle, \cdots, \langle f_{m1}, \ldots, f_{mn_m} \rangle$$

We extend the notion of language of a regular expression to lists of expressions by setting $\mathcal{L}(\langle e_1, \ldots, e_n \rangle) = \mathcal{L}(e_1 \cdots e_n)$, and to multisets of such lists by setting $\mathcal{L}(\langle \Gamma_1 \rangle, \ldots, \langle \Gamma_n \rangle) = \bigcup_i \mathcal{L}(\Gamma_i)$. The hypersequent $\Gamma \to X$ is *valid* if $\mathcal{L}(\Gamma) \subseteq \mathcal{L}(X)$.

If $X = \langle \Delta_1 \rangle, \ldots, \langle \Delta_n \rangle$, we write $\langle \Sigma \rangle X$ for the set $\langle \Sigma, \Delta_1 \rangle, \ldots, \langle \Sigma, \Delta_n \rangle$. When Σ is a singleton $\langle e \rangle$ we simply write eX instead of $\langle e \rangle X$, as an abuse of notation.

The rules of HKA are given in Fig. 3. Notice that these rules satisfy the subformula property. The left logical rules are exactly those of LKA, lifted to hypersequents. The right logical rules slightly differ, to take advantage of the richer structure of the sequents. Weakening and contractions are allowed on the right of the sequents; the identity axiom from LKA is decomposed into an axiom for the empty lists, and a 'modal' rule (k).

Definition 6. *Preproofs and proofs of* HKA *are defined analogously to* LKA; *in particular proofs require fairness of* $*$-l. *We write* HKA $\vdash^\omega \Gamma \to X$ *if* $\Gamma \to X$ *has a regular proof in* HKA, *i.e. one with only finitely many distinct subtrees.*

Remark 7 (Invertibility and cancellation). All rules of HKA except w and k are *strongly* invertible: truth of the conclusion implies truth of all premises in any Kleene algebra. k is not strongly invertible, even in its atomic form, due to the possible existence of 0-divisors. It is however weakly invertible when e is atomic: the validity of the conclusion implies the validity of the premiss.[3] On the other hand, the non-invertibility of w turns out to be crucial for completeness, from a complexity theoretic point of view, cf. Sect. 7.

---

[3] Note that atomicity of e really is required for this, even in the usual rational language model. For instance, we have $\mathcal{L}(a^*ab) \subseteq \mathcal{L}(a^*b)$, but $\mathcal{L}(ab) \nsubseteq \mathcal{L}(b)$.

Left logical rules:

$$0\text{-}l \frac{}{\Gamma, 0, \Delta \to} \qquad 1\text{-}l \frac{\Gamma, \Delta \to X}{\Gamma, 1, \Delta \to X} \qquad \cdot\text{-}l \frac{\Gamma, e, f, \Delta \to X}{\Gamma, e \cdot f, \Delta \to X}$$

$$+\text{-}l \frac{\Gamma, e, \Delta \to X \quad \Gamma, f, \Delta \to X}{\Gamma, e + f, \Delta \to X} \qquad *\text{-}l \frac{\Gamma, \Delta \to X \quad \Gamma, e, e^*, \Delta \to X}{\Gamma, e^*, \Delta \to X}$$

Right logical rules:

$$1\text{-}r \frac{\Gamma \to X, \langle \Delta, \Sigma \rangle}{\Gamma \to X, \langle \Delta, 1, \Sigma \rangle} \qquad \cdot\text{-}r \frac{\Gamma \to X, \langle \Delta, e, f, \Sigma \rangle}{\Gamma \to X, \langle \Delta, e \cdot f, \Sigma \rangle}$$

$$+\text{-}r \frac{\Gamma \to X, \langle \Delta, e, \Sigma \rangle, \langle \Delta, f, \Sigma \rangle}{\Gamma \to X, \langle \Delta, e + f, \Sigma \rangle} \qquad *\text{-}r \frac{\Gamma \to X, \langle \Delta, \Sigma \rangle, \langle \Delta, e, e^*, \Sigma \rangle}{\Gamma \to X, \langle \Delta, e^*, \Sigma \rangle}$$

Identity, modal and structural rules:

$$id \frac{}{\to \langle \, \rangle} \qquad k \frac{\Gamma \to X}{e, \Gamma \to eX} \qquad w \frac{\Gamma \to X}{\Gamma \to X, \langle \Delta \rangle} \qquad c \frac{\Gamma \to X, \langle \Delta \rangle, \langle \Delta \rangle}{\Gamma \to X, \langle \Delta \rangle}$$

Fig. 3. The rules of HKA.

Example 8 (Atomic modal steps). We can reduce k steps to atomic form by regular derivations of HKA. This is proved by structural induction on the modal expression; the key case is for a $*$-formula, where non-wellfoundedness appears:

$$*\text{-}r,w \frac{\Gamma \to X}{\Gamma \to e^*X} \quad *\text{-}r,w \frac{IH \dfrac{*\text{-}l \dfrac{\vdots}{e^*, \Gamma \to e^*X} \bullet}{e, e^*, \Gamma \to \langle e, e^* \rangle X}}{e, e^*, \Gamma \to e^*X} \bullet$$
$$*\text{-}l \frac{}{e^*, \Gamma \to e^*X} \bullet$$

The derivation marked *IH* is obtained from the inductive hypothesis on e.

5   Soundness

We now show that HKA proofs derive only valid sequents. Throughout this section and later, we use standard proof theoretic terminology about *ancestry* in proofs, e.g. from [9].

Theorem 9 (Soundness). *If* HKA $\vdash^\infty \Gamma \to X$, *then* $\mathcal{L}(\Gamma) \subseteq \mathcal{L}(X)$.

Before giving the proof, we need the following intermediate result.

Lemma 10. *If* HKA $\vdash^\infty \Gamma, e^*, \Delta \to X$ *then, for* $n \in \mathbb{N}$, HKA $\vdash^\infty \Gamma, e^n, \Delta \to X$.[4]

---

[4] Strictly speaking, we should bracket e^n as $e(e(\cdots(ee)))$ and set e^0 to 1.

Proof. We define appropriate preproofs by induction on n. Replace every direct ancestor of e^* by e^n, adjusting origins as follows,

$$*\text{-}l\frac{\Gamma,\Delta\to X\quad\Gamma,e,e^*,\Delta\to X}{\Gamma,e^*,\Delta\to X}\quad\mapsto\quad 1\text{-}l\frac{\Gamma,\Delta\to X}{\Gamma,1,\Delta\to X}\quad\text{or}\quad \cdot\text{-}l\frac{\Gamma,e,e^{n-1},\Delta\to X}{\Gamma,e^n,\Delta\to X}$$

when $n = 0$ or $n > 0$, respectively. In the latter case we appeal to the inductive hypothesis. Notice that, on branches where e^* is never principal, this is simply a global substitution of e^n for e^* everywhere along the branch. The preproof resulting from this entire construction is fair since every infinite branch will share a tail with a branch in the proof we began with. □

Now we define a measure with which Theorem 9 will be proved by induction.

Definition 11 (Measure of a sequent). *The $*$-height of a regular expression e, denoted $h_*(e)$, is the maximum nesting of $*$ in its term tree. Formally:*

- $h_*(0) = h_*(1) = h_*(a) = 0$.
- $h_*(e \cdot f) = h_*(e + f) = \max(h_*(e), h_*(f))$.
- $h_*(e^*) = h_*(e) + 1$.

The weighted $*$-height of a list Γ of expressions, denoted $wh_*(\Gamma)$ is the multiset $\{h(e) : e \in \Gamma\}$. We totally order such multisets under a well-known ordering [14]: for two multisets[5] $N, M : \mathbb{N} \to \mathbb{N}$, we set $N < M$ if for any n with $N(n) > M(n)$ there is a $n' > n$ s.t. $N(n') < M(n')$.

Fact 12. *For every rule of* HKA *except $*$-l, the antecedent of each premiss has weighted $*$-height bounded by that of the antecedent of the conclusion.*

For the $*$-l rule also notice that, bottom-up, the maximum $*$-height of an expression in the antecedent does not increase. We now prove our soundness result:

Proof (of Theorem 9). Let π be an HKA proof of $\Sigma \to X$ and let us proceed by induction on the weighted $*$-height of the antecedent Σ. For each infinite branch of π take the least $*$-l step that occurs; their conclusions form a bar B through the infinite tree of π. Since π labels a binary tree, the prefix closure of B must be finite by König's Lemma and thus, if each of the sequents of B is valid then so is the conclusion of π by the soundness of well-founded HKA derivations.

Now, consider a subproof π' that derives a sequent in B. This sequent must have the form $\Gamma, f^*, \Delta \to Y$ where f^* is principal for the concluding $*$-l-step of π'. By construction and Fact 12 notice that $wh_*(\Gamma, f^*, \Delta) \leq wh_*(\Sigma)$. Now, by Lemma 10, π' can be transformed into proofs π'_n of $\Gamma, f^n, \Delta \to Y$ for each $n \in \mathbb{N}$. Since $wh_*(\Gamma, f^n, \Delta) < wh_*(\Sigma)$, each π'_n is sound by the inductive hypothesis. Finally, this means that $\Gamma, f^*, \Delta \to Y$ is valid, by definition of Kleene star for languages, and hence $\Sigma \to X$ is valid after all. □

---

[5] Here we construe multisets as mappings from elements to their multiplicity.

6   Completeness

Infinite non-wellfounded proofs are easily seen to be complete: bottom-up, simply apply left rules forever (they are invertible); the only normal forms of this procedure will have a finite word as the antecedent, whence we may perform the correct finite sequence of right steps to finish proof search.

In this section we give a more sophisticated argument showing that the *regular* fragment of HKA is complete: each valid inclusion has a finite circular proof.

6.1   A Regular Class of Proofs

We first define a class of proofs which can be made regular in a systematic way.

Definition 13. *A preproof is* leftmost *if the principal formula of every logical step is at the beginning of a list, either in the antecedent or the succedent.*

For regularity, the most useful property of a leftmost proof is the following:

Theorem 14. *A leftmost preproof contains only lists of length linear in the size of the end-sequent. Hence only finitely many lists occur in a leftmost preproof.*[6]

Before we can prove this, let us recall some basic notions regarding terms. An *occurrence* in e is a subformula of e together with its position in e. We often omit this positional information when it is unambiguous.

Definition 15 (Total order on occurrences). *Given a fixed term, we define a relation $\preccurlyeq$ on the occurrences in it as follows: $e \preccurlyeq f$ if f contains e, or if e and f are disjoint and e occurs to the left of f.*

Due to the tree structure of a term, any two occurrences in a term are either disjoint or one is contained in the other, so we have the following:

Proposition 16. $\preccurlyeq$ *is a total order on the occurrences in a term.*

In a preproof, let us identify every expression occurring as an occurrence of a term in the end-sequent in the natural way, due to the subformula property and via the usual notions of proof ancestry. In this way, we can meaningfully compare any two expressions in a preproof under $\preccurlyeq$. We have the following:

Lemma 17. *In any leftmost preproof every list is strictly increasing under $\preccurlyeq$.*

Now we can prove the bound on the size of lists in leftmost preproofs:

Proof (of Theorem 14). Every term in a preproof is an ancestor of an occurrence in a term of the end sequent, by the subformula property and usual notions of proof ancestry. Moreover, no occurrence can appear twice in the same list, otherwise we would contradict Lemma 17.   □

---

[6] *A priori*, this could still be exponentially many in the size of the end-sequent.

We still do not quite have regularity, since in the succedent we may have multisets with arbitrarily many occurrences of the same list. Naturally, we appeal to the right structural rules to 'merge' occurrences in such a situation:

Corollary 18. *A leftmost preproof in* HKA *can be transformed into one of the same end-sequent that contains only finitely many distinct sequents.*

Proof. By Theorem 14 only finitely many distinct lists occur in a leftmost preproof. Thanks to contraction and weakening, we can always write succedents with at most two copies of each distinct list, of which there are only finitely many. □

It remains to show that we may place backpointers while preserving correctness:

Corollary 19. *A leftmost proof in* HKA *can be transformed into a regular proof with the same end-sequent.*

Proof. Assuming only finitely many distinct sequents occur, by Corollary 18 above, in each infinite branch some sequent occurs infinitely often, by the pigeonhole principle. This means that, due to fairness, for each infinite branch we may identify two instances of the same sequent with a $*$-l-step in between, whence we may correctly place a backpointer and preserve fairness. □

6.2   Completeness of Leftmost Proofs

Thanks to Corollary 19, for completeness of the regular fragment of HKA it now suffices to show that any valid hypersequent admits a leftmost (possibly infinite) proof. We do so by providing a leftmost proof search strategy for which we need the following important result:

Lemma 20 (Productivity on the right). *Suppose there is a finite* HKA *derivation of right logical rules of the following format,[7]*

$$\Gamma \to X, \langle e^*, \Delta \rangle$$
$$\Big|\pi$$
$$*\text{-}r \, \frac{\Gamma \to Y, \langle \Delta \rangle, \langle e, e^*, \Delta \rangle}{\Gamma \to Y, \langle e^*, \Delta \rangle}$$

such that the list $\langle e^*, \Delta \rangle$ *in the initial sequent is an ancestor of that from the end sequent. If the end sequent is valid, then so is* $\Gamma \to X$.

Proof. Since all right logical rules of HKA are invertible, it suffices to show that $\langle e^*, \Delta \rangle$ in the initial sequent is redundant, i.e. that already $\mathcal{L}(X) \supseteq \mathcal{L}(\langle e^*, \Delta \rangle)$. For this, we appeal to soundness of fair preproofs, Theorem 9, and show that HKA proves the corresponding sequent: $e^*, \Delta \to X$.[8] We construct an appropriate

---

[7] Notice that right logical rules do not branch.

[8] This argument is akin to applying a cut, which is sound since we are only applying it once, and at the meta-level.

proof π' bottom-up by induction on the length of π where, for each right logical rule in π, we apply the analogous left logical rule in π' along the appropriate branch. Each leaf of π' will be of the form $\Sigma \to X$, where Σ is a list occurring in the succedent of the premiss of π, by construction. Now, if $\Sigma \in X$ then we can conclude by weakening, k and identity; otherwise Σ is $\langle e^*, \Delta \rangle$, whence we can conclude by circularity. Notice that π' is fair due to the fact that the bottommost step is a $*$-l due to the analogous $*$-r beneath π.   □

We can now prove our main completeness result:

Theorem 21. *Every valid hypersequent has a leftmost proof in* HKA.

Proof. Construct a leftmost HKA preproof bottom-up as follows:

(i) Apply leftmost left logical rules as long as possible. After this any leaves will be valid, by invertibility of logical rules, and of the form:

$$\to X \quad \text{or} \quad a, \Gamma \to X$$

(ii) Apply leftmost right logical rules until the succedent contains only lists beginning with a $*$-term that have already been decomposed[9] or lists for which no leftmost right logical rule applies. This terminates after finitely many steps due to Theorem 14 and since only $*$-r can increase the length of a list in the succedent. All resulting leaves must be valid, again by invertibility.

(iii) Now we apply w to weaken any appropriate lists in the succedent that have already been decomposed. Leaves remain valid due to Lemma 20 and must be of the form:

$$\to (\langle \ \rangle,) \langle a_1, X_1 \rangle, \ldots, \langle a_n, X_n \rangle \quad \text{or} \quad a, \Gamma \to (\langle \ \rangle,) \langle a_1, X_1 \rangle, \ldots, \langle a_n, X_n \rangle$$

In the former case, since we have preserved validity going upwards, we must have that the empty list occurs in the succedent, whence we can close the branch by several w steps and id.

In the latter case, again since we have preserved validity going upwards, we must be able to weaken any list that begins with an a_i that is not a and preserve validity. Now any remaining leaves are of the form,

$$a, \Gamma \to aX$$

whence we can apply k and preserve validity by Remark 7. Now go back to (i) and repeat the entire procedure.

This procedure will produce a leftmost preproof that is fair since (ii) produces only finite well-founded derivations, and so any infinite branch must either eventually remain in the (i) or (iii) case. For the former, a $*$-l must occur infinitely often since the other left rules shorten the antecedent, and for the latter a k step occurs infinitely often, again meaning that a $*$-l step must occur infinitely often since k also shortens the antecedent.   □

---

[9] Here we mean in the sense that it is identical to a descendant, as in Lemma 20.

Corollary 22. *If* $\mathcal{L}(e) \subseteq \mathcal{L}(f)$ *then* $\mathsf{HKA} \vdash^\omega e \to f$.

Proof. By Corollary 19 and Theorem 21.   □

Example 23. Let us see how the example issues for regularity for LKA we alluded to in Sect. 3 are resolved in HKA. In both cases we use variations of the strategy given in the proof above of Theorem 21.

$$
\cfrac{
  \cfrac{
    id \cfrac{}{\to \langle\,\rangle}
  }{
    \cfrac{}{*\text{-}r,w \; \to \langle(aa)^*\rangle, \langle a,(aa)^*\rangle}
  }
  \qquad
  \cfrac{
    2\text{-}\text{-}r \cfrac{
      k \cfrac{
        *\text{-}l \cfrac{a^* \to \langle a,(aa)^*\rangle, \langle (aa)^*\rangle \; \bullet}{}
      }{a, a^* \to \langle a,a,(aa)^*\rangle, \langle a,(aa)^*\rangle}
    }{a, a^* \to \langle (aa)(aa)^*\rangle, \langle a,(aa)^*\rangle}
  }{*\text{-}r,w \; a, a^* \to \langle (aa)^*\rangle, \langle a,(aa)^*\rangle \; \bullet}
}{
  *\text{-}l \; a^* \to \langle (aa)^*\rangle, \langle a,(aa)^*\rangle
}
$$

$$
\cfrac{
  \cfrac{a^* \to \langle (aa)^*\rangle, \langle a,(aa)^*\rangle}{
    \cdot\text{-}r \; a^* \to \langle (aa)(aa)^*\rangle, \langle a(aa)^*\rangle
  }
}{+\text{-}r \; a^* \to \langle (aa)^* + a(aa)^*\rangle}
$$

$$
\cfrac{
  \cfrac{
    id \cfrac{}{\to \langle\,\rangle}
  }{
    \cfrac{}{*\text{-}r,w \; \to \langle (ba^*)^*\rangle}
    \atop *\text{-}r,w \; \to \langle a^*,(ba^*)^*\rangle
  }
  \quad
  \cfrac{
    k \cfrac{
      *\text{-}l \cfrac{(a+b)^* \to \langle a^*,(ba^*)^*\rangle \; \bullet}{}
    }{a, (a+b)^* \to \langle a, a^*,(ba^*)^*\rangle}
  }{
    *\text{-}r,w \; a, (a+b)^* \to \langle a^*,(ba^*)^*\rangle
  }
  \quad
  \cfrac{
    \cdot\text{-}r \cfrac{
      k \cfrac{
        *\text{-}l \cfrac{(a+b)^* \to \langle a^*,(ba^*)^*\rangle \; \bullet}{}
      }{b, (a+b)^* \to \langle b, a^*,(ba^*)^*\rangle}
    }{b, (a+b)^* \to \langle ba^*,(ba^*)^*\rangle}
  }{
    \cfrac{*\text{-}r,w \; b, (a+b)^* \to \langle (ba^*)^*\rangle}{*\text{-}r,wk \; b, (a+b)^* \to \langle a^*,(ba^*)^*\rangle}
  }
}{
  +\text{-}l \; a+b, (a+b)^* \to \langle a^*,(ba^*)^*\rangle \; \bullet
}
$$

$$
\cfrac{(a+b)^* \to \langle a^*,(ba^*)^*\rangle}{\cdot\text{-}r \; (a+b)^* \to \langle a^*(ba^*)^*\rangle}
$$

Remark 24. Antimirov' *partial derivatives* [3] make it possible to build a non-deterministic automaton whose states are the regular expressions, and such that only finitely many states are reachable from a regular expression. The (finitely many) lists appearing in a leftmost proof, seen as regular expressions, are in sharp correspondence with the partial derivatives of the lists in its conclusion. As a consequence, the proof search procedure of Theorem 21 expresses at a very fine grained level the behaviour of certain coinductive algorithms for language inclusion (equivalence), that explore the reachable states of an Antimirov' automaton and try to build a (bi)simulation [4, 18].

7   Complexity Matters and Algorithms for Proof Search

We present in this section a brief overview of the complexity theoretic aspects of proofs in our calculus HKA.

7.1   Checking Validity of a Regular Preproof

When a preproof is given as a tree with backpointers, it is not difficult to see that checking validity is feasible (i.e. in polynomial time), since we may simply exhaust the paths of the tree, of which there are linearly many, to exclude the existence of a $*$-l-free loop. When the preproof is given as an arbitrary graph the problem is a little more subtle, but remains feasible. Construing sequents as nodes and inference steps as edges, let us delete any edge that corresponds to a $*$-l step. Notice that the original preproof was valid just if there are no infinite paths in the resulting graph, i.e. it is *acyclic*. This can be decided by computing its transitive closure, hence:

Proposition 25. *Validity of a regular* HKA*-preproof, given as an arbitrary directed graph, is polynomial-time decidable.*

Notice that this bound is lower than those for circular proofs in other systems, e.g. [6,15], since logics with more sophisticated fixed points and logical behaviour require a more general correctness criterion reducing to the inclusion of *Büchi automata*, a problem that is PSPACE-complete.

7.2   Complexity of Proof Search

Proof search using HKA yields an optimal bound for deciding equations of Kleene algebra via the induced loop-checking procedure:

Proposition 26. *Proof search in* HKA *induces a* PSPACE *decision procedure for inequalities between regular expressions.*

Proof (sketch). For a leftmost proof we give a polynomial bound on the depth until a loop occurs. Notice that succedents only grow polynomially in depth and $*$-height, by inspection of HKA, and so this indeed yields a PSPACE bound.

Each time a k step is applied, bottom-up, it is on an atom occurrence that may not reoccur, unless we have already formed a loop, namely by unfolding the same $*$-expression, which by construction contains a $*$-l. Every other leftmost step decreases the size of the leftmost term in a list. Thus, any path in a leftmost proof will hit a loop within polynomially many steps.   □

Notice that, while almost every step in HKA is invertible, it is the crucial applications of weakening in the procedure of Theorem 21, justified by Lemma 20, which requires proof search to operate in PSPACE rather than CONP. Indeed, it is the number of w steps along any proof path that allows search complexity to climb up the polynomial hierarchy. This cannot be uniformly bounded since deciding inequalities of regular expressions is known to be PSPACE-complete.

8   Conclusions and Further Work

We proposed a regular and cut-free hypersequent system HKA, which we proved sound and complete for rational language inclusion, and thus for Kleene algebra. We conclude with further comments and directions for future work.

8.1   Richer Systems for Theorem Proving

Now that we have a completeness theorem for HKA, we could envisage enriching the system with more (sound) rules that might be more natural from the point of view of theorem proving. For instance, we might imagine alternative right logical rules for $+$ and $*$ as follows,

$$\frac{\Gamma \to X, \langle \Delta, e_i, \Sigma\rangle}{\Gamma \to X, \langle \Delta, e_1 + e_2, \Sigma\rangle} \quad \frac{\Gamma \to X, \langle \Delta, \Sigma\rangle}{\Gamma \to X, \langle \Delta, e^*, \Sigma\rangle} \quad \frac{\Gamma \to X, \langle \Delta, e, \Sigma\rangle}{\Gamma \to X, \langle \Delta, e^*, \Sigma\rangle} \quad \frac{\Gamma \to X, \langle \Delta, e^*, e^*, \Sigma\rangle}{\Gamma \to X, \langle \Delta, e^*, \Sigma\rangle}$$

Such systems are more expressive since they can encode not only the rules of HKA but also symmetric variants, e.g. unfolding $*$ to the right rather than the left.[10] An illustrative example is the inequality $a^*a \le a^*$, which was one source of irregularity for LKA. Contrast the following two proofs, the left of which follows a leftmost strategy in HKA, the right of which uses the rules above and is acyclic:

$$
\cfrac{
  \cfrac{
    \cfrac{
      \cfrac{
        \cfrac{
          \cfrac{\ \ }{\to \langle\,\rangle}\ id
        }{\to \langle\,\rangle, \langle a, a^*\rangle}\ w
      }{\to a^*}\ *\text{-}r
    }{a \to \langle a, a^*\rangle}\ k
    \quad
    \cfrac{a \to \langle\,\rangle, \langle a, a^*\rangle}{a \to \langle a^*\rangle}\ w
  }{a \to \langle a^*\rangle}\ *\text{-}r
}{a^*a \to \langle a^*\rangle}\ *\text{-}l
$$

$$
\cfrac{
  \cfrac{
    \cfrac{
      \cfrac{
        \cfrac{\vdots}{a^*, a \to \langle a^*\rangle}\ *\text{-}l \ \bullet
      }{a, a^*, a \to \langle a, a^*\rangle}\ k
    }{a, a^*, a \to \langle\,\rangle, \langle a, a^*\rangle}\ w
  }{a, a^*, a \to \langle a^*\rangle}\ *\text{-}r
}{a^*, a \to \langle a^*\rangle}\ \text{--}l \ \bullet
$$

$$
\cfrac{
  \cfrac{
    \cfrac{
      \cfrac{\cfrac{\ \ }{\to \langle\,\rangle}\ id}{a \to \langle a\rangle}\ k
    }{a^*, a \to \langle a^*, a\rangle}\ k
  }{a^*, a \to \langle a^*, a^*\rangle}
}{}
$$

$$
\cfrac{a^*, a \to \langle a^*\rangle}{a^*a \to \langle a^*\rangle}\ \text{--}l
$$

8.2   Extensions of Kleene Algebra

Kleene algebra can be extended with operations such as *meet* [22], *residuals* [32], or *tests* [23]. One can thus ask whether we can obtain regular sequent systems for such extensions. Meets ($\cap$) and residuals ($\multimap$) correspond to additive conjunction and linear implications in (non-commutative) linear logic; they could easily be added to LKA (Palka actually includes them in her system [30]), but it is unclear how to add them to our hypersequent system while preserving regular cut-free completeness. An important difficulty here is that the free model for such structures is not the obvious language model.[11] In contrast, Kleene algebra with tests, whose free model is that of *guarded string* languages [23], could be handled using our approach. It would also be interesting to try adapt our systems to ω-*regular* expressions, which denote languages of *infinite words* and for which automaton models and notions of derivative are well-defined.

---

[10] Notice that the $*$ rules here correspond in fact to an alternative fixed point definition of e^*: $\mu x.(1 + e + xx)$.

[11] Notice also that while it would be natural to enrich the antecedent structure for $\cap$ as we did in succedents for $+$, there is a difficult asymmetry in that $x(y + z) = xy + xz$ but $x(y \cap z) \lesssim xy \cap xz$.

8.3   Cut-Elimination

By completeness, any reasonable 'cut rule' is admissible in the regular fragment of HKA. A natural question is whether one can prove a direct cut-elimination result, using proof theoretic methods. There are several difficulties here: first one has to define a general enough notion of cut for the hypersequent system; second one has to come up with an appropriate correctness criterion for preproofs with cuts (fairness as in Definition 6 is not enough to guarantee soundness); finally, the regular system being complete, one would certainly like to prove that cut-elimination preserves regularity. Such a cut-elimination result would make it possible to interpret Kleene algebra proofs directly into HKA, without going through the free model (languages). This could be helpful to handle extensions of Kleene algebras whose free model is unknown, for instance with meet or with residuals.

8.4   Towards an Alternative Completeness Result for KA

Conversely to the previous comments, an interesting question is whether our completeness result for the regular fragment of HKA can be used to obtain an *alternative* proof of the completeness of Kleene algebra, Theorem 1. Namely, can we prove directly that if HKA $\vdash^\omega e \to f$ then KA $\vdash e \leq f$, in a direct manner? We believe this is possible, by encoding cycles in a leftmost proof as specific instances of the 'induction' axioms (b) and (c) from Sect. 2.[12] For instance a loop in a regular derivation might be transformed as follows:

$$
\cfrac{e^*, f \to g}{\Big| \pi} \qquad \rightsquigarrow \qquad
$$

$$
*\text{-}l\ \cfrac{\cfrac{f \to g \quad e, e^*, f \to g}{e^*, f \to g}}{e^*, f \to g}
$$

$$
cut\ \cfrac{f \to g \quad (b)\ \cfrac{id\ \cfrac{}{g \to g}\ \Big| \pi[g/(e^*,f)] \quad e, g \to g}{e^*, g \to g}}{e^*, f \to g}
$$

Generalising this idea into a full alternative proof of Kozen's and Krob's results is the subject of ongoing work.

References

1. Anderson, C.J., Foster, N., Guha, A., Jeannin, J.-B., Kozen, D., Schlesinger, C., Walker, D.: NetKAT: semantic foundations for networks. In: Proceedings of the POPL, pp. 113–126. ACM (2014)
2. Angus, A., Kozen, D.: Kleene algebra with tests and program schematology. Technical report TR2001-1844, CS Department, Cornell University, July 2001

---

[12] Note that the broader problem of whether cyclic proofs can be simulated by 'inductive' proofs for a certain framework has no known general solution, cf. [6].

3. Antimirov, V.M.: Partial derivatives of regular expressions and finite automaton constructions. TCS **155**(2), 291–319 (1996)
4. Bonchi, F., Pous, D.: Checking NFA equivalence with bisimulations up to congruence. In: Proceedings of the POPL, pp. 457-468. ACM (2013)
5. Braibant, T., Pous, D.: An efficient Coq tactic for deciding Kleene algebras. In: Kaufmann, M., Paulson, L.C. (eds.) ITP 2010. LNCS, vol. 6172, pp. 163–178. Springer, Heidelberg (2010). doi:10.1007/978-3-642-14052-5_13
6. Brotherston, J., Simpson, A.: Sequent calculi for induction and infinite descent. J. Log. Comput. **21**(6), 1177–1216 (2011)
7. Brünnler, K., Studer, T.: Syntactic cut-elimination for common knowledge. Ann. Pure Appl. Log. **160**(1), 82–95 (2009)
8. Brünnler, K., Studer, T.: Syntactic cut-elimination for a fragment of the modal μ-calculus. Ann. Pure Appl. Log. **163**(12), 1838–1853 (2012)
9. Buss, S.R.: An introduction to proof theory. Handb. Proof Theory **137**, 1–78 (1998)
10. Buszkowski, W.: On action logic: equational theories of action algebras. J. Log. Comput. **17**(1), 199–217 (2007)
11. Conway, J.H.: Regular Algebra and Finite Machines. Chapman and Hall, London (1971)
12. Das, A., Pous, D.: A cut-free cyclic proof system for Kleene algebra (2017). Full version of this extended abstract, with appendix https://hal.archives-ouvertes.fr/hal-01558132/
13. Dax, C., Hofmann, M., Lange, M.: A proof system for the linear time μ-calculus. In: Arun-Kumar, S., Garg, N. (eds.) FSTTCS 2006. LNCS, vol. 4337, pp. 273–284. Springer, Heidelberg (2006). doi:10.1007/11944836_26
14. Dershowitz, N., Manna, Z.: Proving termination with multiset orderings. Commun. ACM **22**(8), 465–476 (1979)
15. Doumane, A., Baelde, D., Hirschi, L., Saurin, A.: Towards completeness via proof search in the linear time μ-calculus: the case of Büchi inclusions. In: Proceedings of the LICS, pp. 377–386. ACM (2016)
16. Girard, J.-Y.: Linear logic. TCS **50**, 1–102 (1987)
17. Hoare, C.A.R.T., Möller, B., Struth, G., Wehrman, I.: Concurrent Kleene algebra. In: Bravetti, M., Zavattaro, G. (eds.) CONCUR 2009. LNCS, vol. 5710, pp. 399–414. Springer, Heidelberg (2009). doi:10.1007/978-3-642-04081-8_27
18. Hopcroft, J.E., Karp, R.M.: A linear algorithm for testing equivalence of finite automata. Technical report 114, Cornell University (1971)
19. Jipsen, P.: From semirings to residuated Kleene lattices. Studia Logica **76**(2), 291–303 (2004)
20. Kleene, S.C.: Representation of events in nerve nets and finite automata. In: Automata Studies, pp. 3–41. Princeton University Press (1956)
21. Kozen, D.: A completeness theorem for Kleene algebras and the algebra of regular events. In: Proceedings of the LICS, pp. 214–225. IEEE (1991)
22. Kozen, D.: On action algebras. In: van Eijck, J., Visser, A. (eds.) Logic and Information Flow, pp. 78–88. MIT Press (1994)
23. Kozen, D.: Kleene algebra with tests. Trans. Program. Lang. Syst. **19**(3), 427–443 (1997)
24. Kozen, D.: On Hoare logic and Kleene algebra with tests. ACM Trans. Comput. Log. **1**(1), 60–76 (2000)
25. Kozen, D., Patron, M.-C.: Certification of compiler optimizations using Kleene algebra with tests. In: Lloyd, J., et al. (eds.) CL 2000. LNCS, vol. 1861, pp. 568–582. Springer, Heidelberg (2000). doi:10.1007/3-540-44957-4_38

26. Krauss, A., Nipkow, T.: Proof pearl: regular expression equivalence and relation algebra. JAR **49**(1), 95–106 (2012)
27. Krob, D.: A complete system of B-rational identities. In: Paterson, M.S. (ed.) ICALP 1990. LNCS, vol. 443, pp. 60–73. Springer, Heidelberg (1990). doi:10.1007/BFb0032022
28. Krob, D.: Complete systems of B-rational identities. TCS **89**(2), 207–343 (1991)
29. Lambek, J.: The mathematics of sentence structure. Am. Math. Monthly **65**, 154–170 (1958)
30. Palka, E.: An infinitary sequent system for the equational theory of *-continuous action lattices. Fundam. Inform. 295–309 (2007)
31. Pous, D.: Kleene algebra with tests and coq tools for while programs. In: Blazy, S., Paulin-Mohring, C., Pichardie, D. (eds.) ITP 2013. LNCS, vol. 7998, pp. 180–196. Springer, Heidelberg (2013). doi:10.1007/978-3-642-39634-2_15
32. Pratt, V.: Action logic and pure induction. In: Eijck, J. (ed.) JELIA 1990. LNCS, vol. 478, pp. 97–120. Springer, Heidelberg (1991). doi:10.1007/BFb0018436
33. Schütte, K.: Proof Theory. Grundlehren der mathematischen Wissenschaften, vol. 225. Sprigner, Heidelberg (1977). Translation of Beweistheorie, 1968
34. Wurm, C.: Kleene algebras, regular languages and substructural logics. In: Proceedings of the GandALF, EPTCS, pp. 46–59 (2014)

Integrating a Global Induction Mechanism into a Sequent Calculus

David M. Cerna[1] and Michael Lettmann[2(✉)]

[1] Research Institute for Symbolic Computation,
Johannes Kepler University, Linz, Austria
david.cerna@risc.jku.at
[2] Institute of Information Systems,
Technische Universität Wien, Vienna, Austria
lettmann@logic.at

Abstract. Most interesting proofs in mathematics contain an inductive argument which requires an extension of the **LK**-calculus to formalize. The most commonly used calculi contain a separate rule or axiom which reduces the important proof theoretic properties of the calculus. In such cases cut-elimination does not result in analytic proofs, i.e. every formula occurring in the proof is a subformula of the end sequent. Proof schemata are a generalization of **LK**-proofs able to simulate induction by linking proofs, indexed by a natural number, together. Using a global cut-elimination method a normal form can be reached which allows a schema of *Herbrand Sequents* to be produced, an essential step for proof analysis in the presence of induction. However, proof schema have only been studied in a limited context and are currently defined for a very particular proof structure based on a slight extension of the **LK**-calculus. The result is an opaque and complex formalization. In this paper, we introduce a calculus integrating the proof schema formalization and in the process we elucidate properties of proof schemata which can be used to extend the formalism.

1 Introduction

The schematic construction of objects that forms the basis of proof schemata, as described in this paper, was introduced by Aravantinos et al. [2–7]. Initially, they considered formulas of an indexed propositional logic with a single *free numeric parameter* and with two new logical connectors, i.e. ∨-iteration and ∧-iteration. They developed a tableau based decision procedure for the satisfiability of a monadic[1] fragment of this logic. An extension to a special case of multiple parameters was also investigated by Cerna [13]. In a more recent work,

---

D.M. Cerna—Partially supported by FWF under the project P 28789-N32.

M. Lettmann—Funded by FWF project W1255-N23.

[1] In this fragment the use of schematic constructors is restricted to one free parameter per formula.

R.A. Schmidt and C. Nalon (Eds.): TABLEAUX 2017, LNAI 10501, pp. 278–294, 2017.
DOI: 10.1007/978-3-319-66902-1_17

Aravantinos et al. [6] introduced a superposition resolution calculus for a clausal representation of indexed propositional logic. The calculus provided decidability results for an even larger fragment of the monadic fragment. The clausal form allows an easy extension to indexed predicate logic, though all decidability results are lost. In either case, the refutations producible by the calculus for unsatisfiable clause sets is quite restricted[2].

Nonetheless, these results inspired investigations into the use of schemata as an alternative formalization of induction for proof analysis and transformation. This is not the first alternative formalization of induction with respect to Peano arithmetic [25]. However, all existing examples [11,12,21], to the best of our knowledge, lack a proof normal form or *subformula-like property*[3], i.e. every formula occurring in the proof is a subformula of a formula occurring in the end sequent. What we mean by this is that performing cut-elimination in the presence of induction results in a non-analytic proof: some part of the argument is not directly connected to the theorem being proven. Two important constructions extractable from proofs with the subformula property, *Herbrand sequents* [19,25] and *expansion trees* [22], are not extractable from proofs within these calculi. While Herbrand sequents allow the representation of the propositional content of first-order proofs, expansion trees generalize Herbrand's theorem.

Note that in [20] a finite representation of a sequence of Herbrand sequents is produced, a *Herbrand system*. Of course, such objects are not derivable from a finite set of ground instances, though instantiating the free parameter of a Herbrand systems results in a sequent derivable from a finite set of ground instances. Bounds on the size of these sets of ground instances, in terms of the free parameter, exists [16]. Representing a ground derivation for the Herbrand system as a proof schema itself is still an open problem and is a motivating factor of this paper. In some cases, the resulting Herbrand system is not formalizable as a proof schema in the sense of [16,20] due to the restriction placed on proof schema construction, see [14]. Lifting these restrictions is non-trivial. Our goal is to design a calculus which easily allows one to relax the restrictions.

The first proof analysis carried out using a rudimentary schematic formalism was Baaz et al. [8], where proof analysis of Fürstenberg's proof of the infinitude of primes was successfully performed using **CERES** [9]. The formalism discussed in this paper is an extension of CERES introduced by Dunchev et al. [17]. It allows the extraction of a schema of Herbrand sequents from the resulting normal form produced by cut-elimination in the presence of induction. Problematically, the method of cut-elimination introduced in [17] is not known to be complete, in terms of cut-elimination, and is very difficult to use. For an example of the difficulties see Cerna and Leitsch's work [15]. A much improved version of this

---

[2] A formal analysis has not been performed but through conversations with the authors and their collaborators a polynomial bound on the size of the produced refutations is expected.

[3] A proof fulfilling the subformula property can be referred to as *analytic*. By subformula-like, we mean that the proof is non-analytic, but still allows the extraction of objects important for proof analysis which rely on analyticity.

cut-elimination method has been introduced in [20]. using the superposition resolution calculus of [6]. The method is complete and always produces a schema of Herbrand sequents, but as mentioned earlier, it is quite weak, also in comparison to the method of [17]. It relies on the superposition resolution calculus of [6]. The method of [17] can formalize proof normal forms with a non-elementary length with respect to the size of the end sequent[4].

In both cases, the concept of *proof schema* is designed to encapsulate a sequence of interacting proofs (the proofs are defined using the **LKS**-calculus) [17] which can be joined in a particular way allowing the construction of a valid **LK**-proof for any natural number. The **LKS**-calculus introduces concepts such as *links* but does not place restrictions on what a sound application of the rule is, rather an additional construction, *proof schemata*, provides the soundness conditions. However, as one might expect, most sequences of proofs will result in a invalid proof, multiple proofs when only one is desired, or proofs which are more complex than necessary, i.e. repetition or unnecessary constructions. These issues make extensions of proofs schemata, i.e. adding additional parameters and/or more complexity well-ordering conditions as well as compression and proof optimization, increasingly difficult. However, even more pressing is that the restrictions placed on *proof schemata* avoid sequences which will result in valid **LK**-proof when instantiated. As an example, the schema of Herbrand sequents extracted in [14] from the proof analysis of the infinitary Pigeonhole Principle can not be formulated as a proof schema in the current framework.

In this work we present a novel calculus for proof schemata which provides a better understanding of the restrictions placed on proof schema construction in previous work. The calculus implicitly enforces the sound application of inferences and in doing so it provides an easy mechanism for weakening the soundness conditions. Moreover, we show completeness with respect to the *k-induction* fragment of Peano arithmetic [20], thus showing that the current calculus is equivalent to previous formalisms. However, one of the most interesting results is that *component collections* (an abstraction of sequents used in our calculus) can be interpreted as a sequence of inductions (similar to the fusion method introduced by Gentzen [18]) rather than as a tree of inductions. This is unexpected given that proof schemata enforce a very specific tree structure which is partially what makes introduction of multiple parameters so difficult. This flattened structure allows us to easily consider a *component* as separate from the parameter of the proof schema and separately from the proof schema itself. Taking advantage of this property in order to weaken the current restrictions built into the framework and to formalize multiple parameter schemata is planned for future work.

The rest of this paper is as follows: In Sect. 2, we discuss the necessary background knowledge needed for the results. In Sect. 3 we discuss the evaluation and interpretation of proof schemata. In Sect. 4, we introduce the concept of the calculus. In Sect. 5, we show soundness and completeness of the calculus. In Sect. 6, we conclude the paper and mention possible applications, future work, and open problems.

---

[4] See Orevkov's proof [23] or Boolos' proof [10].

2   Preliminaries

In this section, we provide a formal construction of proof schemata.

2.1   Schematic Language

We work in a two-sorted version of classical first-order logic. The first sort we consider is ω, in which every term normalizes to a *numeral*, i.e. a term inductively constructable by $N \Rightarrow s(N) \mid 0$, such that $s(N) \neq 0$ and $s(N) = s(N') \rightarrow N = N'$. We will denote numerals by lowercase greek letters, i.e. α, β, γ, etc. Furthermore, the omega sort includes a countable set of parameter symbols $\mathcal{N}$. For this work, we will only need a single parameter symbol which in most cases we denote by n. We use k, k' to represent numeric expressions containing the parameter. The parameter symbol n will be referred to as the *free parameter*.

The second sort ι (individuals) is a standard first-order term language extended by *defined function symbols* and *schematic variable symbols*. To distinguish defined and uninterpreted function symbols we partition the functions of ι into two categories, *uninterpreted function symbols* $\mathbf{F_u}$ and *defined function symbols* $\mathbf{F_d}$. Defined function symbols will be denoted with $\widehat{\cdot}$. Schematic variable symbols are variables of the type $\omega \rightarrow \iota$ used to construct sequences of variables, essentially a generalization of the standard concept of a variable. Given a schematic variable x instantiated by a numeral α we get a variable of the ι sort $x(\alpha)$.

Formula schemata, a generalization of formulas including defined predicate symbols, are defined inductively using the standard logical connectives from uninterpreted and defined predicate symbols. Analogously, we label symbols as defined predicate symbols with $\widehat{\cdot}$. A *schematic sequent* is a pair of two multisets of formula schemata Δ, Π denoted by $\Delta \vdash \Pi$. We will denote multisets of formula schemata by uppercase greek letters unless it causes confusion.

Note that we extend the **LK**-calculus [25] to the **LKE**-calculus [17] by adding an inference rule for the construction of defined predicate and function symbols and a set of convergent rewrite rules $\mathcal{E}$ (equational theory) to our interpretation. The rules of $\mathcal{E}$ take the following form $\widehat{f}(\bar{t}) = E$, where $\bar{t}$ contains no defined symbols, and either $\widehat{f}$ is a function symbol of range ι and E is a term or $\widehat{f}$ is a predicate symbol and E is a formula schema.

Definition 1 (LKE). *Let $\mathcal{E}$ be an equational theory.* **LKE** *is an extension of* **LK** *by the $\mathcal{E}$ inference rule*

$$\frac{S(t)}{S(t')} \; \mathcal{E}$$

where the term or formula schema t in the sequent S is replaced by a term or formula schema t' for $\mathcal{E} \models t = t'$.

Example 1. Iterated version of $\vee$ and $\wedge$ (the defined predicates are abbreviated as $\bigvee$ and $\bigwedge$) can be defined using the following equational theory:

$$\bigvee_{i=0}^{0} P(i) = \bigwedge_{i=0}^{0} P(i) = P(0), \qquad \bigvee_{i=0}^{s(y)} P(i) = \bigvee_{i=0}^{y} P(i) \vee P(s(y)), \qquad \bigwedge_{i=0}^{s(y)} P(i) = \bigwedge_{i=0}^{y} P(i) \wedge P(s(y)).$$

2.2 The LKS-Calculus and Proof Schemata

Schematic proofs are a finite ordered list of *proof schema components* which can interact with each other. This interaction is defined using so-called *links*, a 0-ary inference rule we add to **LKE**-calculus: Let $S(k, \bar{x})$ be a sequent where $\bar{x}$ is a vector of schematic variables. By $S(k, \bar{t})$ we denote $S(k, \bar{x})$ where $\bar{x}$ is replaced by $\bar{t}$, respectively, and $\bar{t}$ is a vector of terms of appropriate type. Furthermore, we assume a countably infinite set $\mathcal{B}$ of *proof symbols* denoted by $\varphi, \psi, \varphi_i, \psi_j$. The expression

$$\frac{(\varphi, k, \bar{t})}{S(k, \bar{t})}$$

is called a link with the intended meaning that there is a proof called φ with the end-sequent $S(k, \bar{x})$. Let k be a numeric expression, then $\mathcal{V}(k)$ is the set of parameters in k. We refer to a link as an *E-link* if $\mathcal{V}(k) \subseteq E$. Note that in this work $E = \{n\}$ or $E = \varnothing$.

Definition 2 (LKS). *LKS is an extension of **LKE**, where links may appear at the leaves of a proof.*

Definition 3 (Proof Schema Component). *Let $\psi \in \mathcal{B}$ and $n \in \mathcal{N}$. A proof schema component $\mathbf{C}$ is a triple $(\psi, \pi, \nu(k))$ where π is an **LKS**-proof only containing $\varnothing$-links and $\nu(k)$ is an **LKS**-proof containing $\{n\}$-links. The end-sequents of the proofs are $S(0, \bar{x})$ and $S(k, \bar{x})$, respectively. Given a proof schema component $\mathbf{C} = (\psi, \pi, \nu(k))$ we define $\mathbf{C}.1 = \psi$, $\mathbf{C}.2 = \pi$, and $\mathbf{C}.3 = \nu(k)$.*

If $\nu(k)$ of a proof schema component $(\psi, \pi, \nu(k))$ contains a link to ψ it will be referred to as *cyclic*, otherwise it is *acyclic*.

Definition 4. *Let $\mathbf{C}_1$ and $\mathbf{C}_2$ be proof schema components such that $\mathbf{C}_1.1$ is distinct from $\mathbf{C}_2.1$ and $n \in \mathcal{N}$. We say $\mathbf{C}_1 \succ^* \mathbf{C}_2$ if there are no links from $\mathbf{C}_2$ to $\mathbf{C}_1$ and all links that call $\mathbf{C}_1$ or $\mathbf{C}_2$ are $\{n\}$-links of the following form:*

$$\frac{(\mathbf{C}_1.1, k, \bar{a})}{S(k, \bar{a})} \qquad\qquad \frac{(\mathbf{C}_2.1, t, \bar{b})}{S'(t, \bar{b})}$$

where t is a numeric expression such that $\mathcal{V}(t) \subseteq \{n\}$, k' is a sub-term of k, and $\bar{a}$ and $\bar{b}$ are vectors of terms from the appropriate sort. $S(k, \bar{a})$ and $S'(t, \bar{b})$ are the end sequents of components $\mathbf{C}_1$ and $\mathbf{C}_2$ respectively.

Let Ψ be a set of proof schema components. We say $\mathbf{C}_1 \succ \mathbf{C}_2$ if $\mathbf{C}_1 \succ^* \mathbf{C}_2$ and $\mathbf{C}_1 \succ^* \mathbf{D}$ holds for all proof schema components $\mathbf{D}$ of Ψ with $\mathbf{C}_2 \succ^* \mathbf{D}$.

Definition 5 (Proof Schema [17]). *Let* $\mathbf{C}_1, \cdots, \mathbf{C}_m$ *be proof schema components such that* $\mathbf{C}_i.1$ *is distinct for* $1 \leq i \leq m$ *and* $n \in \mathcal{N}$. *Let the end sequents of* $\mathbf{C}_1$ *be* $S(0, \bar{x})$ *and* $S(k, \bar{x})$. *We define* $\Psi = \langle \mathbf{C}_1, \cdots, \mathbf{C}_m \rangle$ *as a proof schema if* $\mathbf{C}_1 \succ \ldots \succ \mathbf{C}_m$.

We call $S(k, \bar{x})$ *the end sequent of* Ψ *and assume an identification between the formula occurrences in the end sequents of the proof schema components so that we can speak of occurrences in the end sequent of* Ψ. *The class of all proof schemata will be denoted by* Υ.

For any proof schema $\Phi \in \Upsilon$, such that $\Phi = \langle \mathbf{C}_1, \cdots, \mathbf{C}_m \rangle$ we define $|\Phi| = m$ and $\Phi.i = \mathbf{C}_i$ for $1 \leq i \leq m$. Note that instead of using *proof schema pair* [17,20] to define proof schemata we use proof schema components. The only difference is that proof schema components make the name explicit. All results concerning proof schemata built from proof schema pairs carry over for our above definition.

Example 2. Let us consider the proof schema $\Phi = \langle (\varphi, \pi, \nu(k)) \rangle$. The proof schema uses one defined function symbol $\widehat{S}(\cdot)$ to convert terms of the ω sort to the ι sort The equational theory $\mathcal{E}$ is as follows:

$$\mathcal{E} = \left\{ \widehat{S}(k+1) = f(\widehat{S}(k)) \; ; \; \widehat{S}(0) = 0 \; ; \; k + f(l) = f(k+l) \right\}.$$

We abbreviate the context as $\Delta = \{P(\alpha + 0), \forall x. P(x) \to P(f(x))\}$. The proofs π and $\nu(k)$ are as follows:

$$\pi = \quad \cfrac{\cfrac{P(\alpha + 0) \vdash P(\alpha + 0)}{\Delta \vdash P(\alpha + 0)} \; w:l}{\Delta \vdash P(\alpha + \widehat{S}(0))} \; \mathcal{E}$$

$$\nu(k) = \quad \cfrac{\cfrac{\cfrac{\cfrac{\cfrac{\overline{(\varphi, n, \alpha)}}{\Delta \vdash P(\alpha + \widehat{S}(n))} \quad P(f(\alpha + \widehat{S}(n))) \vdash P(f(\alpha + \widehat{S}(n)))}{\Delta, P(\alpha + \widehat{S}(n)) \to P(f(\alpha + \widehat{S}(n))) \vdash P(f(\alpha + \widehat{S}(n)))} \; \to:l}{\Delta, \forall x. P(x) \to P(f(x)) \vdash P(f(\alpha + \widehat{S}(n)))} \; \forall:l}{\Delta, \forall x. P(x) \to P(f(x)) \vdash P(\alpha + f(\widehat{S}(n)))} \; \mathcal{E}}{\Delta, \forall x. P(x) \to P(f(x)) \vdash P(\alpha + \widehat{S}(n+1))} \; \mathcal{E}}{\Delta \vdash P(\alpha + \widehat{S}(n+1))} \; c:l$$

Note that π contains no links, while $\nu(k)$ contains a single $\{n\}$-link.

3   Evaluation and Interpretation

Proof schemata are an alternative formulation of induction. In [20], it is shown that proof schemata are equivalent to a particular fragment of the induction arguments formalizable in Peano arithmetic, i.e. the so called *k-simple induction*. More specifically, *k*-simple induction limits the number of inductive eigenvariables[5] to one. In previous work [17,20], **LKE** was extended by the following induction rule instead of links:

---

[5] Inductive eigenvariables are eigenvariables occurring in the context of an induction inference rule.

$$\frac{F(k), \Gamma \vdash \Delta, F(s(k))}{F(0), \Gamma \vdash \Delta, F(t)} \ \textbf{IND}$$

where t is an arbitrary term of the numeric sort. The result is the calculus **LKIE**. To enforce k-simplicity we add the following constraint: let ψ be an **LKIE**-proof such that for any induction inference in ψ, $V(t) \subseteq \{k\}$ for some k. In [17,20], the authors show that the following two proposition hold, and thus define the relationship between k-simple **LKIE**-proofs and proof schemata. Given that our calculus can be used to construct proof schemata, the relationship can be trivially extended to proofs resulting from our calculus.

Proposition 1. *Let Ψ be a proof schema with end-sequent S. Then there exists a k-simple **LKIE**-proof of S.*

Proof. See Proposition 3.13 of [20].

Proposition 2. *Let π be a k-simple **LKIE**-proof of S. Then there exists a proof schema with end-sequent S.*

Proof. See Proposition 3.15 of [20].

Unlike the induction proofs of the **LKIE**-calculus, proof schemata have a recursive structure and thus require an evaluation ("unrolling"), similar to primitive recursive functions. When we instantiate the free parameter, the following evaluation procedure suffices.

Definition 6 (Evaluation of proof schema [17]). *We define the rewrite rules for links*

$$\frac{(\varphi, 0, \bar{t})}{S(0, \bar{t})} \Rightarrow \pi \qquad\qquad \frac{(\varphi, k, \bar{t})}{S(k, \bar{t})} \Rightarrow \nu(k)$$

for all proof schema components $\mathbf{C} = (\varphi, \pi, \nu(k))$. Furthermore, for $\alpha \in \mathcal{N}$, we define $\mathbf{C}\,[k \setminus \alpha] \downarrow$ as a normal form of the link

$$\frac{(\varphi, \alpha, \bar{t})}{S(\alpha, \bar{t})}$$

under the above rewrite system extended by the rewrite rules for defined function and predicate symbols, i.e. the equational theory $\mathcal{E}$. Also, for a proof schema $\Phi = \langle \mathbf{C}_1, \ldots, \mathbf{C}_m \rangle$, we define $\Phi\,[n \setminus \alpha] \downarrow = \mathbf{C}_1\,[k \setminus \alpha] \downarrow$.

Example 3. Let Φ be the proof schema of Example 2 and Δ defined equivalently. For $1 \in \mathbb{N}$ we can write down $\Phi\,[n \setminus 1] \downarrow$ as follows:

$$\cfrac{\cfrac{P(f(\alpha + \hat{S}(0))) \vdash P(f(\alpha + \hat{S}(0)))\quad \cfrac{\cfrac{P(\alpha + 0) \vdash P(\alpha + 0)}{\Delta \vdash P(\alpha + 0)}\ w:l}{\Delta \vdash P(\alpha + \hat{S}(0))}\ \mathcal{E}}{\cfrac{\cfrac{\Delta, P(\alpha + \hat{S}(0)) \to P(f(\alpha + \hat{S}(0))) \vdash P(f(\alpha + \hat{S}(0)))}{\Delta, \forall x.P(x) \to P(f(x)) \vdash P(f(\alpha + \hat{S}(0)))}\ \forall:l}{\cfrac{\cfrac{\Delta \vdash P(f(\alpha + \hat{S}(0)))}{\Delta \vdash P(\alpha + f(\hat{S}(0)))}\ \mathcal{E}}{\cfrac{\Delta \vdash P(\alpha + \hat{S}(0 + 1))}{\Delta \vdash P(\alpha + \hat{S}(1))}\ \mathcal{E}}\ \mathcal{E}}\ c:l}\ \to:l}$$

The described evaluation procedure essentially defines a rewrite system for proof schemata with the following property.

Lemma 1. *The rewrite system for links is strongly normalizing, and for a proof schema Φ and $\alpha \in \mathcal{N}$, $\Phi\,[n \setminus \alpha] \downarrow$ is an **LK**-proof.*

Proof. See Lemma 3.10 of [20]. $\qquad\qquad$

Proposition 3 (Soundness [17]**).** *Let $\Phi = \langle \mathbf{C}_1, \ldots, \mathbf{C}_m \rangle$ be a proof schema with end-sequent $S(n, \bar{x})$ and let $\alpha \in \mathcal{N}$. Then $\Phi\,[n \setminus \alpha] \downarrow$ is an **LK**-proof of $S(n, \bar{x})$.*

Essentially, Proposition 3 states that $\mathbf{C}_1\,[k \setminus \alpha] \downarrow$ is an **LK**-proof of the end-sequent $S(n, \bar{x})\,[k \setminus \alpha] \downarrow$ where by $\downarrow$ we refer to normalization of the defined symbols in $S(n, \bar{x})$.

4 The $\mathcal{S}i$LK-Calculus

The $\mathcal{S}i$LK-calculus ($\mathcal{S}$chematic $i$nduction **LK**-calculus, see Tables 1 and 2) allows one to build a proof schema component-wise. We call the set of expressions in between two | a *component group*. Note that, unlike proof schemata we do not need proof symbols nor ordering because it is implied by the construction. Each component group consists of a multiset of *component pairs* which are pairs of **LKS**-sequents. A set of component groups is referred to as a *component collection*. Even though all auxiliary components (or component groups) are shifted to the left, we do not intend any ordering, i.e. writing, for instance, ($\top : A \vdash A$) to the right of Π in $Ax_1 : r$ in Table 1 does not change the rule.

Table 1. The basic inference rules of the $\mathcal{S}i$LK-calculus.

$$\frac{\Pi}{(\,\top \,\dot{:}\, A \vdash A\,)\mid\Pi}\ Ax_1:r \qquad\qquad \frac{\Gamma\mid\Pi}{(\,\top\,\dot{:}\,A \vdash A\,),\Gamma\mid\Pi}\ Ax_2:r$$

$$\frac{(\,\top\,\dot{:}\,[\,\mathbf{s}\,]\,),\Gamma\mid\Pi}{(\,A \vdash^{f(n)} A\,\dot{:}\,[\,\mathbf{s}\,]\,),\Gamma\mid\Pi}\ Ax:l \qquad\qquad \frac{(\,\top\,\dot{:}\,\mathbf{s}\,),(\,\top\,\dot{:}\,\mathbf{s}\,),\Gamma\mid\Pi}{(\,\top\,\dot{:}\,\mathbf{s}\,),\Gamma\mid\Pi}\ c_c:r$$

$$\frac{(\,\mathbf{Q}\,\dot{:}\,[\,\mathbf{s}\,]\,),(\,\mathbf{Q}\,\dot{:}\,[\,\mathbf{s}\,]\,),\Gamma\mid\Pi}{(\,\mathbf{Q}\,\dot{:}\,[\,\mathbf{s}\,]\,),\Gamma\mid\Pi}\ c_c:l \qquad\qquad \frac{(\,\mathbf{Q}\,\dot{:}\,[\,\mathbf{s}\,]\,),\Gamma\mid\Pi}{(\,\top\,\dot{:}\,[\,\mathbf{s}\,]\,),\Gamma'\mid\Pi}\ br$$

$$\frac{(\,\top\,\dot{:}\,\mathbf{Q}\,),\Gamma\mid\Pi}{(\,\top\,\dot{:}\,[\,\mathbf{Q}\,]\,),\Gamma\mid\Pi}\ cl_{bc} \qquad\qquad \frac{(\,\top\,\dot{:}\,[\,\mathbf{Q}\,]\,)\mid\Pi}{(\,[\,]\,\dot{:}\,[\,\mathbf{Q}\,]\,)\mid\Pi}\ cl_{LKE}$$

$$\frac{(\,(\Pi \vdash^\alpha \Delta)\,[n\setminus\alpha]\,\dot{:}\,[\,(\Pi \vdash \Delta)\,[n\setminus 0]\,]\,)\mid\Pi}{(\,[\,(\Pi \vdash \Delta)\,[n\setminus\alpha]\,]\,\dot{:}\,[\,(\Pi \vdash \Delta)\,[n\setminus 0]\,]\,)\mid\Pi}\ cl_{sc}$$

$$\frac{(\,\mathbf{Q}\,\dot{:}\,[\,\mathbf{s}\,]\,),(\,\mathbf{R}\,\dot{:}\,[\,\mathbf{s}\,]\,),\Gamma\mid\Pi}{(\,\mathbf{Q}'\,\dot{:}\,[\,\mathbf{s}\,]\,),\Gamma\mid\Pi}\ \rho_2^{sc} \qquad\qquad \frac{(\,\mathbf{Q}\,\dot{:}\,[\,\mathbf{s}\,]\,),\Gamma\mid\Pi}{(\,\mathbf{Q}'\,\dot{:}\,[\,\mathbf{s}\,]\,),\Gamma\mid\Pi}\ \rho_1^{sc}$$

$$\frac{(\,\top\,\dot{:}\,\mathbf{s}\,),(\,\top\,\dot{:}\,\mathbf{R}\,),\Gamma\mid\Pi}{(\,\top\,\dot{:}\,\mathbf{s}'\,),\Gamma\mid\Pi}\ \rho_2^{bc} \qquad\qquad \frac{(\,\top\,\dot{:}\,\mathbf{s}\,),\Gamma\mid\Pi}{(\,\top\,\dot{:}\,\mathbf{s}'\,),\Gamma\mid\Pi}\ \rho_1^{bc}$$

To enforce correct construction of proof schema components we introduce a *closure* mechanism similar to *focusing* [1] (see the inferences cl_{bc}, cl_{LKE}, and cl_{sc} in Table 1). Let us consider a component pair $\mathbf{C} = (\mathbf{Q} : \mathbf{S})$ where $\mathbf{Q}$ is a sequent, a sequent in square brackets, or $\top$ and $\mathbf{S}$ is a sequent or a sequent in square brackets. The left side $\mathbf{Q}$ is the stepcase and the right side $\mathbf{S}$ is the basecase. We use pairs of sequents rather than individual sequents on different branches to enforce the dependence between the stepcase and the basecase, that is, the both have the same end-sequent. The configuration $\mathbf{Q} = \top$ means that we are still allowed to apply rules to the basecase. If $\mathbf{S}$ is closed, i.e. $\mathbf{S}$ is of the form $[\Delta \vdash \Pi]$ for an arbitrary sequent $\Delta \vdash \Pi$, we have closed the basecase (using inference rule cl_{bc}) and essentially fixed its end-sequent. Therefore, $\mathbf{Q}$ is always equal to $\top$ as long as the basecase is not closed. If $\mathbf{S}$ is closed we are allowed to apply rules to the stepcase. This fixing of the end-sequent essentially fixes the sequent we are allowed to introduce using the inference rule $\circlearrowright$.

Apart from schematic proofs, simple **LKE**-proofs can be constructed by keeping the stepcase equal to $\top$. If we instead intend to construct a schema of proofs we have to build a stepcase. The end sequent $(\Pi \vdash \Delta)[n \setminus 0]$ characterizes the stepcase sequent modulo the parameter value, i.e. $(\Pi \vdash^{\alpha} \Delta)[n \setminus \alpha]$ where α depends on the applications of $\circlearrowright$ - or $\curvearrowright$ -inferences (see Table 2). The point of this labelling α of the sequents is to indicate what value of the free parameter must be produced in order to close the component. Normally $\alpha = n'$, or the successor of n. Note that $f(n)$, $g(n)$, and $h(n)$ are intended to be arbitrary primitive recursive functions and may be introduced as an extension of the equational theory.

When a component group contains a single component pair and the end sequents of the basecase and stepcase are the same modulo the substitution of the free parameter we can close the component group using cl_{sc} (see Table 1). Alternatively, we can close a group by applying cl_{LKE} if the stepcase is equal to $\top$. We refer to such a group as a *closed group* and any group which is not closed is referred to as an *open group*. As a convention, inference rules can only be applied to open groups. Concerning $\curvearrowright$ (see Table 2), it may be the case that the closed group whose end sequent we use to introduce a link has free variables other than the free parameter. We assume correspondence between the free variables of the closed group and the main component, meaning that in a call

$$\left((\Lambda \vdash^{f(n)} \Gamma) [n \setminus g(n)] [\bar{x} \setminus \bar{t}] : [\mathbf{S}] \right)$$

of a component with free variables $\bar{x}$ all occurrences of $\bar{x}$ in the proof of

$$([(\Lambda \vdash \Gamma) [n \setminus h(n)]] : [\mathbf{R}])$$

are replaced with $\bar{t}$. Essentially, this rule is inductive lemma introduction. $h(n)$ is used to represent a non-standard instantiation of the free parameter, i.e. other than n'. Though, non-essentially for this work, in future work when we consider more complex inductive definitions and orders, thus such concepts will be necessary.

An $\mathcal{S}i\mathbf{LK}$-derivation is a sequence of $\mathcal{S}i\mathbf{LK}$ inferences rules ending in a component collection with at least one open component group. A $\mathcal{S}i\mathbf{LK}$-proof ends in a component collection where all components are closed. As we shall show, not every derivation can be extended into a proof.

Table 2. The linking rules of the $\mathcal{S}i\mathbf{LK}$-calculus.

$$\frac{(\top : [(\varPi \vdash \varDelta)[n\backslash 0]]), \ulcorner \mid \varPi}{((\varPi \vdash^{(n+1)} \varDelta)[\bar{x}\backslash \bar{t}] : [(\varPi \vdash \varDelta)[n\backslash 0]]), \ulcorner \mid \varPi} \circlearrowright$$

where $\bar{x}$ is the vector of all free variables of $(\varPi \vdash \varDelta)$ and $\bar{t}$ is an arbitrary vector of terms which has the same length as $\bar{x}$.

$$\frac{(\top : [\mathbf{s}]), \ulcorner \mid \varDelta \mid ([(\varLambda \vdash \varGamma)[n\backslash h(n)]] : [\mathbf{R}]) \mid \varPi}{((\varLambda \vdash^{f(n)} \varGamma)[n\backslash g(n)][\bar{y}\backslash \bar{t}] : [\mathbf{s}]), \ulcorner \mid \varPi'} \curvearrowright$$

where $\bar{y}$ is the vector of all free variables of $(\varLambda \vdash \varGamma)$ and $\bar{t}$ is an arbitrary vector of terms which has the same length as $\bar{y}$. Also, g and h are arbitrary primitive recursive functions.

We also consider a special case of $\mathcal{S}i\mathbf{LK}$-derivations (proofs) which we refer to as *pre-proof schema normal form*. A $\mathcal{S}i\mathbf{LK}$-derivation (proof) is in pre-proof schema normal form if for every application of $Ax_1 : r$ the context $\varPi$ is a $\mathcal{S}i\mathbf{LK}$-proof. This enforces a stricter order on the construction of components than is already enforced by the use of the $\curvearrowright$-inference which can be used to construct proof schemata.

Let $\mathcal{I}$ be the customary evaluation function of sequents, i.e. $\mathcal{I}(\varDelta \vdash \varGamma) \equiv \bigwedge_{F \in \varDelta} F \rightarrow \bigvee_{F \in \varGamma} F$ for an **LKE**-sequent $\varDelta \vdash \varGamma$ and assume an $\mathcal{S}i\mathbf{LK}$-proof ending in the component collection

$$\mathbf{C} \equiv ([\mathbf{Q}_0] : [\mathbf{S}_0]) \mid \cdots \mid ([\mathbf{Q}_m] : [\mathbf{S}_m])$$

such that $([\mathbf{Q}_0] : [\mathbf{S}_0])$ is the last component group closed in the proof of C (In the following we will refer to this component as the *leading component*). We extend the evaluation function to the schematic case and define the *evaluation function* of a closed component collection similar to [18] by

$$\mathcal{I}_{\mathcal{S}i\mathbf{LK}}(\mathbf{C}) \equiv \mathcal{I}(\mathbf{S}_0),$$

if $\nu_0 \equiv \top$ and $\mathcal{I}_{\mathcal{S}i\mathbf{LK}}(\mathbf{C}) \equiv$

$$\bigwedge_{i=0}^{m} \mathcal{I}(\mathbf{S}_i) \wedge \forall.x \Big(\bigwedge_{i=0}^{m} (\mathcal{I}(\mathbf{Q}_i [n \backslash x]) \rightarrow \mathcal{I}(\mathbf{Q}_i [n \backslash (x+1)])) \Big) \rightarrow \forall x.(\mathcal{I}(\mathbf{Q}_0 [n \backslash x]),$$

otherwise. Implicitly, the closure rules imply an order. In general, all closed component groups are considered lower in the implied ordering than open component groups. Essentially, the ordering comes from the $\curvearrowright$-rule which can only be applied if the auxiliary component is closed. For example, a component may be forced to be closed last, and thus, would be consider the top of the implied ordering.

We use the following denotations for construction of our inference rules. Context variables within schematic sequents will be denoted by uppercase greek letters Δ, Π, etc. Context variables within component groups will be denoted by blackboard bold uppercase greek letters $\mathbb{A}, \mathbb{\Pi}$, etc. Context variables within the component collection will be denoted by fat bold uppercase greek letters, $\boldsymbol{\Delta}, \boldsymbol{\Pi}$, etc. We use bold uppercase latin letters to denote schematic sequents, $\mathbf{R}, \mathbf{S}$, etc. The inference rules ρ_1^{sc}, ρ_2^{sc}, ρ_1^{bc}, ρ_2^{bc} apply an **LKE** inference rule ρ to the auxiliary sequents to get the main sequent. By the subscript we denote the arity of the inference rule. For example, $(\forall : l)_1^{sc}$ applies the universal quantifier rule to the left side of the stepcase. And finally, we use the following abbreviations:

$$\Gamma' \equiv (\Gamma, (\ \mathbf{Q} : [\mathbf{S}]\ ))\,, \text{ and}$$

$$\boldsymbol{\Pi}' \equiv \boldsymbol{\Delta}, (\ [\ (\Lambda \vdash \Gamma)\{n \leftarrow \alpha\}\ ] : [\ \mathbf{R}\ ]\ ) \ \Big|\ \boldsymbol{\Pi}.$$

The following example illustrates the construction of a simple $\mathcal{S}i\mathbf{LK}$-proof.

Example 4. For the construction of the following $\mathcal{S}i\mathbf{LK}$-proof we use the equational theory $\mathcal{E} \equiv \{\widehat{f^0}(x) = x;\ \widehat{f^{s(n)}}(x) = f\widehat{f^n}(x)\}$ and the abbreviations

$$\Delta \equiv P(0), \forall x.P(x) \rightarrow P(f(x)) \text{ and } \mathbf{S} \equiv \Delta \vdash P(\widehat{f^0}(0)).$$

By applying the evaluation function $\mathcal{I}_{\mathcal{S}i\mathbf{LK}}$ we get

$$\mathcal{I}_{\mathcal{S}i\mathbf{LK}}\left(\left(\,[\,\Delta \vdash P(\widehat{f^{s(n)}}(0))\,]:[\,\mathbf{S}\,]\,\right)\right) \equiv$$

$$\left(\left((\Delta' \to P(\widehat{f^0}(0)))\right) \wedge \forall x.\left((\Delta' \to P(\widehat{f^x}(0))) \to (\Delta' \to P(\widehat{f^{x+1}}(0)))\right)\right) \to$$

$$(\Delta' \to \forall n.P(\widehat{f^n}(0)))$$

where $\Delta' \equiv P(0) \wedge \forall x.P(x) \to P(f(x))$. Essentially, what we have proven with this $\mathcal{S}i\mathbf{LK}$-proof is the sequent

$$P(0), \forall x.P(x) \to P(f(x)) \vdash \forall n.P(\widehat{f^n}(0)).$$

By extending the equational theory and by applying the $\curvearrowright$-inference we can easily strengthen the provable sequent of Example 4.

Example 5. Let $\mathcal{E}$ be the equational theory of Example 4, Π the proof of Example 4 and

$$\Delta \equiv P(0), \forall x.P(x) \to P(f(x)),$$

$$\Gamma \equiv \left(\,[\,\Delta \vdash P(\widehat{f^{s(n)}}(0))\,]:[\,\Delta \vdash P(\widehat{f^0}(0))\,]\,\right),$$

$$2 \equiv s(s(0)),$$

$$\mathbf{S}' \equiv \Delta \vdash P(\widehat{f^{2^0}}(0)),$$

$$\mathcal{E}' \equiv \mathcal{E} \cup \{\widehat{f^{2^0}}(x) = f(x), \widehat{f^{2^{s(n)}}}(x) = \widehat{f^{2^n}}\widehat{f^2}(x)\}.$$

Notice that we were able to get a much stronger theorem without significantly extending the proof. Though, the instantiation of the second proof will be exponentially larger than an instantiation of the first proof for the same value of n, the second proof is only double the number of inferences. This is precisely the method one can use to formalize either Orevkov's proof [23] or Boolos' proof [10].

4.1   From $\mathcal{S}i\mathbf{LK}$-Proof to Proof Schema

It is possible to construct a proof schema from any $\mathcal{S}i\mathbf{LK}$-Proof, though it is much easier to perform the translation from $\mathcal{S}i\mathbf{LK}$-Proof in pre-proof schema normal form. We now show that every $\mathcal{S}i\mathbf{LK}$-Proof has a pre-proof schema normal form.

Lemma 2. *Let Φ be a $\mathcal{S}i\mathbf{LK}$-Proof of a component collection* **C**. *Then there exists a $\mathcal{S}i\mathbf{LK}$-Proof Φ' of* **C** *in pre-proof schema normal form.*

Proof. We prove the statement by rearranging the application of the $\mathcal{S}i\mathbf{LK}$ rules. Let

$$\mathbf{C} \equiv (\,[\,\mathbf{Q}_0\,]\ :\,[\,\mathbf{S}_0\,]\,) \ \Big| \ \cdots \ \Big| \ (\,[\,\mathbf{Q}_m\,]\ :\,[\,\mathbf{S}_m\,]\,)$$

be the ending component collection of Φ. We identify each component group $\mathcal{CG}_i = (\,[\,\mathbf{Q}_i\,]\ :\,[\,\mathbf{S}_i\,]\,)$ with its ancestors in Φ, i.e. all component groups that are connected via a $\mathcal{S}i\mathbf{LK}$ rule, exempting the closed component groups of the $\curvearrowright$ rule, to $\mathcal{CG}_i$. Afterwards, we find the component group $\mathcal{CG}_i$ which is closed first, i.e. reading top to bottom the component group to which cl_{st} or cl_{LKE} is applied first. Since there is no other component closed earlier there are no $\curvearrowright$ rule identified with $\mathcal{CG}_i$, thus we can consider all rules identified with $\mathcal{CG}_i$ to be independent. This implies that we can rearrange Φ such that all rules identified with $\mathcal{CG}_i$ are at the top[6]. This part of the proof will not change any more. Now, we look again for the topmost cl_{st} or cl_{LKE} rule apart from the one we already considered. The corresponding component group $\mathcal{CG}_j$ and its identified rules contain only $\curvearrowright$ rules that link to components that are already rearranged and, hence, we can shift all rules identified with $\mathcal{CG}_j$ directly after the already rearranged ones. If we repeat this procedure, we end up with a proof in pre-proof schema normal form.

The important property of pre-proof schema normal form is that the construction of components is organized such that between any two closure rules is an **LKS**-proof.

Theorem 1. *Let Φ be an $\mathcal{S}i\mathbf{LK}$-Proof of the component collection*

$$(\,[\,\mathbf{Q}_0\,]\ :\,[\,\mathbf{S}_0\,]\,) \ \Big| \ \cdots \ \Big| \ (\,[\,\mathbf{Q}_m\,]\ :\,[\,\mathbf{S}_m\,]\,)$$

such that $\nu_0 \neq \top$ is the leading component, then there exists a proof schema $\langle \mathbf{C}_0, \mathbf{C}_1, \cdots, \mathbf{C}_k \rangle$, for $k \leq m$, where for every $0 \leq i \leq k$ there exists $0 \leq i \leq j \leq m$, where the end sequents of $C_i.2$ and π_j match as well as the end sequents of $C_i.3$ and ν_j.

---

[6] In general, the context is not empty. Since the rules, exempting the $\curvearrowright$, are independent from the context, we can always adjust the context.

Proof. By Lemma 2 we know that Φ has a pre-proof schema normal form Φ'. Note that, in a pre-proof schema normal form the leading component, i.e. ν_0, is the leftmost component. In Φ', we delete all component groups whose stepcase is equal to [ ] and get Ψ which contains k component groups. This is allowed because $\curvearrowright$ cannot link to component groups with stepcase [ ]. We construct the proof schema directly from Ψ where each proof schema component corresponds to a component group of Ψ. A proof schema component $\mathbf{C}_i$ is constructed from a component proof $\mathcal{CG}_j = ([\mathbf{Q}_j] : [\mathbf{S}_j])$ as follows: $\mathbf{C}_i.2$ is the proof containing all rules that are identified with $\mathcal{CG}_j$ and that are applied at the top of cl_{bc}. $\mathbf{C}_i.3$ is the proof containing all rules that are identified with $\mathcal{CG}_j$ and that are between cl_{bc} and cl_{sc}. We translate each component group according to the order of the pre-proof schema normal form, i.e. from right to left, to a proof schema component and construct thereby the proof schema of the theorem.

5   Properties of the Calculus

In this section we discuss the decision problem for validity, soundness of the calculus, and completeness with respect to k-simple proof schemata.

5.1   Decidability

Following the formalization of our calculus, we can state a semi-decidability theorem. This follows from our choice to distinguish between component collections where the leading component is equal but there is a variation in the other components.

Theorem 2. *Let Π be a collection of closed components that has a $\mathcal{S}i\mathbf{LK}$-proof then we find the proof in a finite number of inferences.*

Proof. By Lemma 2 we can construct proofs from right to left. In general, the basecase is an **LKE**-sequent that is itself semi-decidable. The rightmost component cannot contain any $\curvearrowright$-inferences in the stepcase such that it behaves as an **LKE**-proof plus an additional theory axiom for the $\circlearrowleft$-rule and is, therefore, semi-decidable. In the next component's stepcase, we consider all $\curvearrowright$-rules again as theory axioms, such that we end up in a semi-decidable fragment again. By the finite number of components the semi-decidability of Π follows.

The more interesting decidability property is of course whether we are able to extend the number of components on the right of a given component such that the new collection of components has a $\mathcal{S}i\mathbf{LK}$-proof. To see that this is not even semi-decidable we will formalize Robinson arithmetic [24] in our system.

Theorem 3. *Let C be a closed component group. Then deciding if there exists a closed component collection Π such that $C \mid \Pi$ is $\mathcal{S}i\mathbf{LK}$-provable is undecidable.*

Proof. The ω sort obeys the axioms of Robinson arithmetic concerning successor and zero. We can add the addition and multiplication axioms to the equational theory. The most important axiom of Robinson arithmetic $\forall x(x = 0 \lor \exists y(s(y) = x))$ is intrinsically part of the link mechanism. Because Robinson arithmetic is *essentially undecidable* then showing that there is an extension of a given component collection to a $Si\mathbf{LK}$-provable collection must be as well.

5.2   Soundness and Completeness

We provide a proof of soundness using our translation procedure of Sect. 4.1.

Theorem 4 (Soundness of the $Si\mathbf{LK}$-calculus). *If a closed component collection C is $Si\mathbf{LK}$-provable then it is valid.*

Proof. Let Φ be an $Si\mathbf{LK}$-proof of C. By Sect. 4.1 we can transform Φ to a pre-proof schema normal form Φ' and then construct a proof schema Ψ from it. By Proposition 3, we show the validity of the leading component and, therefore, of the evaluation itself, i.e. the $Si\mathbf{LK}$-calculus is sound.

To show completeness we technically need a conversion from proof schemata to $Si\mathbf{LK}$-proofs which can be easily derived given the procedure defined in Sect. 4.1. One needs to construct a closed component group for each component of the proof schema whose proofs can be read off from the proofs of the component's stepcase and basecase. The links are replaced by applications of the $\curvearrowright$-rule or the $\circlearrowleft$-rule. Due to space constraints we avoid formally defining the procedure.

Theorem 5 (Completeness). *If a close component collection C represents a valid n-induction statement then it is $Si\mathbf{LK}$-provable.*

Proof. By the theorems and definitions of Sect. 3, we know that if C represents a valid n-induction statement then a proof can be found in the $\mathbf{LKIE}$-calculus. Any $\mathbf{LKIE}$-proof can be transformed into a proof schema Φ (Sect. 3). We have not shown that Φ can be transformed into $Si\mathbf{LK}$-proofs, but it is quite obvious that the procedure defined in Sect. 4.1 is reversible. Thus, there is a $Si\mathbf{LK}$-proof for C.

6   Conclusion

In this paper we introduce a calculus for the construction of proof schemata the $Si\mathbf{LK}$-calculus which elucidates the restriction found in the formalism of [17] and provides a mechanism to weaken them. Initially, proof schemata were formalized by first defining an extension of the calculus $\mathbf{LK}$, the calculus $\mathbf{LKS}$, which adds so called links and an equational theory rule. Using this extended calculus a formal definition for proof schemata was developed over sequences of proofs. While interesting results followed [20], the results of proof analysis using the method of [17] could not be formalized within the same framework as the original proof [14]. Also, restrictions on the ordering used, the type of induction, and number of parameters are not easy to relax in the existing framework. By flattening the tree structure of proof schema, separating the instantiation of a proof from its definition, and removing the implicit ordering of components which complicates construction of schema with multiple parameters or mutual recursion, we can easily consider extensions of proof schemata and plan to do so in future work.

References

1. Andreoli, J.-M.: Logic programming with focusing proofs in linear logic. J. Log. Comput. **2**(3), 297–347 (1992)
2. Aravantinos, V., Caferra, R., Peltier, N.: A schemata calculus for propositional logic. In: Giese, M., Waaler, A. (eds.) TABLEAUX 2009. LNCS (LNAI), vol. 5607, pp. 32–46. Springer, Heidelberg (2009). doi:10.1007/978-3-642-02716-1_4
3. Aravantinos, V., Caferra, R., Peltier, N.: A decidable class of nested iterated schemata. In: Giesl, J., Hähnle, R. (eds.) IJCAR 2010. LNCS (LNAI), vol. 6173, pp. 293–308. Springer, Heidelberg (2010). doi:10.1007/978-3-642-14203-1_25
4. Aravantinos, V., Caferra, R., Peltier, N.: Decidability and undecidability results for propositional schemata. J. Artif. Intell. Res. **40**(1), 599–656 (2011)
5. Aravantinos, V., Caferra, R., Peltier, N.: Linear temporal logic and propositional schemata, back and forth. In: Proceedings of TIME 2011, pp. 80–87. IEEE (2011)
6. Aravantinos, V., Echenim, M., Peltier, N.: A resolution calculus for first-order schemata. Fundamenta Informaticae **125**, 101–133 (2013)
7. Aravantinos, V., Peltier, N.: Schemata of SMT-problems. In: Brünnler, K., Metcalfe, G. (eds.) TABLEAUX 2011. LNCS (LNAI), vol. 6793, pp. 27–42. Springer, Heidelberg (2011). doi:10.1007/978-3-642-22119-4_5
8. Baaz, M., Hetzl, S., Leitsch, A., Richter, C., Spohr, H.: Ceres: an analysis of Fürstenberg's proof of the infinity of primes. Theoret. Comput. Sci. **403**(2–3), 160–175 (2008)
9. Baaz, M., Leitsch, A.: Cut-elimination and redundancy-elimination by resolution. J. Symb. Comput. **29**, 149–176 (2000)
10. Boolos, G.: Don't eliminate cut. J. Philos. Log. **13**(4), 373–378 (1984)
11. Brotherston, J.: Cyclic proofs for first-order logic with inductive definitions. In: Beckert, B. (ed.) TABLEAUX 2005. LNCS (LNAI), vol. 3702, pp. 78–92. Springer, Heidelberg (2005). doi:10.1007/11554554_8
12. Brotherston, J., Simpson, A.: Sequent calculi for induction and infinite descent. J. Log. Comput. **21**, 1177–1216 (2011)
13. Cerna, D.: A tableaux-based decision procedure for multi-parameter propositional schemata. In: Watt, S.M., Davenport, J.H., Sexton, A.P., Sojka, P., Urban, J. (eds.) CICM 2014. LNCS (LNAI), vol. 8543, pp. 61–75. Springer, Cham (2014). doi:10.1007/978-3-319-08434-3_6
14. Cerna, D.M.: Advances in schematic cut elimination. Ph.D. thesis, Technical University of Vienna (2015). http://media.obvsg.at/p-AC12246421-2001
15. Cerna, D.M., Leitsch, A.: Schematic cut elimination and the ordered pigeonhole principle. In: Olivetti, N., Tiwari, A. (eds.) IJCAR 2016. LNCS, vol. 9706, pp. 241–256. Springer, Cham (2016). doi:10.1007/978-3-319-40229-1_17

16. Dunchev, C.: Automation of cut-elimination in proof schemata. Ph.D. thesis, Technical University of Vienna (2012)
17. Dunchev, C., Leitsch, A., Rukhaia, M., Weller, D.: Cut-elimination and proof schemata. J. Log. Lang. Comput. **8984**, 117–136 (2013)
18. Gentzen, G.: Fusion of several complete inductions. In: Szabo, M.E. (ed.) The Collected Papers of Gerhard Gentzen, Studies in Logic and the Foundations of Mathematics, vol. 55, pp. 309–311. Elsevier, Amsterdam (1969)
19. Hetzl, S., Leitsch, A., Weller, D., Woltzenlogel Paleo, B.: Herbrand sequent extraction. In: Autexier, S., Campbell, J., Rubio, J., Sorge, V., Suzuki, M., Wiedijk, F. (eds.) CICM 2008. LNCS, vol. 5144, pp. 462–477. Springer, Heidelberg (2008). doi:10.1007/978-3-540-85110-3_38
20. Leitsch, A., Peltier, N., Weller, D.: Ceres for first-order schemata. J. Log. Comput. (2017, to appear)
21. Mcdowell, R., Miller, D.: Cut-elimination for a logic with definitions and induction. Theoret. Comput. Sci. **232**, 91–119 (2000)
22. Miller, D.A.: A compact representation of proofs. Stud. Log. **46**(4), 347–370 (1987)
23. Orevkov, V.P.: Proof schemata in Hilbert-type axiomatic theories. J. Sov. Math. **55**(2), 1610–1620 (1991)
24. Robinson, R.M.: An essentially undecidable axiom system. In: Proceedings of the International Congress of Mathematics, pp. 729–730 (1950)
25. Takeuti, G.: Proof Theory, Studies in Logic and the Foundations of Mathematics, vol. 81. American Elsevier Publisher, Amsterdam (1975)

Realizability in Cyclic Proof: Extracting Ordering Information for Infinite Descent

Reuben N.S. Rowe[1]([✉]) and James Brotherston[2]

[1] School of Computing, University of Kent, Canterbury, UK
r.n.s.rowe@kent.ac.uk
[2] Department of Computer Science, University College London, London, UK
J.Brotherston@ucl.ac.uk

Abstract. In program verification, measures for proving the termination of programs are typically constructed using (notions of size for) the data manipulated by the program. Such data are often described by means of logical formulas. For example, the cyclic proof technique makes use of semantic approximations of inductively defined predicates to construct Fermat-style infinite descent arguments. However, logical formulas must often incorporate explicit size information (e.g. a list length parameter) in order to support inter-procedural analysis.

In this paper, we show that information relating the sizes of inductively defined data can be automatically extracted from *cyclic* proofs of logical entailments. We characterise this information in terms of a graph-theoretic condition on proofs, and show that this condition can be encoded as a containment between weighted automata. We also show that under certain conditions this containment falls within known decidability results. Our results can be viewed as a form of *realizability* for cyclic proof theory.

Keywords: Approximation semantics · Cyclic proof · Entailment · Inductive predicates · Infinite descent · Realizability · Sequent calculus · Weighted automata

1 Introduction

In program verification, it is well known that proving *termination* of a particular program depends on identifying a well-founded measure that decreases monotonically during the program's execution. Thus, since the measure cannot decrease infinitely often, no execution of the program can be infinite. In practice, termination measures are typically derived from the data manipulated by the program itself (cf. *size-change termination* [14]), and in particular from notions of the *size* of its data structures.

For example, consider the following code, which "shuffles" a linked list with head pointer x, using an auxiliary list reversal procedure rev:

```
proc shuffle(*x) { if (x != nil) { y := [x]; rev(y); shuffle(y); } }
```

© Springer International Publishing AG 2017
R.A. Schmidt and C. Nalon (Eds.): TABLEAUX 2017, LNAI 10501, pp. 295–310, 2017.
DOI: 10.1007/978-3-319-66902-1_18

where the syntax [x] denotes pointer dereferencing. The termination of the shuffle(x) procedure can be deduced by taking as termination measure the length of the list from x. The call to rev and the recursive call to shuffle both take place on the pointer y to the tail of the list. However, we also crucially rely upon the fact that the reversal procedure rev *does not increase* the size of the list. In a Hoare-style verification, this information is needed when we employ the sequential composition rule:

$$\frac{\{P\}\,\mathtt{rev(y)}\,\{Q\} \quad \{Q\}\,\mathtt{shuffle(y)}\,\{R\}}{\{P\}\,\mathtt{rev(y)}\,\mathtt{;shuffle(y)}\,\{R\}}$$

Here, the information that rev maintains the size of the list must be reflected in the relationship between its pre- and postconditions P and Q (which are logical formulas). Typically, this must be done by endowing these formulas with explicit size information; e.g., we could write an *inductive predicate* $\mathsf{list}(y, n)$ representing linked lists in memory, with an explicit length parameter (cf. [3]).

In this paper, we show that this kind of information, relating the sizes of inductively defined data, can often be extracted automatically from *cyclic proofs* of logical entailments. Cyclic proofs can be seen as formalising proof by regular infinite descent [7]; they are derivation trees with "backlinks" from (some) leaves to interior nodes, subject to a global soundness condition ensuring that all infinite paths correspond to sound infinite descent arguments. Cyclic proof systems have been developed for a wide variety of settings ranging from pure logic [4,5] to Hoare-style logics for program termination [6,17] and other temporal properties [9]; the common denominator is the presence of logical data defined using fixed points. The soundness of cyclic proofs relies on infinite descent over the semantic *approximations* of these fixed points, which can be seen as capturing a notion of size for the corresponding data. Suitable entailments for which to construct these cyclic proofs may be formulated by procedures for verifying the correctness of (fragments of) programs. For example, a procedure to verify the Hoare triple $\{\mathsf{list}(y)\}\ \mathtt{rev(y)}\ \{\mathsf{list}(y)\}$ might result in the entailment $y \mapsto x * \mathsf{list}(x) \vdash \mathsf{list}(y)$ of *separation logic* [11,16]. Such entailments are commonly referred to as verification conditions, since they must be discharged independently.

Relationships between the sizes of inductive data are reflected by *inclusions* between the approximations of the fixed point semantics. To infer these inclusions, we formulate a novel condition on the structure of cyclic entailment proofs (Definition 8) which is sufficient to extract this information (Theorem 2). This condition is equivalent to an inclusion between weighted automata that can be constructed from the cyclic proofs (Theorem 3), and, when the cyclic proof is suitably structurally well-behaved, this inclusion becomes decidable (Theorem 4). For simplicity, we present our results for the well-known cyclic proof system CLKID$^\omega$ for first order logic with inductive definitions [4,7]. However, we stress that our results are not limited to this setting: in a separate technical report we formulate and prove our results for a general, abstract notion of

$$\Rightarrow N\,0$$
$$N\,x \Rightarrow N\,sx$$
$$\Rightarrow E\,0$$
$$O\,x \Rightarrow E\,sx$$
$$E\,x \Rightarrow O\,sx$$

$$\cfrac{\cfrac{E\,x \vdash N\,x}{E\,z \vdash N\,z}\;(\text{Subst})}{\cfrac{E\,z \vdash N\,sz}{\cfrac{y = sz, E\,z \vdash N\,y}{O\,y \vdash N\,y}\;(\text{Case O})}\;(\text{=L})}\;(N\,R_2)$$

$$\cfrac{\cfrac{}{\vdash N\,0}\;(N\,R_1)}{x = 0 \vdash N\,x}\;(\text{=L}) \qquad \cfrac{\cfrac{\cfrac{O\,y \vdash N\,y}{O\,y \vdash N\,sy}\;(N\,R_2)}{x = sy, O\,y \vdash N\,x}\;(\text{=L})}{}\;(\text{Case E})$$

$$E\,x \vdash N\,x$$

Fig. 1. Inductive definitions of N, E, and O, and cyclic proof of $E\,x \vdash N\,x$.

cyclic proof [18]. Consequently our results also hold, e.g. for separation logic with inductive predicates [5,6], and so can be deployed in our cyclic proof framework for proving program termination based on this logic [17].

The remainder of this paper is structured as follows. First, Sect. 2 gives an introductory example motivating our new structural condition for extracting size relationships from cyclic proofs. Section 3 then reprises the basics of first-order logic with inductive predicates and its cyclic proof system CLKID^ω from [4,7]. In Sect. 4 we formulate our structural condition on cyclic proofs and prove its soundness. In Sect. 5 we show how this condition can be encoded as an inclusion between weighted automata and formulate further graph-theoretic conditions on cyclic proofs under which this is decidable. Section 6 concludes.

For space reasons, we elide the detailed proofs of the results in this paper, but they can be found in our longer technical report [18].

2 Motivating Example

Figure 1 gives inductive definitions of predicates N, E and O (intended to capture the properties of being a natural number, even number and odd number respectively) and a cyclic proof of the sequent $E\,x \vdash N\,x$. Note that E and O are mutually defined. The $(N\,R_i)$ rules indicate a right-unfolding of the N predicate, and the (Case E) and (Case O) rules a left unfolding (or *case analysis*) on the predicates E and O respectively. This cyclic proof is sound since its only infinite path contains an infinite, unbroken "trace" of the E and O predicates in the antecedent of each sequent that "progresses" infinitely often as these predicates are unfolded.

This condition ensures that the proof is valid because it can be related to *approximations* of the semantics $[\![\cdot]\!]$ of the predicates, which form an ordinal-indexed chain $[\![\cdot]\!]_0 \le [\![\cdot]\!]_1 \le \dots \le [\![\cdot]\!]_\alpha \le \dots \le [\![\cdot]\!]$. If $E\,x \vdash N\,x$ is invalid then, by local soundness of the rules, so is every sequent on the infinite path in the proof.

The trace along this path then corresponds to a non-increasing subsequence of the ordinals in this chain, which strictly decreases when the trace progresses. Since the trace progresses infinitely often, we obtain an infinitely decreasing chain of ordinals, which is a contradiction.

Interestingly, it turns out that, by examining the structure of this cyclic proof more closely and also considering the (right) unfoldings of N, we can deduce that the αth approximation of E is also included in the αth approximation of N, i.e., $[\![E\,x]\!]_\alpha \subseteq [\![N\,x]\!]_\alpha$. Intuitively, this is because on every maximally finite path in the proof along which N is unfolded, the mutually defined E and O are together unfolded at least as often as N. Thus when x is included in some approximation of E, it is already included in the corresponding approximation of N. Later, in Sect. 4, we will formalise this intuition as an additional syntactic, trace-based condition on cyclic proofs. The upshot is that we may form "traces", as described above, between instances of $E\,t$ and $N\,t$ (for any term t) in the antecedent of sequents, even though they are not related by their inductive definitions.

3   Cyclic Proofs for First Order Logic

In this section we summarise a variant of CLKID$^\omega$, a cyclic proof system for first order logic with inductive predicates [4,7].

3.1   First Order Logic with Inductive Definitions.

We assume the standard syntax and semantics of first order logic. For simplicity, we take models to be valuations of term variables to objects in the semantic domain. A *sequent* $\Gamma \vdash \Delta$ comprises two sequences of formulas: an *antecedent* Γ and a *consequent* Δ. For a sequent $S = \Gamma \vdash \Delta$, we write $m \models S$ to mean that the model m satisfies at least one formula in Δ whenever it satisfies all fomulas in Γ. Conversely, we write $m \not\models S$ to mean that m satisfies all formulas in Γ and *no* formula in Δ. A sequent S is *valid* when $m \models S$ for all models m.

We give the semantics of predicate symbols in the signature by means of sets of inductive *productions*, in the style of Martin-Löf [15].

Definition 1 (Inductive Definition Set). *An* inductive definition set Φ *is a finite set of* productions, *each of the form* $P_1\,t_1, \ldots, P_j\,t_j \Rightarrow P_0\,t_0$, *consisting of a finite set of predicate formulas called* premises *and a predicate formula called the* conclusion. *We say that* $P_1\,t_1, \ldots, P_j\,t_j \Rightarrow P_0\,t_0$ *is a production for* P_0.

Predicate *interpretations* X are functions from predicate formulas to sets of models. We write $[\![P\,t]\!]_X$ to denote $X(P\,t)$. An inductive definition set Φ induces a *characteristic operator* φ_Φ on predicate interpretations, which applies (substitution instances of) the productions in Φ, as follows (where θ is a substitution of terms for variables):

$$\varphi_\Phi(X)(P\,t\,\theta) = \{m \mid P_1 t_1, \ldots, P_j t_j \Rightarrow P\,t \in \Phi$$
$$\text{and } m \in [\![P_i t_i \theta]\!]_X \text{ for all } i \in \{1, \ldots, j\}\}$$

We define a partial ordering $\leq$ on the set of predicate interpretations $\mathcal{I}$ by $X \leq X' \Leftrightarrow \forall F.\ X(F) \subseteq X'(F)$. One can note that $(\mathcal{I}, \leq)$ is a complete lattice and the least element, denoted by $X_\perp$, maps all predicate formulas to the empty set. Moreover, characteristic operators are *monotone* with respect to $\leq$, thus admitting the following (standard) construction that builds a canonical interpretation via a process of *approximation* [1,7]:

Definition 2 (Interpretation of Inductive Definitions). *We interpret an inductive definition set Φ as the least prefixed point of its characteristic operator, $\mu X.\varphi_\Phi(X)$. This least prefixed point, denoted by $[\![\cdot]\!]^\Phi$, can be approached iteratively being the supremum of the (ordinal-indexed) chain $X_\perp \leq \varphi_\Phi(X_\perp) \leq \varphi_\Phi(\varphi_\Phi(X_\perp)) \leq \ldots \leq \varphi_\Phi^\alpha(X_\perp) \leq \ldots;$ each $\varphi_\Phi^\alpha(X_\perp)$ is an approximation of $[\![\cdot]\!]^\Phi$ and is denoted by $[\![\cdot]\!]_\alpha^\Phi$. When the specific inductive rule set is not of immediate relevance we leave it implicit, writing $[\![\cdot]\!]$ and $[\![\cdot]\!]_\alpha$.*

3.2   The Cyclic Proof System

The proof system is essentially Gentzen's sequent calculus, LK, in which derivations are permitted to contain cycles. To the standard proof rules of LK with equality and substitution we add introduction rules for the inductive predicate symbols, derived from their productions. Each predicate P has a single left introduction rule, (Case P), which performs a case split over the full set of productions for P, and every i^{th} production for P induces a distinct right introduction rule (P R_i). Furthermore, we remove the right introduction rules for implication and negation since they invalidate the soundness of our realizability condition (specifically, not all instances of these rules satisfy Property 1, in Sect. 4 below). Although this system is actually quite weak, we believe these particular rules do not play a crucial role in deriving entailments between inductive predicates in general. Note we do not need them in our examples.

We view a cyclic derivation (or *pre-proof*) as a directed graph; each sequent is a node of the graph, and edges go from conclusion to premise. To track sequences of decreasing approximations, we use the notion of a trace in a pre-proof $\mathcal{P}$.

Definition 3 (Traces).

(i) *A* trace value *is a predicate formula (e.g. $E\,x$).*

(ii) *A* left-hand *(resp.* right-hand*)* trace *is a possibly infinite sequence τ of trace values in which those of each successive pair, (τ_i, τ_{i+1}), occur in the antecedents (resp. consequents) of successive nodes in $\mathcal{P}$, and either:*

(a) $\tau_i = \tau_{i+1};$

(b) τ_i *and* τ_{i+1} *occur as part of the conclusion and premise of a substitution rule and τ_i is the result of applying the rule's substitution to $\tau_{i+1};$ or*

(c) τ_i *and* τ_{i+1} *occur as part of the conclusion and premise of a (Case P) or (P R_i) rule, with τ_i of the form $P\,t$ and τ_{i+1} derived from the body of the production for P associated with the premise of the rule (i.e. τ_{i+1} is derived from the unfolding of τ_i).*

$$
\cfrac{
\cfrac{
\cfrac{
\cfrac{
\cfrac{\quad}{(5)\ \vdash \underline{E\,0}, \neg E\,0}\ (E\,R_1)
\qquad
\cfrac{
\cfrac{
\cfrac{\quad}{(8)\ \vdash E\,0}\ (E\,R_1)}
{(7)\ \neg E\,0 \vdash}\ (\neg L)}
{(6)\ \neg E\,0 \vdash \overline{O\,0}}\ (WR)
}{(4)\ \vdash \underline{E\,0}, \overline{O\,0}}\ (Cut)
}{(2)\ x = 0 \vdash \underline{E\,x}, \overline{O\,x}}\ (=L)
\qquad
\cfrac{
\cfrac{
\cfrac{
\cfrac{
\cfrac{
\cfrac{(1)\ N\,x \vdash \overline{E\,x}, O\,x}{(12)\ N\,y \vdash \overline{E\,y}, O\,y}\ (Subst)}
{(11)\ N\,y \vdash O\,y, \overline{E\,y}}\ (PR)}
{(10)\ N\,y \vdash O\,\underline{y}, \overline{O\,sy}}\ (OR)}
{(9)\ N\,y \vdash E\,\underline{sy}, \overline{O\,sy}}\ (E\,R_2)}
{(3)\ x = sy, N\,y \vdash \underline{E\,x}, \overline{O\,x}}\ (=L)
}
{(1)\ N\,x \vdash \underline{E\,x}, \overline{O\,x}}\ (Case\ N)
$$

Fig. 2. A cyclic proof of the entailment $N\,x \vdash E\,x, O\,x$; each node is numbered uniquely, and the consequent trace pairs are indicated using under- and overlines.

We call each pair (τ_i, τ_{i+1}) a *trace pair*. In the case that (c) holds, we say the trace *progresses* at point i and call (τ_i, τ_{i+1}) a *progressing* trace pair.

(iii) For finite traces τ, we write $|\,\tau\,|$ for the length of the trace and denote by $\mathrm{prog}(\tau)$ the number of progression points in τ, which we call the *sum* of τ.

(iv) For an inference rule $r = \langle S_0, (S_1, \ldots, S_n) \rangle$ with trace values τ and τ' occurring in the conclusion S_0 and j^{th} premise S_j, respectively, we write $\delta^A_{(r,j)}(\tau, \tau')$ (resp. $\delta^C_{(r,j)}(\tau, \tau')$) if (τ, τ') forms a left-hand (resp. right-hand) trace. We call δ the *trace pair relation*.

When the meaning is clear from the context, we may sometimes simply write $\delta_r(\tau, \tau')$. In an abuse of notation we write $\delta_r(\tau, \tau') = 1$ to indicate that (τ, τ') is a progressing trace pair, and $\delta_r(\tau, \tau') = 0$ otherwise. When τ occurs in the conclusion of rule r, but there are no j and τ' such that $\delta_{(r,j)}(\tau, \tau')$ is defined, then we say τ is *terminal* for r.

Example 1. In Fig. 2 we show a cyclic proof of $N\,x \vdash E\,x, O\,x$, i.e. that every natural number is either even or odd. Each $N\,t$ in an antecedent is related to the $N\,t'$ in its premise(s); the trace pair relation for the consequent trace values is more complex, and we indicate it visually using under- and overlines.

A pre-proof is valid if it satisfies the following condition on traces.

Definition 4 (Global Soundness). *A pre-proof is globally sound when every infinite path has some tail that is followed by a left-hand trace which progresses infinitely often; when this holds we say that it is a (cyclic) proof.*

The global soundness of a pre-proof can be checked using Büchi automata.

Proposition 1 ([7, Proposition 7.4]). *It is decidable if a pre-proof is globally sound.*

Example 2. The pre-proof in Fig. 1 has only one infinite path (along the cycle), and there is a left-hand trace along this path formed by the alternating occurrences of the E and O predicates in the antecedent of each sequent. This progresses at two points around each cycle on traversing the (Case) rules and therefore the pre-proof is globally sound. A similar argument shows the pre-proof in Fig. 2 is also globally sound: the (unique) infinite left-hand trace progresses once each time around the loop.

We may think of models as *realizers* of trace values. We define a trace *realization* function to specify which models realize trace values and how *quickly* they realize them.

Definition 5 (Trace Realization Function). *The* trace realization function Θ *maps models to the* least *approximations of trace values in which they appear:*

$$\Theta(\tau, m) \overset{def}{=} \min\left(\{\alpha \mid m \in [\![\tau]\!]_\alpha\}\right)$$

The value assigned by Θ corresponds to the ordinal position of this approximation in the chain constructed in Definition 2. Notice that a model may not necessarily satisfy a given predicate formula, so Θ is partial and we write $\Theta(\tau, m)\downarrow$ to indicate that Θ is defined on (τ, m).

The global soundness condition ensures the validity of cyclic proofs because the trace realization function enables us to relate traces to descending chains of approximations. If a cyclic proof were to contain invalid sequents then the trace realization function could be used to derive an infinite descending chain of ordinals and hence a contradiction.

Theorem 1 ([7, Proposition 5.8]). *If $\Gamma \vdash \Delta$ has a cyclic proof then it is valid.*

4   Extracting Semantic Inclusions from Cyclic Proofs

We are aiming to deduce inclusions between the semantic approximations of predicates (viz. trace values), e.g. that whenever there is a model $m \in [\![E\,x]\!]_\alpha$ then also $m \in [\![N\,x]\!]_\alpha$ (cf. Fig. 1). We can express this using the trace realization function as $\Theta(N\,x, m) \leq \Theta(E\,x, m)$, since predicate approximations increase monotonically. We will deduce such relationships from sequents $\Gamma[\tau] \vdash \Delta[\tau']$ in cyclic proofs (where $\Gamma[\tau]$ indicates that the trace value τ occurs in Γ), and so in general we deduce such orderings within a context, Γ. Thus we will write $\Gamma : \tau' \leq \tau$ to mean:

for all models m, if $m \models \Gamma$ and $\Theta(\tau', m)\downarrow$ then $\Theta(\tau', m) \leq \Theta(\tau, m)$,

where $m \models \Gamma$ denotes that m satisfies all the formulas in Γ. We formulate an additional trace condition for cyclic proofs (Definition 8, below) and show that the existence of a proof satisfying this extra condition is sufficient to guarantee this ordering. We say that such a proof *realizes* the ordering, and so refer to the new trace condition as the *realizability condition*.

This realizability condition will express that for every right-hand trace of a certain kind, we can find a left-hand trace which 'matches' it in a sense that we will make precise below. We specify the kinds of right-hand traces of interest using the following concepts.

Definition 6 (Maximal Right-Hand Traces). *A finite right-hand trace τ $(|\tau| = n)$ following a path in a cyclic proof is called* maximal *when it cannot be extended any further, i.e. there is no trace value τ' and premise of the final node in the trace for which $\delta_r(\tau_n, \tau')$ is defined (where r is the rule used to derive the final node). If the final node in the trace is derived using an axiom, then we say the trace is* partially maximal; *otherwise it is called* fully maximal.

Fully maximal traces are ones whose final trace value is introduced by an inference rule, e.g. weakening, as in node (6) of the proof in Fig. 2.

Definition 7 (Groundedness and Polarity). *We call a trace value derivable using a base production (i.e. a production without premises)* ground, *e.g. $N\,0$ or $E\,0$. A* grounded *trace is one whose final trace value is ground. When the antecedent of a sequent contains the negation of a ground predicate instance, we say that it is* negative. *A* positive *sequent is one with no such negated predicate. A* negative (resp. positive) *trace is one whose final sequent is negative (resp. positive).*

For example, in Fig. 2 the right-hand trace $(1, E\,x)$, $(2, E\,x)$, $(4, E\,0)$, $(5, E\,0)$ is grounded, but $(1, O\,x)$, $(2, O\,x)$, $(4, O\,0)$, $(6, O\,0)$ is not. Moreover, the latter trace is negative. Note that, by definition, all models m must satisfy ground predicate instances τ and $\Theta(\tau, m) = 1$. Thus no models may satisfy the antecedent of a negative sequent. This means that we can exclude negative traces when considering the realizability of trace value orderings. We can now formulate the realizability condition itself.

Definition 8 (The Realizability Condition). *We write $\mathcal{P} : \tau \leq \Gamma[\tau']$ when $\mathcal{P}$ is a cyclic proof containing a node $\Gamma[\tau'] \vdash \Delta[\tau]$ satisfying the following: for every positive maximal right-hand trace τ starting at τ, there exists a left-hand trace τ' starting with τ' and following some prefix of the same path in the proof such that:*

1. $\mathsf{prog}(\tau) \leq \mathsf{prog}(\tau')$ *and*
2. *either a) τ is grounded; or b) τ is partially maximal, $|\tau'| = |\tau|$, and the final trace values in τ and τ' match.*

Consider the proof $\mathcal{P}_1$ in Fig. 2.

Example 3 ($\mathcal{P}_1 : E\,x \leq N\,x$). The right-hand trace from $E\,x$ following the path (1) (2) (4) (5) is positive, maximal and grounded. The left-hand trace (1) follows this path and the sum of both traces is 0. The next longest maximal right-hand trace traverses the cycle once, following the path (1) (3) (9) ... (12) (1) (2) (4) (6) along the right-hand side of the (Cut) rule. However, this trace is *negative* and so we need not consider it. The other positive maximal traces are obtained by following the cycle an even number of times before ending at node (5); the progression points occur at $(E\,R_2)$ on the odd-numbered traversals and $(O\,R_2)$ on the even-numbered ones, which is matched by progressions in the corresponding left-hand trace at the (Case) rule. These traces also suffice to demonstrate that $\mathcal{P}_1 : O\,x \leq N\,x$ holds.

Notice that we can obtain a globally sound cyclic proof of $N\,x \vdash E\,x, O\,x$ without using (Cut), by immediately closing node (4) with $(E\,R_1)$. In this case the now (partially) maximal right-hand trace from $O\,x$ in node (1) to $O\,0$ in node (4) is *positive* and so would have to be considered. Unfortunately this trace is *not* grounded, nor does there exist a matching left-hand trace of equal length ending with $O\,0$, and so this simpler (and arguably more natural) proof does not satisfy the realizability condition.

It may seem odd that we cannot use the simpler proof to realize the ordering. We must discount the right-hand traces ending with $O\,0$ since they have no models; yet it is not possible in general to determine syntactically when predicate instances do *not* have models. Our approximation, using negative traces, works at the level of entire sequents and thus the traces ending with $E\,0$ (which we do consider) must be separated from those ending in $O\,0$ (which we must not). This highlights the syntactic nature of our results.

Now consider the proof $\mathcal{P}_2$ of $E\,x \vdash N\,x$ in Fig. 3, which is a modified version of the proof in Fig. 1 that accommodates an additional production for O.

Example 4 ($\mathcal{P}_2 : N\,x \leq E\,x$). The right-hand trace following (1) (2) (4) is maximal, positive and grounded and the left-hand trace $(1, E\,x)$ follows (a prefix of) the same path; the sum of both of these traces is 0. Similarly, the positive right-hand trace following (1) (3) (5) (6) (7) (9) (10) is not grounded, but is partially maximal and there is a left-hand trace of equal length following this same path with a matching final trace value. The sum of both traces in this case is 2: the right-hand trace progresses once at each instance of the $(N\,R_2)$ rule; the left-hand one at the (Case) rules. Other maximal right-hand traces obtained by prefixing the cycle (1)...(12) to the two already considered; notice the left-hand trace following the cycle progresses an equal number of times.

Soundness of Realizability. To show that the realizability condition is sufficient to realize trace value orderings, we extend the concept that models realize trace values and use sequences of models to realize *traces*. We say that a sequence of models m realizes a left-hand trace τ when for every sequent $\Gamma_i[\tau_i] \vdash \Delta_i$ in the corresponding path we have that $m_i \models \Gamma_i$ and $\Theta(\tau_{i+1}, m_{i+1}) + \delta(\tau_i, \tau_{i+1}) \leq \Theta(\tau_i, m_i)$. Dually, m realizes a right-hand trace τ when $m_i \models \Delta_i$ and $\Theta(\tau_{i+1}, m_{i+1}) + \delta(\tau_i, \tau_{i+1}) \geq \Theta(\tau_i, m_i)$ for every sequent $\Gamma_i \vdash \Delta_i[\tau_i]$ in the path. Trace realizers guarantee the following.

Lemma 1. *If m realizes a trace τ of length n then $\Theta(\tau_n, m_n) + \mathsf{prog}(\tau) \leq \Theta(\tau_1, m_1)$ holds if τ is a left-hand trace, and $\Theta(\tau_n, m_n) + \mathsf{prog}(\tau) \geq \Theta(\tau_1, m_1)$ if τ is a right-hand trace.*

$$\cfrac{\cfrac{\cfrac{\cfrac{\overline{(10)\ \mathrm{N\,ss0} \vdash \mathrm{N\,ss0}}\ \text{(Ax)}}{(9)\ \mathrm{N\,ss0} \vdash \mathrm{N\,sss0}}\ (\mathrm{N\,R_2})}{(7)\ y = \mathrm{sss0}, \mathrm{N\,ss0} \vdash \mathrm{N}\,y}\ (=\mathrm{L})\quad\quad \cfrac{\cfrac{\cfrac{(1)\ \mathrm{E}\,x \vdash \mathrm{N}\,x}{(12)\ \mathrm{E}\,z \vdash \mathrm{N}\,z}\ \text{(Subst)}}{(11)\ \mathrm{E}\,z \vdash \mathrm{N\,s}z}\ (\mathrm{N\,R_2})}{(8)\ y = \mathrm{s}z, \mathrm{E}\,z \vdash \mathrm{N}\,y}\ (=\mathrm{L})}{(6)\ \mathrm{O}\,y \vdash \mathrm{N}\,y}\ \text{(Case O)}}{}}{}$$

Fig. 3. A cyclic proof of the entailment $\mathrm{E}\,x \vdash \mathrm{N}\,x$, accommodating the extra production $\mathrm{N\,ss0} \Rightarrow \mathrm{O\,sss0}$ for O.

We say a rule instance is *valid* when its conclusion and premises are all valid sequents.[1] We note the following property of the trace realization function.

Property 1 (Descending Model Property). For all valid, non-axiomatic rule instances $r = \langle \Gamma[\tau] \vdash \Delta[\tau'], (S_1, \ldots, S_n) \rangle$ and models $m \models \Gamma$, there exists some $S_j = \Sigma \vdash \Pi$ and a model $m' \models \Sigma$ such that: either τ' is terminal for r, or there exists τ'' with $\delta_{(r,j)}(\tau', \tau'')$ defined; furthermore, for all trace values τ'':

1. if $\delta^A_{(r,j)}(\tau, \tau'') = \alpha$ and $\Theta(\tau, m)\downarrow$, then $\Theta(\tau'', m')\downarrow$ and $\Theta(\tau'', m') + \alpha \leq \Theta(\tau, m)$
2. if $\delta^C_{(r,j)}(\tau, \tau'') = \alpha$ and $\Theta(\tau', m)\downarrow$, then $\Theta(\tau'', m')\downarrow$ and $\Theta(\tau'', m') + \alpha \geq \Theta(\tau', m)$

This property asserts that the trace pair relation soundly *bounds* the difference in how quickly models realize trace pairs. In the case of antecedents this difference is bounded from above, and for consequents from below. The descending model property guarantees every model of a consequent trace value in a globally sound cyclic proof corresponds to a realizer of a positive maximal right-hand trace.

Lemma 2 (Trace Realization). *If $\mathcal{P}$ is a globally sound cyclic proof containing a node $\Gamma[\tau'] \vdash \Delta[\tau]$ and m is a model such that $m \models \Gamma$ and $\Theta(\tau, m)\downarrow$, then there exists a positive, maximal right-hand trace $\boldsymbol{\tau}$ starting from τ and a sequence of models $\boldsymbol{m}$ with $m_1 = m'$ that realizes it; moreover, $\boldsymbol{m}$ realizes all left-hand traces following the same path starting from τ'.*

As a result, the realizability condition is sufficient to guarantee trace value orderings (see the technical report for a detailed proof [18, Theorem 22]).

Theorem 2 (Soundness of Realizability). *If $\mathcal{P} : \tau \leq \Gamma[\tau']$ then $\Gamma : \tau \leq \tau'$.*

---

[1] Note this is a stronger property than local soundness, which only requires the conclusion to be valid whenever all the premises are.

5   Computing Realizable Orderings Using Weighted Automata

In this section, we demonstrate a close connection between cyclic proofs and weighted automata. Under this correspondence, the realizability condition can be seen to be equivalent to an inclusion between particular weighted automata, allowing us to make use of known decision procedures in the world of weighted automata for deciding the realizability condition.

Weighted automata generalise standard finite state automata, assigning to words over alphabet Σ values from a semiring $(V, \oplus, \otimes)$ of weights (see [8]).

Definition 9 (Weighted Automata). *A weighted automaton $\mathscr{A}$ is a tuple (Q, q_I, F, γ) consisting of a set Q of states containing an initial state $q_I \in Q$, a set $F \subseteq Q$ of final states, and a weighting function $\gamma : (Q \times \Sigma \times Q) \to V$.*

A *run* of $\mathscr{A}$ over a (finite) word $\sigma_1 \ldots \sigma_n \in \Sigma^*$ is a sequence of states $q_0 \ldots q_n$ such that $(q_{j-1}, \sigma_j, q_j) \in \mathsf{dom}(\gamma)$ for each σ_j. We write $\rho : q_0 \xrightarrow{w} q_n$ to denote that ρ is a run over w. The value $\mathsf{V}(\rho)$ of the run is the (left-to-right) semiring product of the weight $\gamma(q_{j-1}, \sigma_j, q_j)$ of each transition. If $q_0 = q_I$ and $q_n \in F$ then ρ is called an *accepting* run. The value of a word is the semiring sum of the values of all the accepting runs of that word, and is undefined if there are no such runs. Sum automata are weighted automata over the max-plus semiring $(\mathbb{N}, \mathsf{max}, +)$, which is also referred to as the arctic semiring. The (quantitative) language $\mathcal{L}_{\mathscr{A}}$ of an automaton $\mathscr{A}$ is the (partial) function over Σ^* computed by the automaton. The standard notion of inclusion between regular languages extends naturally to quantitative languages:

Definition 10 (Weighted Inclusion). $\mathcal{L}_1 \leq \mathcal{L}_2$ *if and only if for every word w such that $\mathcal{L}_1(w)$ is defined, $\mathcal{L}_2(w)$ is also defined and $\mathcal{L}_1(w) \leq \mathcal{L}_2(w)$.*

The inclusion problem for sum automata is known to be undecidable [2,13], but has recently been shown to be decidable for *finite-valued* sum automata, for which a finite bound can be given on the number of distinct values for runs over a given word [10].

5.1   Cyclic Proofs as Sum Automata

Given a node $n = \Gamma[\tau] \vdash \Delta[\tau']$ in a cyclic proof $\mathcal{P}$ we construct two sum automata $\mathscr{A}_{\mathcal{P}}^\tau$ and $\mathscr{C}_{\mathcal{P}}^{\tau'}$ called left-hand and right-hand *trace automata*, respectively. Each state (n, τ) of a trace automaton corresponds to a particular trace value τ in some node n of $\mathcal{P}$, and the transitions are given by the trace pair relation. That is, there is a transition from (n, τ) to (n', τ') with weight $k \in \{0, 1\}$ precisely when n and n' are the conclusion and j^{th} premise, respectively, of a rule instance r with $\delta_{(r,j)}(\tau, \tau') = k$. The letter accepted on the transition is the node n'. Thus, a run of one of these automata corresponds to a trace in $\mathcal{P}$, and the word accepted by the run is the path followed by the trace.

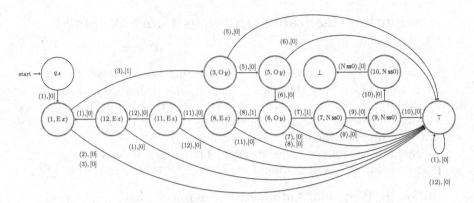

Fig. 4. The left-hand trace automaton $\mathscr{A}_{\mathcal{P}}^{Ex}$ for the proof of $Ex \vdash Nx$ in Fig. 3.

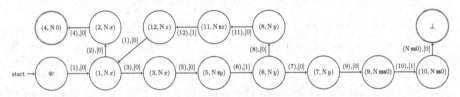

Fig. 5. The right-hand trace automaton $\mathscr{C}_{\mathcal{P}}^{Nx}$ for the proof of $Ex \vdash Nx$ in Fig. 3.

For lack of space, we elide the formal definition of the automata construction (see [18, Definition 23]), but in Figs. 4 and 5 we show the trace automata corresponding to the proof in Fig. 3. Accepting states are indicated by a double circle, and for each transition we show the node accepted in parentheses and the weight of the transition in brackets. We draw attention to the following:

- The left-hand trace automaton also includes (zero-weight) transitions to a state $\top$ with a self-transition accepting any node. Thus, the weight it computes for a path is the maximum value of $\mathsf{prog}(\tau)$ over all traces τ following a *prefix* of that path. In contrast, the right-hand automaton considers only traces following the *full* path.
- Each automaton also includes a state $\bot$, the transitions to which accept a trace value rather than a node. The effect of this is that any word $w = n_1 \ldots n_k \tau$ accepted by the right-hand automaton corresponds to a *partially* maximal right-hand trace ending in τ. If the left-hand automaton also accepts w, then we know there is a matching left-hand trace of equal length (cf. Definition 8).
- The accepting states of right-hand trace automata (excluding $\bot$) correspond to *terminal* trace values in non-axiomatic rules instances; when each such trace value is ground, we say the trace automaton is *grounded*.

This construction results in automata polynomial in the size of the proof $\mathcal{P}$, and allows the realizability condition to be encoded by the inclusion of the right-hand trace automaton within the left-hand one.

Theorem 3. $\mathcal{P} : \tau \leq \Gamma[\tau']$ *holds if and only if* $\mathscr{C}_{\mathcal{P}}^{\tau} \leq \mathscr{A}_{\mathcal{P}}^{\tau'}$ *and* $\mathscr{C}_{\mathcal{P}}^{\tau}$ *is grounded.*

5.2 Decidability of the Realizability Condition

We now demonstrate that under certain conditions our trace automata become *finite-valued,* and so we can decide inclusion between them in polynomial time [10].

Remark 1. The trace pair relation δ satisfies an injectivity property[2]. Namely, if both $\delta_{(r,j)}(\tau', \tau)$ and $\delta_{(r,j)}(\tau'', \tau)$ are defined, then $\tau' = \tau''$. This means that, along any given path, traces may only branch and never converge. Consequently, there is at most one trace along a given path between an initial and final trace value. This immediately gives the following result.

Lemma 3. *Every right-hand trace automaton* $C_{\mathcal{P}}^{\tau}$ *is finite-valued.*

Unfortunately, because left-hand trace automata include the state $\top$ and associated transitions, they are not in general finite-valued. When a proof contains a (left-hand) trace cycle (of the form $(n_1, \tau_1) \dots (n_j, \tau_j)$ with nodes $n_1 = n_j$ and trace values $\tau_1 = \tau_j$), the resulting left-hand trace automaton will contain the following configuration of states:

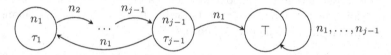

That is, there are runs $(n_{j-1}, \tau_{j-1}) \xrightarrow{w} (n_{j-1}, \tau_{j-1})$, $(n_{j-1}, \tau_{j-1}) \xrightarrow{w} \top$, and $\top \xrightarrow{w} \top$ with $w = n_1 \dots n_{j-1}$. This results in the automaton being infinitely ambiguous [19, Sect. 3] and thus when the weight of the cycle is non-zero it is also infinite-valued.

To avoid this we modify our construction to produce a series of *approximate* left-hand trace automata $\mathscr{A}[k]_{\mathcal{P}}^{\tau}$, where $k > 0$ is called the *degree* of approximation. These refine the 'sink' state $\top$ into a finite chain of k sink states for each node (thus, these approximate automata are a factor of k larger than the original automaton). Once a run enters a chain of sink states $\top_n^{1..k}$, only a finite number of further occurrences of the node n are accepted. In contrast, the full automaton accepts paths with any number of further occurrences. This construction approximates the original one and results in finite-valued automata.

Lemma 4. *Every approximate left-hand trace automaton* $\mathscr{A}[k]_{\mathcal{P}}^{\tau}$ *is finite-valued.*

Lemma 5 (Soundness of Approximate Automata). *For each* $k > 0$, *the inclusion* $\mathscr{A}[k]_{\mathcal{P}}^{\tau} \leq \mathscr{A}_{\mathcal{P}}^{\tau}$ *holds.*

---

[2] Excepting certain instances of the (=L) rule, e.g. $P x, P x \vdash \Delta \Rightarrow P x, P y, x = y \vdash \Delta$. However, note that one can check whether any given instance of (=L) satisfies the injectivity property, and exclude proofs containing such instances from consideration.

The following further restrictions on proofs allow a relative completeness result. They are expressed in terms of *simple* trace cycles (containing no repeated trace values other than the first and last). A *binary* trace cycle is a pair of trace cycles following the same path.

Definition 11. *Let* $S = \Gamma[\tau'] \vdash \Delta[\tau]$ *be a node in a cyclic proof* $\mathcal{P}$. *We say* $\mathcal{P}$ *is* dynamic *(w.r.t. S) when* $\mathsf{prog}(\tau) > 0$ *for every simple left- and right-hand trace cycle* τ *reachable from* τ' *and* τ, *respectively. We say* $\mathcal{P}$ *is* balanced *(w.r.t. S) when* $\mathsf{prog}(\tau_1) = \mathsf{prog}(\tau_2)$ *for every simple left-hand binary cycle* (τ_1, τ_2) *reachable from* τ'.

Checking whether a proof is balanced and dynamic requires finding the simple cycles, which can be done in time $\mathsf{O}((N + E)(C + 1))$, where N, E, and C are the number of nodes, edges and basic cycles in the graph, respectively [12]. The number of basic cycles in a *complete* graph is factorial in the number of nodes, thus the worst case complexity is super-exponential. Notwithstanding, cyclic proofs are by nature sparse graphs, so we expect the average runtime complexity to be much lower. All of our example proofs are both balanced and dynamic.

When a balanced, dynamic proof satisfies the realizability condition, its positive fully-maximal right-hand traces are always matched by left-hand traces that can be recognised by an approximate left-hand automaton whose degree of approximation can be bounded by the following two graph-theoretic quantities (which are polynomially bounded in the size of $\mathcal{P}$).

(a) The *trace width* $\mathbf{W}(\mathcal{P})$ is the maximum number of trace values occurring in the antecedent or consequent of any node in $\mathcal{P}$. Any trace visiting a given node more than $\mathbf{W}(\mathcal{P})$ times *must* contain a cycle.

(b) The binary left-hand *cycle threshold* $\mathbf{C}(\mathcal{P})$ is the number of distinct pairs of left-hand trace values occurring in $\mathcal{P}$. Any pair of left-hand traces following the same path of length greater than $\mathbf{C}(\mathcal{P})$ *must* contain a binary cycle.

Lemma 6 (Relative Completeness). *If* $\mathcal{P} : \tau \leq \Gamma[\tau']$ *and* $\mathcal{P}$ *is both dynamic and balanced with respect to* $\Gamma[\tau'] \vdash \Delta[\tau]$, *then* $\mathscr{C}_{\mathcal{P}}^{\tau} \leq \mathscr{A}[N]_{\mathcal{P}}^{\tau'}$ *and* $\mathscr{C}_{\mathcal{P}}^{\tau}$ *is grounded, where* $N = 2 + \mathbf{W}(\mathcal{P}) \times (\mathbf{C}(\mathcal{P}) + 1)$.

From this, a qualified form of decidability follows. Note that when $\mathcal{P}$ is not balanced and dynamic we still have a semi-decision procedure.

Theorem 4. *If* $\mathcal{P}$ *is dynamic and balanced with respect to* $\Gamma[\tau'] \vdash \Delta[\tau]$, *then it is decidable whether* $\mathcal{P} : \tau \leq \Gamma[\tau']$ *holds.*

6   Conclusions and Future Work

In this paper, we have demonstrated that cyclic proofs of entailments involving inductively defined predicates implicitly contain information about the relationship between the semantic approximations of these predicates. This information is useful because indexing ordinals for these approximations can be used, e.g., as (components of) ranking functions in a program termination proof. We have shown that this information can be made explicit via a novel trace condition, and furthermore we have proved this condition to be decidable via a construction using weighted automata. Although different in form, we have drawn tacit parallels between our work and the (intuitionistic) concept of realizability because we extract the semantic information directly from the proofs themselves.

Our results also increase the expressive power of the cyclic proof technique. For example, if we can deduce from the proof of $\Gamma, P\,t \vdash \Sigma, Q\,u$ that $Q\,u \leq P\,t$ then we can safely form a well-founded trace across the active formula in the cut application

$$\frac{\Gamma, P\,t \vdash \Sigma, Q\,u \quad \Sigma, Q\,u \vdash \Delta}{\Gamma, P\,t \vdash \Delta}$$

from $P\,t$ in the conclusion to $Q\,u$ in the right-hand premise, and therefore witness the validity of cyclic pre-proofs that do not satisfy the existing global soundness condition for cyclic proofs.

An obvious direction for future work is to implement our decision procedure and integrate it with existing cyclic proof-based program verifiers, such as [17] which currently relies on explicit ordinal variables to track approximations. A question of practical importance is whether entailment proofs typically encountered in program verification fall under the conditions for decidability of the trace condition. It is interesting to consider whether weaker conditions exist that still guarantee decidability. There are also wider theoretical questions to consider. Our trace condition is sound, but it is also natural to ask for completeness: if $\Gamma : \tau \leq \tau'$ holds does there also exist a proof $\mathcal{P}$ for which $\mathcal{P} : \tau \leq \Gamma[\tau']$ holds?

Acknowledgements. We extend thanks to Radu Grigore, Carsten Fuhs, and the PPLV group at UCL for useful discussions and invaluable comments. We are grateful to Alexandra Silva for suggesting to investigate weighted automata. This work was supported primarily by EPSRC grant EP/K040049/1, and also by EPSRC grant EP/N028759/1.

References

1. Aczel, P.: An introduction to inductive definitions. In: Barwise, J. (ed.) Handbook of Mathematical Logic, pp. 739–782. North-Holland, Amsterdam (1977)
2. Almagor, S., Boker, U., Kupferman, O.: What's decidable about weighted automata? In: Bultan, T., Hsiung, P.-A. (eds.) ATVA 2011. LNCS, vol. 6996, pp. 482–491. Springer, Heidelberg (2011). doi:10.1007/978-3-642-24372-1_37
3. Berdine, J., Cook, B., Distefano, D., O'Hearn, P.W.: Automatic termination proofs for programs with shape-shifting heaps. In: Ball, T., Jones, R.B. (eds.) CAV 2006. LNCS, vol. 4144, pp. 386–400. Springer, Heidelberg (2006). doi:10.1007/11817963_35

4. Brotherston, J.: Cyclic proofs for first-order logic with inductive definitions. In: Beckert, B. (ed.) TABLEAUX 2005. LNCS, vol. 3702, pp. 78–92. Springer, Heidelberg (2005). doi:10.1007/11554554_8
5. Brotherston, J.: Formalised inductive reasoning in the logic of bunched implications. In: Nielson, H.R., Filé, G. (eds.) SAS 2007. LNCS, vol. 4634, pp. 87–103. Springer, Heidelberg (2007). doi:10.1007/978-3-540-74061-2_6
6. Brotherston, J., Bornat, R., Calcagno, C.: Cyclic proofs of program termination in separation logic. ACM SIGPLAN Not. **43**, 101–112 (2008). doi:10.1145/1328438.1328453. POPL-35. ACM
7. Brotherston, J., Simpson, A.: Sequent calculi for induction and infinite descent. J. Log. Comput. **21**(6), 1177–1216 (2011). doi:10.1093/logcom/exq052
8. Droste, M., Kuich, W., Vogler, H.: Handbook of Weighted Automata. Monographs in Theoretical Computer Science. Springer, Heidelberg (2009). doi:10.1007/978-3-642-01492-5
9. Tellez, G., Brotherston, J.: Automatically verifying temporal properties of pointer programs with cyclic proof. In: de Moura, L. (ed.) CADE 2017. LNCS, vol. 10395. Springer, Cham (2017). doi:10.1007/978-3-319-63046-5_30
10. Filiot, E., Gentilini, R., Raskin, J.-F.: Finite-valued weighted automata. In: FSTTCS-34. LIPICS, vol. 29, pp. 133–145 (2014). doi:10.4230/LIPIcs.FSTTCS.2014.133
11. Ishtiaq, S., O'Hearn, P.W.: BI as an assertion language for mutable data structures. In: Proceedings of the POPL-28, pp. 14–26. ACM (2001). doi:10.1145/373243.375719
12. Johnson, D.B.: Finding all the elementary circuits of a directed graph. SIAM J. Comput. **4**(1), 77–84 (1975). doi:10.1137/0204007
13. Krob, D.: The equality problem for rational series with multiplicities in the tropical semiring is undecidable. IJAC **4**(3), 405–426 (1994). doi:10.1142/S0218196794000063
14. Lee, C.S., Jones, N.D., Ben-Amram, A.M.: The size-change principle for program termination. In: POPL-28, pp. 81–92. ACM (2001). doi:10.1145/373243.360210
15. Martin-Löf, P.: Hauptsatz for the intuitionistic theory of iterated inductive definitions. 2nd Scandinavian Logic Symposium. Studies in Logic and the Foundations of Mathematics, vol. 63, pp. 179–216. North-Holland, Amsterdam (1971)
16. Reynolds, J.C.: Separation logic: a logic for shared mutable data structures. In: Proceedings of the LICS-17, pp. 55–74. IEEE (2002). doi:10.1109/LICS.2002.1029817
17. Rowe, R.N.S., Brotherston, J.: Automatic cyclic termination proofs for recursive procedures in separation logic. In: CPP-6, pp. 53–65. ACM (2017). doi:10.1145/3018610.3018623
18. Rowe, R.N.S., Brotherston, J.: Size relationships in abstract cyclic entailment systems. Technical report (2017). https://arxiv.org/abs/1702.03981
19. Weber, A., Seidl, H.: On the degree of ambiguity of finite automata. Theor. Comput. Sci. **88**(2), 325–349 (1991). doi:10.1016/0304-3975(91)90381-B

Cyclic Proofs with Ordering Constraints

Sorin Stratulat[(✉)]

LORIA, Department of Computer Science, Université de Lorraine,
57000 Metz, France
sorin.stratulat@univ-lorraine.fr

Abstract. CLKID$^\omega$ is a sequent-based cyclic inference system able to reason on first-order logic with inductive definitions. The current approach for verifying the soundness of CLKID$^\omega$ proofs is based on expensive model-checking techniques leading to an explosion in the number of states.

We propose proof strategies that guarantee the soundness of a class of CLKID$^\omega$ proofs if some ordering and derivability constraints are satisfied. They are inspired from previous works about cyclic well-founded induction reasoning, known to provide effective sets of ordering constraints. A derivability constraint can be checked in linear time. Under certain conditions, one can build proofs that implicitly satisfy the ordering constraints.

1 Introduction

CLKID$^\omega$ [9] is the *de facto* standard sequent-based cyclic inference system for performing lazy induction reasoning on specifications based on first-order logic with inductive definitions (FOL$_{ID}$). The CLKID$^\omega$ proofs are represented as finite derivation trees with nodes labelled by sequents. A particular feature is that cycles can be built by establishing connections between terminal and non-terminal nodes labelled with identical sequents. The soundness of CLKID$^\omega$ proofs is entailed from some global trace condition by using Infinite Descent induction arguments [20]. This condition requires that, for every infinite path in the cyclic derivation of a false sequent, all successive steps starting from some point are decreasing and certain steps occurring infinitely often are strictly decreasing w.r.t. some semantic ordering.

CLKID$^\omega$ has been implemented in the CYCLIST prover [8]. Since the global trace condition is an ω-regular property, CYCLIST can check it during the proof construction or *post hoc* as an inclusion between two Büchi automata by calling an external model checker. It turns out that the inclusion test may be costly. Indeed, for any proof P, the approach requires the construction of the automaton complementary to that accepting strings over infinite progressing traces in P, based on a complementation method for Büchi automata as described in [11]. The method ensures that, for every automaton with n states, the generated complementary automaton has at least $2^{O(n \log n)}$ states [12]. In case of failure of the inclusion test, previous proof steps should be reconsidered, requiring that

© Springer International Publishing AG 2017
R.A. Schmidt and C. Nalon (Eds.): TABLEAUX 2017, LNAI 10501, pp. 311–327, 2017.
DOI: 10.1007/978-3-319-66902-1_19

existing connections be broken, proof steps cancelled or different inference rules applied. Hence, it may happen that the test be executed several times during the proof construction. For the proofs of the toy examples from [8], the percentage of time taken by the soundness check include values from 0% to 44%.

Example 1.1. The 'P and Q' example [20] is specified in [8] using the following mutually dependent inductive predicates P and Q defined over naturals:

$$\Rightarrow P(0) \ (1) \qquad\qquad\qquad \Rightarrow Q(x, 0) \ (3)$$
$$P(x) \wedge Q(x, s(x)) \Rightarrow P(s(x)) \ (2) \qquad P(x) \wedge Q(x, y) \Rightarrow Q(x, s(y)) \ (4)$$

where 0 and s are the usual constructor symbols for naturals. Let N define the set of naturals by the productions:

$$\Rightarrow N(0) \qquad\qquad (5) \qquad\qquad N(x) \Rightarrow N(s(x)) \ (6)$$

According to Table 1 from [8], CYCLIST can prove the sequent $N(x), N(y) \vdash Q(x, y)$ in about half a second, by building a proof tree with only 13 nodes. The validation process required 181 calls to the external model checker, among which 171 calls are failing. 31% of the time is spent on the soundness check.

On the other hand, a different approach based on ordering constraints has been proposed in [15,17] for performing cyclic well-founded induction to check inductive consequences of conditional specifications. The proofs generated by this approach are normalized to sets of tree derivations and represented as directed graphs (for short, digraphs) allowing some terminal nodes to be connected to root nodes. The minimal cycles resulting by following the arrows in the digraph are denoted as cyclic lists of paths leading a root to a terminal node in the same tree derivation. The ordering constraints for checking the proof soundness involve only comparisons between instances of root formulas. Their number is given by the number of paths from the minimal cycles and does not depend on the length of these paths. Cyclic well-founded induction proofs have been validated in [16] by certifying environments as Coq [19].

This approach is rather general and helps to define *reductive* inference systems [5,15], as those based on implicit induction [4]. They can build automatically proof derivations whose soundness is implicitly guaranteed by the proof method, hence no validation steps are required. Lacking the inconvenients presented by the on-the-fly/*post-hoc* soundness tests or backtracking steps, they allow for an effective proof generation and help to deal with industrial-size applications [3,14].

This paper, structured in four sections, presents an effective solution to validate the global trace condition for proofs generated with $CLKID_N^\omega$, a restricted version of $CLKID^\omega$ using ordering constraints, in the same line as for cyclic well-founded induction proofs. Section 2 is a quick presentation to the logical framework based on FOL_{ID} and an introduction to $CLKID_N^\omega$. In Sect. 3, we define proof strategies that guarantee the global trace condition for $CLKID_N^\omega$ proofs satisfying a set of ordering and derivability constraints. An ordering constraint consists of a comparison between two sequents, defined as a multiset extension of an ordering $<_a$ over literals. It can be decided in polynomial time in the size of the sequents if the $<_a$-relations can also be decided in polynomial time. The derivability constraints can be checked in linear time provided that the 'history' of some atoms from the compared sequents is preserved. We took as running example the conjecture from Example 6 of [8], whose proof required the maximal time percentage for the soundness check. We provide a CLKID$_N^\omega$ proof of it and show that its soundness check needs only two ordering constraints. A link with the reductive reasoning techniques is established; as a proof of concept, we define proof strategies that can build a reductive proof of $N(x), N(y) \vdash Q(x,y)$ and show that the ordering constraints are implicitly satisfied. The conclusions and future work are given in the last section.

2   The Logical Framework

The logical setting relies on FOL$_{\mathrm{ID}}$ with equality, as presented, e.g., in [7,9].

Syntax. Let Σ be a (countable) language built on a finite alphabet of arity-fixed function symbols $\mathcal{F}$ and predicate symbols, and $\mathcal{V}$ an enumerable set of variables. Each predicate symbol is either *inductive* (i.e., defined by axioms as below) or *ordinary* (i.e., not inductive). Terms and formulas are defined as usual. $(t_1, \ldots, t_n)$ denotes a vector of terms and $P(t_1, \ldots, t_n)$ an *inductive atom*, where P is an inductive predicate symbol and $t_1, \ldots, t_n$ are terms. $\equiv$ represents the syntactic equality. A substitution σ is a finite non-empty set of mappings of distinct variables to terms $\bigcup_{i=1}^{n} \{x_i \mapsto t_i\}$, also denoted as $\{\overline{x} \mapsto \overline{t}\}$, where $\overline{x} \equiv (x_1, \ldots, x_n)$ and $\overline{t} \equiv (t_1, \ldots, t_n)$. $t[\sigma]$ denotes the *instance* of a term t built with the substitution σ; we also say that $t[\sigma]$ *matches* t. Similarly, we can apply substitutions and build instances for atoms, formulas and (multi)sets of formulas. $FV(S)$ denotes the set of free variables from the set of formulas S.

Each inductive predicate symbol P is defined by a finite inductive definition set of productions (axioms) consisting of implication formulas of the form

$$\left(\bigwedge_{m=1}^{h} Q_m(\overline{u}_m) \wedge \bigwedge_{m=1}^{l} P_{i_m}(\overline{t}_m) \right) \Rightarrow P(\overline{t}), \tag{7}$$

where $h, l, i_1, \ldots, i_l$ are naturals and $Q_1, \ldots, Q_h$ (resp., $P_{i_1}, \ldots, P_{i_l}$) are ordinary (resp., inductive) predicate symbols. (7) is an *unconditional* production if $h = 0$ and $l = 0$. If not, (7) is a *conditional* production and $\bigwedge_{m=1}^{h} Q_m(\overline{u}_m) \wedge \bigwedge_{m=1}^{l} P_{i_m}(\overline{t}_m)$ is its *condition*. Φ denotes the set of productions defining each inductive predicate symbol.

Orderings. Let $(\mathcal{E}, \leq)$ be a non-empty poset. The strict part of the partial order $\leq$, referred to as *ordering*, is denoted by $<$. A binary relation R is *stable under substitutions* if whenever $s\,R\,t$ then $(s[\sigma])\,R\,(t[\sigma])$, for every substitution σ and terms/formulas s and t. Given two finite multisets A and B of elements from $\mathcal{E}$, we say that $\ll$ is the *multiset extension* of $<$ and write $B \ll A$ if there are two finite multisets X and Y such that $B = (A - X) \uplus Y$, $X \neq \emptyset$ and $\forall y \in Y, \exists x \in X, y < x$ holds, where $\uplus$ (resp., $-$) is the union (resp., difference) on multisets. In practice, X (resp., Y) is A (resp., B) after having deleted pairwisely the common elements.

The CLKID$_N^\omega$ Inference System. CLKID$_N^\omega$ consists of a finite set of inference rules that process sequents [10] of the form $\Gamma \vdash \Delta$, where Γ and Δ are finite multisets of first-order formulas and referred to as *antecedents* and *succedents*, respectively. An inference rule transforms a sequent, called *conclusion*, into a (potentially empty) multiset of sequents, called *premises*; they are separated by a horizontal line followed by the name of the rule. Most of the CLKID$_N^\omega$ inference rules transform one (principal) formula from the conclusion. In this case, it is explicitly represented in the sequent. A more detailed presentation of the sequent calculus can be found elsewhere, e.g., [13].

$$\frac{}{\Gamma \vdash \Delta} \; \Gamma \cap \Delta \neq \emptyset \; (Ax) \qquad \frac{\Gamma' \vdash \Delta'}{\Gamma \vdash \Delta} \; \Gamma' \subseteq \Gamma, \Delta' \subseteq \Delta \; (Wk) \qquad \frac{\Gamma \vdash F, \Delta \quad \Gamma \vdash G, \Delta}{\Gamma \vdash F \wedge G, \Delta} \; (\wedge R)$$

$$\frac{\Gamma \vdash F, \Delta}{\Gamma, \neg F \vdash \Delta} \; (\neg L) \qquad \frac{\Gamma, F \vdash \Delta}{\Gamma \vdash \neg F, \Delta} \; (\neg R) \qquad \frac{\Gamma, F \vdash \Delta \quad \Gamma, G \vdash \Delta}{\Gamma, F \vee G \vdash \Delta} \; (\vee L)$$

$$\frac{\Gamma \vdash F, G, \Delta}{\Gamma \vdash F \vee G, \Delta} \; (\vee R) \qquad \frac{\Gamma, F, G \vdash \Delta}{\Gamma, F \wedge G \vdash \Delta} \; (\wedge L) \qquad \frac{\Gamma \vdash F, F, \Delta}{\Gamma \vdash F, \Delta} \; (contrR) \qquad \frac{\Gamma \vdash \Delta}{\Gamma[\theta] \vdash \Delta[\theta]} \; (Subst)$$

$$\frac{\Gamma \vdash F, \Delta \quad \Gamma, G \vdash \Delta}{\Gamma, F \Rightarrow G \vdash \Delta} \; (\Rightarrow L) \qquad \frac{\Gamma, F, F \vdash \Delta}{\Gamma, F \vdash \Delta} \; (contrL) \qquad \frac{\Gamma, F[\{\overline{x} \mapsto \overline{t}\}] \vdash \Delta}{\Gamma, \forall \overline{x} F \vdash \Delta} \; (\forall L)$$

$$\frac{\Gamma \vdash F, \Delta}{\Gamma \vdash \forall \overline{x} F, \Delta} \; \overline{x} \cap FV(\Gamma \cup \Delta) = \emptyset \; (\forall R) \qquad \frac{\Gamma, F \vdash \Delta}{\Gamma, \exists \overline{x} F \vdash \Delta} \; \overline{x} \cap FV(\Gamma \cup \Delta) = \emptyset \; (\exists L)$$

$$\frac{\Gamma \vdash F, \Delta \quad \Gamma, F \vdash \Delta}{\Gamma \vdash \Delta} \; (Cut) \qquad \frac{\Gamma \vdash F[\{\overline{x} \mapsto \overline{t}\}], \Delta}{\Gamma \vdash \exists \overline{x} F, \Delta} \; (\exists R) \qquad \frac{\Gamma, F \vdash G, \Delta}{\Gamma \vdash F \Rightarrow G, \Delta} \; (\Rightarrow R)$$

Fig. 1. Sequent-based rules for classical first-order logic.

CLKID$_N^\omega$ consists of the rules displayed in Fig. 1, the rules that process equalities from Fig. 2, as well as the 'unfold' and 'case' rules. $(= L)$ is an instance of the corresponding CLKID$^\omega$ rule for which x can also be a non-variable term.

$$\frac{}{\Gamma \vdash t = t, \Delta} \; (= R) \qquad \frac{\Gamma[\{x \mapsto u\}] \vdash \Delta[\{x \mapsto u\}]}{\Gamma, x = u \vdash \Delta} \; x \text{ is not a variable of } u \; (= L)$$

Fig. 2. Sequent-based rules for equality reasoning.

The unfold rule unrolls the definition of the inductive symbol to transform some succedent atom of a sequent. We denote the unfolding of $P(\overline{t}')$ with the production (7), when $P(\overline{t}') \equiv P(\overline{t})[\sigma]$, by

$$\frac{\Gamma \vdash Q_1(\overline{u}_1)[\sigma], \Delta \quad \cdots \quad \Gamma \vdash Q_h(\overline{u}_h)[\sigma], \Delta \qquad \Gamma \vdash P_{i_1}(\overline{t}_1)[\sigma], \Delta \quad \cdots \quad \Gamma \vdash P_{i_l}(\overline{t}_l)[\sigma], \Delta}{\Gamma \vdash P(\overline{t'}), \Delta} \ (R.(7))$$

The *case* rule is a left-introduction operation for inductive predicate symbols:

$$\frac{\text{case distinctions}}{\Gamma, P(s_1, \ldots, s_n) \vdash \Delta} \ (Case \ P)$$

Every production of the form (7) for which $\overline{t} \equiv (t_1, \ldots, t_n)$ produces the *case distinction*

$$\Gamma, s_1 = t_1, \ldots, s_n = t_n, Q_1(\overline{u}_1), \ldots, Q_h(\overline{u}_h), P_{i_1}(\overline{t}_1), \ldots, P_{i_l}(\overline{t}_l) \vdash \Delta \qquad (8)$$

Each variable y from (7) is fresh w.r.t. the *free variables* from the conclusion of the rule (y can be renamed to a fresh variable, otherwise). $P_{i_1}(\overline{t}_1), \ldots, P_{i_l}(\overline{t}_l)$ are *case descendants* of $P(s_1, \ldots, s_n)$.

CLKID$_N^\omega$ Pre-proof Trees. A *derivation tree* for some sequent S is built by successively applying inference rules starting from S. The terminal nodes in the tree can be either leaves or buds. A *leaf* is labelled by a sequent that is the conclusion of a 0-premise inference rule. A *bud* is every node labelled by a sequent that is the conclusion of no rule. For each bud, there is a *companion*, i.e., an internal node having the same sequent labelling. If a companion is annotated by some sign (e.g., † or ∗), then the buds related to it are uniquely annotated by that sign followed by a number.

Definition 2.1 (pre-proof tree, induction function for tree). *The pair* $(\mathcal{D}, \mathcal{R})$ *denotes a* pre-proof tree *of some sequent S, where $\mathcal{D}$ is a finite derivation tree whose root is labelled by S and $\mathcal{R}$ is a defined* induction function *assigning a companion to every bud in $\mathcal{D}$.*

Example 2.2. A CLKID$_N^\omega$ pre-proof tree of $N(x), N(y) \vdash R(x, y)$ is

$$\frac{\dfrac{\dfrac{\dfrac{Nx' \vdash R(x', 0) \ (\dagger 1)}{Nx'' \vdash R(x'', 0)} \ (Subst)}{\dfrac{Nx'' \vdash R(sx'', 0)}{} \ (R.(10))}{\dfrac{Nx' \vdash R(x', 0) \ (\dagger)}{Nx' \vdash R(sx', 0)} \ (R.(10))} (Case\ N) \quad \dfrac{\dfrac{\dfrac{Nx, Ny \vdash R(x, y) \ (\ast 1)}{Nssx', Ny' \vdash R(ssx', y')} \ (Subst)}{\dfrac{Nx', Ny' \vdash R(ssx', y')}{Nx', Ny' \vdash R(sx', sy')} \ (R.(11))} (Cut)}{Nx', Ny \vdash R(sx', y)}}{Nx, Ny \vdash R(x, y) \ (\ast)} (Case\ N)$$

where the inductive predicate R is defined, as in [8], by the productions

$$\Rightarrow R(0, y) \ (9) \quad R(x, 0) \Rightarrow R(sx, 0) \ (10) \quad R(ssx, y) \Rightarrow R(sx, sy) \ (11)$$

For lack of horizontal space, we have unambiguously omitted the parentheses and commas when denoting some natural and atom $N(t)$, i.e., $s(t)$ (resp., $N(t)$)

becomes $s\underline{t}$ (resp., $N\underline{t}$), where $\underline{t}$ is the notation of t without parentheses. This alternative notation will be used in the following, when necessary.

The double line means that $(= L)$ was applied on each premise of $(Case)$. The (Cut) premise $Nx' \vdash Nssx'$ is suppressed on the right-hand branch as in Example 6 of [8]. The principal formula for each $(Case)$ application is underlined. Finally, the induction function $\mathcal{R}$ is defined such that the companion of the bud denoted by $(*1)$ (resp., $(\dagger 1)$) is $(*)$ (resp., $(\dagger)$).

Semantics. The semantics for FOL_{ID} with equality is defined as in [9]. Prefixed points of a monotone operator issued from Φ [1] help to interpret inductive predicates. A standard model for (Σ, Φ) is a first-order structure defined by the least prefixed point, approached by an iteratively built *approximant* sequence.

Definition 2.3. (validity of a sequent). *Let M be a standard model for $(\Sigma, \Phi), \Gamma \vdash \Delta$ a sequent and ρ a valuation which interprets in M the free variables from the sequent. We write $\Gamma \models_{\rho}^{M} \Delta$ if whenever G holds in M using ρ, for all $G \in \Gamma$, there is some $D \in \Delta$ that holds in M using ρ. We say that $\Gamma \vdash \Delta$ is M-true if $\Gamma \models_{\rho}^{M} \Delta$, for every ρ. When M is implicit from the context, true is used instead of M-true.*

A rule is *sound*, or preserves the validity, if its conclusion is true whenever its premises are true. Hence, the conclusion of every 0-premise sound rule is true.

Theorem 2.4. *The $CLKID_N^{\omega}$ inference rules are sound.*

Definition 2.5 (sound pre-proof tree). *A pre-proof tree of a sequent S is sound if S is true.*

3   Checking the Soundness of Pre-proofs

Not every pre-proof tree is sound. A very simple example of unsound pre-proof tree can be built for every false sequent S by firstly adding a copy of some antecedent formula using $(contr L)$ then deleting it using (Wk). Since the resulting sequent is identical to S, its node is a bud. This finishes the pre-proof tree.

We intend to apply an approach similar to that used for building well-founded (Noetherian) induction-based proofs [15] to check the soundness of pre-proof trees. In this setting, a cycle is uniformly represented as a set of paths from root companions to bud nodes. When a node of the pre-proof tree plays the role of bud *and* companion, it is duplicated by some transformation operation such that the roles are played separately by each copy. The normalization process consists in the exhaustive application of the transformation operations that convert a pre-proof tree to a set of pre-proof trees, for short *pre-proof tree-sets*.

In this section, we briefly explain the transformation operations and show how to build digraphs from pre-proof tree-sets. Then, we prove that a pre-proof tree is sound if the minimal cycles from the digraph of the pre-proof tree-set resulting from its normalization satisfy certain ordering and derivability constraints. Finally, we present some strategies for directly building sound pre-proof tree-sets.

3.1 Defining the Checking Criteria

The first transformation operation applies on an internal node labeled by some premise of *(Subst)*:

$$
\frac{\vdots \quad \Gamma \vdash \Delta}{\Gamma[\sigma] \vdash \Delta[\sigma]} \; (Subst) \qquad \text{produces} \qquad \frac{\Gamma \vdash \Delta \; (*1)}{\Gamma[\sigma] \vdash \Delta[\sigma]} \; (Subst) \qquad \frac{\vdots}{\Gamma \vdash \Delta \; (*)} \quad \text{(new tree)}
$$

The node is duplicated; one of its copies is detached together with the subtree derivation rooted by the node to become a new tree derivation. The two occurrences of the duplicated bud establish a new relation bud-companion by extending the definition of the induction function for trees to sets of trees.

The second transformation rule is performed on a non-root companion of $n - 1$ $(n > 1)$ buds and annotated by $(*)$, of the form

$$
\frac{\vdots}{\Gamma \vdash \Delta \; (*)} \qquad \text{to give} \qquad \frac{\vdots}{\Gamma \vdash \Delta \; (*n)} \qquad \frac{\vdots}{\Gamma \vdash \Delta \; (*)} \quad \text{(new tree)}
$$

The companion $(*)$ is duplicated such that the subtree derivation rooted by it becomes a new pre-proof tree and the copy of $(*)$ becomes a bud annotated by $(*n)$. A new relation bud-companion is created between $(*n)$ and $(*)$.

Example 3.1. The application of the second transformation on the companion annotated by $(\dagger)$ in the pre-proof tree given in Example 2.2 generates a normalized pre-proof tree-set, as shown in Fig. 3.

Definition 3.2 (pre-proof tree-set, induction function for tree-set). *The pair $(\mathcal{MD}, \mathcal{MR})$ denotes a pre-proof tree-set, where $\mathcal{MD}$ is a multiset of pre-proof trees and $\mathcal{MR}$ is a defined induction function assigning a companion to every bud from $\mathcal{MD}$.*

Lemma 3.3. *The normalization process terminates.*

Lemma 3.4. *Let $(\mathcal{MD}, \mathcal{MR})$ be the pre-proof tree-set obtained by the normalization of some pre-proof tree of a sequent S. Then, MD*

(i) has a pre-proof tree rooted by a node labelled by S, and
(ii) is built from pre-proof trees for which the premises of all (Subst) rules are bud sequents.

$$\cfrac{
\cfrac{
\cfrac{\quad}{Ny \vdash R(0,y)}\ (R.(9))
\qquad
\cfrac{
\cfrac{
\cfrac{Nx' \vdash R(x',0)\ (\dagger 1)}{Nx' \vdash R(sx',0)}\ (R.(10))
\qquad
\cfrac{
\cfrac{Nx,Ny \vdash R(x,y)\ (*)}{Nssx',Ny' \vdash R(ssx',y')}\ (Subst)
}{
\cfrac{Nx',Ny' \vdash R(ssx',y')}{Nx',Ny' \vdash R(sx',sy')}\ (R.(11))
}\ (Cut)
}{Nx',Ny \vdash R(sx',y)}\ (Case\ N)
}{Nx,Ny \vdash R(x,y)\ (*)}\ (Case\ N)
}$$

$$\cfrac{
\cfrac{\quad}{\vdash R(0,0)}\ (R.(9))
\qquad
\cfrac{
\cfrac{Nx' \vdash R(x',0)\ (\dagger)}{Nx'' \vdash R(x'',0)}\ (Subst)
}{Nx'' \vdash R(sx'',0)}\ (R.(10))
}{Nx' \vdash R(x',0)\ (\dagger)}\ (Case\ N)
$$

Fig. 3. The normalized pre-proof tree-set.

Any pre-proof tree-set can also be represented as a *digraph* of sequents using nodes from its tree-set and arrows annotated with substitutions. Let $S(N)$ denote the sequent labelling N, for every node N. A solid arrow leads a node N^1 to a node N^2 if there is a rule applied on $S(N^1)$ and $S(N^2)$ is a premise of the rule. It is annotated with the *identity substitution* for $S(N)(\equiv \Gamma \vdash \Delta)$, denoted by $\sigma_{id}^{S(N)}$ and defined as $\bigcup_{x \in FV(\Gamma \cup \Delta)}\{x \mapsto x\}$, if N is not a ($= L$)-node. When not ambiguous, the identity substitutions are omitted. If N is a ($= L$)-node whose principal formula is $x = u$, the arrow leaving N is annotated by the *equality substitution* $\{x \mapsto u\}$. On the other hand, a dashed arrow leads a bud B to its companion and is annotated with a substitution written in boldface. If $S(B)$ is the premise of a ($Subst$) rule using the substitution θ, this substitution is θ. Otherwise, it is $\sigma_{id}^{S(B)}$.

For convenience, the sequent $\Gamma \vdash \Delta$ labelling a node N^i in the digraph is indexed by i as $\Gamma \vdash_i \Delta$.

Example 3.5. Figure 4 shows the digraph of the pre-proof tree-set from Fig. 3.

A *path* is a (potentially infinite) list of nodes built by following the arrows in the digraph. It is ($Subst$)-free if none of the sequents labelling its nodes is the premise of some ($Subst$)-rule.

Definition 3.6 (cumulative substitution). *A ($Subst$)-free path $[N^1, \dots, N^n]$ ($n > 0$) is annotated by the* cumulative substitution $\sigma_{id}^{all}\sigma_1 \cdots \sigma_{n-1}$, *where σ_i is the substitution annotating the solid arrow leading N_i to N_{i+1}, for each $i \in [1 \dots n-1]$, and σ_{id}^{all} is the overall* identity substitution $\bigcup_{N \in [N^1,\dots,N^n]}\{x \mapsto x \mid x \in FV(\Gamma \cup \Delta)$ *and* $S(N) \equiv \Gamma \vdash \Delta\}$.

Example 3.7. The cumulative substitution for the ($Subst$)-free path $[N^1, N^3, N^5, N^6, N^7]$ from Fig. 4 is $\{x \mapsto sx'; y \mapsto sy'\}$, which is the composition of the overall identity substitution $\{x \mapsto x; y \mapsto y\}$ with the substitutions $\{x \mapsto sx'\}, \{y \mapsto sy'\}$, and other identity substitutions.

The digraph $\mathcal{P}$ of a pre-proof tree-set $(\mathcal{MD}, \mathcal{MR})$ can be partitioned in a set of *strongly connected components* (SCCs). Some of them may have only one node. The SCCs with more than one node have at least one *cycle*, i.e., a path built along its nodes where the nodes are repeated. A *minimal* cycle does not contain other cycles.

Definition 3.8 (n-cycle). *Every minimal cycle in $\mathcal{P}$ can be represented as a n-cycle, defined as a finite circular list $[N_1^1, \ldots, N_1^{p_1}], \ldots, [N_n^1, \ldots, N_n^{p_n}]$ of n (> 0) paths leading root nodes to buds such that $N_{next(i)}^1 = \mathcal{MR}(N_i^{p_i})$, for any $i \in [1 \ldots n]$, where $next(i) = 1 + (i \bmod n)$.*

The standard method for checking the soundness of pre-proof trees, e.g. [9], is based on a 'proof by contradiction' approach. Let us assume that the root sequent of some pre-proof tree is false. It is sufficient to show that some global trace condition is satisfied for every infinite path in the pre-proof tree, built by visiting nodes labelled by false sequents if the root sequent is false. This condition stipulates that all successive steps starting from some point in the path are decreasing and certain steps occurring infinitely often are strictly decreasing w.r.t. some semantic ordering underlying ordinals. The trace is a list of *inductive antecedent atoms* (IAAs) of the sequents labelling the nodes from the path. Let $P(\bar{t})$ be one of these atoms. Since P can be generated by a sequence of approximants $(P^\gamma)_{\gamma \geq 0}$, the measure value for $P(\bar{t})$ used by this ordering is the smallest ordinal γ such that $P^\gamma(\bar{t})$ holds for some suitable interpretation. The well-foundedness property of the ordering contradicts the fact that the path is infinite.

The question of whether a pre-proof tree is sound is decidable (see e.g. Proposition 7.4 from [9]), by using a decision procedure based on the automata-based complementation method. On the other hand, the computational and combinatorial complexity of the validation of the global trace condition can be reduced for pre-proof trees of certain structure, e.g., for those having *trace manifolds* [6,7].

The trace manifold condition can be checked only on pre-proof trees in *cycle normal form*, for which the companion of every bud B is also an ancestor of B. Any pre-proof tree can be transformed in a cycle normal form. Mainly, it is unfolded into an infinite pre-proof tree, then the infinite branches are folded to get an equivalent normalized pre-proof tree. An improved complexity bound can be achieved by an iterative 'untangling' process of the pre-proof tree. By Theorem 6.3.6 from [7], if a derivation tree has n nodes, the equivalent normalized derivation tree has no more than $n^{2^{n/2}}$ nodes.

In the same quest to reduce the complexity of the validation process, we adapt the approach for building well-founded induction proofs [15] to generate pre-proof trees that *implicitly* guarantee the validity of the global trace condition. For this, we denote by $\leq_\pi$ a partial ordering defined over the set of instances of every sequent labelling root nodes from some SCC π with cycles. Its strict part is denoted by $<_\pi$ and its equivalence part by $\sim_\pi$. Contrary to [15], $<_\pi$ is not required to be well-founded. We assume that $<_\pi$ is built as the multiset extension of a 'stable under substitutions' ordering $<_a$ defined over IAAs and used to compare instances of the root sequents from π. Hence, $<_\pi$ is also stable under substitutions [2]. We also assume that $\sim_\pi$ is stable under substitutions. Like $<_\pi$, $<_a$ does not need to be well-founded. For each node N in π and every instance S of $S(N)$, we denote by A_S the measure value (weight) of S, represented as a multiset of IAAs of S and used in the comparisons of S with other sequent instances w.r.t. $\leq_\pi$.

Definition 5.4 of [9] for a trace in a pre-proof tree can be adapted for a digraph $\mathcal{P}$ and simplified to take into account the restricted version of $(= L)$.

Definition 3.9 (trace). *A trace following some (potentially infinite) path p in $\mathcal{P}$, denoted by $[N^1, N^2, \ldots]$, is a sequence $(\tau_i)_{(i \geq 0)}$ such that:*

- $\tau_i = P(\bar{t})$, *where $P(\bar{t})$ is an IAA of $S(N^i)$;*
- *if $\Gamma_i \vdash \Delta_i$ is the conclusion of (Subst) then $\tau_i = \tau_{i+1}[\rho]$, where ρ is the substitution associated with the rule instance;*
- *if $\Gamma_i, x = u \vdash \Delta_i$ is the conclusion of $(= L)$, then $\tau_{i+1} = \tau_i[\{x \mapsto u\}]$;*
- *if $S(N^i)$ is the conclusion of a (Case)-rule, then either (i) $\tau_{i+1} = \tau_i$, or (ii) τ_i is its principal formula and τ_{i+1} is a case descendant of τ_i. In this case, i is called a progression point;*
- *if $S(N^i)$ is the conclusion of any other rule, then $\tau_{i+1} = \tau_i$.*

We say that an IAA τ_j derives from an IAA τ_i using the trace $(\tau_k)_{(k \geq 0)}$ if $i < j$. Given two arbitrary substitutions γ and δ, we also say that $\tau_j[\gamma]$ derives from $\tau_i[\delta]$ using $(\tau_k)_{(k \geq 0)}$. Let π be a SCC from $\mathcal{P}$ and $<_a$ the 'stable under substitutions' ordering defined over the set of instances of the IAAs from the root sequents inside π. We can define $<_\pi$ as the multiset extension of $<_a$ that satisfies some derivability constraints.

Definition 3.10 ($<_\pi$-derivability). *Let N^i and N^j be two nodes occurring in some path p from an SCC π, θ and δ two substitutions, and $A'_{S(N^i)[\theta]}$ (resp., $A'_{S(N^j)[\delta]}$) the multiset resulting from $A_{S(N^i)[\theta]}$ (resp., $A_{S(N^j)[\delta]}$) after the pairwise deletion of all common IAAs from $A_{S(N^i)[\theta]}$ and $A_{S(N^j)[\delta]}$. Then, $S(N^j)[\delta]$ is $<_\pi$-derivable from $S(N^i)[\theta]$ along p if (i) for each $l \in A'_{S(N^j)[\delta]}$, there exists $l' \in A'_{S(N^i)[\theta]}$ such that $l' >_a l$ and l derives from l' using some trace following p, and (ii) for each $l \in A_{S(N^j)[\delta]} \setminus A'_{S(N^j)[\delta]}$, there is some $l' \in A_{S(N^i)[\theta]} \setminus A'_{S(N^i)[\theta]}$ such that $l \equiv l'$ and l derives from l' using some trace following p.*

Lemma 3.11. *In Definition 3.10, for each IAA l from $S(N^j)[\delta]$ there is an IAA l' from $S(N^i)[\theta]$ such that l derives from l' using some trace following p.*

We give below some useful properties of the $<_\pi$-derivability relation.

Lemma 3.12. *$S <_\pi S'$ if S is $<_\pi$-derivable from S' along some path p in π.*

Lemma 3.13. *The '$<_\pi$-derivability' relation is stable under substitutions. It is also transitive, i.e., if S is $<_\pi$-derivable from S' along p and S' is $<_\pi$-derivable from S'' along p then S is $<_\pi$-derivable from S'' along p, for some path p in π.*

We are ready to introduce the ordering constraints that help to discharge induction hypotheses by n-cycles.

Definition 3.14 (induction hypothesis (IH), IH discharged by an n-cycle, IH-node). *Let π be an SCC with cycles and C an n-cycle $[N_1^1,\ldots,N_1^{p_1}],\ldots,[N_n^1,\ldots,N_n^{p_n}]$ from π. The instances $S(N_j^{p_j})[\delta_j]$ $(j \in [1\ldots n])$ are called* induction hypotheses (IHs), *where δ_j annotates the dashed arrow starting from $N_j^{p_j}$ in C. For all $i \in [1\ldots n]$, let θ_i^c be the cumulative substitution annotating $[N_i^1,\ldots,N_i^f]$, where the* IH-node N_i^f *is either (i) $N_i^{p_i}$ if $[N_i^1,\ldots,N_i^{p_i}]$ is (Subst)-free, or (ii) $N_i^{p_i-1}$, otherwise. The IHs $S(N_j^1)[\delta_j]$ $(j \in [1\ldots n])$ are discharged* by C *if, $\forall i \in [1\ldots n]$, $S(N_i^{p_i})[\delta_i]$ is $<_\pi$-derivable from $S(N_i^1)[\theta_i^c]$ along $[N_i^1,\ldots,N_i^{p_i}]$.*

Definition 3.14 is well-formed; the cumulative substitution can be computed for the case (ii) because, for each $i \in [1\ldots n]$, $[N_i^1,\ldots,N_i^{p_i-1}]$ is a (Subst)-free path, by following the claim (ii) of Lemma 3.4. By construction, $S(N_i^f)$ is the IH $S(N_{next(i)}^1)[\delta_{next(i)}]$, for all $i \in [1\ldots n]$. For every IAA l of a sequent bud corresponding to some τ_i from a trace $(\tau_k)_{(k\geq 0)}$ following a path from some minimal cycle, we define the *history* of l as the subtrace $(\tau_k)_{(k<i)}$. If each such IAA stores its history during the proof construction, every derivability constraint can be decided in linear time w.r.t. the size of the history, by visiting one by one each element in the history.

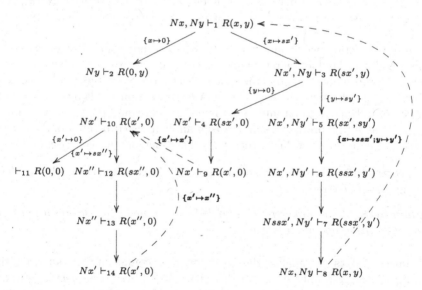

Fig. 4. The digraph of the pre-proof tree-set from Fig. 3.

Example 3.15. The digraph from Fig. 4 has two SCCs with cycles. One of them, denoted by π, consists of the 1-cycle $[N^{10},N^{12},N^{13},N^{14}]$. The other, denoted by π', is made of the 1-cycle $[N^1,N^3,N^5,N^6,N^7,N^8]$. No cycle has the bud N^9.

We define the measure value for any sequent instance of the form $S(N^{10})[\{x' \mapsto t; \ldots\}]$ (resp., $S(N^1)[\{x \mapsto t_1; y \mapsto t_2; \ldots\}]$) as $\{N(t)\}$ (resp., $\{N(t_2)\}$). $<_\pi$ and $<_{\pi'}$ are multiset extensions of an ordering $<_a$ over the IAAs of the form $N(t)$ and whose measure value is $\{t\}$, for any term t. $<_a$ is the multiset extension of the 'stable under substitutions' rpo ordering [2], denoted by $<_{rpo}$ and based on the symbol precedence establishing that 0 is smaller than s.

Every IH from these 1-cycles is discharged. The IH $S(N^{10})[\{x' \mapsto x''\}]$ is $<_\pi$-derivable from $S(N^{10})[\{x' \mapsto sx''\}]$ along the (Subst)-free path $[N^{10}, N^{12}, N^{13}, N^{14}]$, by using the trace $[Nx', Nx'', Nx'', Nx']$ for the IAA Nx' of $S(N^{10})$. Similarly, the IH $S(N^1)[\{x \mapsto ssx'; y \mapsto y'\}]$ is $<_{\pi'}$-derivable from $S(N^1)[\{x \mapsto sx'; y \mapsto sy'\}]$ along the (Subst)-free path $[N^1, N^3, N^5, N^6, N^7, N^8]$, by using the trace $[Ny, Ny, Ny', Ny', Ny', Ny]$ for the IAA Ny of $S(N^1)$. The two comparisons hold as $z <_{rpo} sz$, for every variable z.

Definition 3.16 (proof). *A proof is every pre-proof tree-set whose digraph has only n-cycles that discharge their IHs.*

Theorem 3.17 (soundness). *The root sequents from every proof are true.*

Proof (Sketch). It follows the general structure of the soundness proof for some cyclic well-founded inference systems, e.g., see Theorem 5.11 from [17]. Mainly, we define a partial ordering $<_{\mathcal{R}}$ over the root nodes from the digraph $\mathcal{P}$ of a proof such that, for every two distinct root nodes N^1 and N^2, we have $N^1 <_{\mathcal{R}} N^2$ if (i) N^1 and N^2 are not in the same SCC, and (ii) N^1 can be joined from N^2 in $\mathcal{P}$.

By contradiction, we assume that there exists a root node N such that $S(N)$ is false. A classical induction reasoning using $<_{\mathcal{R}}$ allows to explore all possibilities for N to be considered as one of the root nodes from $\mathcal{P}$. The most difficult case is when N is part of some SCC with cycles. A contradiction yields by showing that there exists a trace with an infinite number of progression points, using similar arguments as in the proof of Lemma 5.7 [9] and witnessed by an infinite strictly decreasing sequence of ordinals, thanks to the $<$-derivability constraints.   □

Theorem 3.17 is the key argument for proving that our approach allows indeed to verify pre-proof trees.

Lemma 3.18. *A pre-proof tree is sound if the pre-proof tree-set resulting from its normalization operation is a proof.*

Validation Costs. We analyse the worst-case time complexity for validating the soundness of a pre-proof tree of n nodes with p ($< n$) buds occurring in minimal cycles. The number of transformation operations during the normalization step is given by the sum of non-root companions and non-terminal (Subst)-nodes, which is smaller than $2n$. The cost of a transformation operation, including the node duplication and the creation of a bud-companion relation, is assumed to be some constant c. Hence the cost of the transformation operations is smaller than $2nc$. If c' is the constant representing the cost for annotating a substitution, the cost for building the digraph of the normalized pre-proof tree-set is smaller than nc'. The partition of a digraph in SCCs can be done in linear time [18].

If B denotes a bud occurring in a minimal cycle, the IH that instantiates $S(B)$ is unique because B has only one companion and at most one companion can be the root of the tree including B. The number of $<$-derivability constraints is that of their buds, i.e., p. In the worst case, p is $n-1$. The validation cost of a $<$-derivability constraint is the sum of the costs of derivability and ordering constraints. The time complexity for checking whether an IAA l derives from another IAA l' is linear w.r.t. the size of the history of l, which is a value smaller than n. The time complexity for checking a multiset extension relation is $O(rq)$, where r and q are the number of IAAs from the measure value of the compared sequents. In the worst case, when all bud IAAs have their history of length n and p is $n-1$, the time complexity for checking the derivability constraints is $O(n^2k^2)$, where k is the maximal cardinality of a sequent's measure value. Similarly, the worst-case validation cost of the ordering constraints is polynomial in k, the maximal size of a literal and n, if the time complexity for comparing two IAAs is at most polynomial, for example by using a Knuth-Bendix ordering [2].

3.2   Strategies for Directly Building Proofs

Theorem 3.17 suggests that sequents can also be proved by directly building sound pre-proof tree-sets. For this purpose, we adapt the DRaCuLa strategy [15]. Mainly, the trees from a pre-proof tree-set are developed by applying the CLKID$_N^\omega$ rules, as usual, with the following exceptions:

- when applying a (*Subst*)-rule, the premise becomes a bud sequent, as shown for the first transformation of the normalization procedure. The next step is to develop a new tree rooted by the companion of the bud;
- when a bud is about to be created, several scenarios may happen. As a preliminary step, if its companion is a non-root node the second transformation of the normalization procedure is applied. If the bud candidate is part of an n-cycle that discharges its IHs, the bud is created (scenario 1). If it is not yet the case, either (i) the strategy tries to build an n-cycle, by developing parts from other trees (scenario 2), or (ii) the n-cycle does not discharge its IHs (scenario 3); in this case, a backtracking step is required either to redefine the ordering at the SCC level, or to redo previous steps, or to continue to develop the proof by applying a CLKID$_N^\omega$ rule on the sequent labelling the bud candidate.
  For (scenario 1), not only the current bud candidate is created, but all the bud candidates from the n-cycle are built, hence *simultaneous* induction is performed.

Example 3.19. The above strategy can build the pre-proof tree from Example 2.2. The progression in its construction can be retraced by following the indexes of the sequents from the digraph in Fig. 4.

This proof strategy uses heuristics based on ordering constraints, different from the iterative depth-first search heuristics used by CYCLIST.

Example 3.20. One could have built a new bud of (*) from the pre-proof tree of Example 2.2, by developing (†) such that $N0$ is added as IAA, then (*Subst*) applied conveniently. The new 1-cycle from its digraph is part of the SCC π' of the digraph from Example 3.15. However, it cannot discharge its IH because the induction ordering is now $<_{\pi'}$ instead of $<_\pi$.

Sound pre-proof trees can also be directly generated to satisfy implicitly the ordering constraints, similar to implicit induction proofs, by using a *reductive* proof strategy based on a unique induction ordering $<$. Such strategy guarantees that, for every two successive nodes N^i and N^{i+1} from each path p, of the form $[N^1, \ldots, N^n]$ and occurring in the definition of some minimal cycle of its digraph, and $i \in [1 \ldots f - 1]$, we have either $A_{S(N^{i+1})[\theta^c_{i+1}]} \equiv A_{S(N^i)[\theta^c_i]}$ or $S(N^{i+1})[\theta^c_{i+1}]$ is $<$-derivable from $S(N^i)[\theta^c_i]$ along p, where f is the index of the IH-node in $[N^1, \ldots, N^n]$ and θ^c_j is the cumulative substitution for the path $[N^j, \ldots, N^f]$ ($j \in [1 \ldots f]$). The derivability constraints are satisfied if the syntactic equality relation is not satisfied at least once along p. Indeed, knowing that the $<$-derivability relation is transitive (Lemma 3.13), we have that $S(N^f)$ is $<$-derivable from $S(N^1)[\theta^c_1]$ along p, as required. If the rule applied at step i is different from (= L), we have that $\theta^c_i \equiv \theta^c_{i+1}$. In this case, it is sufficient to ensure instead that $A_{S(N^{i+1})} \equiv A_{S(N^i)}$ or $S(N^{i+1})$ is $<$-derivable from $S(N^i)$ along p, due to the 'stability under substitutions' property of $<$-derivability (again Lemma 3.13).

Example 3.21. As a proof of concept, we define the derived rule (*DCase*):

$$\frac{S_1 \ldots S_n}{\Gamma, P(\overline{x}) \vdash \Delta} \; (DCase\ P) \quad \text{as}$$

$$\frac{\dfrac{S_1}{\text{case distinction}}\,(=L) \quad \cdots \quad \dfrac{S_n}{\text{case distinction}}\,(=L)}{\dfrac{\dfrac{\Gamma, P(\overline{x}), P(\overline{x}) \vdash \Delta}{}\,(Case\ P)}{\Gamma, P(\overline{x}) \vdash \Delta}\,(contrL)}$$

where $\overline{x}$ is a vector of variables. We also define the (*Bud*) rule:

$$\frac{\text{(bud sign)}}{\Gamma \vdash \Delta}\,(Bud) \quad \text{as} \quad \frac{\dfrac{\dfrac{\Gamma' \vdash \Delta' \;\text{(bud sign)}}{\Gamma'[\sigma] \vdash \Delta'[\sigma]}\,(Subst)}{\Gamma \vdash \Delta}\,(Wk)}{}$$

if $\Gamma' \vdash \Delta'$ *subsumes* $\Gamma \vdash \Delta$ with substitution σ, i.e., $\Gamma'[\sigma] \subseteq \Gamma$ and $\Delta'[\sigma] \subseteq \Delta$. Different variants of the subsumption operation are widely employed by the current theorem provers, CYCLIST being one of them.

By using the alternative notation without parentheses, a pre-proof of $Nx, Ny \vdash Q(x,y)$ is built below by firstly trying to apply the unfold rules followed by (*Bud*), then (*Del*) and, finally, (*DCase*). (*Del*) is a restricted version of the (*Wk*) rule that deletes the IAAs of the form $N(t)$ if none of the inductive succedent atoms from the conclusion has t as argument. It can be noticed that the history of every IAA occurring in each premise of any rule r from the above rules but (*Bud*) has one of the IAAs from the conclusion of r.

$$\dfrac{\dfrac{\dfrac{\dfrac{\dfrac{\dfrac{(*1)}{Nsz, Nz \vdash Pz}\;(Bud) \quad \dfrac{(\dagger 2)}{Nz, Nsz \vdash Qzsz}\;(Bud)}{Nsz, Nz \vdash Psz}\;(R.(2))}{}\;}{Nsz, Nz \vdash Psz}\;(DCase\ N) \quad}{}\;}{}\;}{}$$

The full derivation:

$$
\cfrac{
  \cfrac{
    \cfrac{
      \cfrac{
        \cfrac{(*1)}{Nsz, Nz \vdash Pz}(Bud)
        \quad
        \cfrac{(\dagger 2)}{Nz, Nsz \vdash Qzsz}(Bud)
      }{Nsz, Nz \vdash Psz}(R.(2))
    }{}
  }{\cfrac{N0 \vdash P0}{}}(R.(1))
}{}
$$

$\dfrac{\quad}{N0 \vdash P0}(R.(1))$

$\dfrac{\dfrac{(*1)}{Nsz, Nz \vdash Pz}(Bud) \qquad \dfrac{(\dagger 2)}{Nz, Nsz \vdash Qzsz}(Bud)}{Nsz, Nz \vdash Psz}(R.(2))$

$\dfrac{\dots}{Nsz, Nz \vdash Psz}(DCase\ N)$

$\dfrac{Nx \vdash Px\ (*)}{Nx, Nz, Nsz \vdash Px}(Del)$

$\dfrac{\quad}{Nx, N0 \vdash Qx0}(R.(3))$

$\dfrac{(\dagger 1)}{Nx, Nz, Nsz \vdash Qxz}(Bud) \;\; (R.(4))$

$\dfrac{Nx, Nz, Nsz \vdash Qxsz}{}(DCase\ N)$

$\dfrac{\dots}{Nx, \underline{Ny} \vdash Qxy}\ (\dagger)$

The proof strategy is reductive if the measure value for each sequent of the form $\Gamma, N(t) \vdash P(t)$ (resp., $\Gamma, N(t_1), N(t_2) \vdash Q(t_1, t_2)$ is the multiset of IAAs $\{N(t), N(t)\}$ (resp., $\{N(t_1), N(t_1), N(t_2)\}$) and $<$ is defined as the multiset extension of the ordering $<_a$ over IAAs from Example 3.15. It can be checked that the $<$-derivability constraints are satisfied, by taking into account that the unique SCC with cycles of the digraph associated to its normalized pre-proof tree-set is built from the union of two 1-cycles, $[(*), \dots, (*1)]$ and $[(\dagger), \dots, (\dagger 1)]$, and one 2-cycle $[(*), \dots, (\dagger 2)], [(\dagger), \dots, copyof(*)]$.

By Theorem 3.17, our approach allows to prove several conjectures *simultaneously*. This is a feature specific to formula-based Noetherian induction reasoning [15] as that employed by the implicit induction inference systems. It is particularly useful when the proofs of the conjectures are mutually dependent.

Example 3.22. The normalization step for the pre-proof tree from Example 3.21 can be avoided if the pre-proof trees of $Nx \vdash Px$ and $Nx, Ny \vdash Qxy$ are developed simultaneously.

4   Conclusions and Future Work

We have presented a new method to validate a class of $CLKID^\omega$ pre-proof trees by converting them to pre-proof tree-sets, then showing that the global trace condition is implicitly satisfied if some ordering and derivability constraints hold. Every infinite path p from a pre-proof tree normalized to a proof (tree-set) can be built by concatenating path segments from the definition of the minimal cycles of its proof. These constraints ensure that there is an infinitely progressing trace following some tail of p. Our approach allows more flexibility; a different induction ordering can be defined for each SCC with cycles from the digraph of the proof. This is not the case from the unique induction ordering defined over the buds of a pre-proof tree with trace manifolds [6,7]. Also, our approach does not require pre-proof trees to be in cycle normal form that are, in the worst case, exponentially bigger.

The soundness check can be done in polynomial time provided that the time complexity for comparing two IAAs is at most polynomial. We defined proof strategies ensuring that the number of ordering constraints equals that of the induction hypotheses that are really required in the proof. In practice, their number is generally small even for proofs concerning real-size applications. For example, every cyclic induction proof from [15] (see Table 1) includes at most 8 induction hypotheses and 4 minimal cycles.

The ordering constraints are implicitly satisfied by reductive proof strategies. In the future, we plan to define new (derived) rules and proof strategies that *automatically* generate more compact reductive proof derivations and provide a better control of the proof development. The main challenge of our approach remains to find the 'good' induction orderings.

References

1. Aczel, P.: An introduction to inductive definitions. In: Barwise, J. (ed.) Handbook of Mathematical Logic, pp. 739–782. North Holland, Amsterdam (1977)
2. Baader, F., Nipkow, T.: Term Rewriting and All That. Cambridge University Press, Cambridge (1998)
3. Barthe, G., Stratulat, S.: Validation of the JavaCard platform with implicit induction techniques. In: Nieuwenhuis, R. (ed.) RTA 2003. LNCS, vol. 2706, pp. 337–351. Springer, Heidelberg (2003). doi:10.1007/3-540-44881-0_24
4. Bouhoula, A., Rusinowitch, M.: Implicit induction in conditional theories. J. Autom. Reason. **14**(2), 189–235 (1995)
5. Bronsard, F., Reddy, U.S., Hasker, R.W.: Induction using term orderings. In: Bundy, A. (ed.) CADE 1994. LNCS, vol. 814, pp. 102–117. Springer, Heidelberg (1994). doi:10.1007/3-540-58156-1_8
6. Brotherston, J.: Cyclic proofs for first-order logic with inductive definitions. In: Beckert, B. (ed.) TABLEAUX 2005. LNCS (LNAI), vol. 3702, pp. 78–92. Springer, Heidelberg (2005). doi:10.1007/11554554_8
7. Brotherston, J.: Sequent calculus proof systems for inductive definitions. Ph.D. thesis, University of Edinburgh, November 2006
8. Brotherston, J., Gorogiannis, N., Petersen, R.L.: A generic cyclic theorem prover. In: Jhala, R., Igarashi, A. (eds.) APLAS 2012. LNCS, vol. 7705, pp. 350–367. Springer, Heidelberg (2012). doi:10.1007/978-3-642-35182-2_25
9. Brotherston, J., Simpson, A.: Sequent calculi for induction and infinite descent. J. Logic Comput. **21**(6), 1177–1216 (2011)
10. Gentzen, G.: Untersuchungen über das logische Schließen. I. Mathematische Zeitschrift **39**, 176–210 (1935)
11. Kupferman, O., Vardi, M.: Weak alternating automata are not that weak. ACM Trans. Comput. Logic (TOCL) **2**(3), 408–429 (2001)
12. Michel, M.: Complementation is more difficult with automata on infinite words. Technical report, CNET (1988)
13. Negri, S., von Plato, J.: Structural Proof Theory. Cambridge University Press, Cambridge (2001)
14. Rusinowitch, M., Stratulat, S., Klay, F.: Mechanical verification of an ideal incremental ABR conformance algorithm. J. Autom. Reason. **30**(2), 53–177 (2003)
15. Stratulat, S.: A unified view of induction reasoning for first-order logic. In: Voronkov, A. (ed.) Turing-100 (The Alan Turing Centenary Conference). EPiC Series, vol. 10, pp. 326–352. EasyChair (2012)
16. Stratulat, S.: Structural vs. cyclic induction: a report on some experiments with Coq. In: SYNASC International Symposium on Symbolic and Numeric Algorithms for Scientific Computing, pp. 27–34. IEEE Computer Society (2016)

17. Stratulat, S.: Mechanically certifying formula-based Noetherian induction reasoning. J. Symb. Comput. **80**(Part 1), 209–249 (2017)
18. Tarjan, R.: Depth-first search and linear graph algorithms. SIAM J. Comput. **1**(2), 146–160 (1972)
19. The Coq development team: The Coq Reference Manual. INRIA (2017)
20. Wirth, C.-P.: Descente infinie + deduction. Logic J. IGPL **12**(1), 1–96 (2004)

Formalization and Complexity

A Mechanizable First-Order Theory of Ordinals

Peter H. Schmitt[(⊠)]

Department of Informatics, Karlsruhe Institute of Technology (KIT),
Am Fasanengarten 5, 76131 Karlsruhe, Germany
`pschmitt@ira.uka.de`

Abstract. We present a first-order theory of ordinals without resorting
to set theory. The theory is implemented in the KeY program verification
system which is in turn used to prove termination of a Java program
computing the Goodstein sequences.

1 Introduction

A number of automated reasoning systems have been put to the task to prove
theorems about ordinal numbers. Here is a fair selection of pertinent papers:
[4,5,9,15] for the Isabelle proof assistant, [6,8] for Coq, [3] for OTTER. All these
efforts have in common that they start with a semantic definition of ordinals as
sets with special properties. Of a different flavor are the papers [13,14], that
present algorithms implemented in the ACL2 system for solving problems in
ordinal arithmetic working on a normal form representation.

In this paper, we will present a first-order theory Th_{Ord} of ordinals. The
models of Th_{Ord} are of the form $\mathcal{M} = (U, \dot{0}, \dot{\omega}, +1, \dot{<})$ with universe U, constants
$\dot{0}$, and $\dot{\omega}$, the unary successor function $+1$ and the order relation $\dot{<}$. The logic
itself contains the binary operator $sup_{x<n}m$ binding variable x. Its interpretation
in $\mathcal{M}$ is the supremum of $\{m^{\mathcal{M}}(\alpha) \mid \alpha \in U \text{ and } \alpha \dot{<} n^{\mathcal{M}}\}$. Typically, the term
m will contain the free variable x and $t^{\mathcal{M}}(\alpha)$ stands for the evaluation of m
in $\mathcal{M}$ with x instantiated to the element $\alpha \in U$. The operator $sup_{x<n}m$ is the
only construct in our axiomatization with a set theoretic flavor. This operator
is, however, definable in the standard first-order logic; a proof of this result for
variable-binders in general is available in Ulbrich's PhD thesis [22].

Already in 1965 Gaisi Takeuti presented in [20] a first-order theory $\mathcal{O}$ of
ordinal numbers. His interest were in proof theoretic properties. The theory $\mathcal{O}$
allows to define an inner model of Zermelo-Fraenkel (ZF) set theory. Thus, a
formula ϕ is derivable from $\mathcal{O}$ iff a canoncial translation of ϕ is derivable in ZF
set theory. The vocabulary of $\mathcal{O}$ is much richer than ours: it contains e.g., already
in its axiomatic basis coding and decoding functions for pairs of ordinals. As a
consequence the theory $\mathcal{O}$ is not very well suited as the basis for automated
reasoning on ordinals.

It is well-known that the Peano axioms, PA, for the natural numbers are
incomplete. This did and does not cause much alarm since the examples of true
statements not derivable in PA were consider too arcane to be of any pratical

© Springer International Publishing AG 2017
R.A. Schmidt and C. Nalon (Eds.): TABLEAUX 2017, LNAI 10501, pp. 331–346, 2017.
DOI: 10.1007/978-3-319-66902-1_20

relevance. This is beginning to change as these examples get more and more accessible. We present, based on [10], a Java program with less than 20 lines of code, computing the Goodstein sequences, such that termination of one of its two methods cannot be proved in PA. Still, there is no reason to be alarmed since termination can be proved in Th_{Ord}, which is a simple, plausible extension of PA as can be seen by scrutinizing the axioms in Fig. 1 below.

1. $\forall x, y, z(x < y \wedge y < z \rightarrow x < z)$ transitivity
2. $\forall x(\neg x < x)$ strict order
3. $\forall x, y(x < y \vee x \doteq y \vee y < x)$ total order
4. $\forall x(0 \leq x)$ 0 is smallest element
5. $0 < \omega \wedge \neg\exists x(\omega \doteq x + 1)$ ω is a limit ordinal
6. $\forall y(0 < y \wedge \forall x(x < \omega \rightarrow x + 1 < y) - > \omega \leq y)$ ω is the least limit ordinal
7. $\forall x(x < x + 1) \wedge \forall x, y(x < y \rightarrow x + 1 \leq y)$ successor function
8. $\forall z(z < n \rightarrow m[z/x] \leq sup_{x<n}m)$ def of supremum, part 1
9. $\forall u(\forall z(z < n \rightarrow m[z/x] \leq u) \rightarrow sup_{x<n}m \leq u)$ def of supremum, part 2
10. $\forall x(\forall y(y < x \rightarrow \phi(y/x)) \rightarrow \phi) \rightarrow \forall x\phi$ transfinite induction scheme

Fig. 1. The axioms of the core theory

The first automatic termination proof for Goodstein sequences was recorded in [23]. In that paper a finite rewrite system is presented whose termination encodes the termination of these sequences and termination of the rewrite system is proved. A termination proof using the higher-order logic proof assistant Coq can be downloaded from [7] as part of the Coq project on ordinal notation [6]. Hereditary multisets, a variant of nested multisets, offer a convenient representation of ordinals below ϵ_0. A formalization of hereditary multisets in the Isabelle/HOL proof assistant is available from the Archive of Formal Proofs [5] also containing a termination proof for Goodstein sequences. A corresponding publication is pending [4]. The theory Th_{Ord} has been implemented in KeY, a first-order theorem proving and program verification system based on the sequent calculus [1]. This implementation has been put to use to obtain a machine assisted termination proof of the Java program mentioned above. This seems to be the first termination proof for Goodstein sequences using a first-order reasoning system.

2   A Theory of Ordinals

In the first subsection, we start out with a very simple core theory Th_{Ord}^0. This plays the same role here as Peano's theory for the arithmetic of natural number. In the next subsection, the final theory Th_{Ord} is obtained as a definitional extension of Th_{Ord}^0.

2.1   The Core Theory

The vocabulary Σ^0_{Ord} of the core theory contains the following symbols
  predicate $<$ binary
  functions $+1$ unary
        $0, \omega$ constants

Terms and formulas are defined as usual in first-order logic with the exception that we include a term building operator sup:

  if n, m are terms and x is a variable that does not occur free in n, then

$$sup_{x<n}m$$

is a term.

Two operations, (1) start with 0 and (2) add one, suffice to generate all finite ordinals. We use $x + 1$ to denote the immediate successor of x to avoid the introduction of an additional symbol. In set theory, a third operation is added to generate all transfinite ordinals: (3) for any set X of ordinals, there is a least ordinal not less than all $\alpha \in X$. Here we avoid set theory and restrict this operation to sets X that can be obtained as instances of one term m, where furthermore only instantiations up to a bound n are allowed. This motivates the term constructor $sup_{x<n}m$. The term m will typically contain the variable x.

In most presentations of Peano arithmetic, the order relation $<$ is not part of the core theory, but it is later added as a definitional extension. It would have been extremely cumbersome to do so in our setting. So, we sacrificed on minimality and included $<$ from the outset.

The intended meaning of symbols in Σ^0_{Ord} is fixed by the axioms in Fig. 1.

We thus see that $<$ is to be interpreted as a strict, total, order relation. We use $x \leq y$ as a shorthand for $x \doteq y \vee x < y$. From the axioms, we see that 0 is the least element with respect to $<$ and ω is the first infinite ordinal. Without the two axioms 5 and 6 for ω, the natural numbers with strict order and successor would be a model of the remaining axioms and nothing would have been gained over Peano's theory. Axioms 8 and 9 establish the intended meaning of the supremum operator as explained in the introduction. We use the notation $m[z/x]$ to denote the term that arises from m by replacing x by z everywhere. Note that the way we defined sup, the formulas $sup_{x<0}m \doteq 0$ and $sup_{x<1}m \doteq m[0/x]$ can be derived.

The last and most powerful axiom is the axiom scheme of transfinite induction that is an extension the course-of-value induction scheme in finite arithmetic. Let ϕ be a formula that typically would contain x as a free variable and let $\phi(y)$ stand for the formula obtained from ϕ by replacing x by y (assuming of course that y does not occur in ϕ, neither free nor bound). If we can prove for every x the transfinite induction step $\forall y(y < x \rightarrow \phi(y)) \rightarrow \phi$, then we conclude that ϕ is true for all x.

One could ask whether the sup operator should have been omitted from the core vocabulary and added later as a definitional extension. The answer is no! Since we follow the usual set-up of first-order logic all functions are total. Consequently, inclusion of a function symbol in the vocabulary already implies an implicit existence axiom: the function values exist for all arguments. Adding *sup* is not a definitional extension since the associated existence claim could not be proved in the theory without *sup*.

An alternative would have been to include the following axiom scheme instead of the two parts of the definition of *sup*

$$\forall y(\exists z(\forall x(x < y \rightarrow t \leq z)))$$

A possible instantiation could be $\forall y(\exists z(\forall x(x < y \rightarrow \omega^x \leq z)))$. Then, it would have been possible to show, using transfinite induction, that adding the *sup* operator is a definitional extension of this version of the core theory. The adopted approach is more straightforward.

2.2 The Full Theory

The full vocabulary Σ_{Ord} of the theory Th_{Ord} is shown in Fig. 2.

predicates	$>, \leq$	binary
	lim	unary
functions	$0, 1$	constant
	max	binary
	$+, *, \hat{\ }$	binary

Fig. 2. The full vocabulary Σ_{Ord}'

The axioms of Th_{Ord} are Th_{Ord}^0 plus the definitions of the new symbols in Figs. 3 and 5.

$\forall x, y(x \leq y \leftrightarrow x \doteq y \vee x < y)$ (less or equal relation)
$\forall x(lim(x) \leftrightarrow 0 < x \wedge \neg\exists y(y + 1 \doteq x))$ (limit ordinal)
$\forall x, y(max(x,y) \doteq \text{if } x \leq y \text{ then } y \text{ else } x)$ (maximum operator)

Fig. 3. Definitional extension: axioms for auxiliary predicates

The three axioms in Fig. 3 define the auxiliary symbols $\leq$ and *max* plus the important concept of a limit ordinal. In contrast to other presentations, 0 is not a limit ordinal in our set-up.

Figure 4 shows a sample of lemmas that can already be derived at this point from the axioms considered so far. The lemmas are grouped together according to the syntactical symbols involved. This does not reflect the order in which the lemmas can or need to be proved.

Lemma 1 in Fig. 4 is the least number principle, a well known equivalent to the induction axiom scheme. It is instructive to figure out why this lemma is true even if x does not occur as a free variable in ϕ. Lemma 2 in Fig. 4 is the

1. $\exists x\phi \to \exists x(\phi \wedge \forall y(y < x \to \neg\phi[y/x]))$
2. $\phi[0/x] \wedge$
   $\forall x(\phi \to \phi[x+1/x]) \wedge$
   $\forall x(lim(x) \wedge \forall y(y < x \to \phi[y/x]) \to \phi)$
   $\to \forall x\phi$
3. $\forall x(lim(x) \to sup_{y<x}\, y \doteq x)$
4. $\forall x(sup_{z<x+1}\, t \doteq max(sup_{z<x}\, t, t[x/z]))$
5. $\forall x(\forall y(y < x \to t_1[y/z] \doteq t_2[y/z]) \to sup_{z<x}\, t_1 \doteq sup_{z<x}\, t_2)$
6. $\forall x_1, x_2(\ \forall x(x < x_1 \to \exists y(y < x_2 \wedge t_1[x/z] \le t_2[y/z])) \wedge$
   $\qquad\qquad \forall y(y < x_2 \to \exists x(x < x_1 \wedge t_2[y/z] \le t_1[x/z]))$
   $\qquad\quad \leftrightarrow sup_{z<x_1}\, t_1 \doteq sup_{z<x_2}\, t_2)$
7. $lim(x) \leftrightarrow x \ne 0 \wedge \forall y(y < x \to (y+1) < x)$

Fig. 4. Some lemmas derivable from the axioms considered so far

$\forall x(x + 0 \doteq x)$
$\forall x, y(x + (y+1) \doteq (x+y) + 1)$
$\forall x, y(lim(y) \to x + sup_{z<y}z \doteq sup_{z<y}(x+z))$
$\forall x(x * 0 \doteq 0)$
$\forall x, y(x * (y+1) \doteq (x*y) + x)$
$\forall x, y(lim(y) \to x * y \doteq sup_{z<y}(x*z))$
$\forall x(x^0 \doteq 1)$
$\forall x, y(x^{y+1}) \doteq (x^y) * x)$
$\forall x, y(lim(y) \wedge x \ne 0 \to x^y \doteq sup_{z<y}(x^z))$
$\forall y(lim(y) \to 0^y \doteq 0)$

Fig. 5. Definitional extension: axioms for arithmetic operations

equivalent rephrasing of the transfinite induction scheme 10 in Fig. 1 that is most frequently employed: If a formula ϕ with free variable x is true for $x = 0$ (base case), if for all z we can prove that $\phi[z+1]$ follow from $\phi[z]$ (successor induction step), and if we can prove for every limit ordinal λ, when $\phi[z/x]$ is true for all $z < \lambda$ then $\phi[\lambda/x]$ follows (limit induction step), then we have proved $\forall x\phi$.

Lemma 3 could be rephrased as: if x is a limit ordinal then x is the least ordinal that is greater or equal than all ordinals that are strictly less than x. This is not true for successor ordinals x. In this case, we have $sup_{y<x+1}\, y \doteq x$ instead. Lemma 4 is useful in proving statements involving the sup operator via induction. Lemma 5 helps to show that two suprema are equal especially in the case when equality between t_1 and t_2 is not obvious.

For the purpose of this paragraph we look at a term t that contains z as a sequence t_z. We say that a sequence $t_{z<x_1}$ is confinal in $s_{z<x_2}$ if for every $x < x_1$ there is $y < x_2$ with $t[x/z] \le s[y/z]$. If two sequences are mutually confinal in one another, then they share the same supremum. This is Lemma 6 in Fig. 4. Note, that we get equality of two suprema with different bounds x_1, and x_2. Lemma 7 gives an alternative definition of a limit ordinal.

The second installment of the axioms extending Th^0_{Ord} to Th_{Ord} is listed in Fig. 5. They give the usual recursive definitions of ordinal addition, multiplication and exponentiation.

2.3 Derived Lemmas

In this subsection, we will in Figs. 6, 7, 8 and 9 list and comment on a selection of lemmas derivable from Th_{Ord}.

1. $\forall x, y(y \neq 0 \rightarrow x < x + y)$
2. $\forall x, y(x \leq x + y)$
3. $\forall x, y(y \leq x + y)$
4. $\forall x, y, z(x < y \rightarrow z + x < z + y)$
5. $\forall x, y, z(x \leq y \rightarrow x + z \leq y + z)$
6. $\forall x, y, z(x + y < x + z \rightarrow y < z)$

Fig. 6. Lemmas involving addition and order relations

Figure 6 lists lemmas that are needed as intermediate stepping stones in the proofs of the properties of ordinal arithmetic.

Lemma 1 in Fig. 6 extends the axiom $\forall x(x < x+1)$ from Fig. 1 where we now add on the right side an arbitrary number greater than or equal to 1 instead of just 1. This is, of course, proved via transfinite induction. Lemma 2 is an easy variant of Lemma 1. Addition of ordinals is not commutative, so we cannot conclude from Lemma 1 that $\forall x, y(x \neq 0 \rightarrow y < x + y)$. Indeed, $y = \omega, x = 1$ is a counterexample. But the version for $\leq$ instead of $<$ is provable. This is Lemma 3. Lemma 4 is also proved using transfinite induction. We remark that $\forall x, y, z(x < y \rightarrow x + z < y + z)$ is not true, as can be seen by the instantiation 0 for x, 1 for y, and ω for z. But the relaxed version with $\leq$ instead of $<$ is derivable. This is Lemma 5. Lemma 6 is the reverse of Lemma 4.

Figure 7 gives lemmas on ordinal addition. Since ordinal addition is in general not commutative Lemma 1 in Fig. 7 may not be immediately obvious, but it can be easily proved using ordinal induction. Lemma 3 is a fact on ordinal addition that we have referred to already above. Lemma 4 is a useful lemma formalizing the intuition that the property of being a limit ordinal is determined by the right *end part* of the ordinal regardless of what comes before. Lemma 5 gives a first general representation theorem for ordinals. In [21, Theorem 8.13] it is proved using set comprehension. This is not available in our setting. Fortunately, it turned out that there is a much simpler proof using ordinal induction. Lemma 6 required the most complex proof so far. The basic idea, however, is quite simple. As a witness for z take b, the least ordinal such that $y \leq x + b$. It can easily be seen that such a number exists by the least number principle (Lemma 1 in Fig. 4). Then, a case distinction $b = 0, b \doteq b_0 + 1$ for some b_0, or $lim(b)$ leads to success. Lemma 7 is the wellknown associative law. Lemmas 8 and 9 correspond to the Peano axioms for the natural numbers, which say that 0 is not a successor

1. $\forall x (0 + x \doteq x)$
2. $\forall x, y (x + y \doteq 0 \leftrightarrow x \doteq 0 \wedge y \doteq 0)$
3. $\forall x (x < \omega \rightarrow x + \omega \doteq \omega)$
4. $\forall x \forall y (lim(y) \rightarrow lim(x + y))$
5. $\forall x (\omega \leq x \rightarrow \exists y, n (lim(y) \wedge n < \omega \wedge x \doteq y + n))$
6. $\forall x, y (x \leq y \rightarrow \exists z (x \doteq y + z))$
7. $\forall x, y, z (x + (y + z) \doteq (x + y) + z)$
8. $\neg \exists x (x + 1 \doteq 0)$
9. $\forall x, y ((x + 1) \doteq (y + 1) \rightarrow x \doteq y)$
10. $\forall x, y, z ((z + x) \doteq (z + y) \rightarrow x \doteq y)$
11. $sup_{z<x} (i+t) \doteq i + sup_{z<x} t$ if z does not occur in i and $x > 0$
12. $i + j \doteq j$ if $\omega \leq j$ and $i < \omega$

Fig. 7. Lemmas on addition

and the successor function is injective. Lemma 10 shows that addition on the right, with fixed left summand, is injective. Lemma 11 resisted for a while all my attempts to prove it. Since I could also not find it in [21], I was, at some point, even in doubt wether it is true at all. The inequality, $sup_{z<x} (i+t) \leq i + sup_{z<x} t$ is simple. For the reverse inequality a proof by contradiction turned out to be the right way of attack. So assume $sup_{z<x} (i+t) < i + sup_{z<x} t$ and try to find a contradiction. The key to the solution was the case distinction $sup_{z<x} (i+t) < i$ or $i \leq sup_{z<x} (i+t)$. Notice that in the first case, we arrive at the contradiction $i \leq i+t[0/z] < sup_{z<x} (i+t) < i$. Here also the assumption $x > 0$ comes in. In the second case, there is by Lemma 5 an ordinal k such that $i+k \doteq sup_{z<x} (i+t)$. By the proof-by-contradiction assumption, this yields $i+k < i+sup_{z<x} t$ and further by Lemma 7 in Fig. 6 $k < sup_{z<x} t$. By the definition of sup there, is $\lambda < x$ with $k \leq t[\lambda/z]$. This leads to the contradiction $i+k \leq i+t[\lambda/z] < sup_{z<x} (i+t)$. The *commuted* version of Lemma 11, i.e., $sup_{z<x} (t + i) \doteq (sup_{z<x} t) + i$, provided z does not occur in i and $x > 0$, is – as you would have expected –not true: $\omega \doteq sup_{z<\omega} (z + 1) \doteq (sup_{z<\omega} z) + 1 \doteq \omega + 1$. Lemma 12 shows a dramatic failure of commutativity for ordinal addition: A left finite ordinal summand is simply absorbed if the right summand is infinite. We found it helpful to split the proof of Lemma 12 in the cases $\omega \doteq j$ and $\omega < j$.

Figure 8 shows derivable properties of ordinal multiplication. Lemma 1 shows that the strict order relation is preserved by multiplication on the left, provided that the left multiplyer is not 0. Multiplication on the right only preserves $\leq$, as Lemma 4 shows. Lemma 2 is the reverse implication from Lemma 1. Lemma 3 states that multiplication on the right, with a fixed multiplicand on the left, is an injective function. Lemma 7 is crucial for the proof of distributivity (Lemma 8) and multiplicative associativity (Lemma 9).

After all the preparations the proof of multiplicative associativity is now straightforward. Let us for once give a detailed proof sketch in this exemplary case. We use ordinal induction (Lemma 2 in Fig. 4) on the variable k. The base case is trivial. The successor induction step is proved as follows:

1. $\forall x, y, z((0 < z \wedge x < y) \rightarrow z * x < z * y)$
2. $\forall x, y, z(z * x < z * y) \rightarrow (0 < z \wedge x < y))$
3. $\forall x, y, z(0 < z \wedge z * x \doteq z * y \rightarrow x \doteq y)$
4. $\forall x, y, z(x \leq y \rightarrow x * z \leq y * z)$
5. $\forall x, y(x \neq 0 \rightarrow y \leq x * y$
6. $\forall x(0 < x < \omega \rightarrow x * \omega \doteq \omega)$
7. $sup_{z<x} (i * t) \doteq i * sup_{z<x} t$
8. $\forall i, j, k(i * (j + k) \doteq i * j + i * k)$
9. $\forall i, j, k((i * j) * k \doteq i * (j * k))$
10. $\forall z, x((lim(z) \wedge 0 < x < \omega) \rightarrow x * z \doteq z)$
11. $\forall i, j(1 < i \wedge 1 < j \rightarrow i + j \leq i * j)$
12. $\forall i, z(0 < i \wedge lim(z) \rightarrow lim(i * z))$
13. $\forall i, z(0 < i \wedge lim(z) \rightarrow lim(z * i))$

Fig. 8. Lemmas on multiplication

$$
\begin{aligned}
i * (j * (k + 1)) &\doteq i * (j * k + j) && \text{definition of } * \\
&\doteq i * (j * k) + i * j && \text{distributivity (Lemma 8)} \\
&\doteq (i * j) * k + i * j && \text{induction hypothesis} \\
&\doteq (i * j) * (k + 1) && \text{definition of } *
\end{aligned}
$$

The induction step in the limit case is shown next. We us λ instead of k to signal that k is a limit ordinal:

$$
\begin{aligned}
i * (j * \lambda) &\doteq i * sup_{x<\lambda} j * x && \text{definition of } * \\
&\doteq sup_{x<\lambda} i * (j * x) && \text{Lemma 7} \\
&\doteq sup_{x<\lambda} (i * j) * x && \text{induction hypothesis} \\
&\doteq (i * j) * \lambda && \text{definition of } *
\end{aligned}
$$

Lemma 10 (we are still talking about Fig. 8) is a strengthening of Lemma 6: multiplicative absorbtion on the left of finite ordinals not only holds for ω, but for any limit ordinal. Lemma 11 states when addition of two ordinals is less than their product. The restrictions are necessary as can be seen by the following simple examples:

$$
\begin{aligned}
j &= 0 + j \not\leq 0 * j = 0 \\
1 + j &\not\leq 1 * j = j \\
i &= i + 0 \not\leq i * 0 = 0 \\
i + 1 &\not\leq i * 1 = i
\end{aligned}
$$

Finally, we turn to the lemmas on exponentiation in Figure 9. Note that the restriction on x in Lemma 1 is necessary since by definition $0^0 \doteq 1$. Also the restrictions in Lemma 2, which says that exponentiation is strictly increasing in the left argument, are necessary as can be seen by the following examples $2 \not< 2^0 \doteq 1, 2 \not< 2^1 \doteq 2, 0 \not< 0^2 \doteq 0$, and $1 \not< 1^2 \doteq 1$. It is only weakly increasing on the right, Lemma 3. The strict inequality is far from being true, as Lemma 4 shows. Exponentiation is also strictly monotone in the second argument, as Lemma 5 shows. The reverse implication is also true, as stated by

1. $\forall x(0 < x \rightarrow 0^x \doteq 0)$
2. $\forall x, y(1 < x \wedge 1 < y \rightarrow x < x^y)$
3. $\forall x, y(1 < x \rightarrow y \leq x^y)$
4. $\forall x, y(1 < x \wedge x < \omega \rightarrow x^\omega \doteq \omega)$
5. $\forall x, y_1, y_2(1 < x \wedge y_1 < y_2 \rightarrow x^{y_1} < x^{y_2})$
6. $\forall x, y_1, y_2(1 < x \wedge x^{y_1} < x^{y_2} \rightarrow y_1 < y_2)$
7. $\forall x_1, x_2, y(x_1 < x_2 \rightarrow x_1^y \leq x_2^y)$
8. $\forall x, y(0 < x \wedge lim(y) \rightarrow lim(y^x))$
9. $\forall x, y(1 < x \wedge lim(y) \rightarrow lim(x^y))$
10. $\forall x, y, z(x^{y+z} \doteq x^y * x^z)$
11. $\forall x, y, z((x^y)^z \doteq x^{y*z})$
12. $\forall b((0 < b \wedge \forall x(x < b \rightarrow 0 < j)) \rightarrow sup_{x<b}(i^j) = i^{sup_{x<b}(j)})$
     for all terms i, j such that x does not occur in i.

Fig. 9. Lemmas on exponentiation

Lemma 7. In the first argument exponention is only weakly monotone, as stated by Lemma 7. A counterexample to strict monotonicity is given by the instantiations $x_1 = 2, x_2 = 3$, and $y = \omega$. Lemmas 8 and 9 show how the property of being a limit ordinal is propagated by exponentiation. Lemmas 10 and 11 are laws of exponentiation familiar from finite arithmetic. Lemma 12 is in fact a lemma scheme. Note that in typical applications x is a free variable in j. It states an indispensable continuity property for exponentiation.

The theory Th_{Ord} has been implemented in the KeY system. Interactive proof for over 170 lemmas found in the set theory textbooks [2,11,12,21] have been obtained documenting the strength of Th_{Ord}.

3   Termination of Goodstein Sequences

The sequences under investigation were first introduce by Goodstein in [18]. In fact, Goodstein considered in his paper more general sequences involving a non-decreasing function $f : \mathbb{N} \rightarrow \mathbb{N}$ as a parameter. The Goodstein sequences considered here, these are the same as the ones considered by Kirby and Paris, are obtained by the choice $f(i) = i + 2$. Kirby and Paris showed in their highly acclaimed paper [10] that termination of Goodstein sequences cannot be proved in Peano arithmetic, stronger principles, like e.g., ordinal induction, are needed. We will use ordinal induction, as provided by the theory Th_{Ord} presented in Sect. 2, to prove termination of a Java program computing the Goodstein sequences in Subsect. 3.3.

3.1   Injecting Natural Numbers

The termination proof in Subsect. 3.3 will be done using the program verification system KeY. KeY employs a many-sorted first-order logic. For ease of presentation the theory Th_{Ord} was formulated in Sect. 2 as a one-sorted theory. In the implementation of Th_{Ord} within the KeY prover, Ord is used to name the sort of ordinals. Among the other sorts present in the KeY prover, there are mathematical integers int. It is essential for the intended proof to relate non-negative integers to the finite ordinals. To this end, we add a function $onat : int \rightarrow Ord$.

Figure 10 shows an axiomatisation of the function $onat : int \rightarrow Ord$ that maps the non-negative integers into corresponding ordinals less than ω. Obviously, $onat$ is a partial function. The KeY system deals with partial function by underspecification. That means that $onat$ is a total function, but the axioms do not include any commitment on the values for negative arguments.

Definitional Extension

1. $onat(0) \doteq 0$
2. $\forall n (0 \leq n \rightarrow onat(n+1) \doteq onat(n) + 1)$

Derived Lemmas

3. $onat(1) \doteq 1$
4. $\forall n, m (0 \leq n \wedge 0 \leq m \rightarrow onat(n+m) \doteq onat(n) + onat(m))$
5. $\forall n, m ((0 \leq n \wedge 0 \leq m) \rightarrow (onat(n) \doteq onat(m) \rightarrow n \doteq m))$
6. $\forall n, m ((0 \leq n \wedge 0 \leq m) \rightarrow (onat(n) < onat(m) \leftrightarrow n < m))$
7. $\forall n (0 \leq n \rightarrow onat(n) < \omega)$

Fig. 10. Positive integers as ordinals

Figure 10 also shows useful derived lemmas. We use in this figure and also later on overloaded syntax. Thus, whether 0 denotes an integer or an ordinal, whether + is ordinal addition or addition of non-negative integers can be found out by looking at the type information.

3.2   Definition of Goodstein Sequences

We start with an informal explanation. First, the auxiliary concept of a hereditary base-n notation is needed. This makes only sense for $n \geq 2$. The hereditary base-n notation for a natural number m is obtained from its ordinary base-n notation

$$m = m_k \cdot n^k + m_{k-1} \cdot n^{k-1} + \ldots m_1 \cdot n + m_0, \quad 0 \leq m_i < n, m_k \neq 0$$

by also writing the exponents $k, k-1, \ldots$ in base-n notation and again the thus arising exponents, and so on.

Example 1.   base-2 $35 = 2^5 + 2^1 + 2^0$
              hereditary base-2 $35 = 2^{2^2+1} + 2 + 1$
              base-3 $100 = 3^4 + 2 \cdot 3^2 + 3^0$
              hereditary base-3 $100 = 3^{3+1} + 2 \cdot 3^2 + 1.$

The Goodstein sequence $G_k(m)$ with initial value m is computed as follows

$G_1(m) = m$

$G_2(m) = $ in the hereditary base-2 representation of m
        replace every occurence of 2 by 3 and subtract 1

$\ldots$

$G_k(m) = $ in the hereditary base-k representation of $G_{k-1}(m)$
        replace every occurence of k by $k+1$ and subtract 1

Example 2. The Goodstein sequence for $m = 3$

$G_1(3)$	By definition		3
$G_2(3)$	Write 3 in her. base 2 notation	$2^1 + 1$	
	Replace 2 by 3 minus 1	$3^1 + 1 - 1$	3
$G_3(3)$	Write 3 in her. base 3 notation	3^1	
	Replace 3 by 4 minus 1	$4^1 - 1$	3
$G_4(3)$	Write 3 in her. base 4 notation	3	
	Replace 4 by 5 minus 1	$3 - 1$	2
$G_5(3)$	Write 2 in her. base 5 notation	2	
	Replace 5 by 6 minus 1	$2 - 1$	1
$G_6(3)$	Write 1 in her. base 6 notation	1	
	Replace 6 by 7 minus 1	$1 - 1$	0

Example 3. Initial part of the Goodstein sequence for $m = 4$

		4	
2^{2^1}	$3^{3^1} - 1$	26	ω^ω
$3^2 * 2 + 3^1 * 2 + 2$	$4^2 * 2 + 4^1 * 2 + 2 - 1$	41	$\omega^2 * 2 + \omega * 2 + 2$
$4^2 * 2 + 4^1 * 2 + 1$	$5^2 * 2 + 5^1 * 2 + 1 - 1$	60	$\omega^2 * 2 + \omega * 2 + 1$
$5^2 * 2 + 5^1 * 2$	$6^2 * 2 + 6^1 * 2 - 1$	83	$\omega^2 * 2 + \omega * 2$
$6^2 * 2 + 6^1 * 1 + 5$	$7^2 * 2 + 7^1 * 1 + 5 - 1$	109	$\omega^2 * 2 + \omega + 5$
$7^2 * 2 + 7^1 * 1 + 4$	$8^2 * 2 + 8^1 + 1 + 4 - 1$	139	$\omega^2 * 2 + \omega + 4$
$8^2 * 2 + 8^1 * 1 + 3$	$9^2 * 2 + 9^1 * 1 + 3 - 1$	173	$\omega^2 * 2 + \omega + 3$
$9^2 * 2 + 9^1 * 1 + 2$	$10^2 * 2 + 10^1 * 1 + 2 - 1$	211	$\omega^2 * 2 + \omega + 2$
$10^2 * 2 + 10^1 * 1 + 1$	$11^2 * 2 + 11^1 * 1 + 1 - 1$	253	$\omega^2 * 2 + \omega + 1$
$11^2 * 2 + 11^1 * 1$	$12^2 * 2 + 12^1 * 1 - 1$	299	$\omega^2 * 2 + \omega$
$12^2 * 2 + 11$	$13^2 * 2 + 10$	348	$\omega^2 * 2 + 11$
		1058	
$23^2 * 2$	$24^2 * 2 - 1$	1151	$\omega^2 * 2$
$24^2 + 24 * 23 + 23$	$25^2 + 25 * 23 + 23 - 1$	1222	$\omega^2 + \omega * 23 + 23$

Example 3 shows the Goodstein sequence with initial value 4 upto its 25-th term. The last column should be ignored on first reading. We will come back to it in the next subsection. Also $G_k(4)$ will eventually reach 0, but for k in the order of magnitude of $10^{121210700}$.

The following mathematical formalization of these informal explanations differ in detail greatly from those in the paper [10]. Intuitively the value of the function $\mathrm{oHNf}(n, m)$ is obtained by computing the hereditary base-n representation of m and replacing all occurences of n by $n + 1$. This is turned into the following recursive definition:

Definition 1 ($\mathrm{oHNf}(n.m)$). *For* $n \geq 2, m \geq 0$

$$\mathrm{oHNf}(n, m) = \begin{cases} m & \text{if } m < n \\ (n+1)^{\mathrm{oHNf}(n,k)} * a + \mathrm{oHNf}(n, c) & \text{if } m = n^k * a + c \text{ with} \\ & 1 \leq k \wedge 0 < a < n \wedge c < n^k \end{cases}$$

This is a complete definition since we can easily prove:
$$\forall m, n(2 \leq n \wedge n \leq m \rightarrow \exists r, a, c \, (m = n^r * a + c \ \wedge$$
$$1 \leq r \wedge 0 < a \wedge a < n \wedge c < n^r \wedge 0 \leq c))$$

Definition 2 ($G_n(m)$). *For* $n \geq 2$ *and* $m \geq 0$
$$G_1(m) = m$$
$$G_k(m) = \mathrm{oHNf}(k, G_{k-1}(m)) - 1$$

3.3   Termination Proof

Close inspection showed that the original termination proof of Goodstein sequences in [10] is more complicated than necessary. We follow instead the idea of a short proof of the termination of general Goodstein sequences from [16,17]. Figure 11 shows the Java program to be verified. Since in the default setting the KeY system treats Java integers as mathematical integers this is what we need. Running this program, however, would yield wrong results as soon as maxInt is reached. Since exponention is not part of the Java language, the method intPow had to be implemented. Since this is a standard task, the code is not shown here.

We do not assume that every reader is familiar with program verification and will complement the code with explaining comments. Figure 11 contains the Java code plus annotations in the Java Modeling Language (JML). A lucid introduction to JML can be found in [1, Chap. 7]. The following comments should, we hope, be sufficient to provide the reader with a clear understanding of the central points. JML annotations needed to guide the system but not essential for the casual human reader have been omitted, i.e., replaced by ....

JML allows to add specifications enclosed between special comments /*@...@*/ to a Java program. Formal verification then provides a mathematical proof that the code meets its JML specifications.

JML provides method contracts. These are placed immediately before the method code. The crucial method in Listing 11 is GoodsteinSequence in lines 5–14. Its method contract spans lines 2–4. The requires clause states a precondition that must be met to guarantee the postcondition. Here the precondition requires the initial value for the Goodstein sequence to be strictly positive. The postcondition is - in this case - hidden in the keyword normal_behaviour. This says that the method GoodsteinSequence terminates and no uncaught exceptions

```
1   public class Goodstein{
2     /*@ normal_behavior
3       @   requires startM > 0;
4       @*/
5     public void GoodsteinSequence(int startM){
6       int base = 2; int m = startM;
7         /*@ loop_invariant
8           @   m >= 0 & base >= 2;
9           @   ...
10          @   decreases \dl_oGS(base,m);
11          @*/
12        while   (m > 0) {
13              m = nextExpand(m,base);
14              m = m-1;
15              base = base+1;} }
16    /*@ normal_behavior
17      @ requires m >= 0 & oldBase >= 2;
18      @ ...
19      @ ensures \result ==  \dl_oHNf(oldBase,m);
20      @ ensures \dl_oGS(oldBase,m)==\dl_oGS(oldBase+1,\result);
21      @ measured_by m;  @*/
22    public int nextExpand(int m, int oldBase){
23        if (oldBase > m) { return m;}
24        else { int exp=0; int factor=1; int base=oldBase;
25        /*@ loop_invariant
26          @   factor == intPow(oldBase,exp) &  ... ;
27          @   decreases (m - factor);
28          @*/
29      while (m>=factor*oldBase){exp=exp+1; factor=factor*oldBase;};
30            int a = 1; int c = 0;
31    /*@ normal_behavior
32      @ ensures m == \dl_pow(oldBase, exp) * a + c &
33      @ 2<=oldBase&1<=exp&0<a&a<oldBase&c<\dl_pow(oldBase,exp)&c>=0;
34      @ ...
35      @*/
36          {a =  m/factor; c = m - factor*a;};
37      int r = intPow(oldBase+1,nextExpand(exp,oldBase))*a;
38          r = r + nextExpand(c,oldBase);
39      return r;
40          }}}
```

Fig. 11. Goodstein program for verification

are thrown. The code of the method consists of a simple while loop computing the Goodstein sequence and breaking out when 0 is reached. Now, a second type of JML contracts comes into play namely, loop contracts. The first part of the loop contract in lines 7–11 requires that the formula m >= 0 & base >= 2 be true before entering the loop and after each iteration of the loop body. This is easy. The crucial part of the loop contract is the decreases clause that gives a quantity in some well-founded ordering that is strictly decreased with every loop iteration. Here in line 10 the function $oGS(n, m)$ provides an ordinal for this purpose. The KeY prover knows about the function oGS, but it is by no means part of standard JML. The escape sequence \dl_oGS triggers the JML parser to pass oGS directly to the underlying logic. The same applies for the functions oHNf and *pow*. In line 19 the JML keyword \result for the first time. It denotes the return value of the method the annotation belong to, in this case the return value of nextExpand.

The definition of $oGS(n, m) : int \times int \to Ord$ lies at the very heart of the termination argument. Informally, $oGS(n, m)$ is computed by replacing in the hereditary base-n expansion of m every occurence of n by ω.

Definition 3. *For $n \geq 2$, $m \geq 0$*

$$oGS(n, m) = \begin{cases} onat(m) & \text{if } m < n \\ (\omega)^{oGS(n,k)} * onat(a) + oGS(n, c) & \text{if } m = n^k * a + c \text{ with} \\ & 1 \leq k \wedge 0 < a < n \wedge c < n^k \end{cases}$$

Examples of oGS for an initial segment of the Goodstein sequence with initial value 4 are displayed in the last column in Example 3. The next lemma lists the crucial properties of oGS, that have also been interactively verified with the KeY prover.

Lemma 1

1. $\forall n, m_1, m_2 (2 \leq n \wedge 0 \leq m_1 < m_2 \to oGS(n, m_1) < oGS(n, m_2))$
2. $\forall n, m (2 \leq n \wedge 0 \leq m \to oGS(n, m) = oGS(n + 1, oHNf(n, m)))$

We conclude the subsection by revealing the plan to prove that oGS decreases. An arbitrary loop iteration starts with $oGS(base, m)$. After normal termination of the loop body, the decreasing function evaluates to $oGS(base+1, \result - 1)$, where \result is the return value of the call to method nextExpand in line 13. The method contract for nextExpand guarantees that $oGS(base, m)$ and $oGS(base + 1, \result)$ are equal (line 20). By Lemma 1(1), *oSG* is strictly monotone in its second argument. Thus, $oGS(base + 1, \result - 1)$ is strictly smaller than $oGS(base + 1, \result)$ in the ordinal ordering. Bingo.

In this argument, we have made use of the method contract for nextExpand, but we also need to establish it. It turns out that for this we need to know that the return value is $oHNf(oldBase, m)$, Line 19 and Lemma 1(2) will come into play at this point.

4   Concluding Remarks

What are the limits of Th_{Ord}? Let ϵ_0 be the first epsilon ordinal, i.e., the least ordinal ϵ with $\omega^\epsilon = \epsilon$. Let $\mathcal{M}_{\epsilon_0}$ be the structure with all ordinals less than ϵ_0 as universe and the standard interpretation of Σ_{Ord}. It can be easily checked that $\mathcal{M}_{\epsilon_0}$ is a model of Th_{Ord}. Closure under *sup* is the crucial part. This shows that $\exists x (\omega^x = x)$ cannot be derived in Th_{Ord}. It can furthermore be shown that for a model $\mathcal{M}$ of Th_{Ord} that does not contain nonstandard natural numbers $\mathcal{M}_{\epsilon_0}$ is a substructure of $\mathcal{M}$. In a way, Th_{Ord} is the analogon of Peano arithmetic for

$\mathcal{M}_{\epsilon_0}$. Precise formulations of these claims and complete proofs can be found in the technical report [19].

If we had only intended to present a machine assisted proof of the mathematical theorem that all Goodstein sequences terminate, this could already have been obtained from Lemma 1. We wanted – however – to make the point that there are simple Java programs whose termination cannot be proved in Peano arithmetic, but Th_{Ord} is strong enough to prove it.

Runable Java code, saved proofs and the version of the KeY system needed can be downloaded or "webstarted" from https://www.key-project.org/papers/ordinal-numbers/.

References

1. Ahrendt, W., Beckert, B., Bubel, R., Hähnle, R., Schmitt, P.H., Ulbrich, M. (eds.): Deductive Software Verification - The KeY Book - From Theory to Practice. LNCS, vol. 10001. Springer, Cham (2016). doi:10.1007/978-3-319-49812-6
2. Bachmann, H.: Transfinite Zahlen. Ergebnisse der Mathematik und ihrer Grenzgebiete, vol. 1, 2nd edn. Springer, Heidelberg (1967). doi:10.1007/978-3-642-88514-3
3. Belinfante, J.G.F.: On computer-assisted proofs in ordinal number theory. J. Autom. Reason. **22**(2), 341–378 (1999)
4. Blanchette, J.C., Fleury, M., Traytel, D.: Nested multisets, hereditary multisets, and syntactic ordinals in isabelle/hol (under submission)
5. Blanchette, J.C., Fleury, M., Traytel, D.: Formalization of nested multisets, hereditary multisets, and syntactic ordinals. Archive of Formal Proofs, November 2016. http://isa-afp.org/entries/Nested_Multisets_Ordinals.shtml. Formal proof development
6. Castéran, P., Contejean, E.: On ordinal notations. https://github.com/coq-contr ibs/cantor
7. Castéran, P., Contejean, E.: On ordinal notations. https://coq.inria.fr/V8.2pl1/ contribs/Cantor.epsilon0.Goodstein.html
8. Grimm, J.: Implementation of three types of ordinals in Coq. Research report RR-8407, CRISAM - Inria Sophia Antipolis (2013)
9. Huffman, B.: Countable ordinals. Archive of Formal Proofs, November 2005. http://afp.sf.net/entries/Ordinal.shtml. Formal proof development
10. Kirby, L., Paris, J.: Accessible independence results for Peano arithmetic. Bull. Lond. Math. Soc. **14**(4), 285–293 (1982)
11. Klaua, D.: Kardinal- und Ordinalzahlen, Teil 1. Wissenschaftliche Taschenbücher: Mathematik, Physik. Vieweg Braunschweig (1974)
12. Klaua, D.: Kardinal- und Ordinalzahlen, Teil 2. Wissenschaftliche Taschenbücher: Mathematik, Physik. Vieweg Braunschweig (1974)
13. Manolios, P., Vroon, D.: Algorithms for ordinal arithmetic. In: Baader, F. (ed.) CADE 2003. LNCS (LNAI), vol. 2741, pp. 243–257. Springer, Heidelberg (2003). doi:10.1007/978-3-540-45085-6_19
14. Manolios, P., Vroon, D.: Ordinal arithmetic: algorithms and mechanization. J. Autom. Reason. **34**(4), 387–423 (2005)
15. Norrish, M., Huffman, B.: Ordinals in HOL: transfinite arithmetic up to (and beyond) ω_1. In: Blazy, S., Paulin-Mohring, C., Pichardie, D. (eds.) ITP 2013. LNCS, vol. 7998, pp. 133–146. Springer, Heidelberg (2013). doi:10.1007/978-3-642-39634-2_12

16. Rathjen, M.: Goodstein revisited. ArXiv e-prints, May 2014
17. Rathjen, M.: Goodstein's theorem revisited. In: Kahle, R., Rathjen, M. (eds.) Gentzen's Centenary, pp. 229–242. Springer, Cham (2015). doi:10.1007/978-3-319-10103-3_9
18. Goodstein, R.L.: On the restricted ordinal theorem. JSL **9**, 33–41 (1944)
19. Schmitt, P.H.: A first-order theory of ordinals. Technical report 6, Department of Informatics, Karlsruhe Institute of Technology (2017)
20. Takeuti, G.: A formalization of the theory of ordinal numbers. J. Symb. Logic **30**, 295–317 (1965)
21. Takeuti, G., Zaring, W.M.: Introduction to Axiomatic Set Theory. Graduate Texts in Mathematics, vol. 1. Springer, New York (1971). doi:10.1007/978-1-4684-9915-5
22. Ulbrich, M.: Dynamic logic for an intermediate language: verification, interaction and refinement. Ph.D. thesis, Karlsruhe Institute of Technology, June 2013
23. Winkler, S., Zankl, H., Middeldorp, A.: Beyond Peano arithmetic–automatically proving termination of the goodstein sequence. In: van Raamsdonk, F. (ed.) 24th International Conference on Rewriting Techniques and Applications (RTA 2013). Leibniz International Proceedings in Informatics (LIPIcs), Dagstuhl, Germany, vol. 21, pp. 335–351. Schloss Dagstuhl–Leibniz-Zentrum fuer Informatik (2013)

Issues in Machine-Checking the Decidability of Implicational Ticket Entailment

Jeremy E. Dawson and Rajeev Goré[(✉)]

Research School of Computer Science,
Australian National University, Canberra, Australia
rajeev.gore@anu.edu.au

Abstract. The decidability of the implicational fragment $T_{\to}$ of the relevance logic of ticket entailment was recently claimed independently by Bimbó and Dunn, and Padovani. We present a mechanised formalisation, in Isabelle/HOL, of the various proof-theoretical results due to Bimbó and Dunn that underpin their claim. We also discuss the issues that stymied our attempt to verify their proof of decidability.

1 Introduction

Sequent calculi are useful in many areas of logic, particularly for decidability arguments. Here, we consider the complications that arise when dealing with a substructural logic where one or more of the rules of associativity, commutativity, weakening and contraction are missing. We focus on the implicational fragment $T_{\to}$ of the substructural logic of "ticket entailment", recently claimed as decidable independently by Bimbó and Dunn [BD13], and by Padovani [Pad11].

As is well-known, pen-and-paper proofs about sequent calculi are notoriously tedious and error-prone [GR12], particularly when the authors elide proofs because "the proof is similar". The proofs of Bimbóand Dunn are intricate, some requiring a triple induction over the "grade", "height" and "contraction degree" of the instance of cut. They state in a footnote that these complicated inductions appear to be necessary [BD12, Footnote 9]. Moreover, they use the "dangerous" phrases described above, so how can we be sure that their proofs are sound?

To check, we first formulate the various sequent and "consecution" calculi from [BD12, BD13]. We then describe how we encoded these calculi into the interactive proof-assistant Isabelle/HOL and how we mechanised the various proof-theoretical results of these various calculi. We then explain the issues that stymied our attempt to verify the proof of their main theorem in Isabelle/HOL.

Previously, we have machine-checked various types of calculi: multiset-based sequent calculi with explicit structural rules [DG10], display calculi [DG02], and (shallow and deep) nested sequent calculi [DCGT14]. Here, we needed two novelties: singletons on the right and (non-display) "consecution" calculi built from

---

J.E. Dawson—Supported by Australian Research Council Discovery Grant DP120101244.

R.A. Schmidt and C. Nalon (Eds.): TABLEAUX 2017, LNAI 10501, pp. 347–363, 2017.
DOI: 10.1007/978-3-319-66902-1_21

"structures" (binary trees) where all internal nodes contain a non-commutative and non-associative binary operator " ; " and where all leaves are formulae.

Notation: we use A, B, C for formulae, use $\Gamma, \Gamma_1, \Gamma_2$ for multisets, use U, V, X, Y, Z for structures, and use $X\{Y\}$ instead of $\mathfrak{A}[\mathfrak{B}]$. We use π and τ for the transformations on derivations, but use δ for derivations instead of Δ.

2   Summary of Various Calculi of Bimbó and Dunn

The formulae of our logics are built from an infinite supply of atomic formulae using the BNF grammar below where p is any atomic formula and $\mathbf{t}$ is a constant:

$$A ::= p \mid \mathbf{t} \mid A \to A$$

The superscript $\mathbf{t}$ determines whether or not the verum constant $\mathbf{t}$ is in the syntax. As usual, we drop parentheses and write $A \to B \to C$ for $A \to (B \to C)$. The various logics are defined in Fig. 1 [BD12].

Name	Axioms	Logic			
		$T_\to$	$T^{\mathbf{t}}_\to$	$R_\to$	$R^{\mathbf{t}}_\to$
(A1)	$A \to A$	✓	✓	✓	✓
(A2)	$(A \to B) \to (C \to A) \to (C \to B)$	✓	✓	✓	✓
(A3)	$(A \to B \to C) \to (B \to A \to C)$			✓	✓
(A4)	$(A \to A \to B) \to (A \to B)$	✓	✓	✓	✓
(A5)	$(A \to B) \to (B \to C) \to (A \to C)$	✓	✓		
Name	Rules of Inference				
(R1)	from $A \to B$ and A, deduce B	✓	✓	✓	✓
(R2)	$\vdash A \; // \; \vdash \mathbf{t} \to A$		✓		✓

Fig. 1. Axiomatisations of various logics

A sequent $\Gamma \vdash C$ consists of a finite, possibly empty, multiset Γ of formulae and a formula C. We prefer Greek letters in keeping with modern usage in sequent calculi. The specific sequent calculi that we deal with are tabled in Fig. 2. The "consecution" calculi of Bimbó and Dunn use structures where: every

	(id)	$(\to\vdash)$	$(\vdash\to)$	$(W\vdash)$	$(\mathbf{t} \vdash)$	$(\vdash \mathbf{t})$	$[\to\vdash]$
$LR_\to$	✓	✓	✓	✓			
$LR^{\mathbf{t}}_\to$	✓	✓	✓	✓	✓	✓	
$[LR_\to]$	✓	✓	✓				✓
$[LR^{\mathbf{t}}_\to]$	✓	✓	✓		✓	✓	✓

Fig. 2. Various sequent rules

formula is a structure, and if X and Y are structures then so is $(X \mathbin{;} Y)$. Note: there is no empty structure [BD12]! A consecution $X \vdash C$ consists of a structure X and a formula C. We write $X \mathbin{;} Y \mathbin{;} Z$ for $((X \mathbin{;} Y) \mathbin{;} Z)$ [BD12].

A structure is thus a binary tree where all internal nodes contain " $;$ " and the leaves contain formulae. Suppose X is such a structure (tree) and let Y be the substructure that appears at some particular node in this tree: written $X\{Y\}$. If we now replace this occurrence of Y by an occurrence of the structure Z, we obtain the structure $X\{Z\}$. In the rules shown in Fig. 3, the premises locate the node at which a particular substructure appears in a larger structure. The conclusion shows the result of replacing the substructure occurrence at that node by some structure occurrence, as just described. We use $X\{Y\}$ instead of the $X[Y]$ used by Bimbó and Dunn since the latter can cause confusion with the use of brackets to capture limited contraction in the $[\to\vdash]$-rule from Fig. 2.

$$LT^{t}_{\to}$$

$$(\text{id;}) \ \frac{}{A \vdash A} \qquad\qquad\qquad (\text{W}\vdash;) \ \frac{U\{X \mathbin{;} Y \mathbin{;} Y\} \vdash C}{U\{X \mathbin{;} Y\} \vdash C}$$

$$(\to\vdash;) \ \frac{V \vdash A \qquad U\{B\} \vdash C}{U\{A \to B \mathbin{;} V\} \vdash C} \qquad (\vdash\to;) \ \frac{U \mathbin{;} A \vdash B}{U \vdash A \to B}$$

$$(\text{B}\vdash;) \ \frac{U\{X \mathbin{;} (Y \mathbin{;} Z)\} \vdash C}{U\{X \mathbin{;} Y \mathbin{;} Z\} \vdash C} \qquad (\text{B}'\vdash;) \ \frac{U\{X \mathbin{;} (Z \mathbin{;} Y)\} \vdash C}{U\{Z \mathbin{;} X \mathbin{;} Y\} \vdash C}$$

$$(\text{KI}_t \vdash;) \ \frac{U\{Y\} \vdash C}{U\{\mathbf{t} \mathbin{;} Y\} \vdash C} \qquad (\text{M}_t \vdash;) \ \frac{U\{\mathbf{t} \mathbin{;} \mathbf{t}\} \vdash C}{U\{\mathbf{t}\} \vdash C}$$

$$LR^{t}_{\to} \ := \ LT^{t}_{\to} \ + \ (\text{C}\vdash;) \ = \ LT^{t}_{\to} \ + \ (\text{CI}\vdash;)$$

$$(\text{C}\vdash;) \ \frac{U\{X \mathbin{;} Z \mathbin{;} Y\} \vdash C}{U\{X \mathbin{;} Y \mathbin{;} Z\} \vdash C} \qquad (\text{CI}\vdash;) \ \frac{U\{Y \mathbin{;} X\} \vdash C}{U\{X \mathbin{;} Y\} \vdash C}$$

$$LT^{\circledt}_{\to} \ := \ LT^{t}_{\to} \ + \ (\text{K}_t \vdash;) \ + \ (\text{T}_t \vdash;)$$

$$(\text{K}_t \vdash;) \ \frac{U\{Y\} \vdash C}{U\{Y \mathbin{;} \mathbf{t}\} \vdash C} \qquad (\text{T}_t \vdash;) \ \frac{U\{Y \mathbin{;} \mathbf{t}\} \vdash C}{U\{\mathbf{t} \mathbin{;} Y\} \vdash C}$$

Fig. 3. Various consecution rules

3   Our Isabelle Mechanisation

Our mechanisation builds on our previous work on mechanising traditional sequent calculi [DG10]. That work is a deep embedding of rules and of the variables in them, which permits explicit substitution functions for the variables in a small finite set of rules: see [DG10] for our understanding of what this means, and for more details. Here, we have a deep embedding of rules but a shallow embedding of variables, which means that where we set out the text of a "rule", Isabelle interprets this as all instances of (the variables in) that rule. We define a rule as a data structure, a pair of a list of premises and a conclusion, and Isabelle provides the infinitely many substitution instances of these rules.

3.1   Formalising Formulae, Sequents and Sequent Rules

We first encode the grammar for recognising formulae as below:

```
datatype formula = BImp formula formula ("_ -> _" [61,61] 60)
                 | T
                 | FV string            (* formula variable *)
                 | PP string            (* primitive proposition *)
```

Here, there are four type constructors BImp, T, FV and PP. The first two encode the implication connective $\rightarrow$ and the verum constant t while the second two encode formula variables such as A and primitive propositions (atomic formulae) such as p and q. The constructor BImp takes two formulae as arguments while FV and PP each take one string argument which is simply the string we want to use for that variable or atomic formula. The code at the end of the first line declares -> as an alternative symbol for BImp. For example, BImp (FV "A") (PP "q") encodes $A \rightarrow q$, but it can also be written as (FV "A") -> (PP "q").

Structures are encoded using a parameter 'f as a type variable:

```
datatype 'f structr = Sf 'f
           | SemiC "'f structr" "'f structr" ("_; _" [20,21] 20)
```

Thus Sf f forms an atomic structure from a formula f, while SemiC s1 s2 forms a binary structure from two substructures. A shorthand notation for SemiC allows us to write ((FV "A" -> FV "B") ; (PP "q")) for $((A \rightarrow B) ; q)$.

A sequent is encoded using two parameters 'l and 'r as type variables:

```
datatype ('l, 'r) sequent =
         Sequent "'l" "'r"               ("((_)/ |- (_))" [6,6] 5)
```

An alternative is to replace the prefix Sequent with an infix |-. So the sequent $A, B \vdash C$ is represented as Sequent {A,B} C or as {A,B} |- C. The HOL expression formula multiset captures the type of formula multisets.

A rule type psc is represented as a pair consisting of a list of premises and a conclusion over some parametric type using the type variable 'a:

```
types 'a psc = "'a list *'a"
```

Using it, we can define the ($\rightarrow\vdash$) rule as below:

```
consts impL :: "(formula multiset, formula) sequent psc set"
inductive "impL"
   intrs I "([alpha |- A,                      mins B beta |- C],
             mins (A -> B) alpha + beta |- C) : impL"
```

Here, we first declare that `impL` accepts only sequents built from an antecedent multiset and a single formula succedent: thus 'a must be `((formula multiset, formula) sequent)`. The function `mins` stands for "multiset insert". The function `+` returns the multiset union of its two arguments, where the number of occurrences of each item is the sum of the number of occurrences in the two multisets. So `mins B alpha + beta` forces `alpha` and `beta` to be of type multiset, and returns the result of inserting one occurrence of B into their multiset-union. The sequents `alpha |- A` and `mins B beta |- C` are separated by a comma and enclosed in `[` and `]` to create a list as the first component of the pair formed using (_ , _). The conclusion `mins B alpha + beta |- C` is the second component of this pair, thus forming a rule. The word `inductive` declares `impL` as the smallest set constructed from such pairs (using all possible values for A, B, C, `alpha` and `beta`), which also explains the final `set` in its type declaration.

We now explain our encoding of the "square bracket" conditions in rule [$\rightarrow\vdash$]:

```
consts sqbr ::"'a =>'a multiset =>'a multiset set"
inductive "sqbr dist fmls"
   intrs I "cms <= mins dist fmls ==>
            set_of (mins dist fmls) = set_of cms ==>
            ALL fml. count fmls fml <= Suc (count cms fml)
                       ==>   cms : sqbr dist fmls"
```

Here, `sqbr` accepts two arguments: `dist` of type 'a and `fmls` of multisets over type 'a. It returns a set of multisets over type 'a. The line beginning `intrs` declares that the conclusion multiset `cms` is a submultiset of the multiset obtained by inserting one occurrence of the distinguished formula `dist` into the multiset `fmls`. The next line declares that, as sets, the objects `cms` and `mins dist fmls` are identical: they differ only in the number of occurrences of some formulae in them, including `dist`. The third line declares that if n is the number of occurrences of any formula `fml` in `fmls` and m is the number of occurrences of `fml` in `cms` then $n \leq m + 1$: in other words, $n - 1 \leq m \leq n$ if `fml` $\neq$ `dist` else $n - 1 \leq m \leq n + 1$ if `fml` = `dist`. The rule [$\rightarrow\vdash$] is then encodes as `sbimpL`:

```
inductive "sbimpL" intrs
   I "cms : sqbr (A -> B) (alpha + beta) ==>
            ([alpha |- A, mins B beta |- C], cms |- C) : sbimpL"
```

Thus premises `alpha |- A` and `mins B beta |- C` and conclusion `cms |- C` must obey the definition of `sbimpL`, where `A -> B` is `dist` and `alpha + beta` is `fmls`, given that `cms` is some possible set in `sqbr (A -> B) (alpha + beta)`.

We define the other rules in a similar way, giving rise to our various calculi. Here is the definition of the calculus $LR_{\rightarrow}$.

Definition 1 (LRi). *The rule instance* `psc` *is in the sequent calculus* `LRi` *if it is an instance of any of the rules* `iid_rls`, `impL`, `impR` *and* `lctr_rls`:

```
inductive "LRi"
intrs
    id    "psc : iid_rls  ==> psc  : LRi"
    impL  "psc : impL      ==> psc  : LRi"
    impR  "psc : impR      ==> psc  : LRi"
    W     "psc : lctr_rls ==> psc  : LRi"
```

Here, `LRi` is the smallest set of instances of premises-conclusion pairs that obeys the four clauses `id`, `impK`, `impR`, and `W`. Each clause checks whether a premises-conclusion pair is an instance of some rule: for example `impL`. If so, then it adds that premises-conclusion pair to the set of instances in `LRi`.

Formalising structures, consecutions and consecution rules is similar, except that our basic types are structures, rather than multisets, built from formulae.

3.2   Derivability Predicates `derrec` and `derl`

We also use some general functions to describe derivability. An inference rule of type `'a psc` is a list `ps` of premises and a conclusion `c`. Then `derl rls` is the set of rules derivable from the rule set `rls` while `derrec rls prems` is the set of sequents derivable using rules `rls` from the set `prems` of premises. The special case `derrec rls {}` when `prems` is the empty set `{}` captures the set of `rls`-derivable end-sequents. We defined these functions using Isabelle's package for inductively defined sets, and a more detailed expository account of these, with many useful lemmas, is given elsewhere [Gor09].

```
    derl     :: "'a psc set =>'a psc set"
    derrec   :: "'a psc set =>'a set =>'a set"
```

3.3   Inductive Multi-cut Admissibility via `gen_step2`

Suppose the conclusions `cl` and `cr` have respective derivations as shown below:

$$\frac{\mathrm{pl}_1 \; \cdots \; \mathrm{pl}_n}{\mathrm{cl}} \rho_l \qquad \frac{\mathrm{pr}_1 \; \cdots \; \mathrm{pr}_m}{\mathrm{cr}} \rho_r$$
$$\overline{}_{?} \; (cut \; ?)$$

The bottom-most rules of the respective derivations are the rules ρ_l and ρ_r with respective premises $\mathrm{psl} = [\mathrm{pl}_1, \cdots, \mathrm{pl}_n]$ and $\mathrm{psr} = [\mathrm{pr}_1, \cdots, \mathrm{pr}_m]$. Since some premises may be identical, the constructs `set psl` and `set psr` return the sets of premises formed from the respective lists. Suppose now that we want to prove an arbitrary property `P` of these derivations, such as (multi)cut-admissibility for a cut-formula `A`. In previous work, we have shown how to generalise cut-admissibility proofs using a predicate called `gen_step2sr` [DG10]. Here we use a slight variant of this principle which we call `gen_step2` as described next.

Definition 2 (gen_step2). *For property P, formula A, a subformula relation sub, two sets of sequents dls and drs, inference rules (psl, cl) and (psr, cr), the property gen_step2 holds iff P A (cl, cr) holds whenever all of the following hold: P A' (dl, dr) holds for all subformulae A' of A and all sequents dl in dls and dr in drs; for each pl ∈ psl, pl ∈ dls and P A (pl, cr) holds; for each pr ∈ psr, pr ∈ drs and P A (cl, pr) holds; cl ∈ dls and cr ∈ drs.*

```
gen_step2 ?P ?A ?sub (dls, drs) ((psl, cl), (psr, cr)) =
    (ALL A'. (A', ?A) : ?sub -->
        (ALL dl:dls. ALL dr:drs. ?P A' (dl, dr))) -->
            (ALL pl:set psl. pl : dls & ?P ?A (pl, cr)) -->
                (ALL pr:set psr. pr : drs & ?P ?A (cl, pr)) -->
                    cl : dls --> cr : drs --> ?P ?A (cl, cr))
```

Given two sequents cl and cr, suppose we want P A cl cr to capture cut-admissibility of a particular cut-formula A. By letting dls and drs be the set of derivable sequents, the definition of gen_step2 captures that we can assume:

(a) cut admissibility holds in respect of a smaller cut-formula A'
(b) cut admissibility holds between the sequent cr on the right and the preceding sequents psl in the derivation on the left
(c) cut admissibility holds between the sequent cl on the left and the preceding sequents psr in the derivation on the right.

The main theorem gen_step2_lem below for proving an arbitrary property P states that if seqa and seqb are derivable, and gen_step2 P holds generally, then P A holds between seqa and seqb. In this theorem, the constructions derrec ?rlsa {} and derrec ?rlsb {} are respectively the set of sequents recursively derivable from the empty set {} of premises using the rule sets rlsa and rlsb, which potentially could be different rule sets, but are both the same in our case.

Theorem 1 (gen_step2_lem). *An arbitrary property P holds of an arbitrary formula B, and a pair of arbitrary sequents seqa and seqb if: B is in the well-founded part of the subformula relation; sequent seqa is rlsa-derivable; sequent seqb is rlsb-derivable; and for all formulae A, and all rlsa-rules (psl, cl) and rlsb-rules (psr, cr), our induction step condition gen_step2 ?P A ?sub (derrec ?rlsa {}, derrec ?rlsb {}) ((psa, ca), (psb, cb)) holds:*

```
[| ?B : wfp ?sub ;
    ?seqa : derrec ?rlsa {} ; ?seqb : derrec ?rlsb {} ;
    ALL A. ALL (psa, ca):?rlsa. ALL (psb, cb):?rlsb.
        gen_step2 ?P A ?sub (derrec ?rlsa {}, derrec ?rlsb {})
            ((psa, ca), (psb, cb)) |] ==> ?P ?B (?seqa, ?seqb)
```

Next we define the general property P to be that the sequent that results from multi-cutting cl and cr on cut-formula A is rls-derivable.

Definition 3 (mcd rls). *The predicate mcd ?rls ?A (?cl, ?cr) means that the conclusion $Xl, Xr \vdash B$ of a multicut-instance is recursively derivable from the empty set of premises using rule set rls if $cl = X_l \vdash A$ and $cr = X_r, A^n \vdash B$, where $n > 0$, are the left and right premises, respectively, of the multicut:*

```
mcd ?rls ?A (?cl, ?cr) = (ALL Xl Xr n B.
     ?cl = (Xl |- ?A) & ?cr = (Xr + times (Suc n) {#?A#} |- B)
                    --> (Xl + Xr |- B) : derrec ?rls {})
```

Multicut admissibility is mca, which requires that cl and cr are derivable.

Definition 4 (mca). *For any rule set* rls, *any formula* A, *and any sequents* cl *and* cr, *the predicate* mca rls A (cl, ?cr) *means: if* cl *and* cr *are* rls-*derivable then* mcd rls A (cl, cr) *holds:*

```
mca ?rls ?A (?cl, ?cr) = (?cl : derrec ?rls {} -->
          ?cr : derrec ?rls {} --> mcd ?rls ?A (?cl, ?cr))
```

Using multicut instead of cut avoids the difficulty caused by the contraction rule.

3.4   Modular Multicut Instances

The file LRica.ML is relevant here. Bimbó and Dunn [BD12] begin with the sequent calculus $LR_\rightarrow$ and its slight extension $LR^t_\rightarrow$. Now when admissibility of cut, or of any other rule, holds of a calculus, it does not necessarily hold in a larger calculus. But each proof-step in cut-admissibility for $LR_\rightarrow$ is mimicked in $LR^t_\rightarrow$, requiring extra steps only for the extra rules contained in $LR^t_\rightarrow$.

From Theorem 1, proving cut-admissibility requires proving gen_step2 (mcd rls) for each possibility of the last rules used to derive the premises of the proposed cut. We now show how to express these results in a way which allows them to be used for any containing logic. We refer to the diagram above Definition 2.

Lemma 1 (gsm_impR_R). *If the rule set* rls *contains* $(\vdash\rightarrow)$, *and the rule* ρ_r *on the right is an instance of the* $(\vdash\rightarrow)$ *rule, then* gen_step2 (mcd rls) *holds:*

```
impR <= ?rls
    ==> gen_step2 (mcd ?rls) ?A ?any (?drsl, derrec ?rls {})
        ((?psl, ?cl), ([mins ?G ?alpha |- ?H], ?alpha |- ?G -> ?H))
```

Notice that it does not matter how the left premise cl is derived, just that (as contained in the definition of gen_step2) cut-admissibility (in the sense of mcd, not mca), holds between it and the premises psr of the final rule ρ_r on the right. The term ?drsl is derrec ?rls { } in this proof: see Definition 2.

The form of the theorem indicates which part of the inductive hypothesis is used: for example, the third argument of gen_step is either ?any or ipsubfml depending on whether or not cut-admissibility for subformulae is needed.

4   Various Machine-Checked Results

The Calculi $LR_\rightarrow$ and $LR^t_\rightarrow$

Definition 5 (LRit). *A rule instance* psc *is in the calculus* LRit $(LR^t_\rightarrow)$ *if it is in the calculus* LRi $(LR_\rightarrow)$ *or is an instance of the rule* $(t \vdash)$ *or* $(\vdash t)$:

```
inductive "LRit"
intrs
   LRi "psc : LRi ==> psc : LRit"
   tL  "psc : tL  ==> psc : LRit"
   tR  "psc : tR  ==> psc : LRit"
```

Theorem 2 (mca_LRi). *The sequent calculus* $LR_\rightarrow$ *enjoys multi-cut admissibility:* mca LRi ?A (?cl, ?cr).

Theorem 3 (mca_LRit). *The calculus* LRit *enjoys multicut-admissibility:*
   mca LRit ?A (?cl, ?cr).

Corollary 1 (Theorem 2.2 of [BD12]). *The single-cut rule is admissible in* $LR_\rightarrow$ *and* $LR^t_\rightarrow$: *if* $\Gamma_1 \vdash A$ *and* $\Gamma_2, A \vdash C$ *are derivable then so is* $\Gamma_1, \Gamma_2 \vdash C$.

The Calculi [$LR_\rightarrow$] **and** [$LR^t_\rightarrow$]. The file LRisbcca.ML is relevant here.

These calculi modify $LR_\rightarrow$ and $LR^t_\rightarrow$ by deleting the contraction rule ($W \vdash$), but modifying the ($\rightarrow\vdash$) rule into a new rule called [$\rightarrow\vdash$] that allows a limited amount of contraction. Bimbó and Dunn [BD12, Theorem 2.4] state that the cut rule is admissible, by a proof similar to that for $LR^t_\rightarrow$ [BD12, Theorem 2.2]. We were unable to prove the result in this way but we were able to prove contraction-admissibility instead using a technique similar to that for cut-admissibility, but simpler, as it is a property of one sequent, not two. Again, there are two versions.

Definition 6 (lcd). *For any rule set* rls, *and any formula A, and any sequent c, the predicate* lcd rls A c *means: for all multisets X and all formulae B, if c is* $X, A, A \vdash B$ *then the sequent* $X, A \vdash B$ *is* rls-*derivable.*

```
lcd ?rls ?A ?c == ALL X B. ?c =
(X + {#?A#} + {#?A#} |- B) --> (X + {#?A#} |- B) : derrec ?rls {}
```

Definition 7 (lca). *For any rule set* rls, *and any formula A, and any sequent c, the predicate* lca rls A c *means: for all multisets X and all formulae B, if c is* rls-*derivable then c enjoys* lcd rls A c:

```
lca ?rls ?A ?c == ?c : derrec ?rls {} --> lcd ?rls ?A ?c
```

Definition 8 (LRisb and LRitsb). *The rules of the sequent calculus* LRisb *(resp.* LRitsb*) are those of* LRi, *Definition 1 (resp.* LRit, *Definition 5) omitting the* (($W\vdash$)) *rule, and changing the* ($\rightarrow\vdash$) *rule to the rule* [$\rightarrow\vdash$] *(see Fig. 2)*

```
inductive "LRisb"
intrs id      "psc : iid_rls ==> psc : LRisb"
      sbimpL "psc : sbimpL  ==> psc : LRisb"
      impR   "psc : impR    ==> psc : LRisb"


inductive "LRitsb"
intrs LRisb "psc : LRisb ==> psc : LRitsb"
      tL    "psc : tL    ==> psc : LRitsb"
      tR    "psc : tR    ==> psc : LRitsb"
```

Theorem 4 (lca_LRisb and lca_LRitsb). *The contraction rule is admissible in the calculi LRisb and LRitsb:* lca LRisb ?A ?c *and* lca LRitsb ?A ?c.

Having proved contraction admissibility for LRisb and LRitsb, we prove their equivalence to LRi and LRit respectively as follows.

Theorem 5 (LRi_LRisb, LRisb_LRi, LRisb_eqv_LRi). *Each rule from LRi/ LRisb is admissible/derivable in LRisb/LRi. So LRi and LRisb are equivalent.*

Theorem 6 (LRit_LRitsb, LRitsb_LRit). *Each rule from LRit/LRitsb is admissible/derivable in LRitsb/LRit, so LRit and LRitsb are equivalent.*

These give part of [BD12, Lemma 2.5] and give [BD12, Lemma 2.4].

Theorem 7 (mca_LRisb and mca_LRitsb). *Both LRisb and LRitsb enjoy multicut-admissibility:* mca LRisb ?A (?cl, ?cr) *and* mca LRitsb ?A (?cl, ?cr).

Corollary 2 (Kripke 1959). *The single-cut rule is admissible in* $[LR_{\rightarrow}]$ *and* $[LR^t_{\rightarrow}]$: *if* $\Gamma_1 \vdash A$ *and* $\Gamma_2, A \vdash C$ *are derivable then so is* $\Gamma_1, \Gamma_2 \vdash C$.

The Calculi $LT_{\rightarrow}$ **and** $LT^{\oplus}_{\rightarrow}$. The file LTitca.ML is relevant here. We now need to encode structures with a hole and encode consecutions and rules built from consecutions where the action happens at the hole. We have explained how to achieve this for nested sequent calculi elsewhere [DCGT14] and so the sequel is rather terse. The main point here is that all the action happens in the antecedent and so we concentrate on the relation holding between such contexts.

Definition 9 (sctxt). *If (a, b)* $\in$ *r then (a, b)* $\in$ *sctxt r. Every (a, b)* $\in$ *sctxt r can be extended by prefixing/postfixing with an arbitrary context C.*

```
consts sctxt :: "'f structr relation trf"
(* closure of rule structure relation under context *)
inductive "sctxt r" intrs
    scid "(a, b): r ==> (a, b) : sctxt r"
    scL  "(a, b): sctxt r ==> (C;a, C;b) : sctxt r"
    scR  "(a, b): sctxt r ==> (a;C, b;C) : sctxt r"
```

A structure with a hole (a context) is turned into a consecution by simply adding a turnstile and a singleton on the right as follows. The relation between the antecedents is also retained.

Definition 10 (lctxt). *The set lctxt r is the smallest set of rule instances obtained by extending every pair (As, Bs)* $\in$ *sctxt r into the rule instance ([As |- E], Bs |- E) with premise As |- E and conclusion Bs |- E.*

```
consts lctxt ::
    "'f structr relation => ('f structr,'f) sequent psc set"
inductive "lctxt r" intrs
    I "(As, Bs) : sctxt r ==> ([As |- E], Bs |- E) : lctxt r"
```

We define LTit_lc as the pairs (X, Y) giving us rules of the form
at right. Then lctxt LTit_lc is the set of such deep structural
rules in LTit. First, LTit_lcsub are the pairs (X, Y) which form
rules of the form at right where X and Y consist only of substitutable structure variables (i.e. unlike the rules involving t).

$$\frac{U\{X\} \vdash C}{U\{Y\} \vdash C}$$

Definition 11. *LTit_lcsub is the smallest set of left-context action (pairs of
structural transformations) instances of the (combinator) permutations below.*

```
inductive "LTit_lcsub" (* fully substitutable rules *)
intrs B   "psc : lcB ==> psc : LTit_lcsub"
      Bd  "psc : lcBd ==> psc : LTit_lcsub"
      W   "psc : lcW ==> psc : LTit_lcsub"
```

Here, we define lcB, lcBd and lcW to give us the rules (B⊢;), (B′ ⊢;) and (W⊢;).
Next, we define the separate relation lcC to give $(C \vdash;)$ similarly:

```
inductive "lcB"  intrs I "(Bs; (Cs; Ds), Bs; Cs; Ds) : lcB"
inductive "lcBd" intrs I "(Bs; (Cs; Ds), Cs; Bs; Ds) : lcBd"
inductive "lcW"  intrs I "(Bs; Cs; Cs, Bs; Cs)        : lcW"
inductive "lcC"  intrs I "(Bs; Cs; Ds, Bs; Ds; Cs)    : lcC"
```

Here, we elide parentheses by associating to the left and writing (Bs; (Cs;
Ds), Bs; Cs; Ds) instead of ((Bs; (Cs; Ds)), (Bs; Cs; Ds)). So we now
have the permutations that correspond to the actions that happen at the hole.
We now need to turn these actions into rules formed from consecutions.

Definition 12 (LTit_lc). *LTit_lc is the smallest set of rule instances psc
formed by extending hole permutation pairs into consecution rules*

```
inductive "LTit_lc"
   intrs sub "psc : LTit_lcsub ==> psc : LTit_lc"
         KIt "psc : KIt T ==> psc : LTit_lc"
         Mt  "(Sf T; Sf T, Sf T) : LTit_lc"
inductive "KIt fml" intrs I "(Bs, Sf fml; Bs) : KIt fml"
```

Here, the construction Sf T casts the formula T into an atomic structure.
    We now need to turn these pairs into proper rules built out of consecutions
and also add the usual logical rules.

Definition 13 (LTit). *LTit is the smallest set of rule instances psc which are
instances of the logical rules lcid, lcimpR, lcimpL, and of the structural rules
corresponding to the combinator permutations B, Bd and W:*

```
inductive "LTit" intrs
     id      "psc : lcid ==> psc : LTit"
     impR    "psc : lcimpR ==> psc : LTit"
     impL    "psc : lcimpL ==> psc : LTit"
     lcrules "psc : lctxt LTit_lc ==> psc : LTit"
```

Here, we have omitted the definitions of the consecution rules lcid, lcimpR, lcimpL. Similar definitions to LTit allows us to compose the rule sets LRitsc, and LTitc (omitted) corresponding to the consecution calculi $LR^t_\rightarrow$ and $LT^{\textcircled{t}}_\rightarrow$.

4.1 A Structural Analogue of Multicut

Since these calculi contain a contraction rule we prefer to show admissibility of multicut rather than cut. Following Dunn [Dun73], given premise sequents $X \vdash A$ and $Y \vdash B$, we consider the "multicut" that replaces each one of n (rather than all) occurrences of A in Y by an X, to give Z (say):

$$(\text{multicut}) \quad \frac{X \vdash A \qquad Y\{A\}\{A\}\cdots\{A\} \vdash B}{Y\{X\}\{X\}\cdots\{X\} \vdash B}$$

The relationship between Y and Z described above, is encoded as strrep.

Definition 14 (strrep)

```
consts strrep ::"'f structr pair set =>'f structr pair set"
inductive "strrep S" intrs
    same "(s, s) : strrep S"
    repl "p : S ==> p : strrep S"
    sc   "(u, v) : strrep S ==>
            (x, y) : strrep S ==> (u; x, v; y) : strrep S"
```

This introduces the issue that where $P\{A\}$ and $C\{A\}$ are (say) the antecedents of the premise and conclusion of a rule, and $(P\{A\}, C\{A\}) \in$ sctxt r for a relation (set of pairs) r, e.g. r = (B;(C;D), B;C;D) (for the $(B \vdash;)$ rule), and multicutting with $X \vdash A$ would give $C\{X\}$, i.e. $(C\{A\}, C\{X\}) \in$ strrep $\{(\text{Sf } A, X)\}$, then we need to "close the box" with $P\{X\}$, where $(P\{A\}, P\{X\}) \in$ strrep $\{(\text{Sf } A, X)\}$ and $(P\{X\}, C\{X\}) \in$ sctxt r. The easiest instance is where r is a set of pairs which are entirely substitutable: for example the pair {(B;(C;D), B;C;D)} for $(B \vdash;)$, rather than the pair {A, (t;A)} for $(KI_t \vdash;)$.

Lemma 2 (strrep_sctxt_lcsub)

```
[| (?PA, ?CA) : sctxt LTit_lcsub ;
   (?CA, ?CX) : strrep {(Sf ?A, ?X)} |] ==>
                        EX PX. (?PA, PX) : strrep {(Sf ?A, ?X)}
                        & (PX, ?CX) : sctxt LTit_lcsub
```

Here LTit_lcsub from Definition 13 is the set of pairs of the form found in the rules $(B \vdash;), (B' \vdash;), (W \vdash;)$ from $LT^t_\rightarrow$.

For the verum constant T, the corresponding result is (for example):

Lemma 3 (strrep_sctxt_KIt)

```
[| (?PA, ?CA) : sctxt (KIt T); ?A ~= T;
        (?CA, ?CX) : strrep {(Sf ?A, ?X)} |] ==> EX PX.
   (?PA, PX) : strrep {(Sf ?A, ?X)} & (PX, ?CX) : sctxt (KIt T)
```

So the multicut-admissibility property we prove inductively is mclcd.

Definition 15 (mclcd). *The predicate mclcd means: if* cl $= Xl \vdash A$ *and* cr $=$ $Xr \vdash B$ *and* Y *is obtained from* Xr *by replacing some instances of* A *by* Xl, *then* $Y \vdash B$ *is rls-derivable.*

```
mclcd ?rls ?A (?cl, ?cr) =
  (ALL Xl Xr Y B. ?cl = (Xl |- ?A) --> ?cr = (Xr |- B) -->
  (Xr, Y) : strrep {(Sf ?A, Xl)} --> (Y |- B) : derrec ?rls {})
```

The version conditional on cl and cr being derivable is

Definition 16 (mclca). *The predicate mclca says that if* cl $= Xl \vdash A$ *and* cr $= Xr \vdash B$ *are rls-derivable, and* Y *is obtained from* Xr *by replacing some instances of* A *by* Xl, *then* $Y \vdash B$ *is rls-derivable.*

```
mclca ?rls ?A (?cl, ?cr) = (?cl : derrec ?rls {} -->
                 ?cr : derrec ?rls {} --> mclcd ?rls ?A (?cl, ?cr))
```

4.2   Results for Consecution Calculi

The next result is an example of many results (omitted) expressed to apply to a rule set which is a superset of a given set. Thus it and the omitted results are useful for all of the consecution calculi $LT^t_{\rightarrow}, LR^t_{\rightarrow}$ and $LT^{\circledt}_{\rightarrow}$. In fact we combined all these results to get

Lemma 4 (gsmcl_LTit). *If* rls *contains LTit and rules* (psl, cl) *and* (psr, cr) *are from LTit then* gen_step2 (mclcd rls) *holds:*

```
[| LTit <= ?rls ; (?psl, ?cl) : LTit ; (?psr, ?cr) : LTit |]
  ==> gen_step2 (mclcd ?rls) ?A ipsubfml
      (derrec ?rls {}, derrec ?rls {}) ((?psl, ?cl), ?psr, ?cr)
```

Theorem 8 (mclca_LTit). *The consecution calculus* $LT^t_{\rightarrow}$ *enjoys multi-cut admissibility: if the consecution* $V \vdash A$ *and the consecution* $U\{A\}\{A\} \cdots \{A\} \vdash$ C *are derivable then the consecution* $U\{V\}\{V\} \cdots \{V\} \vdash C$ *is derivable.* mclca LTit ?A (?cl, ?cr).

We obtain the single-cut admissibility result for $LT^t_{\rightarrow}$ which is only asserted by Bimbó and Dunn [BD12, line 10, p. 500] since it is proved elsewhere.

Corollary 3 (Bimbó and Dunn line 10, p. 500 [BD12]). *The single-cut rule is admissible in* $LT^t_{\rightarrow}$: *if the consecutions* $V \vdash A$ *and* $U\{A\} \vdash C$ *are derivable then so is the consecution* $U\{V\} \vdash C$.

Extending the proof to the other calculi was quite easy since we only needed to deal with the cases involving a few additional rules on either side.

Theorem 9 (mclca_LTitc and mclca_LRitsc). *The consecution calculi* $LT^{\circledt}_{\rightarrow}$ *and* $LR^t_{\rightarrow}$ *enjoy multi-cut admissibility: if the consecution* $V \vdash A$ *and consecution* $U\{A\}\{A\} \cdots \{A\} \vdash C$ *are derivable then so is* $U\{V\}\{V\} \cdots \{V\} \vdash C$.

```
mclca LTitc ?A (?cl, ?cr)
mclca LRitsc ?A (?cl, ?cr)
```

Corollary 4 (Bimbó and Dunn Theorem 3.2 and Theorem 5.2 [BD12]).
*The single-cut rule is admissible in $LR^t_\to$, and $LT^{\circledcirc}_\to$: if the consecutions $V \vdash A$
and $U\{A\} \vdash C$ are derivable then so is the consecution $U\{V\} \vdash C$.*

5   A Proof Plan of the Crucial Lemma 11

A putative constructive proof plan of [BD13, Lemma 11] is in Fig. 4.

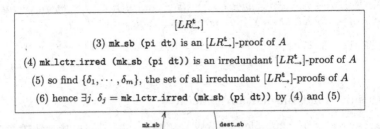

$[LR^t_\to]$

(3) `mk_sb (pi dt)` is an $[LR^t_\to]$-proof of A

(4) `mk_lctr_irred (mk_sb (pi dt))` is an irredundant $[LR^t_\to]$-proof of A

(5) so find $\{\delta_1, \cdots, \delta_m\}$, the set of all irredundant $[LR^t_\to]$-proofs of A

(6) hence $\exists j. \delta_j = $ `mk_lctr_irred (mk_sb (pi dt))` by (4) and (5)

mk_sb   dest_sb

$LR^t_\to$ and $(\vdash \mathbf{t})$-free $LR^t_\to$

(2) `pi dt` is an $LR^t_\to$-proof of A

dest_sb turns $\delta_1, \cdots, \delta_j, \cdots, \delta_m$ into $LR^t_\to$-proofs $\delta'_1, \cdots, \delta'_j, \cdots, \delta'_m$ of A

mk_tRfree turns $\delta'_1, \cdots, \delta'_j, \cdots, \delta'_m$ into $(\vdash \mathbf{t})$-free $LR^t_\to$-proofs $\delta''_1, \cdots, \delta''_j, \cdots, \delta''_m$ of A

(7) so `dest_sb (mk_lctr_irred (mk_sb (pi dt)))` is an $LR^t_\to$-proof of A

(8) `mk_tRfree (dest_sb (mk_lctr_irred (mk_sb (pi dt))))` is a $(\vdash \mathbf{t})$-free $LR^t_\to$-proof of A

(9) $\exists j. \delta''_j = $ `mk_tRfree (dest_sb (mk_lctr_irred (mk_sb (pi dt))))`

π τ

$LT^t_\to \subset LT^{\circledcirc}_\to$

(1) `dt` is one of an infinite number of $LT^t_\to$-proofs of A

$\tau(\delta''_j) \subseteq \bigcup_{i=1}^m \tau(\delta''_i)$ by definition

(10) hence $\tau(\delta''_j) \subseteq$ `tau (mk_tRfree (dest_sb (mk_lctr_irred (mk_sb (pi dt)))))`

(11) hence $\exists$ `dtt` $\in$ `tau (mk_tRfree (dest_sb (mk_lctr_irred (mk_sb (pi dt)))))`

(12) but we cannot see why `dtt` must be an $LT^t_\to$-proof of A

Fig. 4. Proof plan

Assertion 1. *If there is an $LT^t_\to$-proof dt of A then there exists an $[LR^t_\to]$-proof
dtsb of A and there exists an $LT^t_\to$-proof dtt of A.*

Proof Plan: We start with (1) some given $LT^t_\to$-proof `dt` of A. Applying π gives
us (2) there is some $LR^t_\to$-proof `pi dt` of A. By completeness of $[LR^t_\to]$, (3) there

is an $[LR^t_\to]$-proof mk_sb (pi dt) of A. Then, (4) there must be an irredundant such $[LR^t_\to]$-proof mk_lctr_irred (mk_sb (pi dt)) of A. Then (7) the function dest_sb transforms an $[LR^t_\to]$-proof into an $LR^t_\to$-proof by replacing the rule $[\to\vdash]$ with an instance of the $(\to\vdash)$ rule followed by the appropriate number of explicit applications of the contraction rule $(W \vdash)$ thereby "destroying the square brackets". Then (8) the function mk_tRfree transforms the resulting $LR^t_\to$-proof into a $(\vdash t)$-free $LR^t_\to$-proof. Finally, tau transforms this $(\vdash t)$-free $LR^t_\to$-proof into possibly many $LT^\circledcirc_\to$ proofs, hence (11) there must exist some $LT^\circledcirc_\to$-proof dtt of A. But (12) why should (any such) dtt be an $LT^t_\to$-proof of A?

So, how to complete our proof plan? The first point is that the existence of dt must lead to a dtt. There are two plausible approaches:

(a) dtt is equal, similar or somehow related to dt
(b) τ must produce enough proofs to guarantee that if there is an $LT^t_\to$-proof for A, then τ will give us one. To guarantee this, we may have to apply τ to all $[LR^t_\to]$-proofs of A (after applying dest_sb and mk_tRfree to them).

The discussion by Bimbó and Dunn regarding π mentioned in the last two lines of the proof of their Lemma 11 seems only relevant to (a) above. The only relevance of π can be for an argument along the lines shown in Fig. 4.

However, the proof of Lemma 11 of Bimbó and Dunn does not start with a given $LT^t_\to$-proof dt of A, but appears to follow option (b) outlined above. That is, it uses their Lemma 5 to deduce that A being a theorem of $T^t_\to$ implies the existence of some $[LR^t_\to]$-proof of A. So it starts by (5) finding **all** irredundant $[LR^t_\to]$-proofs of A, transforming them into $LR^t_\to$-proofs by simply making contractions explicit, then transforming them to remove all applications of the $(\vdash t)$ rule, and turning the resulting proofs into $LT^\circledcirc_\to$-proofs by applying τ. Their argument that one of these must be an $LT^t_\to$-proof requires considering "all permutations" of the structures involved. But this whole procedure starts with only those proofs which have the contractions allowed by the "square bracket" calculi. Moreover, the decision procedure starts at point (5), but the proof of its completeness starts at point (1), at the hypothesis that A is a theorem of $T^t_\to$.

Our proof plan and their proof align if at (5) we find all irredundant $[LR^t_\to]$-proofs of A, and then (6) one of them, say δ_j, must be the one we are focusing on. So (8) the result of applying both dest_sb and mk_tRfree to δ_j is a $(\vdash t)$-free $LR^t_\to$-proof δ'_j of A and (9) δ''_j must be one of the proofs obtained by doing these transformations to all of the proofs from (5). Finally, τ transforms any one of these $(\vdash t)$-free $LR^t_\to$-proofs into possibly many proofs and hence dtt is in $\tau(\delta''_j)$. But again, (12), we cannot see why this final proof has to be an $LT^t_\to$-proof.

Indeed (12), and our proof plan would hold if we could prove that dt = dtt.

Assertion 2 (tau_irr_sb_pi). *If dt is an $LT^t_\to$-proof of A then*
dt $\in$ tau (mk_tRfree (dest_sb (mk_lctr_irred (mk_sb (pi dt))))).

We cannot see why this assertion should hold. Allowing that it would be true that dt is in $\tau(\pi(\text{dt}))$, we should consider the differences between the proofs $\pi(\mathtt{dt})$ and `mk_tRfree` `(dest_sb` `(mk_lctr_irred` `(mk_sb` `(pi` `dt))))`. Now `mk_lctr_irred` excises parts of a proof and uses height-preserving contraction admissibility, so it (probably) simplifies a proof. Also, `mk_tRfree` makes changes which are probably insignificant. But the `dest_sb` `(... mk_sb ...)` combination moves contractions around, relative to occurrences of $(\rightarrow\vdash)$, since `mk_sb` must remove contractions that are not immediately below $(\rightarrow\vdash)$, and then make up for their removal by inserting appropriate contractions immediately below the $(\rightarrow\vdash)$ rules. But π alone does not do such movements by [BD13, Lemma 6].

6   Conclusions

We have machine-checked all of the proof-theoretic claims made by Bimbó and Dunn [BD12,BD13] including the three lemmata which are at the heart of the decidability argument [BD13, Lemmata 8, 9, 10]. However, we were not able to prove them in that order as our proof of Lemma 9 depends upon our proof of Lemma 10. Moreover, we are yet to be convinced of the correctness of Lemma 11 which ensures that no $LT_\rightarrow^t$ derivation is lost in the transformations of proofs which correspond to $[LR_\rightarrow^t]$-proofs: see Fig. 4. Our files are at http://users.cecs.anu.edu.au/~jeremy/isabelle/2005/bimbo-dunn/ and the URL address http://users.cecs.anu.edu.au/~jeremy/isabelle/2005/ bimbo-dunn/ticket-instructions.html contains instructions for running them.

Acknowledgements. We are grateful to Katalin Bimbó, Michael Dunn and John Slaney for their helpful comments. All remaining errors are our own.

References

[BD12]   Bimbó, K., Dunn, J.M.: New consecution calculi for $R_\rightarrow^t$. Notre Dame J. Formal Logic **53**(4), 491–509 (2012)

[BD13]   Bimbó, K., Dunn, J.M.: On the decidability of implicational ticket entailment. J. Symb. Logic **78**(1), 214–236 (2013)

[DCGT14] Dawson, J.E., Clouston, R., Goré, R., Tiu, A.: From display calculi to deep nested sequent calculi: formalised for full intuitionistic linear logic. In: Diaz, J., Lanese, I., Sangiorgi, D. (eds.) TCS 2014. LNCS, vol. 8705, pp. 250–264. Springer, Heidelberg (2014). doi:10.1007/978-3-662-44602-7_20

[DG02]   Dawson, J.E., Goré, R.: Formalised cut admissibility for display logic. In: Carreño, V.A., Muñoz, C.A., Tahar, S. (eds.) TPHOLs 2002. LNCS, vol. 2410, pp. 131–147. Springer, Heidelberg (2002). doi:10.1007/ 3-540-45685-6_10

[DG10]   Dawson, J.E., Goré, R.: Generic methods for formalising sequent calculi applied to provability logic. In: Fermüller, C.G., Voronkov, A. (eds.) LPAR 2010. LNCS, vol. 6397, pp. 263–277. Springer, Heidelberg (2010). doi:10. 1007/978-3-642-16242-8_19

[Dun73]   Dunn, J.M.: (abstract only) A 'Gentzen system' for positive relevant implication. J. Symb. Logic **38**, 356–357 (1973)

[Gor09] Goré, R.: Machine checking proof theory: an application of logic to logic. In: Ramanujam, R., Sarukkai, S. (eds.) ICLA 2009. LNCS, vol. 5378, pp. 23–35. Springer, Heidelberg (2008). doi:10.1007/978-3-540-92701-3_2

[GR12] Goré, R., Ramanayake, R.: Valentini's cut-elimination for provability logic resolved. Rew. Symb. Logic **5**(2), 212–238 (2012)

[Pad11] Padovani, V.: Ticket entailment is decidable. CoRR, abs/1106.1875 (2011)

Parameterized Provability in Equational Logic

Mateus de Oliveira Oliveira[(✉)]

University of Bergen, Postboks 7803, 5020 Bergen, Norway
mateus.oliveira@uib.no

Abstract. In this work we study the validity problem in equational logic from the perspective of parameterized complexity theory. We introduce a variant of equational logic in which sentences are pairs of the form $(t_1 = t_2, \omega)$, where $t_1 = t_2$ is an equation, and ω is an arbitrary ordering of the positions corresponding to subterms of t_1 and t_2. We call such pairs *ordered equations*. With each ordered equation, one may naturally associate a notion of width, and with each proof of validity of an ordered equation, one may naturally associate a notion of depth. We define the width of such a proof as the maximum width of an ordered equation occurring in it. Finally, we introduce a parameter b that restricts the way in which variables are substituted for terms. We say that a proof is b-bounded if all substitutions used in it satisfy such restriction.

Our main result states that the problem of determining whether an ordered equation $(t_1 = t_2, \omega)$ has a b-bounded proof of depth d and width c, from a set of axioms E, can be solved in time $f(E, d, c, b) \cdot |t_1 = t_2|$. In other words, this task is fixed parameter linear with respect to the depth, width and bound of the proof. Subsequently, we show that given a classical equation $t_1 = t_2$, one may determine whether there exists an ordering ω such that $(t_1 = t_2, \omega)$ has a b-bounded proof, of depth d and width c, in time $f(E, d, c, b) \cdot |t_1 = t_2|^{O(c)}$. In other words this task is fixed parameter tractable with respect to the depth and bound of the proof, and is in polynomial time for constant values of width. This second result is particularly interesting because the ordering ω is not given a priori, and thus, we are indeed parameterizing the provability of equations in classical equational logic. In view of the expressiveness of equational logic, our results give new fixed parameter tractable algorithms for a whole spectrum of problems, such as polynomial identity testing, program verification, automated theorem proving and the validity problem in undecidable equational theories.

1 Introduction

Equational logic is a fragment of first order logic in which all variables are implicitly universally quantified and in which the only relation is equality between terms. Besides playing a central role in the meta-mathematics of algebra [16], equational logic finds several applications in the verification of programs [8,9,15,19], in the specification of abstract data types [6], in automated theorem proving [3] and in proof complexity [4,11]. The success of most of these

© Springer International Publishing AG 2017
R.A. Schmidt and C. Nalon (Eds.): TABLEAUX 2017, LNAI 10501, pp. 364–380, 2017.
DOI: 10.1007/978-3-319-66902-1_22

applications relies on a tight correspondence between equational logic and term rewriting systems. Indeed, with each set of equations E, one can associate a term rewriting system $R(E)$ such that an equation $t_1 = t_2$ is valid in the equational theory induced by E, if and only if there exists a term u to which both t_1 and t_2 can be reduced by the application of rewriting rules from $R(E)$. In many cases of theoretical and practical relevance, completion techniques such as the Knuth-Bendix method [12] or unfailing completion [2] are able to produce rewriting systems that are both Noetherian (terminating) and Church-Rosser (confluent). In these systems each term t has a unique normal form $n(t)$ that is guaranteed to be found in a finite amount of time. Therefore determining whether an equation $t_1 = t_2$ follows from a set of axioms E amounts to verifying if the normal forms $n(s)$ and $n(t)$ are syntactically identical.

Completion techniques have witnessed a success in equational theorem proving [1,2,17], where for instance the EQP theorem prover was able to positively settle Robbin's conjecture [14,18], a problem in boolean algebra that had been open for several decades. Another successful example is the Waldmeister theorem prover which has won for several consecutive years the first place in equational theorem proving competitions [10]. However, completion techniques also have some drawbacks. The main drawback is that there exist very simple finitely presented algebraic structures for which the validity problem is undecidable [13]. Additionally, there exist even examples of finitely generated universal algebras, such as the free modular lattice on five generators [7], which have undecidable word problems.

In this work we study the validity problem in equational logic from the perspective of parameterized complexity theory. Our approach differs substantially from techniques based in term rewriting, since our parameterization can be used to tackle the validity problem in both decidable and undecidable theories, and irrespectively of whether these theories can be associated with confluent and terminating rewriting systems. On the other hand, our approach differs substantially from exhaustive search since we do not impose any upper bound on the size of the largest equation occurring in an equational logic proof. In view of the wide applicability of equational logic, our results yield new parameterized algorithms for a series of hard problems that can be reduced to the validity problem in equational theories, such as, polynomial identity testing, program verification, automatic theorem proving, etc.

1.1 Main Results

Our point of departure is the introduction of *ordered equational logic*, a syntactic variant of classical equational logic. Instead of equations of the form $t_1 = t_2$, sentences in ordered equational logic are *ordered equations* of the form $(t_1 = t_2, \omega)$, where ω is an ordering of set of positions indexing subterms of t_1 and of t_2. Despite such a seemingly technical definition, an ordered equation can be represented just like a classical equation, but with a number above the leading symbol of each of its subterms, as exemplified in Eq. 1. The number above the leading symbol of each subterm is the order of the position corresponding to that subterm.

$$\overset{6}{f}\,(\overset{5}{x},\overset{1}{g}\,(\overset{8}{y},\overset{2}{x}))=\overset{4}{h}\,(\overset{7}{x},\overset{3}{y}) \tag{1}$$

We will parameterize the provability of an ordered equation $(t_1 = t_2, \omega)$ with respect to three measures: *depth*, *width*, and *bound* of a proof. The first parameter, the *depth*, is simply the height of a proof tree for $(t_1 = t_2, \omega)$. The second parameter, the *width*, is defined with basis on a graph theoretic representation of ordered equations. With each ordered equation $(t_1 = t_2, \omega)$ one may naturally associate a digraph $G(t_1 = t_2, \omega)$ by taking the union of the tree representations of t_1 and t_2 and by adding special edges tagged as "variable edges" connecting vertices corresponding to the same variable. The width of an equation $(t_1 = t_2, \omega)$ is the cut-width of $G(t_1 = t_2, \omega)$ with respect to the ordering induced by ω on its vertices. A proof of an ordered equation has width c if all ordered equations used in the proof have width at most c. Finally, the third parameter, the *bound*, is used to restrict the way in which the reflexive axiom, and the substitution rules are applied. We say that a proof is b-bounded if all applications of the reflexivity and substitution rules are b-bounded. Let $|t_1 = t_2|$ denote the total number of positions in t_1 and t_2. If E is a finite set of equations then we write $E_d^{c,b} \vdash (t_1 = t_2, \omega)$ to indicate that the ordered equation $(t_1 = t_2, \omega)$ can be inferred from E via a b-bounded proof of depth d and width c. Our main result is formally stated in Theorem 1.1 below.

Theorem 1.1. *Let E be a finite set of equations and let $d, c, b \in \mathbb{N}$. There is a function $f(E, d, c, b)$ such that for each ordered equation $(t_1 = t_2, \omega)$, one may determine in time $f(E, d, c, b) \cdot |t_1 = t_2|$ whether $E_d^{c,b} \vdash (t_1 = t_2, \omega)$.*

In other words, Theorem 1.1 says that the problem of determining whether an ordered equation has a b-bounded proof of depth d and width c, is fixed parameter linear with respect to all three parameters. Next, in Theorem 1.2 we will state a variant of Theorem 1.1 which can be used to address the validity of equations in classical equational logic. Intuitively, this variant addresses the problem of automatically determining the existence of an ordering ω such that $E_d^{c,b} \vdash (t_1 = t_2, \omega)$.

Theorem 1.2. *Let E be a finite set of equations and $d, c, b \in \mathbb{N}$. There is a function $f(E, d, c, b)$ such that for each classical equation $t_1 = t_2$, one may determine in time $f(E, d, c, b) \cdot |t_1 = t_2|^{O(c)}$ whether there exists an ordering ω such that $E_d^{c,b} \vdash (t_1 = t_2, \omega)$.*

In other words, for constant values of c, one can determine in polynomial time whether a classical equation $t_1 = t_2$ admits an ordering ω such that the ordered equation $(t_1 = t_2, \omega)$ has a b-bounded proof of depth d and width c. The following proposition says that Theorem 1.2 provides a true parameterization for the provability in classical equational logic, in the sense that such an ordering ω is always guaranteed to exist provided the parameters c and b are sufficiently large.

Proposition 1.3. *Let E be a finite set of equations. An equation $t_1 = t_2$ is derivable from E in depth d in classical equational logic if and only if there exists an ordering ω of $t_1 = t_2$ and $c, b \in \mathbb{N}$ such that $E_d^{c,b} \vdash (t_1 = t_2, \omega)$.*

2 Ordered Equational Logic

In this section we will introduce *ordered equational logic*, a variant of equational logic in which sentences are ordered equations. For clarity we will start by defining classical equational logic, and then lift it to its ordered version by making minor adaptations.

2.1 Classical Equational Logic

Let Φ be an alphabet of function symbols and constant symbols and let $\mathbb{X}$ be a set of variables with $\Phi \cap \mathbb{X} = \emptyset$. With each function symbol $f \in \Phi$ we associate an arity $\mathfrak{a}(f)$, which intuitively indicates the number of input arguments of f. Constant symbols may be regarded as function symbols of arity 0. The set $Ter(\Phi, \mathbb{X})$ of *terms* over $\Phi \cup \mathbb{X}$ is inductively defined as follows: if x is a variable in $\mathbb{X}$ then x is a term in $Ter(\Phi, \mathbb{X})$, if a is a constant symbol in Φ then a is a term in $Ter(\Phi, \mathbb{X})$ and finally if $f \in \Phi$ is a function symbol of arity $\mathfrak{a}(f) \geq 1$ and $t_1, \ldots, t_{\mathfrak{a}(f)}$ are terms in $Ter(\Phi, \mathbb{X})$, then $f(t_1, \ldots, t_{\mathfrak{a}(f)})$ is a term in $Ter(\Phi, \mathbb{X})$. The positions $Pos(t)$ of a term t are sequences of integers defined inductively as follows: If t is a variable or a constant symbol, then $Pos(t) = \{\varepsilon\}$, where ε denotes the empty string. If f is a function symbol of arity $\mathfrak{a}(f) \geq 1$ and $t = f(t_1, t_2, \ldots, t_{\mathfrak{a}(f)})$, then $Pos(t) = \{\varepsilon\} \cup \bigcup_{i=1}^{\mathfrak{a}(f)} \{ip \mid p \in Pos(t_i)\}$. The sequences in $Pos(t)$ are used to index subterms of t. The subterm of t at position p is denoted by $t[p]$ and is inductively defined as follows: in the basis case we have $t[\varepsilon] = t$. Now if $t = f(t_1, t_2, \ldots, t_{\mathfrak{a}(f)})$ then $t[ip] = t_i[p]$ for $1 \leq i \leq \mathfrak{a}(f)$. We denote by $var(t)$ the set of variables appearing as sub-terms of t. A substitution is a function $\sigma : \mathbb{X} \to Ter(\Phi, \mathbb{X})$ assigning to each variable $x \in \mathbb{X}$ a term $\sigma(x)$ in $Ter(\Phi, \mathbb{X})$. The action t^σ of σ on a term $t \in Ter(\Phi, \mathbb{X})$ is inductively defined as follows: $x^\sigma = \sigma(x)$ for each variable $x \in \mathbb{X}$; $a^\sigma = a$ for each constant symbol $a \in \Phi$; $f(t_1, \ldots, t_{\mathfrak{a}(f)})^\sigma = f(t_1^\sigma, \ldots, t_{\mathfrak{a}(f)}^\sigma)$ for each function symbol $f \in \Phi$ of arity $\mathfrak{a}(f) \geq 1$ and terms $t_1, t_2, \ldots, t_{\mathfrak{a}(f)} \in Ter(\Phi, \mathbb{X})$. The *support* of a substitution σ is the set $supp(\sigma) \subseteq \mathbb{X}$ of all variables that are *not* mapped to themselves. In this work we will only be concerned with substitutions with finite support. A substitution σ is *pure* if $var(\sigma(x)) \cap var(\sigma(y)) = \emptyset$ for $x \neq y$. Additionally, we assume that whenever a pure substitution σ is applied to an equation $t_1 = t_2$, $[var(t_1) \cup var(t_2)] \cap var(\sigma(x)) = \emptyset$ for every $x \in \mathbb{X}$, meaning that in a pure substitution all introduced variables are new. A substitution $\rho : \mathbb{X} \to \mathbb{X}$ in which each variable is mapped to another variable is called a *renaming of variables*. We notice that we allow several variables to be mapped to the same variable, and thus we do not require a renaming of variables to be injective, as it is often assumed in other contexts. Also, as opposed to pure substitutions, when applying a renaming of variables ρ to an equation $t_1 = t_2$, we allow $\rho(x) \in var(t_1) \cup var(t_2)$. Any substitution α can be cast as $\alpha = \rho \circ \sigma$ where σ is a pure substitution and

ρ a renaming of variables. Thus unless explicitly stated otherwise, whenever we use the term substitution we will mean a pure substitution.

Let E be a finite set of equations. Then the equational theory $T(E)$ induced by E is the smallest set of equations containing E and which is closed under the following rules of inference:

$$\frac{}{\forall t_1 = t_2 \in E, \, \overline{t_1 = t_2}} \; Eq \qquad \frac{}{t = t} \; Ref \qquad \frac{t_1^1 = t_2^1 \quad \cdots \quad t_1^{a(f)} = t_2^{a(f)}}{f(t_1^1, \ldots, t_1^{a(f)}) = f(t_2^1, \ldots, t_2^{a(f)})} \; Cong$$

$$\frac{t_1 = t_2}{t_2 = t_1} \; Sym \qquad \frac{t_1 = t_2 \quad t_2 = t_3}{t_1 = t_3} \; Tr \qquad \frac{t_1 = t_2}{t_1^\sigma = t_2^\sigma} \; Sub \qquad \frac{t_1 = t_2}{t_1^\rho = t_2^\rho} \; Ren$$

In the rules of inference above, f is an arbitrary function symbol in Φ, σ is any pure substitution and ρ is any renaming of variables. Observe that the substitution rule defined above together with the renaming rule are equivalent to the substitution rule that is usually found in the literature, and which does not require substitutions to be pure. The only reason we consider a split version of the substitution rule is the fact that in this way some proofs will be simplified.

2.2   Ordered Terms and Ordered Equations

An *ordered term* is a pair (t, ω) where t is a term in $Ter(\Phi, \mathbb{X})$ and $\omega : Pos(t) \to \{1, \ldots, |Pos(t)|\}$ is a bijection associating with each position p in $Pos(t)$ an order $\omega(p)$. If $T = \{t_i\}_{i \in I}$ is an indexed set of terms in $Ter(\Phi, \mathbb{X})$ for a finite set $I \subseteq \mathbb{N}$ of indexes, then the set of positions of T is defined as $Pos(T) = \bigcup_{i \in I} \{ip \mid p \in Pos(t_i)\}$.

If $ip \in Pos(T)$ then we set $T[ip] = t_i[p]$. An indexed subset of T is an indexed set $T' = \{t_j\}_{j \in J}$ for $J \subseteq I$. A *subterm ordering* of T is a bijection $\omega : Pos(T) \to \{1, \ldots, |Pos(T)|\}$. If T is an indexed set of terms, T' is an indexed subset of T and ω is a subterm ordering of T then we let $\omega|_{T'}$ be the subterm ordering induced by ω on $Pos(T')$. In other words, $\omega|_{T'}$ is the unique subterm ordering of $Pos(T')$ such that for each two positions p_1, p_2 in $Pos(T')$, we have that $\omega|_{T'}(p_1) < \omega|_{T'}(p_2)$ if and only if $\omega(p_1) < \omega(p_2)$.

If t is a term then the leading symbol $ls(t)$ is defined as follows: If $t = x$ for a variable x then $ls(t) = x$ otherwise, if $t = f(t_1, t_2, \ldots, t_k)$ then $ls(t) = f$. We say that two terms t and t' are syntactically equal if $Pos(t) = Pos(t')$ and if $ls(t[p]) = ls(t'[p])$ for each $p \in Pos(t)$. We will write $t_1 \stackrel{\triangle}{=} t_2$ to denote that t_1 is syntactically equal to t_2. An ordered equation is a pair $(t_1 = t_2, \omega)$ where $t_1 = t_2$ is an equation and $\omega : Pos(\{t_1, t_2\}) \to \{1, \ldots, |Pos(\{t_1, t_2\})|\}$ is a subterm ordering of $\{t_1, t_2\}$. In Eq. 2 below, we show an ordered equation $(f(x, g(z, x)) = g(x, y), \omega)$ and the subterms orderings induced by ω on $Pos(f(x, g(z, x)))$ and on $Pos(g(x, y))$ respectively. The order of the position corresponding to each subterm is indicated by a number over the leading symbol of such subterm.

$$\overset{6}{f} (\overset{5}{x}, \overset{1}{g} (\overset{8}{z}, \overset{2}{x})) = \overset{4}{g} (\overset{7}{x}, \overset{3}{y}) \qquad \overset{4}{f} (\overset{3}{x}, \overset{1}{g} (\overset{5}{z}, \overset{2}{x})) \qquad \overset{2}{g} (\overset{3}{x}, \overset{1}{y}) \tag{2}$$

We denote by $ord(t)$ the set of all subterm orderings of a term t; by $ord(T)$ the set of all subterm orderings of a set of terms T; and by $ord(t_1 = t_2)$ the set of all subterm orderings of $\{t_1, t_2\}$. An ordered substitution is a pair (σ, Ω) where σ is a substitution and Ω is a function that associates with each variable $x \in supp(\sigma)$ a subterm ordering Ω_x of the term $\sigma(x)$. In this sense, the pair $(\sigma(x), \Omega_x)$ is an ordered term for each $x \in \mathbb{X}$. If T is a set of terms, and x is a variable in $\mathbb{X}$ then we let $Pos(T, x)$ be the subset of positions in $Pos(T)$ corresponding to the variable x. More precisely,

$$Pos(T, x) = \{p \in Pos(T) \mid T[p] = x\}.$$

2.3 Ordered Equational Logic

Now we are in a position to introduce *ordered equational logic*. In this logic sentences are ordered equations. The rules of inference in ordered equational logic mimic very closely the rules of inference in classical equational logic, except for some minor adaptations to make these rules meaningful in the ordered setting.

Equation Rule:

$$\frac{}{(t_1 = t_2, \omega)} \; o\text{-}Equation \qquad \text{for each } t_1 = t_2 \in E \text{ and each } \omega \in ord(\{t_1, t_2\})$$

Observe that the only difference with respect to the Equation rule in classical equational logic is that, since an equation can be ordered in several ways we need to consider all such orderings.

Reflexivity Rule:

$$\frac{}{(t_1 = t_2, \omega)} \; o\text{-}Reflexivity \qquad \text{provided that } t_1 \stackrel{\Delta}{=} t_2, \; \omega \in ord(t_1 = t_2) \text{ and } \omega|_{\{t_1\}} = \omega|_{\{t_2\}}$$

For instance, while the ordered equation $\overset{1}{f} (\overset{3}{x}, \overset{5}{y}) = \overset{2}{f} (\overset{4}{x}, \overset{6}{y})$ is an axiom because the restriction of the ordering to both sides yields the ordered term $\overset{1}{f} (\overset{2}{x}, \overset{3}{y})$, the ordered equation $\overset{1}{f} (\overset{4}{x}, \overset{5}{y}) = \overset{3}{f} (\overset{2}{x}, \overset{6}{y})$ is not an axiom because the restriction to the left term yields $\overset{1}{f} (\overset{2}{x}, \overset{3}{y})$ while the restriction to the right term yields $\overset{2}{f} (\overset{1}{x}, \overset{3}{y})$.

Symmetry Rule:

$$\frac{(t_1 = t_2, \omega)}{(t_2 = t_1, \omega)} \; o\text{-}Symmetry$$

For instance if $\overset{1}{f} (\overset{4}{x}, \overset{5}{y}) = \overset{3}{g} (\overset{2}{x}, \overset{6}{y})$ then we can infer that $\overset{3}{g} (\overset{2}{x}, \overset{6}{y}) = \overset{1}{f} (\overset{4}{x}, \overset{5}{y})$.

Transitivity Rule:

$$\frac{(t_1 = t_3, \omega_1) \quad (t_3 = t_2, \omega_2)}{(t_1 = t_2, \omega_3)} \; o\text{-}Transitivity$$

provided $\exists\, \omega \in ord(\{t_1, t_2, t_3\})$ such that $\omega_1 = \omega|_{\{t_1, t_3\}}$, $\omega_2 = \omega|_{\{t_2, t_3\}}$, and $\omega_3 = \omega|_{\{t_1, t_2\}}$. For instance, the following is a valid application of the transitivity rule

$$\frac{\overset{5}{f}\,(\overset{1}{x},\overset{6}{y}) = \overset{3}{g}\,(\overset{2}{y},\overset{4}{z}) \qquad \overset{2}{g}\,(\overset{1}{y},\overset{4}{z}) = \overset{5}{h}\,(\overset{6}{z},\overset{3}{w})}{\overset{5}{f}\,(\overset{1}{x},\overset{6}{y}) = \overset{3}{h}\,(\overset{4}{z},\overset{2}{w})}$$

since the ordering on each equation above is induced by the following ordered triple of terms:

$$\{\overset{8}{f}\,(\overset{1}{x},\overset{9}{y}),\ \overset{3}{g}\,(\overset{2}{y},\overset{5}{z}),\ \overset{6}{h}\,(\overset{7}{z},\overset{4}{w})\}$$

Congruence Rule:

$$\frac{(t_1^1 = t_2^1, \omega_1) \quad \cdots \quad (t_1^{\mathfrak{a}(f)} = t_2^{\mathfrak{a}(f)}, \omega_{\mathfrak{a}(f)})}{(f(t_1^1, \ldots, t_1^k) = f(t_2^1, \ldots, t_2^k), \omega)} \quad o\text{-}Congruence$$

provided $\omega|_{\{t_1^i, t_2^i\}} = \omega_i$ for each $i \in \{1, \ldots, \mathfrak{a}(f)\}$.

In other words when restricting the ordering ω to the positions of each pair of subterms $\{t_1^i, t_2^i\}$, this restriction should be equal to the original ordering ω_i assigned to $t_1^i = t_2^i$. The following is a valid application of the congruence rule.

$$\frac{\overset{1}{a}\,(\overset{3}{x}) = \overset{2}{b}\,(\overset{4}{x}) \qquad \overset{2}{c}\,(\overset{1}{y}) = \overset{4}{d}\,(\overset{3}{y})}{\overset{2}{f}\,(\overset{1}{a}\,(\overset{7}{x}),\overset{5}{c}\,(\overset{3}{y})) = \overset{8}{f}\,(\overset{4}{b}\,(\overset{9}{x}),\overset{10}{d}\,(\overset{6}{y}))}$$

Substitution Rule:

We recall that according to the notation introduced in Sect. 2.2, $\{t_1, t_2\}[p]$ denotes the subterm of either t_1 or t_2 at position p. If $p = 1p'$ for some p' then $\{t_1, t_2\}[p]$ denotes the subterm $t_1[p']$ of t_1. Otherwise, if $p = 2p'$ then $\{t_1, t_2\}[p]$ denotes the subterm $t_2[p']$ of t_2. We also recall that $Pos(\{t_1, t_2\}, x)$ denotes the set of all the positions p of $\{t_1, t_2\}$ in which instances of the variable x occur. Therefore, if σ is a substitution, and $p \in Pos(\{t_1, t_2\}, x)$, then the subterm $\{t_1^\sigma, t_2^\sigma\}[p]$ is (syntactically) equal to $\sigma(x)$. Let (σ, Ω) be an ordered substitution. The ordered substitution rule is defined as follows.

$$\frac{(t_1 = t_2, \omega)}{(t_1^\sigma = t_2^\sigma, \omega')} \quad o\text{-}Substitution$$

provided that

(i) $\omega = \omega'|_{\{t_1, t_2\}}$.
(ii) For each $p \in Pos(\{t_1, t_2\}, x)$, $(\{t_1^\sigma, t_2^\sigma\}[p],\ \omega'|_{\{t_1^\sigma, t_2^\sigma\}[p]}) = (\sigma(x), \Omega_x)$

Condition (i) says that the subterm ordering induced by ω' on the positions of the original equation $t_1 = t_2$ is precisely ω. In other words, ω' is an extension of ω to the positions of $t_1^\sigma = t_2^\sigma$. Note that since $Pos(\{t_1, t_2\}) \subseteq Pos(\{t_1^\sigma, t_2^\sigma\})$,

Condition (i) is well defined. Condition (ii) says that if a term $\sigma(x) = u$ is substituted for a variable x, then the ordering induced by ω' on each substituted instance of u in $t_1^\sigma = t_2^\sigma$ is equal to the ordering Ω_x. For instance, if (σ, Ω) is an ordered substitution such that $supp(\sigma) = \{x\}$ and $\sigma(x) = \overset{1}{h}(\overset{2}{z}, \overset{3}{w})$, then the following is a valid inference step,

$$\frac{\overset{1}{f}(\overset{3}{x}, \overset{5}{y}) = \overset{2}{g}(\overset{6}{y}, \overset{4}{x})}{\overset{1}{f}(\overset{3}{h}(\overset{5}{z}, \overset{7}{w}), \overset{9}{y}) = \overset{2}{g}(\overset{10}{y}, \overset{4}{h}(\overset{6}{z}, \overset{8}{w}))}$$

Note that the ordering induced by $\overset{1}{f}(\overset{3}{h}(\overset{5}{z}, \overset{7}{w}), \overset{9}{y}) = \overset{2}{g}(\overset{10}{y}, \overset{4}{h}(\overset{6}{z}, \overset{8}{w}))$ on each instance of $h(z, w)$ is equal to $\overset{1}{h}(\overset{2}{z}, \overset{3}{w})$.

Renaming Rule:

$$\frac{(t_1 = t_2, \omega)}{(t_1^\rho = t_2^\rho, \omega)} \ o\text{-}Renaming$$

In other words, when renaming a variable x with a variable y in an equation $t_1 = t_2$, the numbering assigned to each occurrence of y in the new equation is the same as the number assigned to the corresponding occurrence of x in $t_1 = t_2$. For instance, if $\rho(x) = y$ then the following is a valid inference step.

$$\frac{\overset{1}{f}(\overset{4}{x}, \overset{5}{y}) = \overset{3}{f}(\overset{2}{x}, \overset{6}{y})}{\overset{1}{f}(\overset{4}{y}, \overset{5}{y}) = \overset{3}{f}(\overset{2}{y}, \overset{6}{y})}$$

2.4 Proof Trees and b-boundness

Let E be a finite set of equations and $(t_1 = t_2, \omega)$ be an ordered equation. A proof tree for $(t_1 = t_2, \omega)$ is a tree $\mathfrak{T} = (\mathfrak{V}, \mathfrak{E}, \mathfrak{l})$ where $\mathfrak{V}$ is the set of nodes, $\mathfrak{E}$ is the set of arcs, and $\mathfrak{l}$ is a function that labels the nodes in $\mathfrak{V}$ in such a way that the following conditions are satisfied.

1. If $\mathfrak{v}$ is a leaf, then $\mathfrak{l}(\mathfrak{v})$ is either an ordered version of an axiom in E or it is an equation of the form $(t_1 = t_2, \omega)$ where $t_1 \overset{\Delta}{=} t_2$ and $\omega|_{t_1} = \omega|_{t_2}$.
2. If $\mathfrak{v}$ is an internal node then the ordered equation $\mathfrak{l}(\mathfrak{v})$ is obtained by the application of some rule of inference to the equations labeling $\mathfrak{v}'s$ children.

The depth of $\mathfrak{T}$ is defined as the size of the longest path from the root of $\mathfrak{T}$ to some leaf of $\mathfrak{T}$. We say that an ordered equation $(t_1 = t_2, \omega)$ can be proved in depth d if there exists a proof tree for $(t_1 = t_2, \omega)$ of depth at most d.

b-boundedness

Let $T = \{t_1, \ldots, t_r\}$ be a set with r instances of a term t. In other words, for each $i \in \{1, \ldots, r\}$ we have that $t_i \overset{\Delta}{=} t$. We say that a subterm ordering ω of T is b-bounded if for each position $p \in Pos(t)$ and each $i \in \{1, \ldots, r - 1\}$ we have that $|\omega(ip) - \omega([i+1]p)| \leq b$. In other words, the order assigned to the position p of the term t_i is at most b apart from the order assigned to the position p of the term t_{i+1}. For instance, the subterm ordering $\{\overset{1}{h}(\overset{4}{z},\overset{7}{w}), \overset{2}{h}(\overset{5}{z},\overset{8}{w}), \overset{3}{h}(\overset{6}{z},\overset{9}{w})\}$ is 1-bounded. We say that a reflexivity axiom $(t_1 = t_2, \omega)$ is b-bounded if ω is a b-bounded subterm ordering of $\{t_1, t_2\}$. Let (σ, Ω) be an ordered substitution. We say that an application $(t_1 = t_2, \omega) \overset{(\sigma,\Omega)}{\longrightarrow} (t_1^\sigma = t_2^\sigma, \omega')$ of the substitution rule is b-bounded if for every variable $x \in supp(\sigma)$, the restriction of ω' to the set $\{\{t_1^\sigma, t_2^\sigma\}[p]\}_{p \in Pos(t_1 = t_2, x)}$ is b-bounded. In other words, for each variable x in $supp(\sigma)$, if we restrict the ordering ω' to all those instances of $\sigma(x)$ in the new equation $t_1^\sigma = t_2^\sigma$, then this restricted ordering is b-bounded. For instance, let $\overset{1}{g}(\overset{2}{x},\overset{3}{y}) = \overset{4}{g}(\overset{5}{y},\overset{6}{x})$ be an ordered equation, and let $x \to \overset{1}{h}(\overset{2}{z},\overset{3}{w})$ be a substitution that replaces the variable x with the ordered term $\overset{1}{h}(\overset{2}{z},\overset{3}{w})$ then the derivation

$$\overset{1}{g}(\overset{2}{x},\overset{3}{y}) = \overset{4}{g}(\overset{5}{y},\overset{6}{x}) \longrightarrow \overset{1}{g}(\overset{2}{h}(\overset{7}{z},\overset{9}{w}),\overset{3}{y}) = \overset{4}{g}(\overset{5}{y},\overset{6}{h}(\overset{8}{z},\overset{10}{w})) \tag{3}$$

is 1-bounded because if we restrict the ordering of the resulting equation to the two instances of $h(z, w)$ we get the 1-bounded ordering $\overset{1}{h}(\overset{3}{z},\overset{5}{w}) = \overset{2}{h}(\overset{4}{z},\overset{6}{w})$.

2.5   Graphs Associated with Terms and Equations

In this section we will associate digraphs with ordered terms and equations. This association has two motivations. The first motivation is to eliminate the need of using variable names. Two nodes of such a digraph represent the same variable if and only if they are connected by a path. Indeed, since variables in equations are implicitly universally quantified, equations that differ only up to an injective renaming of variables are deemed equivalent. Two such equivalent equations are associated with the same digraph. The second motivation is that, by representing ordered equations as digraphs, we will be able to define and manipulate infinite sets of equations within the framework of slice languages which will be introduced in Sect. 3.

Let (t, ω) be an ordered term, x be a variable occurring in t, and p be a position in $Pos(\{t\}, x)$. We denote by $next_{t,\omega}^x(p)$ the position in $Pos(\{t\}, x)$ with smallest order after p. In other words $\omega(next_{t,\omega}^x(p)) > \omega(p)$ and there is no other position $p' \in Pos(\{t\}, x)$ such that $\omega(next_{t,\omega}^x(p)) > \omega(p') > \omega(p)$. Analogously, if $(t_1 = t_2, \omega)$ is an ordered equation, x a variable occurring in $t_1 = t_2$, and p a position in $Pos(\{t_1, t_2\}, x)$, we let $next_{t_1=t_2,\omega}^x(p)$ denote the position in $Pos(\{t_1, t_2\}, x)$ with smallest order after p.

Graph Associated with a Term: The digraph $G(t, \omega) = (V, E, \lambda, \xi)$ associated with an ordered term (t, ω) is defined as follows: The vertex set V has a vertex v_p for each position $p \in Pos(t)$. If $t[p] = f(t_1, t_2, \ldots, t_{a(f)})$ for some function symbol f, then we let λ label v_p with f and add the directed edges (v_p, v_{pi}) to E for $1 \leq i \leq a(f)$. Each such edge (v_p, v_{pi}) is labeled by ξ with the number i, indicating that t_i is the i-th argument of f. If $t[p] = x$ for a variable $x \in \mathbb{X}$ then the vertex v_p is labeled by λ with the tag *"var"* indicating that v_p is a variable vertex. We note however that v_p is not labeled with the variable x itself. Now we add edges connecting vertices that correspond to the same variable. More precisely, to each variable x and each two positions $p, p' \in Pos(t, x)$ we add an edge $(v_p, v_{p'})$ if and only if $p' = next^x_{t,\omega}(p)$. Each such edge $(v_p, v_{p'})$ is labeled with the tag *inner-var* indicating that it is an inner variable edge. In other words, the graph $G(t, \omega)$ is constructed by taking the tree representation of the term t and connecting the leaves of this tree corresponding to the same variable by a sequence of inner-variable edges. Finally, the root vertex v_ε is tagged by λ as being a "root".

Graph Associated with an Equation: The graph $G(t_1 = t_2, \omega)$ associated with an ordered equation $(t_1 = t_2, \omega)$ is intuitively constructed by taking the disjoint union of the graphs $G(t_1, \omega|_{t_1})$ and $G(t_2, \omega|_{t_2})$, and by adding edges to connect vertices that represent the same variable. Formally the construction proceeds as follows: Let $G(t_1, \omega|_{t_1})$ and $G(t_2, \omega|_{t_2})$ be the graphs associated with the ordered terms $(t_1, \omega|_{t_1})$ and $(t_2, \omega|_{t_2})$ respectively. Let $L(G(t_1, \omega|_{t_1}))$ be the graph derived from $G(t_1, \omega|_{t_1})$ by tagging all its edges and vertices with the left symbol L, and $R(G(t_2, \omega|_{t_2}))$ be the graph derived from $G(t_2, \omega|_{t_2})$ by tagging all its edges and vertices with the right symbol R. Now consider the disjoint union $L(G(t_1, \omega|_{t_1})) \dot{\cup} R(G(t_2, \omega|_{t_2}))$ of these two graphs. Finally, we connect the vertices of both graphs corresponding to the same variable using outer-variable edges. More precisely, for each variable x and each two positions p, p' in $Pos(t_1 = t_2, x)$ we add an edge $(v_p, v_{p'})$ if and only if $p' = next^x_{t_1=t_2,\omega}(p)$. We label each such edge with the tag *"outer-var"*, indicating that this edge is an outer-variable edge. Observe that while the inner variable edges connect the vertices in increasing order with respect to $\omega|_{t_1}$ and $\omega|_{t_2}$ respectively, the outer-variable edges connect the vertices in increasing order with respect to the whole ordering ω. Observe that if ω and ω' are two distinct orderings of an equation $t_1 = t_2$, then the graphs $G(t_1 = t_2, \omega)$ and $G(t_1 = t_2, \omega')$ may differ, since the disposition of the variable edges depends on the ordering assigned to $t_1 = t_2$. In Fig. 1 we show the graphs associated with the equation $x \cdot (y + z) = x \cdot y + x \cdot z$ according to two possible orderings.

Width of Equations: If $G = (V, E)$ is a digraph, then for each two sets $V_1, V_2 \subseteq V$ we let $E(V_1, V_2)$ be the set of edges of G with one endpoint in V_1 and another endpoint in V_2. If $\omega = (v_1, v_2, \ldots, v_n)$ is an ordering of the vertices of G then the cut-width of G with respect to ω is defined as

$$\mathbf{cw}(G, \omega) = \max_j |E(\{v_1, \ldots, v_j\}, \{v_{j+1}, \ldots, v_n\})|.$$

If $(t_1 = t_2, \omega)$ is an ordered equation then the ordering ω induces an ordering ω_G on the vertices of the graph $G(t_1 = t_2, \omega)$ by setting $\omega_G(v_p) < \omega_G(v_{p'})$ if and only if $\omega(p) < \omega(p')$. The width $\mathbf{w}(t_1 = t_2, \omega)$ of an ordered equation $(t_1 = t_2, \omega)$ is defined as the cut-width of the graph $G(t_1 = t_2, \omega)$ with respect to the ordering ω_G. More precisely, $\mathbf{w}(t_1 = t_2, \omega) = \mathbf{cw}(G(t_1 = t_2, \omega), \omega_G)$.

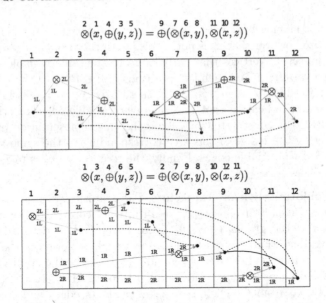

Fig. 1. Two ordered versions of the equation $\oplus(x, \otimes(y,z)) = \oplus(\otimes(x,y), \otimes(x,z))$ expressing that the function symbol $\oplus$ is distributive with respect to $\otimes$, and their respective associated graphs. The edges represented by full bold lines are inner-variable edges. The edges represented by dashed lines are outer variable edges. The width of both ordered equations is 6.

3   Equational Slice Languages

We will represent infinite families of equations using the framework of slice languages [5]. Let Φ be a ranked alphabet. Let $\Gamma_1(\Phi) = \Phi \cup \{var, L, R,$ $root, connector\}$ where $var, L, R, root, connector$ are the tags defined in Sect. 2.5 to indicate that a vertex of a graph is a variable vertex, a left vertex, a right vertex, a root vertex or a connector vertex respectively. Analogously let $\Gamma_2(\Phi) = \{1, \ldots, \mathfrak{a}(\Phi)\} \cup \{inner - var, outer - var, L, R\}$ where $\mathfrak{a}(\Phi)$ denotes the largest arity of a function symbol in Φ and $inner\text{-}var, outer\text{-}var, L$ and R are the tags defined in Sect. 2.5 to indicate that an edge is an inner-variable edge, an outer-variable edge, a left edge and a right edge respectively. Let $c \in \mathbb{N}$.

A (c, Φ)-*slice* is a digraph $\mathbf{S} = (V, E, \lambda, \xi, s, t, [C, I, O])$ comprising a set of vertices V, a set of edges E, a vertex labeling relation $\lambda \subseteq V \times \Gamma_1(\Phi)$, an edge labeling relation $\xi \subseteq E \times \Gamma_2(\Phi)$, and total functions $s, t : E \to V$ associating with each edge $e \in E$ a source vertex $s(e)$ and a target vertex $t(e)$. Alternatively, we say that $s(e)$ and $t(e)$ are the endpoints of e. The vertex set V is partitioned into three disjoint subsets: an in-frontier $I \subseteq V$ a center $C \subseteq V$ and an out-frontier $O \subseteq V$. A slice is subject to the following restrictions.

1. Each frontier vertex in $I \cup O$ is tagged by λ with a number in $\{1, \ldots, c\}$ in such a way that no two vertices in the same frontier are tagged with the same number. Additionally, no frontier vertex receives more than one tag.

2. Each frontier vertex in $I \cup O$ is the endpoint of exactly one edge.
3. No edge has both endpoints in the same frontier.

We say that $\mathbf{S}$ is *initial* if its in-frontier is empty and *final* if its out-frontier is empty. We say that $\mathbf{S}$ is a *unit slice* if $|C| = 1$. We denote by $\Sigma(c, \Phi)$ the set of all unit (c, Φ)-slices. Note that $\Sigma(c, \Phi)$ has at most $2^{O(c \log c)}$ slices where the hidden constant in the exponent depends on the size of Φ. We denote by $\Sigma(c, \Phi)^*$ the set of all finite sequences of (c, Φ)-slices.

Let $\mathbf{S}$ be a slice with frontiers (I, O). Let v be a vertex in I labeled with number i. Then we denote by $e(\mathbf{S}, I, i)$ the unique edge which has v as endpoint. Analogously, if $v \in O$ is labeled with i, then we let $e(\mathbf{S}, O, i)$ be the unique edge that has v as endpoint. A slice $\mathbf{S}_1 = (V_1, E_2, \lambda_1, \xi_1, s_1, t_1, [C_1, I_1, O_1])$ with frontiers (I_1, O_1) can be glued to a slice $\mathbf{S}_2 = (V_2, E_2, \lambda_2, \xi_2, s_2, t_2, [C_2, I_2, O_2])$ with frontiers (I_2, O_2) provided the following conditions are satisfied: (i) $\lambda_1(O_1) = \lambda_2(I_2)$; (ii) for each $i \in \lambda(O_1)$, $\xi_1(e(\mathbf{S}_1, O_1, i)) = \xi_2(e(\mathbf{S}_2, I_2, i))$; and (iii) for each $i \in \lambda(O_1)$, either the target of $e(\mathbf{S}_1, O_1, i)$ lies in O_1 and the source of $e(\mathbf{S}_2, I_2, i)I_2$, or the source of $e(\mathbf{S}_1, O_1, i)$ lies in O_1 and the target of $e(\mathbf{S}_2, I_2, i)$ in I_2. If $\mathbf{S}_1$ can be glued to $\mathbf{S}_2$, then we let $\mathbf{S}_1 \circ \mathbf{S}_2$ be the slice obtained by merging, for each $i \in \lambda_1(O_1)$, the edge $e(\mathbf{S}_1, O, i)$ with the edge $e(\mathbf{S}_2, I, i)$ into a single edge $e(\mathbf{S}_1, \mathbf{S}_2, i)$.

A unit decomposition over $\Sigma(c, \Phi)$ is a sequence $\mathbf{U} = \mathbf{S}_1 \mathbf{S}_2 ... \mathbf{S}_n \in \Sigma(c, \Phi)^*$ where $\mathbf{S}_1$ is an initial slice, $\mathbf{S}_n$ is a final slice and for each $i \in \{1, ..., n-1\}$, $\mathbf{S}_i$ can be glued to $\mathbf{S}_{i+1}$. With each unit decomposition $\mathbf{U}$ we may associate a graph $\overset{\circ}{\mathbf{U}} = \mathbf{S}_1 \circ \mathbf{S}_2 \circ ... \circ \mathbf{S}_n$ which is obtained by gluing each two consecutive slices in $\mathbf{U}$. We say that $\mathbf{U}$ is compatible with an ordered equation $(t_1 = t_2, \omega)$ if $\overset{\circ}{\mathbf{U}} = G(t_1 = t_2, \omega)$ and for each position $p \in Pos(\{t_1, t_2\})$, the vertex v_p of $G(t_1 = t_2, \omega)$ is the center vertex of the slice $\mathbf{S}_{\omega(p)}$.

A slice language is a subset of $\mathcal{L} \subseteq \Sigma(c, \Phi)^*$ consisting only of unit decompositions. If all unit decompositions in $\mathcal{L}$ are compatible with some ordered equation, then we say that $\mathcal{L}$ is an *equational slice language*. The set of all ordered equations derived from an equational slice language $\mathcal{L}$ is defined as

$$\mathcal{L}_{eq} = \{(t_1 = t_2, \omega) \mid \exists \mathbf{U} \in \mathcal{L} \text{ such that } \mathbf{U} \text{ is compatible with } (t_1 = t_2, \omega)\}.$$

A *slice automaton* is a finite automaton $\mathcal{A}$ over $\Sigma(c, \Phi)$ whose language $\mathcal{L}(\mathcal{A})$ is a slice language. A *slice regular expression* is a regular expression over $\Sigma(c, \Phi)$ whose language $\mathcal{L}(\mathcal{E})$ is a slice language (Fig. 2). We let $\mathcal{L}_{eq}(\mathcal{A})$ and $\mathcal{L}_{eq}(\mathcal{E})$ be the set of equations compatible with unit decompositions in $\mathcal{L}(\mathcal{A})$ and $\mathcal{L}(\mathcal{E})$ respectively.

3.1 Equational Operators

Let $\mathcal{L}$ be a slice language over $\Sigma(c, \Phi)$ representing a set $\mathcal{L}_{eq}$ of ordered equations. Below, we will define equational slice languages $\mathbf{Sy}^c(\mathcal{L})$, $\mathbf{Co}^c(\mathcal{L})$, $\mathbf{Tr}^c(\mathcal{L})$, $\mathbf{Re}^c(\mathcal{L})$ and $\mathbf{Su}^{c,b}(\mathcal{L})$, which represent the set of all ordered equations of width c that can

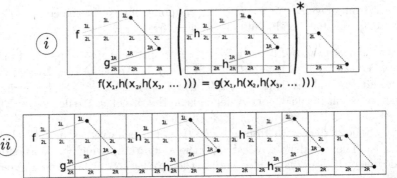

Fig. 2. An example of how to represent infinite sets of equations via regular slice languages. (i) A regular expression over slices. (ii) A unit decomposition obtained after two iterations of the expression between parenthesis. This unit decomposition represents the equation $f(x_1, h(x_2, h(x_3, x_4))) = g(x_1, h(x_2, h(x_3, x_4)))$.

be obtained from $\mathcal{L}_{eq}$ by an application of the symmetry rule, congruence rule, transitivity rule, renaming rule and b-bounded substitution rule, respectively.

$$\mathbf{Sy}^c(\mathcal{L}) = \{\mathbf{U} \in \mathcal{L}(t_2 = t_1, \omega) \mid \omega \in \mathrm{ord}(t_1 = t_2, c), \ \mathcal{L}(t_1 = t_2, \omega) \cap \mathcal{L} \neq \emptyset\}$$

For each function symbol $f \in \Phi$ of arity $\mathfrak{a}(f)$, let

$$\begin{aligned}\mathbf{Co}_f^c(\mathcal{L}) = \{\mathbf{U} \in \mathcal{L}(f(\overline{t_1}) = f(\overline{t_2}), \omega) \mid \overline{t_1} = (t_1^1, \ldots, t_1^{\mathfrak{a}(f)}), \ \overline{t_2} = (t_2^1, \ldots, t_2^{\mathfrak{a}(f)}), \\ \omega \in \mathrm{ord}(f(\overline{t_1}) = f(\overline{t_2}), c), \forall i \in \{1, \ldots, \mathfrak{a}(f)\} \ \mathcal{L}(t_1^i = t_2^i, \omega|_{\{t_1^i, t_2^i\}}) \cap \mathcal{L} \neq \emptyset \}.\end{aligned}$$

The slice language $\mathbf{Co}^c(\mathcal{L})$ is obtained by taking the union of $\mathbf{Co}_f^c(\mathcal{L})$ over all function symbols $f \in \Phi$.

$$Co^c(\mathcal{L}) = \bigcup_{f \in \Phi} Co_f^c(\mathcal{L}).$$

$$\begin{aligned}\mathbf{Tr}^c(\mathcal{L}) = \{\mathbf{U} \in \mathcal{L}(t_1 = t_2, \omega|_{\{t_1, t_2\}}) \mid \exists \ t_3, \text{ such that } \omega \in \mathrm{ord}(\{t_1, t_2, t_3\}), \ \omega|_{\{t_1, t_2\}} \in \\ \mathrm{ord}(t_1 = t_2, c), \ \mathcal{L}(t_1 = t_3, \omega|_{\{t_1, t_3\}}) \cap \mathcal{L} \neq \emptyset, \ \mathcal{L}(t_3 = t_2, \omega|_{\{t_2, t_3\}}) \cap \mathcal{L} \neq \emptyset\}\end{aligned}$$

$$\begin{aligned}\mathbf{Re}^c(\mathcal{L}) = \{\mathbf{U} \in \mathcal{L}(t_1^\rho = t_2^\rho, \omega) \mid \rho \text{ is a renaming of variables}, \\ \omega \in \mathrm{ord}(t_1^\rho = t_2^\rho, c), \mathcal{L}(t_1 = t_2, \omega) \cap \mathcal{L} \neq \emptyset\}\end{aligned}$$

Below we write $(t_1 = t_2, \omega) \xrightarrow{(\sigma, \Omega)} (t_1^\sigma = t_2^\sigma, \omega')$ to indicate that an ordered equation $(t_1^\sigma = t_2^\sigma, \omega')$ follows from $(t_1 = t_2, \omega)$ by an application of the ordered substitution rule (σ, Ω).

$$\begin{aligned}\mathbf{Su}^{c,b}(\mathcal{L}) = \{\mathbf{U} \in \mathcal{L}(t_1^\sigma = t_2^\sigma, \omega') \mid (\sigma, \Omega) \text{ is a } b\text{-bounded ordered substitution}, \\ \mathcal{L}(t_1 = t_2, \omega) \cap \mathcal{L} \neq \emptyset, \ \omega' \in \mathrm{ord}(t_1^\sigma = t_2^\sigma, c), \ (t_1 = t_2, \omega) \xrightarrow{(\sigma, \Omega)} (t_1^\sigma = t_2^\sigma, \omega')\}\end{aligned}$$

Let E be a finite set of equations over an alphabet Φ of function symbols. We denote by $\mathcal{L}_{ref}^{c,b}(E)$ the set of all unit decompositions over $\Sigma(c, \Phi)$ that are compatible with some ordered equation $(t_1 = t_2, \omega)$ in which $t_1 \overset{\Delta}{=} t_2$ and in which ω is a b-bounded ordering of $t_1 = t_2$. We let $\mathcal{L}(E, d, c, b)$ denote the set of all unit decompositions in $\mathcal{L}(\Sigma(c, \Phi))$ that can be deduced from E by an ordered equational logic proof of depth d, width c and bound b. The set $\mathcal{L}(E, d, c, b)$ can be inductively defined as follows:

$$\mathcal{L}(E, 0, c, b) = \mathcal{L}_{ref}^{c,b}(\Phi) \ \cup \bigcup_{t_1 = t_2 \in E} \mathcal{L}(t_1 = t_2, c) \tag{4}$$

$$\begin{aligned}
\mathcal{L}(E, d, c, b) = \ &\mathcal{L}(E, d-1, c, b) \cup \mathbf{Sy}^c(\mathcal{L}(E, d-1, c, b)) \\
&\cup \mathbf{Tr}^c(\mathcal{L}(E, d-1, c, b)) \\
&\cup \mathbf{Co}^c(\mathcal{L}(E, d-1, c, b)) \\
&\cup \mathbf{Re}^c(\mathcal{L}(E, d-1, c, b)) \\
&\cup \mathbf{Su}^{c,b}(\mathcal{L}(E, d-1, c, b))
\end{aligned} \tag{5}$$

Intuitively, the language $\mathcal{L}(E, 0, c, b)$ contains all unit decompositions of width at most c corresponding to equations in E, together with all unit decompositions compatible with a b-bounded ordered versions of equations of the form $t_1 \overset{\Delta}{=} t_2$ (i.e. reflexivity axioms). For each $d \in \mathbb{N}$, the language $\mathcal{L}(E, d, c, b)$ consists of all unit decompositions that are compatible with ordered equations of width at most c which can be inferred from equations in $\mathcal{L}_{eq}(E, d-1, c, b)$ by one application of the symmetry rule, transitivity rule, congruence rule, renaming rule or b-bounded substitution rule.

4   Proofs of Our Main Results

In this section we will prove Theorems 1.1 and 1.2. Recall that Theorem 1.1 states that one can determine in time $f(E, d, c, b) \cdot |t_1 = t_2|$ whether an *ordered* equation $(t_1 = t_2, \omega)$ has a b-bounded proof of depth d and width c. On the other hand, Theorem 1.2 states that one can determine in time $f(E, d, c, b) \cdot |t_1 = t_2|^{O(c)}$ whether a *classical* equation $t_1 = t_2$ can be proved by a b-bounded *oriented* proof of depth d and width c. The following Lemma, whose proof is quite intricate, states that the equational operators $\mathbf{Sy}^c, \mathbf{Tr}^c, \mathbf{Co}^c, \mathbf{Re}^c$ and $\mathbf{Su}^c$ can be effectively realized on slice automata.

Lemma 4.1 (Equational Operators Lemma). *Let Φ be an alphabet of function symbols, $\mathfrak{a}(\Phi)$ be the largest arity of a function symbol in Φ and $\mathcal{L}$ be an equational slice language over $\Sigma(c, \Phi)$ accepted by a slice automaton $\mathcal{A}$.*

1. *One can construct an automaton $\mathbf{Sy}^c(\mathcal{A})$ on $O(|\mathcal{A}|)$ states accepting $\mathbf{Sy}^c(\mathcal{L})$.*
2. *One can construct an automaton $\mathbf{Tr}^c(\mathcal{A})$ on $O(|\mathcal{A}|^2)$ states accepting $\mathbf{Tr}^c(\mathcal{L})$.*
3. *One can construct an automaton $\mathbf{Co}^c(\mathcal{A})$ on $|\Phi| \cdot 2^{O(c \log c)} \cdot |\mathcal{A}|^{\mathfrak{a}(\Phi)+1}$ states accepting $\mathbf{Co}^c(\mathcal{L})$.*

4. One can construct an automaton $\mathbf{Re}^c(A)$ on $2^{O(c\log c)} \cdot |A|$ states accepting $\mathbf{Re}^c(\mathcal{L})$.

5. One can construct an automaton $\mathbf{Su}^{c,b}(A)$ on $2^{O(c\log c)} \cdot |A|$ states accepting $\mathbf{Su}^{c,b}(\mathcal{L})$.

Lemma 4.2 below states that the set of all unit decompositions representing b-bounded reflexivity axioms can be effectively represented by a slice automaton.

Lemma 4.2. Let Φ be an alphabet of function symbols and $c, b \in \mathbb{N}$. Then the b-bounded reflexive language $\mathcal{L}_{ref}^{c,b}(\Phi)$ can be generated by a slice automaton $\mathcal{A}^{ref}(\Phi, c, b)$ over $\Sigma(c, \Phi)$ on $2^{O(b \cdot c \log c)}$ states.

Finally, we are in position to prove Theorem 1.1 using a combination of Lemmas 4.1 and 4.2.

Proof of Theorem 1.1: As a first step, we construct an automaton $\mathcal{A}(E, d, c, b)$ accepting the slice language $\mathcal{L}(E, d, c, b)$ defined in Eq. 5. In other words, $\mathcal{A}(E, d, c, b)$ accepts a unit decomposition $\mathbf{U}$ if and only if it represents an ordered equation that can be proved from E by a b-bounded proof of depth d and width c. The construction of $\mathcal{A}(E, d, c, b)$ is by induction on d. In the base case, $d = 0$. In this case we have that

$$\mathcal{L}(E, 0, c, b) = \mathcal{L}_{ref}^{c,b}(\Phi) \cup \bigcup_{t_1 = t_2 \in E} \mathcal{L}(t_1 = t_2, c).$$

Let $l(E)$ be the maximum size of an equation in E. Since E has $|E|$ equations, and since each equation can be ordered in at most $l(E)! = 2^{O(l(E)\log l(E))}$ ways, we have that there is a slice automaton on $|E| \cdot 2^{O(l(E)\log l(E) + c\log c)}$ states generating the slice language $\bigcup_{t_1 = t_2 \in E} \mathcal{L}(t_1 = t_2, c)$. Additionally, by Lemma 4.2, the b-bounded reflexivity language $\mathcal{L}_{ref}^{c,b}(\Phi)$ can be generated by a slice automaton on $2^{O(b \cdot c \log c)}$ states. Therefore, $\mathcal{L}(E, 0, c, b)$ can be generated by a slice automaton $\mathcal{A}(E, 0, c, b)$ on $r = 2^{O(b \cdot c \log c)} + |E| \cdot 2^{O(l(E)\log l(E) + c\log c)}$ states.

Now suppose that for $d \geq 1$, the slice language $\mathcal{L}(E, d - 1, c, b)$ can be generated by a slice automaton $\mathcal{A}(E, d - 1, c, b)$ on s states. Then using Eq. 5, together with Lemma 4.1, we can construct a slice automaton $\mathcal{A}(E, d, c, b)$ on $2^{O(a(\Phi) \cdot c \log c)} \cdot s^{O(a(\Phi))}$ states generating the slice language $\mathcal{L}(E, d, c, b)$. Therefore, using the fact that $\mathcal{A}(E, 0, c, b)$ has r states, and by induction on d, we have that $\mathcal{A}(E, d, c, b)$ has $f(E, d, c, b) = 2^{O(c \cdot \log c) \cdot a(\Phi)^{O(d)}} \cdot r^{a(\Phi)^{O(d)}}$ states.

We note that the slice language $\mathcal{L}(E, d, c, b)$ is vertically saturated. Thus, for each ordered equation $(t_1 = t_2, \omega)$ in the equation language $\mathcal{L}_{eq}(E, d, c, b)$, we have that each unit decomposition $\mathbf{U}$ compatible with $(t_1 = t_2, \omega)$ belongs to the slice language $\mathcal{L}(E, d, c, b)$. Therefore, to determine whether an ordered equation $(t_1 = t_2, \omega)$ has a b-bounded proof of depth d and width c it is enough to select in linear time an arbitrary decomposition $\mathbf{U} = \mathbf{S}_1 \mathbf{S}_2 \ldots \mathbf{S}_n$ compatible with $(t_1 = t_2, \omega)$, and then verify whether $\mathbf{U}$ is accepted by $\mathcal{A}(E, d, c, b)$. Since $\mathcal{A}(E, d, c, b)$ has $f(E, d, c, b)$ states, we can decide whether $\mathbf{U}$ is accepted by $\mathcal{A}(E, d, c, b)$ in time $f(E, d, c, b) \cdot |\mathbf{U}| = f(E, d, c, b) \cdot |t_1 = t_2|$. □

Theorem 1.1 concerns the provability of ordered equations. In other words, to ask about the provability of an equation $t_1 = t_2$ we need to specify an ordering ω a priori. On the other hand, Theorem 1.2 states that at the expense of a moderate increase in the running time we can address the provability of classical equations, in the sense that a suitable ordering ω that yields the provability of $t_1 = t_2$ in depth d, width c and bound b, may be determined automatically. Before proving Theorem 1.2, we need to state an auxiliary lemma. Lemma 4.3 below says that for any given equation $t_1 = t_2$ one may construct in time $|t_1 = t_2|^{O(c)}$ a slice automaton generating precisely the set of unit decompositions of width at most c that are compatible with ordered versions of $t_1 = t_2$. Recall that $\mathrm{ord}(t_1 = t_2, c)$ denotes the set of all orderings of $t_1 = t_2$ of width at most c.

Lemma 4.3. *Let $t_1 = t_2$ be an equation and $c \in \mathbb{N}$. Then one may construct in time $|t_1 = t_2|^{O(c)}$ a vertically saturated slice automaton $\mathcal{A}(t_1 = t_2, c)$ over $\Sigma(c, \Phi)$ generating the following slice language:*

$$\mathcal{L}(t_1 = t_2, c) = \bigcup_{\omega \in\, \mathrm{ord}(t_1 = t_2, c)} \mathcal{L}(t_1 = t_2, \omega)$$

Proof of Theorem 1.2: First, we construct the slice automaton $\mathcal{A}(E, d, c, b)$ accepting the set $\mathcal{L}(E, d, c, b)$ of all unit decompositions that can be proved from E in depth d, width c, and bound b. Subsequently, we construct the slice automaton $\mathcal{A}(t_1 = t_2, \omega)$ accepting the set of all unit decompositions of width at most c compatible with some ordered version of the equation $t_1 = t_2$. To verify whether $t_1 = t_2$ admits an ordering ω, such that $(t_1 = t_2, \omega)$ can be proved from E in depth d, width c and bound b, it is enough to verify whether $\mathcal{A}(E, d, c, b) \cap \mathcal{A}(t_1 = t_2, \omega)$ accepts a non-empty language. Since $\mathcal{A}(E, d, c, b)$ has $f(E, d, c, b)$ states, and $\mathcal{A}(t_1 = t_2, \omega)$ has $|t_1 = t_2|^{O(c)}$ states, this test can be performed in time $f(E, d, c, b) \cdot |t_1 = t_2|^{O(c)}$.

References

1. Bachmair, L., Dershowitz, N.: Equational inference, canonical proofs, and proof orderings. J. ACM (JACM) **41**, 236–276 (1994)
2. Bachmair, L., Dershowitz, N., Plaisted, D.A.: Completion without failure. In: Resolution of Equations in Algebraic Structures, Rewriting Techniques, vol. 2, pp. 1–30. Academic Press (1989)
3. Bachmair, L., Ganzinger, H., Lynch, C., Snyder, W.: Basic paramodulation. Inf. Comput. **121**(2), 172–192 (1995)
4. Buss, S., Impagliazzo, R., Krajíček, J., Pudlák, P., Razborov, A.A., Sgall, J.: Proof complexity in algebraic systems and bounded depth frege systems with modular counting. Comp. Complex. **6**(3), 256–298 (1996)
5. de Oliveira Oliveira, M.: Reachability in graph transformation systems and slice languages. In: Parisi-Presicce, F., Westfechtel, B. (eds.) ICGT 2015. LNCS, vol. 9151, pp. 121–137. Springer, Cham (2015). doi:10.1007/978-3-319-21145-9_8
6. Ehrig, H., Mahr, B.: Fundamentals of Algebraic Specification 1. Equations and Initial Semantics. Monographs in Theoretical Computer Science. An EATCS Series. Springer, Heidelberg (1985). doi:10.1007/978-3-642-69962-7

7. Freese, R.: Free modular lattices. Trans. Am. Math. Soc. **261**, 81–91 (1980)
8. Goguen, J.A., Lin, K.: Specifying, programming and verifying with equational logic. In: We Will Show Them!, vol. 2, pp. 1–38. College Publications (2005)
9. Goguen, J.A., Malcolm, G.: Algebraic Semantics of Imperative Programs, 1st edn. MIT, Cambridge (1996)
10. Hillenbrand, T., Buch, A., Vogt, R., Löchner, B.: Waldmeister-high-performance equational deduction. J. Autom. Reas. **18**(2), 265–270 (1997)
11. Hrubes, P., Tzameret, I.: The proof complexity of polynomial identities. In: 24th Conference on Computational Complexity, pp. 41–51 (2009)
12. Knuth, D.E., Bendix, P.: Simple word problems in universal algebras. In: Leech, J. (ed) Comput. Probl. Abstr. Algebra, 263–297 (1970)
13. Matijasevic, J.V.: Simple examples of undecidable associative calculi. Sov. Math. (Dokladi) **8**(2), 555–557 (1967)
14. McCune, W.: Solution of the Robbins problem. J. Autom. Reas. **19**(3), 263–276 (1997)
15. Meinke, K., Tucker, J.V.: Universal algebra. In: Handbook of Logic in Computer Science, Vol 1, pp. 189–409. Oxford University Press (1992)
16. Pigozzi, D.: Equational logic and equational theories of algebras, Technical report. Purdue University (1975)
17. Plaisted, D.A., Zhu, Y.: Equational reasoning using AC constraints. In: IJCAI, pp. 108–113. Morgan Kaufmann (1997)
18. Wampler-Doty, M.: A complete proof of the Robbins conjecture. Archive of Formal Proofs (2010)
19. Wechler, W.: Universal Algebra for Computer Scientists. Springer, Berlin (1992)

Author Index

Printed in the United States
By Bookmasters